Consumer Economic Issues in America

8th Edition

E. Thomas Garman
InCharge Institute of America

THOMSON

CUSTOM PUBLISHING

Editor: Robert LaManna
Publishing Services Supervisor: Christina Smith
Manufacturing Supervisor: Garris Blankenship
Graphic Designer: Krista Pierson
Rights and Permissions Specialist: Kalina Ingham Hintz
Project Coordinator: Brian Schaefer
Marketing Manager: Sara L. Hinckley

Thomson Custom Publishing
5191 Natorp Blvd.
Mason, Ohio 45040
USA

For information about our products, contact us:
1-800-355-9983
http://www.thomsoncustom.com

International Headquarters
Thomson Learning
International Division
290 Harbor Drive, 2nd Floor
Stamford, CT 06902-7477
USA

UK/Europe/Middle East/South Africa
Thomson Learning
Berkshire House
168-173 High Holborn
London WCIV 7AA

Asia
Thomson Learning
60 Albert Street, #15-01
Albert Complex
Singapore 189969

Canada
Nelson Thomson Learning
1120 Birchmount Road
Toronto, Ontario MIK 5G4
Canada
United Kingdom

Visit us at www.thomsoncustom.com and learn more about this book and other titles published by Thomson Learning Custom Publishing.

0-759-32018-7

The Adaptable Courseware Program consists of products and additions to existing Custom Publishing products that are produced from camera-ready copy. Peer review, class testing, and accuracy are primarily the responsibility of the author(s).

Table of Contents at a Glance

Table of Contents

Part One: Some Perspectives

Chapter 1   What is the Consumer Interest?   1

Part Two: Facing Consumer Problems Successfully

Chapter 3   Consumer Rights, Responsibilities and
Remedies   45

Chapter 4 Rip-offs and Frauds in the Marketplace   71

Part Three: The Challenging Marketplace

Chapter 6 The Capitalistic American Marketplace   161

Chapter 7 Economic Concepts Critical to Consumer Success   189

Chapter 9 Government Regulation of Economic Interests   **237**

Chapter 10   Government Regulation of Consumer Interests

265

Part Four: Information Processing

Chapter 11 Policymaking and Consumer Issues 287

Chapter 13 The Planned Buying Process   337

Part Five: Consumer Economic Issues

Chapter 14   Food Issues   367

Chapter 16   Product Safety Issues   **421**

Chapter 18   Insurance and Investment Issues   479

Preface

It is always a pleasure for me to take the opportunity to update *Consumer Economic Issues in America*. Yes it is a lot of work, but writing this book also is a labor of love. I am very fortunate to be able to create a coherent presentation of the consumer economics curriculum for people unfamiliar with the subject—students—so that professors have a base of comprehensive material to draw upon in making more sophisticated observations of their own.

This book is the instructor's **second voice** to communicate with students, and it enhances the teaching and learning process. It is my hope that the instructor and this book will bring the subject of consumer economics to students in such a way as to motivate them to lead lives that are more personally fulfilling because of a newly acquired pro-consumer perspective, and to encourage them to help improve the economic marketplace so it will better serve all consumers.

Thanks to the support of instructors and students around the United States and in several other countries, the eighth edition of *Consumer Economic Issues in America* is a reality. You must share the belief that consumer issues are important and that all consumers must be empowered with sufficient—not superficial—knowledge about consumer economics. Such information helps consumers clarify their values, goals, interests, and priorities about how the world works, what needs to be done to improve it, and how they can do their part to help make it better.

These times are bringing positive changes to the consumer's world. While the consumer movement has long been interested in strengthening the power of consumers in the seller-consumer relationship, this emphasis continues to gather steam, particularly in light of the many recent scandals in corporate America. Over 200 large corporations are being sued by consumer shareholders for "cooking the books," also called accounting problems. This country is experiencing increased citizen activism among students, and energetic and informed participation by consumers regarding the issues of the day is becoming a form of patriotism.

In the years ahead, the consumer movement will continue to address such issues as improving government regulation, breaking up large corporate monopolies, demanding more accuracy in advertising, increasing the availability of useful purchasing information, preventing frauds and misrepresentations, keeping unsafe foods, drugs and dangerous consumer products out of the marketplace, improving automobile safety, developing better remedies for those who have consumer problems, and providing consumers with a greater voice in government and corporate policy matters.

While the consumer movement continues to broaden and mature around the world, individual consumers will continue to ask such questions as **"How can I get my money's worth?" "How can I live the good life?"** and **"How can I personally help improve the world in which I live?"**

Students already possess some experience in answering these questions. Each student is now probably in the first part of what is expected to be a long life of consumer decision-making. Most decisions will be good, but some will not. A sound understanding of the principles and concepts of consumer economics is absolutely vital if students are to avoid the pitfalls of poor consumer decision-making and learn to deal effectively with the marketplace. At the very least, students need to know what questions to ask. Accordingly, I believe it is essential to provide much more than a simplistic "how to" approach to consumer economics.

I want students to learn enough to **become knowledgeable and assertive** consumers who are able to efficiently and effectively satisfy personal needs and wants. I want students to be prepared to help improve the functioning of the American economic marketplace for all consumers. I want students to be sufficiently well-informed—not fooled by materialism and the good life—to protect their own interests. What students learn should be practical and have a favorable impact on the resources, health, and safety of consumers.

Ralph (the Nation's Consumer Advocate) and Tom (Your Author) on Consumer Education

Ralph Nader observes that **"We don't grow up civic—we grow up corporate."** In the schools we learn how to sell...We don't learn anything about how to be a skilled consumer or skilled citizen." He is right! And, how stupid it is that fewer than 5 percent of secondary school and college students have access to a course in consumer education. The need for consumer education is so obvious that it is difficult to imagine why the subject is not required instruction everywhere. Instead, the status quo in education continues.

Today's schools do not emphasize **living skills**. They ostensibly prepare students to go on for higher education or to get jobs. But they do not prepare students to live life. (See www.wa.gov/ago/youth/.) Hans B. Thorelli once observed that "We need more consumer education—and notably for the underprivileged. Without education there is no motivation or receptivity; indeed, no basis for informed consumership."

Consumers today live in the capitalistic American economic marketplace; the other economic system, socialism, failed over a decade ago. We realize that our market economy does not function perfectly and that it never will. In the meantime, consumers are faced with a marketplace that contains anti-competitive practices and numerous rip-offs and deceptions. Consumers make **poor buying decisions and inefficient tradeoffs** based on insufficient and sometimes inaccurate information. The U.S. marketplace, therefore, makes it hard for consumers to get their money's worth. This book tries to remedy that situation.

A citizenry better educated on consumer information and issues can greatly **help themselves and all other consumers** live a better quality of life. Consumers must be educated to understand market conditions that can affect them negatively, to know how to go about effectively buying within the American marketplace, and to appreciate the mechanisms to help them change the market while securing, protecting, and asserting their consumer rights. Informed consumer-citizens are needed to help make the American marketplace function more effectively.

Studying consumer economics means that **students will learn to become involved in societal issues** and, in addition to doing well in life, they will do some good. Consumer economics is a subject that encourages students to calculate the benefits and costs of alternatives. I also argue that consumer economics has to do with honor, kindness, decency, fairness, and compassion. Actor and comedian Bill Cosby says when talking about education "It doesn't mean anything if you can't take what you know and make America a better place."

Promotes the Consumer interest

In order to think systematically and properly function as a consumer-citizen, one first needs to understand the concept of consumer interest. The **consumer interest** involves efforts to secure, protect, and assert consumer rights in the marketplace in order that all consumers receive an acceptable quality of goods and services at fair or low prices. The consumer interest is first and foremost concerned with price and quality, and it is also concerned with questions of equity. Accordingly, this book emphasizes fundamental, real-life consumer issues and problems.

Takes a Normative, Pro-Consumer Viewpoint

Experts agree that consumer economics must include emphasis on buying skills, money management, and consumer-citizenship responsibilities. I strongly agree! One cannot become an effective citizen-consumer without being aware of the facts, understanding and applying principles and concepts, developing favorable attitudes and a personal code of ethics, and making a commitment to help create positive changes in the economic marketplace.

This book *rejects* the assumption that consumer economics should be value-free knowledge. There are no correct answers because knowledge and truth are qualitative. Society was created by humans and is subject to change by them. Consumer economics demands that consumers become involved in the quality of lives of the people in society. The **normative approach to consumer economics** asks that students respond to the high expectations that the best of America holds for them.

The viewpoint taken in *Consumer Economic Issues in America* is **pro-consumer and normative**, and it reveals the vested economic interests of businesses, governments, and consumers. This book also is appropriately critical of each interest, and this perspective becomes apparent as the book pursues, illuminates, and illustrates the consumer interest in over 100 consumer issues.

The author pleads guilty to "ranting and raving" on page after page of this book because the reader is being offered dozens of normative perspectives to accept, reject, or consider for a while longer. Your author has lived his life in the world of consumer issues, and he believes that we all can do better. He subscribes to the lyrics of Don Quixote in *The Quest*, "To dream the impossible dream...to fight the unbeatable foe...to fight the impossible fight...to right the unrightable wrong...this is my quest."

Develops informed Citizen-Consumers

Knowledge and information is power. Consumers need to **get that knowledge and information**, and use it to their advantage to make better consumption decisions and to discipline and improve the economic marketplace. Consumers must learn that they have many important responsibilities as well as rights. This empowerment permits consumers to foment change as well as create forces for change. Accordingly, this book seeks to develop informed citizen-consumers who have a right and a duty to protect their own interests as well as those of other consumers. Informed citizen-consumers who make wise decisions in the marketplace ultimately help raise the level of living for all consumers while also contributing to improvement in the morality of the marketplace.

Uses Economic Concepts to Develop Higher-Order Thinking

This book **depends on economics**—presented in an uncomplicated manner—because applying economic concepts is a form of **higher-order thinking**. The term describes the process of learning how to learn. One's success in life depends less on what is learned in school and more on learning how to apply what is known in a world that is constantly changing. Thus, to help develop higher-order thinking skills in consumer economics, it is important for students to find structure in what appears to be disorder. This mode of thinking encourages students to analyze consumer issues, deal effectively with complex public policy proposals, recognize different approaches to thinking and problem solving, and be able to develop multiple solutions when appropriate. A special effort is made to introduce basic economic concepts that anyone can understand as they apply to consumer decision-making situations and analysis of issues.

Uses an Issues Approach

Consumer Economic Issues in America examines basic issues between consumers and sellers. Although the short-run interests of consumers and sellers are different, and often very much at odds, they are interdependent. Consumers and sellers have to cooperate for long-run satisfaction and economic survival. In effect, the consumer movement desires to maintain a "creative friction" between consumers and sellers where both accept certain responsibilities to effectively resolve consumer issues for the betterment of all.

This book focuses on many important consumer issues. It also tries to go **beyond concern about today's "issue of the moment."** An attempt is made to expose the underlying forces, interests, and problems among consumers, sellers, and governments. This book tries to clarify the scope and depth of consumer issues, and to suggest what direction the future likely holds for resolution of the concerns.

The approach is to provide a book that contains adequate treatment of most all consumer interest topics in order that **students are well informed**. Students need to be familiar with a breadth of consumer concerns in order to develop a full understanding of how to effectively protect and promote the consumer interest. Also included is a discussion of the analysis and resolution of consumer issues so that students can appreciate the process of constructive cooperation.

Includes Chapters Plus Appendices

As part of an important conceptual approach, some chapters have one or more appendices. This allows flexibility. The reader can simply read each chapter as presented and gain the essentials in consumer economics. The appendices then supply supplementary material that offers more depth in subject matter or provides additional practical advice.

Goals of This Text

Two broad goals define the efforts in writing *Consumer Economic Issues in America*: (1) to develop competence in understanding consumer economic issues, and (2) to develop confidence in dealing with consumer economic concerns.

To Become Competent

To become competent in understanding consumer economic issues, students must be provided a wide scope of subject matters. I have successfully endeavored to make this the most comprehensive textbook available by including all traditional topics and some of particular importance (such as health and product safety issues). The book attempts to make clear the nature of the issues as well as current and proposed solutions.

A unique learning feature appearing throughout the text to help build competence is called **"Consumer Update."** These are brief inserts, typically two to three paragraphs in length, that provide **up-to-date information** on approximately one hundred consumer problems and issues. Sometimes these offer relevant asides or additional details that add depth to the topics examined. Another competence-building feature is a **"Did You Know?..."** series of boxed inserts offering interesting data related to consumer topics.

Competence also requires an **in-depth examination** of a subject. Students need to understand how the economic marketplace is designed to serve consumers as well as how it sometimes fails to serve them. Students must comprehend the nature of the economic system and its impact on them as consumers. Supportive of this understanding is an underpinning of **technically correct legal information** on dozens of federal, state, and local consumer protection laws and regulations.

This book also helps **bridge the differences in viewpoints** between consumers and sellers. This book encourages rational decision-making. After completing this book, readers should **be prepared to dialogue intelligently** on the issues with government personnel, businesspersons, consumer activists, and "real" everyday consumers.

WHAT STUDENTS SAY IS THE MOST IMPORTANT THING A CONSUMER SHOULD KNOW

Here are the words of some consumer economics students: "I don't have to accept less than adequate products, services, or business/government inattention to the interests of consumers. That goes for me and everyone else out there. I demand better quality and prices, and my fellow consumers deserve the same. The status quo is unacceptable. Together, we can make the institutions of society better attend to the interests of consumers."

To help readers become competent in understanding consumer economic issues, this book **provides some perspectives** on the changing economic marketplace and some **useful tools** for success as consumers. Students need to decide what personal economic goals are important and go about achieving them. Thus, students have to come face to face with their values, goals, and dreams and then give them priorities so that they can manage their choicemaking in those directions. *Consumer Economic Issues in America* helps students learn how to manage their resources to reach their goals. It also can serve as a useful reference for the future.

To Become Confident

To become confident in dealing with consumer economic concerns, students need to be led **through**, not simply **to**, the material. This book attempts to acquaint students with the subject matter **logically** and to offer no unanticipated surprises. Assuming that most students in consumer economics have little background in economics, family economics, and sociology, the book **provides appropriate background knowledge** when necessary. **Numerical examples** are always explained parenthetically, and I have endeavored to discuss the **benefits and costs** of different consumer decisions.

Key words and concepts—which are printed in bold type—are clearly and completely defined when they first occur in the text and again in later chapters, in case the chapters are read out of sequence. Many standard terms are defined too, in recognition of the fact that American English is not the native tongue of many students. This book emphasizes the importance of understanding **new vocabulary and basic concepts**, since these are the tools used to confidently master the principles of consumer economics.

"**Already highlighted**"is a new feature to this edition. Most of the important points that a student would likely highlight with a pen as "important" and "might be on a test" have **already been marked in bold type**. This way the student will be much less likely to miss comprehending

Throughout the text there are a number of **tables, charts, and illustrations** to aid understanding. These make the text more **enjoyable to read** and provide visual clarification of important concepts.

Objectives open each chapter to bolster student confidence in the subject matter of consumer economics by focusing on what is important. The "Review and Summary of Key Terms and Concepts" questions at the end of each chapter emphasize **applying** the concepts and principles to **everyday real-life** consumer decision-making situations. **Principles** that are well learned, particularly in applied situations, have long lives.

To help build personal understandings of the material, a feature is offered called **"Issue for Debate..."** a boxed insert that describes a controversial consumer issue. Information is provided to help the student better comprehend the topic, and each issue is concisely framed for analysis.

A **new feature** to this edition is **Key Topic in Consumer Economics**. These boxed inserts by their title are intended to communicate that the content is critically important, so please pay careful attention. Also new are **400+ websites** listed at the end of each chapter that zero in to provide additional information on topics contained in each chapter.

As students **better understand themselves, their economic and political belief systems and why and how they believe what they do,** they develop more expertise in analyzing consumer economic issues. These students become more **informed citizen-consumers** who are better able to advocate the consumer interest.

Organization and Topical Coverage

I surveyed many instructors across the country and conducted focus groups to discover what they wanted in a quality textbook on this subject. The clearest message I heard was that instructors wanted a straightforward book to **emphasize the fundamental consumer economic issues affecting all consumers**.

Consumer Economic Issues in America has a bias toward consumer economic issues that help the American marketplace become more **competitive, free, and fair** for the benefit of sellers and consumers alike. I believe in supporting **the self-regulatory efforts** of business and at the same time looking carefully at what government is doing and can do for consumers. This book emphasizes **understanding our American economic system, the concepts of consumer sovereignty and the consumer interest, evaluative criteria** by which products and services are judged, tools for living, how to analyze issues, money management, and factors that affect buying decisions. This book includes consideration of **environmental issues** because many consumer decisions in the marketplace have environmental aspects which are thought to be important. This book provides coverage of the **consumer protection efforts by federal, state, and local governments**.

As can be seen in the table of contents, this book approaches topical coverage in a manner that provides a **full explanation of the fundamentals** of a topic before commencing further study. While each of the eighteen chapters has a place in the overall sequence, **each**

chapter also is complete in itself. Thus, the chapters can be rearranged to be read in another developmental sequence with minimal loss of comprehension.

Part One provides an introduction to consumer economics by offering **Some Perspectives**. Chapter 1 focuses on the question "What is the consumer interest?" Surprisingly, no other textbook addresses this question meaningfully. Chapter 2 provides an overview of the problems, concerns, and issues faced by the consumer movement over the past 100 years, and suggests future directions for these changing times.

Part Two, **Facing Consumer Problems Successfully**, contains three chapters. Chapter 3 discusses the rights and responsibilities of consumers as well as the remedies available to consumers when seeking to correct any wrongs encountered. Chapter 4 provides a virtual encyclopedia of information on avoiding rip-offs and frauds in the American marketplace. Chapter 5 offers an "appendix format" of about 70 key laws and regulations that protect consumers and help them obtain redress.

Part Three, **The Challenging Marketplace**, contains five chapters. Chapter 6 examines capitalism and how resources are allocated in the unique American marketplace. Chapter 7 details a number of economic concepts critical to consumer success. Both chapters 6 and 7 are especially useful for readers who may not have completed a course in economics. Chapter 8 examines consumers in a global economic marketplace, as it surveys the related topics of free trade, industrial policy, regional trading agreements, and the international consumer movement. Chapter 9 examines the vital function of government in regulating economic interests while Chapter 10 overviews government regulation of the interests of consumers.

Part Four, **Information Processing**, has three chapters. Chapter 11 presents an introduction to the breadth of current concerns of consumer interest and offers a framework to help analyze and resolve consumer issues. Chapter 12 focuses on rational decision-making and how this process is affected by factors such as concerns about the environment and advertising. Chapter 13 provides a detailed illustration of the planned buying process for major expenditures, using an automobile purchase as an example.

Part Five, consisting of five chapters, focuses on **Consumer Economic Issues**. Chapter 14 is aimed at helping students better understand the food issues affecting consumers and how to deal with them, and it explains the laws, regulations, and agencies protecting the consumer interest. Health care issues are examined in Chapter 15, including the effects of using tobacco and alcohol.

No consumer economics book would be complete without a chapter focusing on product safety issues, the subject of Chapter 16. In this chapter, the effectiveness of two government agencies is scrutinized: the Consumer Product Safety Commission and the National Highway Traffic Safety Commission. Chapter 17 focuses on consumer problems and such issues in banking, credit, and housing, as basic banking, the infamous savings and loan scandal, redlining, and other forms of access discrimination. Chapter 18 examines consumer problems and issues in insurance and investments, including ideas to confront overpricing of automobile insurance, what happens when insurance companies go bankrupt, and some dangers to the employer-sponsored pension plans of working consumers.

Revisions and Learning Aids

Hundreds of substantive changes were made to the eighth edition to make the book more up-to-date, focus more tightly on consumer issues, facilitate student readability, and shorten its length. More than a thousand sources were utilized.

- **"Updates"** were made to every chapter to reflect these changing times. Substantive revisions and **new material** exists on the following topics in the chapters listed below:

  Consumer Rights, Responsibilities and Remedies: privacy in consumer transactions is under threat; boycotts and class-action lawsuits;

  Rip-offs and Frauds in the Marketplace: economic fraud is rampant among big corporations; Internet frauds and scams; identity theft insurance rip-off; income tax refund anticipation loan rip-off; unfair or deceptive advertising; hidden product prices that are deceptive; title loans; moving company state laws;

  Laws that Help Consumers: do-not-call registry; bank insurance sales regulations; recent antitrust examples;

  The Capitalistic American Marketplace: capitalism is full of shortcomings;

  Consumers in the Global Market: the future of trade and globalization; global market reforms; income inequality; profit protection for the sugar industry;

  Government Regulation of Economic Interests: historical culture of U.S. government regulation; ways big business gets government to help them overcharge consumers; unfair methods, acts and deceptive practices;

  Government Regulation of Consumer Interests: regulations are negotiated; how lawmakers strengthen consumer protection laws or undercut and weaken them;

  Policymaking and Consumer Issues: do corporations own American politics?

  Decision-making: global warming and the Asian brown cloud;

  The Planned Buying Process: auto dealer ploys to get you to pay more money; compromise effect of buying;

  Food Issues: questionable and confusing food selling practices; food products that deceive; vendor hush-hush payments; organic food labeling;

  Health Care Issues: young people overpay; reform proposals; medical malpractice damages; dietary supplements, lies and dangers;

  Product Safety Issues: sellers of unsafe products; needed product safety regulations; needed vehicle safety regulations; product liability lawsuits under assault by conservatives;

  Banking, Housing and Credit Issues: ugly fees and penalties for bouncing checks; banks hate credit unions; the unbanked; privacy in consumer transactions; late fees, penalty interest rates and overcharges; card blocking may create penalties; new bankruptcy law; predatory lending; kickback fees and upcharges;

  Insurance and Investment Issues: non-competitive insurance industry; buying insurance on the Internet; pay-per-mile auto insurance; fraud and thievery in investments; retirement plans at risk;

- **"Objectives"** begin each chapter.

- **"Narrative Introductions"** give a rationale for study and preview the contents of each chapter.

- **"Already Highlighted"** is a **new feature** to this edition. Most of the important points that a student would likely highlight with a **pen as "important" and "might be on a test"** have **already been marked in bold type**. This way the student will be much less likely to miss comprehending key points.

- **"End-of-Chapter Review of Key Terms and Concepts"** that allows the student to **apply** the concepts presented and gain confidence in using the knowledge outside the classroom. Students responding to these questions will have reviewed **all important**

concepts in each chapter. These are appropriate for instructors to use in class when orally reviewing the material.

- **"End-of-Chapter 'What Do You Think?' Questions"** offer three or four ideas to consider in view of reading the chapter. Students respond with their emotions, values and critical thinking.

- **"End-of-Chapter 'Useful Resources for Consumers'"** offers **over 400 websites**. Many more websites are cited in the chapter narrative, too.

- New **"Key Topic in Consumer Economics"** are boxed inserts that by their title are intended to communicate to the reader that *"this content is critically important, so please pay careful attention."*

- New **"Top Ten"** Lists about the **big corporations that have defrauded and ripped off** consumers. Topics include:

  "Top Ten Corporations Caught Lying to Investors"
  "Top Ten Greedy Credit Card Companies"
  "Top Ten Corporations Caught Using False Advertising"
  "Top Ten Corporate Price-Fixers"
  "Top Ten Corporations that Lied to Fleece Consumers"
  "Top Ten Sellers of Unsafe Products"
  "Top Ten Product Liability Lawsuits"

- **"Issue for Debate..."** is a series of boxed inserts on controversial consumer issues. Information is provided to help the student better understand the topic, and each debate issue is concisely framed for analysis. Examples include:

  "Sealed Court Records By Greedy Corporations Should be Prohibited by Law"
  "Genetically Engineered Food Should be Labeled as Such"
  "Schools Should Publish Quality Indicators for Students"
  "The State Lottery Rip-off is Against the Consumer Interest"
  "Americans Should Reject Materialism"
  "Raise Taxes on Cigarettes to Discourage Consumption"
  "Motorcycle Safety Helmets Should be Mandatory"
  "Food Health Claims Should Be Better Regulated"
  "The U.S. Should Require Daytime Running Lights on Vehicles"

- **"Consumer Update" Boxed Inserts** spotlight important information and present it in a concise manner. They add emphasis and stimulate interest as they offer excellent tips, identify consumer problems, focus on important concepts in consumer economics, and provide observations about society.

  Boxes that offer *"excellent tips"* **include:**

  "CLUE Reports on Homes"
  "Estimate Your Retirement Needs"
  "The Poor Pay More for All Financial Services"
  "Your FICO Credit Score"
  "Bad Credit Boosts Insurance Costs"
  "Consolidate Student Loans"
  "Bad Credit Records Plague Consumers, Especially African-Americans
  "Alternatives for Getting Out of Debt"
  "Government Housing Program Assists the Poor and Some New College Graduates"
  "Medical Privacy Protections"
  "Judging Quality with Brand Names, Store Brands and Generic Brands"

"Dealer Ploys to Get You to Pay More Money"
"Buy Textbooks on the Internet"
"Be Aware of Identity Theft"
"Gripe Sites for Complaints on the Internet"
"Rule #1 of Life–When in Doubt About a Purchase, Put It on Your Credit Card"
"Vehicle Rollover Risk Ratings"
"Get a Copy of the *Consumer's Action Handbook*"
"How to Successfully Move a Consumer Issue Forward"
"Toy Safety Recommendations for Gift Givers"
"Do You Have to Mail in the Warranty-Registration Card?"
"How to Get Out of a Contract"
"Gifts and Prizes...What They Really Are"
"Some Rebate Cards and Frequent-Buyer Programs are Good Deals"
"Questions to Ask Your Health Care Provider"
"Products with the Largest Advertising Expenses"

Boxes that identify *"consumer problems"* include:

"Advertising Drugs: Illegal, Unethical or Both?"
"A Dozen Ways Big Business Gets Government to Help Them Overcharge Consumers"
"Advertising Food to Kids on Television"
"Privacy in Consumer Transactions is Under Threat"
"Food Safety"
"False Auto Price Advertising"
"Telemarketing Crooks Can Get Your Cash"
"Many Infomercials are Rip-offs"
"Bridgestone/Firestone Tires/Ford Explorer SUV Tire Blowouts Scandal Shows that NHTSA Needs More Powers to Police the Market"
"SUVs Should be Efficient or Taxed, Just Like Automobiles"
"Women and African-Americans Pay Higher Prices"
"Young Shoppers are Discriminated Against"
"Job-Search Companies: Rip-offs?"
"Classified Ads are Full of Lies"
"The Five Biggest Lies Told to Consumers"
"Referral Rebate Sales are Illegal Pyramid Schemes"
"Chain Letters are Illegal Pyramid Schemes"
"Telemarketing Recovery Room Scams"
"Unhealthy Theater Popcorn"
"Community Reinvestment Act Ratings"
"Global Warming and the Asian Brown Cloud"
"Automobile Bumpers Remain Weak"
"Cartels Overcharge Consumers"
"Poor Consumers are Disadvantaged in the Marketplace"
"The Poor Pay More for Food"
"Examples of Discrimination"
"Responsibilities of Consumers in Product Safety"

Boxes that focus on *"important concepts"* in consumer economics include:

"Ralph Nader, the Nation's Leading Consumer Advocate"
"Consumer Protections Threatened by Trade Agreements"
"Consumers Sometimes Lack 'Standing' to Sue"
"Consumer Power Disciplines and Improves the Marketplace"
"Antitrust Tools to Promote Fair Competition"
"On the Difference Between an Environmentalist and a Consumer Advocate"
"Coalition for Environmentally Responsive Economies"

"The Costs of Government Regulation are Paid by Consumers"
"The Historical Culture of U.S. Government Regulation"
"General Motor's Price on Fire Deaths Used to be $2.40"
"Indicators of Economic Confidence"
"Why Learn About Food and Health?"

Boxes that offer on *"observations about society"* **include:**

"Consumers Accept the False Promises of Television Commercials"
"Taxes are Low on Low- and Middle-income People"
"Social Change is an Evolutionary Process"
"Consumer Movement is Strong"
"Capitalism is Full of Shortcomings"
"Bush's Gigantic Federal Budget Deficits"
"Capital Flight Hurts Less Developed Countries"
"Developing Countries Make Good Trading Partners"
"The U.S. Exports 'Its Values' Around the World"
"Why Government Takes on So Many Jobs"
"Some Things that Government Does Right!"
"Communitarian: A Political Ideology *Between* Conservatism and Liberalism"
"Humorist P. J. O'Rourke on Democrats and Republicans"
"Why Do Some People Persist in Harming Their Health"

"Did You Know?..." is a series of **boxed inserts** that offer interesting **insights and data** related to consumer topics:

"Insurance Company Don't"
"Divorced Women's Right to Ex-husband's Pension"
"How to Opt Out of Junk Calls, Mail and E-mail"
"New Bankruptcy Law"
"What Some Confusing Warranty Phrases Really Mean"
"Your Insurance May Already Cover the Liability for Lost Credit and Debit Cards"
"How to Get a Copy of Your Credit Report"
"Refuse to Pay Punitive Interest Rates"
"Going to College has Opportunity Costs"
"Safety Ratings and Repair Cost Estimates Available"
"How Much Does It Cost to Drive?"
"Take the Auto Dealer's Cash Rebate or a Low Interest Rate Loan?"
"Vehicle Death Rates"
"How to Report Discrimination"

- **"An Economic Focus On..."** is a series of boxed inserts that describe and illustrate a **single economic concept** important to understanding the chapter. These explanations—written by experts from the U.S., Canada and China—are presented in a **non-technical manner** so that all students can understand the essence being presented. Examples include:

"Discrimination Harms Consumers and Sellers"
"Stages in the Economic Cycle"
"The Propensity to Consume"
"Indifference Curve and Budget Line Analysis"
"The Consumer Interest in International Trade"
"How the Supply of and Demand for Labor Affect Wage Rates in Developing Countries"
"China's Consumer Movement"
"Large-Scale Production and Price Regulation"
"Information Search in the Buying Process"
"The Supply and Demand for Housing"

"Usury Laws and the Supply and Demand for Consumer Credit"
"The Life Cycle and Permanent Income Hypotheses"
"Standard and Level of Consumption and Living"
"The International Consumer Movement and the Consumer Interest"
"The Medical Care Market has Characteristics that Make It Difficult to Reform"
"The Geistfeld Model of Consumer Decision-Making"

- **"Key Terms and Concepts"** are reinforced in several ways. All key terms—over 1,200—are **highlighted in bold type** the first time they are used, then they are clearly defined! In the index, the key words and the numbers of the pages on which they are defined and discussed are in **bold** in the index.

- **"An Index"** appears at the end of the book and it is the most thorough of all books on the market—over 3,000 entries in all.

- **"Headings and Subheadings"** in bold print, four levels in all, are used to improve readability and reinforce the organization of the topics.

Supplements to Text

Accompanying this text is an **Instructor's Manual with Test Bank**, **Multi-media PowerPoint[1] Presentations** for *All* Textbook Chapters, and a special **Powerpoint Presentation on Consumer Frauds and Rip-offs** suitable for classes as well as general audiences. The **Instructor's Manual with Test Bank** contains several components:

- **"Organizing the Course"** Suggested course syllabi and outlines are offered to emphasize four different approaches to the subject matter, descriptions of eight methods of instruction and five types of reports/projects, suggestions on how to guide students who are doing class presentations, and numerous audio-visual and print resources for instructors.

- **"Computerized Test Bank"** of over 2,000 new and revised objective questions from the *Instructor's Manual with Test Bank* available to adopters.

- **"Answers to End-of-chapter Questions."**

---

[1] Microsoft® PowerPoint® Presentation Graphics Program is a registered trademark of Microsoft Corporation. Hereafter, this proprietary trademark is indicated by following the capitalization style used by the manufacturer.

Acknowledgments

I realize that an instructional text of this breadth and depth could not be created without the assistance of many people. A number of reviewers offered helpful suggestions and criticisms of the text while it was being developed and revised. The text has unquestionably been strengthened by their contributions. I am deeply appreciative of the generous assistance for the suggestions given by:

Ralph H. Alexander, Jr., former Executive Director, National Advertising Review Board
Anne W. Bailey, Professor, Miami University
William Bailey, Professor, University of Arkansas
Peggy S. Berger, Professor, Colorado State University
D. Douglas Blanke, Office of the Attorney General of Minnesota
Mary Ann Block, Professor, Tarleton State University
Jan Bowman, Professor, Louisiana State University
Stephen J. Brobeck, Executive Director, Consumer Federation of America
Gregory E. Brown, Professor, Central Missouri State University
James Brown, Director, Center for Consumer Affairs, University of Wisconsin
John R. Burton, Professor, University of Utah
Patrick Butler, Director, Insurance Project, National Organization for Women
Marilyn L. Cantwell, Professor, Louisiana State University
Nina Collins, Professor, Bradley University
Ellen Daniel, Professor, Harding University
Joye J. Dillman, Professor, Washington State University
Elizabeth Dolan, Professor, University of New Hampshire
Judith Durrand, Professor, University of Houston
Sidney W. Eckert, Professor, Appalachian State University

Judy A. Farris, Professor, South Dakota State University

Linda Kirk Fox, Professor, University of Idaho

Stephen Gold, Editor, Tax Foundation

Victoria Marie Gribschaw, Professor, Seton Hill College

Gong-Soog Hong, Professor, Utah State University

Virginia Junk, Professor, University of Idaho

Lauren Leach, Professor, State University of New York College at Oneonta

Irene Leech, Professor, Virginia Tech

Patricia Luvano, University of Michigan, National Election Studies Center for Political Research

Meredith M. Layer (deceased), Senior Vice President of Public Policy (deceased), American Express

Mary Ellen Fise, Director, Product Safety, Consumer Federation of America

Vicki Schram Fitzsimmons, Professor Emeritus, University of Illinois

Raymond E. Forgue, Professor, University of Kentucky

Steve Hamm, Administrator, Department of Consumer Affairs, South Carolina

Barbara Heinzerling, Professor, University of Akron

Donna Iams, Professor, University of Arizona

Jane Kolodinsky, Professor, University of Vermont

Virginia H. Knauer, Special Assistant for Consumer Affairs to President Ronald W. Reagan, President Gerald R. Ford, and President Richard M. Nixon

Jeffrey H. Krasnow, Attorney at Law, Roanoke, Virginia

Fran C. Lawrence, Professor, Louisiana State University

Carole J. Makela, Professor, Colorado State University

Drew E. Mattson, Professor, Anoka-Ramsey Community College

Martin Machowsky, Vice President, Issue Dynamics Incorporated

Carol B. Meeks, Professor and Dean, Iowa State University

James L. Morrison, Professor, University of Delaware

Kathleen Morrow, Professor, Syracuse University

Richard L.D. Morse (deceased), Professor Emeritus, Kansas State University

Martin Nyberg, Instructor, Virginia Tech

Jeffrey O'Connell, Professor, University of Virginia

Joseph G. Painter, Jr., Attorney at Law, Blacksburg, Virginia

Claudia Peck, Professor and Associate Dean, University of Kentucky

Esther Peterson (deceased), Special Assistant for Consumer Affairs to President John F. Kennedy, President Lyndon B. Johnson, and President Jimmy Carter

R. David Pittle, Technical Director, Consumers Union

Aimee D. Prawitz, Professor, Northern Illinois University

Mary E. Pritchard, Professor and Department Head, Northern Illinois University

Warren J. Prunella, Chief Economist, Consumer Product Safety Commission

S. Lee Richardson, Jr., Professor and G. Maxwell Armor Eminent Scholar, University of Baltimore

Mary Ellen Rider, Professor, University of Nebraska

Margaret Sanik, Professor, The Ohio State University

David Schmeltzer, Associate Director of Compliance and Administrative Litigation, Consumer Product Safety Commission

Jane Schuchardt, Program Director, United States Department of Agriculture Cooperative Extension Service

William B. Schultz, Senior Attorney, Public Citizen Litigation Group

Mark Silbergeld, Director of the Washington Office, Consumers Union of the United States

Mary Frances Stephanz, former Executive Director, Better Business Bureau of Western Virginia

James S. Turner, Attorney, Swankin and Turner

Sue Unger, Professor, Pittsburgh State University
Clinton Warne, Professor, Cleveland State University
Dorothy West, Professor, Michigan State University
Lynn B. White, Professor, The Texas A&M University System
Richard Widdows, Professor, The Ohio State University
Jing-jian Xiao, Professor, The University of Rhode Island

A number of experts have taken considerable time to generously contribute to this book by writing boxed inserts titled "An Appendix Issue," "A Consumer Update On...," "An Economic Focus On...," or selected pages of text narrative. Each has strengthened the text. The insightful and generous contributors include:

Patrick Butler, Director, Insurance Project, National Organization for Women
Raymond E. Forgue, Professor, University of Kentucky
Helen Foster, Professor, State University of New York at Oneonta
Lucy S. Garman, Registered Dietician, Orlando, Florida
Mohamed Abdel Ghany, Professor, University of Alabama
Paul S. Forbes, President, The Forbes Group
Loren V. Geistfeld, Professor, The Ohio State University
Sherman Hanna, Professor, The Ohio State University
Gong-Soog Hong, Professor, Utah State University
Robert Kerton, Professor, University of Waterloo
Joan Kinney, Professor, University of Wisconsin-Madison
Joan Koonce Lewis, Professor, University of Georgia
Carole J. Makela, Professor, Colorado State University
Julia Marlowe, Professor, The University of Georgia
Robert N. Mayer, Professor, The University of Utah
E. Scott Maynes, Professor Emeritus, Cornell University
Tamra Minor, Assistant to the Vice President, The Ohio State University
W. Kurt Schumacher, Board of Governors of the Federal Reserve System
Mark Silbergeld, Director, Washington Office, Consumers Union of the United States
Carol Ann Walker, Personal Finance Manager/Air Force Aid Officer, Peterson Air Force Base, Colorado
Jing-jian Xiao, Professor, The University of Rhode Island
Zhiming Zhang, Economist, People's Republic of China

In addition, I wish to thank the thousands of students who for the past thirty years have had the opportunity to read, critique, and provide inputs for *Consumer Economic Issues in America*. Some have written letters and e-mails offering suggestions as well as criticism, and I deeply appreciate each communication.

Also deserving of thanks are the many instructors of consumer economics who have been generous enough to share their views on what should and should not be included in a high-quality textbook. A number of suggestions have come from directors of **Centers for Economic Education**, directors of state **Offices of Consumer Affairs**, and **Media Consumer Affairs Experts**, especially News 5 reporter **Elizabeth Owen** in Nashville, Tennessee. I have attempted to meet the collective needs in every way possible.

Appreciation is also due to the mentors of my academic and professional life: *John Binnion, William Boast*, and *Ronald West*. By their examples in life and collegiate instruction, they have given me motivation, dedication, direction, and the tools to seek excellence. Thanks are due also to *William McDivitt* for allowing me to register for college with less than a dollar in my pocket on two separate occasions. Ray Forgue always deserves my thanks for both his long friendship and his brilliant questions that get my mind thinking at a higher level.

Finally, *Lucy S. Garman* has helped me clarify my thoughts on many consumer issues (especially in nutrition and health) over our candlelit, evening meals together every night. She has regularly added to the quality of this book and my life. As my partner forever, she has been wonderful in her genuine support of my passion to write *Consumer Economic Issues in America.*

Former *Senator Charles Percy* once wrote of this book that, "*Consumer Economic Issues in America* is a challenge. It is controversial. It is informative. It is factual. It is honest. It is a book to be selected by instructors who care deeply about their students and want them to read newspapers, watch public television, listen to National Public Radio, and become involved in understanding issues of concern to consumers around the world." Senator Percy is right!

I believe that the approach of this book will make the reader an informed consumer who in turn will help shape a continually improving world for others. I also believe that this is an interesting text that students will enjoy reading. I hope I have succeeded because I have the strong bias that students need to learn consumer economic concepts and principles thoroughly so that they make better individual consumer decisions. This will improve their personal levels of living as well as the lives of other consumers.

E.T.G.

P.S. Dear Students: If you are going to save any of your college textbooks, be certain to save this one. Especially valuable are the chapters on consumer protection laws and how to remedy wrongs against consumers. Also, you may want to present the book as a gift to a significant other, spouse, or parent. My e-mail address is tgarman@bellsouth.net.

Foreword by Virginia H. Knauer*

We are a nation of nearly 300 million consumers. Whatever type of work we do, wherever our homes may stand, whoever we are, we are all consumers. Although our needs and desires are diverse, this common role causes us to share many interests. Underlying these is the sincere belief that our moral and ethical consumer rights are as important as our legal rights. We expect equal standing with sellers in marketplace transactions. And we hope for a marketplace that is guided by principles, rules, and standards of good conduct, whether fashioned by business or government. In short, we want to shop in a marketplace that knows right from wrong.

We are also realists. We recognize a natural tension between consumers, who want the best value for their money, and sellers, who want to make as much profit as they can and stay in business. Yet we know that without consumers to buy products and services, there is no market for the products and services that manufacturers and sellers promote. So we can see that if we become informed consumers, if we learn and exercise our marketplace rights, then we can help shape the competitive marketplace to meet our needs. This, then, is how we pursue our consumer interest.

Consumer Economic Issues in America represents a breakthrough in communicating to the public perspectives of what the consumer interest is truly about. It looks broadly at the important responsibilities of business, government, private voluntary groups, and individual consumers in helping to promote and protect the consumer interest. It provides insights into the essence of consumerism and presents both its history and a glimpse of its future. It explains the government decision-making process so that consumers can become more involved in the formation of public policy. It provides useful everyday tools consumers can use to help analyze consumer issues and better understand their own rational (and sometimes irrational) decision-making. And it details many key consumer responsibilities that accompany consumer rights in the marketplace.

The overwhelming majority of businesses in America are trying honestly and diligently to meet the needs of consumers today. Increasing competition from foreign marketers, better-informed consumers, and rapid developments in advanced technology—in short, the realities of the modern marketplace dictate this posture. Evidence of this long-term trend is found in the increased emphasis on customer service, proactive complaint-handling, better-quality products, and the development of partnerships between consumers, business, and government aimed at searching out and meeting consumers' needs.

When fraud does occur, however, the consumer must be well prepared to spot it, avoid it, and help prevent it from victimizing others. The material in the chapters on frauds and misrepresentations is frightening upon first reading. The staggering number and variety of fraudulent schemes are limited only by the creativity of the scam artists behind them. However, the purpose is not to frighten, but to enlighten; to boost consumers' awareness of the signs of fraud so that they will do a little checking before they believe an offer that sounds too good to be true. This will reduce the number of people who fall victim to these scams and, in turn, the number of scams out there.

Another important element of this book is its detailed attention to the many current consumer issues. No book of this type would be complete without a detailed discussion of food and health issues. American consumers want to know about such topics as how to acquire good eating habits, how to use nutritional and diet-food labeling, where to learn about additives in food, which government agencies and programs are designed to help consumers, how to find information about the services of alternative health care providers, when to buy generic drugs, and how tobacco and alcohol products affect the body. *Consumer Economic Issues in America* addresses these and many other topics.

Indeed, dozens of important issues are examined in this book. It is not necessarily a neutral presentation, and perhaps not all would subscribe to the author's endorsements. But this book strives to offer all sides of the issues. For instance, the importance of self-regulation in product safety and effectiveness is made clear along with suggested appropriate roles for governments and consumers. This book also carefully examines the issues of benefit-cost analysis, product liability laws, disclosure laws, warnings, and ingredient labeling; it discusses criticisms of product safety efforts. The same degree of depth is seen in every chapter of *Consumer Economic Issues in America*.

This book plays an important role in advancing the consumer interest. It can be a major contribution to our universal goal of a competitive marketplace that works, a nation of businesses and governments that are able to satisfy consumers, and a country of consumers who are able and willing to cooperate with businesses and governments in positive partnership efforts where consumer interests are paramount in the marketplace.

If you are a student, I recommend this book to you. And when you have finished reading it, I urge you to further your studies with a look at consumerism in other nations. Our marketplace is increasingly global in nature, and the decisions and issues affecting governments in far corners of the world—whether they concern trade policy, agricultural policy, safety regulations, or whatever—have everyday implications for the marketplace choices we enjoy in America. Once this becomes clear, you will begin to see that consumerism changes and matures as economies develop. And you will recognize that an adequate consumer education requires more than one course. It is a lifelong process. This excellent book is but a strong beginning for your own consumer education.

Virginia H. Knauer

*Virginia H. Knauer is former White House Special Assistant for Consumer Affairs for President Ronald W. Reagan, President Gerald R. Ford, and President Richard M. Nixon. Mrs. Knauer is currently a member of Anderson, Benjamin, Read & Haney, a Washington, D.C. consulting firm that boasts a nationally recognized consumer relations program.

About the Author E. Thomas Garman

E. Thomas Garman is an advisor and author, based in Orlando, Florida, and Professor Emeritus at Virginia Tech, where he concluded a long teaching career and served as executive director of the university's National Institute for Personal Finance Employee Education. He also was a Fellow in the university's Center for Organizational and Technological Advancement. Research studies conducted under his direction have won seven national awards.

He received his bachelor's and master's degrees in business administration from the University of Denver and his doctorate in economic education from Texas Tech University. Garman's employment includes work for a United States Senator in Washington, retail sales management in Colorado, and management of an economic development project in West Africa. He taught in 8 states and 3 countries, including 15 workshops for 10 universities, and several "Consumer Issues in Washington" classes in the nation's capital. Virginia Tech recognized him an excellent teacher.

Garman is an elected Distinguished Fellow in both the American Council on Consumer Interests and the Association for Financial Counseling and Planning Education. He served as president of those organizations as well as of the Consumer Education and Information Association of Virginia. Garman was awarded the Louis M. Linxwiler Award by the National Foundation for Credit Counseling for his outstanding contributions to consumer credit education. Garman received the Stewart E. Lee Consumer Education Award from the American Council on Consumer Interests in recognition of his lifetime achievements in consumer education.

Garman has served on the Consumer Advisory Council of the Board of Governors of the Federal Reserve System, Board of Trustees for the National Foundation for Credit Counseling, Consumer Credit Counseling Service of Southwest Virginia, National Advertising Review Board, the National Advisory Council on Financial Planning for the International Board of Standards and Practices for Certified Financial Planners, and the Food and Drug Administration. He has served on the board of directors of the American National Standards Institute and a number of other organizations.

Garman has authored 200 academic articles and 28 books, including *Consumer Economic Issues in America, Regulation and Consumer Protection, Rip-offs and Frauds: How to Avoid and How to Get Away* (winner of a journalism award), *The Mathematics of Personal Financial Planning* (all published by International Thomson/Southwestern Publishing), and *Personal Finance* and *Personal Finance Handbook* (both with Houghton Mifflin).

His work has been featured in hundreds of publications, including *Journal of Consumer Affairs, Advancing the Consumer Interest, Journal of Consumer Studies, Financial Counseling and Planning, Journal of Compensation and Benefits, HR Today, Employment Relations Today, Ticker, USA Today, Wall Street Journal, The Washington Post, Los Angeles Times, The Chicago Tribune, Reader's Digest,* and *U.S. News & World Report.* He appeared on National Public Radio and *NBC Nightly News.*

Garman and his wife, Lucy, live in Orlando, Florida, and they stay in contact with their children, their respective spouses and significant others, and grandchildren: Dana, Jim, Jeff, Julia, Scott, David, Alieu, Isatou, Kumba, Alimatou, Ousman. Garman may be e-mailed at tgarman@bellsouth.net. See www.EThomasGarman.net for research, speeches and publications.

Part One:

SOME PERSPECTIVES

Chapter 1

What is the Consumer Interest?

OBJECTIVES

After reading this chapter, you should be able to

1. Describe the basic economic activities performed by consumers.

2. Discuss why consumers are not sovereign in the economic marketplace.

3. Realize that consumer problems exist in a world of imperfectly competitive markets.

4. Understand that the consumer interest is about value for money and equity for all consumers.

5. Recognize eight important consumer rights.

6. Recognize that the consumer interest is a special-interest group.

7. Appreciate how the interests of consumers differ from the interests of business and the public.

In order to understand better the consumer interest and your role in it, you need to understand what the consumer interest is. Many confuse the narrow interests of consumers with the broader concerns of the general public. It is crucial for those teaching or studying consumer economic issues, as well as for those working in the consumer interest, to have a clear understanding of the perspectives because the consumer interest and the public interest differ sharply. In addition, it is important for all of us to understand our multiple roles in the social-political-economic marketplace as well as know something about the other major players in the economy.

This chapter begins by reviewing how consumers satisfy their economic goals in the economy: earning, consuming, borrowing, saving, investing, taxpaying and utilizing. The question of consumer sovereignty versus producer sovereignty is then examined. Next, the problems of consumers are examined in the context of a world where the interests of sellers and consumers will always conflict. Then the consumer interest is differentiated from both business and public interests through an examination of a price-quality continuum, a useful but incomplete perspective. The consumer interest is then carefully defined, explained and more correctly viewed in a value-for-money/equity model. How consumers attempt to achieve their consumer interests is by securing, protecting, and asserting their several consumer rights. It then becomes apparent that the consumer interest is a special-interest group and consumers themselves must pursue their own consumer interest objectives because no one else can do it as well as they can. Further clarifications are also made on the interests of consumers, governments and businesses, especially in a capitalistic form of an economic system. The chapter concludes with some reflections about how consumers go about pursuing their special interests.

Upon completion of this chapter, you should clearly understand the agendas of business, government and the public. Once the consumer interest is clear in your mind—value for money and equity for all consumers—you can then spend the rest of your life looking out for your own and your fellow consumers' interests.

Economic Activities Performed by Consumers

The American marketplace is where we satisfy our personal economic goals. It is a **market price system** where the economy is driven by supply and demand and that is what determines which goods and services are produced and the prices at which they are sold. Individuals in society play three roles in economic life: (1) citizen, (2) worker, and (3) consumer. As a citizen, you are expected to be concerned about policies and laws that affect your country, community, family, and others in society and the world. As a worker, you are probably concerned about having a job, employment conditions, and future growth of income. As a consumer, you are likely interested in spending, saving, investing, and the rising cost of goods.

As we go through life, each of us is **constantly engaged in economic activities**, such as earning an income, spending money on food and borrowing money to finance an automobile or a home. We can seek and reach our personal economic goals in the marketplace more easily when we understand and use a few useful concepts related to our economic activities.

A **consumer** is one who acquires goods and services for ultimate consumption or use by a person, family, or household. Consumers go shopping and purchase goods and services in their efforts to accomplish their own economic goals. The ultimate purpose of all economic activity is to satisfy consumer wants. **Satisfaction** is defined individually by each person when his or her desires and needs are fulfilled or gratified. Consumers must be involved in economic activities in order to accomplish their personal goals and achieve satisfactions.

People's personal economic **goals are often in conflict**, and sometimes consumers must make difficult decisions among alternatives. For example, as an earner, you may want to demand a higher salary. This conflicts with your desire to not spend too much because prices are pushed up by increasing labor costs. While you may want the government to put ceilings on interest rates for consumer loans to reduce your borrowing costs, this conflicts with your desire to earn a high interest rate on your savings account. The economic activities performed by consumers are described below.

Earning

Earning, a basic economic activity for most people, is the gain derived from the performance of service, labor, or work, such as the salary or wages of a person, the profits of a business enterprise, and returns from an investment. Earning is production in the marketplace. The median **household income** in the U.S. is about $43,000 (that is, half of all the 110 million households had incomes above $42,200 and half below). Since consumer goods and services cost money, most people work to earn money income so that they can spend.[1] American earners are tremendous producers of goods and services. The typical U.S. worker puts in 39.5 hours a week and has a vacation of two weeks. Workers in other major industrial nations work fewer hours per week (Germany [31], France [33], United Kingdom [34], Japan [37]).

Consuming

Consumption is the expenditure made by consumers and nonprofit institutions for goods and services. At the consumer level, consumption is the acquisition and utilization of goods, such as commodities and services, directly to satisfy wants. This is a natural and fundamental act by consumers.

Consumers are the driving force in the American economy, making up **65 percent of total spending**. Business investment is 18 percent and government spending (excluding services provided like welfare or Social Security payments) makes up 17 percent. Americans are the greatest consumers in the world as they use (and dispose) enormous quantities of goods and services. This high level of consumption, more than $6 trillion annually, occurs because the level of living for so many people is quite high.

Consumption by consumers helps **provide guidance** to the economy. More than 200 years ago, philosopher Adam Smith wrote that "Consumption is the sole end and purpose of production and the interest of the producer ought to be attended to, only so far as it may be necessary for promoting that of the consumer."

---

[1] Household production, while extremely valuable to the family and to society in general, does not produce money income or earnings in the traditional economic sense.

It is in their role as consumers that Americans typically consume for 70 to 80 years of their lifetimes, while their economic role of earning often lasts for less than 40 years. (During the earliest years of life, when they are too young to work, the sole task of humans is to consume.) Consumers, therefore, by the observable essence of their marketplace behavior, are **strongly interested** in pursuing their consumer interest in seeking an acceptable quality of goods and services at fair or low prices.

Utilizing

Utilizing can be defined as using for a certain purpose. In an economic sense, it is effectively making use of all of one's economic and non-economic resources. Utilizing involves disposing of material resources, such as money and property, as well as using up the nonmaterial resource of time. Utilizing also involves the reaping of benefits of personal economic activities. In our affluent American society, time becomes scarcer with increasing material consumption. In economist Staffam Burenstam Linder's classic book *The Harried Leisure Class*, he observed that consumers have time pressures to earn more money to buy more goods, which then take, care, and maintenance. Consumers are always faced with **choices and tradeoffs** on how to effectively utilize.

Borrowing

Most consumers must borrow at one time or another. **Borrowing** is obtaining or receiving something with the promise to return it or its equivalent. About two-thirds of all Americans own their homes, and most had to borrow to make the purchase. Nearly three-quarters of the adults finance their automobile purchases with a loan or lease. Half of all Americans use credit cards, another form of borrowing, to make consumer purchases. Of these, about 40 percent pay off their credit card balance **in full every month**; about one-quarter say they hardly ever do.

Saving

Saving is the act of setting aside for future use, and in an economic sense, it is income not spent for consumption. Consumers save by putting money into a savings or checking account at a financial institution, buying a government savings bond, putting cash into a money market fund, or buying a certificate of deposit (CD). People also save by putting money into retirement accounts, stocks, bonds, mutual funds, and homes, that may be sold and used for consumer purchases. Only about 30 percent of households have saved to have cash on hard and 50 percent have saved for retirement. As a nation, the savings rate is about four percent of annual income. The government's definition of **personal savings rate** excludes gains on money invested in the stock market (although it includes taxes paid on capital gains), and this understates the real savings rate, which is higher.

Investing

Investing is committing money or property to a productive use (such as for equipment and machinery) to be used in producing goods or services in order to profit in the form of interest, dividends, rent, capital gains, or other income. Investment adds to the nation's stock of capital goods. Savings is not the same as investing, since the former arises from not spending and the latter results from putting money into productive use. The intent of investing is to increase future income and help maximize enjoyment of life. Investments have an element of risk, since money is placed in assets that **do not guarantee** return of principal or earnings. About half of all Americans directly invest in the stock market or do so indirectly through retirement savings plans. Half have yet to begin saving for retirement.

Taxpaying

Taxpaying is another economic activity performed by consumers. This is the payment of taxes to any number of governments. **Taxes** are compulsory charges imposed by a government on people. In the United States, approximately 32 percent of personal income goes for taxes: federal income, social security, state (and sometimes local) income, sales, use (e.g., gasoline, cigarettes, liquor, highway tolls), real estate, personal property, and gift and estate. Despite political rhetoric to the contrary, American consumers pay much less in total taxes than those in other major industrialized countries.

The wealthiest 1 percent of Americans pays 35 percent of all federal income taxes; the **wealthiest 5 percent pays 54 percent**. The bottom 50 percent of earners pays only 4 percent of federal income taxes. More than 80 percent of revenue for the U.S. federal government comes from personal income taxes and Social Security taxes. Total government spending (federal, state and local) for a family of four in the U.S. is about $5,000 annually.

Consumer Sovereignty in the Marketplace

Consumers are people like you and me. We purchase goods and services for our personal and family use. **Consumer choice** is a market condition that exists when a consumer is presented with options from which he or she can choose to buy or not. If consumers have the freedom to decide what to buy and how to use it, then consumer choice exists.

Consumer sovereignty is a market situation where consumers have the power to ultimately decide which products and services society will produce and consume. Neither producers nor politicians dictate consumer tastes, rather, as economists like to say, "the consumer is king." When consumer sovereignty exists, production in the economy is directed by millions of consumers making buying decisions with their dollar votes. You can have consumer choice but not consumer sovereignty when laws require consumers to buy automobile insurance and to acquire driver's licenses.

Another view of consumer decision making is called **producer sovereignty**. Here the producers have the power to decide which products and services society will produce and consume. Some believe that consumers are mere puppets who are easily manipulated into spending their economic dollars on products and services for which manufacturers create demand. This view holds that the consumer is a pawn to be directed and exploited.

Which theory of consumer participation in the market is **correct**? Is the consumer sovereign in the marketplace where the consumer is king? Or is the consumer led, directed, and manipulated by artificial demand where the consumer is no more than a puppet?

Consumer Problems in an Imperfectly Competitive Market

Consumers **need to be sophisticated**, demanding, discriminating, and concerned about getting their money's worth. Otherwise they will pay too much money for the values received and sometimes be harmed. Consumers confront a variety of problems when shopping in a market-driven economic system impacted by economic deregulation from the government, technological advances, and intensive marketing. Consumer problems exist because markets are imperfectly competitive and because the interests of sellers and consumers differ.

What Are "Consumer Problems"?

Consumer problems exist in the marketplace. Mayer defines **consumer problems** as "conditions that cause dissatisfaction in the process of selecting, using, or disposing of goods and services."[2] Four consumer problems exist:

1. **The inability, or unwillingness, of producers to fully satisfy consumer needs and interests.**[3] This, says Thorelli, results in things consumers do not want, such as dangerous and defective products, price gouging, product performance failures, delivery failures, deceptive advertising, dishonored promises and warranties, and frauds and rip-offs.
2. **A lack of consumer information on important matters, such as** performance, durability, likelihood of defects, and health and safety threats. It is difficult to get your money's worth in a marketplace that often offers insufficient information for effective choice making. Consumers experience problems in making healthy food choices, selecting good medical care, finding adequate and fairly-priced housing and transportation, avoiding high costs for banking and credit, and any number of services where quality is difficult to objectively measure. Information is crucial for consumers because it empowers them to effectively pursue their interests.
3. **A market system that does not resolve consumer grievances very easily or effectively,** as observed by Maynes.[4]
4. **Under-representation of the consumer interest in government** occurs to the point where many public policy decisions overly favor producers to the detriment of consumers.[5]

Consumers Shop in Imperfect Markets

Consumer problems always have existed in part because the world always has had imperfectly competitive markets. **Characteristics of failing markets** are:

1. **Insufficient competition in the marketplace** due to seller efforts to restrict "a consumer's freedom of choice among goods and services;[6]

---

[2] Mayer, R. N. (1991), Gone today, here today: Consumers issues in the agenda-setting process, *Journal of Social Issues.* 47, 21.

[3] Thorelli, H. (1988), *The Frontier of Research in The Consumer Interest*, 525.

[4] Maynes, E. S. (1976), *Decision-Making for Consumers* (MacMillan), 256-257.

[5] *Ibid.*

[6] Titus, P. A., & Bradford, J. L. (1996), *loc cit.*

2. **Seller profiteering that encourages misrepresentations, deceptions and frauds**;

3. **Imperfect information** due to seller control of valuable information, such as data on the frequency of products needing repair;

4. **Consumers who are unable to possess sufficient knowledge** to make wise purchase decisions;

5. **Products that put consumers at greater risk than can be readily foreseen**, such as unsafe toys and vehicles with poor safety records;

6. **Morally questionable marketing**,[7] such as promoting products that are inappropriate for certain age levels, making unnecessary emotional claims, and using scare techniques;

7. **Negative externalities are overprovided and difficult to avoid**, such as produce from farmers who use techniques that cause erosion and deplete natural resources, as well as pesticides that cause water pollution; and

8. **Positive externalities are underprovided**, such as information, safety, representation of consumers, competition, and redress of wrongs.

To address these **market failures**, consumers tend to demand a fairer marketplace. They support laws and regulations to combat misrepresentations and deceptions as well as to mandate disclosures of information, enforce antitrust standards, obtain health and safety protection, and seek regulation of economic interests. Businesses, the sellers, typically resist government intervention unless they believe it will help them or hurt their competitors. These imperfections in the marketplace and "maldistributions of power" are precisely "what brought the consumer movement into being."[8] Informed consumers should realize that the enemy is always the **status quo** because today's marketplace need to be made better for tomorrow's consumers.

The Seller-Consumer Conflict Will Always Exist

The market system is organized to **promote private financial gain**, not to promote public welfare or consumer well-being. While sellers and consumers are mutually dependent on each other, the essence of the relationship is that they have different motivations. Sellers are interested in revenues and profits. Consumers are interested in satisfying their needs, with little, if any, regard for the interests of the sellers. Thus, a **seller-consumer conflict** will always be present in market transactions, suggests Feldman.[9]

Also, sellers and consumers usually **perceive consumer issues differently**. Getting agreement on or even defining the nature and extent of a consumer problem is often difficult. The differences are apparent when consumers and sellers work together to find suitable remedies for problems. Many people in business, for example, endorse a model of our marketplace that is not reality, but rather is an ideal. The premise is that competitive forces are sufficient to regulate the relationship between sellers and consumers in the marketplace. This model is based on the assumption that any seller who offers shoddy products or services

---

[7] *Ibid.*

[8] Galbraith, John Kenneth (1995, March 17), Esther Peterson and the Consumer Movement, address to the Consumer Federation of America and the American Council on Consumer Interests, Washington, DC.

[9] Part of the logic in developing this section was taken from L. P. Feldman (1980), *Consumer Protection: Problems and Prospects*, 2nd ed., West, 21-34.

or who treats customers poorly will lose out to competitors. In reality, this almost never happens! One reason is that most businesses try to attract new customers and do not necessarily need to retain all their previous customers. Another reason is that few consumers or even consumer advocacy groups are influential enough in spending their economic dollars to force manufacturers to change their perspective. Consumers **are not truly sovereign**.

The viewpoints of sellers and consumers will never be fully reconciled. The challenge, therefore, is to **reduce the level of the conflict** to the point where they calmly talk with each other to find areas of agreement where both interests can benefit.

The Consumer Interest

An **interest** in the sense examined here is a regard for one's benefit or advantage; a self-interest. An interest can be exhibited by a person, group, organization or government.

A Price-Quality Model is Useful but Incomplete

The process of consumption at its most fundamental level involves consumers buying products and services in the marketplace. Each player in the market, every single buyer and seller, is hoping to get a **good deal**. The sellers hope to get the most they can for what they have to sell. The buyers hope to pay as little as possible for what they buy. This dynamic interaction of economic advantage is at the heart of understanding the consumer interest.

Consumer advocate and attorney James S. Turner describes one major aspect of the consumer interest using a **price-quality model**, as illustrated in Table 1-1. He suggests that one can readily see that the *consumer interest* (assuming for a moment that there is only a single consumer interest) is to obtain goods and services of the highest quality at the lowest possible prices. The *business interest*, on the other hand, is to try to sell goods and services at the highest price possible for the lowest quality. The *public interest*, suggests Turner, involves selling goods and services of fair quality (including safe use) at fair prices. ("Fair" and "low" are normative terms and subject to change over time.) Turner argues further that the idea of fair price for fair quality "is the generic objective of an entire local, national and global economy with production and consumption working in tandem."[10] In short, this model suggests that the consumer interest lies in getting value for money spent; therefore, it focuses upon **consumer efficiency in marketplace transactions**.

	Consumer	Public	Business
Price	Low	Fair	High
Quality	High	Fair	Low

TABLE 1-1   **Price-Quality Model Illustrating Differences Among Interests**

---

[10] A broader discussion of these concerns can be found in J. S. Turner (1984), Whither consumerism? *At Home With Consumers* (The Direct Selling Education Foundation), *5*(4).

This price-quality model demonstrates the **fundamental differences in perspectives** and agendas of business, consumers, and the public by drawing attention to the basic importance of price and quality in marketplace transactions. However, observation of reality suggests that the interests of businesses and consumers are not quite as compartmentalized as presented in this model. For example, businesses sell goods and services of low, medium, and high quality and they do so at **a variety of prices**. Therefore, the **business interest**, more accurately than suggested above, is to sell goods and services of whatever quality at the highest possible prices given the competitive forces at work in the marketplace. The price-quality model is further limited because it focuses solely on a concern for personal consumer efficiency. The consumer interest embraces **more than value for money**.

The Consumer Interest is About Value for Money *and* Equity

Specifically, the **consumer interest** is concerned with securing, protecting, and asserting consumer rights primarily in marketplace transactions in order that all consumers receive an acceptable quality of goods and services at fair or low prices. Thus, the consumer interest has to do with both value for money for oneself and equity for others. The emphasis of the definition on the consumer interest occurring "primarily in marketplace transactions" is because that is where consumers predominately do what they do when they perform the consuming function. Also note that each consumer has his or her own definition of **acceptable quality**. Thus, one consumer might only purchase goods that are considered friendly to the environment or made by someone who was paid a fair wage. Another consumer might demand that the worker be employed in safe working conditions by a socially responsible company that did not discriminate in hiring practices or neglect the needs of the economically disadvantaged. Yet another consumer might ignore such considerations when making a purchase. Further, each consumer has his or her own definition of a **fair** or **low price**, and these vary over time for each product or service purchased.

Consumer Interest #1: Seeking Value for Money

Americans spend a lot of time in their consuming role, such as going to shopping malls, buying groceries, eating meals in restaurants, buying automobiles, paying for gasoline, and living in homes. They are looking for good values for their money. In that search, consumers constantly make tradeoffs between price and quality in marketplace transactions where there is imperfect information available to consumers (virtually all the time). A **tradeoff** is the act of giving up one good or activity in order to obtain another good or activity. This involves an exchange of one thing in return for another, especially a giving up of something desirable as a benefit or advantage for another benefit or advantage regarded more desirable.

While pursuing value for money in the marketplace, consumers often make **inefficient tradeoffs**. Here consumers make poor quality and/or price decisions. This occurs because consumers operate in a complex and technological marketplace where, during marketplace transactions, they are often lacking in legal strength, product knowledge, capacity, resources, organization, and willingness. Thus, they frequently operate at a disadvantage to the sellers who are experts in sophisticated production and selling techniques. Misrepresentations and deceptions exist that confound consumers in the marketplace. Consumer advocate Esther Peterson said that many of them "are simply enthralled with the worst that mass marketing and communications has to offer...that sell false glamour, false fears of personal failure, and false choices between ten different kinds of denture cleaners and twenty different antacids."[11] In sum, consumers occupy a weak position relative to producers, distributors, advertisers and retailers. This reduces the consumer's success in obtaining value for money.

Not all consumers think it imperative that they always pay the lowest price. A **"fair price"** or a "somewhat low price" is oftentimes acceptable and usually desirable, given a certain minimum amount of quality. A number of consumers seem to have an inclination towards preferring to pay high prices, although few consumers ever tell a seller to "Please sell me something at the highest price you want to charge" or to "Please take this amount of money and sell me any level of quality."

Probably everyone occasionally makes an **irrational consumer decision**. There are some areas where consumers have "persistently biased perceptions of risk, or notions about what cost to count. They may not believe the odds in a gamble even if they are told."[12] All of this suggests that consumers cannot make good decisions for themselves unless they are educated so they know **how to act on appropriate information**.

Consumer Interest #2: Seeking Equity for All Consumers

Equity is what is right and what is wrong. Equity is about the ideals of justice, impartiality and fairness. A consumer inequity occurs when benefits and burdens are not distributed fairly. For example, a fully loaded tractor-trailer weighs about the same as 25 automobiles, yet, while causing as much damage to highways as 10,000 cars, the truck pays only a small fraction of its fair share in road taxes. An emphasis on equity for all consumers encourages consideration of a *morality aspect* to the consumer interest. This suggests that **consumers should possess a moral perspective** and concern about the economic marketplace. Mayer says that the concept of consumerism is beneficial for people to understand because as consumers seek to improve their self interest (get value for money expended) they also improve their social consciousness.[13]

Kroll contends that an equity aspect of the consumer interest has to do with opportunity rights and benefit rights as solutions to consumer problems.[14] **Opportunity rights** are those that improve "the opportunity for effective exercise of individual responsibility in securing benefits" such as the right to information and choice and disclosures for product ingredients, product life, care instructions, comparative prices, comparative performance, and health and safety warnings. **Benefit rights** are those that "provide benefits to members of some group without the exercise of individual responsibility," such as mandated automobile safety standards and low-cost banking services. The consumer interest has to do with **non-economic concerns** (e.g., health, safety, quality, ethics, equity) and **economic concerns** (e.g., buying efficiency, credit availability).

Thus, the equity aspect of the consumer interest focuses first on asserting consumer rights for individual consumers and their families. The equity interest then **broadens** to include encouraging access to acceptable goods and services for all consumers. Examples of this are check cashing at banks by economically poor non-depositors, availability of lower-cost

---

[11] Peterson, E. (1994, March 10), Speech to the Consumer Federation of America, Washington, D.C.

[12] Morgan, James N. (1985), What is in the consumer's interest? In K. P. Schnittgrund (Ed.) *The Proceedings of the American Council on Consumer Interests*, University of Missouri, 3.

[13] Mayer, R. N. (1989), *The Consumer Movement: Guardians of the Marketplace* (Twayne Publishers), 9 and 31.

[14] Kroll, R. J. and R. W. Stampfl (1981), The new consumerism, *Proceedings of the American Council on Consumer Interests*, 97-98; and Kroll, R. J. and R. W. Stampfl (1986), Orientations toward consumerism: A test of a two-dimensional theory, *Journal of Consumer Affairs*, 20,2, 214-230.

generic prescription drugs for the elderly, and subsidized housing loans for low-income families.

In sum, the consumer interest has to do with seeking equity between sellers and buyers through a **mutual recognition of several consumer rights** as well as with pursuing equity for all consumers in their access to acceptable goods and services at fair or low prices. Table 1-2 offers a model of the consumer interest using the constructs of **both value for money and equity**.

VALUE-FOR-MONEY INTERESTS	EQUITY INTERESTS
Obtaining an acceptable quality of goods and services at fair or low prices	Seeking equity between sellers and buyers provided by a mutual recognition of several consumer rights
Expecting the benefits of a competitive marketplace	Pursuing equity for all consumers in their access to acceptable goods and services

TABLE 1-2   The Value-for-Money/Equity Model of the Consumer Interest

Eight Important Consumer Rights

Consumers try to achieve their interests by securing, protecting, and asserting their consumer rights. These rights[15] are important aspects of the consumer interest and they have been suggested by several American presidents and other people and organizations. Consumer rights are not simply given to people. Once articulated and secured for consumers, the **rights must be protected and asserted**.

1. **Choice**, where consumers have the right to make an intelligent choice among products and services;

2. **Information**, where consumers have the right to accurate information on which to make a free choice, thus they are provided access to the facts with which to make informed choices while also being protected against fraudulent, deceptive, and misleading information, advertising, labeling, and related practices;

3. **Safety**, where consumers have the right to expect the health and safety of the buyer will be taken into account by those seeking patronage; thus consumers should be able to assume that products will perform as intended without being hazardous to health or life;

4. **Voice** (or the right to be heard), where the interests of consumers will be given full and fair consideration in government policy-making situations;

---

[15] As human rights are more fundamental to civilized society than consumer rights, these are excluded from this list. **Human rights** are those factors fundamental to civilized humanity, such as the rights of all people to food, clothing, shelter, health care, sanitation, education, employment, worker safety, fair wages, safe environment, and peace.

5. **Redress** (or the right to remedy), where consumers are provided with easily accessible, understandable and cost-efficient mechanisms through which consumer grievances and dissatisfactions can be addressed;

6. **Environmental health**, where consumers may consume in an environmentally sound manner and be protected from the ill effects of pollution of the air, earth, and water while performing everyday marketplace transactions;

7. **Service**, where consumers may expect convenience, courtesy, and responsiveness to consumer needs and problems and all the steps necessary to ensure that products and services meet the quality and performance levels claimed for them. This helps all consumers to maximize their resources, become more effective in the marketplace and achieve personal satisfaction in consumption.

8. **Consumer education**, where consumers are provided the right to consumer education, without which consumers cannot gain the full benefit of the other seven consumer rights.

The Consumer Interest as a Special Interest Group

Equity for consumers is **first defined** by each individual consumer, who also is the *true* spokesperson for the consumer interest. Different perceptions about the consumer interest are held by various individuals and organizations. The consumer interest in equity issues (as well as value-for-money issues) is also determined by many concerned groups, including consumer activist organizations, unions, churches, state governments, and a number of consumer protection organizations. Each organization brings its unique perspective to consumer issues.

The equity outlook also suggests that consumers can be **paternalisticly forced to accept some protection** against negative consequences of their own behaviors because their choices may be restricted or prohibited. For example, the only rotary lawnmowers available in the marketplace today are those that adhere to government-mandated safety standards. As another example, low-income consumers have no choice other than to purchase the same three-pronged electrical safety extension cords as do more affluent consumers. Also, people of all income levels buy new automobiles that meet government safety standards. Thus, the less affluent are forced to accept certain benefits (such as safety or information) whether or not they want to pay for them.

This equity aspect of the consumer interest is generally limited to situations where the majority of consumers will themselves experience only very low additional costs or very small decreases in quality in order to provide access benefits to other consumers through **cross-subsidization** or **cost-shifting**. This is the process of shifting the costs of supporting one segment of a business with the income from another. Typically, cross subsidization supports a service for the less affluent (such as rural telephone customers) with the income or tax revenues from the affluent (urban telephone customers, in this example).

A **special-interest group** is a group of persons who attempts to influence the statutory, regulatory, economic, and political decisions of government as it appeals for special consideration for its particular concerns. The concerns of special-interest groups center around **economic self-interest**. Groups with a special interest include computer chip manufacturers (who want protection from foreign competition), physicians (who want to keep their incomes high), prescription drug manufacturers (who want the legal right to market their inventions for a number of years), and hundreds of others. As former U.S. Senate Commerce Committee

Chairman Warren Magnuson used to say after a long day of listening to lobbyists, **"All anyone ever wants is a fair advantage!"**

The consumer interest can be advocated by individuals in **daily marketplace transactions**, as well as in the public policy arena of government decision making. The consumer's special-interest perspective is that of a **self-interested economic player** who first wants value for money. The consumer interest in equity for all consumers has its roots in the community values of truth, reciprocity, trust, fair dealing, equality, value for money and social justice.

These goals are pursued by **citizen-consumers**, people who seek to promote the interests of consumers by striving to improve the betterment of their community and society. The special-interest perspectives of the civil rights and environmental movements are similar in that regard. In this role, active citizen-consumers become political persons who try to influence laws, regulations, and the allocation of public goods. It is good for a society to have an active citizenry and good for consumers to live by values embedded in the consumer interest.

Consumers and consumer groups get particularly awakened when business or government disregards, ignores, forgets, or **overrides the consumer rights** of special groups of consumers, such as women, minorities, children, the elderly, the physically handicapped, and the poor. When the consumer interest **is not properly attended to**, and that is often, consumers and consumer groups are quick to challenge decision-makers to be certain that the consumer interest is protected.

The Interests of Consumers Differ from Public and Business Interests

The preamble to the U.S. Constitution states that the purpose of the federal government is to, "provide for a more perfect union." Government does this by providing for the national defense, making social welfare programs accessible to many, caring for the needy, subsidizing space research, and providing for other public needs. Government provides the people with **public goods**. These are goods (or services) that have the attributes, or benefits, of shared consumption and non-exclusion. Examples include clean air, ample supplies of water, state recreation parks, radio and television broadcasts, police protection, and national defense. The **public** is all of us—consumers, taxpayers, business people, government employees, children, elderly, physicians, sugar beet growers, computer chip manufacturers, and others.

ECONOMIC INSIGHT:
Discrimination Harms Consumers and Sellers*

In the absence of discrimination, all consumers in the market for a particular good x face the **same market Demand**, D_t, and Supply, S_t, curves. The resulting equilibrium Price is P_t as shown in Figure 1-1. (The vertical axis represents the increase in price while the horizontal axis represents the increase in quantity, as one moves away from 0.) With discrimination, some sellers **will not sell** to the group of consumers (group A) that they are discriminating against. In this case, those being discriminated against face a reduced Supply, S_a. The result of this reduced supply is that consumers being discriminated against must pay a higher Price, P_a, than they would without discrimination in order to purchase what they desire.

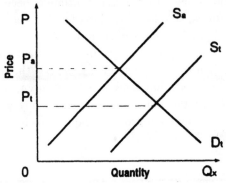

Figure 1-1: Discrimination Against Group A

There is evidence that blacks and Hispanics **face higher prices** with respect to low-income rental housing as a result of discrimination. See Chapter 17. Discrimination also hurts sellers, because those sellers who refuse to sell to a particular group face a decreased Demand curve, D_b; see Figure 1-2. Consumers not being discriminated against (group B) pay a lower Price, P_b. Thus, the seller receives a lower price in order to satisfy his/her "taste for discrimination."

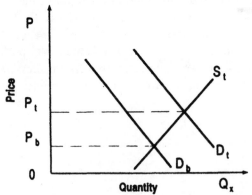

Figure 1-2: No Discrimination Against Group B

*Julia Marlowe, Associate Professor, and Joan Koonce Lewis, Associate Professor, The University of Georgia

---

ISSUE FOR DEBATE:
Young Shoppers are Discriminated Against

Many stores discriminate against high school and college-age consumers. Store employees in expensive stores, **especially in malls**, seem to believe that every young person wearing jeans, looking young, sounding loud, and carrying a backpack is going to steal everything in sight. Sometimes the discrimination is based on skin color. New York City became the first city to prohibit such unfair discrimination. Violators may be reported to the Human Rights Commission.

More often than not, young consumers **have money to spend**. Many have their parents' credit cards; some have their own. More than one young shopper has said, "Whenever I'm carefully watched in a store, I take my business elsewhere." Responsible young shoppers who are unfairly discriminated against should complain to store supervisors, mall managers and community human rights commissions.

The Public Interest

Consumers have a special-interest perspective on matters affecting them that often is very different from the public interest. The **public interest** is concerned with generally accepted, socially shared standards and practices pertaining to the welfare of *all* those in the community. To be in the public interest, policies must promote the interests of individuals that are collective. As a result, decisions made by government in the public interest should, theoretically, **supersede the concerns of all** special-interest groups. In fact, the public interest should serve as a counterweight to special-interest groups seeking exclusive benefits. The public interest often requires resolving issues among consumers (but not private matters or conflicts), various consumer organizations, different businesses, competing unions, several levels of government, and other groups (e.g., business managers, local government officials, police officers, church leaders, military personnel, secretaries, postal employees, the poor, the elderly, women, students, and children).

The public interest should be concerned with the **welfare of all** those in the community rather than cater to private matters or interests. Note, further, that when markets are insufficient by themselves to protect consumer health, promote safety, provide social equity, safeguard vulnerable consumers, and protect the environment, government must step in to secure the public interest. Examples of public interest goals are safeguarding the environment, seeking fairness in taxation, encouraging quality housing, feeding the hungry, saving endangered species, protecting workers from employment hazards, providing housing for the homeless, assuring universal access to health care, and guarding our nation from potential adversaries. The difficult and broad task of serving the public interest involves **compelling and competing challenges**.

One's Consumer and Public Roles Differ

One's consumer and public roles for people sometimes differ and can even be in conflict. **Consumers** are people who acquire goods and services for ultimate consumption or use by a person, family, or household. Consumers go shopping and purchase goods and services in their efforts to accomplish their own economic goals. Thus, the interests of consumers is **primarily focused upon consumption**.

As members of the public, our interests are **broader and more diverse**. Each of us probably supports the goals of several special-interest groups, such as family, church, neighborhood, community, employer, local government, etc. In such efforts, Americans typically visualize themselves as having **citizen roles**, such as taking primary responsibility for their own affairs, adhering to certain standards of morality and ethics, participating in community affairs, and voting. These are some of our citizen roles that we take as members of **a democratic American society**.

Names

Consumer advocate James S. Turner adds that we are consumers when we cast our **dollar votes (economic votes)** on a daily basis and we are citizens when we cast our **political votes** on other concerns about once a year, and both are vital to responsible citizenship. In our consumer role, spending money counts as a **yes vote**: "Make more of these products please" and "I want to give repeat business to this seller." Not purchasing counts as a **no vote**: "The product I bought before was inferior," "My previous experience with the seller was not pleasurable, so I'll never buy here again," and "My conscience will not allow me to buy," and "This particular seller should be boycotted."

Business and the Consumer Interest

Typically, **businesses try hard** to meet the needs of consumers by providing **fairly priced goods** and services when and where desired; otherwise they may wind up without customers and go out of business. Turner reminds us that, "business people are fond of saying they are consumers too." They are, says Turner, except in the one area of economic activity when they are carrying out their business. The primary responsibility of a businessperson is to **advance the interests of the business**. This is not incompatible with advancing the consumer interest," but oftentimes it is in conflict. **When forced by government regulations**, business is able to disclose standardized information to consumers in a much more meaningful way than when business volunteers some information. Examples include nutritional labeling, written warranties, and Truth in Lending disclosure requirements.

Gronmo suggests that an example of a **common interest** of businesses and consumers is, "supporting neighborhood stores in their competition with larger companies"...that "are favored by the concentration tendencies in the distribution system."[16] It is in the consumer interest when companies provide **high-quality goods at low prices**, and some companies do that better than others. This is why Wal-Mart has become the largest and most successful retailer in the world. Founder Sam Walton practiced "trying to squeeze the lowest possible price from the people who sell to you, and then pass the savings on to the consumer."

The interests of sellers and consumers similarly **overlap** when business provides **informational advertisements** (rather than use sex, love, or other emotional claims) and strongly supports the practices of the self-regulatory Better Business Bureau. In general, businesses are willing to help people assert their consumer rights (such as maintaining an efficient complaint-handling system, for example) only when (1) it will not cost too much, (2) the competition is doing it so the business might lose market share if it doesn't do it too, or (3) not doing it will have a negative effect on the "bottom line" of business profits.

---

[16] Gronmo, S. (1987), Relationships among consumer interests and other interests: Some implications for consumer policy, *Proceedings of the American Council on Consumer Interests*, 302.

Government Often Promotes the Consumer Interest

Societies need **effective public oversight of markets** when sellers lack effective incentives to responsibly regulate their own conduct. Government safeguards and oversight also are needed when "health, safety, and other special concerns are at issue."[17]

The task of government should be to **attempt to reconcile the views of many** special-interest groups and make policy determinations in favor of what is perceived by politicians and bureaucrats as the good of all. James Madison stated it another way in *The Federalist Papers* when he wrote that the task of enlightened legislators is to refine the public's views **to ascertain the true interests of the country**. Inevitably these decisions require compromises by government that depend upon the tenor of the times, the politics of the day, the state of the economy, the strength of arguments offered by the special interest groups, the economic clout of affected groups, and the type of economic/political system in operation. Government must **maintain a balance** between popular pressures of the day and a larger concept of our national interest.

Consumer interest issues are more **narrow in focus** than public interest issues. The consumer interest tends to center on their economic consuming role in marketplace transactions. If consumers had their way, they would like to purchase a loaf of bread for ten cents, but it has been determined by the powers that be in the United States that it is not in the public interest for government to control the supply and demand of bakery goods by heavily subsidizing bread prices, as is the practice in a number of underdeveloped countries.

Government has **long been interested** in protecting consumer interests in selected ways by **preventing fraud, maintaining competition and promoting health and safety**. For decades we have had postal inspectors, licensing of trades and professions, antitrust laws, food safety standards, and a variety of product safety standards. Government also requires ingredient nutritional labeling of most foods, requires credit reporting agencies to tell consumers when information in their files has been used to deny them credit, and provides "lemon laws" to help consumers get their vehicles repaired satisfactorily in a reasonable length of time.

Conflicts Between the Public and Consumer Interests

Conflicts between the public interest and the consumer interest typically arise when the **costs** of providing increased safety and protection for all consumers is likely to push certain **prices up** (and that is not in the consumer interest) and/or additional consumer problems might be created by approval of a particular proposal (and most often these are attempts to reduce consumer rights).

1. **Potential Price Increases.** When consumers buy low-priced imported products, such as cotton shirts and blouses, from developing countries, their low-price consumer interest conflicts with the public concern to protect American textile jobs. Other examples include requiring no-fault automobile insurance (that limits the public's ability to sue) and requiring impact-resistant doors on vehicles (that increases purchase costs).

2. **Consumer Rights.** While many will argue that the consumer interest is to have a 100 percent safe food supply, government acts in the public interest by permitting approved limits of dozens of chemical and incidental additives in foods that may be unsafe in high

---

[17] Guest offers lessons for the consumer movement (2002, April), CFA News, 2.

concentrations, typically because such chemicals substantially increase the harvest. Similarly, requiring automatic passive restraint systems on new vehicles saves the lives of many people (over 3,000 annually), but it also increases purchase costs for the buyers.

How Consumers Pursue Their Interests

In the aggregate, the voices of about 290 million consumers are heard in the American economic marketplace in their **daily decisions to buy or not to buy**. Consumers need to be responsible in pursuing their interests. In doing so, people will improve their own consumer education and that will help them make better future choices because they will "not regret them, and would not do so even if they had better information or understanding."[18]

In a market-oriented capitalistic economy, only one group has as its **primary function to consume**—consumers. Therefore, consumers should organize to better represent their own interests, to more effectively pursue one perceived set of consumer interests over those of other consumer groups, and to encourage governments to support the consumer interest more often as they act in the public interest. Turner observes that "it is very difficult for an individual or household to do much by themselves, therefore, they **must get into groups** to demand better prices and quality."[19]

Turner says that "the thrust for **participatory democracy** is the ideological background of the consumer movement."[20] Deeply rooted in American history, consumerism is like the American revolution in its belief that "power ought to flow from the bottom up (that is, from the people up) rather than from the top down (from the King down)." Thus, sellers need to meet regularly with consumers to provide participatory access for them to make inputs into the corporate decision making process. Those being affected by decisions, consumers, ought to be a part of the process of **decision making** in corporations and governments. Turner concludes that, "Consumers are to economics what voters are to politics; consumers with rights enhance the wealth of the nation."

The great majority of consumers, probably 60 percent of the total, go about their consuming with a **less than perfect understanding** of how to find acceptable-quality goods and services at fair or low prices. They muddle through the marketplace often spending too much money for the values received.

There are only a relatively small number of consumers—perhaps only 20 percent—who are **well informed** in many areas of buying. They are "a minority who are engaged, educated, enlivened by choices and wise and considered actions."[21] many of these are **aggressive-assertive consumers** because in addition to knowing about their consumer rights they vigorously pursue getting their money's worth in the marketplace. These sophisticated consumers are the ones most likely to get redress when wronged by businesses because they are savvy, assertive and empowered. Their actions help police the marketplace and such efforts help improve markets for all consumers.

Vulnerable, or **disadvantaged, consumers** need special **protection**. The president of Consumers Union, publisher of *Consumer Reports* magazine, says that vulnerable consumers

---

[18] Morgan, James N. (1985), What is in the consumer's interest? In K. P. Schnittgrund (Ed.), *Proceedings of the American Council on Consumer Interests*, 2.

[19] Turner, James S. (1994, July 18), Speech to University of Georgia "Consumer Issues in Washington" class in Washington, D.C.

[20] Nasibitt, J. (1982), *Megatrends* (Warner Books), 177.

[21] *Ibid.*

cannot "afford the basic necessities of life" and they have to "fight for affordable goods and services, fair financial practices, and a society in which all Americans and their families have a fair chance at a decent living." They include people who are economically poor, young children, mentally retarded, severely handicapped, non-English speaking, and some elderly people. This group, comprising perhaps 20 percent of the population, experiences varying degrees of difficulty in buying. Unsophisticated consumers, when **left unprotected** in the marketplace, are the **targets of unscrupulous and unethical business practices**.

It is a **challenge** to be an effective consumer pursuing the consumer interest. While it is easy to simply "go out and spend money," the real effort comes in obtaining good quality for a fair or low price. It is challenging to take actions to secure, protect, and assert our consumer rights. It takes **time and effort** to complain to a store manager or to a government agency about a problem. It takes personal commitment to become actively involved in local, state, and national consumer organizations that work to protect the rights of consumers. Nevertheless, the voices of consumers need to be heard on matters that affect them in the regulatory and political arenas in Washington, in state capitals, and in town meetings across America.

Joining consumer organizations is one of the very **best ways** to improve one's consumer education. They usually publish a useful newsletter. In addition, the financial dues paid to a consumer organization help support the goals of all consumers. Consumers are encouraged to join Public Citizen (www.publiccitizen.org) as well as a local or state consumer action organization..

Consumer advocates are people who work for nonprofit organizations that seek to influence public policy to the benefit of consumers. They **monitor** the activities of regulatory agencies and legislatures to ensure that consumer interests are recognized and safeguarded. They conduct **research**, communicate with legislators, talk with the press, build coalitions, and activate grass-roots networks to **support particular consumer-interest positions**. Some advocates focus their efforts at the state level, while others specialize in federal government activities. Stephen Brobeck, executive director of the Consumer Federation of America, the nation's largest consumer organization, says that "The greatest success of the consumer movement is that **millions of people** today consider themselves consumer advocates."[22]

Consumer advocate Ralph Nader says that, "there can be no daily democracy without **daily citizenship**. If we do not exercise our civic rights, who will? If we do not perform our civic duties, who can? The fiber of a just society in the pursuit of happiness is a thinking, active citizenry. That means you!"

The academic field of consumer economics utilizes economic concepts and principles, along with **normative analysis**, as it makes value judgments about the formulation and evaluation of public policies from the viewpoint of the consumer interest. The standards being applied, products of moral reasoning that differ from person to person, are those rooted in the consumer interest. Thus, many consumer economics instructors and their students are active in pursuing the consumer interest.

Millions of us go about trying to pursue the consumer interest every day in our **own varied ways**, sometimes informed and sometimes not. We are just ordinary people who want to get our money's worth while asserting our rights in marketplace transactions and we want to make sure that all consumers are treated equitably. As individual consumers, it is our task and our responsibility to better understand the consumer interest and to seek it!

---

[22] Brobeck, Stephen (1997, March 20), speech to the Consumer Federation of America, Washington, DC.

Review and Summary of Key Terms and Concepts

1.   What is a **consumer**?

2.   List the fundamental **economic activities** performed by consumers.

3.   Distinguish between **consuming** and **utilizing** as economic activities.

4.   Distinguish between **saving** and **investing** as economic activities.

5.   Briefly discuss why consumers do not have **consumer sovereignty** in the economic marketplace.

6.   List two key **consumer problems** that exist in society.

7.   What is the **seller-consumer conflict**, and why will it always be present?

8.   Explain the statement that informed consumers should realize that the enemy is always the **status quo.**

9.   Briefly summarize one fundamental aspect of the consumer interest using a **price-quality model**.

10.   Summarize how the consumer interest can be explained correctly using a **value-for-money/equity model**.

11.   Define the **consumer interest** and explain the two key aspects of acceptable quality and fair or low prices.

12.   Briefly explain the concept of **value-for-money** as it relates to the consumer interest.

13.   Briefly explain the concept of **seeking equity** for all consumers as it relates to the] consumer interest, and comment on the idea of inefficient tradeoffs.

14.   Distinguish between **opportunity rights** and **benefit rights**.

15.   Identify two of the eight **consumer rights**.

16.   Summarize the critical role of the **right to information**.

17.   Explain why the consumer interest is a **special-interest group**.

18.   Compare and contrast the **public interest** with the consumer interest.

19.   What happens to supply and price for consumers when **discrimination** occurs in the economic marketplace?

20.   Give some examples of how **business and government** sometimes support the consumer interest.

21.   What are the two primary reasons why **conflicts** occur between the consumer interest and the public interest?

22.   Summarize why **consumers themselves** must look out for the consumer interest.

23.   List two actions by businesses and governments that **sometimes help consumers**?

24.   List two ways that consumers **pursue their interests**?

25.   What do you think is the **major challenge** of being an effective consumer?

Useful Resources for Consumers

Consumer Information Center
www.pueblo.gsa.gov

Consumer Federation of
America
www.consumerfed.org

Consumers Union
www.consumersunion.org

Federal government agencies
www.consumer.gov

First Gov (20,000 federal
government web sites)
www.firstgov.gov

National Consumers League
www.ncl.org

National Fraud Information
Center
800-876-9060
www.fraud.org

National Institute for Consumer
Education
www.emich.edu

Public Citizen
www.publiccitizen.org

"What Do You Think" Questions

1. Why is it vitally important for you and other consumers to understand and pursue the **consumer interest**?

2. Select one of the eight important **consumer rights** and explain why it is important both to you and to other consumers.

3. Explain why the concept of equity sometimes requires a **paternalistic attitude** that encourages protection of certain kinds of consumers.

4. What types of actions do you think American society should take to help consumers make more **efficient marketplace decisions**?

5. The term **acceptable quality** can have many definitions. What do you generally think that word means to you in your marketplace transactions? Also, explain how that definition might change for different products and services you purchase.

6. What kinds of actions can you suggest to sellers that would encourage them to more often **serve the consumer interest**?

7. Do you think **student consumers** are discriminated against in the business community where you live? Offer some ideas on how students might go about changing the attitudes of business owners and their sales personnel on discrimination against students.

Chapter 2

The Consumer Movement

OBJECTIVES

After reading this chapter, you should be able to

1. Summarize the changing times of the consumer economic marketplace for Americans.

2. Provide examples of events during the consumerism era of the 1960s and 1970s.

3. Summarize the responses of government and business to the consumerism era.

4. List social and economic factors that make consumer movements successful.

5. Describe today's consumer movement.

T he idea of consumerism is embedded in American history. Consumers during the early part of the 20th century organized against tenement housing, unsafe working conditions, unwholesome food, and a host of other consumer problems. Americans in the 1960s began to rebel against similar problems and ushered in the decade of consumerism. Today's consumer movement in the 21st century serves as an important means to achieve a just and fair society.

This chapter looks at the changing consumer movement, suggests why the role of the consumer has changed and predicts how it will continue to evolve. The chapter begins with a historical review of the early periods of the consumer movement and the consumerism era of the 1960s and early 1970s. Next the responses of businesses and governments to the surges of interest in the consumer movement are examined. This includes a description of social change as an evolutionary process that provides insight into today's mature and successful consumer movement.

The Early Periods of the Consumer Movement

The first three periods of the consumer movement occurred before 1890 (awakening to consumer problems), from the 1890s to 1929 (early consumer movement), and from 1929 through the 1950s (renewed consumer interest).

Awakening to Consumer Problems: Before 1890

The first organized consumer revolt in the United States occurred before the country was founded. Settlers in the 1760s fought to **reverse imperial policies** by boycotting imported goods. The colonists protested British taxes on stamps, glass, paint, paper and tea. Over a 12-year period, many consumers gave up imported tea, liquor, ribbons, laces, and silks. These actions also induced long lasting preferences for American-made products. Thus, the American colonial era gave birth to the traditions of its consumer movement.[1]

In 1776, the population of the 13 colonies was about 2 ½ million. People then lived a highly **individualistic life**. They wanted freedom and independence and were extremely self-reliant. They were basically self-sustaining, cooperative, and giving. The welfare of consumers depended in part on the honesty and buying skills of both themselves and a few local shopkeepers. Retail stores consisted of itinerant peddlers, rural general stores, specialized city shops and auction sales. If the shopkeepers were smart enough to purchase good-quality products, then consumers who bought from them at least had access to good products.

The range of products available to consumers was quite small, and "locally produced items accounted for the majority of purchases."[2] The products were generally simple in design and were in everyday use. Buyers were faced with **few products** that were not within their range of experience. Intelligent buyers, therefore, had the expertise to make a reasonable evaluation of most products. Most consumers were thrifty and frugal.

Most goods had no trademarks, and few had brand names. The wise consumer knew the merchandise and tried to avoid shoddy products. However, consumers had almost no

---

[1] Witkowski, T. H. (1989), Colonial consumers in revolt: Buyer values and behavior during the nonimportation movement, 1764-1776, *Journal of Consumer Research*, 216-226.
[2] *Ibid*, p. 217.

protection against merchants who raised prices needlessly, and they could do little to stop frauds, such as misbranding and adulteration. The prevailing consumer motto was **caveat emptor**, meaning "let the buyer beware."

By the 1890s, the effects of a rapidly growing society changed the role of the consumer. **Industrialization**, along with population growth, brought 40 percent of the population to the cities. A nationwide system of railroads served the needs of those who had moved into urban areas, where employment opportunities and local trolley transportation systems thrived.

The ensuing congestion also led to "urban poverty, tenement housing, immigrant ghettos, municipal corruption, hazardous working conditions, sweat shops, child labor and a variety of consumer problems."[3] To fight these problems, people, particularly women, banded together. The numerous **reform organizations** created were concerned with political change. Newly created workers' unions sought equity for people of the working class. Populists and progressives promoted economic and social change to correct "the imbalances, injustices, and inequities of an economic system that contained too much exploitation of the weaker and poorer by the stronger and richer."[4] Volunteer groups of "do-gooders" concerned themselves with local issues, such as child labor and food adulteration.

Early Consumer Movement: The 1890s through the 1920s

The power to regulate commerce was reserved to the States until passage of the **Interstate Commerce Act** in 1887. Following upon this federal authority, the Federal Meat Inspection Service was established in 1891. The years from the 1890s through the 1920s were a time when most people in the U.S. still lived on farms in rural areas, and these years can be described as the early consumer movement. This initial movement was an extension of other social movements (labor, cooperatives, and women's groups) that provided the foundations for today's consumer activities. The first Consumers' League was formed in 1891, and eight years later the National Consumers League was founded to fight marketplace injustices. Branch offices were quickly established in 20 states. During these years, Congress passed over 50 consumer protection laws. A feeling for the times can be seen in typical newspaper headlines (shown on the following page.)

During what became World War I, patriotic fever and wartime shortages, and then postwar readjustments, diverted much attention from consumer problems. After the war, during the early 1920s, **consumer incomes rose** sharply. Mass-production techniques were developed bringing consumers more and newer products such as automobiles, radios, telephones, and movies. Advertising expenditures that had been criticized as serving no useful purpose, quickly exceeded $3 billion annually. Buyers were confused by the growing array of products, and it is no wonder that consumer outrage books became best sellers, such as *Counterfeit, Not to Be Broadcast, 40,000,000 Guinea Pig Children, The American Chamber of Horrors*, and *100,000,000 Guinea Pigs*. The books illustrated dozens of instances of misbranding, mislabeling, and unsafe practices being committed by large, well-respected companies that injured or cheated consumers.

---

[3] Herrmann, R. O. (1970), *The Consumer Movement in Historical Perspective* (Pennsylvania State University, Department of Agricultural Economics and Rural Sociology), 1.

[4] Turner, James S. The consumer interest in the 1990's and beyond: The 1995 ACCI Colston Warne Memorial Lecture, *Consumer Interests Annual*, 41, 1-11.

> STANDARD OIL "TRUST" SUCCEEDS THROUGH BRIBERY, GRAFT, FRAUD, VIOLENCE, AND THE DESTRUCTION OF COMPETITION
>
> AGRICULTURE DEPARTMENT DOCUMENTS 1400 PAGES OF FOOD ADULTERATION
>
> FORMALDEHYDE USED AS FOOD PRESERVATIVE
>
> GROUPS OPPOSE FOOD AND DRUG LEGISLATION, INCLUDING AMERICAN MEDICAL ASSOCIATION
>
> PRESIDENT ROOSEVELT INVESTIGATES FOODS
>
> PURE FOOD AND DRUG LAW PASSES CONGRESS
>
> CHICAGO HOUSEWIVES LEAGUE FORMED TO CHECK SANITARY CONDITIONS IN FOOD STORES
>
> CONGRESS PASSES ANTITRUST LAWS TO PROMOTE COMPETITION
>
> U.S. ENTERS WORLD WAR

 In 1929, an **independent product testing organization**, Consumers Research, was formed by F. J. Schlink, author of the best-selling *Your Money's Worth* (subtitled "A Study in the Waste of the Consumer's Dollar"). CR published *Consumers' Research Magazine*. During these years, a number of product-testing laboratories, some of which were run by department stores and trade associations, were established to provide the public buying information. The federal Bureau of Standards established a national system of weights and measures.

At that time, **trusts** were combinations of firms that got together to reduce competition and control supplies and/or prices throughout a geographic area or industry. Trusts existed in fuel, sugar, whiskey, and matches. The consumer battle against the trusts established the Federal Trade Commission Act in 1914. The consumer fight for pure food resulted in passage of the Pure Food and Drug Act of 1906. These events, along with rising prices and an increasing torrent of advertising, helped make the public aware of their special interests as consumers as distinguished from their interests as workers, property owners or voters. Thus, a "consumer consciousness" developed in the United States.

Renewed Consumer Interest: 1929 through the 1950s

A variety of circumstances brought on a renewed interest in consumer issues from 1929 through the 1950s, which also was a time of population migration to the cities. Early on, the Great Depression of the 1930s came. Typical headlines illustrate the times (as shown below). Demand for consumer goods was almost totally **depressed for 15 years**, from 1930 to 1945, first because of the Depression and next because of World War II. Food and drug laws were broadened in the 1930s, and the Wheeler-Lea amendment to the Federal Trade Commission Act empowered the FTC to investigate "unfair" as well as deceptive practices.

The postwar period of the late 1940s and into the 1950s saw strong economic growth and **rising consumer incomes** for our primarily blue-collar society. During the 1950s, thousands took advantage of the educational opportunities offered to World War II veterans, that pushed them up the economic ladder and helped gradually transfer the U.S. into a better educated and increasingly white-collar society. Magazine circulation for the popular buying information magazine *Consumer Reports*, published by Consumers Union, Inc., grew to almost half a million by 1950. The National Association of Consumers, a small consumer group, merged with the Council on Consumer Information.

ONE-THIRD OF LABOR FORCE UNEMPLOYED

BARGAIN SALES OF PRE-DEPRESSION MERCHANDISE

CONSUMERS SHOULD BEWARE OF SHODDY MERCHANDISE

IS ADVERTISING RESPONSIBLE FOR THE WASTEFUL PROLIFERATION OF BRANDS AND COSTING CONSUMERS MORE?

"USE IT UP, WEAR IT OUT, MAKE IT DO, OR DO WITHOUT"—NEW CONSUMER SLOGAN

PICKETING DETROIT HOUSEWIVES FORCE MEAT PRICES TO ROLL BACK 20 PERCENT

EMPLOYEES ON STRIKE AT CONSUMERS' RESEARCH, INC.

NEW TESTING GROUP ORGANIZED—CONSUMERS UNION, INC.

PURE FOOD AND DRUG LAW NOW OUTDATED

NEW SULFA "WONDER DRUG" KILLS NEARLY 100 PEOPLE

IMPROVED FOOD AND DRUG LAW PASSES CONGRESS

During the 1950s, the increased use of **installment credit** for household products and vehicles and newly available amortized mortgage loans for new homes (payable in monthly installments, instead of a single lump sum) motivated schools to offer courses to help improve consumers' buying skills. They taught the hows and whys of buying until the Soviet Union sent up the first satellite, Sputnik, in 1957. This event rapidly turned attention away from life adjustment courses as schools began to emphasize science and mathematics.

Some consumer issues still caught the headlines, however. In *The Hidden Persuaders*, Vance Packard argued that the public was being **manipulated by advertisers**. Things were rather quiet on the consumer front because the nation's attention was focused on the relative economic prosperity of the 1950s, Senator Joseph McCarthy's campaign against so-called communists, and the growing interest in space and national defense.

Consumerism: The 1960s and Early 1970s

By the 1960s, Americans were much **more aware** of the marketplace. Television made every consumer an expert, because for the first time in history people were constantly exposed to product claims. The decade of the 1960s saw a social movement evolve in that more economically informed Americans (better than their parents) expressed dissatisfaction with the existing social, economic, and structural systems. Such disharmony helped people develop a **greater social conscience**, and they demanded social change. As members of an increasingly wealthy industrial society that met most of its people's basic needs, Americans could afford to turn their attention to social concerns, such as race relations, consumer problems, pollution cleanup, product safety, and social justice. Since both the economic marketplace and government were inadequately addressing these concerns, American consumers perceived this inattention as a violation of the public trust and demanded action. This **consciousness revolution** recast American values with deepening concerns about helping others solve difficult societal problems.

People became more open to **self-criticism** regarding social and economic problems. Some of the best-selling books were Rachel Carson's *The Silent Spring* (1962, environment), Michael Harrington's *The Other America* (1962, poverty), Jessica Mitford's *The American Way of Death* (1963, funerals), David Caplovitz's *The Poor Pay More* (1963, poverty and credit), Maurine Neuberger's *Smoke Screen: Tobacco and the Public Welfare* (1963, cigarettes), and Richard Harris' *The Real Voice* (1964, drug safety). The nation was becoming more aware of its problems, and this ushered in the loosely organized era of activist consumerism, that lasted until the mid-1970s.

During these years, **consumerism** was a label put on the efforts of a growing number of consumer advocates who questioned the **inadequacies of the marketplace** and the unwillingness of business and government to deal with important consumer needs and demands. Concerns included: (1) the increasing complexity of products confronting consumers in the marketplace, (2) frustration with the growing specialization of services that were difficult to assess, (3) false advertising, (4) empty warranties, (5) selling that was impersonalized, (6) serious automobile, health, and product safety problems, and (7) stopping government decisions that ignored the viewpoints of consumers.

Consumerism emerged because many people concluded that making money should not be the only objective of the capitalistic economic system. Many Americans began to question the logic of commitments to maximizing economic growth that were crucially important to earlier generations. People demanded **justice and fair play** in the marketplace and that represented a significant shift in the national value system. Americans began to realize that fulfilling the consumer interest, as suggested by Adam Smith in his 1776 book *The Wealth of Nations*, is the best means to enhance the wealth of the country.

The term **consumer movement** characterizes the organized activities of a loose coalition of groups of people working toward the achievement of a number of related goals that (1) protect consumer rights (such as health and safety), (2) help consumers gain power to control critical factors in their lives (i.e., competent choice-making and appropriate redress), and (3) limit marketplace abuses.

Thus, the consumer movement seeks **honest packaging**, accurate labeling, truthful advertising, fair pricing, and improved safety standards. An effective consumer movement encourages the competitive economic system of capitalism to reward those companies that produce better products. People involved in the consumer movement come from several areas of society: community, senior citizen, cooperatives, labor unions, foundations, academics, consumer information, consumer advocacy, and consumer affairs professionals in business and government.

Consumer advocate Lee Richardson says that, "The *consumer movement* is what consumer activists do." Stephen Brobeck, Executive Director of the Consumer Federation of America, defines **consumer activists** or **consumer advocates** as "those persons affiliated with nonprofit organizations who seek to influence public policy to the benefit of consumers." Arch W. Troelstrup, then a professor at Stevens College, says of the *consumer movement* that, "It punctures false claims, it spreads knowledge of new quality products, it harnesses science for the service of the buyer." He argues that the consumer movement also helps restore the capacity of the competitive system to reward those companies that are producing better products. "The central aim of the consumer movement," says Troelstrup, "is to help organize the economy in ways that will best serve the consumer interest."

The **beginning** of the consumer movement of the 1960s probably began with a boycott by a group of housewives in Denver, Colorado, who picketed local supermarkets protesting high prices. With nationwide publicity of this event and others, the consumer movement grew and began to make its strength felt in America. Numerous groups with an interest in consumer concerns began to spring up.

In March 1962, John F. Kennedy presented the first presidential message to Congress directed at consumer concerns. He asked for legislative action and new programs in several areas. The most important aspect of this message, however, was the now famous **Consumer Bill of Rights**. Kennedy stated that consumers have four rights: (1) the right to safety, (2) the right to be informed, (3) the right to choose, and (4) the right to be heard. This message provided a great surge of interest in consumer concerns.

Consumer problems remained in the news. President Kennedy established a **Consumer Advisory Council** to assist his Council on Economic Advisors. The thalidomide drug scandal resulted in the birth of over 20,000 deformed babies around the world, although few occurred in the United States. The congressional hearings prior to passage of the Kefauver-Harris Drug Amendments revealed scandalous information about large numbers of ineffective and useless drugs being sold to unsuspecting Americans.

In 1964, President Lyndon B. Johnson created a **new White House position**, Special Assistant to the President for Consumer Affairs. He appointed Esther Peterson to this post. She was well qualified, and she had previously served as director of the Department of Labor's Women's Bureau under the Kennedy Administration. With White House visibility, consumer concerns became front-page news. Later that year, Johnson sent a consumer message to Congress urging passage of several new laws. These indeed were exciting times for consumers and consumer advocates, and the liberal landslide in the 1964 election gave strength to those calling for reforms. Ralph Nader's call for volunteers to come to Washington to research and become active on consumer issues resulted in hundreds of people joining what *The Washington Post* writer William Greider called **"Nader's Raiders."**

The **consumerism era** brought on a number of events: (1) housewives boycotting supermarkets because of high meat prices, (2) exposés in the form of books, news articles, and radio and television programs, (3) the formation of numerous local consumer-action groups, (4) a flurry of legislative action on national and state levels, (5) scandals concerning fabrics, drugs, food, credit, and product safety, (6) further presidential support by Lyndon B. Johnson and Richard M. Nixon through more consumer messages, (7) introduction of consumer education courses into many schools, (8) an increased media interest in consumer issues as news, (9) Nader's Network of consumer organizations, and (10) a general broadening of support for consumer concerns.

In 1968, the **Consumer Federation of America** was formed. Its strength came from the nearly 200 other consumer organizations that were members. It lobbied for consumers and pushed for more government intervention in the marketplace. The premise was that consumers needed more than information to make wise decisions; they needed strong voices to speak and leaders to fight for them. These years saw the **"ism"** in consumerism become appropriate as once-quiet consumers organized and spoke out on many issues of justice and fairness. Active leaders were almost militant in promoting the moral and ethical rights of consumers.

Responses to Consumerism

Business and government had different responses to the demands of consumers through the years. Business tended not to listen, took few positive actions, and typically remained disinterested in consumerism issues. Government listened and took a number of actions to help consumers.

Business Response

The social consciousness of the early 1960s, rising incomes of consumers, and higher expectations of quality (suggested primarily by advertising) were signs that could have predicted the consumerism of the times. A greater number of Americans had money and wanted quality goods and services. Substantial numbers of Americans had little money but still wanted those same goods and services. Businesses tried to provide what consumers wanted, but good quality and **low prices were difficult to find**.

In the early 1960s, the typical business response was "ignore the demands of the consumer activists and they will go away." Fear was the reason. Some business persons said, **"Fight the consumerists!** Save our free enterprise system!" The food industry reacted violently against Esther Peterson's modest proposal for a truth-in-packaging law, accusing her of being anti-American. Business views about consumer issues were often grudging and negative. The overall response of business to consumer demands for change in the 1960s was negative. The typical business response was concisely stated by the editors of *Business Week* in 1969:

> **Deny everything**. Nearly everyone goes through a phase of shock when hallowed business practices are questioned, and this is the automatic response.
>
> **Blame wrongdoing** on the small marginal companies. In any industry where fragmentation and ease of entry are the rule, the argument is popular that the major companies are blameless, but that the small outfits must cut corners to survive.
>
> **Discredit the critics**. "Hell," says one congressional staff man, "I've had publishers, worried about circulation sales, conducting an investigation down here peddling stuff on the communist nature of consumerism based on 1942 documents."
>
> **Hire a public relations person**. A big campaign to modify public opinion is alluring. But as one PR man says, "There's no sense in a PR campaign if you have nothing to say."
>
> **Defang the legislation**. Trade associations and Washington law firms are specialists in this, and it [passing weak regulatory laws] is often effective, at least for a while. It worked for the tobacco industry in 1965. It also worked in respect to the truth-in-packaging law.
>
> **Launch a fact-finding committee** to find out whether anything really needs to be improved in the way the company does business. The food industry is deeply involved in this now.
>
> **Actually do something**, whether you think you are guilty or innocent.[5]

Increasing inflation, beginning in the mid-1960s, and rising unemployment, combined with the louder voices of consumer advocates, finally convinced business that consumerism was a force to be reckoned with. Business had to be dragged into the realities of the times. Because of the reactionary attitudes of business, by the mid-sixties the historical business motto of **caveat emptor**, in existence since the 1500s, had changed to **caveat venditor** "let the seller beware!" Big business was worried because consumers were upset and would not take it anymore! By 1972, big business decided to form a coalition of their chief executive officers, the CEOs, to gain political power—the Business Roundtable. In 1978, that group

---

[5] Reprinted from the September 6, 1969, issue of *Business Week* by special permission, copyright by McGraw-Hill, Inc.

DID YOU KNOW?
Ralph Nader is the Nation's Leading Consumer Advocate

Ralph Nader today is best known for being responsible for **getting George W. Bush elected** President of the United States. Nader is a liberal idealist who had zero chance of getting elected president in 2000 on the Green Party ticket, but refused to opt out even though his inclusion on the ballot was sure to drain votes away from presidential candidate Al Gore. Nader received three percent of the vote. As a result, the conservative, pro-business Bush is president today rather than the more liberal, pro-consumer Gore. One political scientist wrote that Nader's decision ushered in "four years of reduced environmental protection, fiscally irresponsible tax-cuts, and conservative political hegemony...with Supreme Court appointments that will create a dark age of socially repressive rulings...."[1]

Nader is America's **most famous** consumer advocate. To many he is "Saint Ralph, the consumer's knight in shining white armor." Nader has spent his life helping ordinary consumers defend themselves against corporate negligence and government indifference. To the pro-business newspaper, *The Wall Street Journal*, and many business groups, such as the National Association of Manufacturers, he is a whining moralizer. Nader earns $200,000 to $300,000 a year making speeches, but lives on $25,000; he donates 80+ percent of his income to non-profit organizations.

Nader is **a crusader**, a muckraker and a person of enormous integrity. His combat has always been against the might of unelected and unaccountable corporate power. Who controls society, asks Nader? Business. Who makes the decisions? Business. Who owns America? Business. Who has a voice and access in politics? Business. Who pays the bills? Not business, but consumers!

In 1965, shortly after graduating from Harvard Law School, Ralph Nader wrote a book entitled ***Unsafe at Any Speed: The Designed-in Dangers of the American Automobile*** that indicted the auto industry for habitually subordinating safety to style and specifically criticized the design safety of the General Motor's Corvair automobile. The book became a best seller only after it was revealed that General Motors had investigated Nader's background in an attempt to discredit both the man and book. The resulting controversy led to an apology by the chairman of the board of General Motors during televised congressional hearings. Ralph Nader became an instant "folk hero," and the public's response prompted passage of the National Traffic and Motor Vehicle Safety Act later that year. Nader deserves credit for getting government to require automakers to install seat belts, air bags, and other safety equipment.

Nader's lawsuit against General Motors gave him the then-large sum of $425,000 in an out-of-court settlement. He used this money to establish several new consumer organizations, such as the Center for the Study of Responsive Law, Public Citizen, and Center for Auto Safety. The money also paid for summer interns to work on various ad hoc task force projects. These people became known as **Nader's Raiders** in part because of the excellent quality of their investigative research that typically resulted in a written report or book followed by changes in government laws and policies. Ralph Nader moved the idea of consumerism (then primarily concerned with bargain shopping and redeeming supermarket cents-off coupons) completely off the women's pages of the newspapers to the front pages. Nader has made major contributions to American society, particularly in the form of serving as a catalyst to pass laws and regulations to protect and empower consumers.

Nader and his various satellite organizations, including Essential Information, continue to combat practices that are hostile to consumer's interests. They conduct quality research and get good press coverage in an effort to force businesses and governments to do more of what is right for consumers. Nader wants America **to live up to its democratic ideals**—to make the free enterprise system work as it is supposed to—by helping consumers to more effectively participate in the American economic and political systems.

---
[1] Mayer-Blackwell, K. (2003). Nader: The life of the party, *The Journal of Consumer Affairs*, p. 180.

was credited with defeating the creating of an independent consumer protection agency within the federal government.

On the positive side, some businesses started going along with the demands of consumers, especially when those calls for change did not cost much money. Only a **few business leaders** viewed the consumerism movement as an opportunity. Those who did sought help from consumer advocates, knowing that such action would, at the very least, help improve their public relations images and perhaps also result in improved sales.

By the early 1970s, over 1000 regional and national businesses had hired **consumer affairs professionals (CAPs)**, people trained to represent the interests of both consumers and their employing organizations. A significant number of the appointments were for high-level positions, such as consumer manager or vice president for consumer affairs. This all started when Esther Peterson left the Johnson administration to become an in-house consumer advocate on her own terms for Giant Food. She had complete freedom to speak out according to her convictions, both publicly and within the company. Giant Food was the only food company that was accessible during the truth-in-packaging controversy. During this time, a professional association was established, the Society of Consumer Affairs Professionals in Business (www.socap.org). Collectively, the corporate consumer affairs professionals, particularly those in positions of high authority, played an important role in getting an increasing number of businesses to respond in a favorable way to consumer demands for change. Business has continued to embrace the consumer profession and today there are 3000 business CAPs.

Government Response

As consumer problems with price and quality persisted and complaints continued about the disparity between claims and performance, consumers looked for ways to fix the systematic poor attitudes of sellers. When the growing dissatisfactions were not met by corporations, consumers **took their grievances to government**.

During the 1960s and early 1970s, the over-arching belief was that informed consumers are essential to the fair and efficient functioning of a free-market economy. Congress chose **affirmative disclosure** (encouraging assertions of accurate information about products and services) as a major technique for regulating business. Local, state, and federal legislation became the primary governmental response to consumer problems. If a problem arose, it seemed logical and not expensive to write a new law or regulation, start a special agency, and/or create a commission to study the matter and make recommendations. Ralph Nader speculated that consumer legislation was likely to be enacted only under one configuration of interests: divided business groups and united consumer groups. Dozens of consumer protection bills were proposed and many were passed, although most were cosmetic gestures, like the Truth-in-Packaging Law, to appease constituents.

Many states and localities **passed a number of laws** and regulations in an effort to protect consumers. Examples include civil and criminal penalties against offenders, injunctions against unethical merchants, licensing of business services (such as television and automobile repairs), mandatory posting of octane ratings for gasoline, prohibition of pyramid sales promotions, banned advertising of any items when sufficient quantities were not readily available, and "little FTC" laws making it unlawful to use fraud, deception, or false pretense in the sale or advertising of merchandise.

However, putting laws on the books is one thing and providing effective consumer protection is another. **Weak and unenforced consumer legislation** results in inadequate consumer protection.

DID YOU KNOW?
Social Change is an Evolutionary Process

Social change has been described as an eight-stage evolutionary process:

1. **Situational evolution**—awareness of the changes starts to dawn slowly on those affected;
2. **Growing frustration**—quiet dissatisfaction slowly develops, but people do not know what to do about it;
3. **The lonely voice**—someone articulates the developing situation and seizes the public attention that serves to alert "astute managers with an invaluable early warning system for detecting emerging social change";
4. **Dissatisfaction coalesces**—people succeed in giving voice and shape to the growing frustration below the surface that has not yet been focused;
5. **Action/reaction**—public support evolves into a mass movement where demands for change are made, compromises are few, requests for voluntary change are resisted, and obstinacy fuels the demands for change;
6. **Political action**—leaders of the movement organize their followers, who have the votes, to put pressure on politicians for mandated changes, but the latter are supported by the status quo that results in passage of a watered-down version of the demanded reforms;
7. **Institutionalization**—supporters of the change gradually win institutional acceptance (at the economic, political, and social levels) as responsible leaders are appointed to political office and hired by corporations to administer the programs, and
8. **Incremental change**—"supporters of the new changes work for gradual, incremental improvements that ultimately achieve most of what the mass movement had demanded," demonstrating that the changes are mainstream ideas and part of the national agenda.[1]

---

[1]Private correspondence from Paul S. Forbes. Reprinted with permission.

The federal legislative rush to protect consumers during the 1960s and early 1970s resulted in more than **500 bills being proposed,** many for political reasons only. Less than 30 were made into law, and enforcement was typically weak. Still, Congress had passed laws that confronted **all the major problem areas** facing consumers: credit, warranties, product safety, cosmetics, medical devices, appliance energy labeling, real estate, drugs, and food. More consumer protection laws were passed between 1965 and 1975 than during the previous 75 years. In addition, four regulatory agencies were established: Consumer Product Safety Commission, National Highway Traffic Safety Administration, Occupational Safety and Health Administration, and Environmental Protection Agency. In addition, the existing government organizations tried to do a better job. By the end of the decade, there were 42 complaint departments in agencies of the federal government and more than 225 county and city consumer protection offices. Since the 1970s, government support for consumer issues has largely depended upon which political party held the presidency. Republican presidents and conservative members of Congress largely have been **anti-consumer** while democrats typically have supported the consumer agenda.

What Makes Consumer Movements Successful?

The history of the consumer movement in America provides insights as to why, on occasion, consumer interests seem to rise and fall and then rise again. Six social and economic factors seem associated with interest in consumer problems.

Rising Expectations of Consumers

Interest in consumer issues is so strong that it is now a part of the **American psyche**, the unconscious soul or spirit and behavior of the American population. Consumerism has become part of the social fabric of American life. People today demand and expect refunds for products that don't live up to their expectations. They want "somebody" to fix their problems "right now," and they want a "good buy." Today's consumers demand that business and government **pay attention to consumer issues**, and lately that includes more tangible concerns about banking, insurance, health care, and pensions. Interest in consumer issues is now accepted by custom and by law. People today believe that consumerism is synonymous with "free-market democracy" in that it gives people a voice in the economic and political decisions that affect them as consumers. Informed consumers encourage the competition that is needed to discipline the capitalistic marketplace.

Scandals and Dramatic Crises

Print media during the 1800s, radio during the 1920s and 1930s, television in the late 1940s and 1950s, and all mass media in the more recent decades have provided a ready outlet for scandals. Scandals, such as price fixing, bribery, adulterated foods, unsafe automobiles, bankrupt pension plans, bureaucratic incompetence, and dangerous chemicals, are viewed by consumers as violations of the public trust. These occasional lapses by business serve as a recurring **impetus that fuels the consumer movement**. Best-selling books and journalistic exposés of political and commercial corruption by investigative reporters quickly gain and hold the attention of Americans. When enough consumers are upset about a particular scandal, they demand corrective action by government officials.

Today's investigative television shows "60 Minutes" and "20/20" can keep the entire country talking about a story for weeks. The media helps sustain the consumer movement. Important in some scandals are **whistleblowers**, employees in government or business who cry out against injustice by exposing fraud, waste and mismanagement at their place of work. Congress has passed laws to protect whistleblowers from the risk of reprisals by their employers. Wronged whistleblowers can collect attorney fees in court if they win.

Without media attention, scandals and dramatic crises would have little or no impact. Many Americans were shocked and outraged by Upton Sinclair's book *The Jungle*, that while simultaneously offering a call to workers to unite and create a utopian vision of society, exposed the **scandalous and unhealthy conditions** of the meat-packing plants and led to a new food and drug law. The Chase and Schlink book, *Your Money's Worth*, resulted in the formation of several product-testing organizations. The liquid form of a drug called Elixir Sulfanilamide caused a national crisis when it killed nearly 100 people, and this, in part, resulted in improved drug and food legislation in 1938. Another drug scandal involved thalidomide, that caused birth defects in thousands of babies and led to further drug amendments in the 1960s.

Consumers often have the **support of the media** in their efforts. Today there are "Action Line" (callforaction.org) columns in over 100 newspapers in the United States, as well as consumer "Call for Action" lines on 20 radio and television stations. Several hundred newspapers and television and radio stations also employ reporters who uncover unfair business practices and disseminate valuable consumer information to the public. A major problem with media exposes is, however, that they rarely provide the aroused viewer, listener or reader with information (telephone number and address) on how to learn more about the topic, how to offer assistance, or how to join a group.

Ralph Nader's book *Unsafe at Any Speed* did not sell well until the **televised congressional hearings** disclosed the scandalous investigation of Nader by General Motors. The publicity made him into something of an American hero, and he soon became the nation's leading spokesperson for consumers. Nader's book also contributed to passage of major automobile safety legislation later that year.

Charismatic People

Certain people have a special quality of personal magnetism or charm and a demonstrated ability to win the devotion of large numbers of people. This **charisma** carries over into their leadership styles.

Throughout each consumer era, a few **individuals have inspired others** to listen, to think, and to act. People followed Theodore Roosevelt, and when, as President, he called for food and drug legislation, the country responded. Schlink's writing led to the formation of Consumers' Research, Inc., that published its findings in a periodical (now called *Consumers' Research Magazine*) to which thousands subscribed. People also responded to the leadership of Colston Warne, who founded *Consumer Reports* magazine in 1936, with a readership of hundreds of thousands. Warne's large physical size added to his charismatic presence when he spoke out supporting the consumer interest to groups around the world. *Consumer Reports* is now the nation's most popular consumer magazine, with a circulation of about 5 million copies monthly (see www.consumerreports.com/).

Vance Packard was a popular author throughout the 1950s, and when he appeared on television talk shows and addressed consumer issues, people really took notice. John F. Kennedy was legendary for his charismatic personality, and his famous **Consumer Bill of Rights** heralded a new era of consumer interest. Esther Peterson was such a tremendous spokesperson for consumers that businesses unsuccessfully pressured President Johnson to remove her. Ralph Nader's charisma from the 1960s continues today as he fights against overpriced automobile insurance and other issues.

Active Government Organizations

Federal, state, and local government organizations have much to do with promoting the consumer interest. They have the political power, after all, to propose and/or enforce laws and regulations. Government agencies strengthen the consumer movement by their very presence because they **institutionalize** the effort. Once a governmental agency is created, it is difficult to eliminate—thus the constituency (consumers in this instance) is likely to be served forever.

An *active* government organization is one that is **vigorously pursuing its mission** rather than just existing. Good leadership can make a difference. In the 1890s, for example, Dr. Harvey W. Wiley of the Department of Agriculture got excellent news coverage when he dramatized the food adulteration problem. He created a "poison squad" of 12 men who were fed adulterants common to the diet of most Americans to establish the "influence of food preservatives and artificial colors on digestion and health." None died, although some became ill. The publicity led to improved legislation.

During the 1920s, the Federal Trade Commission was responsible for the strong enforcement of the laws that mandated the breakup of business trusts that illegally conspired to fix prices. The importance of **antitrust efforts continues** today as federal judge Harold H. Greene said, "If the United States is today a consumer and consumption society, rather than one dominated by cartels with price-fixing abilities, it is largely because of the antitrust laws."

The drug thalidomide **deformed children worldwide** in the 1960s, but not in the U.S. because the Food and Drug Administration prohibited its sale. The FDA's Dr. Francis Kelsey was most active and vocal in her disapproval of this drug, and she was almost singlehandedly responsible for the refusal to allow thalidomide to be marketed in this country. Strong leadership at the Consumer Product Safety Commission in the 1970s resulted in a prohibition of the sale of flammable sleepwear for children.

State and local governments actively sustain the consumer interest in a number of ways. In all states, the **attorney general represents** both consumer and public interests. In most states, the representation consists of a full staff of lawyers and professionals. Since it is usually good politics to be pro-consumer, most state attorneys general support consumer interests. Each state also has a Weights and Measures Department that is charged with the responsibility to safeguard the interests of consumers.

Throughout the country every state has a **state office of consumer affairs (OCA)** to help consumers in complaint-handling (see /www.pueblo.gsa.gov/crh/state.htm.) Most of the time the OCA is under the office of the attorney general, but sometimes it is attached to the office of the governor. Public service announcements to advertise the OCA toll-free complaint hotline and appearances by committed government officials go a long way toward supporting the interests of consumer. All states have a consumer services mission in their state insurance and banking departments that offer information, education and complaint-handling.

Some states have employed **state-paid consumer advocates** to actively pursue the consumer interest before its governmental regulatory commissions, such as the state public utility commission (PUC) and the state agriculture department. In this way, the state's concern for the public interest is balanced against the special interests of consumers.

For many years, personnel in the White House acted to help sustain the consumer interest through its U.S. Office of Consumer Affairs, but it was closed in the 1990s. Thus, **no one in the executive branch** of the federal government is designated to forcefully project the interests of consumers to Congress, government agencies and the general public.

Active Private Organizations

A number of private organizations have helped to sustain interest in consumer matters. In 1891, a New York City action group **whitelisted** shops that treated employees fairly. This was in contrast to **blacklisting** stores that treated employees poorly by creating a list of persons or organizations that are disapproved or boycotted or suspected of disloyalty. Whitelisting encouraged patronage of those businesses that "paid fair minimum wages, had reasonable working hours, and decent sanitary conditions." By 1903, the National Consumer's League (NCL) had 64 branch offices in 20 states focusing on consumer and workplace issues. Today, NCL specializes in providing the consumer perspective on child labor, privacy, food, safety, and medication information. Today's largest consumer action group, the **Consumer Federation of America (CFA)**, represents about 280 national, state, and local pro-consumer organizations, with a combined membership exceeding 50 million people. It actively represents the consumer interest on key issues before governmental policy-making and regulatory bodies and the courts. CFA specializes in the issues of finance, food and agriculture, health care, privacy, safety and environmental health, and utilities.

Every state today has a **statewide consumer action group** and many larger states have multiple organizations. These groups typically charge a small membership fee, such as $10, produce an informative newsletter, and actively lobby in the state legislature and before regulatory agencies. Particularly strong consumer groups exist in California and Ohio. Some cities and even neighborhoods are well organized, too. Many private complaint-handling and mediation organizations also exist, such as Automobile Consumer Action Panels (AUTOCAPs) in cities across the country. One useful Internet portal for consumers is Consumer World.

Other privately organized groups include Ralph Nader's Center for the Study of Responsive Law, a relatively small group of lawyers and technical specialists who work on reform issues, and numerous offshoot organizations (the **"Nader Network"**). Nader contributes money, support, and advice to many of these groups but no longer has an active role: Public Citizen, whose members support a staff of 60 working in several sections (Congress Watch, Health Research Group, Litigation Group, Critical Mass Energy Project, and Buyers Up); U.S. Public Interest Research Groups (organizations in 35 states); Clear Water Action; Center for Auto Safety; Pension Rights Center; Center for Science in the Public Interest (1 million subscribers); Essential Information; National Association for Public Interest Law; Trial Lawyers for Public Justice; National Insurance Consumer Organization; Aviation Consumer Action Project; and Telecommunications Action and Research Center. Altogether these groups employ about 1,500 people and **serve 4 million members**.

Citizen utility boards (CUBs) are funded by member dues to serve as watchdog organizations that intervene in rate cases and legislative hearings on electric, gas and telephone matters. They represent the views of consumers and small businesses before public service commissions. CUBs were inspired by Ralph Nader, and they exist in a number of states. (For example, see the Illinois CUB at www.citizensutilityboard.org.)

Perhaps the most powerful private consumer organization is **Consumers Union (CU)**, the publisher of *Consumer Reports* magazine (www.consumerreports.org). The publication is authoritative, respected, and well read by millions of Americans. Consumers Union also has something historically uncommon among consumer groups, and that is money. Although not affluent, its profitable ventures allow CU to donate funds to fledgling consumer organizations to help them succeed. CU also funds advocacy offices in Austin, Texas, San Francisco, California, and the nation's capital. Also powerful is the **Consumers International**, headquartered in London, that represents **250 affiliated consumer organizations in 115 countries**.

Consumer organizations often work to achieve their goals with the help of other organizations. A **coalition** is an alliance, particularly temporary ones, of people or groups to accomplish some single effort that is a jointly held goal of each. Since coalitions have more than one organization involved, it is easier to create public awareness of a concern and/or push for action to change. Consumer groups have found it beneficial to work with other organizations, often with government, labor, and environmental organizations, and sometimes even with traditional business opponents to move toward a particular goal. For example, even though a union might be seeking higher wages that could raise prices and hurt the consumer interest of low prices, a consumer organization and a union might work together to support a law requiring disclosure of prescription drug prices to be posted inside drug stores that consumers could read and perhaps compare with other sellers. The JumpStart Coalition for Personal Financial Literacy supports consumer education in the schools.

Consumer groups work with unions, chambers of commerce, **cooperatives** (businesses that belong to the people who use them), credit unions, Better Business Bureaus, and businesses. Coalition organizations have included the Credit Union National Association, National Council of Better Business Bureaus, and leading companies such as American Express, Avon Products, and J.C. Penney. The Coalition for Health and Safety is a partnership of consumer, health and insurer groups.

The American Council on Consumer Interests (ACCI), successor to the Council on Consumer Information, is the professional association for academics in the consumer field. The Michigan-based National Institute for Consumer Education serves educators at all levels. The National Association of Consumer Advocates (NACA) is a nationwide association of more than 800 attorneys and consumer advocates. The **National Association for Consumer Agency Administrators (NACAA)** is an organization of 150 state and local consumer affairs professionals representing consumer protection offices. The Society for Consumer Affairs Professionals in Business serves a similar function for people working in business.

Poor Economic Conditions

When the economy experiences high unemployment and/or rising prices, consumers feel the pressure. They become acutely interested in what happens to their dollars, they get upset, and **they organize**. As a result, consumer protection efforts often succeed.

The inflationary period of the early 1900s helped give rise to the union movement. The Depression of the 1930s had an official unemployment rate of 25 percent, although historians say the jobless rate was more like 40 to 50 percent. Such eras of serious economic troubles saw consumer education courses brought into the schools and forced the federal government to legislate food and drug protection, employment programs, Social Security, and establish regulatory agencies, like the Securities and Exchange Commission (SEC). The **consumer voice was recognized** for the first time by government in the 1930s through its Consumer Advisory Board. High inflation in the 1960s and 1970s provided the impetus for passage of much consumer legislation, including the Real Estate Settlement Procedures Act, Emergency Petroleum Act, and Motor Vehicle Information and Cost Savings Act.

Today's Consumer Movement

Today's consumer movement exists in challenging times, particularly when conservative Republican policy-makers use **budget cuts** of consumer protection regulatory agencies "to reduce the burden of government regulation." Such efforts protect the interests of businesses over consumers. However, today's consumer movement is mature, well-organized, active, effective, and productive. Public opinion polls consistently show very strong support for consumer issues, especially those related to health, safety, and the environment. Added to that list are current consumer questions about privacy, errors in data files, bias, and fairness.

The consumer organizations in the consumer movement that fight for the consumer interest are constant in number, forceful in strength, and financially stable. They tend to have **growing memberships**, increasing participation, salable ideas, effective fund raising techniques, and high organizational credibility. There are over three hundred grassroots state and local consumer organizations and dozens of national groups that focus on consumer concerns.

Many are quite able to aggressively address consumer issues. **Powerful consumer groups** that make a difference in people's lives include the Consumer Federation of America, National Consumer's League, Public Citizen, the Center for the Study for Responsive Law, and the Center for Auto Safety. The constituents of these organizations, consumers themselves, seem to be quite willing to help finance the efforts.

Consumer organizations are quite capable of developing and presenting **well-prepared arguments** and mobilizing resources and support. They often use the federal Freedom of Information Act as a tool to obtain information from agencies of the government. When appropriate, consumer groups initiate lawsuits to force government to act more promptly, particularly when the Administration seems uninterested in enforcing consumer protection laws and regulations. Consumer groups also use direct-ballot initiatives to pass pro-consumer legislation.

ECONOMIC INSIGHT:
What Does the Consumer Movement Do?

The consumer movement is strong, and it is primarily concerned with:

1. **Fighting consumer problems** to protect consumers from such things as rip-offs and frauds, dangerous and defective products, unsafe food, price gouging, product performance failures, delivery failures, deceptive advertising, dishonored promises and warranties, and discrimination.

2. **Strengthening redress systems**, especially for consumers who have access problems in the marketplace (i.e., elderly, children, poor, new immigrants).

3. **Securing equity** for consumers in purchasing transactions.

4. **Increasing the quantity and quality of objective and useful information** about products and services as well as safety and environmental concerns.

5. **Improving the effectiveness of existing laws and regulations** to protect consumers.

6. **Cultivating strong consumer organizations** to more clearly articulate and champion the consumer interest.

7. **Motivating the vast powers of government** to assist (or at least not block) efforts to improve the way the capitalistic economy works so that it better supports the interests of consumers.

8. **Trying to fix the political system** itself by limiting political action committees (PACs), prohibiting legislators from accepting honoraria, and financing elections with public funds.

9. **Mobilizing and empowering citizens** to effectively participate in our democracy.

Consumer organizations continue to have excellent **access to the media**, and CFA's Stephen Brobeck says that is "the greatest strength" of consumer groups. Even the *Wall Street Journal* recognizes the credibility of various consumer organizations when, for example, it once noted, "When Consumer Federation of America talks, congressmen listen."

Most consumer organizations have a clear view when pursuing the consumer interest that is not simply an out-of-date anti-business, anti-government or anti-future perspective. Consumer organizations value the opportunity to **directly deal with corporations** because they see it as an appropriate way to resolve problems without confrontation. Consumer groups that have historical roots with the labor movement often remain "ambivalent when it comes to the interest of consumers at the short-run expense of labor."[6] Taking stands against big labor in favor of consumers risks losing the support of their labor membership.

Consumer groups often form **informal coalitions** with individual firms, business trade associations or entire industries on questions of consumer policy when a pro-consumer position is supported by a segment of the business community. Advocates for Highway and Auto Safety, for example, includes a number of top consumer activists and insurance company executives. It attempts to "save lives and reduce costs from motor vehicle crashes." The benefits of consumer-business coalitions are enormous.

CFA's Stephen Brobeck says that **public support is vital** to the future success of consumer organizations. He notes that the support "can be sustained only if two conditions are met: the public must continue to recognize that their interests as consumers are at risk; and they must remain convinced that consumer advocates effectively defend and promote their interests."

Traditional consumer organizations, such as the Consumer Federation of America, National Consumers League, and Consumers Union, remain successful in retaining the financial support of consumers. Such groups have found that people want to join consumer organizations that provide **tangible benefits**, rather than just making them feel good. Thus, consumer groups often offer redress assistance and buying information. The Consumers' Checkbook organization in Washington, DC, for example, provides reports on the attributes of service providers in the community, including physicians, television and auto repair dealers, and plumbers.

The causes of consumerism are **no longer the exclusive domain** of the traditional consumer groups. The 33-million-member AARP advocates improved benefits in areas such as health, telecommunications, and financial information for women. The Gray Panthers group also advocates the interests of older Americans. The AFL/CIO has promoted consumer education among its members for years as has the National Credit Union Association. The Association of Community Organizations for Reform Now organizes low- and moderate-income consumers to improve their communities. A number of consumer issues are also vital to the interests of the National Organization for Women and the National Association of Attorneys General. Today's consumer movement is fragmented by a plethora of groups supported by a diverse set of constituencies and such **variety provides part of the strength** and vigor of the consumer movement.

Businesses and consumers are increasingly **working together** to resolve problems and to seek opportunities for compatible beneficial interest. One method of collaboration is through **consumer advisory panels**. These are corporate-sponsored meetings where businesspeople meet regularly with consumer leaders, usually activists and academics, to share concerns and explore ways the company can better serve consumers.

Many businesses and governments have created a **consumer affairs department**. Whether in the corporation or government agency, most consumer affairs departments are organized to centrally manage consumer complaints. Many have an 800-number telephone service, a consumer/community outreach program, a system to track consumerism issues, and a consumer information and education program. These offices are usually staffed by consumer affairs professionals (CAPs).

Consumers today **are generally aware** that they have certain rights to help them avoid getting ripped off or cheated. They may not be aware about a specific law or regulation that

---

[6] McGowan, D. A. (1992, Spring), Gloves off consumer economics, *Advancing the Consumer Interest*, 4, 19.

can apply but they "know" there is probably some corporate office or government agency that will help. Consumers today in the United States inherently believe both that they have consumer rights and the power to assert them. American consumers live in a society that has permanently imprinted the consumer interest in the mentality of its people, as well as in many of the mechanisms of business and government. Consumers seek not only a more equal buyer-seller role but a **consumer-citizenship role** in society.

Review and Summary of Key Terms and Concepts

1. Give some examples of what the **economic marketplace** looked like for American consumers before the year 1890.

2. Illustrate the **kinds of problems** consumers had during the early consumer movement from the 1890s through the 1920s.

3. What were some of the circumstances that led to a renewed interest in the consumer movement **between 1929 and the 1950s**?

4. Provide some illustrations of what happened during the consumerism **era of the 1960s and 1970s**.

5. What did the terms **consumerism**, **consumer movement** and **consumer advocates** mean during the 1960s and 1970s?

6. Explain why **Ralph Nader** was and remains a leading consumer spokesperson.

7. Summarize the **responses of governments** in the 1970s and 1980s to consumerism.

8. Distinguish between **caveat emptor** and **caveat venditor**.

9. What is meant by the term **affirmative disclosure**, and why did it occur?

10. Summarize what is meant by **"social change is an evolutionary process."**

11. What does **rising expectations of consumers** have to do with making consumer movements successful?

12. Explain how **scandals and dramatic crises** contribute to making consumer movements successful, and include an explanation of **whistleblowers** in your response.

13. Identify illustrations of how **active government organizations** contribute to making consumer movements successful, and include an explanation of **state-paid consumer advocates** in your comments.

14. Provide illustrations of how **active private organizations** contribute to making consumer movements successful, and include an explanation of the terms **blacklisting, citizen utility boards** and **coalition** in your response.

15. List three of the **primary concerns** of today's consumer movement.

16. Summarize how **consumer organizations** contribute toward helping to shape the future of the consumer movement.

Useful Resources for Consumers

Association of Community Organizations for Reform Now
www.acorn.org/

American Council on Consumer Interests
www.consumerinterests.org

Advocates for Highway and Auto Safety
www.saferoads.org

Better Business Bureau
www.bbb.org

Federal Trade Commission Bureau of Consumer Protection
www.ftc.gov/consumer.htm

Call for Action
www.callforaction.org

Center for Auto Safety
www.autosafety.org

Center for Study of Responsive Law
www.csrl.org

Consumer Action
www.consumer-action.org/

Consumer Federation of America
www.consumerfed.org

Consumer World
www.consumerworld.org

Consumers' Checkbook
www.checkbook.org/

Consumers International
www.consumersinternational.org

Consumers Union
www.consumersunion.org

Essential Information
www.essential.org/about.html

Federal Consumer Information Center
www.pueblo.gsa.gov/crh/state.htm

Gray Panthers
www.graypanthers.org/

JumpStart Coalition for Personal Financial Literacy
www.jumpstart.org

National Association of Attorney's General
www.naag.org/

National Association of Consumer Advocates
www.naca.net

National Association of Consumer Agency Administrators
www.nacaanet.org/

National Institute for Consumer Education
www.nice.emich.edu/

National Consumers League1
www.nclnet.org

National Organization for Women
www.now.org

Ralph Nader (The Nader Page)
www.nader.org

U.S. Public Interest Research Group
www.uspirg.org

Public Citizen
www.citizen.org

Society of Consumer Affairs Professionals in Business
www.socap.org/

"What Do You Think" Questions

1.   Thinking about Ralph Nader's comments on **citizen empowerment**, list some examples of activities that college students might do to help reform and improve American society.

2.   Choose any issue of interest (e.g., abortion, prostitution, overseas economic aid, legalizing drugs) and consider the **eight steps** presented in the text on the topic of social change as an evolutionary force. (A) Where along the eight steps do you believe the issue is now? (B) What do you think must occur for the issue to continue towards change?

3.   Your life is already full of consumer experiences, some satisfying and others not so. Thinking about your personal experiences and about society's needs, what are three consumer topics, concerns or issues that you believe **need improvement** to make life for consumers better?

Part Two:

FACING CONSUMER PROBLEMS SUCCESSFULLY

Chapter 3

Consumer Rights, Responsibilities and Remedies

OBJECTIVES

After reading this chapter, you should be able to

1. Understand how to use the legal rights available to consumers.

2. Appreciate the moral rights that consumers possess.

3. Cite examples of consumer responsibilities and identify why people often do not complain.

4. Recognize that the complaining process should follow sequential levels and channels and what damages to ask for when suing.

5. Describe how to use a small claims court.

6. Consider using various "techniques of last resort" to fight back and win.

T he American economic marketplace is unquestionably the best in the world. Reasons include the enormous supply of high-quality goods and services, the multitude of choices available, the large number of competitors, the belief and trust in self-regulation instead of heavy government intervention, the emphasis on safety standards for virtually all products and services, and a serious concern for the environment. Another reason the American marketplace is so good is the existence of a strong consumer interest perspective in society—people want to get their money's worth. Besides, when there is a problem with a product or service, the American consumer wants it resolved, and resolved right now!

Americans are fortunate to have a number of legal and moral rights available. Consumers need to understand how to use their rights. To be effective advocates of their interests and to help provide part of the discipline necessary to keep the marketplace honest, consumers must become knowledgeable and empowered. Consumers have a responsibility to not be a victim, but if they do become a casualty of a rip-off, they must know and exercise their rights.

This chapter accepts that challenge by examining consumers' legal and moral rights as well as the important consumer responsibilities associated with these rights. Some people do not complain, and this void hurts both consumers and sellers; the chapter examines why people do not complain. The last part of the chapter details the remedies available to consumers who seek to correct wrongs encountered. One appendix is included at the end of the chapter on "Writing a Letter of Complaint."

Legal Rights of Consumers

A **right** is an entitlement to something or to be treated in some particular way. Rights of consumers are important because they empower people to protect themselves in the economic marketplace. Consumers have three types of legal rights: (1) **Implied warranties** that arise from common law or by operation of law and need not be specified by the parties,[1] (2) **Express warranties** that arise from contracts (and largely governed in the states by the Uniform Commercial Code and by the federal Magnusson-Moss Warranty Act), and (3) dozens of **statutory rights** that are provided in the details of written laws and regulations.

Implied Warranty Rights are Powerful Legal Rights

A **warranty** or **(guarantee)** is a written or oral assurance by the seller of property that the goods or property is of the quality represented or will be as promised. It generally means that the seller will repair or replace a defective product or service within a specified period of time. The **cost of a warranty** is included in the price of the product. A person who purchases a new clothes dryer, buys a stereo system, or pays for auto repairs that later fail to function properly has the right to get the problem corrected. If it is not fixed, the consumer has the right to get the product or service replaced or obtain a refund of money paid. When no remedy occurs, the consumer can bring legal action against the seller. This is a powerful legal right.

---

[1] **Common law** is a system of laws originated and developed in England based on court decisions, on the doctrines implicit in those judgments, and on customs and usages, rather than on codified written laws.

All states have similar warranty laws mandating an implied warranty *every* time goods are sold by merchants to consumers. Thus, the law requires that merchants provide implied warranties when they sell clothing or bicycles or whatever, but a neighbor selling similar goods at a garage sale does not have to provide such warranties. An **implied warranty** is a written or unwritten promise that the manufacturer implicitly asserts that the product is usable and will not fail during normal use. There are two types:

Warranty of Merchantability

The first type of implied warranty is a **warranty of merchantability**. This means that the consumer has a right to expect that the product is reasonably fit for the ordinary purposes for which the goods are expected to be used. This means that the goods, such as a used vehicle, should be in **proper condition for sale** and that it will **perform as intended**. For example, a vacuum cleaner is expected to function properly and clean dirt from carpets and rugs. It should vacuum, not just sweep, as with electric brooms. Note that in a number of states, courts have ruled that home builders are responsible for any defects in their work, even if there is no written contract or warranty that makes responsibilities clear. Authority for such a ruling comes under the concept of an implied warranty of merchantability, and this legal right can be upheld even *after* a written warranty has expired. The U.S. Supreme Court ruled that manufacturers could not unreasonably and unconscionably put short time limits on warranties. Thus, **if a consumer believes** a new product should have a warranty longer than its written warranty, it probably does.

Warranty of Fitness for a Particular Purpose

The second type of implied warranty is **warranty of fitness for a particular purpose**. Here the seller is presumed to know the particular purpose for which a buyer is purchasing the goods *and* knows that the buyer has relied upon the seller's knowledge, skill, and judgment to select and sell appropriate goods. In order for a warranty of fitness for a particular purpose to be created between the seller and the buyer, the seller should have **"reason to know"** the buyer's purpose for purchasing the product and the buyer must rely on the seller's skill or judgment in selecting the goods.

This important legal right of warranty of fitness for a particular purpose protects consumers who go to buy a product or service from a merchant and trust the advice they receive, buy it, and then suffer because it does not perform as anticipated. For example, Jean Johnson, from Logan, Utah, goes to an electronics store to buy a television antenna and tells the salesperson that she wants to pick up the Salt Lake City stations. After installing it on the roof, she finds that the television works, but the pictures coming from the Salt Lake stations are just not clear. This is a simple case of **breach of implied warranty**. The store created the contract when Jean relied on the advice of the salesperson, and it is violated because she cannot receive the television picture desired. The store owes her a refund, even if the product has scratches from putting the mast up on the roof.[2]

The same legal rights **apply to all types of services**. For example, if one is charged $8 for dry cleaning services, it is understood that the soiled clothes should be returned clean. The proprietor has a legal obligation to stand by the quality of the work. If the clothing is

---

[2] Sellers that correctly practice the concept of implied warranties by establishing a formal policy of satisfaction guaranteed include McDonalds's, L. L. Bean, Orvis, Craftsman, and Cross.

not cleaned properly, either they should be processed again or the cost should be refunded. To avoid the warranty of fitness for a particular purpose, some dry cleaners are careful to tell customers that they do not remove "stubborn stains."

Express Warranty Rights

In the area of warranties, express warranties are covered by both statutory and common law. An **express warranty** can be created by written or verbal words or by demonstration as it sets out the specific assurances by the manufacturer or seller. Once created, an express warranty is extremely difficult to destroy. **Written express warranties** are statements that specify the name and address of the warrantor, the product or parts covered, the duration of the warranty, what the warrantor will do, and who will pay for it. Each state has provisions under the Uniform Commercial Code that regulate implied and express warranty rights.

There is a federal statute in the area of warranties also. Sellers who offer warranties on consumer products that cost $15 or more are required to comply with various standards under the Magnusson-Moss Warranty Act. Basically, this federal law demands that a warranty should mean what it says and that the details should be spelled out in easy-to-understand language. The law requires that guarantees be conspicuously designated as either **full** or **limited**. This immediately gives consumers an indication of the degree of warranty coverage provided. The law also encourages the use of an informal dispute procedure whenever warranty problems arise between sellers and buyers. Consumers who successfully file state or federal lawsuits against warrantors may be awarded their purchase costs, attorney fees, and damages. (More information on consumer rights and remedies under the provisions of the Magnusson-Moss Warranty Act is in Chapter 5.)

As a defense against a warranty claim, a seller may argue that the buyer was given an opportunity for reasonable inspection that was disclaimed by the buyer's inaction. Sellers also sometimes **try to disclaim** or repudiate warranties to make them void. For example, some state laws permit a warranty of merchantability to be disclaimed legally if it is done in clear, conspicuous, and specific language. A popular example is when a used automobile is sold **as is**, or with all its faults.

CONSUMER UPDATE:
Do You Have to Mail in the Warranty-Registration Card?

Many products come with warranty-registration cards that are to be mailed back to the manufacturer. Most contain irrelevant requests for personal information, such as income, age, and motivations for purchase; facts often used for marketing purposes. Failure to mail in the warranty-registration **does not void** the warranty because the sales receipt is proof of purchase.

Many computer and software sellers, however, will provide technical assistance only to those who have registered, and they often offer free or discounted upgrades to their registered customers. Consumers may choose to send in the warranty-registration card without responding to the personal questions, so they can **be notified** about product defects or recalls.

KEY CONSUMER ECONOMIC CONCEPT:
Rule #1 of Consumer Life—When in Doubt About a Purchase,
Always Put it on Your Credit Card

Consumers have the legal right not to pay for the **cost of a disputed purchase** made on a credit card when they complain about it to the merchant and the creditor. This right is provided in the Fair Credit Billing Act. Let your credit card company—VISA, MasterCard, American Express, Discover, whatever—help you fight the merchant or unscrupulous scam operator that provided you with an "unsatisfactory purchase" that you charged on your card. Those credit card users who dispute charges have an excellent chance of getting their money back; those who **paid with cash** or a check may never again see their money. See Chapter 5 for details.

Other Legal Rights Exist

While consumers have many moral rights they prefer to have the support of explicit statutory laws. Consumers have been pushing unsuccessfully to have **more legal statutes** enacted to better protect them, such as making into law an airline passenger bill of rights. Dozens of federal, state, and local laws, regulations, and ordinances are available to protect consumers, and many of them will be described in Chapter 5. For example, consumers have the legal right to find out the reason why they are turned down for credit based on information provided by a credit-reporting agency under provisions of the Fair Credit Reporting Act.

Moral Rights of Consumers are Legitimate Expectations

In addition to legal rights, consumers have moral rights in the marketplace. **Moral rights** are expectations of consumers that the marketplace will be guided by principles, rules, and standards of good conduct that arise from conscience or a sense of right and wrong.

General Moral Rights

Some general moral rights include:

- Being treated equitably in the marketplace
- Being treated courteously by salespersons when shopping even though a purchase may not be made
- Being given an opportunity to compare prices and products inside stores without interference
- Being able to buy goods and services with socially acceptable minimum standards of quality
- Being sold products that are safe, both to the consumer and the environment
- Being assured of honesty from merchants in every transaction

- Being assured of a certain degree of privacy

- Being given fair treatment by sellers regardless of economic, political, religious, racial, ethnicity, gender, or youthful appearance

President Kennedy's Consumer Bill of Rights

President John F. Kennedy took the idea of moral rights for consumers a major step forward when he formally proclaimed a "Consumer Bill of Rights" in a speech before the Congress of the United States. The rights as President Kennedy set them down in 1962 are:

- The right to choose

- The right to safety

- The right to be informed

- The right to be heard

Subsequent presidents have confirmed to the nation that consumer rights in America are here to stay.

Consumer Rights for All Americans

There are eight important consumer rights:

1. **The right to choice**, by which consumers have the right to be assured, wherever possible, access to a variety of products and services at competitive prices. In those industries in which competition is not workable and government regulation is substituted, consumers have the right to an assurance of satisfactory quality and service at fair prices. Having choices is sometimes more complicated than not having choices, but consumers do benefit from the availability of choices.

2. **The right to information**, by which consumers have the right to be given accurate and adequate information upon which to make free and intelligent decisions as well as be protected against fraudulent and misleading information, advertising, labeling, and other deceptive marketing practices.

3. **The right to safety**, by which consumers have the right to expect that their health and safety—as well as financial well-being—will be properly and effectively protected in the marketplace.

4. **The right to voice**, by which the interests of consumers will be given full and fair consideration in government policy-making situations and expeditious treatment in its administrative tribunals.[3]

---

[3] The right to voice is guaranteed in the first amendment to the U.S. Constitution that provides citizens with freedom of speech. This right was tested when the Texas cattlemen tried to silence Oprah Winfrey's comments about mad cow disease. Many observers called this a **"SLAPP suit"** (Strategic Litigation Against Public Participation) intended to intimidate Winfrey and discourage others from defaming food products. She won. Such so-called **veggie libel** state laws are agricultural defamation statutes that, if appealed all the way to the U.S. Supreme Court, will eventually be found to be unconstitutional.

5. **The right to redress or remedy**, by which consumers are provided a full and fair hearing in any case of dissatisfaction and, wherever possible, the complaint is satisfactorily resolved.

6. **The right to environmental health**, by which consumers may consume in an environmentally sound manner and be protected from the ill effects of pollution of the air, earth, and water that may occur in the performance of everyday marketplace transactions.

7. **The right to service**, by which consumers may expect convenience, courtesy, and responsiveness to consumer needs and problems as well as all steps necessary to ensure that products and services meet the quality and performance levels claimed for them.

8. **The right to consumer education**, by which consumers are provided the right to continuing consumer education without which consumer-citizens cannot enjoy the full benefit of the other enumerated rights.

ISSUE FOR DEBATE:
Schools Should Publish Quality Indicators for Students

The typical situation in higher education is that students often have little more than word-of-mouth information from other students about the quality of instructors. While that information is useful, it often is not accurate or reliable. In fact, all schools have quality indicators about their faculty. **Quality indicators** that schools already possess, but generally keep under wraps, that they would find relatively inexpensive to provide students, if asked, include average class sizes, data on over-enrolled required courses, teaching scores for instructors, retention rates for each major every academic year, graduation rates, percent of majors that go on for graduate study, employment rates of graduates (including how many are still flipping burgers for McDonald's), and median salaries of graduates (starting salaries, plus figures after one and five years). One website of the many that rates professors is www.ratemyprofessors.com.

Responsibilities of Consumers

The first responsibility of consumers is to **assert their consumer rights** when seeking value for money in marketplace transactions. A second responsibility is to know what questions to ask and ask them. A third responsibility is to complain when not satisfied. Listed below are several specific responsibilities that are related to consumer rights.

Regarding *the right to choose*, consumers have the responsibility to

- Understand their personal motivations for buying certain products and services.
- Recognize persuasive selling techniques.
- Compare products for both price and quality.
- Exercise independence of judgment in decision-making.
- Avoid buying by habit.
- Choose carefully from whom they buy.

- Practice comparison shopping in an effort to frequently get a **best buy**; that is a product or service that, in the buyer's opinion, represents acceptable quality at a fair or low price for that quality.
- Consider the cost of time and other resources in decision-making.
- Continue to buy when products and services are satisfactory.
- Refuse to buy when products and services are unsatisfactory.
- Recognize the ecological consequences of choices.
- Be honest in dealings with sellers.
- Encourage sellers and governments to enhance access to choices for all consumers.
- Make purchases from sellers who support consumer rights.

Regarding *the right to safety*, consumers have the responsibility to

- Use products with reasonable caution and care, and report defects.
- Carefully read product labels and use products as intended.
- Read and follow care and use instructions carefully, and respond to recalls.
- Read and heed any warning labels.
- Question sellers about the safety attributes of products.
- Examine merchandise for safety features before buying.
- Assume personal responsibility for normal precautions when using a product.
- Inform retailers, manufacturers, industry trade organizations, and government agencies when a product does not perform safely.
- Support efforts to improve safety for all consumers.

Regarding the right to information, consumers have the responsibility to

- Use available information.
- Seek out accurate information about products and services.
- Read advertisements and promotional materials carefully.
- Analyze and understand performance claims.
- Ask questions of sellers about products and services when complete information is not available.
- Support sellers who make serious efforts to provide useful information to all consumers.

Regarding *the right to voice* (or *to be heard*), consumers have the responsibility to

- Become informed and speak up about issues that affect all types of consumers.
- Seek remedies to consumer problems.
- Seek to right wrongs occurring in the marketplace.
- Assist others in asserting their consumer rights.
- Support efforts to increase the ability of consumers to participate effectively in corporate and government decision-making.
- Boycott by refusing to take part in, deal with, or trade with an unscrupulous seller.

Regarding *the right to redress or remedy*, consumers have the responsibility to

- Know where and how to go about seeking redress.
- Speak up when errors occur, when safety problems are apparent, and when the quality of products or services is inferior.
- Make suggestions for product and service improvements.
- Complain to and compliment sellers as appropriate.
- Seek satisfaction directly from the seller before using other forms of redress.
- Utilize informal dispute mechanisms when available.
- Seek out and utilize third-party complaint-handling procedures where available, such as the state, county, or city office of consumer affairs.
- When appropriate, use the legal system to redress wrongs.
- Support efforts to broaden access to redress mechanisms for all consumers.

Regarding *the right to environmental health*, consumers have the responsibility to

- Become informed about environmental issues.
- Learn the environmental effects of alternative product and service choices.
- Compare products for their effects on the environment.
- Make reasoned and environmentally sound consumption choices.
- Support sellers who practice positive environmental policies.
- Support efforts to stop the use of consumer products that are harmful to the environment and to enhance the availability of goods friendly to the environment.

Regarding the *right to service*, consumers have the responsibility to

- Expect and demand good service.
- Compliment service providers where appropriate.

Regarding *the right to consumer education*, consumers have the responsibility to

- Become more informed about how to get their money's worth in the American economic marketplace.
- Learn how to assert all the consumer rights.
- Become more knowledgeable about the American economic marketplace and the consumer's role in it.
- Learn how to protect and assert the consumer interest.
- Become an educated consumer.
- Support efforts to have more consumer information and education programs accessible to all students and the public.

KEY CONSUMER ECONOMICS INSIGHT:
Privacy in Consumer Transactions is Under Threat

Privacy is the condition of being secluded or isolated from the sight, presence, or intrusion of others. It is under threat. Privacy problems exist in the banking, credit, food, housing, telecommunications, and financial services industries, where a tremendous amount of information is collected and retained on the daily transactions of individual consumers. **Profiling information** about consumers helps sellers suggest things that people might wish to purchase, develop improved products, offer better packaging, and conduct more precise marketing. Creating centralized warehouses of data about an individual's activities and sharing that information for marketing purposes increases the chances for misuse and abuse. Polls show that privacy concerns are the number one consumer issue for the 21st century.

Consumers often inadvertently supply firms with personal information. This occurs when you send in a warranty-registration card; rent a video or order one from a satellite; subscribe to a magazine; use a smart card; invest in stocks and mutual funds; purchase auto health, and life insurance; look at a website (**cookies** record where individuals go online, how often, and for how long); purchase an airline ticket on the Internet; finance or lease an automobile; check into a hospital; apply for a mortgage loan; and use a frequent-purchaser grocery discount card at a supermarket. Every credit card purchase is captured by financial services companies. Some states sell motor vehicle registration information to marketers.

Many consumer products come with tiny computer chips called **RFID tags**, or radio frequency identification tags. These reading sensors have been used for years to track shipping containers, and they are also used at some highway toll roads allowing drivers to bypass the booths. They contain information such as the product's serial number that can be read by a scanner at the checkout counter. Retailers and manufacturers can immediately track what was sold and when, which helps with inventory processes. Privacy becomes a concern when that information is combined with the credit card purchaser's information.

When such data are combined with a person's social security and/or driver's license number(s), the data can be overlaid to develop detailed pictures of almost anyone. This might include employment history, preference for breakfast cereal, list of magazines read, health records, prescription purchases, check-writing history, school records, and more. Making a telephone call to a business that has **"caller ID"** technology identifies callers by telephone number and permits the seller to later match the number with names and addresses. The use of caller ID raises the issue of whose right is more compelling: the caller or the person being called. And, in the broadest sense, who owns the information about each consumer? The answer is that consumers do!

To increase your privacy, see the Federal Trade Commission's privacy page (www.ftc.gov/privacy) for instructions. Privacy laws are explained in Chapter 5. Privacy advocates want a law that provides an **opt-in arrangement** (not opt out) that would require companies possessing data about a person to explicitly get his or her permission before transferring or selling the information to affiliates or other third-party companies. Corporations respond that this would be too expensive. Consumers also should have the right to review a company's **information about themselves**, as well as the right to correct errors.

Why People Don't Complain

More than 200,000 consumers complain annually to the Federal Trade Commission. The top types of consumer fraud complaints were **identity theft** (42%), Internet auctions (10%), Internet services (7%), and shop-at-home and catalogue offers. The top categories of complaints to state and local consumer protection agencies were home improvement (59%), household goods (54%), automotive sales (51%), automotive repairs (46%), credit/lending (42%), business practices (32%), services (24%), telecommunications (20%), and collections, pyramids and business opportunities (all at 17%). (Frauds in all of these areas are examined in Chapter 4.) It is impossible for consumers to go through life without experiencing occasional difficulties in marketplace transactions. Research shows that approximately one out of four purchases results in some type of problem.

Even though sellers are generally receptive to complaints, **many consumers do not complain**. People do not because they think complaining will not be worth their time, because they think that complaining will not do any good, and because they do not know how or where to complain. Many do not because they believe the benefits of complaining will not exceed the costs.

John Goodman, president of Technical Assistance Research Programs (TARP), has research data on customer dissatisfaction. It shows that about one-third of consumer dissatisfaction with a product or service stems from either **unfulfilled expectations** or **lack of knowledge regarding use**. Another one-third stems from company policies and procedures, and a final one-third results from product defects. The percentage of customers experiencing problems with selected products and services who do not complain are 60 percent for high-priced durable goods, 50 percent for medium-priced durable goods, 37 percent for high-priced services, and 45 percent for low-priced services.

For small consumer problems that result in a loss of a few dollars or a minor inconvenience, **only 3 percent** of consumers complain, 30 percent return the product, and nearly 70 percent either do nothing or discard the product. Research from the A. C. Nielsen Company shows that of those people who experience major consumer problems, such as a financial loss of about $150 or more, about one-third never complain.

TARP data revealed that the average business **does not hear from 96 percent** of its unhappy customers. For every complaint received at company headquarters, the average business has another 26 customers with problems, at least six of which are serious concerns. Depending on the industry, between 65 and 90 percent of non-complainers do not buy from particular businesses again and they never tell the business why. In sum, every complaint represents dozens of dissatisfied customers. Complaining consumers who have had their complaints resolved satisfactorily and quickly tell 6 people. In contrast, those who are not satisfied tell 12 to 24 other people.

Enlightened business leaders view customer complaints as **opportunities in disguise**. They invite customer complaints and use complaint data in worthwhile ways, because they see that what consumers think about a company is almost more important than the complaints themselves. It costs a company probably five to 10 times as much to go out and find a single new customer rather than handling a complaint properly in the first place. Smart business people know that if they are totally consumer-focused and deliver what customers want, everything else falls into place, i.e., sales, profits, bonuses, happy employees. From the business perspective, **consumer satisfaction** is when a customer's needs, wants, and expectations are met or exceeded, and that satisfaction results in repurchases and loyalty to the seller.

Remedies to Resolve Consumer Problems

No laws require merchants to offer refunds, exchanges, or credits on merchandise they sell. Before making purchases, shoppers should inquire about the seller's **return policy**. This is the set of procedures used by sellers that explicitly states the conditions under which products can be returned, exchanged, or credited. Policies are often posted inside store premises near the cash register; many states have laws requiring the posting of return policies. Most sellers require that products be returned within a limited time period, in good condition, in the original packaging, and with a sales receipt; others are more flexible in their conditions. Some sellers may require a restocking charge, perhaps 15 percent of the price and/or prior authorization before one can return an item.

If you buy goods or services that are **unsatisfactory**—not at the level of price and quality you expected—ask the seller to take back the goods, if possible, and obtain a refund. If not, ask the seller to reduce the price to accommodate your dissatisfaction. You may ask a seller for a refund or price reduction even if you simply **changed your mind**. Perhaps you don't like the color after all, or it really doesn't fit the decor of the home, or you spent too much money and need the cash for something else.

Sellers are willing to handle the numerous types of consumer complaints for **several reasons**: (1) to fulfill the desire to act fairly and honestly in marketplace transactions and maintain a positive reputation, (2) to obtain early warning signals about defects and possible violations of laws, (3) to learn about problems with products or services, so they can be corrected quickly, (4) to avoid bad publicity, particularly from assertive consumers who write letters to third parties (such as government agencies), (5) to reduce third-party liability claims, (6) to keep customers satisfied and loyal (so they will not go to the competition), (7) to increase profits over the long run by making sales to new customers who receive positive word-of-mouth comments from existing customers, and (8) to avoid government regulation and improve relationships with regulators.

Effective Complaining Should Follow a Sequence

The way to remedy a wrong committed by a seller is to **personally take actions** to resolve it. Simply put, consumers must complain, and if complaining does not work, they should tell lots of people about their bad experiences with that seller. Also, if appropriate, consumers should consider legal action.

Americans should simply **refuse to accept** shoddy products or service. When you have a negative marketplace experience, make sure your complaint does the most good. To be an effective complainer, you must first decide on the objective of the complaint. If your objective is to be treated a little better while in a store, just ask to see the person in charge. This may be the store manager or an assistant manager. Simply and factually report the quality of service received and request that someone more capable be provided so you can spend your money in the store. If your objective is to remedy a wrong, more work is necessary.

Follow these procedures **to complain** effectively: (1) Pursue your complaint as soon as possible after experiencing dissatisfaction, while events are still fresh in your mind; (2) clearly identify the problem and document it with evidence; (3) if possible, register your complaint with the person responsible for the transaction, otherwise go to that person's boss; (4) explain how you want your complaint resolved (i.e., apology, repair, refund); (5) be courteous and show respect, but be firm and persistent (realizing too that even though you were wronged, there are two sides to every story); (6) be willing to compromise, especially if you will not otherwise benefit; and, (7) be prepared to wait a reasonable amount of time for the responsible person to make a decision on your complaint.

Table 3-1 shows the five **sequential levels** of complaining: (1) to business, (2) to manufacturers, (3) to self-regulatory groups, (4) to consumer action personnel, and (5) to the private-action legal arena. If the problem is an illegal fraud, you should, of course, begin by reporting the crooks to the police. You can follow these channels individually or simultaneously, but usually one should begin the complaint process with the seller.

Sequential Levels to Bring Your Complaint	Sequential Channels for a Complaint
1. Local business	Salesperson → supervisor → manager/owner
2. Manufacturer	Consumer affairs department → president and/or chief executive officer (CEO)
3. Self-regulatory organizations	Better Business Bureau → county professional societies → consumer action panels (CAPs)
4. Consumer action agencies	Private consumer action groups → media action lines → government agencies

TABLE 3-1   Complaint Procedure—Sequential Levels and Channels

Note that federal agencies, such as the Food and Drug Administration (www.fda.gov), Consumer Product Safety Commission (www.cpsc.gov) and Federal Trade Commission, (www.ftc.gov) are not included in this table. These agencies can **register consumer complaints**, but they do not have the power to resolve individual consumer problems. Complaining to federal government agencies helps them obtain information to take collective actions against sellers.

Complaints about services should follow the same channels. Each type of service provider (i.e., doctors, chiropractors, lawyers, nursing homes, telephone bills, landlords, tax collectors, pre-schools) has an overseeing self-regulatory body and/or government agency. Appropriate addresses and telephone numbers can be obtained by looking in the front pages of the telephone directory and the blue pages listing government agencies.

1. The Local Business

The best approach in complaining is to give the seller **every opportunity** to right the wrong before taking additional action. For example, a complaint about an unsatisfactory product, such as a faulty Nokia telephone, should be brought to the attention of the merchant. Take the telephone back and talk to a salesperson. If he or she cannot resolve the problem, simply ask to see the supervisor. If you still get no satisfaction, such as a refund, a substitute product, or a repair, ask to see the manager or owner.

2. The Manufacturer

When a problem with a product cannot be resolved satisfactorily directly with a merchant and/or the difficulty is really with the product itself, you can keep your complaint within the business **self-regulatory scheme** by bringing it to the attention of the manufacturer's consumer affairs department at the corporate headquarters.

Product manufacturers provide **toll-free telephone numbers** for consumer inquiries and complaints. Addresses and telephone numbers of companies can be found on warranties, owner's instruction manuals, product hang tags, or on the Internet.

Should you get no resolution from a senior-level manager in the consumer affairs department (don't ever take "no" from a low-level person!), then it is time to communicate with the manufacturer's **president** or chief executive officer (CEO). Simply send a complaint letter addressed to the title "President" or "Chief Executive Officer" and await the response. The chapter appendix explains and illustrates how to write a complaint letter.

DID YOU KNOW?
How to Get a Copy of the *Consumer Action Handbook*

The federal government publishes the *Consumer Action Handbook* every year (www.pueblo.gsa.gov/crh/respref.htm). In addition to offering tips on buying smart, it provides **thousands of addresses and websites** in a consumer assistance directory format. Included are corporations, national consumer organizations, car manufacturers, Better Business Bureaus, trade associations, government consumer protection offices, aging offices, banking authorities, insurance regulators, securities administrators, utility commissions, vocational and rehabilitation offices, weights and measures offices, selected federal agencies, and military commissary and exchange offices. Single copies of the current **Consumer Action Handbook** are available free by writing Handbook, Federal Consumer Information Center, Pueblo CO 81009, calling 1-888-878-3256, or clicking on www.pueblo.gsa.gov/crh/cahform.htm.

---

3. Self-Regulatory Organizations

The role of self-regulatory organizations is to attempt to resolve disputes between consumers and sellers. Should the particular business, manufacturer, or profession not resolve the consumer complaint, then it's time to use sources of assistance outside the business. These are **third-party complaint-handling sources**. For example, county medical societies have judicial committees that handle written complaints against member physicians, usually concerning overcharging or improper treatment.

The largest self-regulatory organization is the Better Business Bureau (BBB) with offices in over 140 large communities. The Better Business Bureau typically has four functions: (1) to provide pre-purchase information to the public on such topics as "Tips on Buying a New Car"; (2) to handle **pre-purchase inquiries** (12 million) by providing reports about businesses to consumers before they spend their money; (3) to mediate disputes (3 million) between consumers and businesses by accepting consumer complaints, forwarding them to the business involved, and encouraging settlement between the parties; and (4) to arbitrate disputes between consumers and participating sellers, often automobile manufacturers.

The BBBOnline Privacy Program (www.bbbonline.org) certifies that certain websites protect consumer privacy. The **BBBonline** symbol conveys assurance that the seller complies with a privacy policy that clearly tells consumers what information is to be collected and how it will be used.

Consumers can obtain a number of useful booklets on consumer topics by visiting a local Better Business Bureau office. Those interested in learning about the **reputation of any business** in the country need only telephone the local Better Business Bureau where the company is located to obtain an oral report. Consumers wanting to complain about a seller must do so in writing to the BBB that then mails a copy to the company, allowing 15 days for a response, or via the Internet. The seller is expected to tell the BBB their side of the story that the BBB then presents to the consumer for reaction.

Mediation is the process of negotiating to resolve differences by a person who acts as an intermediary agent between two or more conflicting parties. Companies that do not respond to complaints or mediate in bad faith can lose their membership in the Better

Business Bureau. Consumers with unresolved problems can still take their complaints to a government consumer protection agency, small-claims court, or an attorney.

Arbitration is a form of adjudication.[4] Here a dispute is resolved by the judgment of an impartial third party who holds a hearing, listens to arguments, examines evidence presented by both sides, and makes a decision or judgment. In addition to the reputable American Arbitration Association, many industry trade associations are involved in arbitrating consumer disputes. Examples include the New York Stock Exchange, Chrysler Customer Arbitration Board, and local Better Business Bureaus. Arbitrators are appointed by mutual consent of the parties involved, by provisions in a consumer contract (such as a credit agreement), or according to statutory provisions. The consumer usually does not pay a fee for arbitration.

The BBB has **arbitration contracts** with most automobile manufacturers as well as other companies. A consumer who complains to an automobile dealer often also complains to the manufacturer. When a dispute cannot be settled, the consumer can then ask the BBB through its Automobile Consumer Action Panel (AutoCAP) to step in on the matter. In an arbitration case, the BBB hears the oral arguments of the consumer and the manufacturer and then makes a decision. Typically, the decision is binding on the manufacturer but not on the consumer. Thus, a still dissatisfied consumer, if he or she desires, may go further and sue in court or ask a government agency for assistance.

Several industries have **consumer action panels** to facilitate handling of complaints on an industry-wide basis. These are complaint-handling boards of impartial people, usually sponsored by an industry trade association, whose purpose is to mediate or arbitrate disputes between consumers and manufacturers or dealers. The people who usually serve on panels are executives from a specific industry plus some consumer representatives. When the consumer action panel receives a complaint from a consumer, it asks the manufacturer or dealer to reinvestigate and report back. The typical panel has the arbitration authority to make a decision that is **binding on the business**, although the consumer can accept or reject it. Complaining to self-regulatory groups gives them the last opportunity to get the business to resolve the problem:

Automotive Consumer Action
Program (AutoCAP)
8400 Westpark Drive
McLean, VA 22102
www.tada.org

Better Business Bureau
Autoline
Council of Better Business
Bureaus
1515 Wilson Boulevard
Arlington, VA 22209
www.dr.bbb.org

Better Business Bureau
National Consumer
Arbitration
Council of Better Business
Bureaus
1515 Wilson Boulevard
Arlington, VA 22209
www.bbb.org

Carpet and Rug Institute
1100 17th Street, NW
Washington, DC 20036
www.carpet-rug.com/

Direct Marketing Association
Mail Order Action Line
1101 17th Street, NW - Suite 705
Washington, DC 20036
www.the-dma.org/

Direct Selling Association
1776 K Street, NW
Washington, DC 20006
www.dsa.org/

International Association for
Financial Planning
www.iafp.org

National Advertising Division
(NAD)
Council of Better Business
Bureaus
www.bbb.com/advertising/

---

[4] Many sales contracts include binding arbitration clauses that require complaining consumers to submit to the seller's arbitration program instead of being allowed to sue in court. See Chapter 18 for more information.

4. Consumer Action Agencies

Consumer action agencies are third-party public and private organizations that purposefully and forcefully represent the interests of consumers, often by accepting individual complaints and taking action to resolve such problems. There are three common types of consumer action agencies: (1) media, such as newspapers, radio, and television stations, (2) government, such as state, county and city offices of consumer affairs as well as state attorneys general offices, and (3) private, such as local, state, and national consumer activist organizations.

In many communities the **media is actively involved** in consumer protection. A number of local newspapers, radio, and television stations have "Action Line" programs whose purpose is to take actions to resolve a variety of problems concerning the public. Sometimes it is getting a pothole fixed on a busy street; often it is a consumer problem. When a consumer's effort has failed to solve a problem, the action line staff investigates and tries to right the wrong. An example of a media action line is Call for Action, a network of radio and television stations that offer resolution for consumer problems. After being contacted by a media action line, many sellers quickly give in to the consumer's position because they fear the possibility of negative publicity.

Government **consumer action agencies** include various consumer affairs departments and the offices of the attorneys general. Usually the Office of Consumer Affairs (OCA) is a state responsibility operating under the legal authority of the Attorney General's office. These organizations have a high success rate in resolving consumer complaints because they can bring civil and criminal actions to enforce laws and regulations, although it is rare to get money back for individual consumers.

CONSUMER UPDATE:
Complain on Internet Gripe Sites

A consumer can try to settle a score with a seller with his/her own Internet website for less than $100 in start-up costs. There are hundreds of websites on the Internet that give consumers an outlet for rage against **well-known sellers**. They yell about lousy service, poor working conditions and policies they believe are wrongheaded. People there commiserate about consumer problems or seek redress for the wrongs. See www.planetfeedback.com, www.Feedbackdirect.com, and www.thecomplaintstation.com. These sites provide helpful hints on complaining as well as government regulations.

Lots of company-specific "gripe sites" have addresses that include the words "sucks" and "I hate". As a result, sellers are listening more and even responding. Many sellers have hired Web monitoring services to listen in on chat rooms, and they are mounting public relations campaigns to try to combat misinformation and **regain customer loyalty**.

Private consumer action organizations exist everywhere. Local consumer action groups are just some of the many special-interest organizations trying to achieve their ends, such as helping senior citizens, improving access to low-income housing, and trying to preserve the environment. State and local consumer action organizations are usually well known to the populations they serve, such as the Consumer Education and Protection Association in Philadelphia and the California Consumers Association. At the national level, particularly active private consumer organizations include the Consumer Federation of America, Public Citizen, Center for Auto Safety, and National Consumers League.

5. Small Claims and Civil Courts

Seeking remedies through the first four channels in the complaint procedures in Table 3-1 can rectify almost all consumer complaints. If these procedures fail, it is possible that the matter can be **pursued in the legal arena**. Few people take consumer complaints to an attorney and file suit against a seller in the regular civil court system because it is quite expensive. Attorney fees vary but easily could amount to $500 or even $1,000 to take a simple case to court. Examples of cases that consumers probably should bring to civil court include a breach of contract situation for a $3,000 faulty air-conditioning system, a $5,000 shoddy remodeling construction job, or a landlord-tenant dispute over $1,500 in rent. People with limited incomes can go to legal-aid societies, usually listed in the telephone book under "Legal Aid" or "Legal Services", for less expensive attorney fees. Suing in small claims court (see below) is very inexpensive.

Use Small Claims Lawsuits to Sue When Necessary

For reasons of cost and convenience, many people choose to use small claims courts to resolve consumer problems. A **small claims court** (or **pro se court**) is one that specializes in adjudicating legal claims involving small amounts of money in a simple and economical manner, with relaxed procedures and rules of incidence, sometimes without the assistance of attorneys. Fully one-fourth of the total civil caseload in the United States is made up of small claims actions. Almost all states have small claims courts, and many courts are open during evening hours as well as weekends. The maximum amount that can be litigated is usually **limited to $1,200**, although a number of states have a jurisdictional limit of $5,000 or higher. Nine states permit jury trials.

Costs are kept low, in part, because a **written transcript is not kept** of the proceedings, although court records are maintained. In most small claims courts, consumers are prohibited from bringing an attorney into the courtroom. The idea is that the consumer can present his or her own legal claim before a judge (or arbitrator) in an informal setting, as some of the more formal legal proceedings are relaxed. The seller-defendant is usually allowed to have an attorney, although they are prohibited in some states. On most military bases and college campuses, free legal assistance is available to offer guidance on small claims cases and on other legal issues.

To file a small claims court action, you would go to the courthouse and inquire as to which court hears small claims. A small fee, perhaps $20, is required, along with fees of normally $10 for each court summons or subpoena. A **summons** is a notice issued to a person summoning him or her to report to court as a juror or witness. A **subpoena** is a legal writ requiring appearance of certain items in court. When you complete the necessary forms, it is important to fill out the full legal name of the **defendant** (the person who allegedly committed the wrong act and is the subject of the litigation), and to carefully describe the action about which the lawsuit is concerned. The court will subpoena all necessary witnesses and the defendant for the day of the trial. The legal summons has a motivational effect on many defendants, since about one-quarter of all small claims cases are settled **out of court** before the hearing date.

The day the case is heard, you, the **plaintiff** (the person who has filed the small claims or civil court case and is suing the defendant), should be well prepared and have a clear understanding of the sequence of events that led up to the claim. Bring all relevant documentation. In most courts, the decision of the judge can be appealed by the loser to a higher court, and that can result in considerable attorney fees and related costs. Small claims court decisions are won by the plaintiff about three-quarters of the time and are not appealed.

Winning a small claims decision does not mean that you automatically get satisfaction. Often the judge makes a compromise decision, perhaps ordering a $200 judgment on a $400 claim. Also, it is sometimes **difficult to collect** from the defendant. The small claims court does not act as a collection agency, rather it issues a **judgment**. This is a judicial decision and determination of a court of law, often creating or affirming an obligation, such as a debt.

If you experience difficulty collecting, you can go back to small claims court to ask the judge to order a **writ of execution**, that is a right to exercise a claim against the defendant's property, bank accounts, personal property (such as a motor vehicle), and wage income. Executions on real estate are not allowed. Going to small claims court takes time and energy, so consumers must weigh the potential benefits of going to court against the potential costs. It is usually much less expensive for a consumer to **picket the seller's place of business**, as described later in this chapter.

Damages to Ask for When Suing

When a consumer goes to small claims or civil court for a breach of contract or deception lawsuit, he or she is suing for relief and/or damages. To remedy the wrong, a consumer asks the court for assistance. Note that if a criminal act occurred during the unfair or deceptive practice, it is incumbent on the federal, state, county or city to seek civil and/or criminal penalties. **Damages** consumer plaintiffs may seek in court include:

1. **Restitution** is the act of restoring to the rightful owner something that has been taken away, lost, or surrendered, such as money given to the seller.

2. **Compensatory damages** are out-of-pocket losses plus the difference between the consumer's expenses and the value claimed by the seller, such as payment for mental anguish, physical pain and suffering, and various incidental expenses (such as taxi fares) and consequential costs (such as losing a day's wages and attorney fees).

3. **Punitive damages** are those awarded by a judge or jury that aim to penalize or inflict punishment on the wrongdoer.

How Consumers Can Break a Contract

When consumers receive goods that do not conform to the express or implied warranty, they can attempt to remedy the situation or break the contract. Four ways are:

1. **Keep the goods and sue the seller for damages.** Here the consumer asks the court to order the defendant to pay the dollar value of the losses.

2. **Revoke acceptance and seek a return of the purchase price.** Here the consumer returns the goods (such as a car) to the seller and formally communicates in writing a revocation of acceptance to the seller. First, however, the consumer must give the seller an opportunity to **cure the difficulty**. Revocation must occur within a reasonable amount of time after discovering that a problem with the product substantially impairs the value of the item to the consumer; minor defects are not

acceptable cause for revocation. (This is the essence of state **lemon laws** that permit revocation of a new car after it has been repeatedly returned to the shop for a series of unsuccessful repairs [this topic is discussed in Chapter 5].) Consumers who return goods to sellers and revoke acceptance run the risk that the seller will then sue the them for non-performance of the contract, although a well-prepared consumer can win with a sympathetic judge.

3. **Ask a court to reform the contract.** When a court orders **reformation** it alters or corrects the contract to remove faults or defects; sometimes the court makes the seller actually do what was promised.

4. **Ask a court to rescind the contract.** If granted by a court, an order of **rescission** annuls the contract and that puts each party back into the position they were in before the alleged unfair or deceptive practice occurred.

DID YOU KNOW:
How to Get Out of a Contract

It is easy to give in to the persuasive powers of a salesperson and sign on the dotted line of a contract. Later you may conclude that you should not have obligated yourself. Getting out of a contract depends upon (1) an appropriate federal or state law, and (2) the goodwill of the seller.

Automobile purchases and leases–You usually can cancel if you have not yet taken possession of the vehicle, before the paperwork for the title gets processed at the state Department of Motor Vehicles, before you have put more than 5 or 10 miles on it, or before the loan or interest rate have been approved. Auto leases are almost impossible to cancel.

Insurance policies–Most states permit a free cancellation period of 10 days; some allow 30 days to change your mind. Nationwide sellers are usually lenient. Follow correct cancellation procedures described in the fine print of the policy. Thus, you may be able to cancel life, health, disability, and credit insurance policies.

Lodging—Most allow same-day cancellations with no penalty, but some require 3 days notice. Still, you should only lose the first day's charges.

Non-refundable Airline Tickets—No refunds, but you can pay $100 per ticket to make another reservation and use the new ticket within one or two years.

Extended Service Contracts–These contracts almost always have a cancellation clause, typically 15 to 60 days. Most can be canceled later with a nominal service charge.

Future Service Contracts—Those who have signed a contract for a buying club, weight-loss center, health spa, or any other **future services contract** (a binding document stating that services will be provided in the future for a certain sum) may get the contract voided. Since state judges do not like businesses who pressure people to sign contracts, especially contracts that are unfair or deceptive, they often let consumers out of those contracts for the sum of $1. Why $1? Because the services have not yet been provided, thus there is no genuine loss for the seller. You often have to go to court to win.

Various federal and state **cooling-off laws** (described in Chapter 5) also permit contract cancellation for health spas, campgrounds, home improvements, and timeshares.

Techniques of Last Resort: How to Fight Back—And Win!—Against Rip-offs and Frauds

When you have been deceived or ripped off, you can fight back using these procedures:

1. **Review the deception and look for actual illegal actions by the seller.** If something illegal occurred, report it to the police, state office of consumer affairs,

or state attorney general. Many college students enjoy the advantage of having a **student attorney** on campus who gives advice and guidance on legal issues, and occasionally files a lawsuit on behalf of a concern that impacts one or more students.[5] Low-income consumers can seek assistance from **legal-aid attorneys** who are available in most communities. In all cases, an attorney offers the appearance that the consumer is quite serious about the matter.

2. **Calculate "the numbers" to determine the likely value that a seller might settle for to get rid of your complaint, and then you can offer them a deal that they very well may accept.** Sometimes it is important to obtain a full refund, so you should push for it. In other instances, 100 percent may not be necessary. Therefore, it is important to know the likely value that a seller might settle for to get rid of your complaint. To begin, know that commissions for door-to-door and telemarketing sales often amount to 1/3 to ½ the total price. This is in contrast to 5 to 10 percent for most retail store sales commissions.

    To illustrate the calculation, assume the bad transaction cost you $200. The salesperson may have earned $80 commission on the deal, while the cost of the product or service may have amounted to a genuine $70 or so, leaving a profit of $50 to the seller. Most sellers are willing to give a complaining consumer the salesperson's commission plus part of the profit, perhaps $130 in this example. Consequently, when communicating with a seller, calculate how much you are willing to compromise. Tell them that for, **"X" dollars, you will walk away satisfied**. If they don't accept, tell them that you have "all the time in the world" to continue to pursue your rights and that you're going to fight back. Tell them that unless your reasonable demands are met, you will soon take a whole host of actions.

3. **Fight back with multiple actions**. If necessary, communicate that you are prepared to do all of the following:

    *   **Write complaint letters** to the Better Business Bureau, Office of Consumer Affairs, and state Attorney General.

    *   **Sue in small claims court**.

    *   **Make a big sign and picket outside the place of business** of the seller or where the seller goes to visit potential customers. Avoid slanderous and libelous words (perhaps just say, "Beware of XYZ Seller") and keep walking (so you do not impede others) and you will break no laws. Before you begin to picket, politely show the seller the sign and again ask for a settlement.[6]

    *   **Prepare a handout on consumer rip-offs** and distribute it while picketing. Be careful not to disparage the seller in a slanderous manner, and share the handout with all your friends, neighbors and co-workers.

    *   **Send your story to media action lines** run by local newspapers and television stations.

---

[5] The Foundation for Individual Rights in Education (www.thefireguides.org) produces a series of guidebooks to help students understand and defend their rights.

[6] Your author recently had to resort to picketing a retailer. After 90 minutes of walking in front of the business, I telephoned the manager to inform him that I would be back the next day to continue picketing and that I would invite a photographer from the local newspaper. The seller gave in and quickly did what he was supposed to do in the first place.)

DID YOU KNOW?
Consumer Power Disciplines and Improves the Marketplace

Consumers have two key powers to discipline and improve the economic marketplace. Any efforts to take away or restrict these powers should be vigorously fought by consumers.

1. **Boycott** A **boycott** is an abstinence from using, buying, or dealing to express protest or coerce. At times, individual consumers will buy selectively by holding back their dollar votes and refusing to patronize a certain seller or product perhaps because they do not like the quality, prices, service, sales atmosphere, or attitude of personnel. They may wish to evidence their ethical or moral displeasure, perhaps because of labor practices, political beliefs, environmental concerns, and/or they want to demand corporate accountability in the marketplace. This is a **personal boycott**.

   Large numbers of consumers occasionally band together in a coordinated manner to encourage others to boycott a certain product or seller. Boycotts are an established form of non-violent blackmail. The potential lost sales usually is not the motivation for the seller to capitulate; rather it is a **fear of controversy** and the accompanying negative publicity. At any point in time, there are more than 60 groups simultaneously participating in 200 or more boycotts. Check an Internet search engine for the latest boycotts.

   To **conduct a boycott**: (1) Consider your target (e.g., the industry leader, the worst company, the one most likely to change); (2) Write the company explaining your position and seek a face-to-face meeting with a company official; (3) Should discussions prove fruitless, announce that you are considering a boycott and that you will continue negotiations over a list of demands that you present to the company; (4) Choose which company products to boycott and seek the cooperation of other groups that will support the boycott while sending the company names of boycott co-sponsors; (5) Call a press conference located very close to a company site to distribute your list of demands and use graphic visual aids to help make your points.

2. **Class action lawsuit** Many consumer misrepresentations and deceptions are relatively small in cost, and it is expensive to hire an attorney to recoup losses of being ripped off $10 or even $1,000. Thus, the pooling of small monetary claims is necessary to obtain redress. A **class action lawsuit** permits representative members of a common class, such as consumers who have been similarly wronged, to seek joint redress by suing the defendant, usually a large corporation, for damages (purchase costs, attorney fees and damages) on behalf of themselves and all those similarly situated. A telephone company that overcharges each of its ten million customers $1 per monthly bill would reap a windfall of $120 million annually. Individual consumers in such cases often do not get back a lot of money, perhaps $2 or $3 in this example, in part because of large attorney fees. Consumers are still winners because they have **made the defendant pay** for wrongful behavior and keep the corporation from similarly over-billing others in the future. Also, class action lawsuits deter other potential wrongdoers. Class action lawsuits are consumer's single most powerful weapon to discipline sellers in the marketplace.

   Most large corporations and their conservative pro-business legislative friends are working to pass a law to move all class action lawsuits from state courts to the federal system where judges are hostile to consumer rights.

Review and Summary of Key Terms and Concepts

1. What is a **right**, and what does it have to do with **implied warranties** and **express warranties**?

2. Distinguish among the two types of **implied warranties**: **warranty of merchantability** and **warranty of fitness for a particular purpose**.

3. How are **express warranties** created, and what is a **written express warranty**?

4. Explain the meaning of selling a product **as is**.

5. What is **rule number 1** of consumer life and why does it usually work?

6. Give some examples of **moral rights**, and tell how they differ from President Kennedy's **Consumer Bill of Rights**.

7. Select two of the **consumer rights of all Americans**, and explain what they mean.

8. List some **responsibilities of consumers**.

9. Give three examples of how businesses collect **privacy information** about consumers.

10. Why don't people **complain**?

11. Discuss how many people **complain about certain goods**.

12. Why are **return policies** important?

13. Explain why it is beneficial for consumers and sellers to **get satisfaction**.

14. What are some reasons why **sellers are willing to handle consumer complaints**?

15. Summarize the sequential levels of the **complaining process**.

16. When should a consumer take a problem to a manufacturer's **zone office**?

17. What are **third-party complaint-handling sources**?

18. Distinguish between **mediation** and **arbitration**.

19. What are **consumer action panels**?

20. Explain the term **consumer action agencies**, and give some examples.

21. Summarize the processes followed in a **small claims court**, and in your response define the terms **summons**, **subpoena**, **judgment**, and **writ of execution**.

22. Distinguish between the terms: **restitution** and **compensatory damages**.

23. What are **punitive damages** and why do they occur?

24. Explain two ways that consumers might **get out of a contract**.

25. What two actions in **fighting back** look reasonable to you?

26. What is a **class action lawsuit**, and why is this important to consumers?

27. Explain how a **boycott** works and why companies sometimes give in to the demands of a well organized boycott.

Useful Resources for Consumers

American Bar Association
www.abanet.org

Automotive Consumer Action
Program
National Automobile Dealers
Association
www.nada.org/

Consumer Action Website
Federal Citizen Information
Center
www.consumeraction.gov/

Consumer Action
www.consumer-action.org/

Consumer Action Handbook
www.pueblo.gsa.gov/crh/stat
e.htm

Consumer Information Center
(California)
www.dca.ca.gov/cic/

Council of Better Business
Bureaus
www.bbbonline.org

Federal Trade Commission
www.ftc.gov and
www.ftc.gov/consumer.htm

FindLaw
wwwfindlaw.com

Federal Government's Portal
FirstGov.gov

Foundation for Individual
Rights in Education
www.transparency.org/

Free Advice.com
www.freeadvice.com

National Association of
Attorneys General
www.naag.org

National Consumer Law
Center
www.nclc.org

National Consumers League
www.nclnet.org/

National Fraud Information
Center
www.fraud.org/

Nolo.com
www.nolo.com

Privacy Foundation
Organization
www.privacyfoundation.org

Privacy Rights Clearinghouse
www.privacyrights.org

Transportation, U.S.
Department of
www.dot.gov
www.dot.gov/airconsumer/tellj
udge.htm
www.oig.dot.gov (to log
complaints)
www.ticked.com (tips on
complaining)
www.1travel.com ("their" rules
of air travel)

TARP (Technical Assistance
Research Group)
www.e-satisfy.com/

USLaw.com
www.uslaw.com

"What Do You Think" Questions

1. Consider the term **implied warranty rights** and the views of the Supreme Court on the subject. Think of two examples where the concept of implied warranty rights could help consumers and explain why.

2. Which of the **moral rights** do you think is most important? Why?

3. Select one of the **consumer rights** and tell why it is important to you.

4. The concept of **privacy** is of growing importance to consumers. What are your thoughts on privacy concerns, and in particular, how do you see the balancing of the rights of consumers against the rights of sellers?

5. Think about a recent situation where you or a someone else was ripped off in the marketplace. Review the suggestions on **fighting back**, and record some notes to guide your action to try and resolve the situation.

6. Offer your views on the statement that, **"Students should have the right to quality indicators at their schools."**

7. Many people **fail to complain** about consumer problems. What types of actions can sellers and government take to help get more consumers complaining?

**Appendix Issue 3-A:
Writing a Letter of Complaint**

Don't put up with poor treatment by sellers or government agencies. Do not accept being "brushed off" by someone in authority. If you cannot think clearly when someone is pressuring you, go away and take some time to think. Then sit down and make some notes of things to say. Either go back later and complain or write a letter of complaint.

When writing a consumer complaint letter, type the letter on business-size paper and aim your communication at the right person. Sometimes it's the consumer affairs office, sometimes it's the company president or chief executive officer (CEO). You or a reference section librarian can locate corporate names and addresses. The "Who's Who" books have the home addresses of lots of big name executives.

1. Explain the problem. Be clear and concise in explaining the problem. Be factual, and do not dwell on sensitive issues. Be polite. Avoid being sarcastic or overly emotional; let them know that you are a reasonable person. Try to say it all in one sentence, and add clarifying statements if needed. Also, tell the story of what you have already done in attempting to resolve the problem.

2. Identify your expectations. Be firm and courteous when requesting (don't demand) what it is that you want the seller to do. Do you want something repaired, a product replaced, or a refund? Give choices, if appropriate.

3. Give persuasive reasons. Sellers are people just like everyone else, and they like to be treated with both intelligence and respect. Give logical reasons why the action you want is, first, the right thing to do and, second, also in the best interest of the seller. If you have been a long-time customer, tell the seller, especially if you intend to buy from that seller in the future.

4. Document your request. Few sellers are going to do what you want without a little proof, so include appropriate documentation. Sellers want to see such things as a receipt for proof of purchase, a canceled check, a charge slip, or a service invoice. Never send originals because they may become lost. If such documentation is no longer available, just explain why.

5. Use an action close. The way to get action is to ask for it. Therefore, in a positive way, tell what action you will take next should the seller not respond affirmatively within an appropriate time period. Give a reasonable deadline. Include your address and telephone number.

The second complaint letter (and, if necessary, the third, fourth and fifth) should briefly repeat the problem, remind them that they have not yet responded to your letter (or the response was unsatisfactory), tell them you will now complain to third-party agencies, and enclose a photocopy of your previous correspondence.

SAMPLE COMPLAINT LETTER

Your address
Your city, state, and ZIP code
Today's date

Name of person (if known)
Job title
Company name
Street address
City, state, and zip code

Dear Mr. or Ms. last name (or Dear Reader):

I am writing to tell you of my dissatisfaction with (name of product and its serial number or the service performed), that was purchased (tell where and when). The exact problem is that the product (tell the reasons for the complaint, that it no longer functions, is wrong for the task, or whatever). What I have already done to try and resolve the problem is (tell the story of what occurred as well as the actions and statements of particular salespersons or managers).

In order to resolve this problem, I think that you should (state what specific action or actions you believe the seller should take on your behalf).

In all fairness, your company should (give the refund, exchange the product, or whatever) for the following reasons. (Give two or more reasons whenever possible.)

Enclosed are photocopies of (sales receipt, invoice, previous letters, whatever) that support my request for action. Please note (in one specific document) that (focus the reader's attention on a particular item you want them to be sure and see because it supports your position).

I look forward to receiving your reply providing a speedy resolution to this problem, and I will allow three weeks before complaining to the Better Business Bureau and to the appropriate state and local government consumer protection agencies. Please write to me at the above address or contact me by telephone (give both home and work numbers if it would be difficult to locate you during daytime hours).

Sincerely,

Your name

Enclosures (include copies of appropriate documents)

Chapter 4

Rip-offs and Frauds in the Marketplace

OBJECTIVES

After reading this chapter, you should be able to

1. Explain why rip-offs and frauds exist.

2. List guidelines to help consumers avoid rip-offs and frauds.

3. Examine the suggestion that economic fraud is rampant among big corporations

4. Recognize that the Internet is packed with rip-offs and scams.

5. Understand that almost all rip-offs are not illegal.

6. Distinguish between deceptions and unfair practices.

7. Describe a number of rip-offs and frauds in the areas of telemarketing and mail, buying, vehicle sales and repairs, and investments.

I t would take an encyclopedia to describe all of the rip-offs, misrepresentations, schemes, scams, deceptions, and frauds aimed at taking money from consumers. New ones are invented every year, too. Rip-offs and frauds occur in all societies, because there seems to be an inherent motivation among some people to take advantage of others in economic transactions. The perpetrator's incentive to seek easy profits is only exceeded by consumers who want to take advantage of a really good deal, or better yet, get something for nothing. The informed consumer must learn about the variety of rip-offs and frauds to avoid the come-ons, hooks, and traps used by unprincipled sellers. Consumers also have dimes and dollars stolen from them every day by some large so-called reputable companies through illegal price-fixing and rip-offs.

This chapter begins by examining why rip-offs and frauds exist in the marketplace. Next we overview what rip-offs and frauds have in common. This is followed by a number of guidelines consumers can use to avoid being taken. Importantly, consumers need to understand that rip-offs are legal (at least until a judge says something different) and that there are hundreds. The chapter also focuses on the unique aspects of Internet frauds and scams. Government plays a large role in consumer protection from deceptions and unfair practices, as well as in overseeing bait-and-switch advertising. After listing a number of well-known corporations that commit economic fraud, the chapter provides examples of the popular unscrupulous practices that exist to cheat consumers out of their money. You can recognize the danger signs and avoid being victimized.[1]

Why Rip-offs and Frauds Exist in the Marketplace

Some businesses practice rip-offs and deceptions against consumers. **They lie and cheat**. When this occurs, it places honest sellers at a competitive disadvantage because consumers looking for a bargain buy from the bad sellers rather than the honest ones. The result of rip-offs and frauds is that consumers are **fooled into putting up money** for goods and services of inferior qualities that are not good values, and often are horribly overpriced.

Dishonest sellers promote their schemes and reach their consumer victims in the **same ways used by legitimate firms**—by telemarketing, direct mail, referrals, media advertising, cable television, catalogues, e-mail, web sites, online auctions, and online investment bulletin boards (reached via America Online, CompuServe and Prodigy). Swindlers often place classified advertisements in highly respected newspapers and magazines as well as run local television and radio commercials.

The following illustrates the challenge of fighting to eliminate rip-offs and frauds. A Federal Trade Commission (FTC) study of 300 broadcast, print and Web advertisements on weight-loss and dietary topics found that **55 percent** made at least one false claim. While the major TV networks have for years screened out false advertising, other media do not. As a result, the FTC recently asked all media to police advertisements by refusing ads that are "grossly exaggerated and blatantly false." Media organizations replied saying they are not regulators, they do not have the scientific expertise to determine which ads are valid,

---

[1] A number of additional rip-offs and frauds are examined in other chapters as they more appropriately fit. These include check cashing outlets; payday loans; post-dated checks; auto title loans; auto brokers; pawnshops; sale and lease back; credit repair; sub-prime lenders; risk-based lending; red-lining in credit, housing and insurance; predatory home mortgage lending; price-fixing, anti-group laws, calendar marketing agreements; and timesharing vacation properties.

they are not capable of making these kinds of decisions on a deadline, and that screening ads would have "a chilling effect on otherwise [constitutionally] protected speech." Government agencies are the only institutions that consumers can depend upon to police false advertising, and their budgets have never been generous.

Today, **one in five** Americans reports being **a victim** of a major consumer fraud or swindle at some point, according to a survey by AARP, and three-quarters report having a "bad buying" experience in the past 12 months. The crooks have more than 290 million American shoppers as potential customers to choose from, including two million military personnel and 14 million college students. Therefore, they do not need repeat customers, although the sad fact is that they often get them.

Rip-offs and frauds exist in the American marketplace for a number of reasons:

1. **Sellers are expert, full-time professional specialists in persuasion while consumers are amateurs.**

2. **Consumers are not well informed in many areas of buying.** People cannot possibly be well informed in all necessary areas of buying. Consumers are ignorant about how to shop for best buys. **Ignorance** in this context means a lack of sophistication. Many people are not knowledgeable about buying expensive products and services, and they do not follow rational rules of comparison shopping.

3. **Consumers are quite trusting**, and they are inclined to believe advertisements and statements made by sales personnel.

4. **Consumers believe misleading advertising.** Consumers often think that magazines and newspapers will only accept advertisements from reputable sources. The reality is that if newspapers have no valid reason to suspect an advertiser, they generally print the ad.

5. **Consumers lack knowledge about rip-offs and frauds**, so they can easily be victimized.

6. **Some sellers aim to deceive just like a number of so-called reputable companies.**

7. **Some sellers lie and use high-pressure sales techniques.** Such sellers tell lies on the telephone and in face-to-face conversations. They make false promises, misrepresent costs and describe fictional cancellation policies.

8. **Some consumers are greedy and they have a sweepstakes mentality.** Consumers often have a desire to "win a prize," "get something for nothing" or "get a lot for a little," such as health and wealth. In a recent national survey, 11 percent of the respondents said that the best way to get rich was to play the lottery.

9. **Deception is profitable.** Crooks usually can make a lot of money before the authorities get around to investigation and prosecution. Only about two percent of victims ever complains to the fraudulent sellers, and the latter generally find it easy to satisfy the complaints of the two percent. In addition, this usually can keep the government regulators at bay for several months or even a couple of years. Then the unscrupulous sellers continue to profit by fleecing the next 98 percent who do not complain. Surveys show that fewer than 10 percent of consumers who say they were swindled report the crime to the proper government authorities. Many consumers are too ashamed to complain.

10. **Many scam artists escape by fleeing the boundaries of a state and/or declaring bankruptcy.** Crooks often get away with their illegal schemes by fleeing the boundaries of one state and setting up a new business in another state under a similar but a different name, so they can go on and cheat more victims. The life of some scam businesses is as short as 90 days.

11. **Penalties against deceptions are primarily civil in nature.** When caught, perpetrators sometimes have their bank assets frozen, and such funds may be used to make partial refunds to some consumers. Perpetrators typically negotiate a settlement with a government, pay a civil fine, and move on, all the time avoiding criminal prosecution and jail.

12. **Price-fixing and other illegal forms of collusion exist** to control supply or price, and they are nearly impossible for consumers to recognize. Only government (with expertise in economics, accounting, and marketing) has the ability to identify and stop price fixing.

13. **Limited government resources to combat rip-offs and frauds.** Because of under-funding, government regulators can go after only the most flagrant price fixers and companies that scam consumers; a relative few every year.

General Guidelines to Avoid Rip-offs and Frauds

Here are some guidelines to avoid rip-offs and frauds. Most rip-offs and frauds can be avoided by using common sense and a bit of healthy skepticism.

Be Cautious in Marketplace Dealings

1. Talk to friends and acquaintances to learn about their experiences with particular sellers, products and services.

2. Buy only from reputable sellers that you know or from those who are recommended by someone you trust.

3. Avoid being too courteous with every telephone caller and salesperson and, instead, end the conversation.

4. Stop being so trusting about salespersons because scam artists lie all the time.

5. Be cautious of **testimonials** (endorsements of products) by experts because these people are often paid large sums for their statements. Personal testimonials from regular people are frequently fictitious.

6. Get the names, addresses, and telephone numbers of salespersons and companies.

7. Check out the **reputation** of the seller by contacting the Better Business Bureau, the State Attorney General's Office, or an Office of Consumer Affairs. Telephone the same agencies in the state of any out-of-town sellers.

8. Research the company on the **Internet** or in the library by looking them up in reference volumes, such as Dun & Bradstreet.

9. Try not to be overly sympathetic to salespersons, especially those that pretend to be "your friend," so you can avoid falling prey to frauds using this tactic.

10. Be **wary** of purchasing from door-to-door salespersons. Always ask for proper identification and carefully examine it.

11. Be **cautious** about buying anything over the telephone. Never buy over the telephone unless you originated the call or you know the caller.

12. Realize that a classy Internet web site is no guarantee that the sponsor is legitimate.

13. Say "No," until you receive written information about the offer and any oral promises made by the salesperson.

14. Read and understand sales agreements and contracts before signing. Make sure the terms are the same as those given in the sales presentation, and get a copy of the documents.

15. Read advertisements thoroughly, looking for limitations in the small print.

16. Get an attorney or trusted friend to look over documents and contracts when a substantial amount of money is involved.

ISSUE FOR DEBATE:
Consumers Accept the False Promises of Television Commercials

Esther Peterson, onetime Special Assistant to the President for Consumer Affairs, was always angry about commercial television. She always asked, "Why is it okay to be cynical about government, cynical about personal responsibility, cynical about love, but **reverent toward the marketing** of cars, pain relievers, and just plain junk that is sold daily through television?" Television commercials offer consumers false promises, deductive lies and corrupt fantasies. Why are people, who are cynical about so many things in society, so accepting about what and how products are sold on television? Consumers shouldn't, should they?

Ask Lots of Questions

1. Ask salespersons to explain advertisements, product operations, warranty terms, and so on.

2. Ask to see the company's written policies on refunds and exchanges.

3. Ask to see warranties and read them. Understand the warranty before buying, such as what it covers, for how long, and who will honor it.

4. Ask what your legal **rights** are if you later want to cancel the contract, and get such promises in writing.

5. Ask the seller to give you time to think before you make up your mind, such as overnight.

Things Never to Do

1. Never put yourself in situations where you may be set up to be deceived, such as going to a motel or a sales office to listen to a sales presentation.

2. Never **buy on impulse**.

3. Never allow yourself to be persuaded and **pressured** into hurrying and making a quick decision. Stop and think before buying. Ask yourself the following questions: "Do I really need this?" "Why am I buying this?" "Does something sound a little fishy?" and "Should I ask a trusted friend before buying?"

4. Never take a vehicle home for a one- or two-day tryout because regardless of what the salesperson says, the dealer does not have to take it back should you change your mind.

5. Never reveal **account numbers** or partial account numbers of a credit-card, checking account, driver's license, or social security over the telephone for "identification" or "verification" purposes, unless you initiate the call, have been a satisfied customer of the business in the past, and are certain of the caller's identity.

6. Never send cash, money orders, or checks to a post office address or give such to a courier unless you are positive about the reputation of the company.

7. Never pay for an Internet transaction unless you have high confidence that the escrow or online payment service is legitimate. If it is not a well-known service, don't use it.

8. Never pay money for a prize.

9. Never pay money in advance to obtain a loan.

10. Never pay with **cash**. Put transactions on a credit card or write a personal check. If you pay with a credit card, you may have the legal right to not pay your credit-card company when you are dissatisfied with poor-quality goods and services purchased from a seller. To cancel a check with a **stop payment order** (that is good for only six months, so, if needed, be sure to renew it), telephone your bank before the check is presented there for payment.

Be Informed Before Going Shopping

1. Educate yourself about the product or service you are considering buying and become aware of the likely prices involved. What does it do? What does it not do?

2. Read magazines that contain lots of **useful buying information**, such as *Consumer Reports*, *Kiplinger's Personal Finance Magazine*, *Money*, *Smart Money*, and *Worth*.

3. While learning about a product you expect to buy, try to make up your mind as much as possible before you actually go shopping.

4. Always try to **comparison shop** for product features, price, and service at two or more sellers.

Know Your Rights

1. Know your **legal rights** as a consumer, especially implied warranties, cancellation (recission) of door-to-door purchases, cooling-off periods, and charge-back credit regulations.

2. If you do not like a particular clause in a contract, say so, **cross it out**, and get the initials of all parties next to the crossed out portion evidencing agreement.

Be Alert to Signs of Being Ripped Off

1. Ignore any deal that **sounds too good**.

2. Be alert to commonly used deceptive practices, such as bait-and-switch advertising.

3. No legitimate business will ever force you to make a quick decision or send a courier to your home to pick up money; these are not normal business practices.

4. Know that if you have to send money or buy a product, you have not won anything.

5. Be wary of hot investment tips, especially from acquaintances and fellow members of church and fraternal organizations.

6. High-pressure sales tactics are a strong tipoff that you are the target of a scam.

When in Doubt

1. Realize that nothing is *free*. It is almost impossible to get something for nothing. If the deal **sounds too good** to be true, it is.

2. Realize that you are more likely to be struck by lightning (1 in 700,000) than to be an actual winner of a contest or lottery; therefore, such notifications are almost always false.

3. When you think that you might be the target of a rip-off or fraud, ask for advice from an impartial third person. To **check the reputation** of the seller or caller and to verify claims, telephone the Better Business Bureau, State Attorney General's Office, District Attorney's Office, Consumer Fraud section of the Police Department, or an Office of Consumer Affairs.

4. If you want to check the validity of a telemarketing call, ask the caller to mail you printed information. Once received, you can verify it.

5. Once you say "No" to a seller, stick to your position and leave the premises.

6. On important decisions, wait and talk to a trusted friend or impartial advisor.

7. Always try to get a second estimate for expensive repairs, such as on your vehicle or your home.

8. If you must act "right now" to take advantage of a deal, do not, because this is a tipoff that you are being scammed.

9. When in doubt about any marketplace transaction, don't!

Economic Fraud is Rampant Among Big Corporations

Economic thievery is rampant in American society. Almost every week corporate executives are caught lying and committing criminal actions. Over 300 corporations **restated earning** last year, a polite way of saying the original financial statements contained gross inaccuracies. **Economic frauds** are largely hidden from the public eye, although these corporate executives steal billions every year. Many are instances of **price fixing**, where competing sellers interfere with market forces to eliminate competition, control prices or supplies, and other **deceptive practices**. Many of the world's largest companies have been caught by the Federal Trade Commission, the Antitrust Division of the Attorney General's Office, and/or various state Attorney's General.

These events keep occurring because the rewards of economic fraud are high and the penalties are low. Too many corporate executives realize this and take advantage. In well over 95 percent of instances of **corporate fraud**, the government reaches a **settlement** with the companies and executives who are accused of wrongdoing. Further, as a condition of signing the settlement, there is almost never any finding or admission of wrongdoing on the part of the corporation and the company officers. In essence, they do not admit to breaking any law.

These economic crimes against consumers will **continue forever** until government is empowered and has the budget to investigate and go to court to force wrongdoers to disgorge money obtained illegally and to put the perpetrators into jail. Simply fining corporations does not change corporate behavior. Crooked corporate executives will not stop stealing until they are forced to give back the ill-gotten profits and they are jailed.

Of the **hundreds of big corporations caught** in recent years for doing dishonest deeds, a number of short lists of big corporations that cheated millions of consumers are presented in different chapters in this book. See in this chapter *Top Ten Corporate Liars That Fleeced Consumers by Lying* and *A Dozen Ways Big Business Gets Government to Help Them Overcharge Consumers*; *Top Ten Corporate Price-Fixers* in Chapter 9; *Top Ten Big Corporate Crooks* in Chapter 10; *Top Ten Product Manufacturers With Unsafe Products* in Chapter 16; and *Top Ten Corporate Crooks Caught Stealing Investor's Money* in Chapter 18.

Internet Frauds and Scams

Frauds and deceptions are practiced in classified advertisements in newspapers and magazines (sometimes with expensive full-page advertisements), through the mail, on television, on the telephone via telemarketing, through door-to-door sellers, and by business persons in local communities. The same scams that are conducted by mail and telephone are on the **Internet**. Cyberspace has made it easier and cheaper to scam consumers through unsolicited **e-mails**. Consumers are being swamped with the old tricks on a new medium as con artists have adapted yesterday's old scams to today's technology. In addition, it is very difficult to tell the difference between reputable online sellers and crooks that use the Internet to defraud people. An FTC investigation found that two-thirds of unsolicited commercial e-mails, **spam**, are deceptive (e.g., fake return addresses, false claims, false subject lines), and the perpetrators should be prosecuted.

CONSUMER UPDATE:
Top Ten Corporations that Lied to Fleece Consumers

It is important to note that in these **"settlements"** with government, there is almost never any finding of wrongdoing on the part of the corporation, and the company officers do not admit to breaking any law.

10. **"Miss Cleo" Psychic Readers Network** — Agreed to pay the FTC $5 million and stop collection efforts to forgive $500 million in outstanding charges by consumers.

9. **Home Shopping Network** – Agreed to stop claiming that any stop-smoking product or other similar program works for consumers, unless they secure scientific evidence that any food, supplement or drug can treat a disease or affect a function of the body.

8. **Orkin Pest Control** — Stopped making promises that it won't keep as it refused responsibility for guaranteeing their work by claiming that needed repairs are due to "old damage."$80 million judgment.

7. **AOL** — Paid $3 million to 44 states for misleading consumers on changes in costs and services.

6. **Quaker State's Slick 50** – Agreed to stop false and unsubstantiated advertising claims that tout tests showing improved engine performance and reduced engine wear; 30 million consumers have purchased the product, and no refunds were ordered by the government. The same unsubstantiated claims were made by **Dura Lube Super Engine Treatment**.

5. **General Electric** — Deceived hundreds of thousands of consumers into buying new dishwashers by falsely saying the old ones (ordered recalled by the Consumer Product Safety Commission) could not be repaired. Fined $1 million.

4. **Doan's pills** — Agreed to run advertisements (only the second such FTC order in history) to correct misconceptions by previous misleading claims that their product relieved back pain better than other over-the-counter pain relievers.

3. **Wonder Bread** — Dropped its advertising claim that the calcium in the company's products could make children's minds work better and improve their memories.

2. **Dairy and juice companies** — FTC says that 40% of such products sold to schools are short-filled about an ounce (yes, businesses stole from children).

1. **Sears** — Fined $63 million for knowingly selling defective *Die Hard* auto batteries that it falsely claimed were "long lasting"; Sears caught for auto repair frauds, advertising deceptions and credit card rip-offs.

Internet service providers do not screen messages for misrepresentations. About **10,000** new Web sites are created daily. Federal and state government cyber-cops are stopping scams every month, but more and more pop up every day. If government is not vigilant, cyber-crime will turn the Internet into the Wild West of the 21st century. The National Consumers League's National Fraud Information Center reports that the top ten Internet frauds are:

1. **Online Auctions**—items that were misrepresented or never received after being sold to the highest bidder in a virtual auction. Bogus **escrow and online payment services** exist that promise to act as a legitimate go-between for buyers and sellers of goods from Internet auction sites, but turn out to be outright frauds.

2. **General Merchandise**—anything sold on a Web site (not an auction, and not computer software or hardware) that was misrepresented or never received.

3. **Nigerian Money Offers**—requests for aid from someone claiming to need help to transfer a fortune from Africa.

4. **Computer Equipment/Software**—equipment (not sold on an auction) that was never received or misrepresented.

5. **Internet Access Services**—charges from Internet Service Providers (ISPs) that were never ordered and/or received.

6. **Information/Adult Services**—charges to credit cards or phone bills for services never provided or misrepresented as free.

7. **Work-at-Home Schemes**—kits sold with false promises of profits.

8. **Advance-Fee Loans** —empty promises of loans requiring payment of application and other fees in advance.

9. **Credit Card Offers**—phony promises of credit cards requiring up-front payment of application and other fees.

10. **Business Opportunities/Franchises**—exaggerated claims of potential profits through investments in prepackaged businesses or franchises.

In an AT&T Worldnet study, **almost all** respondents said they received unsolicited e-mail offers from what experts consider scam artists. Thirty-two percent of respondents said they have received credit card offers in their e-mail boxes; 30 percent received loan offers; 30 percent received offers to make money working at home; 27 percent received invitations to visit X-rated sites; and 12 percent received Nigerian money offers. The **Nigerian money scam** is a letter, fax or e-mail communication from someone in a west African country who claims to have amassed a fortune and he or she wants to transfer it to your bank account in the U.S. for safekeeping, ostensibly because it is politically difficult for the perpetrator himself to get the money out of the country. The perpetrator offers you millions of dollars to hold the money in your bank account temporarily. Victims are told to pay attorney's fees, taxes, transfer fees, and other charges, sometimes hundreds of thousands of dollars. It's all lies. NCL advises that, "there is no fortune, and the purpose of the scam is to take money out of your bank account, not put money into it." Also see **econsumer.gov** which is an international multilingual effort to combat Internet fraud and deception. It includes contact information for consumer protection authorities in each country, as well as an online complaint form. The remainder of this chapter describes rip-offs and frauds, and almost all of them operate on the Web. You can protect yourself by learning how to recognize the danger signs of fraud.

Rip-offs—and There Are Many—Are *Not* Illegal

Rip-offs are unfair acts of exploitation of consumers in marketplace transactions. Most rip-offs(believe it or not) are legal unless and **until a judge says** that it is fraud. Many rip-offs have consumers paying prices that are way too high. Other rip-offs permit little recourse when consumers are caught in an unfavorable situation. All rip-offs result in people **not getting their money's worth**. Some examples:

• Paying $6,000 for a used car that's really worth only $4,000.

• Signing a contract to "pay a few dollars a month" for a **multi-year contract** to receive several magazines that could have been bought at lower prices elsewhere.

• Ordering $49.95 worth of vitamins advertised to "heal cold sores, reduce hangover symptoms, and increase energy," only to discover that the claims were false.

- Saying "yes" to a caller asking you to buy light bulbs or another household product to benefit disabled persons only to later discover that the charity is a rip-off.

- To get your tax refund a little faster, you pay $300 to take out a $900 **tax refund anticipation loan** from a tax service that files returns electronically.

- Paying $39 on the Internet for 8 ounces of "Dream Thigh Cream" that is supposed to melt away unsightly fat in days, only to realize that the **product does not work**.

- Wasting 20 cents per gallon paying for high octane gasoline ($100 a year) when only 5 percent of today's cars require higher octane gas to perform correctly.

- Being persuaded to pay for an **extended service contract** on a new television, VCR or automobile that pays off less than 2 percent of the time.

Price gouging is one form of rip-off, and it occurs when a seller charges an exorbitant price in a situation where the buyer has little, if any, option except to pay. For example, consumers staying at a hotel who find that the soda machine down the hall sells Pepsi for $2 a can. Another is having no choice at a sporting event except to pay $6 for popcorn and $5 for a drink.

ISSUE FOR DEBATE:
The State Lottery Rip-off is Against the Consumer Interest*

Americans spend $600 billion annually on gambling, which is more than what is spent on clothes or vehicles or groceries. Of the industry's profits of $50 billion, $13 million went to political campaigns to maintain the status quo.

All but three states have some form of gambling. The worst gambling game for consumers is the state lottery. Three-quarters of the states have **state-sponsored lotteries**, and all but a few of these states participate in multi-state lotteries. **Lotteries** are games of chance in which consumers buy instant scratch (daily winners), numbers (bet on an unpredictable numeral), or lotto tickets (jackpots grow until there is a winner) for a low per unit price.

States see lotteries as an easy way to **increase revenues, a voluntary tax**. Rhode Island leads the nation in per capita sales per year; over $800. A lottery is a monopoly. The state has exclusive control over the product, its sale, and prizes awarded. The state operates, advertises, and promotes the lottery, collects revenues, and names an oversight board.

Consumer safeguards are granted for an essential good, such as energy produced by a monopoly. However, similar protections are not available to consumers who purchase lottery tickets.

In a lottery, the consumer buys a ticket from the state through a third-party vendor who is paid a commission often including incentives for high levels of sales. Consumer and vendor must accept the state's rules to participate. A consumer's favorite game may change if lottery officials decide revenue generation would be enhanced through a different package or product. Rules may be imposed on vendors and consumers on a take-it-or-leave-it basis.

As a monopoly, **choice is limited**—the only lottery in town is the state's. Other gambling opportunities exist but one cannot buy a lottery ticket from a competitor. In a state lottery, consumers risk their dollars for very low odds of winning at lower pay-outs than other types of gambling (i.e., slot machines, blackjack).

Misleading advertising is the norm. Do consumers know that the odds of winning your state lottery vary from 1 in 3.5 million (Missouri and Oregon) to 1 in 18 million (California), while most are 1 in 7 million? Powerball odds against winning are 80 million to 1. In contrast, the odds of being struck by lightning are 3 million to 1.

Do advertisements state that **98 percent of tickets are losers**? Do advertisements indicate how much is spent to operate and promote the lottery? Is it clear that the jackpot is paid out over 20 or more years and due to inflation, loses purchasing power the whole time? Do advertisements report that the state is not paying out the full amount, but is purchasing an annuity for the winner costing a fraction of the stated amount? Does anyone request and read a state's annual lottery report? Even if this information were readily available, would consumers understand it? Perhaps most important, does the state want consumers to understand crucial information about its lottery? The answers are "no" because the state's objective is to **maximize revenues** and therefore ticket sales. It is useful to ask, "If consumers knew and understood how a lottery really works, what effect would this have on ticket sales?"

So far, states' revenue generation has overshadowed attention to consumer rights. Lotteries are not in the consumer interest.

*Carole J. Makela, Professor, Colorado State University

Rental Cars—A Scumball Industry that Rips Off Consumers

Beware of the rental car industry because it is **full of rip-offs**, particularly in three areas: rental prices, pre-paid gas and hidden fees, and insurance.

Rental Car Prices that "Take You for a Ride"

"Rental car prices industry-wide change **thousands of times a day**," says industry consultant Neil Abrams. Prices for the same vehicle can vary $12 or more throughout the day. You sometimes can get the best rental car price (even lower than the corporate rate) by ignoring the so-called discounts and telephoning around to make some cost comparisons. Once you have a price quote and reservation in hand, simply show up at the rental car counter of a competitor and ask for a better price. This is known as the **walk-up price**. Try it and you may get a better price or a nicer vehicle, or both.

Prepaid Gas Option and Hidden Fees are Rip-offs

If the rental clerk offers to fill the gas tank upon your return for a price per gallon that seems like a good deal, say "No," even though it is convenient. The reason is that the charge that will show up on your credit card receipt next month will be for a **full tank**. The rental car companies charge customers whatever the vehicle manufacturer says the tank can hold, not how much gas is actually put into the tank. That's what the small print says in the contract and this is a crooked way to do business!

The typical rental car company assesses **umpteen fees** in the small print of the contract, such as charges for exceeding mileage limits, returning the vehicle late, city surcharges (taxes), convention center taxes, airport surcharges (fees), additional-driver fees, frequent-flyer miles tax, under-age surcharges, child's car seat fees, bike rack charges, and transporting fees to take customers from airports to and from rental offices. The companies also assess a "voluntary concession recovery fee" (the fee the company pays to do business at the airport); it's "voluntary" unless you inquire and then refuse to pay it. These charges may add as much as 40 percent to the overall bill, yet they are never mentioned in the advertised rental rates.

Overpriced, Unneeded Insurance

Rental car companies often use questionable selling techniques to peddle horribly overpriced insurance to consumers who often do not need the coverage. **Rental car insurance** is a contract sold through rental car companies designed to protect the consumer from bills if a rented vehicle is damaged or stolen. Rental car insurance has been called "a classic consumer rip-off" by the U.S. Public Interest Research Group because the coverage sold, sometimes using high-pressure sales techniques, is expensive ($2 to $25 per day). The coverage often duplicates the customer's private insurance coverage (auto and home), as well as coverage provided automatically through credit cards and motor club memberships.

Rental car companies generally sell five types of overpriced insurance to consumers: (1) **Collision-damage waiver (CDW)** pays if your rental car is damaged or stolen (and most drivers know it as collision insurance). This coverage has been banned in New York and Illinois, which wisely restrict the liability of drivers to $100 and $200. And, contrary to impressions received by many consumers, CDW does not cover bodily injury or personal property damage. (2) **Loss of use (LOU) waiver**, sometimes called **loss-damage waiver**, pays the rental car company for each day that the damaged rental car is in the repair shop instead of being rented to someone else. (3) **Personal accident insurance (PAI)** that pays for injuries to the driver or passengers. (4) **Personal effects coverage (PEC)** that protects against the theft of any personal items left in the vehicle. (5) **Additional liability insurance** that is an umbrella policy that provides up to $1 million for bodily injury and property damage caused to others in an accident.

Smart consumers should take the following actions:

1. **Telephone your insurance agent** and find out if your personal auto policy covers the potential types of losses that are possible when renting a vehicle, because almost all policies do. Obtain a copy of your policy with the appropriate section marked by the agent to show if needed; a copy is required for overseas rentals. Also confirm that your homeowner's (or renter's) insurance policy covers theft of items taken from inside rental cars. If your present auto insurance policy does not provide adequate protection, ask your insurance agent to add a **rider** to your policy to cover collision and loss-of-use costs in rental cars. The cost? Only $20 to $30 a *year*.

2. **Telephone your credit-card companies** to inquire about their automatic **secondary collision-damage** and **loss-of-use coverage** that provide insurance when a vehicle is rented using their credit card. Some credit-card companies, such as Diner's Club, American Express, MasterCard, and Visa, pay for the portion of damage to a wrecked rental car not covered by your personal auto insurance. However, most credit card companies do not cover pickup trucks, off-road vehicles or rental cars valued at over $50,000.

The only people who should consider purchasing insurance coverage sold through rental car companies are people without any auto insurance (such as urban dwellers who **do not own a vehicle**), car owners who dropped the collision/loss coverage on their auto insurance policy, foreign visitors, and people who do not want to report a rental-car accident to their own insurance companies.

Smart Money magazine says that the rental car company's insurance **may not pay for a covered loss** anyhow because of clauses in the contracts. For example, Hertz and Budget don't pay "unless you are wearing your seat belt." Those two, plus Avis, Enterprise and Thrifty void the coverage "if the doors were not locked or keys were left in the car when the car was damaged or stolen." Enterprise voids the collision coverage if you use the vehicle "in an imprudent manner." The practices described above in the rental car industry are not illegal, but they are immoral.

Credit- and Debit-Card Registration Services—Rip-offs?

In case of lost credit and debit cards, the cardholder should notify debit and credit card companies to avoid legal liability for fraud and misuse. Some firms sell a **card registration service** that registers all the credit- and debit-card numbers of a consumer and arranges for cancellation and replacement of any lost or stolen credit cards. For $49 to $99 a year, you only need to make one telephone call to report all card losses. This is a **wasteful purchase decision** because it's easy to keep one's own list. Plus, consumers are not liable for illegal use of a lost credit card for two days and after that, the liability is only $50 per card.

Virtually no credit card issuers assess the $50 fee since they would rather be nice and keep people as customers.

Identity Theft Insurance—Rip-off?

Identity fraud, discussed in detail later in this chapter, occurs when a thief co-opts some pieces of someone's personal information and steals and misuses an individual's financial assets. Companies are selling insurance policies to protect people against losses incurred if they fall victim to **identity theft**. Policies cost $59 to $180 a year. The coverage pays for costs associated with re-claiming one's identify, such as long-distance telephone calls and the cost of hiring an attorney. If you have a renter's or homeowner's insurance policy, it is likely that you already have this coverage. In addition, you cannot be held liable for more than $50 in fraudulent credit card purchases, and most creditors waive that fee (see Chapter 5). This is another **rip-off insurance policy** that consumers do not need.

Diet, Health and Fitness Products—Rip-offs?

The Food and Drug Administration (FDA) describes **heath fraud** as "articles of unproven effectiveness that are promoted to improve health, well-being or appearance." Health products are an especially appealing area for schemes as people are quite susceptible to health-related misrepresentations offering quasi-scientific claims like: "End arthritis pain with this stylish copper bracelet!" "Scrub away cellulite with ancient ingredient!" "Bleaching cream brightens your skin!" "Eliminate skin cancer in days," "Spray Slender Mist into your mouth to depress your appetite!" "Weight-loss secret from the Orient!" "Melt fat away while you sleep!" "Miracle cure for cancer!" "Bee pollen formula cures herpes!" "Magnets that eliminate pain!" "Magnetic mattress pads cure back pain," "Herbal dietary supplement works wonders!"

There is no reputable research to back up the claims, only testimonials and personal stories. Gullible consumers believe the claims, especially when they experience a **placebo effect** that occurs when any new treatment is started because it is "expected" to work. These effects disappear over time. Advertisements promise a "money-back" guarantee, although few consumers get their money back before the promoters take their profits. For more information on health frauds, see www.fda.gov/fdac/features/1999/699_fraud.html.

Opting for such unproven pills, potions, drinks, gadgets, and programs may **waste precious time** that could be used for proven remedies and therapies. You can only be sure of four things in health quackery: (1) the product will not do what is promised, (2) your health may be harmed, (3) you will have wasted your money, and (4) you will not get a refund.

Weight-Loss Products and Centers—Rip-offs?

About 50 million Americans will go on a diet this year. While some will succeed in taking off weight, very few—about **five percent**—will manage to keep all of it off. A National Institutes of Health panel reviewing industry-supplied data found that dropout rates for weight loss centers go as high as 80 percent. The Federal Trade Commission says that only five percent of people manage to keep the weight off for longer than one year. The only way to lose weight and keep it off is to eat fewer calories or use more calories. This can be done by eating less food, exercising more, or both. There is no magic bullet to eliminate fat from the system.

Quackery and false advertising succeed in this $30 billion industry because there are so many customers who are willing to try some new diet book, pill, cream, or something they think might work. Examples include diets that focus on one particular food, such as grapefruit; pills, such as starch blockers advertised as diet aids; electrical muscle stimulators; body wraps, preceded by application of some cream or lotion; and capsules that promise to burn, block, flush or otherwise obliterate fat. The FTC says, "Whether pills, potions, or lotions, the only thing these quick-fix products leave lighter are **consumers' wallets**."

For useful information, see www.healthyweightnetwork.com. Companies recently fined by the FTC include General Nutrition Centers Inc., New Directions, UWCC Permance Program, HMR Fasting Program. **Each year** the FTC brings about ten cases against marketers of fraudulent weight-loss products.

Weight-loss centers are a problem industry, too. They should be required to provide clear and **comparable information** about a program's cost, length, effectiveness, and safety, as well as the qualifications of the staff. The FTC has issued voluntary guidelines for weight loss centers, but they do not mandate the reporting of the **success rate**. Only Connecticut requires weight-loss centers to report outcomes.

CONSUMER UPDATE:
Job-Search Companies—Rip-offs?

Unscrupulous sellers also take advantage of consumers who are seeking employment. Because people may be experiencing difficulty in locating a job, they sometimes turn to private employment agencies. The process works like this: The person completes an application form and signs a contract to register interest in certain types of jobs. The **job-search company** then provides some career counseling, helps improve the person's resume, and tries to locate suitable job positions for which the person can interview. Most headhunters, executive recruiters, management consultants, and outplacement firms are reputable businesses; some are not.

The way some of these companies make money is to **charge a fee**, often $500, $1,000, $2,000, or more, for trying to place someone in an employment position. Ads tucked away in classified sections entice consumers by claiming they can open hidden jobs or boasting about secret connections, sometimes with overseas employers. Most of the disreputable firms offer nothing more than sloppily done resumes and outdated lists of corporate contacts. Some firms **go through the motions** of forwarding your resume in an attempt to help you find a job; others require that you send out your resumes. The small print in the signed contract spells out the limitations, such as printing costs are an extra charge and that the firms do not guarantee jobs for clients. The job seeker must pay any remaining fees "when the person accepts a job of his or her choice," no matter how it was found.

Legitimate employment agencies collect **no advance fees** from those looking for work. They only get paid when the person finds employment for which the agency arranged an interview. Reputable agencies typically collect their entire fee from the employer, not the new employee.

Supplemental Insurance (Health, Cancer, Life)—Rip-offs?

Mail-order insurance is largely a world of schlock. Advertisements in the Sunday newspapers, in magazines, and on television make **fantastic claims** about the need for insurance protection against the likelihood of death, cancer, and other dread diseases.

Usually a celebrity, movie star, or athlete makes the promotion. And they may get $100,000 or more for one day of taping commercials.

All too often these people are pitching **nearly worthless** health and life insurance policies. Suggestions that, "One out of three people will get cancer" and that "The average hospital stay for cancer victims is 2 months" are pure fabrications. Companies tell such lies to create illusions and fears that they promise to fix. They may claim that, "Cash benefits are paid directly to you" or "No one can be turned down for life insurance." Then they set artificial time limits, such as, "You must apply by October 15!" or, buried in the small print, "No benefits for two years."

The products being advertised are called **supplemental insurance**, as the policies are intended to add to one's existing insurance coverage. The ads mention the initial benefits, such as guaranteeing acceptance, and then fail to tell crucial details—what several insurance commissioners describe as serious misrepresentations and omissions. The state of Washington has tough advertising standards and has prohibited the broadcast of commercials from many of these companies, arguing that they were "false, deceptive, or misleading advertisements." These types of policies simply do not provide the insurance protection that consumers think they are getting. Such policies are just rip-offs.

Most advertised health policies **duplicate coverage** that consumers already have, restrict the conditions for paying a claim, do not pay for preexisting conditions for the **first two years** the policy is in effect, pay minuscule benefits, and pay nothing until the insured has been in the hospital 14 days. Cancer policies, for example, cover only 1/10 or 1/20 of one's risk. Consumers who have major medical coverage as part of their health insurance plan are adequately covered for illness, including cancer. If needed, major medical coverage can be added to most health insurance policies for perhaps another $50 per month.

The National Association of Insurance Commissions (NAIC) reports an industry-wide payout ratio of 43 percent for supplemental health insurance policies. A **payout ratio** is the proportion of premium dollars paid out as benefits to insurance purchasers. This means for every dollar paid in premiums policyholders only receive 43 cents through claims. This low return does not come close to the **NAIC payout ratio standard** of 65 percent for policies sold directly to consumers and 75 percent for policies sold to groups. Policies with low pay-out ratios are rip-offs.

Sales of life insurance is similarly a poor value. Robert Hunter, insurance expert for the Consumer Federation of America, says that most of these life insurance policies pay nothing if the policyholder dies within the first two years. Upon the non-accidental death of a 60-year-old man, these policies generally pay about $1,500. To keep the premiums level, the benefits also drop further with age. For example, the policy advertised by one television actor pays only $500 at age 65 and only $350 at age 70. A study by the state of Wisconsin found that **only three policyholders in 1,000** collect in the first seven years. Those who have life insurance coverage through their employment or who already have a private policy do not need supplemental policies. See "Tips on Buying Life Insurance" in Chapter 17 for information on buying excellent policies at fair or low prices.

Credit-Life, Disability- and Unemployment-Insurance

If you have a car loan or lease, you might have signed up for credit life insurance coverage for $15 or $25 a month. Most consumers are asked when they complete and sign a credit agreement whether or not they want to purchase **credit-life insurance**, **credit-disability**, and/or **credit-unemployment insurance**. These are add-on, high-priced policies that are sold to consumers who are financing vehicles, furniture, and appliances. Should the borrower die, become disabled or unemployed (according to the narrow definition in the policy), the insurance pays off the unpaid balance of the consumer debt.

Credit life insurance is the **nation's worst rip-off**, reports the Consumer Federation of America. An estimated $500 million is wasted annually on overcharges. Sellers and finance companies have "sold" this overpriced product to 60 million customers who simply do not understand the poor logic of their decision to purchase. The reason the product is **"sold"** is that sales commissions average 40 percent of the premium. Some consumers do not even realize that they have purchased such insurance; others are mistakenly led to think that they cannot borrow without purchasing the insurance. If a lender requires coverage to secure a loan, the law says that the consumer need not purchase insurance from the lender or from lender-recommended sources.

Insurance sellers in some states have a **payout ratio of 12**, where as little as 12 cents of every premium dollar collected goes to pay claims. That's 88 cents in profit for every $1 in premium! What a rip-off business!

Term life insurance can be purchased from a local insurance agents as well as on the **Internet**, where a policy costs about 1/6 to 1/10 of the car dealer's policy. Credit disability and unemployment insurance policies are equally costly. It is not uncommon for consumers to unnecessarily pay $2,000 in premiums over the life of an installment loan for life, disability, and unemployment insurance. These monthly premiums can add up to a lot of wasted money.

Income Tax Refund Anticipation Loans—Rip-offs?

Refund anticipation loans (RALs) are short-term loans, often for less than two-weeks, from a tax-preparation service that are secured in the amount the taxpayer can expect from the government as an income tax refund. The loan is repaid when the refund is received in a temporary bank account set up by the lender.

RALs carry **outrageous interest rates and fees**. A Consumer Federation of America study found that rates range from 67% to 774%. In New York, the attorney general found that a person who gets a RAL of $500 paid $197. That included $30 in interest charges at 522% annual percentage rate, if repaid a year later, plus a "peace of mind guarantee" for $129 and a filing fee of $38, even though electronic filing is free. RALs are not illegal; they are just very bad deals. The result of a local government lawsuit was that H&R Block provided restitution of $4.2 million in overcharges to 62,000 New Yorkers.

You can file electronically yourself and receive your refund through a direct bank deposit in as little as ten days. However, the software provided free by various companies supporting the IRS **Free File** webpage (accessed at www.irs.gov or www.firstgov.gov) is confusing and clunky. Think about it: Why would the private sector provide the IRS with free, easy-to-use tax-filing software (on the IRS webpage) for taxpayers to use that competes with the polished commercial software that they sell? Perhaps the IRS will eventually conclude that it should develop its own software.

A LIST OF PROBABLE RIP-OFFS

Rip-off	The Promise Explained	The Reality
Fake Checks	The check made out to you; also stamped "This is not a check"	Can only be used to purchase over-priced products from a catalog
False Gold and Platinum Credit Cards	$49.95 membership fee for a "similar" card	Can only be used to purchase over-priced products from a catalog
Low-Interest Credit Card	$99 permits you to transfer other credit balances to the low-interest card	If a real Visa or MasterCard is received, the rate will rise later; most often the consumer receives a booklet explaining how to apply for a card
Unordered Merchandise	Company mails something with the hope that receiving party will pay	You may keep anything shipped to you and then you can assess the sender storage fees and charges to return the goods
Phony Bills	Bill comes in the mail, perhaps for a deceased relative	A likely fraud; ask for copy of a signature on order form
Unclaimed Funds	Letter on official-looking stationery saying a "routine audit" has determined that you are owed money; send $35 for processing fees	Only scam artists charge processing fees
Photo Clubs	Lifetime supply of film and development	Required to swap film on a 1-for-1 basis; cannot order 10 rolls; club costs $1,000+
Home Improvements and Repairs	Promises high-quality work and must have X dollars as a down payment	Unlicenced repairpeople take the money and run; sometimes they just do shoddy work with poor materials
Free Baby Photos	Company offers free baby photos but pressures the consumer to buy expensive photo packages	Take the free photos and pay an inexpensive service charge; skip the package deal
Magazines	Young people sell magazines pretending that they are working their way through school; also you have "won" a subscription for three years	Shipping and Handling fee of $50+; also "salesperson" disappears with the money
Vacuum Cleaners, Sewing Machines, Encyclopedias, and Fire Extinguishing Systems	Usually legitimate door-to-door sales of consumer goods	Often horribly overpriced and the merchandise is not needed

(continued)

A LIST OF PROBABLE RIP-OFFS

Rip-off	The Promise Explained	The Reality
Campground Memberships	Consumer signs 25-year lease to use same plot in campground for two weeks every year	Overpriced and not really needed; companies often go bankrupt
Health Club Spas, Weight-Loss Center, Martial Arts Facilities, and Dance Lessons	Consumer signs a contract for a series of services and some success is quickly achieved	Firm often cannot deliver what was promised; many companies go bankrupt
Freezer Meat	Very low advertised price for frozen meat	Meat sold at "hanging weight" before fat is cut off; poor quality meat is substituted when packed
Frozen-Food Freezer Plan	Bulk purchase of meat delivered regularly and it includes purchase of freezer	Freezer is overpriced; quality of food is excellent in the beginning, then declines
Degree Mills	Sell diplomas for a price with an extreme minimum of on-site educational experiences	Such diplomas do not meet the standards of the genuine accrediting associations
Term Papers	Sell term papers on any topic	Poorly written and referenced essays that if turned in to a school will result in disciplinary action
Publishing Songs, Poetry and Books	Promise to publish your work and you can expect to make royalties on the sales	Firm collects substantial upfront fee that pays the cost of production; profits never exist
Phony Bank Examiner	Asks for help in identifying teller who is embezzling funds by having consumer make withdrawal from that teller	The receipt from the "bank examiner" is worthless because he really does not work for the bank
Pigeon Drop	Person "finds" money in a bag or envelope and offers to share it with a nearby consumer	After taking "pigeon's" good-faith money to a lawyer's office for safe-keeping, the bag of money is switched; a partner is often used and the lawyer does not exist
Work at Home	Advertisements for huge profits for at-home tasks, such as stuffing envelopes	Products completed at home often refused by seller; sometimes the "deal" requires consumer to run similar ads to get money from other consumers

---

KEY TOPIC IN CONSUMER ECONOMICS:
Be Aware of Identity Theft

Identity fraud occurs when a thief co-opts some pieces of someone's personal information and appropriates it without the person's knowledge to pretend to merchants, creditors and other sellers that they are in fact that person. The objective is to commit fraud or to steal and misuse financial assets.

The thief fraudulently **obtains your credit report** (that lists account numbers) by posing as a landlord, employer or someone else who may have a legitimate need for— and a legal right to—the information. Once identity thieves have your information, perhaps from a stolen wallet, they may open new accounts or lines of credit -- under your name, and then run up big credit balances and take cash advances. ID thieves can open new checking accounts in your name and write bad checks, and they can call credit card issuers to change your mailing address. Some ID thieves open new cell phone accounts and run up thousands of dollars in charges.

Perpetrators use a **variety of tactics** to obtain enough personal information about a victim to then drain that person's finances. Some thieves look in trash bins for unshredded credit applications, canceled checks or other bank records. Others "shoulder surf" at an ATM or phone booth to get your PIN code.

Sometimes it is months before the victim is aware of being a victim. When you get turned down for credit, a car loan, or a mortgage on your dream house because you've got a bad credit rating and you know you've paid your bills on time, it is likely that an identity thief stole your identity. Victims take an estimated **200 hours** and $1,100 to correct and clear their credit records, and this effort can take months or even years.

Here are some **steps to help prevent falling victim** to identity theft. Be cautious about sharing personal information with anyone. Be watchful in public by concealing private information. Place complicated passwords on your credit card, bank and phone accounts. Secure personal information in your home, especially if you have roommates, employ outside help or are having service work done in your home. Secure your mailbox. Shred non-essential identify information. Closely review your credit card bills and bank statements to check the accuracy of all transactions. Give your SSN only when absolutely necessary. Do not let your state use your Social Security number for your driver's license number. Periodically **order a copy of your credit report** from each of the three major credit reporting agencies (Experian [888-397-3742; www.experion.com], Trans Union [800-888-4213; www.transunion.com], and Equifax [800-685-1111; www.equifax.com]) to look for new account numbers and late payments that do not belong to you. Remove your name from mailing lists (see Chapter 5.) **Opt out** of the phone number service of www.google.com; to do so, begin by typing in your phone number and search.

If you''ve been a victim of identity theft, first report it immediately to the police. Second, report the fraud to one of the three major credit bureaus, because they will notify the other two. Third, call the FTC's Identity Theft Hotline toll-free at 1-877-IDTHEFT (438-4338). Counselors will take your complaint and advise you on how to deal with the credit-related problems that could result. In addition, the FTC, in conjunction with banks, credit grantors and consumer advocates, has developed the ID Theft Affidavit to help victims of ID theft restore their good names. The **ID Theft Affidavit**, a form that can be used to report information to many organizations, simplifies the process of disputing charges with companies where a new account was opened in your name. For a copy of the ID Theft Affidavit, visit the ID Theft Website at www.consumer.gov/idtheft.

Negative Option Buying Plans—Rip-offs?

A **negative option plan** is a legal sales agreement between a consumer and a company that periodically delivers merchandise, such as books, compact discs, and videos. The contract **obligates the consumer** to accept and pay for an item unless he or she notifies the company within a specified time period that a particular item is unwanted. The advertisement may read, "Eight compact discs for $1!" When the offer is accepted, the consumer typically agrees to buy additional purchases under the club's negative option plan. If you want the selection offered, you do nothing; it will be shipped to you automatically.

If you do not want the selection, you must tell the seller not to send it. The difficulty for consumers occurs when the negative option notice appears at their home address while they are away on vacation or they simply neglect to return the notice, and it results in them having to pay for goods not wanted. This is known as "stop-us-before-we-mail-you-more-merchandise marketing." Rip-off![2]

A variation of the negative option technique is the **soft-sell** used by some of the nation's best-known companies who offer you either a free trial membership or complimentary copies of magazines. When the trial period is over, they assume that you want the membership or subscription service because you have not contacted them to say that you do not want it to continue. Then they bill you for an entire year. This is **trickery**.

Deceptions and Unfair Practices

Rip-offs are not illegal. Neither are scams, misrepresentations, deceptions and frauds *unless and until* a judge says so. The dictionary says that a "deception" is a form of **trickery** involving the selling of goods or services to consumers and a **fraud** is an intentional perversion of truth in order to induce another to part with something of value. Governments at the federal, state and local levels attempt to police the market to help keep it free of dishonest practices.

The Federal Trade Commission Act allows the FTC to act in the interest of all consumers to prevent deceptive and unfair acts or practices. The government's interpretation of **Section 5** of the FTC Act is "that a representation, omission or practice is **deceptive** if it is likely to (1) mislead consumers and (2) affect consumers' behavior or decisions about the product or service." In addition, an act or practice is "**unfair** if the injury it causes, or is likely to cause, is substantial, not outweighed by other benefits, and not reasonably avoidable."

Unfair or Deceptive Advertising

Advertisements for products and services are subject to self-regulation, such as the Council of Better Business Bureaus' **"Code of Advertising"** (see www.adcouncil.org/), as well as the laws and regulations of federal, state and local governments. The Federal Trade Commission Act prohibits **unfair or deceptive advertising** in any medium. In essence, advertising must tell the truth and not mislead consumers. (Chapter 12 examines advertising and consumer decision making, the types of truth and exaggeration in advertising, and advertising to children.)

An **advertising claim** can be "**misleading** if relevant information is left out or if the claim implies something that is not true." Advertising claims "must be **substantiated**, especially when they concern health, safety, or performance." The seller should have documentation that provides evidence on the product, the claims, and whatever facts experts

---

[2] Once you fulfill the commitment to purchase so many items, you can request that you be switched to a **positive-option plan**. Then you get the catalog but do not have the obligation to return a postcard unless you want to purchase something.

believe necessary.[3] The advertising agencies or website designers are responsible for reviewing the substantiation information to be assured that the claims are substantiated. An agency or catalog marketer shall be held liable by the FTC depending upon the extent of the agency's participation in the preparation of the challenged ad and whether the agency knew or should have known that the advertisement included false or deceptive claims. Agencies should be especially cautious "when it comes to extravagant performance claims, health or weight loss promises, or earnings guarantees."

Proving Deceptions and Unfair Practices

In a court of law, the burden of proving deception or fraud is upon the consumer. Because proof is very difficult to show (such as an intention to deceive the victim), consumers in such situations can turn to governments for help. Both the local government **Office of Consumer Affairs** and the state government **Office of the Attorney General** have the authority to pursue consumer deceptions. While the federal government also investigates and prosecutes deceptions; it does not have the authority to seek redress for individual consumers. For example, the Federal Trade Commission logs in complaints, conducts inquiries and investigations, and when appropriate takes legal action on behalf of all consumers. Refunds are rarely obtained for individual victims, although many companies are fined for illegal behaviors. On very rare occasions, a perpetrator is jailed for defrauding consumers.

Many state **consumer protection acts** define **deception** more broadly than the Federal Trade Commission. Their standard is "a tendency or capacity to deceive consumers, even if they do not actually deceive." This more generous definition allows many state and local governments to try to protect normal consumers *as well as* the uninformed, the ignorant, those with poor language skills, those whose first language is not English, those of low intelligence, and even children. Using this broad standard to protect all consumers, states do not have to prove actual deception or definite injury to consumers. The state may find practices to be deceptive "if the ignorant, the unthinking, and the credulous" could be deceived. Thus, many **states have more power** than the federal government to close down deceptive practices.

Historically, the Federal Trade Commission regulates unfair and deceptive marketplace practices as well as advertising claims on a **case-by-case basis**, one bad seller at a time, and occasionally with industry-wide trade regulations. Both approaches have proved extremely slow.

The state attorneys general fight deceptions and unfair practices that escape the attention or authority of the FTC. Neither **online advertising** nor **infomercials** (program-length advertisements) are regulated effectively by government. Thus, such advertisements should not be believed.

---

[3] **Political advertisements** are subject to no regulation of any kind. Unscrupulous political advertising techniques, such as reliance on innuendo, half-truths, fear-mongering (including racism), negative assaults, distortions, and outright falsehoods, are protected as "free speech" by the First Amendment of the Constitution of the United States.

CONSUMER UPDATE:
The Five Biggest Lies Told to Consumers

The "Five Biggest Lies Told to Consumers," reports the **U.S. Postal Service** are (1) "You are a guaranteed winner of one of five valuable prizes," (2) "You have been selected to receive a fabulous vacation," (3) "Stuff envelopes at home and earn big $$$,"(4) "This chain letter is perfectly legal," and (5) "Your humble assistance is highly solicited in transferring millions of dollars...All we need is your bank account number."

Puffery Statements are Legal

Puffery advertisements make unsupported, subjective favorable opinions, and exaggerated statements concerning the quality, value, or goodness of a product offered for sale that is not made as a representation of fact. Puffing is **not considered fraud** in the eyes of the law, since everyone knows a seller will tend to exaggerate a bit. Sellers are allowed some leeway in describing attributes of their products, and such overstatements are typically considered innocent misrepresentations. Statements such as, "This is the finest-quality wool coat money can buy" and "This is the most powerful vacuum cleaner made in America" should not be taken seriously by consumers. The words *better*, *best*, *greatest*, and *finest* are typically employed. Consumers view puffery advertisements "through a filter of protective skepticism," says *Advertising Age*.

Bait and Switch Advertising is Illegal

Bait and switch advertising is defined as an alluring but insincere offer to sell a high-quality product or service at a bargain price that the advertiser does not intend or want to sell. This idea is to lure a great number of shoppers and **sell them a substitute**. The seller then pushes an inferior substitute at an exorbitant price. The bait is the product or service advertised at the apparently low sale price in order to attract the customer into the store. The well-meaning consumer wants to take advantage of the bargain, but the salesperson almost steadfastly refuses to sell the product, for such reasons as..."There aren't any left," "You can't get delivery for three months," "Many people who bought it aren't satisfied," and "The product just isn't very good." The salesperson tries to persuade the customer to buy a similar but more expensive item. This is the switch. Many sellers of mattresses, appliances and vehicles sometimes use bait and switch tactics. One reason why bait and switch works is that once consumers have experienced the search costs of shopping they typically **do not want to bother** to look elsewhere.

Do not confuse bait and switch with **trading up**. This is a perfectly proper sales technique where a salesperson encourages a customer to buy a higher-priced item in order for the salesperson to make a bigger sale, earn a larger commission, and/or better fill the customer's needs and wants. Grocery stores that give **rain checks** for merchandise that is sold out similarly are not using bait and switch advertising because their ads say that there are limited quantities.

CONSUMER UPDATE:
Classified Advertisements are Full of Lies

Classified advertisements placed in newspapers and at the back of magazines are almost never investigated for truthfulness by the owner of the publication. As a result, this form of advertising attracts unscrupulous sellers.

Popular scams regularly seen in classified ads include:

- **Overseas employment opportunities** (you pay an **up-front fee** [also called an **advance fee**] for a list of names of potential employers who supposedly are hiring)

- **Summer jobs in Alaska** (you buy an overpriced reference that lists potential employers)

- **Loans for consumers with poor or no credit history** (hefty advance fees are charged, and if a victim gets a loan it will be at a very high interest rate)

- **Stuff envelopes at home** (promoter sends you a letter telling you to place the same ad in newspapers and magazines)

- **Earn money by working at home** (promoter sells overpriced goods for victim to work on and then the seller does not buy the products when completed)

- **Earn money by reading** (promoter sells overpriced reference that tells how to sell editing services to publishers)

- **Scholarships for college** (victim pays for an outdated reference listing scholarships that are defunct, past deadline, or for which the student will not qualify)

You can be confident of two things when responding to a classified advertisement: (1) the reality will not be the same as what was advertised, and (2) you will not get your money back, even though the promoter "guarantees" that refunds are available.

Telemarketing and Mail Scams

Several types of rip-offs, misrepresentations, and deceptions regularly use mail and telecommunication as ways to reach consumers.

Mail Fraud

The U.S. Postal Service reports that the average American gets **550 pieces** of junk mail, mostly advertising materials, every year. That amounts to about 40 pounds of catalogs, political flyers, charitable solicitations, sweepstakes packets, magazine subscription offers, coupons, food samples, investment opportunities, and the like. More than half of all adults in the United States purchase something by mail every year, and millions of them are victims of mail fraud. **Mail fraud**, according to the 1872 Postal Service Law, is the use of the mail for "any scheme to defraud, or for obtaining money or property by means of false or fraudulent pretenses."

To avoid mail fraud, the consumer has to know it when he or she sees it. (See www.usps.gov/websites/depart/inspect/consmenu.htm.) The most familiar tactic in mail fraud is misleading or false advertisements by which the perpetrators use the mails to lure consumers into their scams. Consumers are led to believe that they are **getting a really good deal**, perhaps something free. The consumer unwittingly puts up money expecting a product of excellent quality, but instead receives something of poor quality and of **little or no value**.

Lack of physical contact with victims makes identification of mail-order and Internet crooks difficult. Also, the geographic distance between the victim and the perpetrators makes apprehension more difficult and expensive. Because of the usual small amount of money that is lost, many consumers are willing to chalk up the loss to experience **rather than report it** to authorities. The U.S. Postal Service manages to obtain convictions against about 1,000 swindlers each year.

Telemarketing to Get Your Money

Telemarketing is selling a product or service over the telephone. Many worthwhile products are marketed using telecommunications, such as up-to-date financial news, stock quotations, insurance company financial-soundness ratings, legal aid by the minute, sample music cuts, and critiques of latest films. When you answer the telephone or make a call, the telemarketer has a convincing sales pitch.

The government reports that over 140,000 telemarketing firms are in operation and that about **14,000** of them deliberately practice fraud. The National Fraud Information Center estimates one-half of all telemarketing calls to consumers' homes are from crooks trying to defraud the public. Solicitors of all kinds telephone more than 18 million Americans every day. The average loss to a telemarketing scam is $822, reports the National Consumers League.

The term **telefrauds** describes what unscrupulous telephone salespeople do—use the telephone for non-legitimate sales. Many people describe the proliferation of legitimate and unscrupulous telemarketing techniques as **junk calls**.

The National Fraud Information Center reports that the most popular telemarketing frauds are **phony credit card offers**, work-at-home, prizes and sweepstakes, and advance-fee loans. Almost anything can be sold by unscrupulous sellers over the telephone, including bad deals on prize offers, penny stocks, office supplies, magazine subscriptions, credit repair, job opportunities, precious metals, travel packages, art, business ventures, travel clubs, coupon books, lotteries for wireless cable and cellular phones, investments, business opportunities, precious gems, refund companies, living trusts, timeshares, buying-club memberships, water treatment units, travel certificates, and vacations.

Both good and bad telemarketing sellers use 800-numbers and 900-numbers to market goods and services. An **800-number** (also 888, 877, 866 ... 822) is a toll-free long-distance telephone line (except for audio entertainment or information services). About 40 percent of all long-distance calls are made to 800-numbers. A **900-number** is a caller-paid long distance service that allows consumers and businesses to access information over the telephone. (Local callers dial **976-numbers** the same way.) The caller pays for telephone numbers with 900 and 976 prefixes. After 15 years of profiting, AT&T decided to no longer bill their customers for 900 calls. Watch out when responding to advertisements that give an area code that seems unfamiliar, such as 809 (in the Caribbean) because it may be an international number that is long-distance, and the toll charges are likely to be enormous.

One indicted telemarketing promoter was quoted as saying that, "If you ask 100 people any question, **at least 3 of them will say 'yes'**. With the right pitch, you can sell 15 of every 100 people you telephone." AARP estimates that telephone marketing swindlers cheat American consumers out of $40 billion annually.

Many telemarketing scams originate out of **boiler rooms**. This is a place (historically in the basement next to the heating unit) where a number of people use high-pressure telephone sales tactics to sell stock, commodities, petroleum partnerships, unmined gold, re-opened oil wells, land, travel clubs, and other so-called opportunities.

CONSUMER UPDATE:
Telemarketing Crooks Can Get Your Cash

A telemarketer does not need a person's signature granting permission to withdraw funds from one's bank account (**automatic debiting**) if they get the consumer's express verifiable authorization. Never answer a telemarketer's questions with a simple "yes" or "no," because they may be taping your "permission." Laws also do not prohibit the use of **unsigned checks** without first getting explicit authorization from the consumer. Consumer protection regulations do not prohibit **courier pickups** of payments. The truth is that persuasive crooks have an easy time getting thousands of consumers every day to inadvertently agree to allow funds to be withdrawn from their accounts or picked up from their homes.

Sweepstakes

A **sweepstakes** is an advertising or promotional device where consumers get a chance to win a prize without having to know anything or pay anything. Prizes are awarded to participating consumers by chance, with no purchase or entry fee required in order to win. One's chances of winning are determined by the number of participants and the number of prizes to be awarded. Some sweepstakes sponsors, especially those who are marketing products and services, put up all the prize money themselves.

Marketers use sweepstakes because they are **extremely effective** in generating attention for the sponsoring companies. By federal law, competitors in sweepstakes competitions must have an equal chance of winning. Also, a sweepstakes sponsor must disclose the odds of winning.

In contrast to a sweepstakes, in a **lottery** the consumer has to pay to have a chance at winning a prize. Here the participants' contributions form a fund to be awarded as a prize to the winner or winners. Only states and certain exempt charitable organizations may conduct lotteries; all other lotteries are illegal.

The highly publicized sweepstakes contests by Publisher's Clearinghouse, Reader's Digest, and American Family Publishers are designed to sell magazines. These sellers **lure consumers into buying** magazines by implying that they are more likely than non-purchasers to win big prizes. Publisher's Clearinghouse recently settled charges of deceptive marketing with 50 states and paid fines of $52 million. American Family Publishers also settled with the states.

These well-known companies do give away all the prizes, although you probably will not win, since you are much more likely to die in a fireworks accident at a fourth of July celebration. American Family Publishers' odds are typical. The chances of winning $1,000 to $60,000 are **1 in 122.5 million**; you have 1 chance in 12.5 million of winning $500, 1 chance in 4.9 million of winning $100, 1 chance in 2.45 million of winning $50, and 1 chance in 2,869 of winning $5. Columbia University statistics professor Herbert Robbins calculated the odds. Late Show comedian David Letterman once accurately joked that, "the odds of winning Publisher's Clearinghouse are about the same as not entering at all."

Fake Sweepstakes Clubs

A variation of the fraudulent sweepstakes occurs when the winners (or should that be "losers"?) are invited to join a fake **sweepstakes club**, perhaps for only $5 a month. The "winners" are promised that the company will use its "special formula" to identify the sweepstakes—that are held monthly—that offer them the greatest odds of winning; then the company signs them up. Victims—often the elderly—are later talked into joining a number of similar clubs. Losses of $1,000 to $3,000—a month!—are common.

Some crooks telephone consumers to tell them that they have won the Reader's Digest Sweepstakes or some other sweepstakes or contest. Then they say that the winnings **cannot be released** until a certified check in the amount of $500, or even $10,000, is sent to cover shipping, handling, and taxes. The bad guys often send a courier service to the conned consumer's home to pick up the money that will never be seen again. One crook had his 42 sweepstakes companies closed by the federal government, but not before he grossed $82 million in a single year.

Prizes and Free Gifts

Nearly all consumers in the United States have received (and probably will again in the future) at least one official-looking "notice" or telephone call stating that they are the **"guaranteed winner"** of one of the "following four prizes worth thousands of dollars," including a glamorous vacation and a new automobile. Such claims are always lies. Prizes and free gifts offered by sellers are simply come-ons. Unscrupulous businesses use these marketing techniques because they work; so do legitimate sellers.

Prizes are a popular way to interest consumers into buying home fire-prevention systems, raw land for investment purposes, vacation condominium time shares, home security systems, water treatment systems, vitamins, and a host of other products they are not likely to buy without some encouragement. Gifts and prizes are used to **get consumers to the telephone** or into the showroom so the persuasive sales force can interest them in overpriced products and services. The values of the prizes, such as jewelry, are truly cheap and often grossly misrepresented, but nothing requires that good-quality prizes must be given away. The truth is that you always win the cheapest prize.

One of the gambits commonly used by scam telemarketing operators is the guise of **marketing research** in combination with prizes and awards. The promoters ask you to help their market research by "testing a product." To encourage participation, consumers are offered fabulous gifts and prizes with inflated values, either free or at substantial discounts, such as a motor boat or a motorcycle. To receive the prize, the consumer is coaxed into paying an up-front "processing fee," "redemption fee," or a "shipping-tax-and-handling fee." It turns out that the fee, perhaps $295, is much higher than the value of the product.

CONSUMER UPDATE:
Gifts and Prizes ... What They *Really* Are*

Sellers try hard to convince consumers that the "prize" they have won is **worth a lot of money**. Consumers are enticed to "send money for shipping and handling" or "come and listen to a one-hour sales presentation with no obligation." In actuality, the prizes and gifts are simply **worthless**.

- "½ Carat Diamond Ring" ... A zirconia stone valued at $10

- "1 Carat Genuine Semi-precious Stone" ... A cheap gemstone valued at $3

- "Big Screen Television" ... A big-screen projection system that reflects a fuzzy picture from your TV screen that is enlarged against a wall, valued at $10

- "$500 Savings Bond" ... A zero-coupon bond of a corporation currently valued at $5 because the company is near bankruptcy and won't be around 30 years later to pay the $500

- "35 Millimeter Camera" ... An all-plastic camera worth about the price of a roll of film

- "Food processor" ... A hand-operated food chopper

- "Stereo system" ... A plastic toy that fits in your hand

- "Genuine Leather-Like Luggage" ... A cheap plastic bag shaped like luggage with metal brackets so weak that they would collapse if a child sat on it

- "Clock" ... Made of cardboard or plastic

- "Vacation cruise" ... You must send in a redemption fee of $295

- "Motorcycle" ... A plastic replica suitable for a very small child

- "Full-size Motor Boat" ... A five-foot inflatable rubber raft powered by a small battery-activated motor

*Carol Ann Walker, Personal Finance Manager/Air Force Aid Officer, Peterson Air Force Base, Colorado

---

Contests

The U.S. Postal Service once sent out pink-colored "contest announcement postcards" to 200,000 consumers telling them that, "You are a contest winner! Congratulations!!" The card then listed "five wonderful prizes." Over **55,000 people called** the toll-free number to claim their prize. "Winners" were played a tape recording advising them to be more careful about phony sweepstakes solicitations. This study means that about 30 percent of consumers reply to contest scams. A national survey by Louis Harris indicated that **29 percent** of people contacted by the guaranteed prize postcard scheme have responded.

Many contests purposely have very easy, **simple solutions**. Once the consumer mails in his or her solution, he or she is sent a prize for winning, although it is usually something of low quality and little value. Some sewing machine and vacuum manufacturers, for example, encourage potential buyers with contest prizes. They award books, cameras, and jewelry to winners of "easy-to-win" or "everybody-really-wins" contests. To claim a prize, a consumer need only respond correctly to the promoter's question(s), mail in some postal card response, telephone the seller, or visit the sales showroom.

In a related scam, you, the "lucky winner," might be told that you are eligible to enter a **tie-breaker contest** where, for an additional fee, you are allowed to compete for a much larger prize. Crooks typically offer a series of fake tie-breaker contests, offering the hope of winning some grand prize. Of course, no one wins a prize.

Some contest scams require that as a winner all you have to do is to telephone the company's **900-number** to collect the prize. Using 900-numbers costs the calling consumer lots of money, often $25 to $100 to simply call up and ask about the prize. To entice people to respond, slick telemarketers sometimes allow victims to call toll-free 800-numbers where they get a recording saying that in order to receive the prize they must call another number, and yes, it is a 900-number.

A variation of the contest scam occurs when one calls to say that "as a credit card holder you have won." The caller then asks for **your credit card number** for "verification" purposes. If you do give them your number, your next month's credit card bill is likely to reveal substantial unauthorized charges to your account.

Many Charities Are *Not* What They Claim to Be

There are approximately 1.8 million charities in the United States. About 4 in 5 American households make charitable donations each year, averaging $800 a year or about $450 per person. However, the generous American public winds up giving part of that money—over $150 billion annually—to fraudulent or **quasi-charities**. These are charities that have not yet been closed down by a government agency, but they are unscrupulous because they spend an excessively high proportion of their income on administrative expenses and fund-raising and give very little money to those really in need. The major activity of such quasi-charities is **"program services" and "education"** for the public by mailing out solicitation letters for more money. That, plus mailing costs, fat salaries, and overhead, eats up most of the money raised. The operators are greedy, self-serving crooks. The executive director of one Better Business Bureau states that, "It happens all the time, and unfortunately, there's not much that the law can do." There are no laws governing how much officers should be paid or how much must be spent for charitable program activities.

Many of the so-called well-known legitimate charities pay exorbitant fees to **professional fund-raisers**, or commercial telemarketers, to collect for them. A study by the Connecticut Attorney General says that telemarketer's fees average 70 percent! The fund-raisers sometimes keep 90 percent of the money collected.. For example, Telemarketing Associates kept about $6 million of the $7 million it raised for VietNow, a so-called non-profit group that raises money for injured and homeless veterans. The Marketing Corporation of America raised over $12 million for the March of Dimes, although **less than half** went to the charity.

The U.S. Supreme Court ruled in 2003 in the VietNow case that state attorneys general "can sue telemarketers that mislead donors about how much of a contribution will be turned over to charity." States are expected to try to stop fund-raisers from deluding donors into believing that a substantial portion of their contribution will actually go to specific charitable programs when the reality is they keep most of the money for themselves.

The worst charities **spend the least** on genuine program services. *Worth* magazine recently published a list using data from charity-ranking organizations, including the state of South Carolina. Among the worst are American Deputy Sheriffs Association (only 1% spent on programs!), Veterans of Foreign Wars of the U.S. Southern Conference (7%), Children's Wish Foundation International (8%), American Foundation for Disabled Children (10%), Firefighters Charitable Organization (11%), Fraternal Order of State Police Lodge (13%), and Dogs Against Drugs/Dogs Against Crime (14%), Defeat Diabetes (15%), National Park Trust (23%), Feed the Children (25%), and Humane Society of the United States (53%). Charities that consistently rank among the worst are: Vietnow, National Caregiving Foundation, Oblate Missions, Walker Cancer Research Center, Help

Hospitalized Veterans, Dakota Indian Foundation, Cancer Fund of America, Retired Enlisted Association, North Shore Animal League, and Marine Toys for Tots Foundation. Plus, there are over 200 organizations soliciting donations by promising to send terminally ill children to DisneyWorld, and **most are scams**.

A **"good" charity** has at least 75 percent of its expenses going to program services; otherwise it is inefficient. To be certain that your money goes to the charity and not a fund-raising firm, research the charity; otherwise you may be throwing most of your contribution to fundraisers.

Two **watchdog groups** can provide reports (sometimes free) on fund-raising costs for national charities: (1) The Philanthropic Advisory Service of the Council of Better Business Bureaus (www.give.org), and (2) American Institute of Philanthropy (www.charitywatch.org/). Electronic images of the IRS Form 990 disclosure forms for 400,000 charities may be viewed at GuideStar (a national database of nonprofit organizations; www.guidestar.org) and National Center for Charitable Statistics (nccs.urban.org). Churches and other religious organizations are exempted from filing IRS Form 990. Too many charities are just fronts to steal money from generous people and they are not illegal; they are just rip-offs.

The Federal Trade Commission has no jurisdiction over non-profit organizations because, like charities, they are not engaged in commerce, although they can prosecute professional fund raisers. Individual **states**, therefore, are left to supervise charities.

CONSUMER UPDATE:
Telemarketing Recovery Room Scams

A **recovery room scam** (reloading scam or double-scamming) occurs when victims of previous investment schemes are targeted again by the same or another promoter offering, for a fee, to recover lost funds or the product or prize never received. Consumers who have lost money through prize promotions, merchandise sales, investment swindles, and so-called charity drives often have their names put on a **"sucker's list"** that is sold to other crooks so they can be victimized again.

The crooks sometimes will call claiming to **represent a government agency** (U.S Attorney or FBI) or consumer organization and report that the thieves have been caught and that their remaining assets have been frozen. The salesperson then says, "For only $250 (or $1,000) in attorney's fees (or a charitable donation), we can 'recover' at least one-half of the money you originally lost, and perhaps all of it." Other promoters state that they already are holding the money for you. When the swindler disappears with the recovery fee, the consumer has been scammed a second time.

Pricing and Buying Rip-offs

Numerous misrepresentations and scams exist in the pricing of products and services. By cautiously looking for what is wrong with such deals you can try to avoid being victimized.

Hidden Product Prices Deceive Consumers

Consumer prices for many products and services are **hidden**, thus consumers are disadvantaged in the buyer-seller relationship. Prices are disguised behind the fine print and last-minute add-ons. Studies of consumer buying behavior show that most people ignore the extra costs when purchasing. As a result, shoppers think that product prices are less expensive than they really are. Such faulty conclusions hurt the consumer interest.

Areas of commerce where consumers are confronted with **hidden prices** include concert tickets (don't forget to pay Ticketmaster its three fees), magazine subscriptions (plus postage and handling), motels and hotels (sales tax plus local occupancy fee, whatever that is), online shopping (sales taxes are not added on until checkout), rental cars (the originator of the hidden fee), and telephone service.

The pricing market for long-distance, cellular and local **telephone services** is purposeful **total confusion**. Why? Because the status quo allows the sellers to overcharge most consumers. Six out of 10 consumers are paying the highest long-distance rates their companies offer. Prices vary widely, from 60 cents per minute down to 3 cents. Those who frequently make long-distance calls should sign up for one of the various "discount" programs. Otherwise, for example, you will pay MCI $2 a minute for a long-distance call and $5 a minute for an overseas call. The companies offer cash and some free long-distance minutes to consumers who will switch from one carrier to another. Every year nearly 20 percent of U.S. households switch telephone companies. (To compare long-distance carriers, visit TollChaser.com, SaveOnPhone.com, GetConnected.com, www.trac.org/WebPricer, or consumerreports.telebright.com/consumerreportsLd.htm). Some of telecommunications customers are illegally switched from one company to another without their permission. This is called **slamming**.

Advertised monthly prices for cell phones are a **total deception**. No one gets a monthly bill for the advertised $35-a-month because the companies are not required to tell the truth about universal service fees, surcharges, sales taxes, federal taxes, 911-service tax and local taxes that often push the bill up another 20 to 25 percent, or $42 to $44.

In many places, it costs more to make in-state telephone calls, perhaps 25 to 35 cents a minute, than for coast-to-coast calls, less than a nickle a minute. State regulators set rates for in-state calls and competition among telephone companies for local service is minimal. The monthly charges for major local phone services are rapidly escalating. Services like caller ID, voice mail and directory assistance that individually cost $3 a month three years ago have jumped to over $5.50 today. TNS, a market research firm, reports that monthly local phone bills in the U.S. average almost **$40**, up 16 percent from three years earlier. The lack of competition in local markets gives the regional Bell companies little incentive to drop prices.

In the U.S., only cigarettes, gasoline, and airline tickets **must be advertised** with tax included. Consumer advocates want government regulations to bring some truth-in-advertising to the many hidden prices in the marketplace. Even with the taxes included, airline pricing is almost impossible for consumers to understand because prices change many times throughout each day. To make matters worse, the Airline Deregulation Act of 1978 exempted airlines from state laws that prohibit deceptive practices.

Another type of phone company also hides its prices. **Alternate operator services (AOS)** are companies that charge very high prices for long-distance telephone services for consumers who make credit-card and third-party billing calls. Their prices are high because the AOS companies share their excessive profits with the owners of the businesses with whom they contract. AOS companies lease long-distance lines from the major carriers and enter into contracts with businesses such as hotels, motels, airports, hospitals, and universities to **resell** standard intrastate and interstate long-distance telephone services. AOS companies charge exorbitant prices, often from **two to ten times** the traditional cost of making a long-distance telephone call through companies such as AT&T, MCI, or U.S. Sprint. Their pricing information is hidden in spite of the fact that a Federal Communications Commission (FCC) order requires AOS companies in interstate commerce to inform users of the services and how much calls will cost. AOS companies are required by regulation to put **identification on or near the telephone**. The FCC also ordered them to not block callers from using other long-distance carriers, if the customer requests. So far, the FCC has chosen not to regulate rates. When in doubt dial 0 to reach a local telephone company or 00 to reach a long-distance operator; then ask about the cost of the call.

AOS overcharges occur even if you call collect or charge the call to your telephone credit card. If you are ripped off by these companies, you can complain to your **local telephone company** and refuse to pay the exorbitant amounts charged. The local companies that are required to do the billing for the AOS companies can offer credits to complaining customers. Local companies cannot cut off service for non-payment of bills if customers have "legitimate" and "bona fide" disputes with a long-distance provider.

Buying Clubs

A **buying club** is a company that purports to offer consumers goods and services at prices lower than department and discount stores. Products can be offered through retail stores, like Sams or BJs, as well as catalogues. The **catalog buying clubs** are the problem area. Consumers complain about high shipping costs, setup charges, non-delivery of merchandise, delays in shipping, unavailability of goods, substitution of goods for out-of-stock items, unavailability of the latest models, difficulties in returning goods, long-term contracts, firms going bankrupt, and warranty service. Many duped consumers plunk down their money failing to realize that they can get the **same products for equal or better prices** at local discount stores.

Promoters of **buying clubs** often use telemarketing to entice people to come to their sales office that is usually a suite of motel rooms rented for a few weeks. Consumers are given so-called valuable gifts for being willing to "just listen to an explanation about our exciting membership buying program."

The Federal Trade Commission recently settled charges of deception with a group of buying clubs, including Triad Discount Buying Service Inc., a Boca Raton-based business, its dozens of related companies, and their operator, Ira Smolev. Triad will pay more than $9 million to settle charges that they misled consumers into **accepting trial club memberships** and obtained consumers' billing information from telemarketers without the consumers' knowledge or authorization. Consumers then were enrolled in the clubs and charged up to $96 in yearly membership fees.

The FTC charged the Triad companies with deceptively signing up buying club members through more than 100 **contract telemarketers**. These telemarketers generally advertised products such as kitchen gadgets and diet pills to consumers via outbound calls and through media advertising, direct mail, or catalogs that result in inbound calls. After consumers provided their credit card number to pay for the telemarketer's product, the telemarketer pitched a 30 day "no obligation" free trial in Triad's buying club. Once consumers agreed to the free trial, and in many instances even when they did not agree, their names and credit card numbers were transferred by the contract telemarketer to the Triad companies. Within 45 days, the Triad companies charged membership fees to the consumers' credit cards without their knowledge or authorization unless they had called to cancel their trial membership. Triad, of course, has **filed for bankruptcy** after bilking thousands and thousands of consumers.

Coupon Books

You may think you are getting a good deal when you buy a book of coupons purporting to offer excellent values. With **coupon books**, the consumer is offered free or discounted prices on goods and services. The coupon book might cost $39.95 for several discounted restaurant meals in a community or $149.95 for several nights of lodging at various motels. While some companies are legitimate, such as Entertainment, many are fly-by-night operations.

Three problems are common: (1) the coupons have **restrictions** as to times and locations that may not be convenient, (2) the coupon book promoters often sell many more than the participating merchants have been led to believe, and later the merchants may be unwilling to honor all the requests, and (3) some of these operators get a few businesses to agree to participate and then lie about the others. As the complaints start to come in, the promoter quickly leaves town to go elsewhere seeking more victims.

Vacation Certificates

Promoters of **vacation certificates** claim that for only $59.95 or perhaps $129.95, you are eligible for, "Three days and two nights of free lodging at excellent hotels in vacation spots like Las Vegas, Miami, New Orleans, or even Hawaii." Vacation certificates typically include discount or free coupons for a handful of hotels, selected restaurants, and certain attractions in a resort area. The deal is that you pay many dollars for **something of little value**, and, because of certain reasons described below, it is likely that you will not be able to use the certificate anyhow. The American Society of Travel Agents reports that of all the travel vouchers sold, only ten percent provided customers with actual vacations.

To receive a free vacation certificate, you may be **required to attend** a sales presentation. Sometimes there are minimum age and income conditions, or a requirement that you be accompanied by your spouse or significant other, so that you both will be there to sign on the dotted line of a contract.

The **lure of a free vacation** certificate is often used in advertising to draw people to the seller's sales site with the goal of selling a specific product or service. Vacation certificates are used by time-share resorts, membership campgrounds, automobile dealers, and solar energy companies as prizes. Some vacation certificate promoters ask for a major credit-card number to validate a complimentary vacation and then illegally charge fees on the consumer's credit-card account.

Winners of vacation certificates sometimes are required to pay a **non-refundable processing and handling fee**, or a refundable deposit from $50 to $100 to reserve each vacation time request. And, of course, they say "Yes, we can charge the amount to your credit card!" They promise that the deposit will be returned upon your arrival at the place of lodging or after the vacation is complete. It won't be.

Complaints about these deals include: the written information given after the sales presentation is different from what was promised, the available lodging is typically at cheap hotels that have names that sound like the better hotels, the hotel accommodations can only be obtained through the promoter, reservations are hard to confirm, rooms are available only on a space-available basis, the hotel price is a daily rate based on occupancy of several days, airline reservations are almost impossible to obtain, the cost for the second airfare ticket is over $1,000, there are substantial charges for extra fees, and the certificates are limited to use during off-season time periods, with perhaps 80 percent of the year being considered the peak season. Furthermore, such vacations are not free when you have to pay for part or all of the **transportation**, meals, drinks, taxes, and miscellaneous expenses.

Rent-to-Own

The **rent-to-own industry** (also known as the **rental-purchase industry**) consists of dealers that rent furniture, appliances, home electronics, and jewelry to consumers. People respond to advertisements that say, "No credit hassle!" "No long-term commitment!" "No down payment!" and "Free service in your home!" There are no down payments or credit checks required.

Rent-to-own (RTO) transactions provide immediate access to household goods for a relatively low weekly or monthly payment, typically without any down payment or credit check. Consumers enter into a self-renewing weekly or monthly lease for the rented merchandise, and are under no obligation to continue payments beyond the current weekly or monthly period. The contract provides the **option to purchase** the goods, either by continuing to pay rent for a specified period of time, usually 12 to 24 months, or by early payment of some specified proportion of the remaining lease payments. These terms are attractive to consumers who cannot afford a cash purchase, may be unable to qualify for credit, and are unwilling or unable to wait until they can save for a purchase.

The goods purchased in this way are extremely expensive, often costing **two or three times the cash price**. For example, Kevin rents a 23-inch color TV (valued at $300) and he pays $19 a week for 52 weeks for a total of $988 ($300 + 52 X $19).Consumers pay these high prices because they have no choice; they cannot buy the same goods at another store on credit. A rent-to-own contract can be compared fairly to a credit contract. If rent-to-own payments were considered interest, the effective annual rate in this example would be over 250 percent.

Rent-to-own customers who miss a payment may have their goods **repossessed**. To get them back, they have to pay a repossession fee and begin renting again. Rent-to-own companies are aggressive collectors of past-due amounts and frequently repossess goods. The FTC found that **one-quarter** of RTO customers are dissatisfied with the buying experience. Consumers need protection from such high fees and exploitive product prices.

Unfortunately, the rent-to-own industry has succeeded in getting **weak laws** passed in 46 states that regulate the transactions as leases. The industry, along with their Republican conservative friends, is trying to get Congress to pass a law to preempt the other four strong laws (MN, NJ, WS & VT) that regulate rent-to-own as credit transactions. New Jersey limits rent-to-own contracts to a maximum of 30 percent interest, the same limit that applies to other small loans. That's strong consumer protection!

Vehicle Sales and Repairs

The automobile industry is one of the last bastions of **hard selling**, where the customer must be "sold" something by highly persuasive practices.

High-Balling the Value of the Trade-in Allowance

High-balling is a technique used by an automobile salesperson who offers a shopper an extra-high trade-in allowance on his or her present car to create interest in a vehicle even though the offer may later be repudiated by the salesperson's manager. The high offer is made in an effort to keep the potential customer on the sales lot seriously interested in purchasing a newer vehicle.

This is the way the scheme works. The buyer desires a new car with a list price of $20,000 and wants to trade in his or her own vehicle worth only $1,500. The salesperson offers the buyer an inflated trade-in value of perhaps $3,000 toward the new car, and the buyer expects to pay only $17,000 ($20,000 – $3,000). The salesperson writes up the contract, gets the person's signature on it, and goes to find the manager, who must okay all sales. The salesperson soon **reappears with the manager close behind** who explains to the shopper that he will not okay the contract because the salesperson mistakenly misquoted the trade-in price. Because the shopper was so committed to the purchase, he now can be convinced to buy the car at a still-too-high price, perhaps $19,500. And he goes home feeling good about the price he or she paid for the car and glad he or she could help the salesperson out of the predicament with the manager.

Low-Balling the Price of a New Vehicle

Low-balling is an unscrupulous technique used by a salesperson who offers to sell a shopper a product at an unusually low and unrealistic price that will not be honored by the sales manager when the customer wants to make the purchase. The suggestion of a low-price deal is made in an effort to **keep the customer in the showroom**. Again the salesperson returns with a contract rejected by the sales manager. Then the price rises, after the customer has had his or her heart set on that particular vehicle. Many times the customer still goes ahead and buys at a price somewhat higher than it would have been with good bargaining.

Automobile Repair Scams

Surveys show that the odds of being cheated in an auto repair are 50-50! Auto repair scams occur in part because **most people know little** about the operational aspects of an automobile, hence they are especially vulnerable to automobile repair deceptions. For example, if a transmission specialist showed you metal filings that purportedly came from the transmission pan, would you know whether the transmission actually needs replacing? If a service station attendant along the interstate highway points out what appears to be an oil leak on a shock absorber, would you know if the car really needed new shocks? Consumers with vehicles that need repair usually have more success patronizing businesses that have mechanics **certified** in specialties by the National Institute for Automotive Excellence, an independent voluntary certification program for mechanics.

Another auto deception has to do with a popular method of diagnosing a vehicle's problem, known as, "**RCI**," or **remove, check, and install**. Consumers wind up paying $75 to $250 in RCI charges and perhaps another $300 to $2,000 for repairs. This occurs frequently at repair shops dealing with vehicle transmissions, brakes, shock absorbers, and struts. They say they cannot give an estimate for repairs until after they do an RCI procedure that sometimes is unnecessary. Other recurring problems in this industry include **making unnecessary repairs** and charging for work not performed.

Well-known companies caught by governments and investigative news reporters for scamming consumers, primarily by selling unnecessary parts and services, include Sears Auto Centers, Pep Boys, Goodyear, Tuneupmasters, Purrfect Auto Service, Midas Muffler & Brake Shops, Econo Lube N' Tune, Kmart, Goodyear Auto Centers, Tuneup Masters. See www.carinfo.com for additional information.

Investment Swindles

A **swindler** is an unscrupulous promoter who concocts an investment scheme that has zero possibility of making money for anyone other than the schemer. Swindlers cheat people out of money or property, and many of them are very good at it. Some swindlers are outright crooks. Others start out to be honest people but wind up sacrificing their ethics for the fast buck of an investment scam.

The result of all swindles is the same—the investing **consumer loses**. Swindlers try to convince consumer-investors of several things: (1) the plan will produce large profits, (2) there is low risk, (3) they are confident you are going to make money, and (4) it is urgent that the consumer act right now.

The Investment Swindler's Game

Investing consumers should be highly skeptical when an investment opportunity emphasizes:

- Low risk

- Big profits

- A quick return

- Return of the invested amount is guaranteed

- Approved by the Internal Revenue Service (IRS) or the Securities and Exchange Commission (SEC)

- A once-in-a-lifetime opportunity

- It is urgent that the consumer invest now

- They are confident that the investor is going to make money

- No experience is necessary

- This is the chance to "get in on the ground floor"

Offers for "financial opportunities of a lifetime" are usually exactly that—the consumer's one good chance to lose a lot of money. Most such offers **promise high profits** for those with little or no business experience. Unfortunately, the investing consumer ends up with the experience, while the promoter earns the high profits. The top investment fraud is **unlicenced individuals selling securities** (such as stocks, bonds and mutual funds), insurance policies, and fake promissory notes, supposedly issued by certain banks or countries.

Among the many scams are those for **so-called "investments"** in rare coins; art; precious metals; gold and silver contracts; commodities; foreign currencies; off-shore investment funds; "prime" bank notes; oil and gas lease programs; wireless cable television; interactive video and data service television licenses; cellular telephones; specialized mobile radio licenses; invention promotion kits; Rembrandt prints; land sales; gum ball machines; pay telephones; electronic games; popcorn vending machines; and display racks for greeting cards, telephone cards or compact discs. Nearly worthless collectibles are popular investment scams, too, such as 1957 Chevy miniatures, china dolls, and painted dishes. Some schemes employ holy themes, including divinely inspired investment advice.

CONSUMER UPDATE:
Many Infomercials are Rip-offs

Infomercials are late-night and mid-morning feature-length radio and television commercials, or sales pitches, often with too-good-to-be-true claims for products and services. Infomercials typically include testimonials from satisfied customers." Examples of such infomercials include products to grow hair; lose weight without exercising or dieting; cleaning one's body of "toxic" wastes;" cures" for substance addictions, such as smoking; speed reading; and improving memory. Others tout the opportunity to make money in gold or real estate.

Former Late Late Show host Tom Snyder describes one real estate infomercial by saying that, "The Dave Del Gotto Cash Flow Method is the one where Dave shows you **how the cash flows right from your bank account** into Dave's." They make incredible claims seem believable," says the Federal Trade Commission.

Ponzi Schemes Are Illegal[4]

The Ponzi scheme is named for Charles A. Ponzi, who defrauded hundreds of people in the 1920s by never investing in anything. Instead, he paid off old "investors" with money coming in from new "investors." A **Ponzi scheme** is an investment scam in which the victims are promised an unusually high rate of return in only a few months or weeks and are duped into thinking that they will earn this return for a long time period. A chance to double your money in six months is the usual pitch. The earliest investors actually receive good returns, sometimes with their own money that when paid, attracts more investors. In reality, there is no investment because the promoter is using the money taken from the many later investors to pay high returns to the **few first investors** before absconding with the remaining funds. The Ponzi swindler may operate his or her scheme for some time before disappearing with all the "investments" or revealing the bad news that the investments all went bad.

One of the latest big-time Ponzi scam artist was Reed Slatkin, who bilked his victims for almost $600 million. The first 75 investors in EarthLink Investment profited handsomely, but no one else did for the **next 15 years**. The SEC closed the business. Slatkin was outdone by one Martin Armstrong whose Republic New York Security bilked $700 million victims in only four years. Govenment is slow to close down these scams in part because consumers do not complain early enough.

---

[4] Helpful information for this and the following two sections came from: *Pyramid Schemes: Not What They Seem!* (Direct Selling Education Foundation), *Tips on Multi-Level Marketing (How to Tell a Legitimate Opportunity From a Pyramid Scheme)* (Better Business Bureau), and *How to Avoid Ponzi and Pyramid Schemes* (U.S. Securities and Exchange Commission).

Pyramid Schemes Are Illegal

In a **pyramid scheme**, investors are sold the right to become a sales representative or member with the right to sell the same privilege to others. The sale of a product is sometimes involved but it is always secondary in importance to the recruitment of new participants. It operates on the fallacious assumption that the so-called investors all can make money by getting others to give money to join the operation.

CONSUMER UPDATE:
Referral Rebate Sales are Illegal Pyramid Schemes

Referral rebate sales are a variation of the illegal pyramid scheme. This occurs when a buyer is induced to sign a contract with the promise that he or she will receive a commission, rebate discount for refunds, or other consideration that is dependent on a referred customer who actually contracts to make a similar purchase from the seller. It is illegal for payment to be contingent upon a subsequent sale. For example, a buyer might sign a contract to purchase a $1,000 stereo system with the promise that $50 will be credited to the $1,000 obligation for every person that the buyer refers to the seller who purchases the stereo system.

The **impossible mathematics** of the pyramid scheme is obvious and that is why they are illegal. Usually exempt from these laws are referrals for real estate, automobile and insurance sales, areas where it is traditional for sellers to pay their customers finder's fees for referrals.

In the "Friends Helping Friends Pyramid" scam, you give the "president" of the pyramid $100 to become a member. Then it is your responsibility to **recruit others** (friends, relatives, strangers also known as "victims") to join. When you sign two people up and collect their $100 each, you give it to the president and you move up the pyramid. Once you recruit eight members, you become president of a new pyramid. When your recruiters bring in new members, you are $800 richer. This is illegal. The reason why is illustrated in the following mathematical example.

Month	Participants
1	6
2	36
3	216
4	1,296
5	7,776
6	46,656
7	279,936
8	1,679,616
9	10,077,696
10	60,466,176
11	362,797,056 (far exceeds U.S. population)
12	2,179,782,336
13	13,060,694,016 (more than *double* the world population)

Initially, the progression of a pyramid scheme seems like it can go on forever with all "investors" making money. Pyramid schemes offer the appeal of **quick and enormous profits** to the participants, but the mathematical progression quickly reaches ridiculous numbers. In fact, the number of "investors" that it takes to keep this scheme going quickly exceeds the population of the world. This is shown in the illustration that assumes that the promoter initially sells distributorships to six persons, each of whom brings in an additional six investors every month.

The illustration above also shows why the pyramid scam is so lucrative to the original promoters. Those at the top of the pyramid of "investors" quickly receive a lot of money. The scam works for the promoter because large numbers of people at the bottom of the pyramid pay money to a few people at the top. There is no way the "investors" coming in at the lower levels in a pyramid investment scheme can make any money. No matter how it is described, this pyramid stuff **always collapses**!

Telltale signs of pyramid investment schemes is that (1) they rely upon new investors to pay returns, commissions, or bonuses, (2) there is a need for an inexhaustible supply of new investors, (3) there is a conspicuous absence of a product or substantial efforts to make profits through productive work or the sale of the products, (4) they charge high fees to become a distributor, (5) they require distributors to spend a lot of money up front to buy goods, and (6) they do not offer guaranteed refunds on unused products.

Some pyramid investment schemes are made to look like multi-level marketing businesses. **Multi-level network marketing** (see below) is **a legitimate sales method** that uses a network of independent distributors to sell consumer products, often in consumers' homes and, most importantly, the bulk of income is earned from product sales. These are bona fide business opportunities, such as Mary Kay Cosmetics and Amway.

In an attempt to avoid prosecution by government agencies, pyramid schemes **try to appear to be legitimate** multi-level marketing organizations. Therefore, many pyramid investment schemes do have a line of products to sell while the promoter claims to be in the business of selling the products to consumers. The products often are things like cosmetics, long-distance telephone service, hair care, vitamins, magnets, and exotic miracle cures. After a while, sometimes after years of scamming consumers, the FTC or a state attorney general finally collects enough evidence to close down a pyramid scheme.

CONSUMER UPDATE:
Chain Letters are Illegal Pyramid Schemes

Chain letters involve the sending through the mail, in person or by computer, money or other items of value and promises of a substantial return to the participants. Typically, a letter from some distant city arrives addressed to you with instructions to **send a sum of money** (perhaps $2 or $20) to the top name on an enclosed list of perhaps five names. Then you are to eliminate that name, add your own name and address at the bottom of the list, and mail copies of the new list to all the people on it. The appeal is that your name will be added to a multitude of subsequent lists by other people in the chain and you will receive enormous sums of money within a month or so.

Another chain letter scam says, "Earn $19,500 by buying a $5 computer program called Network!, copy it onto floppy disks, and **send it on to five people**." The letter also says that the five people who receive the copied disk will in turn make five more copies and send them on, and so on, until thousands of people have the program. You will make money because those thousands will send $5 each to the originator of the chain letter. Selling a product, such as a computer disk, is a gimmick to try to avoid the appearance of an illegal pyramid scheme.

The narrative also falsely claims that, "This is a perfectly legal enterprise!" or "Approved by the Postal Service!" Anyone who participates is not only out the $2, $5, or whatever amount (plus the cost of stamps), but his or her name and address are now clearly recorded. That makes it easier for a government fraud unit to identify the consumer should they investigate this particular scam. Chain letters are a form of **gambling that is illegal**, and they operate on the same fallacious principle as pyramid schemes. As a result, the great majority of participants must lose. Chain letters that do not involve money or something or value (such as picture postcards or recipes) are not illegal; however, they are a waste of time, envelopes, and stamps.

Multi-Level Network Marketing Investments Are Legitimate

As a distributor, the investor in a legitimate multi-level marketing opportunity is **an independent business person**, setting working hours, and earning money selling products or services supplied by an established company. In a multi-level business, distributors also have the opportunity to develop and manage their own sales forces by recruiting, training, and supplying others to sell. A distributor's compensation then is based upon fees earned for recruiting others into the business, commissions earned on personal sales, and a percentage of the sales of the recruited sales force. To be legitimate, a multi-level marketing investor must earn the **bulk of his or her profits from product sales**.

Here is an example of how a multi-level marketing opportunity works. An investor puts up $2,000 to buy into and become a dealer of a product line, perhaps some cosmetics. By going door-to-door, the person investing in this business can sell some products that the public might like and make a little money. The investor is further told that if he or she recruits other persons to invest $2,000 each to start up a distributorship, the first investor will receive a $500 **bonus for each recruit** and a 5- to 10-percent commission on the wholesale value of all the sales of the newer investor-distributors.

Key differences between illegal pyramid schemes and multi-level marketing opportunities are: (1) the bulk of the income in a multi-level marketing business comes from product sales, (2) the product are priced comparably with similar items on the market, rather than at inflated figures, (3) legitimate companies sell quality products and **do repeat business** with their customers, (4) start-up fees for legitimate businesses are small, (5) legitimate companies that require inventory purchases (and not in excessive quantities) will usually repurchase any unsold items, and (6) legitimate companies do not promise enormous earnings in a short time for little work, but instead want to make money with the investor and expand the overall market for the business.

Financial Planning Seminars

A growing number of schemes have as their sole purpose to sell overpriced business-type manuals at **financial planning seminars**. People respond to advertising and attend a half-day seminar that are sales presentations in disguise. These are held at a local motel and could be titled, "Low Down Payment Real Estate," "Invest for Success" or "Invest in Viatical Settlements." You may even be sent "complimentary tickets" in the mail. Most meetings are free, although some promoters charge an attendance fee of $10 to $39.

Promoters offer these "free seminars" to **entice potential customers to attend**. As a sales incentive, consumers are given a "rebate check" that may be used to pay part of the cost of any purchase made during the sales presentation. Once in attendance, you will be met by **motivational speakers**, upbeat loud music, and testimonials from others. Some will be **shills**, people who are paid to offer fictional testimonials of success and/or to pretend to purchase by being the first ones to "sign on the dotted line." When the seminar is over, the promoters move on to the next town.

The question is, after paying out the money-to attend the seminar, buy the books, cassettes and videotapes, and perhaps a membership to receive future counseling or advice, "Did the purchaser get his or her **money's worth**?" Some will say "Yes," but almost all, after only a few weeks or months, will reach the opposite conclusion. Instead, they will have paid way too much money for the value received. That's not illegal, it's just another rip-off.

Student Traveling Sales Jobs

Some companies place **classified advertisements** in school newspapers for college students to interview for jobs that promise lavish pay and travel. Callers are told that, "The details can only be provided during an interview." They want to get students in a local motel room for the "hard sell" sales pitch to persuade them to sign a contract. The truth is that the job will entail door-to-door selling of such products as magazines, books, soap, and cleaning fluids. Some promoters even sell bogus "consumer organization memberships."Each worker's hourly wage is based upon an estimate of his or her potential commissions, and the costs for housing and meals may be deducted. The "travel" part of the job usually means being transported to another state to stay at dingy motels. Workers may get dropped off in a neighborhood just after dawn and picked up at dusk. Crew leaders have been known to collect all the money and disappear, **leaving the workers stranded**.

Review and Summary of Key Terms and Concepts

1. Give some reasons "how" rip-offs and frauds **work against consumers**.

2. List four reasons "why" **rip-offs and frauds exist** in the marketplace.

3. Offer six **guidelines to avoid rip-offs and frauds**.

4. Describe two **Internet frauds**.

5. Give examples supporting the argument that consumer **fraud is rampant** among many big corporations.

6. Define **rip-offs** and give three examples.

7. When can a **negative-option buying plan** be a rip-off?

8. Summarize one of the rip-offs present in the **rental car insurance** industry.

9. How effective are the popular **weight-loss programs** over the long term?

10. How can a **job-search company** rip a consumer off?

11. Summarize one of the rip-offs present in the **telephone company industry**.

12. What is the rip-off problem with the **supplemental health insurance policies**?

13. Distinguish between **deception** and **rip-off**.

14. Cite two examples of **lies in classified advertisements**.

15. Choose three examples of recent **economic frauds** committed by large corporations.

16. What is **mail fraud**, and why does it work?

17. Explain how **telemarketing** promotions seem to work.

18. What do **prizes**, **free gifts**, **contests**, and **sweepstakes** have in common as schemes?

19. Explain how to identify fraudulent charities and **quasi-charities**.

20. Summarize why **buying clubs** are bad deals.

21. How does the **rent-to-own industry** function?

22. Why do **coupon books** sometimes turn out poorly for consumers?

23. Why are **vacation certificates** bad deals for consumers?

24. Distinguish between **hard selling** and **high-balling**.

25. Summarize how the "**RCI**" approach to transmission repairs works.

26. What do most **investment swindlers** promise in order to entice consumers to give them money?

27. List three **suggestions on how to avoid getting involved in a bad investment**.

28. How do **Ponzi** schemes work?

29. Briefly distinguish between a **pyramid scheme** and a legitimate **multi-level network marketing** business opportunity.

30. Explain why **chain letters** are illegal.

Useful Resources for Consumers

Alliance Against Fraud in Tele-marketing
www.fraud.org/aaft/aaftinfo.htm

American Institute of Philanthropy
www.charitywatch.org/

Call for Action
www.callforaction.org/

California Department of Consumer Affairs–Bureau of Auto Repair
www.autorepair.ca.gov/stdhome.asp

Consumer Information Center (California)
www.dca.ca.gov/cic/

Consumer Action
www.consumer-action.org/

Consumer Sentinel (cyber frauds)
www.consumer.gov/sentinel/about.htm

Consumer Web Watch
www.consumerwebwatch.com/

College Board Scholarship Fund Finder
www.collegeboard.org

Consumer Action (in California)
www.consumer-action.org/

Council of Better Business Bureaus, Inc.
www.bbb.org/bbb

Cyber Crime (U.S. Department of Justice)
www.cybercrime.gov/

International Internet consumer fraud
www.econsumer.gov

Internet ScamBusters
www.scambusters.org/

Federal Trade Commission
www.ftc.gov/
www.ftc.gov/telemarketing
www.ftc.gov/bcp/scam01.htm

FTC Consumer Publications
www.ftc.gov/ftc/consumer.htm

FTC Diet, Health and Fitness
www.ftc.gov/bcp/menu-health.htm

Financial Crimes Enforcement Network
www.fincen.gov/

Government Agencies (lots of links)
www.publicdebt.treas.gov/cc/ccphony6.htm

GuideStar (database of nonprofit organizations)
www.guidestar.org

Minnesota Attorney General
www.ag.state.mn.us/consumer

National Association of Securities Dealers
www.nasdr.com

National Center for Charitable Statistics www.nccs.urban.org

National Consumer Law Center
www.consumerlaw.org/

National Consumers League
www.nclnet.org/

National Charities Information
Bureau
www.give.org

National Fraud Information
Center
www.fraud.org

North American Securities
Administrators Association
www.nasaa.org/

Philanthropic Advisory
Service of the Council of
Better Business Bureaus
www.charitywatch.org/

Scotland Yard (United
Kingdom)
www.met.police.uk/

Securities and Exchange
Commission
www.sec.gov

Urban Legends Reference
Pages
www.snopes.com/snopes.asp

U.S. Postal Inspection
Service
www.usps.com/websites/depa
rt/inspect/consmenu.htm

U.S. Postal Service
www.usps.com/

U.S. Secret Service
www.secretservice.gov

"What Do You Think" Questions

1. **Frauds** in the marketplace seem rampant, especially in **telemarketing**. Outline a plan that would greatly reduce such deceptions. In your response, be sure to comment on civil and criminal penalties, as well as the right of free speech.

2. The text has "**A List of Probable Rip-offs**." What commonalities do you see occurring time after time in these various scams?

3. **Rent-to-own** businesses argue that they offer needed products and services in the community. Assume that you agree with that position. Then offer suggestions on how the rent-to-own industry might go about providing deals for consumers that would be perceived as being more equitable.

Chapter 5

Laws That Help Consumers

OBJECTIVES

After reading this chapter, you should be able to:

1. **Understand appropriate provisions of laws and regulations that protect consumers and help them obtain redress.**

2. **Appreciate well-constructed sample complaint letters in the chapter appendix.**

U ninformed consumers lose in marketplace transactions. They often pay too much for goods and services, purchase products of inferior quality, and sometimes suffer the consequences of unsafe products and illegal discrimination. Informed consumers also find themselves losing in the economic marketplace. The marketplace where consumers meet sellers is difficult and challenging for all. Fortunately, there are a number of federal, state, and local laws and regulations that serve to protect consumers and help them remedy marketplace wrongs. Most of these laws do more than offer disclosure—instead, the laws empower knowledgeable consumers by giving them a legal right to take action. This chapter is placed early in the book to provide a strong focus on the legal protections available to consumers. It may be read in sequence with the other chapters and/or may be used as a reference.

This chapter focuses on federal and state laws and regulations, with an occasional reference to local ordinances. It describes about 60 legal protections for consumers in the following areas: sales transactions, vehicles, warranties, housing, and credit/debit transactions. Because of space limitations, this chapter excludes some laws that protect consumers (For more information on consumer protection laws, see www.nacaanet.org/legmenu.htm and www.consumerlawpage.com.). Finally, a number of sample complaint letters can be found in the chapter appendix.

Laws on Sales Transactions

There are over twenty laws and regulations in the area of sales transactions.

Telemarketing Regulations

The Federal Communications Commission (FCC) and the Federal Trade Commission (FTC) have issued **national regulations** to comply with the Telephone Consumer Protection Act, Telephone Disclosure and Dispute Resolution Act, Telemarketing and Consumer Fraud and Abuse Prevention Act, and Deceptive Mail Prevention and Enforcement Act. The FTC also has issued telemarketing regulations through the 2003 Telemarketing Sales Rule. Enforcement of the laws is given to the Federal Communications Commission, the Federal Trade Commission, the state attorneys general, and consumers themselves.

In addition to federal officials, state attorneys general now have the power to prosecute fraudulent telemarketers who operate across state lines by suing in federal courts. State officials are allowed to get nationwide **injunctions** that will prevent an unscrupulous seller from moving operations to another state. Fines are $11,000 per violation, and consumers are supposed to receive restitution of losses suffered. The regulations do not preempt stronger state laws where they exist. Also, the **states can sue telemarketers** that mislead donors about how much of a contribution will be turned over to charity, when the reality is they keep most of the money for themselves.

These rules are designed to **help protect consumers** against deceptive and abusive telemarketing sales practices. Rules cover unsolicited telemarketing solicitations, "junk fax," and auto-dialer calls. The rules cover most types of telemarketing calls, including calls to pitch goods, services, "sweepstakes," and prize-promotion and investment opportunities.

"Do Not Call" Registry

Many consumers see telemarketing calls as annoyances, unwanted intrusions into their homes, and invasions of privacy. People who want to stop nuisance calls from telemarketing companies now have relief available through the 2003 FTC regulations under the amended Telemarketing Sales Rule. The Federal Trade Commission regulation establishes a national **"Do Not Call Registry,"** funded by **fees assessed** on the telemarketing industry, that can stop almost all telemarketing calls. Consumers can register online (www.donotcall.gov/) or with a single toll-free telephone call (1-888-382-1222). Registration of one's telephone number, which is free, is good for five years or until the consumer changes his or her telephone number or moves. Cell phone numbers can be registered too. In effect, registration gives consumers the chance to **opt out** of receiving most telemarketing calls.

Consumers **may still receive** telemarketing calls from companies with whom they have an "established business relationship," such as a creditor, bank or telephone company where one has an account. Since the FTC does not have regulatory authority over banks, telephone companies, airlines, insurance companies, credit unions, charities, political campaigns, and political fund- raisers, these groups are exempt from the do not call regulations. However, people can make a **specific request** to any company not to call.

The new FTC rule also requires telemarketers to transmit **Caller-ID information**, so that consumers who subscribe to Caller-ID services will know who is calling. The regulation also bans **unauthorized billing**; thus telemarketers are prohibited from processing any billing information for payment without the consumer's express verifiable authorization to the terms of the transaction.

Further, the FTC rules restrict the practice of **call abandonment,** where a consumer rushes to answer the phone only to find "dead air." Telemarketers who persist in placing unwanted calls to consumers listed on the registry are subject to fines of up to $11,000 per call. Finally, the FTC requires disclosure of all material terms of any offer that involves a **free trial period**, after which the consumer automatically incurs charges, unless he or she takes affirmative action to cancel.

Rules Telemarketers Must Follow

Following are some key provisions of the telemarketing laws and regulations:

1. **Calling times are restricted to the hours** between 8 a.m. and 9 p.m.

2. **Recorded sales pitches** to consumers' homes are prohibited unless the consumer gives permission, or has a business relationship with the company.

3. **Before they make their sales pitch**, telemarketers must "promptly" tell you that it is a sales call, provide the name of the seller, and tell what they are selling.

4. **If the pitch is for a sweepstakes or prize promotion**, they must tell you how to enter the contest, that no purchase or payment is necessary to enter or win, and the odds of winning. They also are required to tell you any restrictions or conditions of receiving the prize. It is illegal to misrepresent the value or nature of a prize.

5. **It is illegal for telemarketers to lie or misrepresent any information**. In the areas of telemarketing of investments, work-at-home, and business opportunity schemes,

for example, it is illegal to lie or misrepresent the facts about the goods or services, the earnings potential, profitability, risk, or liquidity.

6. **Before you pay, telemarketers must tell you the total cost** of the goods or services, as well as any restrictions on getting or using them, or that a sale is final and non-refundable.

7. **Before taking money from your bank account**, they must tell you their plans to access your account and they must use one of three ways to obtain authorization: (a) receive written authorization, (b) tape-record your authorization, or (c) send you a written confirmation *before* debiting your bank account. If they tape-record your voice, you must receive the following information: date of the **demand draft** (processed like a check, but without a signature), amount, the payor's name (who gets the money), the number of drafts (if more than one), a telephone number that you can call during normal business hours, and the date that you are giving your oral authorization.

If they obtain your **written permission**, they must give you all the information required for a tape-recorded authorization *and* explain to you in the confirmation notice the refund procedure you can use to dispute the accuracy of the confirmation and receive a refund.

Charitable Solicitations Regulations

Many states have enacted laws on charitable solicitations. Most provide for relief only **after the consumer has been ripped off**. Fraudulent charities are allowed to stay in business because the U.S. Supreme Court has upheld such solicitations as protected under the guarantee of free speech under the First Amendment. Some state laws require contracts between charities and fund-raisers to clearly specify the **percentage of gross revenue** that the charity will receive; provide the name and address of the charity, and, **upon request**, must inform a potential donor of the percentage of gross revenue that will go to the charity. Charities that lie about the percentage can be charged with fraud.

The FTC's Telemarketing Sales Rule applies to telemarketing firms that use **interstate** telephone calls to solicit charitable contributions. It requires telemarketers to promptly disclose the name of the organization making the request and that the purpose of the call is to ask for a charitable contribution. Thus, consumers will quickly receive key information necessary to enable them to decide whether to prolong the initial intrusion into their privacy or to terminate the call. The rules are designed to protect consumers from deceptive and fraudulent charitable fundraising. Finally, while charitable fundraising calls are exempted from compliance with the national "do not call" registry, the rule does require that such telemarketers accept and adhere to entity-specific "do not call" requests from consumers.

"900-Number" FCC Regulations

Regulations of the Federal Communications Commission implement part of the Telephone Disclosure and Dispute Resolution Act. Consumers who do not want calls made from their telephones to **900-numbers** (pay-per-call services) must be given a block on their telephones. The consumer's local telephone company must list the charges for pay-per-call services separately on the customer's bill.

All pay-per-call services costing more than $2, either on a flat-fee or cost-per-minute basis, are required to begin with a **preamble**, a message disclosing the price and the identity of the company providing the service. They must sound a warning signal telling the consumer that he or she has only three seconds remaining to hang up before another tone begins that lets the caller know the paid service is beginning. Callers must be permitted to hang up early and **not be charged**. Services aimed at children under age 12 are prohibited; services directed to 12- to 18-year-olds must state that parental permission is needed to complete the call. Companies must provide a local number or a toll-free line to call with billing questions.

Rules for settling disputes are similar to credit card regulations. Billing complaints must be acknowledged in writing within 40 days and **resolved within 90 days**. The 900-number companies, or their representatives, have 90 days to eliminate the disputed charges or investigate and demand payment. A consumer's credit rating cannot be penalized until the dispute is addressed.

Although the rates of non-traditional telephone companies are generally **not regulated**, consumers who are ripped off may challenge any and all excessive charges to their local telephone companies. Even though the local telephone company did not cause the problem and is not responsible for its solution, complaining consumers usually get some relief. Local telephone companies are required by law to do the billing for other firms that provide services to their customers. The contract typically states that, "Contested charges by consumers will be **charged back** to the original service provider." As a result, local telephone companies are inclined to give in to consumer complaints. Ask for a supervisor, if necessary.

Switching or "Slamming" Telephone Regulations

The Federal Communications Commission (FCC) issued rules in 1998 to give slamming victims some legal rights. **Slamming** is the illegal practice of switching consumers' long-distance telephone company without their permission. Consumers have up to 30 days to avoid paying long-distance charges when their service is illegally switched. This gives consumers time to revolve the problem and get switched back to their original carrier. If that does not occur and bills continue, the consumer does **not have to pay** the offending seller anything. If the consumer has paid the amount in full, he or she is entitled to a refund or credit of the difference between what they paid and what their original carrier would have charged.

There are three ways to obtain the consent of a consumer **to switch**: (1) a customer letter authorizing the switch, (2) a third-party verifying that the consumer wants to switch, and (3) a toll-free number to call to switch companies.

Do not say you can't fight the phone company. The Federal Communications Commission wants to hear all grievances, so use the online **Consumer Complaint Form** (http://www.fcc.gov/cgb/).

Unordered Merchandise Regulations of the Postal Service

Federal regulations of the U.S. Postal Service state that if you receive merchandise in the mail that you did not order, you may consider it as **a gift**. You are under no legal obligation to pay for it or return it. Postal Service regulations specify that you do not have to pay for unordered merchandise and that it is illegal for the company to bill you for it or send you persistent bill collection communications for unordered merchandise. In fact, the only materials that can be mailed to you without your permission are those clearly marked as free samples and merchandise mailed by charitable groups asking for a contribution. Even in these cases, you can consider any merchandise as a gift.

Of course, you cannot keep something like a video cassette recorder **inadvertently mailed** to your home. You should write or call when such a legitimate shipping error occurs and return it to them providing they pay all costs involved.

If you are sure the merchandise was never ordered, write the sender that you are **keeping it** as a free gift. You may want to send the letter by certified mail and keep the return receipt and a copy of the letter. Say you are sending a copy of your letter to the Office of Consumer Affairs, and do so. A sample complaint letter is at the end of this chapter.

The unordered merchandise regulations state that you can **refuse a shipment** that arrives by U.S. mail simply by not opening it and returning it to the post office. By writing "Refuse to accept" on a package and giving it back to the post office, it is returned to the sender at no cost to the consumer.

If you are not certain that you ordered goods that have arrived by U.S. mail, consider sending the company **a letter** (preferably certified with a return receipt requested) and ask for proof of your order. The small print in sweepstakes promotions often says that you have actually ordered something, like magazines. If you get unordered merchandise by private delivery services, such as UPS or Federal Express, do not accept the shipment. Realize, too, that this unordered merchandise rule offers you no protections. If you have already accepted something from a private delivery service, write the sender a certified letter and get a return receipt. Demand **proof of your order**. If there is no valid proof, tell the sender that unless the merchandise is picked up within 30 days, you will dispose of it. If you return it, be sure you do so at the sender's expense and get a receipt from the carrier.

Negative Option Mail-Order Rule of the FTC

Books, records, compact discs, videotapes, and other items are often sold through membership in a negative-option club. Typically the consumer receives an introductory offer, such as three books for $1, if you agree to purchase more items. A **negative option** is a consumer decision-making situation in which the consumer must notify the company that a particular selection is not desired in order to not receive it. If the company does not receive the negative notification, the consumer will receive the goods according to the previously agreed-to contract.

The Federal Trade Commission (FTC) Negative Option Rule requires that sellers clearly and conspicuously **give consumers certain information** about the plan in any promotional material. For example, the seller must tell: (1) how many selections you must buy, if any, (2) how and when you can cancel your membership, (3) how to notify the seller when you do not want the selection, and (4) when to return the negative option form to cancel shipment of a selection. The regulation requires that the company give consumers at least 10 days to reject the monthly or periodic selection, based upon the **mailing date** (the date the form must be postmarked to the seller) or the **return date** (the date the form must be received by the seller).

FTC's Mail and Telephone Order Merchandise Regulations

The Federal Trade Commission (FTC) has a trade regulation concerning mail-order and telephone merchandise sales. The regulation requires that (1) the buyer should receive any ordered merchandise when the seller promises to deliver it, such as within three weeks, unless the advertisement promises a different shipping time, (2) when no date is mentioned, the seller must ship the merchandise **no later than 30 days** after receiving the order (evidenced by receiving the payment, charging a credit account, or getting the telephone order), and (3) if the consumer does not receive the ordered merchandise by the 30-day deadline, the order can be canceled and the consumer can get his or her money back.[1] The 30-day clock does not begin until the order is received. At least one part of the transaction must take place through the U.S. mail in order for the rule to apply.

The seller has specific responsibilities if the promised delivery date (or 30-day limit) cannot be met. The seller must communicate to the consumer the new shipping date through an **option notice**. The consumer then has the option to cancel the order and obtain a refund or agree to a new shipping date. If paid by charge or credit card, the seller has one billing cycle to credit the account. A free means of response must be provided, such as a postage-paid postcard or a toll-free telephone number. If the consumer fails to reply and if the delay will be less than 30 days, the company can assume the consumer agrees to the delay. For delays over 30 days, money must be **refunded** to consumers who have not given their consent to such a delay. Prepaid orders that are canceled must be refunded within 7 days.

These regulations cover a number of mail and telephone order situations for consumers, mostly affecting transactions with traditional mail-order firms. However, there are **exceptions** to the rules: mail-order photo finishing; magazine subscriptions; serial deliveries (such as negative-option plans, as in book and record clubs), except for the initial shipment; mail-order seeds and plants; COD (cash on delivery) orders; and credit orders that are not charged until the goods are shipped. Note that the regulations do cover orders placed by telephone, fax, as well as on-line.

Refunds for orders paid by check, money order, or cash must arrive at the consumer's mailing address within **7 business days** of the merchant's receipt of the cancellation. For credit-card orders, the consumer's account must be credited within one billing cycle. The FTC defines a **business day** as Mondays through Saturdays, not Sundays or the Mondays following a national holiday.

COD (Cash on Delivery) Rule of the Postal Service

Rules issued by the U.S. Postal Service allow consumers to pay **COD (cash on delivery)** charges with a check made out to the seller instead of the Postal Service. This option enables consumers who are dissatisfied with mail-order merchandise to stop payment on a check before it is cashed. Then the buyer will only be out the bank fee for stopping payment on the check.

FTC's Door-to-Door Sales Cooling-Off-Period Regulations

Purchasing goods and services from door-to-door salespersons (which can include sellers who telephone you at home) may be convenient and appear to be inexpensive, but some tremendous **risks exist** because the seller has you at a disadvantage. First, it is much harder to ask someone to leave your home than to walk out of a retail store. (It's harder to say "no" in your home, too.) Second, most door-to-door sales are conducted by sellers who are not located in your community and often are from out of state. Third, Because these sellers may have no

---

[1] There is one exception to the 30-day rule: If a company does not promise a shipping time, and the consumer is applying for credit, the company has 50 days after receiving the order to ship.

permanent place of business, there is a substantial risk of you **being cheated**. Fourth, once you have given up your money, you may never receive the product, or the quality and quantity of the product may be much less than you expected. As a result, should you need to complain later, it will be **difficult and perhaps impossible** to receive satisfaction.

The Federal Trade Commission (FTC) has a trade regulation under the Truth in Lending Law regarding door-to-door sales. It provides a **cooling-off period** which is a time period during which the consumer has the opportunity to reconsider the wisdom of making a door-to-door contract purchase. During the cooling-off period, a consumer may **change his or her mind**, cancel the contract, and obtain a refund.

The FTC door-to-door regulation applies to sales agreements for $25 or more **made in your home** or at a location that is not the permanent place of business for the seller. Therefore, consumers can cancel agreements for $25 or more made in motel rooms, restaurants, their homes (including dormitory rooms), and the homes of friends or acquaintances. The rule applies whether the consumer invited the seller into the home or the seller made the arrangement. The cooling-off period also applies when your home is used to **secure the loan** no matter where the contract was signed.

The FTC regulation has some **exceptions**. It does not apply to sales made entirely by mail or telephone, for emergency home repairs, maintenance or repairs on personal property, arts and crafts sold at fairs or other locations (such as shopping malls, civic centers, and schools), for vehicles sold at temporary locations when the seller has at least one permanent place of business, for purchases of insurance, securities, or real estate, or for sales made at the seller's normal place of business.

The FTC regulation states that consumers have the right to **cancel most door-to-door contract** purchases (both cash or credit transactions) within 3 days of the original purchase. The FTC regulation requires that on door-to-door sales of $25 or more, the salesperson must verbally tell consumers of this right to cancel a contract, give the consumer a written contract, and give the consumer two copies of a **"notice of cancellation,"** that must be in the same language used in the sales presentation.

The law requires that the notice accompanying the contract be dated, show the name and address of the seller, and include the following **statement**: "You, the buyer, may cancel this transaction at any time prior to midnight of the third business day after the date of this transaction. See the attached notice of cancellation form for an explanation of this right." Consumers have until midnight of the **third business day** after the contract date to cancel. To do so, the consumer either: (1) dates, signs, and mails the form to the address given for cancellation, being sure to retain one of the detachable copies of the cancellation form and to have the envelope properly canceled with the correct date by the Postal Service, or (2) hand delivers it to the same address. If necessary, consumers can make their own cancellation form letter as long as it provides the same types of information found on the proper cancellation form.

The seller has several **responsibilities to perform** within 10 days if a consumer cancels a sales agreement: (1) cancel and return any contract papers signed, (2) refund any money and return any trade-in, and (3) tell the consumer how and where the product not desired will be picked up or returned.

Within 20 days the consumer **must make available** to the seller the item to be returned, and it should be in the same condition as when it was received. The consumer must pay return shipping charges if he or she agrees to do so. Alternatively, the seller might agree to pick up the item and/or pay for the return shipping expenses.

Door-to-Door Sales Cooling-Off-Period Laws in States

There is no general three-day right to cancel all contracts. Most states, however, have their own **specific door-to-door laws** that extend the cooling-off protections offered in the FTC regulation for door-to-door sales. States often allow consumers to cancel sales contracts made for any amount, including those under $25, if the agreement was made away from the seller's regular place of business, such as in the consumer's home or in a motel suite. The contract must have been for personal or household purposes. Most states provide that such contracts can be canceled by midnight of the third business day (Saturday usually counts as a business day). To cancel, follow the instructions on the cancellation form provided as part of the contract. Most states require notice of contract cancellation in the **same language** as the oral presentation. Some states have specific statutes that allow cancellation of magazine contracts sold door-to-door.

Cooling-Off Laws for Health Spas, Timeshares, Campground Contracts, Mortgage Refinancing, Credit Repair

Many consumers are pressured into signing contracts on the spot, in order to take advantage of a one-day-only deal. Most states have specific cooling-off statutes for particular types of contracts no matter where the agreement was signed; in someone's home, in a motel suite, or at the seller's place of business. In general, **cooling-off laws** permit the consumer to reconsider his or her action and exercise a **penalty-free cancellation** of an agreement after thinking about the situation for three to fifteen days. There is no need for any justification.

Laws typically require that the consumer receives notification of the right in writing from the seller. A written notification of cancellation, sometimes called **"Buyer's Right to Cancel,"** should be delivered by certified mail, return receipt requested, or by personal delivery to the address on the contract. If delivered in person, the consumer should have an **employee acknowledge receipt** of the cancellation in writing. Consumers should always keep a copy of any cancellation notice. Other contracts you can cancel under various state laws include dance lessons, seminar sales, dating services, discount buying clubs, hearing aids, rental housing locators, trade and correspondence schools, foreclosure sales, home repairs, martial arts, condominium sales, and multiple magazine subscriptions. A 1997 FTC regulation gives consumers three days to cancel a contract with a **credit repair firm**.

Vehicle Leasing

The Federal Reserve Board's **Regulation M**, effective in 1997, updates the Consumer Leasing Act. The regulations require disclosures on a standardized worksheet of (1) **total gross capitalized cost** of the lease (analogous to the total sales price), (2) **capitalized cost reduction** (analogous to the down payment), (3) how scheduled payments were calculated, including the **value** of the vehicle at the start of the lease as well as its **residual value** (dealer's estimate of the worth of the vehicle at the end of the lease), (3) total amount due at lease-signing, (4) **early termination penalties**, (5) various estimated charges, e.g. financing, taxes, insurance, registration, excessive wear and tear, acquisition fee, (6) depreciation, and (7) **option price** (what you can buy the vehicle for at the end of the lease). The **rent charge** (sometimes called the **lease rate**) is also provided, and this is the dollar amount one really pays for a leased vehicle. Leases still do not have to disclose the equivalent of an annual percentage rate.

Airline Travel Rights

It is frustrating to discover that after you made an airline reservation the price went down. If asked, however, most major airlines **will credit the difference** between the fare you paid and the newer, lower fare. Just ask the agent to check current prices, and if the fare is lower, re-ticket your reservation. They will mail you a travel voucher for the difference in price.

Should your airline go **bankrupt**, Department of Transportation regulations require that competing airlines that have a seat available on the same dates of travel must accept your ticket, plus they cannot charge you more than a $25 fee. Fliers have 60 days to exchange their ticket at another airline.

If you are **late** for a flight, including not being at the gate ten minutes before departure time, the door is almost never reopened. The airline has the right to cancel your reservation for being late and give you a refund. If you still want to fly that day, you will have to buy a new ticket at the higher, last-minute price.

Delayed or Canceled Flights and Missed Connections

Flight schedules are not guaranteed and policies on cancellations of flights differ among airlines. One in four airline flights arrives late. Airlines are required by the government to offer a refund only when the delay, cancellation or diversion is caused by weather or another event **outside their control**.

If the flight is delayed, canceled or diverted because of a problem under the **control of the airline**, such as an equipment breakdown or missing crew, airlines are legally obligated to place the passenger on its next available flight to that person's destination. The airline *may* have a policy to provide some compensation, such as vouchers for meals and access to the airline's first-class lounge. If stranded overnight, passengers may get cash for miscellaneous expenses, taxi costs to and from a motel, the cost of overnight lodging, a coupon to upgrade to first-class, and perhaps a voucher for travel on a future flight.

Usually, only **assertive, polite consumers** who ask get compensation. Frustrated consumers join the line at the gate to reschedule. Because it is faster, smart consumers also use a cell phone while waiting in line to call the airline or their travel agent to re-book. Passengers who verbally abuse airline employees in these situations may be offered only a blanket and a pillow.

Bumping

Over half a million airline passengers are **bumped** (denied boarding because of over-booking) per year. Department of Transportation (DOT) rules do exist for **over-booking** (oversold flights), but these exclude charter flights, commuter flights with 60 or fewer passengers and when the carrier replaces a scheduled aircraft with a smaller plane. If a flight was over-booked and no one volunteers to give up a seat, the last one on is usually the first to get bumped. The U.S. Supreme Court ruled that passengers bumped from oversold flights may sue for compensatory (not punitive) damages for actual injuries in a state court.

Should you be **involuntarily bumped**, you are not entitled to reimbursement when the airline is able to get you to your destination by means of any airline within one hour of your scheduled arrival time. If you arrive at your destination between one and two hours late (four on international flights), the airline must pay you an amount equal to your one-way fare, up to $200. Passengers have the right to accept a travel voucher or a check. If you are more than two hours late, the airline must pay you **twice the amount** of the ticket up to $400. The airline will put you on the next available flight, too. If you are involuntarily bumped, make sure that the alternate ticket is for a confirmed seat, not standby, because you may get bumped again.

Many airlines provide up to $25 in cash or vouchers for food and miscellaneous expenses—if you ask for them—for those who are involuntarily or voluntarily bumped when a flight is seriously delayed. Those who elect to be **voluntarily bumped** (four-fifths of the total number bumped per year) usually receive a voucher for a free domestic round-trip ticket, sometimes some cash, experience a few hours delay at the airport, and continue to their destination on a later flight.[2] For details, see the DOT website (www.dot.gov).

Delayed and Lost Luggage

When airline baggage is delayed, most airlines will make arrangements to **deliver it to you** as soon as possible. Typically, no compensation is offered for the inconvenience and there are no government regulations for delayed luggage. When you have been seriously inconvenienced by the delayed or lost baggage, and if you ask, you may receive cash or vouchers for miscellaneous expenses (often $25 maximum). Should the airline not provide cash, send photocopies of your receipts for toothbrush, clothing or whatever (keep originals) to the airline's consumer affairs office with your complaint letter requesting reimbursement.

Department of Transportation regulations specify that the airlines have a **maximum liability** for lost or damaged baggage of $1,250 on domestic flights and a $1,850 on international flights. However, the regulations do not say what has to be covered. Most airlines do not accept any liability for lost computers, cash, jewelry, antiques, camera equipment, medicine or similar valuables.

Pet Lemon Laws

Some states (AR, CA, CT, FL, NH, NY, VT, VA) have **Pet Lemon Laws**. The "lemon" concept is that when a consumer has purchased a product that soon turns out to be bad, the purchaser is entitled to repair, replacement or refund. The law requires stores to replace animals they sell that are found to have defects or diseases, or to pay for medical treatment. Those who want to keep their unhealthy animal are entitled to receive reimbursement for **limited and reasonable** veterinary expenses. Several states require pet sellers to disclose facts about the animal's health to the purchaser in writing, including the place that the animal came from and its health, immunization record, age, and medical history. Animals usually can be returned within one or two weeks of purchase, although animals suffering from congenital disorders may be returned up to a year from the purchase date.

---

[2] No such regulations exist for hotels and motels, even reservations guaranteed with credit cards and confirmation numbers. A breach of contract situation exists when a hotel tries to turn a consumer away who has confirmed reservations; therefore, insist to the manager that he or she book you elsewhere and pay for the room.

Weight-Loss Center Laws

Some states and localities have statutes to regulate weight-loss centers. For example, New York City's law requires four steps: (1) commercial weight-loss centers must post a prominent "Weight-Loss Consumer Bill of Rights" sign in rooms where sales presentations are made that inform consumers there may be serious **health problems** associated with rapid weight-loss, and that only lifestyle changes (such as eating healthful meals and regular physical activity) promote permanent weight-loss, (2) weight-loss centers must hand out the bill of rights to potential clients, (3) centers must disclose the hidden costs of products or laboratory tests that may be part of the program, and (4) weight-loss centers are required to tell dieters the duration of their recommended program.

Rent-to-Own Laws

In an effort to stop consumers from being overcharged, a number of states have passed laws regulating aspects of rent-to-own contracts. In New York, for example, consumers are allowed a **7-day "cure" period** to make delinquent payments and/or redeem an item that has been repossessed. This action reinstates the original contract with credit for all previous payments. If partial payment is made along with a voluntary return of merchandise, the reinstatement time period can be extended up to 180 days.

New York also requires contracts to disclose: (1) the cash price of an item, (2) the price of the rental option, and (3) the total price (a combination of the first two, which cannot be more than 100 percent greater than the cash price). This information must be attached to each displayed item. Amounts assessed for **late charges are limited**, and consumers are allowed to buy the rented item at any time for the cash price less one-half the total of previous payments. If advertising mentions the possibility of ownership, the total cost of the option must be given.

Deliveries and Installations Laws

Some states protect consumers from having to **wait at home** for hour after hour for deliveries and installations that never happen or occur quite late. California, for example, requires a maximum delivery-installation time period of four hours for cable television companies, utilities, and business firms with 25 or more employees.

Moving Companies

In addition to a weak federal regulation on interstate moving companies, most states have laws regulating movers that haul people's belongings inside the state. It generally requires moving companies to provide written estimates in a contract that cover the **entire costs** of a move and customers must sign the documents before loading the vehicles. Also, movers cannot hold a customer's belongings while trying to get paid for increased or unexpected costs.

The Federal Motor Carrier Safety Administration (FMCSA) expanded its Safety Violation Hotline (888-368-7238) to include consumer **complaints** against *interstate* household goods carriers. You can obtain licensing, complaint and other information about movers by using FMCSA's online Safety and Fitness Electronic Records (SAFER) System.

You can check up on an interstate mover by using it's **"MC" number**, which must appear in advertisements.

Bank Insurance Sales

Under provisions of the Gramm-Leach-Bliley Act, the federal bank regulatory agencies have adopted rules to protect and inform consumers who are considering **buying insurance products** from federally insured banks and savings institutions. Included in the new rules are (1) a prohibition against misleading consumers that an insurance is federally insured, (2) a requirement that insurance sales take place **physically apart** from where deposits are routinely accepted, and (3) a notice to consumers that the institution cannot condition the approval of a loan on the purchase of insurance from that bank or an affiliate. The rules also establish government procedures for handling consumer complaints about bank insurance sales.

Privacy Laws

The Supreme Court has read into the Bill of Rights a **limited constitutional right** of privacy. However, the United States has steadfastly refused to establish generic privacy protection laws. As a result observes Roger Clarke, an expert on privacy laws around the world, "the U.S. is the most over-governed country in the world, despite their rhetoric about being the 'land of the free.' The reason is that every time a new issue hits the airwaves, a new statute results, targeted at this year's major public scandal."

The U.S. has a number of narrow statutes on privacy. These include:

Privacy Act (1974)
Federal Trade Commission Act (1914)
Fair Credit Reporting Act (1970)
Family Educational Rights and Privacy Act, Public Law 93-380, 1974
Cable Communications Policy Act (1984)
Cable Privacy Protection Act of 1984
Electronic Communications Privacy Act (1986)
Computer Matching and Privacy Protection Act (1988)
Tax Reform Act of 1976
The Right to Financial Privacy Act of 1978
Video Privacy Protection Act (1988)
Telephone Consumer Protection Act (1991)
Drivers Privacy Protection Act, PL 103-322 (1994)
Health Insurance Portability and Accountability Act of 1996
Children's Online Privacy Protection Act (1998)
Gramm-Leach-Bliley Act (1999)

Each privacy law typically covers the collection, use and disclosure, quality, and security of personal information. The law gives consumers the right to **access and correct** personal information about themselves. In addition, consumers have the right to make a complaint if they think their personal information has been mishandled.

Opt Out of Offers for Credit Cards and Other Financial Products

Under the Gramm-Leach-Bliley Act, your financial company can provide your personal financial information to **non-affiliated service providers**, including joint marketers. But before it shares your information with other third-party non-affiliates (outside of these exceptions), your financial company must **tell you** about its information-sharing practices and give you the opportunity to opt out. Companies are required to develop a **privacy policy** and make it available to all customers once a year explaining how consumers can prevent the organization from sharing or selling personal data to other businesses, such as banks, insurance companies and brokerage firms. Less than 1 percent of consumers reads the policies.

The **privacy notice** must give consumers the right to **opt out** of having their personal information shared with other institutions or used for promotional purposes. You may do so by using a toll-free number or postage-paid, postcard. In effect, the company must give consumers the chance to decline to have their information shared. The notification responsibility is on the consumer because if one does not opt out, the institution can share the personal data with other companies. An exception to the law is that financial institutions may still share or sell your personal information among *affiliated businesses* if they tell you that they are do so *even though* you communicate that you want to opt out.

To opt out of receiving unsolicited credit and insurance offers for **two years** through a legally mandated system of the major credit bureaus, you can just contact them at 888-5-OPTOUT (888-567-8688). You also may request a form to return that will remove your name forever; however, you may still receive solicitations that do not use credit bureau files.

Opt Out of Mail, Telephone and E-mail (Business Sponsored System)

The Direct Marketing Association (DMA) offers voluntary Mail, Telephone, and E-mail Preference Services. These allow consumers to **opt-out** of direct mail marketing, telemarketing and/or e-mail marketing from many national companies. Use the following DMA links to access information and forms to reduce unsolicited mail (www.dmaconsumers.org/offmailinglist.html), e-mail (www.dmaconsumers.org/emps.html), or telephone calls (www.dmaconsumers.org/offtelephonelist.html).

Internet Privacy Law

An **Internet Privacy Law** exists in Minnesota. Unsolicited e-mail must be identified in the subject line as an advertisement with the letters "ADV" and the e-mail must carry a valid return address or phone number. Also, Internet service providers may not disclose any personally identifiable information without a person's consent. There is no similar federal regulation.

Medical and Banking Privacy Laws

The topic of privacy in consumer transactions is covered in Chapter 3 Medical privacy is examined in Chapter 15.

Privacy Complaints

Privacy complaints to regulators have to go to the **right agency**. For banking issues there are three choices: the Office of the Comptroller of the Currency (www.occ.trea.gov) when a national bank is involved (these include banks with the initials "NA" as part of their name); Department of Health and Human Services for medical privacy; and to the Federal Deposit Insurance Corporation (ww.fdic.gov) S&L issues. The Federal Trade Commission (www.ftc.gov) accepts complaints about advertising and any other misrepresentations or deceptions in consumer transactions. The Federal Communications Commission may be contacted when complaints are about telecommunications. Also, a number of state constitutions include a right to privacy and they sometimes provide **stronger protections** than the federal government.

Laws on Vehicles

There are a number of laws and regulations regarding vehicles.

Odometer Fraud Law

Odometer fraud occurs when an odometer is rolled back or disconnected and when incorrect information is given about the **accuracy** of the odometer reading. The Federal Odometer Law requires that the odometer reading be entered on the vehicle's title in all states. Those who are wronged by odometer fraud may sue the seller and if they win, collect a minimum of $1,500 in compensatory damages, plus treble damages, punitive damages, **and attorney's fees**. Over 450,000 cases of odometer fraud occur annually.

Motor Vehicle "Buyer's Orders" Laws

Several states have laws designed to stop dealer financing arrangements from **being changed** after the customer has agreed to a deal. The situation occurs when a purchaser contracts to buy a vehicle, based on assurances that dealer financing will be obtained at a certain percentage rate. Perhaps a week later the buyer, after **leaving the trade-in car behind** receives a call from the dealer saying that the financing rate is going to be several points higher, meaning higher payments. A number of states require that the sale of a car is not finalized unless the proposed sales contract is approved under the terms agreed to by the purchaser. Also, the consumer can cancel the contract and require any down payment and/or trade-in be returned if anything specified in the contract is changed.

Lemon Laws for New Vehicles

States typically define a **lemon** as a passenger vehicle meant for personal or family use that has been unsuccessfully repaired four or more times (three times in some states) for the same problem that *substantially impairs* the use, value, or safety of the vehicle, or the car has been in the repair shop for a cumulative total of 30 days during the first year. About **three percent** of new vehicles qualify under state laws, and more than 150,000 consumers every year face problems associated with the purchase of a lemon vehicle. To deal with the diagnosis and repair of lemon vehicles can become such a frustrating experience that the new-car buyer may decide to throw in the towel, after absorbing an emotional and financial beating. Thus, lemon laws are designed to offer improved warranty protections to consumers. All states have lemon laws, and such authorities have been upheld by the U.S. Supreme Court. Vehicles with safety related lemon problems also should be reported to the National Highway Traffic Safety Administration.

The lemon-owner would like to return the car and get his or her money back or get a replacement vehicle because the problem is major and has reduced the use, safety, or value of the vehicle. This procedure is called **revocation of acceptance**. It is instigated by returning the vehicle to the dealer and writing a letter to the dealership specifying why this action is being taken. Some states, such as Virginia, provide that if the consumer wins in court, the consumer's attorney and expert witness fees shall be **paid by the manufacturer**. Since returning a vehicle may cause a hardship on consumers, lemon laws do not require lawsuits. Problems with the vehicle must occur within one year, or during the length of the warranty period, whichever is shorter.

The typical lemon law provides that if a newly purchased vehicle is in the shop for a **total of 30 days** during the first year of ownership (or 12,000 miles) or if the same problem is not successfully repaired after three or four attempts, the consumer is entitled to redress. After being notified by the complaining consumer, the manufacturer usually has two choices: (1) refund the purchase price, including all collateral expenses (such as title fees, repairs, mileage to and from the dealer, sales taxes, inspections, and vehicle rental) plus money for loss of use of the original car, less a reasonable charge for the miles driven, or (2) replace the vehicle with a comparable model acceptable to the consumer. Leased vehicles are *excluded* from lemon laws in the following states: AL, CO, MI, MO, NE, NM, OH, OK, PA, and WV.

Consumers exercising their lemon-law rights must first **exhaust remedies** under a manufacturer's informal dispute settlement procedure before going to court. In these cases, the dealer or manufacturer usually has to pay the prevailing consumer-plaintiff's reasonable attorney fees (if any), expert witness fees, and court costs. One provision of many lemon laws creates a state recovery fund that enables lemon vehicle buyers to collect court judgments against automobile dealers or salespeople.

Used Vehicle Lemon Laws

Lemon laws that cover used vehicles are in effect in Connecticut, the District of Columbia, Massachusetts, Minnesota, New York, and Rhode Island. Each law varies as to the age of the vehicle, its mileage, and cost. The Massachusetts law requires mandatory but limited warranty protection on used vehicles for engines, transmissions, steering mechanisms, and brakes. For used vehicles with **less than 40,000 miles** at the time of purchase, the warranty period is 90 days or 3,750 miles; vehicles with between 40,000 and 79,999 miles must be warranted for 60 days or 1000 miles; for those with between 80,000 and 124,999, the warranty must be for 30 days or 750 miles. Before a consumer can get a refund, the dealer must be given three repair attempts for the same defect or the car must be out of service for 11 business days. Massachusetts also requires auto dealers to give a consumer a refund should the vehicle fail state safety inspection within 7 days of purchase and if the inspection-related repairs are expected to cost more than 10 percent of the purchase price. (See infoservice.flasuncoast.com/lemonfr.htm.)

Used Vehicle Lemon Branding Laws

Only 38 states require sellers to label **lemons**, vehicles with serious defects, that have been repurchased under the requirements of state lemon laws. The laws specify that the title of a vehicle be properly branded with a clear indication that the vehicle was a lemon and that disclosure must be made to consumers at the point of sale.

Secret Warranty Disclosure Laws for Vehicles

For many years, automobile manufacturers have offered **secret vehicle warranties** to relatively few consumers that provide free repairs or reimbursement of incurred expenses when persistent problems develop beyond the traditional warranty time period. The problems usually affect the vehicle's performance or safety, but are not the subject of a formal recall. Secret warranties offered by auto manufacturers are disclosed in **technical service bulletins** that are sent to dealers authorizing them to make the repairs. In such cases, the dealers, not consumers, are notified. Historically, the dealers have been allowed to offer to make repairs at their discretion, and only those owners who complain the loudest received the free repairs. About 500 secret vehicle warranties are in effect at any point in time. Manufacturers sometimes call these efforts **policy adjustments** or **goodwill service**. What is especially bad about secret auto warranties is that not all affected consumers benefit since most owners remain unaware of the manufacturer's policies.

Only a few states (CA, CN, VA, and WS) have secret warranty **disclosure laws** for vehicles that require the manufacturers and dealers to notify all affected owners when such repairs will be paid by the manufacturer. These laws typically require auto manufacturers to notify by first-class mail **all owners** who may be affected by a manufacturer's warranty adjustment program. This includes notifying those owners who have already paid for the relevant repairs; therefore, those consumers may obtain reimbursement. Dealers also must tell consumers who have purchased an extended warranty if a particular repair is covered under such a program; dealers also must tell consumers if future repairs could be covered under an extended warranty. In some states, consumers are allowed to sue and collect damages from any auto manufacturer who violates the secret warranty disclosure law.

Federal Trade Commission Used Car Rule

Each year, Americans spend about $100 billion to buy more than **17 million used cars**. If you are buying a used car, the Federal Trade Commission's Used Car Rule may help you.

The rule requires all used car dealers to place a large sticker, called a **buyer's guide**, in the window of each used vehicle they offer for sale. The buyer's guide will state:

- Whether the vehicle comes with a warranty, and if so, what specific warranty protection the dealer will provide.

- Whether the vehicle comes with no warranty (**"as is"**) or with **implied warranties** only.

- That you should ask to have the car inspected by your own mechanic before you buy.

- That you should get all promises in writing.

- What some of the major problems are that may occur in any car.

Whenever you purchase a used car from a dealer, you should receive the original or an identical copy of the **buyer's guide** that appeared in the window of the vehicle you bought. The buyer's guide must reflect any changes in warranty coverage that you may have negotiated with the dealer. It also becomes a part of your sales contract and overrides any contrary provisions that may be in that contract.

Dealers are required to post the buyer's guide on all used vehicles, including used automobiles, light-duty vans, and light-duty trucks. A **used vehicle** is one that has been driven more than the distance necessary to deliver a new vehicle to the dealership or to test drive it. Therefore, "demonstrator" cars are covered by the rule. Motorcycles are excluded.

If you buy a used car from a private individual (for example, through a classified newspaper ad), the **sale is not covered** by the rule. Private sellers do not have to use the buyer's guide. In most private sales, the car is sold "as is." Without a written contract with specific repair provisions, the private seller in most states has no further responsibility for the car. If you have a written contract, the seller must live up to the promises stated in the contract. Depending on its age, the car may be covered by a **manufacturer's warranty or service contract**. Ask the seller to let you examine any unexpired warranty or service contract on the vehicle.

Even without the buyer's guide, when you buy a used vehicle from a private party, you can follow the suggestions given here. For example, refer to the list of potential problems in the buyer's guide. In addition, ask the seller whether you may have the **vehicle inspected** by your own mechanic. It is important to find out about the mechanical condition of the vehicle before you buy it.

If you buy a used car and the sales talk is conducted in **Spanish**, you are entitled to see and keep a Spanish-language version of the buyer's guide. The Used Car Rule includes a text for the Spanish-language version.

Vehicle Repair Laws

Unfair and deceptive practices abound in the auto repair industry. As a result, most states have a vehicle repair law designed to protect consumers from unscrupulous merchants. Generally, such laws provide that on request, a consumer must be given **a written repair estimate** from someone who is going to repair his or her vehicle, unless the business is unwilling to do the repair. The consumer must sign the estimate to indicate that the terms are understood. Later, if the mechanic or body repair person determines that the repairs are going to cost **more than 10 percent** above the estimate, the shop must obtain the consumer's permission to go ahead at the higher price. No charges are allowed for unauthorized work. It is also illegal for repair shops to suggest that certain repairs are necessary or desirable when such is not the case. Finally, a consumer has the right to **get back any parts** removed by the repair shop. If covered by a warranty or rebuilding arrangement, the consumer may view the parts, but may not be able to keep them.

Laws on Warranties

There are a number of laws and regulations on warranties. The major federal law at the federal level is the Magnusson-Moss Warrant Act. All states have warranty laws and oftentimes they give consumers more powers than the federal law.

Magnusson-Moss Warranty Act

The conflicting viewpoints of consumers and sellers have historically resulted in warranty problems. The concept of warranties that used to give consumers dissatisfaction due to a lack of clarity and deceptions perhaps can best be summed up by the old adage, "The bold print giveth and the fine print taketh away." As a result, governments have written laws and regulations to govern warranty situations. The Magnusson-Moss Warranty Act was passed in 1975. It authorized the Federal Trade Commission to write regulations that interpret and implement the law, primarily through an effort to require disclosure of warranty terms. The Magnusson-Moss Warranty Act attempts to restore a sense of **fair play** in the marketplace by giving consumers a warranty **more equal** to that of the sellers.

A **warranty** or (**guarantee**) is an assurance by a seller that the goods or property sold are of the quality represented or will be as promised. Warranties on consumer products are offered by manufacturers as a **promotional device** to help differentiate one product from its competitors. In fact, whole advertising campaigns are sometimes designed around a product warranty.

The seller sees the warranty as something that **limits the firm's liability**, since it legally obligates the manufacturer to limit in dealing with buyers who have problems, while simultaneously inducing particular expectations on the part of the consumer. For example, a written warranty may specify which remedies are available to consumers with problems and may limit how much the company will pay. An **express warranty** is a written guarantee setting out specific assurances by the manufacturer or seller.

The consumer, however, views warranties in a different light. Most consumers accept warranties uncritically, assuming that the act of offering a warranty suggests that **this is a quality product**.

Standards for Companies that Offer Warranties

The Magnusson-Moss law and subsequent regulations do not require that a manufacturer offer a guarantee, but if a manufacturer does offer a written warranty, **it must comply with various standards**. Basically the law demands that a warranty should mean what it says and that the details should be spelled out in **easy-to-understand language**. Therefore, products claiming a "money-back guarantee," suggesting that they are "fully guaranteed," or promising "satisfaction guaranteed or your money back," should do what is promised. Sellers are prohibited from giving something to consumers with the big print and taking it away with the small print.

Warranties must use clear and simple language to tell the following: (1) the name and address of the warrantor, (2) whether the warranty is given only to the original purchaser, (3) a description of exactly **what is warranted** and for how long, (4) an indication that a registration card must be returned if that is the warrantor's procedure, (5) the **procedure** for placing a claim, (6) what the company will do in case of problems, and (7) step-by-step procedures to follow to **settle a dispute** between the buyer and the seller.

To reduce problems with warranties, the Magnusson-Moss law requires that consumers be able to examine warranty coverage **before they make a purchase**. Any product that costs $15 or more is covered under the law and must be made available for inspection. Either sellers can print the warranty on the outside of the product package or retailers must post a sign near products that have warranties indicating where in the store a customer can go to examine the warranty, such as on a shelf at the back of a retail store.

Disclaiming Implied Warranties is Prohibited Except When Something is Sold "As Is"

Importantly, the Magnusson-Moss law **prohibits warrantors from disclaiming implied warranties** unless the product is clearly labeled **"as is"** when sold. This phrase indicates that the product, such as a used vehicle, comes with no warranties, either express or implied. Therefore, when the buyer purchases something marked "as is," he or she assumes **full responsibility** for determining the condition of a product being purchased. It also releases the seller of all legal claims.

Full and Limited Warranties May Be Offered

The law requires that express guarantees be **conspicuously designated** as either full or limited, which immediately gives consumers an indication of the type of warranty coverage provided. To meet the federal standards to be a **full warranty**, the warrantor must: (1) remedy a defective product within a reasonable time and without charge in the event of a defect, malfunction, or failure to conform to the warranty, and (2) after a reasonable number of attempts by the warrantor to remedy defects, the warrantor must give the consumer the option of either a refund or replacement without charge. The latter part of this definition is known as a **lemon clause** because it provides recourse to buyers who are stuck with products that seem to be unrepairable. Replacements must be made **free of charge**, including removal and reinstallation, while warrantors may deduct an amount for depreciation based on actual use when they replace products. In addition, another requirement for full warranties is that the consumer must not have to do anything unreasonable to get warranty service, such as return a heavy product, like a washing machine, to the seller. Full warranties cannot require the return of a warranty registration card either.

The FTC has the authority to define what is a reasonable number of repairs for various products. Consumers with persistent vehicle complaints can use the power of lemon clauses for cars with full warranties, as well as state lemon laws to motivate sellers to make proper repairs. It is also important to note that products offering full warranties cannot place limits on the **duration of implied warranties**; thus a warrantor offering a full warranty is liable for any incidental and consequential damages, such as food, lodging, towing, car rental fees, and food spoilage. Full warranties apply to **both** the original purchaser and subsequent owners during the warranty period.

Limited warranties are much **more widespread** because of the severe obligations placed on sellers offering full warranties. A **limited warranty** is any written guarantee that provides less than a full warranty. If any full warranty requirement is not provided in a warranty, the warranty is classified as a limited warranty. For example, a limited warranty may cover parts only, instead of parts and labor, or it may cover repairs only, instead of replacement or refund. Limited warranties sometimes state that the buyer has to return a warranty card to activate the warranty, although this is not a legal requirement. Many limited warranties provide excellent coverage on consumer products.

DID YOU KNOW?
What Those Confusing Warranty Phrases Mean

The law has improved the opportunity for consumers to understand and practice their warranty rights; however, the language on warranties remains legalistic and perplexing for many. This results in confusion since state laws often offer more protections to consumers than the federal laws. An **implied warranty** is a written or unwritten promise that the seller implicitly asserts that the product is usable and will not fail during normal use. These rights *cannot* be **taken away** unless the product is sold **"as is."** Following are some examples of typical phrases that appear in written warranties which "appear" to take away one's legal rights:

1. *"This warranty gives you specific legal rights, and you may also have other rights which vary from state to state."* This means that the consumer's strong implied warranty rights of merchantability and fitness for a particular purpose may be provided for under the laws of the state where you live.

2. *"Some states do not allow limitations of incidental or consequential damages, so the above limitations may not apply to you."* This also means that the laws of the state where you live may provide more protection.   Many consumers also have trouble understanding such legal concepts as incidental and consequential damages. To illustrate, your warranted vehicle antifreeze may not perform as advertised leading to a frozen engine needing $2,000 in consequential repairs. There also could be incidental towing costs to get the vehicle to the repair shop.

3. *"This limitation or exclusion may not apply to you."* Again, state laws may offer more protection.

4. **"Some states do not allow limitations on how long an implied warranty lasts, so the above limitations may not apply to you."** Here you need to find out if your state provides any limitations on to the length of implied warranty rights.

Although these phrases are accurate and provide important protection for consumers, they seem to confuse rather than clarify the issues. In all warranty situations, you have to **find out for yourself** whether your state laws offer more protection than that provided for in the seller's warranty because a lack of uniformity exists among the states. To complicate matters more, written warranties typically take multiple paragraphs to state the limitations of the seller. To assert these rights under state laws (variations of the Uniform Commercial Code), consumers often have to resort to civil lawsuits.

Informal Dispute Procedures are Encouraged

The Magnusson-Moss Warranty Act encourages the use of an **informal dispute procedure** whenever warranty problems arise between sellers and buyers. Such a procedure allows impartial people to review the arguments and evidence of the complaining consumer and the seller in an attempt to resolve the conflict about warranty service. Warrantors are not required to set up such procedures, but when they do, the procedures must meet minimum standards established by the FTC (known as **Rule 703**) and explain the details in their written warranties. When a warrantor has established an informal dispute procedure, the **consumer must use it** before taking any legal action. Therefore, manufacturers are motivated to set up an informal dispute procedure as an alternative to engaging in costly litigation with consumers with warranty service problems. Rule 703 requires that consumer disputes be settled within a 40-day time period.

Consumers who successfully file state or federal lawsuits against warrantors who do not have an informal dispute procedure may be awarded their purchase costs, attorneys fees, and damages. In addition, consumers injured by a breach of warranty may file a federal class action lawsuit. Few warranty problems meet **all the restrictions** necessary for consumers to economically and successfully pursue a class-action lawsuit under the provisions of the Magnusson-Moss Warranty Act. The Magnusson-Moss Warranty Act does not preempt the field of state warranty law. Instead, it adds another layer of consumer protection while preserving rights and remedies under state law.

Laws on Housing

There are a number of laws and regulations that exist in the area of housing.

Renter's Security Deposits

Almost all states have laws governing security deposits paid by renters to landlords. A landlord usually cannot collect **more than one or two month's rent** as a security deposit. That amount must be held in an interest-bearing bank account, and the interest must be paid to the tenant within 30 days of the yearly anniversary date of tenancy. At the end of the tenancy, the landlord may only deduct for unpaid rent and for "damages beyond **reasonable wear and tear**." Typically, the tenant has a right to be present at the final inspection and be furnished with an itemized list of the damage found. Security deposits must be returned, noting deductions, within 30 days after the tenancy ends; otherwise the renter may be entitled to double or triple damages.

Late Possession of the Rental Property

Sometimes consumers experience difficulty in taking possession of rental housing because the landlord cannot deliver the unit. The problem may be that the previous tenant will not move out or the landlord may find that it will take more time to put the facility into proper condition. Regardless of the reason, this may cost the renter **extra money** in the form of motel expenses until the move can be made.

In all states, consumers so wronged have the right to sue in an attempt to collect damages from the landlord. He or she usually can be forced to **reimburse** the renter for costs of lodging elsewhere, plus any storage expenses. It is easy to win such lawsuits where there is a "damages" clause in the lease contract; such lawsuits will fail if the lease contains a clause that totally absolves the landlord of any liability in such situations. In such cases, the dispute may be resolved by compromises made between the landlord and the tenant.

Habitability of Rental Unit

All states and municipalities provide legal rights to tenants. The habitability of the rental unit must meet some legally **prescribed minimum standard**, such as running water, functional toilets, heat during the winter months, and a working stove. In most states, an implied warranty covers the availability of heat and the safety of access areas, such as stairs. Filing a lawsuit against a landlord for nonperformance is permitted in all states. This is usually done in a small claims court (described in Chapter 3), where for a nominal filing fee (perhaps $15), lawsuits up to a certain dollar amount (perhaps $2,500) can be pursued without an attorney.

Reporting building-code violations to a local government Housing Department, Building Inspector or Mayor's Office is **not just cause** for eviction or for harassment in the form of a rent increase or utility shutoff. Also, joining a tenant organization is not cause for eviction; tenant organizations aim to improve the bargaining power of tenants. In many states, tenants may legally make **minor repairs themselves** and deduct those costs from their next rent payment. This is subject to certain restrictions, such as giving sufficient prior written notification to the landlord.

Community Reinvestment Act

The Community Reinvestment Act (CRA) requires that banking institutions help meet the **credit needs of their communities**, especially low- and moderate-income neighborhoods. The Federal Reserve Board assesses the institutions' records of meeting those credit needs by preparing an evaluation of the institutions along with the assignment of a concluding **CRA rating** supported with facts. These are disclosed to the public. The CRA does not apply to mutual funds, finance companies, mortgage bankers or others outside the banking system.

Fair Housing Act

Discrimination is acting on the basis of bias or intentional prejudice. It is illegal to discriminate in the financing of housing. Various laws prohibit discrimination on the basis of race, color, religion, national origin, sex, parenthood, handicap, or being elderly.

The Fair Housing Act **prohibits discrimination** on the basis of race, color, sex, religion, handicap, familial status, or national origin in the financing, sale, or rental of housing. The Fair Housing Act directly prohibits discrimination in mortgage lending. It empowers the Department of Housing and Urban Development and the Attorney General to help assure non-discriminatory practices in all aspects of the housing market. For example, it is illegal to discriminate against families with children when renting or selling a house or apartment. The Justice Department can ask for compensatory monetary damages for persons victimized and assess civil penalties. The maximum civil penalty for a first finding of discrimination is $50,000, and up to $100,000 for a subsequent violation. (See www.hud.gov/fhe/fheact.html.)

Home Mortgage Disclosure Act

The Home Mortgage Disclosure Act (HMDA) requires certain lending institutions to **report annually** on their mortgage lending practices, including both originations and purchases of homes and home improvement loans, as well as applications for such loans. The type of loan, location of the property, race or national origin, gender, and income of the applicant are reported. Such information, which collectively must be disclosed to the public, can help determine how well institutions are serving the housing credit needs of neighborhoods and communities. Lenders must post a notice of lending availability in their **public lobby**.

These data also **allow others** to check on any discrimination in the pattern of lending. Recent data from the Federal Reserve Board reveal that while 11 percent of white people are rejected for home loans, the figure is 24 percent for blacks. These numbers do not prove that discrimination is occurring in housing lending, but they do suggest that discrimination may be happening. Consumers need to be aware of the housing laws that can be used to protect them.

State Housing Discrimination Laws

In addition to the federal regulations prohibiting discrimination, all states have fair housing laws with similar purposes. The typical state law protects against the following acts: (1) **refusal** to sell or rent or to deal or negotiate with any person, (2) presenting variable terms and conditions to different people for buying or renting housing, (3) advertising that housing is available to certain persons, (4) denying housing is available for inspection, sale, or rent when it really is, (5) **blockbusting**, which is persuasion of owners to sell or rent housing by telling them that minority groups are moving into the neighborhood, (6) denying or making different conditions or terms for home loans by commercial lenders, and (7) **redlining,** which is drawing a red line (or any other color for that matter) around areas of a community and refusing loans to people wanting financing in those areas.

A number of **exclusions** to federal and state laws usually exist. An exclusion usually occurs when a private individual sells or rents a home without employing a real estate broker, without using discriminatory advertising, and without having sold more than one residence in the past 2 years. The laws also are not applicable to the rental of rooms or units in buildings of not more than four families if the owner lives in one of the units and if no discriminatory advertising is used. Also, religious organizations or private clubs may give preferences to their members in housing.

Laws on Credit

There are a number of laws and regulations in the area of credit.

Limited Liability on Credit Cards

The Fair Credit Reporting Act, passed in 1972, limits the liability for unauthorized use of credit cards, including telephone credit cards, and provides other consumer rights. It results in a **maximum liability of $50 per card**. This **credit-card liability** occurs only if you receive notification of your potential liability, you accepted the card when it was first mailed to you, the company provided you with a self-addressed form with which to notify them if the card was lost, and the card was used illegally before you notified them of the loss. If you notify the credit-card company **within two days** of a lost or stolen card, you are **not legally responsible for any charges**. After two days you are liable for only $50 in false charges. In addition, there is no time limit for reporting unauthorized charges when someone has illegally used your credit card; however, you must specify in a complaint letter to the credit card company that it is an **"unauthorized charge."**

Although your financial liability is low, some companies specialize in selling lost credit-card insurance; it is profitable for them and an unnecessary expense for you. Besides, consumers who have renter's or homeowner's insurance typically **already have coverage** that automatically protects them against such losses. As a gesture of goodwill, most companies **waive the $50 charge** for unauthorized use of credit cards. As might be expected, the credit-card insurance companies generally do not offer such information.

Electronic Funds Transfer Act

People often make regular **direct deposits**, such as a paycheck, stock dividends, or Social Security benefits, to financial accounts electronically. You also can authorize your financial institution to pay recurring bills in both regular amounts (such as a mortgage or vehicle loan) and irregular amounts (such as for electric or telephone bills). The federal Electronic Funds Transfer Act (EFTA) permits you to stop a pre-authorized payment by **calling or writing** the financial institution, so that your new order is received at least three days before the payment date. Written confirmation of a telephone notice to stop payment may be required by the institution.

The EFTA Applies to Electronic Transfers, Debit Cards, and Credit Cards Used as Debit Cards

All kinds of electronic transfers occur daily for most consumers. Federal and state regulations have been adopted to provide **protection for EFT users**. (Electronic benefit transfers are currently exempt from the EFT regulations, since most electronic benefits programs are experimental.) The 1978 Electronic Funds Transfer Act is the governing statute and the Federal Reserve Board's "Regulation E" provides the specific guidelines on EFT-card liability. The Electronic Funds Transfer Act affects consumer use of electronic transfers, debit cards, and credit cards used as debit cards.

Rules specify that a **valid card** can be sent only to a consumer who has requested it. Unsolicited cards can be issued only if the card cannot be used until validated and the user is **informed of liability** for unauthorized use as well as other terms and conditions. When you sign up for EFT services, your depository institution must inform you of your rights and responsibilities in a written disclosure statement containing the above information.

Consumers must be offered **written receipts** when withdrawing money or making deposits with an ATM machine or using a point-of-sale terminal to pay for a purchase. These show the amount of the transfer, the date it was made, and other information. General protection of customers' accounts exists in the form of a periodic statement that financial institutions regularly send out. These show all electronic transfers to and from your account, any fees charged, and the opening and closing balances. EFT users should regularly reconcile the information on their periodic statement with the written receipts.

Correcting EFT Errors on Periodic Statements

Should you find an error in your periodic statement, notify the issuing organization in writing **as soon as possible**. Correct notification procedures can be found in the disclosure statement. You have **only 60 days** from the date of the statement or receipt error to notify the financial institution; otherwise the institution has no obligation to investigate. Always telephone and follow up with a letter. If the institution needs more than 10 business days to investigate and correct a problem, generally it must return to your account the amount in question while it finishes the investigation (within a required 45 days). If there were an error, the institution must correct it promptly by making the correction final. If there were no error, the institution must explain in writing why it believes there was no error and let you know that it has deducted any amount temporarily credited during the investigation. However, the institution **must honor withdrawals** against the credited amount for 5 days. You may ask for copies of documents relied on in the investigation and again challenge if a mistake has been made.

Lost EFT Cards

The sooner you report a lost electronic funds transfer (EFT) card, the more likely you will limit your liability if someone uses your card without your permission. Cardholders are liable for only the **first $50** of unauthorized use if they notify the issuing company within 2 business days after the loss or theft of their card or code, unless the consumer was in the hospital or on extended travel. Between 2 and 60 days, cardholder liability for unauthorized use **rises to $500**. If you fail to alert the financial institution within 60 days, you risk **unlimited** loss. Thus, you are liable for every dollar stolen in your account, plus your maximum overdraft line-of-overdraft credit. The logic is that if cardholders examine their monthly statements, they will note unauthorized use of the account. These regulations are for specific EFT cards *and* for other cards used to make an electronic funds transfer (such as a Visa credit card). A number of states (IA, KS, MA, MN, NM, and WS) have capped the liability for unauthorized withdrawals on an ATM or debit card at $50.

It is difficult for consumers to dispute an item with a merchant (for faulty goods, for example) if the merchant has **already been paid** by means of EFT. Because the merchant already has the money, the consumer's only recourse to correct or reverse EFT transactions is to ask for a refund.

DID YOU KNOW?
Your Insurance Likely Already Covers Lost Credit and Debit Cards

Many firms sell a **card registration service**, where for a fee of perhaps $49 a year and upon notification of a missing card or wallet by the consumer, that information will be communicated to all companies with whom the cardholder has accounts. This is a waste of money.

Federal law protects consumers against credit card fraud. You have **zero liability for 2 days** after you have lost your card and if you notify the issuer within that time period you will have zero liability forever. If you fail to tell the credit card issuer, your maximum liability if $50 per card. And virtually no credit card issuer assesses the $50 fee; they would rather keep you as a customer.

Credit card registration services are **bad deals** for consumers because in case of loss, they can notify debit and credit card companies themselves. It's not too difficult to maintain a list of card companies and their 800-numbers. Homeowner's and renter's insurance policies typically cover the liability for the unauthorized use (usually theft) of both debit and credit cards. If such protection is not in your current policy, the coverage generally can be added to a homeowner's or renter's policy for $10 to $15 a year.

Automatic-Billing Disputes

As a matter of convenience, many consumers give their credit card or checking account number to vendors so that regular monthly fees may be automatically charged, or debited, to their accounts. If charges come directly out of a checking account, a problem may occur because your **money is gone** and it is hard to get it back.

Consumers do have protections from *electronic* debits to their bank accounts under the **Automated Clearing House (ACH) rules** governing financial institutions. After receiving a statement, consumers have **15 days** to tell their bank that the charge was unauthorized. It is then the bank's responsibility to prove the validity of the charge, or reverse the debit. However, there are no protections for consumers for *paper* debits. Alternatively, if you permit charges to a credit card you have the protections of the Fair Credit Billing Act (discussed below) that allows consumers to dispute an unauthorized charge up to 60 days after it occurred.

Fair Credit Reporting Act

Most credit reporting is done by **credit bureaus** or **credit reporting agencies**, for-profit agencies that compile information about credit applications and forward such to creditors and others. There are over 2,000 local credit reporting agencies, and most are associated with one of the **"Big Three"** agencies: Equifax, TransUnion, and Experian.

A creditor comes under the Fair Credit Reporting Act (FCRA) only when credit information from one firm **is forwarded to another** and a credit decision is based on that information. The law prohibits access to a credit report without a **legitimate business purpose**; therefore, those who may see your file include employers, landlords, and life insurance companies. Also, it is illegal for an automobile dealer to access your credit report while you are shopping for a vehicle, because you have not yet initiated a credit transaction. The objective of the act is to place certain restrictions on credit-reporting agencies to reduce errors. FCRA, which is enforced by the federal and state governments, gives consumers the right to learn what is contained in their credit records and to correct inaccurate or incomplete information. The FCRA gives consumers **two years** to sue if an error by a credit-reporting agency results in **identify theft** and subsequent fraud. The U.S. Supreme Court, however, says that the two-year clock starts at the time of the error. Since an average of 14 months passes before consumers typically realize that mistakes are uncovered, the time for taking legal action is short.

Consumers Have the Right to Know the Contents of Their Credit File, Including Medical Information

Even if you have not been denied credit, for a **small fee** (usually $8) you can obtain a copy of your credit bureau file. People who are indigent, on welfare, or unemployed and job-hunting can get one free report a year. Some states have laws that either limit the amount of the charge or require that a **free report** be given to residents who request one (CN, CO, GA, MD, MA, and VE). A credit record may be retained for a period of 7 years for judgments, liens, lawsuits, and other adverse information, except for bankruptcies, in which case records may be retained for 10 years.

When you apply for life insurance or employment, a credit bureau is usually paid to compile an **investigative report**. This is a much more detailed report than a regular consumer credit report. It often includes interview comments from neighbors and friends about your lifestyle, morals, character, and reputation. The FCRA requires that you be informed when this kind of report is being compiled.

DID YOU KNOW?
How to Get a Copy of Your Credit Report

Each of the three major national credit bureaus have credit histories on over 100 million people: Equifax (1-800-685-1111; www.equifax.com), Trans Union (1-800-888-4213; www.transunion.com), and Experian (1-888-682-7654; www.experian.com). At CreditPage (www.creditpage.com) or Qspace (www.qspace.com), you may obtain a copy of your credit report in less than 1 minute for $8.

The regulations require that you have the right to **examine your file information** if it led to a denial of *any benefit*, such as renting an apartment, opening a cell phone account, or denied credit, employment, insurance or a security clearance. You have up to 60 days from the denial to request your report.

When information held by a credit bureau plays a role in denying a consumer credit or insurance, he or she **must be informed** of the existence of any pertinent medical records, be able to check the file, and make corrections. The Medical Information Bureau (MIB) is the company that collects and maintains information on consumers' credit history, medical conditions, driving records, criminal activity, participation in hazardous sports, and more. Copies of an MIB report are available for $8; call (617)-426-3660 or write MIB, Box 105, Boston, MA 02112.

Rights Exist if a Poor Credit Report Results in an Adverse Action

A **credit report** is a document that displays information about an individual's personal credit history. It is the single most important piece of information creditors consider when determining whether or not to grant credit to an individual and, if so, how much to give; it also is used to help creditors decide the interest rate that will be charged. Such files are compiled by credit bureaus or credit-reporting agencies, and they are used by lenders, employers and others who have a need to know about someone's credit history and reliability. If, because of a poor credit report, an **adverse action** occurs, such as being rejected for credit, an apartment, a job, a license, an insurance policy or a loan at a favorable rate, the law requires disclosure to you of the name, address and toll-free telephone number (to a human, not a machine) of any credit-reporting agency that supplied information about you. You can then request a copy of your file at the credit-reporting agency without a fee; a **cost-free credit report** must be requested within 60 days of denial.[3] Send a copy of the denial letter with your request. If the information was in error, it must be corrected. Credit bureaus must "consider" your evidence, such as a canceled check, receipt, or letter on creditor's stationery.

If you dispute an item, it **must be reinvestigated**. The law requires credit bureaus to investigate consumer complaints within 30 days, weigh information obtained, correct any inaccurate or unverified information, and notify the complaining consumer of the results. The **burden of proof** is more squarely on the credit bureau, instead of the consumer. Disputed

---

[3] The law permits credit bureaus to hold back one piece of information when providing a copy of a credit file to a consumer: the **"credit score"** and similar predictors used by credit grantors when deciding who gets credit and who is rejected.

data removed from your file may not be reinserted unless it is **"certified"** by the creditor as accurate; evidenced by a letter from the creditor reasserting that the debt is owed. If disputed data does return to your file, the credit bureau is required to notify you and provide you with a new credit report within 5 days of completion.

The regulations also apply to those who furnish information to credit bureaus, such as creditors and retail stores. They must meet the same **30-day standard** for investigating a complaint as well as take reasonable steps to ensure corrected errors do not reappear in a consumer's file.

Also, card issuers are required to conduct a **"reasonable investigation"** before considering any dispute settled. They are required to conduct an **"independent assessment"** of a consumer complaint based on information provided by the merchant and the consumer. Creditors may be sued for violating the FCRA, especially if they don't correct a mistake, verify incorrect data, or reinsert erroneous information.

You also may wish to explain anything that might cause lenders to shy away from you by telling your side of the story about a disputed item by adding, in 100 words or less, an **explanatory consumer statement** to your credit file (see an example of a statement in the chapter appendix). It must be sent to anyone who received a credit report on you in the previous 6 months.

Fair Credit Billing Act

The Fair Credit Billing Act (FCBA) went into effect in 1975 to protect against **billing errors** and the receipt of **unsatisfactory goods** and services when one uses **open-end credit** (credit cards, department store accounts, and others where the amount due each month varies), including charges made by mail or telephone. It establishes procedures for the **prompt correction** of all types of errors on open-end credit accounts.[4] It provides safeguards against unsatisfactory purchases and uncooperative merchants. The law also protects a consumer's credit rating while the consumer is settling a dispute. In the past, complaining about a credit card bill often resulted in delays and in harmful information going into a consumer's credit file. Four sample credit complaint letters are in the chapter appendix.

Under the claims and defenses portion of the law, also known as the **charge back** section, consumers may legally withhold payment for a disputed amount for a number of reasons. Here your credit card company will attempt to "charge back" the disputed amount to the merchant. In essence, the original transaction is rescinded. Consumers **may not be responsible** for a charge on their credit account if it:

1. is in error,

2. was not made by a person authorized to use the account, or

3. is for goods and services that were not provided or delivered according to agreement, or they were "unsatisfactory."

---

[4] The law excludes purchases paid with a cash advance on a credit card as well as a "ready check" or "cash check" associated with a credit card.

To exercise your rights,[5] you must provide **written notification** to your credit card company of your problem within 60 days of the postmark date on the bill in which the charge appeared, i.e., when it was *mailed to you*. A telephone call to the lender will *not* preserve your rights.

The credit card issuer is **required to investigate** such inquiries and respond in writing within 30 days. During the time when the company is looking into the problem, consumers are not required to pay the questioned amount or any finance charges associated with the disputed amount. These rights do not guarantee consumers a refund, but the law does require that the credit card issuer investigate the matter in their effort to resolve the dispute. If the creditor's explanation does not satisfy the consumer, the creditor must be notified in writing **within10 days** to further certain consumer rights. Any reports sent to a credit bureau and other creditors must state that the consumer disputes the charges, and the consumer must be told who receives such reports for the **following six months**. With all challenges to credit card bills if the credit card issuer turns down the challenge, the consumer still owes the amount of the charge, plus any finance costs that have accumulated (but were suspended until the challenge was resolved).

The law is limited to unpaid credit card purchases **totaling over $50** that were made within your home state or within 100 miles of your current address, whichever is farther. The dollar and distance limitations do not apply if the creditor owns the merchant, or the creditor mailed the advertisement for the goods or services, or if the merchandise came from a mail-order catalog. In practice, most credit card companies allow consumers to contest **any charge, regardless of amount or distance from one's home**. While these protections exclude overseas purchases, some U.S. credit card issuers have voluntarily extended the coverage around the world.

If the consumer has already paid the card issuer for a charge before realizing that a problem existed, one's legal leverage has been lost; however, most issuers are willing to work with customers who have been ripped off. Obviously, making payment with a credit card offers consumers **much more protection** than when paying with cash or a check.

The FCBA also states that bills must be mailed to cardholders **at least 14 days** before payments are due. Companies are required to send a reminder of their consumer credit rights under the FCBA to all customers twice a year. Another provision requires that retailers who voluntarily give **price discounts of up to 5 percent to cash customers** must publicly state that information. In this way, cardholders can choose to elect to pay cash and thus avoid the extra costs the merchant imposes on credit accounts.

Consumers Get to Keep $50 of the Disputed Amount if the Credit Card Company Fails to Follow the Rules

Failure of the company to follow all the rules within the proper time limits, allows the cardholder to **keep the first $50** of the amount in dispute and finance charges, even if the bill turns out to be correct. Also, the consumer may sue for damages resulting from the violation, plus twice the amount of any finance charge (not less than $100 or more than $1,000), plus attorney fees and costs.

Reason #1 to Challenge a Credit Bill—Consumers are Not Liable for the Errors of Others

---

[5] These rights exist both in the United States and overseas, although in some foreign countries local laws may limit one's FCBA rights.

A consumer has the right to dispute a charge and temporarily withhold payment for that charge while the credit card company investigates for a **number of reasons**: (1) something you did not buy, (2) something purchased by an unauthorized person, (3) something not properly identified on a bill (i.e., place, description, date), (4) an amount different from the actual purchase price, (5) something not accepted on delivery, (6) something that was not delivered according to agreement (e.g., wrong quantity, incorrect specifications, or unreasonably late), (7) arithmetic errors, (8) failure to reflect a payment or a credit, (9) failure to mail the billing statement to the current address, provided the lender received notice of that address at least 20 days before the end of the billing period, and (10) any item for which a consumer requests additional clarification.

After investigating a challenge, the credit card issuer typically forwards the complaining consumer a **photocopy of the signature** on the credit slip. The issuer's position typically is, "Well, if that is your signature, you still owe us the money, so stop your complaining and pay us what is owed." Consumers should not be taken in by such an attitude and quickly give in and pay the disputed amount. If it is your signature but there is some genuine problem with the bill, write the card issuer again reaffirming the challenge. This time **write to a supervisor** at the credit card issuer, being even more explicit with your explanation. A sample complaint letter to a supervisor at a credit card company is shown in the chapter appendix.

Another good reason to challenge an "error" is that the credit card bill was **received too late** or not received at all. This problem often occurs when people move from one address to another and when the Postal Service loses the mail. In this instance, the consumer simply writes to challenge the finance charges that were incorrectly imposed on the account. Such charges should be credited on the account provided the lender received notice of that new address at least 20 days before the end of the billing period.

If the credit card issuer disagrees with and rejects the challenge, they must tell the consumer why they believe the bill is **not in dispute**. At this point, the consumer may ask for copies of relevant documents and then re-file the complaint (perhaps with more information). Refusal to pay may result in the lender beginning collection procedures, although credit card issuers usually do not begin to send collection letters for 90 days.

Reason #2 to Challenge a Credit Bill—It Appears to be an Unauthorized Charge

If your reason for the challenge is that the charge appears to be unauthorized, the card issuer will forward you a photocopy of the signature on the credit card slip so it can be examined. Should the consumer write back reporting that the signature is not valid, the credit card issuer **must give in** and accept the challenge as legitimate. That means that the challenged amount will immediately be credited. If the amount involved is substantial, the card issuer's fraud investigative unit will contact the consumer in an effort to obtain additional information that might be useful in investigating and catching the culprit who falsified the signature. Sometimes a relative or acquaintance of the family misuses a person's credit card.

Reason #3 to Challenge a Credit Bill—Unsatisfactory Goods

Examples of **unsatisfactory goods** and services include: (1) ordered merchandise was never delivered to your home, (2) stitching in a new jacket ripped out under normal use, (3) fraudulent emergency auto repairs were made to your vehicle while on an out-of-town trip, (4) you did not enjoy a meal at a restaurant about which you complained to the merchant, and (5) you lost a night's sleep in a noisy motel room where you complained to the night manager to no avail. If you are owed a refund by an airline that went bankrupt, the law requires your credit cared issuer to credit your account.

Key to successfully winning a dispute is that **you *must* make a real attempt** to resolve the problem with the merchant. The chapter appendix contains **illustrative letters** that can be sent to the merchant and the credit card issuer. If you attempt to challenge a credit card bill on the grounds that you are dissatisfied without first, or simultaneously, contacting the merchant in an attempt to resolve the matter, the card issuer will very likely refuse your request and reinstate the charge to your account.

When Necessary, Consumers Should Write Firm Letters to Merchants and Credit Card Companies

To properly dispute a credit card charge, first, write the merchant to complain and, if appropriate, **seek a compromise**. Second, write a complaint letter to the credit card company. Provide the credit card company with a chronology and as much documentation as possible, so that they can contact the merchant to try to thrash things out. During that time creditors cannot send **dunning letters** (notices that make insistent demands for repayment) to you or send negative information about your account to a credit bureau without stating additionally that, "Some items are in dispute." Consumers who pay off their bills before realizing a problem exists are *not* entitled to a credit.

When writing, be **pleasant but firm**, state only the important details, and tell them what you want done. Many consumers wisely charge any and all expenses that might later turn out to be a problem, such as air travel and auto repairs while on trips. For travel expenses, the 60-day period to contest a charge begins from the date of the bill, not the date of travel. Three companies have extended the challenge time for travel charges: Visa voluntarily extended the time period from the date of travel, MasterCard 120 days from the date of the bill, and American Express up to a year.

Equal Credit Opportunity Act

Discrimination in lending against women, the elderly, and religious and racial minorities resulted in the passage of the Equal Credit Opportunity Act of 1975, which **prohibits discrimination in granting credit**. Rejecting a credit application due to poor credit history is legal, but rejecting a person on the basis of sex, race, color, age, marital status, religion, national origin, or because the person receives public assistance is not. It also prohibits discrimination because of good faith exercise of any rights under the federal credit laws and regulations. By law, credit applications cannot probe for information that could be used in a biased manner. The Equal Credit Opportunity Act requires creditors to provide to the applicant a written statement, if requested, of the reasons for refusing credit. Should discrimination be proven in court, the lender may be liable for up to $10,000 in fines. (See www.fdic.gov/banknews/fils/1998/fil9840.html.)

Lenders must **use the same criteria** to judge applications from single and married persons. A married man or woman applying for credit need not disclose marital status or a spouse's income unless he or she is dependent on that income, in which case it is used as the basis for granting credit. Several states take exception to this, considering any property acquired by either the husband or wife, known as **community property**, to be jointly owned and equally shared.

Fair Debt Collection Practices Act

This 1977 legislation was aimed at eliminating abusive, deceptive, and **unfair debt collection practices**. It applies to third party debt collectors or those who use a name other than their own in collecting consumer debts. Banks, dentists, lawyers, and others who do their own collecting are exempt. **Collection agencies** attempt to make collections of debt from consumers that could not be obtained through the usual procedures of sellers.

Collection agencies are **prohibited** from harassing debtors, telephoning before 8:00 a.m. or after 9 p.m. on Mondays through Saturdays, making numerous repeated telephone calls during the day, misrepresenting themselves (such as claiming they are attorneys, unless they are, or falsely implying the consumer has committed a crime) or the purpose of their communication, using profane or abusive language, making threats, making racial or ethnic slurs, or spreading rumors that the debtor is a "deadbeat." Collectors may not contact consumers at work if they are told that one's employer disapproves. They may not communicate about outstanding debt with any person other than the consumer or his/her attorney.

Even with these limitations, realize that collection agencies can be **irritatingly persistent** in collecting past-due accounts. If they are not successful they take the consumer to court and seek a default judgment as the last resort.

Debtors have the right to request that collectors **cease communication**, and if debtors are represented by attorneys, all future contact regarding those accounts must be with the attorneys. Should the collector persist, debtors should write a letter and firmly inform the collector to stop. Telephone numbers in your state to call for help against harassment are available at www.usatoday.com.

Fair Credit and Charge Card Disclosure Act

The Fair Credit and Charge Card Disclosure Act of 1988 provides that credit-card issuers must reveal a number of important **pricing details before consumers sign up** for the credit cards. The law requires any direct-mail credit application or solicitation to reveal: (1) the **annual percentage rate (APR)** of interest, including the way the rate is calculated and if the rate is variable, (2) the method used to calculate the monthly account balances against which the company applies interest or finance charges, (3) all fees, including annual fees, minimum finance charges, transaction charges, cash-advance fees, late fees, and fees for going over the credit limit, and (4) the length of time of the grace period, if any. Information such as APR, annual fee, and grace period must be provided in tabular form. Companies that impose an annual fee must provide **disclosures before annual renewal**. Card issuers that offer credit insurance must inform customers of any increase in rate or substantial decrease in coverage should the issuer decide to change insurance providers.

This law enables consumers to comparison-shop for credit cards. Research from the Survey Research Center of the University of Michigan indicates that about **35 percent of us**

shop for the most attractive interest rate on credit cards, so many Americans benefit from this information.

DID YOU KNOW?
Refuse to Pay Punitive Interest Rates

If a bank credit card company raises the interest rate on an existing account (for a legitimate reason or otherwise, a **punitive interest rate**), the consumer has the right in 20 states to reject any commitment to paying the higher rate. To do so, one must notify the card issuer in writing. Various state laws (CA, CO, DE, IL, IA, ME, MD, MO, NE, NH, NY, OK, SC, SD, VT, WS, WY, NJ, PA, WV) allow a bank credit card holder to continue to pay off balances under the terms of the original agreement provided that no additional charges are made on the card and the account is closed. Any continued use of the credit card means that the consumer has accepted the new higher terms.

Home-Equity Loan Consumer Protection Act

Recent data from the Federal Reserve Board reveal that 12 percent of all homeowners, about 7 ½ million people, have established some type of home-equity loan. A **home-equity loan** is an open-ended credit plan **secured by the borrower's principal residence**. Some 40 percent of home-equity loans are used for home improvements, 30 percent are used to repay debts, and the remainder is used for new purchases. Less than ¾ of 1 percent of such loans are delinquent, and this compares to 2 ¼ to 3 percent for other types of consumer loans. Borrowers can lose their homes if they do not repay their home-equity loans. (See www.ag.uiuc.edu/~vista/html_pubs/YOURCRE/homeloan.html.)

The Home Equity Loan Consumer Protection Act of 1988, Regulation Z of the Federal Reserve Board, and a 1994 mortgage disclosure regulation (see below) attempt to **curb some of the abuses** in the growing home-equity loan market by providing borrowers with more information about the costs of such loans. The regulations prohibit lenders from unilaterally changing the terms of a loan after a contract has been signed. They prohibit lenders from calling in loans before the due date, except in cases of fraud or misrepresentation by the borrower in connection with the loan, failure to meet the payment obligations, or borrower behavior that jeopardizes the value of the home.

Advertisements promoting initially low "teaser" rates **must display** the current long-term interest rate with equal prominence. Advertisements must include cost information, such as loan fees, the rate used to compute finance charges, and the maximum potential increase in the rate.

For variable-rate home-equity loans, lenders must link their interest rate formula to a **public index** outside the lender's control. They also must tell applicants the frequency of changes in the annual percentage rate and provide a **15-year historical table** showing how the rate and payments would have been affected by changes in the value of the index.

All borrowers must receive detailed information on the home-equity loans along with the credit application **before any fees are paid**. Lenders have to disclose information on interest rates, fees, interest ceilings, an estimate of fees imposed by third parties, and repayment options, and they must provide an example of a repayment schedule. Should any terms change before the loan is finalized, the consumer has the right to demand a complete refund of all fees paid.

Home Ownership and Equity Protection Act

The Home Ownership and Equity Protection Act (HOEPA) of 1994 amends the Truth in Lending Act and aims to eliminate the **unscrupulous practice of making predatory loans** in the **second mortgage market**. This is also known as the **subprime market** because the borrowers often do not have a good credit rating. **Predatory lending** is a lender action to steer cash-strapped homeowner-borrowers into taking out home-equity loans and mortgages at excessive costs without regard to the homeowner's ability to repay. Oftentimes the middle-income borrowers cannot repay so they lose their homes through **foreclosure** (forced sale).

The Home Ownership and Equity Protection Act (HOEPA) discourages legitimate lenders from making such loans or buying credit contracts from the original holders of the notes. HOEPA also provides remedies for victims of such unethical practices. The law creates regulations for a particular type of closed-end loans. **Closed-end loans** are those with set payment terms, such as 60 monthly payments of $200. (This is in contrast to open-end loans where consumers can tap into a line of credit, like a credit card or a traditional home-equity loan.) A loan that uses a person's home for security will meet the requirements of the law and be defined as a **special home-ownership closed-end loan** when one or more triggers occur: (1) if the annual percentage rate (APR) of the loan is more than 10 percentage points above the yield on certain Treasury securities, and (2) the loan's up-front fee and charges are greater than 8 percent of the total amount of the loan or $400, or more. Exempt from HOEPA regulations are traditional residential mortgage loans, reverse mortgages, and open-end credit transactions.

Lenders now must make a great number of **disclosures** regarding the terms of such loans, and they are prohibited from using certain terms and placing onerous conditions in their contracts.

When violations of the HOEPA law occur, the victims of such high-interest loans have **three *years* to cancel** the transaction. This right of recision is provided in the Truth in Lending Act, and it extends the historic three-day cooling-off period for some credit transactions. The borrower, of course, is required to give back the proceeds of the loan to the lender; however, all obligations to pay interest and closing costs are canceled. These claims may be made against the original lender as well as the current holder of the note. This recision right is expected to be a powerful influence in the market and, it is hoped, force the reduction or elimination of such home-ownership closed-end loan scams.

This all may sound like good consumer protection, but it has **not been enough**. As a result, many states have passed **strong laws** against predatory lending. Many large financial institutions and their Republican conservative pro-business legislative friends are assisting the mortgage lending industry to get a weak federal law passed that would **pre-empt** all the stronger state laws, as well as prohibit non-federal regulation of the industry.

High Cost Mortgage Act

The High Cost Mortgage Act protects consumers when they refinance their home or take out a home-equity loan with rates or fees that qualify as **high cost**. This is a mortgage which carries greater than $400 or 8 percent of the loan amount in fees as part of the financing transaction. Those borrowers must be provided a disclosure statement three days before closing advising that the deal can still be canceled. **Balloon payment plans**, in which regular monthly payments are followed by an extremely large lump-sum final payment of the balance due, are prohibited for loans of fewer than five years (except for **bridge** loans of less than one year used by those who are selling one home and buying another). **Prepayment penalties** (charges for paying off a loan early) are generally prohibited as are **negative amortization plans**. These are loans that allow the unpaid balance (the principal debt) to grow rather than diminish, and if they occur when the repayment amount received by a creditor is less than the amount of interest assessed during a given time period.

Review and Summary of Key Terms and Concepts

1. Why does the federal government have **telemarketing regulations?**

2. Summarize the FTC regulations on the **Do-Not-Call Registry**.

3. List three key portions of the **rules telemarketers** must follow.

4. How can you **fight back** against rip-off telephone charges?

5. Outline the **unordered merchandise regulations** of the Postal Service.

6. List the key portions of the **negative option mail-order rule** of the Federal Trade Commission.

7. What special responsibilities do the **mail- and telephone order merchandise sellers** have if they expect to be slow in forwarding your merchandise ordered by mail?

8. Summarize the federal *and* state **door-to-door sales regulations**. In your response, define the term **cooling-off period**.

9. What are typical limits on **cooling-off** time periods for consumer purchases for **health spas, timeshares, campground contracts, mortgage refinancing and credit repair firms**?

10. Outline the **airline bumping rules**.

11. Choose one of the following and list the consumer protections available: **airline lost baggage regulations, pet lemon laws, weight-loss center laws**.

12. How does New York state regulate **rent-to-own** businesses?

13. What are the provisions of typical **privacy laws** in the U.S.?

14. Explain the term **lemon**, and the typical benefits of **state lemon laws**.

15. What does a good state law on **secret vehicle warranties** do?

16. How do **vehicle repair laws** usually protect consumers?

17. Why do sellers put **confusing phrases** in some warranties?

18. Distinguish between a **full** and a **limited warranty**.

19. What are the typical provisions of a state law governing **renter's security deposits**?

20. From the point of view of a college student, explain the concepts of **late possession** and **habitability**.

21. Define the term **discrimination**, and distinguish between **blockbusting** and **redlining**.

22. Tell how consumers have a **limited liability on credit cards**.

23. Summarize the protections offered by the **Electronic Funds Transfer Act**.

24. What rights do consumers have in **automatic-billing disputes**?

25. What are your rights if a poor credit report results in an **adverse action**?

26. List the consumer benefits of the **Fair Credit Billing Act**, and tell when consumers may properly challenge a charge on their credit bills.

27. What protections are offered under the **Equal Credit Opportunity Act**?

28. Choose one of the following and list the consumer protections: **Fair Debt Collection Practices Act**, **Fair Credit and Charge Card Disclosure Act**, **Home Equity Loan Consumer Protection Act**, **Home Ownership and Equity Protection Act**, and **High Cost Mortgage Act**.

29. Distinguish between **balloon loans** and **negative amortization**.

Useful Resources for Consumers

Board of Governors of the Federal Reserve System
www.federalreserve.gov

Consumer Information Center (*Consumer's Resource Handbook* is free)
www.pueblo.gsa.gov

Consumers Union (publisher of *Consumer Reports*)
www.consumersunion.org

Consumer World (portal)
www.consumerworld.org

Direct Marketing Association
www.the-dma.org/

Direct Selling Association
www.dsa.org/

Federal Aviation Administration
(800)-FAA-SURE
www.faa.gov/

Federal Communications Commission
202-632-7000 (consumer assistance)
www.fcc.gov

202-632-7048 (complaints about radio or television)
www.fcc.gov

Federal Deposit Insurance Corporation 877-ASK-FDIC (or 877-275-3342) toll-free
www.fdic.gov

Federal Trade Commission
202-326-3128 (complaints)
www.ftc.gov/consumer.htm

Laypeople's Law Lounge
www.lectlaw.com/lay.html

Lemon Law America (attorneys and state laws)
www.lemonlawamerica.com

National Association of Consumer Agency Administrators
www.nacaanet.org/

National Association of Regulatory Utility Commissioners
www.naruc.org

National Consumer Law Center
www.consumerlaw.org

National Credit Union Administration
www.ncua.gov

National Highway Traffic and Safety
888-DASH-2-DOT (888-327-4236)
www.nhtsa.dot.gov

National Senior Citizens Law Center
www.nsclc.org

Nolo Press
www.nolo.com

Office of the Comptroller of the Currency
www.occ.treas.gov

Office of Thrift Supervision
800-842-6929 toll-free
www.ots.treas.gov

Privacy Rights Clearinghouse
www.privacyrights.org

U.S. Department of
Transportation
Aviation Consumer Protection
Office
www.dot.gov/

U.S. Postal Service
Inspection Service
www.usps.com/postalinspect
ors/

"What Do You Think" Questions

1.   The text lists over twenty laws and regulations on **sales transactions**. How would you describe the themes of the numerous laws? Offer two reasons why you think there are so many laws.

2.   The **Federal Trade Commission Used Car Rule** offers a number of protections for consumers. Considering your knowledge of the buyer-seller relationship in a used car transaction, offer your views on the necessity for such a regulation.

3.   The problems facing the purchaser of a **lemon vehicle** can be especially serious. Review the typical provisions of **lemon laws**, and offer your views of the degree of protection provided consumers.

Appendix Issue 5-A
Sample Letters Challenging Credit Card Charges

COMPLAINT LETTER CHALLENGING AN ERROR ON A
CREDIT CARD BILL
(Send this letter whenever an error is found on a credit card bill)

Return address
Today's date

Address (the address listed after "Send inquiries to")

Dear reader (use correct name if known):

Subject: Billing Error Notice for Credit Card Charge Account #(put your number here)

I am writing today to complain about a charge that appeared on my recent bill. The amount of (give dollar figure here) that appeared on my bill with a date of (give date here) is in error.

The reason why the amount on my bill is being challenged is that you (made an arithmetic error, failed to reflect a payment or a credit, failed to mail the billing statement to the correct address [provided the company was notified at least 20 days before the end of the billing period], failed to mail the billing statement [and you assume it may have been lost in the mail], it is something that you did not buy, it is something purchased by an unauthorized person, it is something not properly identified on the bill [place, description, date], an amount different from the actual purchase price, it is something not accepted on delivery, it is something that was not delivered according to agreement, an item simply needs clarification, or another good reason). (Explain your side of the situation more fully. If appropriate, explain why you are willing to accept a partial credit rather than a full credit.)

As stated in the Fair Credit Billing Act, I will expect to hear from you within 30 days. I have paid the remainder of my bill, as I am required to do. But I have not made any payment toward the disputed amount. Please attend to this matter.

I expect that (name of credit card company) will immediately credit my account for the challenged amount (and, if appropriate, remove any interest assessed on that particular charge). (If appropriate, also say that you assume that the credit card company will reinvestigate this transaction and send you a letter reporting the findings.) I fully expect that my credit card account with (name of credit card company) will remain credited in the amount of (put amount here).

Thank you for your cooperation in this matter.

Sincerely,

Your Name

Enclosure

COMPLAINT LETTER TO MERCHANT REQUESTING CREDIT FOR AN UNSATISFACTORY PURCHASE
(Send this letter as soon as credit card bill is received)

Return address
Today's date

Name and address of merchant

Dear reader (use correct name if known):

RE: Credit Card Charge Account #(put your number here)

I am writing today to complain about a charge from (name of merchant) that appeared on my recent (name of credit card company) bill. This bill is in error, and I am asking (name of merchant) to credit my account for (amount of credit desired).

The reason for this request is that (it is something that you did not buy, something purchased by an unauthorized person, something not properly identified on the bill [place, description, date], an amount different from the actual purchase price, something not accepted on delivery, something that was not delivered according to agreement, or another good reason). (Explain your side of the situation more fully. If appropriate, explain why you desire a partial credit rather than a full credit. Also, if true, tell them that you intend to do business with them again.)

Therefore, I expect that (name of merchant) will credit my credit card account in the amount of (put amount here) as soon as possible. Thank you for your cooperation in this matter.

(This is an optional paragraph that could be placed immediately preceding the one above.) Should (name of company) not credit my account by the next billing cycle, at that time I will file an official complaint to (name of credit card company) under the rights provided consumers by the Fair Credit Billing Act. That law and the contract between (name of merchant *and* the name of the credit card company) both require that my account be immediately credited for the amount challenged while the credit card company investigates the complaint. Since my facts as described above are correct, the law also says that the credit on my account will remain.

Sincerely,

Your Name

COMPLAINT LETTER TO CREDIT CARD COMPANY ABOUT AN UNSATISFACTORY PURCHASE
(Send this letter on the same day as the letter to the merchant)

Return address
Today's date

Name and address of credit card company

Dear reader (use correct name if known):

RE: Credit Card Charge Account #(put your number here)

I am writing today to complain about a charge from (name of merchant) that appeared on my recent bill. The amount of (give dollar figure here) that appeared on my bill with a date of (give date here) is in error. As you can see from the enclosed letter, I have already attempted to get (name of merchant) to credit my account for (amount of credit desired).

The reason why the amount on me bill is being challenged is that (it is something that you did not buy, something purchased by an unauthorized person, something not properly identified on the bill [place, description, date], an amount different from the actual purchase price, something not accepted on delivery, something that was not delivered according to agreement, or another good reason). (Explain your side of the situation more fully. If appropriate, explain why you are willing to accept a partial credit rather than a full credit.)

Therefore, I expect that (name of credit card company) will immediately credit my account for the challenged amount (and, if appropriate, remove any interest assessed on that particular charge). Plus, (name of credit card company) will reinvestigate this transaction with (name of merchant) and send me a letter reporting your findings. I fully expect that my credit card account with (name of credit card company) will remain credited in the amount of (put amount here).

Thank you for your cooperation in this matter.

Sincerely,

Your Name

Enclosure

COMPLAINT LETTER TO SUPERVISOR AT CREDIT CARD COMPANY
(Send this letter if the credit card company turns down
your request for a credit)

Return address
Today's date

Name and address of credit card company

Dear supervisor of lower-level employee (at credit card company):

RE: Credit Card Charge Account # (put your number here)

Please see the enclosed letters in reference to an incorrect charge of (put amount here) on my (name of credit card company) account. I have asked the merchant to correct the error and I have asked (name of credit card company) to correct the error. Your (name of credit card company person who signed letter saying that upon completion of their investigation they will not credit your account) has made a mistake in writing to me saying that (name of credit card company) has decided not to properly credit my account for (repeat the reason given in their letter); therefore, I am asking that you take corrective action.

(Give your reason[s], such as simply sending you a photocopy of your correct signature does not invalidate your proper claim of defective/shoddy/deficient product or service.)

Should my account not be credited by the next billing cycle and the amount of the original charge remain on the account, I will then file an official complaint to the Federal Trade Commission under the rights provided consumers by the Fair Credit Billing Act. As you know, that law and the contract between (name of merchant *and* the name of the credit card company) both require that my account be credited for any amount challenged while the credit card company investigates the complaint. I contend that your investigation was insufficient and that the facts of the situation, described in the enclosed letters, are correct. The law says that the credit on my account will remain when the merchant is wrong. If (name of credit card company) fails to follow all the government rules within proper time limits, (name of credit card company) is required by law to credit my account for $50 of the amount in dispute. Alternatively, I can sue (name of credit card company) in the local small claims court asking the court for the credit, plus attorney fees and costs.

Further, (name of credit card company) will not lose a penny on this complaint since all you have to do is process your credit against (name of merchant) as detailed in your contractual agreement with that merchant.

If after reinvestigating this complaint, (name of credit card company) still does not credit my account I will close my account. If I close my account, (name of company) will lose approximately (amount of dollars here based upon last year's total finance charges) from interest charges and (amount of dollars here based on three percent of last year's total purchases) from discounts to retailers for each charge. That means (name of credit card company) will lose (total amount of both figures) if my account is not properly credited.

Therefore, I expect that (name of credit card company) will credit my account for the challenged amount (and, if appropriate, remove any interest assessed on that particular charge).

Thank you very much for your cooperation in this matter.

Sincerely,

Your Name

Enclosures

**EXAMPLE OF AN "EXPLANATORY CONSUMER STATEMENT" TO ADD
TO ONE'S CREDIT REPORT TO TELL
THE CONSUMER'S SIDE OF A DISPUTE
(Up to 100 words may be added to one's credit file)**

Return address
Today's date

Name and address of credit bureau (Experian, Equifax, or Transunion)

Dear reader (use correct name if known)

Please add the following consumer statement to my credit file:

"Last year, I co-leased an apartment for one year with a friend. One week before our lease expired, I moved back to my hometown. Prior to my departure, I called the leasing agent for the apartment complex and confirmed that I owed nothing on the lease. However, unbeknownst to me, my former roommate had damaged the apartment in the process of moving out. In addition, he remained in the apartment five days beyond the date of the expiration of the lease. He further chose not to pay the realty agent for those expenses. Six months later, the XYZ Collection Agency notified me that I was responsible for the $300 not paid by my former roommate. I promptly paid them."

After this consumer statement is added to my credit file, please send me a copy of my credit report. Thank you for your cooperation in this matter.

Sincerely,

Your Name

Part Three:

THE CHALLENGING MARKETPLACE

Chapter 6

The Capitalistic American Marketplace

OBJECTIVES

After reading this chapter, you should be able to

1. Give an overview of how the capitalistic American economic system functions.

2. Understand how the U.S. economic system allocates resources

3. Appreciate the key role of government in influencing the U.S. economy, especially through its use of fiscal and monetary policies.

4. Describe the broad social and economic goals of American society.

Many consumers do not understand how the American marketplace functions. It is important for each of us to comprehend how conditions in the socio-political-economic world affect our personal economic opportunities and well-being. We also should know how our own individual behaviors and economic choices will affect the social-political-economic systems. In the United States, these activities occur in a society founded on the twin pillars of representative democracy and free-market capitalism.

This chapter helps consumers better understand how the economic system of capitalism functions, especially as it operates in the United States. This requires an appreciation of how resources are allocated under capitalism as well as recognition of the vital roles that the federal government's fiscal and monetary policies play in attempting to manage the economy. The concepts of scarcity, democracy and capitalism are explored since they are at the essence of American capitalism. The chapter ends with a review of the broad social and economic goals of American society. Consumers need to recognize that these goals are difficult to reach and they are sometimes in conflict with each other.

How an Economic System Functions

At its essence, an **economic system**, or **economy**, is an organization for the production and distribution of goods and services. It provides the way for economic decisions to be made. More descriptively, an *economic system* is an organized set of institutions, laws, technologies, traditions, ideas, and popular attitudes that propel production, the management of resources, and the conduct of business. To work effectively, an economic system depends on the cooperative efforts of several components, including businesses, governments at all levels, and millions of consumers. Together, these forces determine the answers to the **key economic questions**:

!   What kinds of goods and services shall be produced?

!   How will goods and services be produced?

!   How much shall be produced?

!   For whom shall goods and services be produced?

The central economic problem in any economy is how to satisfy unlimited wants with limited resources. **Resources** are things used in the production process, and resources are limited in supply. After all, each country has only so much land, labor, capital, and management expertise. People's wants are unlimited, as well as variable and changing. It is impossible to satisfy all of them with the limited resources available. Therefore, priorities must be established. The field of **economics** is the study of how people and society choose to employ the scarce productive resources among alternative wants to produce various commodities and distribute them for consumption now or in the future. **Economists** analyze the costs and benefits of improving patterns of resource allocation.

The subject matter of economics is divided into positive economics and normative economics. **Positive economics** is concerned with questions of certainty, such as in describing "what is," in a manner somewhat devoid of norms, values, or political overtones.

Normative economics is concerned with questions of "what ought to be" in a manner that encourages use of value judgments, desirable behaviors, standards or goals, and what is best for society. Economists use scientific, historical, descriptive, and quantitative methods to obtain knowledge. Principles, theories, and policies used to analyze economic behavior frequently come from **models** that are abstractions of reality.

Societies differ in the ways they organize production and consumption in order to cope with the same basic problems and find answers to the key economic questions. The economic system established in a country helps **decide the best use** of that society's resources not just for today, but for future generations as well. There are only two dominant types of economic systems, socialism and capitalism.

Socialism as an Economic System

Socialism is an economic system in which the producers possess both political power and the means of producing and distributing goods. Government owns most resources, other than labor, and centralized economic decision making is the norm. Government politicians, typically elected without opposition, not consumers, decide what kinds of goods and services will be produced, how goods and services will be produced, how much will be produced and for whom will they should be produced. Thus, expenditures by **government** (instead of by consumers or businesses) **play the dominant role** in a socialistic economy, often **exceeding 50 percent** of domestic spending.[1] In socialistic countries, employment with the government greatly exceeds that in the private sector.[2] Since money prices do not control supply and demand, rationing of limited amounts and long waiting lines occur.[3] In socialistic countries where limited market reforms are allowed to function, heavy supervision from the state is still typical.

A few socialistic economic systems around the world (China, North Vietnam, Cuba, and North Korea)[4] are run by the **totalitarian** form of government where one person or party exercises absolute control over all spheres of human life and opposing parties are not permitted to exist. Totalitarian decisions are made to reflect the **narrow views** of a single person or ideology. **Communism** is a political party with an ideology that implies a socialistic economic system and totalitarianism in the political sphere, with individuals subservient to the state.

In the ideal socialistic country, the **motives seem worthy**. Economic justice is achieved when people determine their own needs and take from the common product of society. The

---

[1] Sweden, buffeted by a struggling economy, has begun to trim the benefits of its "welfare state" and reduce its public expenditures that account for nearly **75 percent** of all domestic spending.

[2] According to the Organization for Economic Cooperation and Development, employment of government workers in industrialized countries is 9% in Japan, 14% in Great Britain, **15% in the United States**, 16% in Germany, 16% in Italy, 21% in Canada, and 25% in France.

[3] A **traditional economic system** still exists in many developing nations where long-established customs, religious beliefs, and family practices dominate the society's decisions on the key economic questions of *what*, *how*, *how much* and *for whom*. These economies generally reject consideration of alternative ideas.

[4] Gross domestic product **per capita** in capitalistic South Korea is about $9,000 compared to only $1,000 in communist North Korea. With less than twice the population of the north, South Korea has 10 times the North's number of commercial aircraft, 17 times its gross domestic product, 90 times its automobiles, and external trade over 100 times the North's.

socialist Karl Marx's dictum is, "From each according to his ability, to each according to his needs." However, there are few incentives for producers and workers to innovate and economize in a socialistic economic system. Instead, **stagnation and regimentation** prevail and are usually tolerated by the people. Because its deeds were never matched by its ideals, the socialist economies governed by communists caused the loss of personal freedoms and the deaths of more people than any doctrine in history.

The countries of the former Soviet Union have been moving away from socialism and **toward capitalism**, and for most it has been horribly difficult. To illustrate, in the past decade economic output in Russia declined 30 percent and consumer spending dropped 35 percent. Russia was recently designated by the United States as now having a market economy. The U.S. Commerce Department reports that private companies now account for 70 percent of Russia's economic output. Also, the ruble, Russia's currency, is set by market forces and the country is open to foreign investment.

Capitalism as an Economic System

Decisions involving social and economic problems of each society are made within its own particular economic system. The **American market system**, or **socioeconomic system**, is unique in its market-oriented approach based on the traditions and laws of the United States. Americans' secular values are based on democracy, religious pluralism, opportunity, and individual liberty under constitutional law **guided by the courts**, and it depends on capitalism to make decisions on how scarce resources are allocated among alternative uses. **Capitalism** is an economic system characterized by open competition in a free market, in which the means of production and distribution are privately or corporately owned and development is proportionate to increasing accumulation and reinvestment of profits. Banks, capital markets, and contracts support decentralized capitalism.

Capitalism has enabled more people to **experience freedom and prosperity** than any other economic doctrine in history, yet it is often vilified because it is based upon the selfish motives of property rights and profits. Winston Churchill identified the differences in economic systems best: "Capitalism is the unequal distribution of wealth, and socialism is the equal distribution of misery. In the real world, there are winners and losers."

Property Rights

The success of American capitalism hinges on the fact that the United States is a nation of **laws and legal systems**. Private enterprise is achieved through the legal right of private property. **Property rights** can be defined as the right to use, restrict, or dispose of personal, business property and capital as the owner sees fit. For the most part, property is used by its owners to make a profit.

Private ownership capitalism **relies upon a market system** to allocate resources, goods and services to their most highly valued uses. Thus, most productive efforts in the U.S. are carried out by privately owned corporations, partnerships, and individual citizens. There are some exceptions, such as city-owned bus lines, state-owned liquor stores, and the federal government-owned Hoover Dam. However, most of the factors of production in the U.S. economy are privately owned. The greatest difficulty in exporting capitalism has been the absence of and respect for laws protecting property rights of citizens.

Profit Motivation

Profit in an accounting sense is the value of output less the cost of inputs, or income minus expenses. It is an advantageous return or gain received on a business undertaking after all operating expenses have been met. Profit acts as an **incentive** for business entrepreneurs to undertake the production of goods and services for the satisfaction of customer demand. The profit earned by a business becomes the property of the owners. The motivation for profit explains why businesses are so inventive and dynamic.

Economists say that **economic profit** is the difference between the value of output and the opportunity cost of all inputs, including the opportunity cost of the owner's or shareholder's capital. **Excess profits** can also occur. These are profits above those needed to keep all factors of production busily involved in the entrepreneurial effort. It is important to realize that excess profits serve as a motivation for other entrepreneurs to enter the same line of business to compete for profits. The economic question of for whom to produce is made by *prices* and *income* in a capitalistic economy; thus resources in an economy flow **to where profits are highest**.

The desire for profit can be either **positive or negative**. When it is positive, it can have a tremendous effect on one's personal wealth, create jobs in the community, and lead to successful economic development for the country. When it is negative, profit can lead to exploitation of consumers, businesses, and governments; two examples of which are the dumping of toxic wastes and price-fixing.

Competition

In the American capitalistic market system, competition is directly related to the profit motive. **Competition** is the rivalry between two or more businesses striving for the same customers or market. Competition encourages the most skilled, the most ambitious, and the most efficient to be effective and rise to the highest levels of economic performance. Economists like to say that competition exists when a number of firms sell the same goods, but no one firm is large enough by itself to affect the price of the good.

Today businesses compete on price as well as other factors, such as product improvements, methods of selling, service, and advertising. Competition is wonderful for consumers as long as it **gives them choices** among alternatives. Competition is important in the American economy because it ensures the availability of products and services at low costs (which is in the consumer interest) and helps small businesses enter and thrive in the marketplace.

Adam Smith, the father of neoclassical economics, described the importance of competition in his handbook of economic development entitled *The Wealth of Nations*, published in 1776. He argued that the greatest efficiency in an economy can come from specialization, division of labor, and exchange. Smith contended that government **should not interfere** in the market. Such noninterference would allow producers to compete freely with one another as if guided and regulated by the **invisible hand** of price competition to produce the greatest quantity of goods at the lowest possible prices. This is in contrast to the **visible hand** of government regulators, or what economist Milton Friedman calls "the government's invisible foot."

Smith argues that in a competitive market the producer maximizes profit by being **as efficient as possible**. This is done by keeping prices low, improving the product and selling as many as possible. In this way the producer serves the interests of consumers as well as those of the producer. Smith says that the producer's efforts "promote an end that was no part of his intention." Moreover, "Consumption is the sole end and purpose of all production, and the interest of the producer ought to be attended to only as far as it is necessary for promoting that of the consumer." Competition is absolutely essential to create the changes in demand and supply that occur. This is why **public policy** places great attention on maintaining and strengthening competition.

Mixed Economic Systems Predominate Today

Most economic systems are not purely socialistic or capitalistic. Rather, they are mixed. Most often there is a **mix of private and public** ownership and enterprise, such as in Sweden and the United Kingdom. On a continuum, the United States and Canada are illustrative of somewhat pure capitalism while countries like Cuba and China have extremely socialistic economies. These markets also differ in the extent to which competition or monopoly prevails. Depending upon the culture and politics, each economic system offers individuals different degrees of information, mobility and freedom in the marketplace.

Allocating Resources in the U.S. Economy

The economic system in the United States takes a variety of resources and allocates them primarily through the price mechanism in its market-driven economy. How this occurs is discussed below.

Types of Resources

As a nation, the United States has **limited availability of natural resources** (such as coal, oil, and varieties of ore), limited quality of such materials (such as the availability of high-grade ores), and limited technical skills and money for investment in future development. All these things are resources insofar as the economy is concerned. The task of the economic system is to determine the best combinations of the various factors of production to ensure prosperity and well-being for consumers and businesses alike. Consideration must be given to how much is to be produced and for whom. **Production** is the process of creating finished goods by using the factors of production. The four major factors of production are **labor, land, capital, and management**.

The **"old economy"** of business production, primarily based on the use of physical assets, is evolving toward a **"new economy"** that invests in intangibles like talent, innovation, ideas, intellectual property, technology, brand names, customer base, and innovative business models rather than physical assets. The Internet and the associated industries of information and communications technology are the backbone or infrastructure of the new economy. Global companies will be the true business leaders on a worldwide scale.

ECONOMIC INSIGHT:
Capitalism is Full of Shortcomings

No economic **system is perfect**; neither socialism nor capitalism. Yes, capitalism can deliver ample supplies of goods and services to those who can afford them. But it lacks sufficient mechanisms and incentives to attend to the basic needs of low-income people. Consumer advocate Rhoda Kartapkin sums up the problems of a market economy.[1]

Capitalism has **many weaknesses**. It has little interest in providing information to consumers to ensure wise spending decisions. Markets on their own will not ensure safe food, safe drugs, safe products, or safe technologies. In marketing products and services, capitalism will neither guarantee the truthfulness of advertising nor work to assure consumers a fair and just marketplace.

Capitalism, by definition, is **not designed to conserve** natural resources, preserve the environment, or safeguard bio-diversity. And it does not, by itself, deliver justice or ensure redress for injustice or punish unconscionable business conduct. There is little doubt that capitalism is harsh on vulnerable consumers and inefficient workers. In a capitalistic economy, the profit motive sometimes **encourages companies to cheat consumers**, mistreat workers, or ruin the environment.

Marketplace imperfections exist in all capitalistic societies, says Stephen J. Brobeck, executive director of the Consumer Federation of America. Among **its many flaws** are:

1.   Bottlenecks that seriously hinder or prevent competition;

2.   Predatory marketing practices that restrict competition and prey upon the unsophisticated;

3.   Insufficient information or inability to process information that hinders effective competition;

4.   Products containing hidden or delayed adverse health or safety impacts;

5.   Deceptive and unconscionable sales practices (often directed at the least well-informed and lowest-income groups); and

6.   Inadequate marketplace pricing of essential but rapidly depleting natural resources.

Capitalism is **not self-motivated** to ensure that goods are safe, of good quality, fairly priced, and honestly marketed. Capitalism is **not guided by a moral mandate** that includes fairness, equity, or concern for future generations. These are goals of the consumer movement which came into being as a counter force, as a **contravening power** to business, in an attempt to try to offset the built-in failures of the market system .

---

[1]See Rhoda H. Karpatkin (1999, Spring), Toward a fair and just marketplace for all consumers: The responsibilities of marketing professionals, *Journal of Public Policy and Marketing*, 18;1, pp. 118-122. Also see articles on lending institutions, life insurance companies, and shoe manufacturers in the July 1998 issue of *Consumer Reports*.

Resource Availability

Resources available usually remain reasonably stable or decline over time, but the **population keeps growing**.[5] Therefore, sooner or later production falls behind population growth. This will result in a lower level of living unless the supply of resources, including substitutes, increases faster than the population grows. This may occur because of advanced

---

[5] According to the United Nations Population Fund, the world's 6 billion population is likely to nearly double to 9.5 billion by 2025 and to reach 14 billion before the end of the next century, unless birth control use increases dramatically around the world (currently used by 45 percent of women).

technology, the production of synthetic raw materials, the development of new ideas, skills, and research, the accumulation of **capital** (any form of material wealth used or available for the production of more wealth, such as money), and general initiative and creativity. Of course some resources are finite, such as coal and oil, whereas others are renewable, such as timber.

How Resources are Allocated

Key factors that affect how resources are allocated are **supply and demand**, the price mechanism, government and large corporations. Scholars have noted that perhaps the major economic event in the twentieth century in the United States has been the creation of large corporate entities. By their existence, corporations have taken on **many of the characteristics of governments**. The policy decisions that governments and many corporations make create an enormous force in how resources are allocated. For example, the decisions to safeguard the environment have created several new industries concerned with pollution, waste, and related issues.

The supply of and demand for resources are the primary factors that affect the allocation decisions of the market. If a great deal of one resource is needed to make a particular product that is valuable to a society, the allocation of that resource will be **diverted away** from use in products of lesser value that employ smaller amounts of the resource. For example, the high demand for petroleum in the production of plastics is different from the demand for petroleum for use in kerosene in today's market. The premise of supply and demand is that such buying and selling **leads to optimal outcomes**.

Consumers continually demand products through their purchases. If a lawnmower of questionable safety is manufactured, consumers can either accept or reject it. If they buy it, they accept it; if not, they reject it. Essentially, the consumer casts an economic vote for or against the product by this action. An **economic vote (dollar vote)**, therefore, is the spending or non-spending of dollars for products and services.

The Price Mechanism at Work

Price is the exchange value stated in terms of money. Pricing goods is a complex task. Originally, each seller establishes a price based on a primary need to survive in the market—to make a profit. Often firms seek to earn a targeted **return on investment (ROI)**. This is the amount of income earned on an investment and it is often expressed as a percentage. Most companies need to earn an ROI of 20 percent or more to be successful and grow. As an illustration, to achieve this goal using a cost-based approach, a firm might determine that the total cost of manufacturing and marketing 100,000 compact discs is $500,000; that works out to $5 a unit. If the manufacturer seeks a 20 percent profit, the wholesale price will be $6 ($5 × 120%).

A retailer may then price the purchase of 1,000 compact discs at $12, representing a **100 percent markup**, knowing that the average markup might eventually fall to 20 or 30 percent because of price reductions, scratched disks, unsold items and the costs of selling the goods (employee salaries, rent, utilities, financing, etc.). Sellers use a variety of pricing strategies in attempting to achieve their marketing goals. As a general rule, it is to the economic benefit of both sellers and consumers alike to allow prices to be established by **operation of the free market** rather than some government agency or legislation.

AN ECONOMIC FOCUS ON...Standard and Level of Consumption and Living*

The indiscriminate use of the concepts **standard and level of consumption** and **standard and level of living** is prevalent in the spoken word of politicians and the writing of popular media as well as in academic publications. The concept **standard** refers to the level of material and nonmaterial goods and services that an individual or a group *desires to attain*, whereas the concept **level** refers to the *actual situation that has been achieved* and is being experienced.

Even though early academicians did not clearly distinguish between the concepts standard and level of living, they pointed out the importance of these concepts. Watkins wrote "the **standard of life** is the central fact in the dynamics of consumption, and hence is of dominant importance for the theory of economic and social progress".[1] Devine, in stressing the significance of standard of life wrote, "the greatest national asset of any civilized, enlightened, prosperous, and progressive people is the standard of life of its adult population." [2] Devine, who was a sociologist, also defined **standard of living** as "that spiritual atmosphere, that indefinable force, compounded of income and what we buy with it, ideals and tastes and the environment provided by our fellow, that is something different from any of them, a power to which unconsciously we defer in every choice we make, and which we frequently invoke to sustain arguments or justify general policies." [3]

The economist Ely, however, defined the standard of living somewhat differently as "the number and character of the wants that a man considers more important than marriage and family constitute his standard of life." [4] Sumner, a social psychologist, defined **standard of living** as, "the measure of decency and suitability in material comfort (diet, dress, dwelling, etc.) that is traditional and habitual to a subgroup." [5]

It can be seen from the above discussion that early writers defined standard of living differently depending upon their academic orientation. Davis is credited with clearly distinguishing between the concepts standard and level of living. He defined **standard of living** as "the plane of living that an individual or a group earnestly seeks and strives to attain, to maintain if attained, to preserve if threatened, and to regain if lost." [6]

The **level of living** (or **plane of living**), according to Davis, is composed of several things that a person has currently attained: the level of consumption, working conditions, possessions, freedoms, and atmosphere. **Consumption** includes purchased goods and services as well as having access to and using goods provided by either the public sector or the environment without charge.

Working conditions include hours and intensity of work, regularity of employment and security, health benefits, safety, opportunity for advancement, comfort and beauty of the surrounding environment, and congeniality of personal relationships. **Possessions** include tangible physical stocks of goods, intangible ownership of savings and investments, insurance protection. **Freedoms** include those related to expression, speech, movement, association, religion, learning, and earning. Atmosphere includes the feelings of being wanted, loved, secure, and harmony with one's fellows in the home and outside the home.

Note that every variable of these components of the level of living places certain demands upon time and space. These demands may be met or avoided, enjoyed, accepted, or despised.

Linder argues that "a given pattern of consumption is accompanied by a certain way of living, reflected in the amounts of time that an individual allocates to his various consumption goods."[7] Simply stated, consumption itself requires time. Having relatively little time available for consumption may lead to **simultaneous consumption** (the consumption of more than one item at the same time), **successive consumption** (using the item for a short period of time or not consuming it completely before using another item), and/or using a more expensive version of a commodity. Clearly, time is a scarce commodity that should be taken into consideration when defining the level of living.

Space is another very important factor to consider when examining the level of living of an individual or a group. Both time and space set limits on the choices available in human life, and thus constitute the spatio-temporal framework within which people interact. The following three situations illustrate the importance of space as a limiting factor in maximizing satisfaction. First, a person may possess a good and have the time to use it, yet lack the space necessary for use of the good. Imagine yourself having a tennis racket, balls, and the time to play with your partner. But because tennis courts are not available, you can not play. In this type of situation, space may be called **limitational space**.

The second situation may exist when the consumer good is available, but because of the simultaneous use of space by other individuals, additional time is required for consumption. In our crowded cities, this situation is prevalent when driving, especially during rush hour. Because other drivers are using the same streets, travel from one point to another may take longer than if fewer drivers were present. In this type of situation, space may be called **interactional space**.

In the third situation, the good is available, time for consumption is available, but space required for consumption is not available at a desirable location. For example, you may go to the theater to watch a play, only to find that the seat you would prefer to have is already taken. So you select another, less preferred seat. In this case, consumption takes place, but on a lower level of satisfaction than you desired. This situation exemplifies **locational space**.

Given the vital role of time and space in consumption activities, the content of the level of living should not only include consumption, working conditions, possessions, freedoms and atmosphere, but **also the resources of time and space**.

[1]Watkins, G.P. (1915). Welfare as an Economic Quantity (Houghton Mifflin Company), 97.

[2]Devine, E.T. (1915). The Normal Life (Survey Associates), 157.

[3]Ibid, 156.

[4]Ely, R.T. (1923). Outlines of Economics (MacMillan), 378.

[5]Sumner, W.G. (1940). Folkways: A Study of the Sociological Importance of Usage, Manners, Customs, Mores, and Morals (Ginn and Company), 156.

[6]Davis, J.S. (1945). Standards and Content of Living, *American Economic Review*, (35), 10.

[7]Linder, S.B. (1970). The Harried Leisure Class (Columbia University Press), 112.

*Mohamed Abdel-Ghany, Professor, The University of Alabama

As the demand for specific products increases, manufacturers will try to supply more. As these manufacturers use more resources, the market prices of these needed resources will help decide who gets the resources. As a resource in high demand becomes more scarce, the **price normally rises**. Therefore, higher prices ultimately place a restriction on utilization and allocation priorities are established. Prices thus reach a point where demand for a resource is roughly equal to supply. Actual prices, however, are also influenced by custom, tradition, competition, and public authority.

As a resource, energy is very important in today's economy because it is a high-priority item. Energy-producing resources in America are at times in good supply and at other times in short supply. To buy these resources (oil, for example) from other countries is sometimes very expensive. Consequently, prices rise for consumers and become too high for many to afford. In such an instance, priorities are established primarily by the prices charged. Conversely, if **buying power** is low (people have little money to spend for a given resource), regardless of availability, that resource will not be heavily used because there is no demand.

Prices in the supply/demand scenario are originally set by sellers. Maynes states that the **price mechanism** is "a system of motivation and error correction."[6] He explains that a rising price signals that a particular seller is performing well, "other things being equal," and more goods should be produced. A price fall indicates the opposite. Sellers are motivated to respond to price signals by their self-interest in profits, higher wages, interest and rent. Further, over time the market economy is a "system of error correction." A fall in demand for a good, other things being equal, signals that the firm is doing something wrong and that further errors on the part of the firm will lead to financial bankruptcy. Note also that the price signal is a crude device because it communicates failure, but not the causes. The economists' statement **"other things being equal"** comes from the Latin phrase **ceteris paribus**, meaning everything else is held constant. Such assumptions are crucial to the models economists develop when making hypotheses.

The Circular Flow of Economic Activity

The major actors in the American economy are consumers, producers, and government. Figure 6-1 shows the mechanism by which land, labor, capital, and management **resources are allocated** among these components of the economic system. The **circular flow** of economic activity is the process by which a society determines the remuneration to the factors of production and by which it distributes income to the various components of the economy. The figure shows how goods and payment for them move among the various sectors of the American economy. Producers depend on individual employees to do the work, individuals depend on producers to employ them, consumers depend on producers to produce goods and services, producers depend on consumers to buy, and government takes in money through taxes and also makes expenditures. The model shows an oversimplified picture of the real world, but it does provide a useful tool to **visualize the complications** of the economic world in which consumers live.

---

[6]Maynes, E. S. (1992, October 23), *Consumerism* (unpublished paper.)

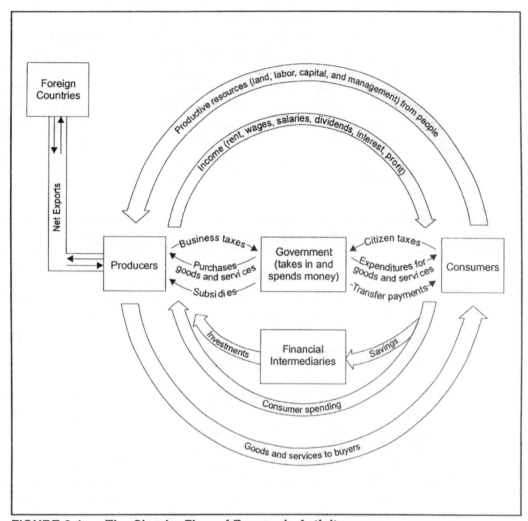

FIGURE 6-1   The Circular Flow of Economic Activity

The Multiplier Effect

Assume for a moment that the government wanted to increase national income by $10 billion so that more people would have jobs resulting in increased tax revenues (because employed people pay taxes). To accomplish this goal, would government have to increase its own autonomous spending by $10 billion? The answer is "No," and the reason is the multiplier effect. The **multiplier effect** is the dollar change in income produced by a change in expenditures made independent of income. It demonstrates that an **increase in one sector** of the economy will result in an **increase elsewhere** in the economy.

For example, an increase in **government spending** of $10 billion on **infrastructure** (the basic facilities, equipment and installations needed for the functioning of a society, such as highways, bridges, dams, and water systems) immediately increases the incomes of construction workers by $10 billion. The construction workers spend $8 billion on domestic goods (80 percent), $1 billion on imported items (10 percent), and $1 billion is saved (10 percent). The $8 billion spent (groceries, rent, clothing, etc.) becomes income for another group of workers who then spend 80 percent of their $8 billion on domestic goods ($6.4 billion), while spending $0.8

billion (10 percent) on imported goods and saving $0.8 billion (10 percent). Each round of spending becomes smaller but the overall **total effect is quite large**.

As one's disposable income rises, consumption and savings rise by a certain proportion. Consumers typically spend 90 percent of any extra income they receive and save 10 percent. The causes of this effect come from the **marginal propensity to consume (MPC)**, the **marginal propensity to import (MPI)** and the **marginal propensity to save (MPS)**. The MPC is the change in consumption as a proportion of change in disposable income; the MPI is the change in consumption due to spending on imported items. The MPS is the change in savings as a proportion of change in disposable income. The **multiplier** (1/MPS + MPI) equals 5 (1/20) when MPS and MPI are both 0.10. Thus, an initial increase in expenditure of $10 billion results in a total change in the economy of $50 billion.

How the U.S. Government Tries to Manage the Economy

Government plays a vital role in the U.S. economy, especially in its use of fiscal and monetary policies. The Congress uses its taxing and spending policies and the Federal Reserve Board uses its monetary policies to help achieve social and economic goals.

Fiscal Policies: Taxing and Spending

To exist and perform its duties, government must **raise taxes and spend money**. By taxing and spending, government influences both the patterns of production and consumption. It does this by purchasing goods and services to provide for the public good and by making **transfer payments** for which it does not expect anything in return. For example, government purchases many goods and services, such as roads and school buildings, teachers' salaries, and defense armaments. Transfer payments include veterans' benefits, welfare payments, and farm subsidies. According to the Office of Management and Budget and the Joint Committee on Taxation, taxpayers spend $55 billion in direct subsidies to business (including $30 billion for agribusiness) and another $59 billion in tax breaks for corporations.

Government also **redistributes wealth** among the population from the taxpayers through a progressive tax system. In general, governments use both progressive taxes and regressive taxes to raise money. For example, federal income tax is a **progressive tax**, since it is a tax that demands an increasing portion of a person's income as income increases. A state sales tax is an example of a **regressive tax**, since it demands a decreasing proportion of a person's income as income increases. To illustrate, a person earning $50,000 has an easier time paying a sales tax of $24 when purchasing a television set than a person earning $12,000, who has to pay the same $24 tax on the same purchase. (See www.el.com/elinks/taxes.)

The taxing and spending policies of the federal government **affect interest rates**, inflation, employment, production, and economic growth. **Inflation** is the value of money in terms of goods and services. As inflation occurs, it reflects rising prices for goods and factors of production, including land, labor, capital, and management. There are two kinds of inflation, and both result from an overheated economy: cost-push and demand-pull. **Cost-push** occurs when rising demand for a commodity such as gasoline or steel pushes prices upward. **Demand-pull** occurs when the supply of goods and services such as people with good skills does not meet demand. Government tries to control the economy by **coordinating** its fiscal and monetary policies.

Fiscal policy is the federal government's policy with respect to taxing, spending, and management of the national debt; it is the government's effort to raise taxes and allocate money. Fiscal policy is a powerful tool for influencing the flow of spending and thus for promoting economic growth and stability. To stimulate demand for goods and services, government can **lower taxes and/or increase its own spending**. Note that when government imposes taxes on citizens and businesses, it lessens the ability of these citizens and businesses to compete or bid for productive resources because they have less money. Lower taxes keep more money in the pockets of consumers and businesses, which they can then use to buy goods and services. Increased government spending causes businesses to expand their production of goods and services to meet the increased demand. Economic expansion and growth are the result. The reverse action is often taken during times of high inflation. Raising taxes and reducing government spending both take money out of circulation. This reduces demand and slows economic growth, which usually lowers inflation.

DID YOU KNOW?
Bush's Gigantic Federal Budget Deficits

The George W. Bush Administration and the Republican Congress have given the nation its **largest spending deficits** in history. Depending upon growth in the economy, the annual budget deficits in the years ahead are projected to be $400+ billion, not including money for the war with Iraq and post-war rebuilding expenses. "Overspending" and "Big Deficits are Okay" is the new mantra of the Republicans. Only a third of the increases in spending go for homeland security and national defense; the remainder goes for things like highways, farm subsidies and tax cuts for the wealthy.

The Republican editor-in-chief of *U.S. News & World Report*, Mortimer B. Zuckerman, says that "In just two years the United States has morphed from a country with a long-term budget surplus, a strong currency, and a decreasing national debt into a country with a long-term budget deficit, a weakening currency, and a spiraling national debt."[1] The federal **national debt** is $6.3 trillion and rising. At the end of the Clinton Administration that had four consecutive **budget surpluses** (the first federal surpluses in almost 30 years), the country had a projected $5.6 trillion surplus over the next ten years.

The Bush Administration's reduction of tax rates for upper-income Americans (dropping the top rate from 38.6 to 35 percent) **eliminated all of the surplus**, and Bush now projects a 10-year deficit of $4+ trillion. The Bush tax cuts will ensure that tax revenues will not go up in Washington to pay down the deficits. This means that eventually the young people in society are going to have to pay much higher taxes to first, stop the deficits, and second, pay for government programs for their elders.

[1]M. B. Zuckerman (May 19, 2003), *U.S. News & World Report*, p. 64.

Monetary Policies: Managing Money and Credit

Monetary policy is the federal government's policy to attempt to manage the supply of money and credit in the economy so as to influence total spending and thus have an effect on general economic stability, consumption, a stable dollar, sustained non-inflationary economic growth, and long-run stability in our international balance of payments. If money is scarce, interest rates go up; **lower interest rates** encourage economic growth.

In the United States, the Federal Reserve System (www.frs.gov) runs the nation's **central banking system**. The Federal Reserve System, commonly called the **Fed**, was created in 1913 and is governed by a management group known as the **Board of Governors**.

Current laws set three primary goals for the Fed: (1) maximize employment, (2) stabilize prices, and (3) maintain moderate long-term interest rates. The Federal Reserve System is the non-political operating arm of the Federal Reserve Board. The System consists of a seven-member Board of Governors with headquarters in Washington, D.C. and twelve Reserve Banks located in major cities throughout the United States. The Fed acts as an **independent regulatory agency** that influences the amount of money and credit utilized by commercial banks.

The Fed performs **many banking services**. In addition to providing checking accounts for the Treasury, issuing and redeeming government securities, and acting as a fiscal agent for the U.S. government, the Federal Reserve System also moves currency and coin into and out of circulation, collects and processes millions of checks each day, and transfers billions of dollars worth of electronic payments.

The Board of Governors of the Federal Reserve System (Fed) uses **three tools** to manage money and credit:

1. Reserve Requirements

The Federal Reserve **sets reserve requirements** for its member banks. **Member banks** include all federally chartered national banks and any state-chartered banks that request to be members. The **reserve requirements (or a reserve rate)** are a percentage of total deposits that depository institutions cannot lend out but must maintain every day in the form of vault cash or as deposits with a Federal Reserve bank. The reserve requirement serves as a backup for the deposits of consumers, businesses and governments. The reserve requirement is currently 10 percent. Each of the nation's 10,000+ depository institutions must take action to maintain the proper reserves on a daily basis. Overall, this is called the **fractional reserve system** because banks keep less than 100 percent of their deposits on hand.

A **low reserve rate** lowers the banks' cost of funds, so they lower the price of loans to businesses and consumers. Thus, a low reserve rate makes it easier for firms to expand and invest. Lower interest rates on credit cards, personal loans and home mortgages make it easier for consumers to spend, which adds to overall spending in the economy.

In effect, lowering the reserve rate **puts dollars into the banking system** that banks can lend and re-lend again. The multiplier effect becomes quite powerful with only a 10 percent reserve ratio. Note, too, that the banking system actually *creates money* as each individual bank can lend its excess reserves (up to the balance of the remaining 90 percent of funds deposited) which are then spent, deposited by others and loaned again. For example, when you are granted a loan, the money just appears as numbers on your bank statement. The **bank creates the money** simply by adding the numerals to your account. Recognize that this created money then disappears as you repay the loan because each repayment is taken out of some other personal account.

A **high reserve rate requirement** has a **contracting effect** on the economy because it reduces the amount of money available for lending. Changes in the reserve requirement occur infrequently; only when very strong action is warranted. During a time of high inflation, the Fed is likely to raise the reserve requirement to tighten the money supply and the ripples of such a policy multiply many times throughout the economy. Member banks then may be forced to either curtail loans or sell securities, and this should slow demand, which should lower prices on goods and services. Since deposits vary daily and the legally-required reserve must be met every day, when a bank runs short it must borrow needed funds (usually only for overnight) from an approved source. When a bank borrows from another commercial bank that has excess reserves to lend, the interest rate paid is called the **federal funds rate**.

2. Open-market Operations

Fine tuning of the money supply is attempted by the Fed when it uses its powers in **open-market operations**. This is the buying and selling of government securities by the Federal Reserve System undertaken to influence the volume of money and credit in the economy. The Fed only buys or sells its own debt instruments: Treasury Bonds, Notes, and Bills. If the Fed wanted to tighten up the money supply, its **Federal Open Market Committee (FOMC)** might direct the **Federal Reserve Bank of New York** (the Fed's trading office) to sell bonds to banks. Money to pay for these bonds flows out of the economy and into the Fed because when the member banks write checks to purchase Treasury securities, they use funds that in effect tie up a larger percentage of total bank funds. Since this money is no longer available for lending, such an action decreases the money supply.

When the Fed wants to increase the money supply, perhaps to help stimulate the economy out of a **recession** (a period of moderate decline in the national economy characterized by decreasing business activity, falling prices, and unemployment), it does the opposite. Here the Fed purchases Treasury securities back from banks, which makes the member banks more liquid and therefore able to make loans.

3. Discount Rate

The Fed also **sets the discount rate.** That is the interest rate at which **member financial institutions may borrow money**, usually for short periods, from a regional Federal Reserve bank. It is called a discount rate because the interest is subtracted up front when the loan is made to a member bank rather than collected later upon repayment. During a time of rising inflation when the economy is overheating, the Fed is likely to "step on the brakes" by raising interest rates, because this will discourage borrowing by banks which then will grant fewer loans to consumers and businesses. Here the Fed tries to engineer a "soft landing" by slowing the economy just enough to avoid higher inflation and to avoid a "hard landing" of a recession. Without "easy credit," homes go unbuilt, vehicles go unsold, and some workers in those industries and others will lose their jobs.

Alternatively, when the economy is sluggish or slowing down, the Fed will "step on the gas" by **lowering the discount rate to encourage economic growth**, because the banks will be inclined to borrow more from the Fed and thus lend more. Changes in the Fed's discount rate often pressure other lenders (e.g., savings and loan associations, credit unions, consumer finance companies) to change their interest rates in the same direction. Rates for automobile and housing loans are quickly affected by changes in the discount rate.

Note that the Fed has researched the issue of its impact on the economy and concluded that over the years, the **velocity of the money supply**, a measure of the number of times money changes hands in the economy, is 1.6527. Every $100 the Fed puts into the economy grows to $165.27 by the end of the year. Thus when the Board of Governors of the Federal Reserve System wants to spark up the economy and encourage economic growth, the Federal Reserve System follows a policy of **easy money**. Reserve requirements are low, interest rates are low, and money and credit are readily available. Thus consumers are encouraged to buy homes, clothing and automobiles, which stimulates further production of such goods. Companies borrow to expand their businesses and hire more people.

Moreover, the fiscal and monetary tools available to the government are fairly blunt instruments, and there is considerable **lag time** before effects can be seen and properly measured. Nevertheless, these are the tools available and government does the best it can. The whole idea is to try to reduce the extremes of the economic cycles: rapid inflation and serious recession or depression.

Scarcity, Democracy, and Capitalism are at the Essence of American Society

The topics of scarcity, democracy and capitalism are examined below. Recognize that these three concepts are at the essence of American society.

Scarcity

To accomplish its economic goals, society must make choices about **how to use** its available resources. The fundamental economic problem facing all societies is that of **scarcity**; that is the short supply of productive resources relative to the ever-increasing needs and wants of the people.

Democracy

In the United States, society is conceptually organized as a **democracy**, which is government by the people, exercised either directly or through elected representatives. In a *true* democracy, however, the majority can do whatever it wants, including **restricting the freedoms of the minority**. The framers of the Constitution of the United States feared a true democracy and instead created a republic to prevent government from imposing forms of tyranny on the citizens. (To verify, check the pledge of allegiance to the flag.) A constitutional government form called a **republic**, such as the one we have in the U.S., provides that the citizens and the government are both subject to certain laws established to protect and enhance—not restrict or deny—citizens' rights to life, liberty, and property. Instead of resorting to violence or threats of violence to make changes, democratic governments submit their ideas and programs to periodic free elections. Laws and representatives rule the U.S., not the people directly.

In a **weak democratic form of government**, policy decisions are often made **in favor** of the strong capitalistic interests in the economy, indulging the interests of business. In a strong democratic government, decisions are made by elected representatives who are occasionally accountable to the multiple interests in society (e.g., church, organized labor, physicians, consumers, environmentalists, abortion rights advocates). The United States has a strong representative democratic form of government operating within a capitalistic or free market- oriented economic/political system. The accountable government tries to solicit the views of all affected special-interest groups. In a democracy like the Republic of the United States, the power in society comes from the bottom up—from the people to the government.

Capitalism

Economic **systems vary** from country to country because people have different traditions and different ideas about how to use their limited resources. Thus, the people in each society make different choices about how they want their economy to operate.

The economic system in America is called **capitalism**, and it is characterized by **open competition** in a free market in which the means of production and distribution are privately or corporately owned. In a **capitalistic economic system**, decisions as to what to produce, how much to produce, whether to produce for the present or the future, and how to distribute production are determined primarily by individuals and businesses.

Broad Social and Economic Goals of American Society

Every economic decision is made in light of certain goals. Public-policy decisions made by societies are based on **broad social values and goals**, while individuals make decisions based on their personal values and goals. A **public policy** is a plan or course of action by a government designed to influence and determine decisions, actions, and other matters concerning or affecting the community or people rather than private affairs or interests.

The United States is firmly committed to a great **variety of worthy economic goals**: stable prices, a balanced budget, no tax increases, a steadily declining trade deficit, and no cuts in benefits to the elderly, the poor, the sick, or anybody else. Achieving such economic goals is very difficult. Public policy making can occur in any branch of government—executive, legislative, or judicial. Public policies are shaped by a number of factors, such as the availability of resources, past experiences of the policy-shaping person or group, and the ideas of concerned public officials and activist citizens.

In its eternal quest to resolve the problem of scarcity and address the key economic questions for its population, each society establishes a number of economic values and goals. The **primary economic goals of American society** are (1) economic freedom, (2) economic efficiency, (3) public well being and safety, (4) full employment, (5) price stability, (6) economic growth, (7) economic productivity, (8) economic security, and (9) economic equity and justice.

Society's economic goals are at times **in conflict** with one another, or at least under substantial tension. When goals conflict, **difficult choices** have to be made. Economic goals give society a sense of direction and a benchmark from which to measure progress.

Primary Goal: Economic Freedom

The first broad social and economic goal of American society is **economic freedom**. Economic freedoms are rights that business, labor, and consumers enjoy in the American economy pertaining to the production, development, and management of material wealth. These freedoms are given to American consumers in the Bill of Rights of the Constitution, along with other rights and freedoms. People are **free to make decisions about the use of resources** under their control.

People decide for themselves if they want to own property, which job or career they want, whether they want to move freely across our land and whether they want to save or spend their money in the marketplace. They make these decisions without being coerced by others. Other economic freedoms include the right of a worker to bargain with his or her employer, to join a union, to go on strike, to change employment, to quit his or her job, or to retire. At the heart of our economic system are **citizens making their own decisions**, not government.

For businesses, the concept of economic freedom means the opportunity to pursue profits and the absence of unnecessary regulation. Privately owned, profit-seeking businesses can be started anew or changed as market forces demand; this is the right to **private** or **free enterprise**. Economic freedom gives businesspeople, merchants, producers, and manufacturers the right to **decide on the nature and method of operation** of their businesses, such as when and where to advertise, and how to market their goods and services.

Consumers have **freedom of choice in the marketplace**—that is, the freedom to buy or not. Consumers have the right to decide what kind of home to live in, what goods to buy, what papers and books to read, and how to manage their towns and cities. Importantly, consumers also have the freedom to make many informed decisions. Each consumer must decide what a purchasing decision means, what it will mean in the short run, and how it will affect others (environmentally and socially) in the long run. Therefore, knowledge is basic to economic freedom.

The founders of the United States believed that the nation could best be served if citizens had the freedom to produce, trade, and consume as they saw fit, with a minimum of regulation by government. This approach of government is called **laissez-faire**. Thus, we use terms like free enterprise, private enterprise, and capitalism to describe the American economic system.

Primary Goal: Economic Efficiency

Another broad social and economic goal of American society is **economic efficiency**. This is a situation where no one in society can be made better off without making someone else worse off. Economic efficiency from a business firm's perspective occurs when it produces a given quantity and quality of goods at the lowest possible cost. Economic efficiency in a market system occurs through the millions of self-interested actions of participants in that system. Efficiency results because people own their resources and will give them to others **only when the exchange makes them better off**.

For individuals and families, **consumer efficiency** is getting value for one's money, making the best of one's abilities, and using one's income, wealth, energy, and limited time to get the greatest benefits. The well-being of individuals and families is greatly dependent on their economic efficiency. Those who are **more efficient have a higher level of living** than others with similar resources.

Primary Goal: To Promote Public Well-being and Safety

A major function of government is to promote public well-being and safety. **Numerous government regulations** exist to help in this endeavor: pure food and drug laws, product safety standards, environmental standards, industrial safety standards, consumer protection regulations, equal opportunity laws, and fair labor practices laws. A variety of federal, state, and local government agencies administer appropriate laws and regulations in these areas.

Primary Goal: Full Employment

American society also holds **full employment** as another economic and social goal, which suggests that all of an economy's resources, particularly labor, are fully utilized. An **unemployment rate** of zero cannot occur because there always is some frictional, structural, and cyclical unemployment resulting from such events as plant closings, career changes and worker mobility. The economist's typical measure of full employment is probably about 5 or 6 percent. The **natural rate of unemployment**, is the minimum level to which unemployment can be reduced without stimulating inflation. That rate is about 4 percent.

The social goal of full employment recognizes the lost output that accompanies high unemployment, the **squandering of human resources**, and the costs to individuals and families because of economic hardships. From an individual perspective, people not only want to get jobs, but they also want to keep them. From society's perspective, it is vital to keep the productive resources of labor at work.

Recall that the **central economic problem** of any society is that productive resources are **scarce relative to the wants of the population**. Therefore, it is a colossal waste to allow some of those productive resources to stand idle. Industrialized nations face the harsh tradeoff between providing low-wage jobs for millions of their less skilled workers or leaving those people with no jobs at all. Those with inadequate skills live in a world that increasingly demands higher levels of skills.

Technological changes and competition from developing nations have **reduced the demand** for some types of skilled workers. This adds to unemployment in many countries and it holds down wages of such workers in the United States.

The **flexible wage system** in the U.S. keeps the costs of low-skilled labor down, so most people can find employment. In European countries such as France, where rigid regulations and expensive benefits programs exist, low-skilled workers are very expensive to hire, and this forces **unemployment rates quite high**: 9% in Great Britain, 11% in Germany, 13% in France and 18% in Spain.

Primary Goal: Price Stability

Another social and economic goal of society is **price stability**. This means that expected changes in the average price level are small enough and gradual enough that they do not materially enter business and household financial decisions. It means the **absence of significant changes in prices**. While reasonable price stability might see prices rising 2 or 3 percent per year, greater increases require consumers, businesses, and governments to make costly adjustments to offset the effects of inflation. Price stability contributes to economic efficiency, in part, by reducing the uncertainties that tend to inhibit investment.

Inflation is signaled by rising prices for goods and increased factors of production. Inflation is caused by too much demand, sharply increasing costs of products and/or too much money circulating in the economy. During times of price inflation, most workers' real incomes will go down. **Real income** is money income relative to the prices of goods and services. It is what one's money will actually buy in contrast to the designated value of the money itself. Although the purchasing power of the dollar has declined over the past 50 years, today we have many more dollars in income. Because **incomes have not kept up with inflation** over the past 20 years, the resulting purchasing power of most consumers has remained flat or declined slightly.

Stages in the Economic Cycle

An **economy** is a system of managing the productive and employment resources of a country, community, or business. Government attempts to regulate the American economy to maintain stable prices (low inflation) and stable levels of employment (low unemployment). The intent is to achieve sustained economic growth. An **economic cycle** (sometimes called a **business cycle**) is a wavelike pattern of economic activity that includes four temporary phases that undulate from boom to bust: expansion, recession, depression, and recovery (Figure 6-2).

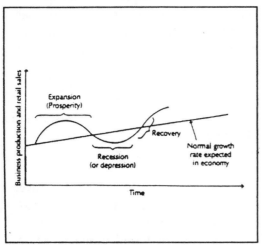

**FIGURE 6-2   Phases of the Economic Cycle:
A Roller Coaster**

The optimal phase of the economic cycle is the **expansion stage**, where production is at high capacity, there is little unemployment, retail sales are high, and inflation and interest rates are low or falling. This makes it easy for consumers to buy homes, cars, and expensive goods on credit; it also encourages businesses to borrow to expand production to meet the increased demand. As the demand for credit increases, short-term interest rates rise because more borrowers want money.

As consumers and businesses purchase more goods, this increase exerts inflationary pressure on prices. Eventually, interest rates and inflation climb high enough to stifle consumer and business borrowing, send stock prices down and choke off the expansion. The result is flat economic growth or even a decline. In such situations the economy often moves toward a **recession**, generally described as a decline in business activity or a downturn in the economy. Many economists further define a recession as two consecutive quarters of a decline in economic activity.[1]

The phases or stages in the economic cycle are officially defined by the U.S. Department of Commerce's Business Cycle Dating Committee within the National Bureau of Economic Research. Its definition of a **recession** is "a recurring period of decline in total output, income, employment and trade, usually lasting from six months to a year and marked by widespread contractions in many sectors of the economy."[2] Especially difficult recessions are

sometimes characterized as **stagflation;** that occurs when the painful combination of slow economic growth and high unemployment simultaneously are confronted with rising inflation. During recessions consumers typically become pessimistic about their future buying plans. The average U.S. recession is an economic decline of 2.2 percent that lasts for 11 months. The decline during the 1990-1991 recession was 1.1 percent; the decline during the 1973-75 recession was nearly 5 percent. The U.S. has had 9 recessions since World War II.

A **depression** is a severe downward phase of the economic cycle where unemployment is very high, prices are very low, purchasing power is sharply decreased, and economic activity has virtually ceased. Depressions do not occur in the American economy anymore (the last one occurred throughout the 1930s and into the early 1940s) because of the existence of so many social and economic safety-net programs, such as insured bank deposits, unemployment benefits and social security. Instead, the U.S. economy now occasionally experiences prolonged periods of sluggish economic growth (such as 1989-1991 and 2001-2002) where it may occasionally experience quarters of very minimal or negative growth. This also can be called a **psychological recession** because very slight economic growth (perhaps 0.5 to 1.5 percent) and persistently high unemployment (6.0 percent or more) can together negate the positive expectations about the future held by consumers and businesses causing them to continue to depress spending that prolongs the negative scenario.[3] Sometimes this pushes the economy back into a technically defined recession.

The slowdown eventually ends and consumers and businesses become more optimistic. The economy moves into the **recovery phase** where levels of production, employment, and retail sales begin to rapidly improve, allowing the overall economy to experience some growth from its previously weakened state. The stock market and new housing starts generally lead the way. To complete the business cycle, the economy moves from the recovery phase into the expansion phase. The whole economic cycle normally takes 3 to 4 years from start to finish.

---

[1] Economist Robert J. Samuelson observes that, "What no one says (but everyone recognizes) is that recessions are a grim sort of industrial policy. They promote efficiency and punish sloppiness."

[2] A **rolling recession** is a term used to describe the fact that while the overall U.S. economy might be enjoying growth there may be one or more geographic regions that are experiencing economic decline. A rolling recession seemingly moves around the country from one geographic region to another.

[3] A **psychological recession** is partly caused by personal experiences of unemployment and the fear of job insecurity. Other causal factors include an omnipresent communications system that constantly offers large doses of negative information, such as violence on television and in movies, alleged "scandals" on tabloid television, and "action" news about death and mayhem on the streets. Americans in recent decades are not and have not been optimistic about the future. Rather, discontent is rampant and many people are anxious about tomorrow.

One gauge of the amount of inflation is calculated monthly as the government's **consumer price index (CPI)**, which is an index of price changes in hundreds of basic commodities and services. The CPI is calculated by the Bureau of Labor Statistics (BLS).

The CPI was revised recently. It now takes into account consumer behavior when people buy a cheaper item if the price of what they prefer has risen. Thus, the CPI no long seriously **overstates the cost of living**. The revised CPI rises about 0.2 percentage points less than those calculated by the former method.

Some people benefit from inflation (most homeowners and investors in stocks), while others suffer economic harm (those living on fixed incomes and taxpayers paying the higher bills). A **cost-of-living adjustment, or COLA**, is an increase in numbers due to increases in the cost of living as determined by the consumer price index. For example, if inflation for one year was 2 percent, the recipients of Social Security benefits would receive an automatic increase in their government checks of that same amount (or a little less depending upon the formula being used.

Deflation is a decrease in the general level of prices, and it too can be a threat to economic price stability. Japan and Hong Kong have struggled with falling prices for years. With deflation, citizens wait to buy many goods because they expect prices to continue dropping, thus economic growth comes to a standstill.

Primary Goal: Economic Growth

One of America's primary social and economic goals is growth. **Economic growth** is a condition of increasing production and consumption in the economy—and hence increasing national income—over the long term. The individual's desire for a better life and the **rising aspirations** of all the American people shape the direction of our economy. The logical deduction is that we must have greater economic growth if everyone is to get ahead and improve their level of living. A great motivator of economic growth is our interest in continuing to increase our standard of living. Growth is measured by economists by finding out **how much is produced** in a given time period. The government regularly announces the annual rate at which the gross domestic product has grown over the previous **quarter**, a time period of 3 months. **Gross domestic product (GDP)** is a measurement of the goods and services produced within the U.S. (regardless of ownership) over a period of time, such as one year, measured in dollars.[7] It excludes earnings on U.S. investments abroad. GDP is the broadest measure of the economic health of the nation as it is composed of the key economic factors of personal consumption, government expenditures, private investment, inventory growth, and trade balance that have occurred within the U.S. borders.

Less than a 2 percent annual increase in GDP is considered **low growth**; more than 3 percent is considered vigorous growth. Economic growth during the 1950s and 1960s averaged 4 percent annually. The U.S. economy grew more than 4 percent annually throughout the 1990s. As long as inflation is held to 3 percent or less, the economy is likely to continue to grow at an annual rate of 2 percent or more.

The GDP, which is reported quarterly, can have a strong effect on government policy because it shows whether the economy is in a recession and whether inflation is out of line. When using GDP as a measure of economic progress, the figure should be corrected for

---

[7] The current GDP is misleading since the expenditures associated with prison building, nuclear waste disposal, crime, divorce, timber sales, and natural disasters are considered economic gains. Some argue for a **genuine progress indicator (GPI)** that would subtract growth for negatives.

price changes and increases in the population. Since prices usually rise every year in the United States, part of an increase in GDP represents some amount of inflation. As a result, the government develops figures that subtract the effect of inflation from GDP, and the result is known as **real gross domestic product**. The population also increases regularly. Therefore, another key economic figure published by government is the **real per capita gross domestic product**, which is a measure of economic growth on a per-person basis after subtracting the effects of inflation. This is perhaps the most valid measure of economic growth. The U.S. real per capita gross domestic product is more than $21,000.

The U.S. Department of Commerce publishes an **index of leading economic indicators (LEI)**, which is a measure designed to **forecast swings in the economy**, such as whether the nation is growing or sliding toward a recession. The LEI is a composite index, reported monthly as a percentage by the Commerce Department, suggesting the future direction of the cyclical economy of the United States. It summarizes 11 components that historically tend to move downward or upward before the economy swings in those directions. Examples are new orders for consumer goods and materials, new business formation, new private housing starts, average weekly claims for initial unemployment benefits, consumer expectations measured by the University of Michigan, and growth of money supply, which taken together generally offer a somewhat reliable prediction about future directions in the economy. A **falling index** for three or more consecutive months is a signal that economic growth will slow in the months ahead, although monthly moves in the index are not nearly as important as the cumulative, long-term trend. These and other economic indicators (see www.census.gov/econ) are used by governments and businesses to help make policy decisions. Since they are so widely reported by the media, such indices also influence consumer buying decisions.

ECONOMIC INSIGHT:
Indicators of Economic Confidence

Two private organizations report on **consumer attitudes toward the economy** in an effort to include the human factor in economic matters. The Conference Board, a New York-based organization, and the University of Michigan's Survey Research Center, frequently measure consumer views regarding the health and direction of the economy. The *Conference Board* tracks in one confidence index (with a sample of 5000) consumers' plans to buy cars, houses, appliances and take vacations. The *Survey Research Center* reports (with a sample of 500) consumers' expectations about personal finances, business conditions, and buying conditions as it tries to get at the psychological reasoning behind consumers' decisions.

Future directions in economic growth are largely affected by personal perceptions that motivate spending and saving decisions. This, in turn, pushes the economy higher or pulls it down. Since consumer spending accounts for **two-thirds** of the nation's gross domestic product, such buying intentions are vital. Evidence clearly shows that **optimism** about future economic conditions breeds consumer confidence and a willingness to buy and to acquire debt. Consumers are quite adept at forecasting future economic events—**3 to 9 months in advance**—such as unemployment, interest rates, inflation, home and vehicle purchases and general business conditions. Such early indicators, especially when they occur for 3 months in succession, give businesses and governments information to help them make better plans and policy decisions.

Primary Goal: Economic Productivity

The single most important factor affecting the economic growth of a country is probably **productivity**, or **economic productivity**. This is the economic output of an hour of labor.

It is the key indicator of a nation's efficiency. Workers' real income and their level of living cannot increase without increases in the productivity of a nation's labor force. Workers' resources of knowledge and skills must keep expanding.

In the United States, **labor represents 70 percent of business costs** while capital represents the remaining 30 percent. Productivity in the U.S. is held back by fewer technological innovations, low business profits, slowdowns in economic growth, increases in inflation, large numbers of young employees, growing numbers of under-skilled workers (including some women returning to the paid work force), and a poorly educated citizenry.[8] Key to improvements in labor productivity are better technology, growing resources, high savings rates, declining government deficits, improving labor quality, low energy costs, and productivity incentives. **Rising productivity** enables businesses to produce more without hiring more workers.

International groups rank the U.S. as the **most competitive economy in the world**, partially because it has the highest productivity. The U.S. has just 5 percent of the world's population although it produces **28 percent of the world's wealth**. A McKinsey Global Institute survey concluded that if the productivity of U.S. workers is ranked at 100, German workers score 90 and Japanese workers score 55.

Productivity increases in the **manufacturing sector** in recent years generally have been 2 to 4 percent per year. The **service sector** economy of the United States—retail stores, restaurants, hotels, real estate, banking, accounting, airlines, and utilities—is vital to economic growth, and it has been climbing more than 2 percent per year.

Job layoffs generally result in a higher level of productivity. This implies that **downsizing**—reducing the size of work forces in businesses and governments—does contribute to better productivity. Firms that have grown inefficient or whose products are no longer desirable must give way to new businesses with new products. Fierce competition, layoffs, and bankruptcies are indicators that productivity increases are soon to arrive. Economic productivity in the U.S. surged so much in recent years that the cost of labor declined (**wage compression**), signaling that the economy may continue to grow without serious inflation pressures.

The U.S. has 83 percent of its 130 million workers in the **service sector** and 15 percent in manufacturing. As the U.S. continues to become a service economy, manufacturing jobs will decline, say the Bureau of Labor Statistics, to a projected 10 percent in 2017.

Increasing productivity in the service sector, by using more computers on the job, retraining adult workers, increasing educational requirements for new hires, working at home (telecommuting), and using just-in-time inventory methods, will result in higher real earnings for those workers. Increased productivity permits wages to go up without those increases being eroded by inflationary price increases.

Productivity increases **raise the real earnings** of workers. Therefore, increasing real productivity is crucial to long-term improvement in the level of living for any population. Higher productivity enables businesses to increase wages without causing inflation. Without improvements in productivity, young people cannot look forward to a better economic life than their parents.

---

[8] According to a Department of Education report, *Adult Literacy in America*, nearly half of the 191 million Americans over age 15 read and write so poorly that they have difficulty holding down their jobs. These Americans do not have the skills they need to earn a living in our increasingly technological society and international marketplace.

Primary Goal: Economic Security

Another social and economic goal of American society is **economic security**. This is the desire for **protection against the economic risks** people face in their lives, such as loss of employment, illness, business bankruptcy, bank failures, poverty, and destitution in old age. Individually, consumers take action to protect themselves by saving money and buying insurance to protect against such events.

To achieve this important goal, labor unions negotiate contracts with employers to provide for job security and pension benefits. **Union membership** as a percentage of nonagricultural employment in the U.S. is 9.1 percent.

Over the years, the middle-class has enhanced its economic security with a **multitude of government benefits**: Social Security, Medicare, mortgage interest tax deductions, veterans' benefits, student loans, farm subsidies, unemployment compensation, roads and bridges, airports and railways, and federally insured bank deposits. Some would call this **middle-class welfare**. One of the big myths in American society is the growth of "big government programs being forced upon unwilling voters"; rather, **most federal spending goes for these popular programs**.

Some Americans, however, remain in **poverty**. The government's official definition of the threshold for the poverty level is $18,000 for a family of four. About thirty million people, or ten percent of the population, are in poverty. The poverty rate today is the lowest in twenty years.

ECONOMIC INSIGHT:
Taxes are Low on Low- and Middle-income People

In the United States, **income taxes are low**, particularly for middle-income taxpayers. According to the Office of Management and Budget and the Congressional Budget Office, when figured as a percentage of gross domestic product, federal tax receipts are at their highest level since World War II. However, when measured as the average rate for a typical family with two children, federal taxes are at the **lowest since 1957**.

According to the House Ways and Means Committee, the top one percent of income-earners **pay 29 percent** of all federal individual income taxes, the top 2 percent pay 40 percent, and the **top 5 percent pay 47 percent** of the total burden. The top 10 percent pay 59 percent, the top 25 percent pay 80 percent, and the top 50 percent pay 95 percent of all federal income taxes. Two-thirds of all taxpayers either pay no federal income tax or pay at a tax rate of 10 percent.

The wealthiest taxpayers in America are paying a large share of the nation's tax burden. This fact is made even clearer when one realizes that the 56 million filers representing the **lower half of income earners pay only 5 percent** of all federal income taxes collected.

Supporters of tax reform in the U.S. argue for greater simplicity and fairness. A "fair tax system," goes the reasoning, would treat everyone and every dollar of taxable income the same. The result would benefit those who have high incomes. President Bush has already eliminated the federal estate tax on inherited wealth and reduced the income tax rates on higher-income taxpayers. When taxes are **reduced on the wealthy**, the poor and middle-income consumers have to pay more or government **services are reduced or eliminated**. Bush's budget deficits are projected to accumulate to $2 trillion over the next 10 years, up from the current $6 billion.

Primary Goal: Economic Equity and Justice

A key social and economic goal of American society is **economic equity** (what is right and wrong) and **economic justice** (when the benefits and burdens are distributed equitably according to some accepted rule). Society has a broad goal of economic equity and justice but there is plenty of room for disagreement about specifics. For example, because it is fair government has a law requiring a minimum wage for employment. Governments also have decided to provide minimal health care for the poor (Medicaid) because it is the moral thing to do, and on the same grounds, governments redistribute income by taxing the wealthy and providing for the needy and the middle class.

Rising incomes throughout the first 75 years of the 20th century brought growing prosperity to more and more Americans. However, increasing **economic equality is no longer happening** in the United States. Since the1970s, more wealth is being concentrated among fewer people. Data from the Federal Reserve show the growing **economic inequality**. The wealthiest **one percent** of U.S. households—those with a net worth of $2.3 million each—**owns nearly 40 percent of the nation's wealth**. The top 20 percent of wealthy taxpayers, those with a net worth above $180,000, have more than 80 percent of the wealth.

Explanations for the growing disparity include low minimum wages, falling real wages for unskilled workers, low tax rates, and the rise in the stock and bond markets, in which wealthy people are heavily invested. (See www.stw.org/ for income inequality numbers.) The high-tech future of society will make the **inequality worse**, says Michael Dertouzos, author of *What Will Be*, because the poor "will tend to under-use information resources because they can't afford them." As a result, poor people will not even be able to get started on the path to economic prosperity either through improved consumption or better employment.

Review and Summary of Key Terms and Concepts

1. Define **economic system**, and identify the **key economic questions** that every society faces.

2. Distinguish among the terms **economics**, **positive economics** and **normative economics**.

3. Summarize the differences between a **socialistic** and a **capitalistic** economic system.

4. What is the **American market system**?

5. Why are **property rights** important to the American market system?

6. Distinguish between **profit** in an accounting sense and **excess profit**.

7. Discuss the concept of **competition** in a market economy, and explain what the **invisible hand** means.

8. What are some of the **defects of capitalism**?

9. Distinguish between **standard of living** and **level of living**.

10. Discuss what is involved in **allocating resources**, focusing upon the **price mechanism**.

11. Summarize the **circular flow** of economic activity and explain how the **multiplier effect** works.

12. Distinguish between one's **marginal propensity to consume**, **marginal propensity to import** and **marginal propensity to save**.

13. Give some examples of **transfer payments**.

14. How do **progressive** and **regressive** taxes differ?

15. Summarize the essence of the term **monetary policy**.

16. Briefly explain how **reserve requirements** work and why our banking system is called a **fractional reserve system**.

17. Distinguish between **open-market operations** and use of the **discount rate** in influencing monetary policy.

18. Distinguish between **velocity of money** and **easy money**.

19. What are the **broad social and economic goals of American society**?

20. Distinguish between a **true democracy** and a **republic**.

21. Define the term **capitalism**, and tell what spurs economic growth in such an economic system.

22. Describe the **central economic problem** in the context of the economic goal of **full employment**.

23. What is meant by the economic goals of **price stability** and **economic growth**?

24. Explain how major research organizations monitor **consumer sentiment**, and how the **index of leading economic indicators** works.

25. Define the term **economic inequality**, and give examples of the concept.

26. Explain how the wealthy already pay a substantial portion of the nation's **income tax burden**.

Useful Resources for Consumers

About Economics
www.economics.about.com/

Board of Governors of the
Federal Reserve System
www.federalreserve.gov

Consumer Federation of
America
www.consumerfed.org

Department of Labor
www.dol.gov/

Economics America
www.economicsamerica.org/

EconEdLink
www.econedlink.org/

Economic Education Web
www.ecedweb.unomaha.edu/

Essential Links
www.el.com/elinks/taxes

National Labor Relations
Board
www.nlrb.gov

Social Science Information
Gateway - Economics
www.sosig.ac.uk/economics/

United for a Fair Economy
www.stw.org/

U.S. Census Bureau
www.census.gov

U.S. Department of
Commerce
www.commerce.gov/

U.S. Department of
Commerce
Economics and Statistics
Administration
www.esa.doc.gov/508/esa/ho
me.htm

U.S. Department of Labor
www.dol.gov

White House Economic
Statistics Briefing Room
www.whitehouse.gov/fsbr/esb
r.html

WWW Economic Resources
in Economics
www.helsinki.fi/WebEc/WebE
c.html

"What Do You Think" Questions

1. How do you think the concept of the **price mechanism** works in reality? Give some examples.

2. Thinking of the community where you are going to school, give some examples of how the **multiplier effect** works in banking, employment and retail sales.

3. Which two of the **broad social and economic goals** do you believe offer high potential for conflicts in making public policy decisions? Explain your reasoning.

4. What do you think about the fact that **high-income taxpayers** pay a rather large portion of the total revenue of the federal government?

Chapter 7

Economic Concepts Critical to Consumer Success

OBJECTIVES

After reading this chapter, you should be able to

1. Explain the concepts of supply, demand, and market equilibrium.

2. Recognize situations where supply and demand do not work.

3. Give examples of income and substitution effects.

4. Summarize how indifference curve and budget line analysis can be used in decision-making.

To effectively participate in society, an individual performing the roles of worker, citizen and consumer must have an understanding of the economic marketplace. Good personal decisions will result when you are able to visualize the economic effects—both for yourself and for society as a whole—of alternative courses of action. Several economic concepts are important in the process of being able to reason rationally. This critical thinking is required to properly analyze consumer issues as well as alternative proposals to resolve consumer problems. This chapter examines the economic concepts of demand, supply, market equilibrium, when supply and demand do not always work, income and substitution effects, and indifference curve and budget line analysis. One appendix is included at the end of the chapter that provides more depth to rational decision- making: The Life Cycle and Permanent Income Hypothesis.

Demand in a Market Economy

The American marketplace is best described as a **market economy** or a **market-oriented economy**. This is an economy that is guided mostly by decisions made in the private sector by consumers and businesses. The American economy is characterized by decentralized decision making. In contrast, China, Cuba, North Vietnam and North Korea have government-controlled, centrally-planned economies.

A **market** is an organized situation in which buyers and sellers register their individual economic demands and make their decisions to buy and sell. They express their demands by **economic voting** which is the spending or non-spending of dollars for products and services. If they buy, they accept; if not, they reject. Consumers, businesses and governments cast economic votes for or against all products and services by such actions.

Each market works in the same way. High profits signal other business firms that more should be produced. As more firms enter a market and compete for the same customers, prices drop, and at the same time, supplies go up until a new equilibrium is reached.

In our modern and complex world there are thousands of markets. Buyers and sellers come together to let supply and demand decide wholesale and retail prices of products, the prices of labor, and the cost of stocks and money. The market system adds up the collective decisions made by millions of buyers and sellers in all the markets and converts them into aggregate forces of supply and demand. The quantities of supply and demand interact with each other and determine the prices of goods and services.

A number of economic concepts affect decision-making, including economic voting, demand, elasticity of demand, supply, market equilibrium, farm prices, price-fixing, price ceilings, income and substitution effects, opportunity cost, marginal cost, diminishing marginal utility, and cost-benefit analysis.

How Demand Affects Prices

When buyers and sellers meet in a market they are very interested in price. They want to know how much each is willing to buy or sell at a particular price. When they agree on a price, it is called the **market price**, what a willing and able buyer is willing to pay a willing seller.

Demand (sometimes called **effective demand**) in a general sense is the willingness and ability of consumers to spend money on certain products and services. The **law of demand**

suggests that as the price increases, the quantity demanded of goods and services will decrease. Conversely, as the price decreases, the quantity demanded will increase. In short, there is an inverse relationship between price and quantity demanded. Common sense and simple observation tell us that this principle is true.

The concept of demand also can be explained in terms of **substitutability** of products. Usually there are a reasonable number of substitutes for any one product. Thus, an increase in the price of one product tends to make consumers substitute other products for it, and this action tends to constrain price increases. Similarly, a decline in the price of a product will make consumers substitute it for other products.

The Demand Curve Slopes Downward and to the Right

Demand is technically defined in economics as a schedule that shows the various quantities of a product that consumers are willing and able to purchase at each specific price in a set of possible prices during a specific period of time. It is difficult to construct a demand schedule for a specific product in advance because we must know exactly how many units people would actually buy at given prices. Still, we know that people will buy more units of a product at a low price than they will at a high price. Although the quantity of a good tends to vary inversely with price, this does not imply that the variation in the amount sold is always proportionate to the change in price. Demand portrays a series of alternatives that can be set down in tabular form.

Table 7-1 reflects the relationship between the price of apples and the quantity that a consumer would be willing and able to purchase at each of the prices. The consumer typically uses price as a reference point; thus the question is "What amounts of products will consumers buy at various prices?" By itself, a demand schedule of a single consumer's buying intentions cannot indicate which of the five possible market prices will actually exist for apples because this price depends on both demand and supply.

Price per Pound	Quantity Demanded per Week
$5	10
4	20
3	35
2	55
1	80

TABLE 7-1   A Single Consumer's Hypothetical Demand for Apples

The inverse relationship between the price of a product and the quantity demanded can be illustrated on a graph that charts quantity demanded on the horizontal axis and price on the vertical axis. The five price-quantity possibilities in Table 7-1 are plotted as appropriate points on the two axes in Figure 7-1. Each of these points represents a specific price and the corresponding quantity that an individual consumer is willing and able to pay during a specific time period. We assume that the same inverse relationship exists between all points as between the ones graphed. This allows us to generalize and draw a curve to represent all price-quantity possibilities within the limitations of the graph. The resulting curve is called a **demand curve**, labeled *DD*, which slopes downward and to the right because the relationship it illustrates between price and quantity is inverse.

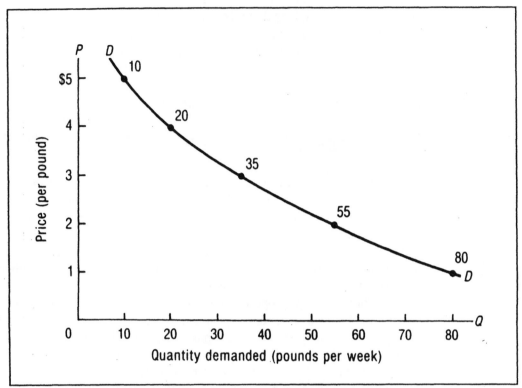

FIGURE 7-1   One Hypothetical Consumer's Demand for Apples

The assumption of competition forces us to make a transition from the illustration of one consumer to that of a large number of buyers in a market. If we sum the demand schedules of each and every consumer at the various prices, we now have a *market* demand curve instead of an *individual* demand curve.

Figure 7-2 illustrates that an increase in demand is reflected as a shift of the demand curve to the right, for example, from *D1D1*, to *D2D2*; the converse occurs with a decrease in demand, resulting in a shift of the demand curve to the left, for example, from *D1D1*, to *D3D3*. A demand schedule may be represented by a curve or a straight line. A change in demand means that there are shifts of the entire demand curve to the right or left.

Notice that one assumption in a demand curve is that price is the most important determinant of the amount of a product purchased by consumers. Thus, economists are fond of saying, **ceteris paribus**, meaning **"other things being equal,"** or everything else held constant. In the real world, however, this is not true. Factors other than price do affect purchases. When **non-price determinants of demand** change, the location of the demand curve shifts to the right or left, as graphed in Figure 7-2 as *D2D2* and *D1D1*, respectively. The non-price determinants of demand include (1) tastes and preferences of consumers, (2) number of consumers in the market, (3) money incomes of consumers, (4) prices of related goods, and (5) expectations of consumers regarding future prices and incomes.

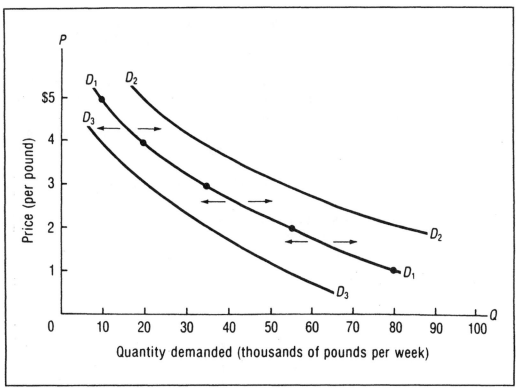

FIGURE 7-2   The Effects of Non-price Determinants on Consumer Demand for Apples

Demand is Characterized by Its Elasticity

Elasticity is a term that expresses the change in one variable in response to a given change in another variable. This concept is useful to sellers when faced with the problem of determining at which price to offer goods for sale. While it is true that a greater number of sales can be made at lower prices, it is questionable whether greater revenue from the larger sales will offset the reduced revenue from the reduced price. Further, the changes are not proportional. **Price elasticity of demand** is a measure of consumer responsiveness to a change in price. How well a seller fares by raising or lowering prices depends on the degree of price elasticity. The demand for some products is such that consumers are relatively responsive to price changes; the demand for such products is said to be **elastic**. For other products, consumers are relatively unresponsive to price changes. When price changes result in only modest changes in the amount purchased, the demand is said to be **inelastic**.

The **elasticity of demand coefficient** E_d (shown in Equation 7.1) is a measure of the degree of elasticity or inelasticity of a particular section of a curve. It refers to the ratio of the percentage change in price to the percentage change in the quantity of a good that will be purchased as a result of the change in price. To calculate the percentage changes, you actually divide the change in price by the original price and the resulting change in quantity demanded by the original quantity demanded. Demand is inelastic if a given percentage change in price is accompanied by a relatively smaller change in the quantity demanded. Demand is elastic if a given percentage change in price results in a larger percentage change in quantity demanded. The formula for the elasticity of demand coefficient is

$$E_d = \frac{\text{percentage change in quantity demanded}}{\text{percentage change in price}} \qquad \text{(Equation 7.1)}$$

The U.S. Department of Commerce publishes the income sensitivity factors for various products. Examples of measures include an elasticity of 3.0 for pleasure boats, 2.0 for new automobiles, 0.5 for gasoline, and 0.2 for electricity.

Elasticity of demand may range from perfect elasticity to perfect inelasticity, as illustrated in Figure 7-3. **Perfectly elastic demand** may occur for a product for which an infinite number could be sold at a given market price. For example, demand curve *D1D1*, (a straight horizontal line) in Figure 7-3 illustrates the situation of a wheat farmer who is able to sell all of his or her product to the government at a special subsidized price. Consumer goods that tend toward greater elasticity include luxuries, large-expenditure durable goods, and substitute goods. Examples of goods that tend toward inelasticity include groceries and vehicle license plates.

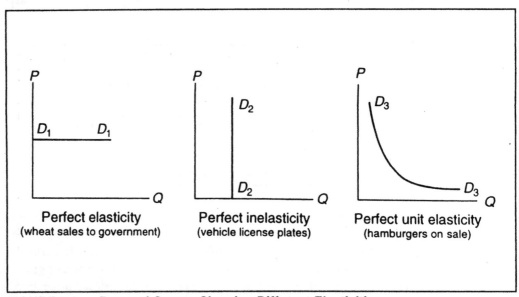

FIGURE 7-3   Demand Curves Showing Different Elasticities

The determinants of elasticity of demand include (1) substitutability (the larger the number of good substitute products available, the greater the elasticity of demand), (2) proportion of income (the products that take a greater bulk of income, that is, expensive goods tend to have a greater elasticity of demand), (3) necessities and luxuries (the demand for necessities tends to be inelastic while the demand for luxuries tends to be elastic), and (4) time (the longer the time period under consideration, the more elastic is the demand for a particular product).

Demand curve *D2D2* (a straight vertical line) in Figure 7-3 is **perfectly inelastic**, indicating that the same quantity of the product will be bought regardless of the price. A change in the price of automobile license plates, for example, results in no change in the quantity demanded. (At some point a rise in price would encourage owners of older automobiles to consider not licensing the vehicles.) Consumer goods that tend toward inelasticity include necessities, small-expenditure perishable goods, and complementary goods.

In the special case of **unit elasticity**, demand curve *D3D3* (a hyperbola) in Figure 7-3 shows an increase or decrease in price will leave total revenue unchanged, since the loss of revenue occurring because of lower prices is offset by the gain in revenue from the increased sales. Thus, changes in price and quantity are proportional throughout the demand curve, resulting in an elasticity coefficient of exactly 1.0, or unity.

Supply Affects Prices

Total **supply** in a general sense is the maximum amount of a product or service available for sale at a given price. The **law of supply** suggests that as the price goes up, so does the quantity supplied. Conversely, as the price goes down, so does the quantity supplied. For example, if the price of apples is rising, more growers will be interested in planting apple trees in hope of future profits. When prices are declining, supplies also drop because fewer sellers will want to provide that product in the market for little anticipated profits.

The Supply Curve Slopes Upward to the Left

Supply is technically defined in economics as a schedule that shows the various amounts of a product that a producer is willing to supply for sale in the market at each specific price in a set of possible prices during some specific time period. A supply schedule portrays a series of alternative possibilities, as shown in Table 7-2, for a single producer of apples. The farmer uses supply as a reference point, thus the question is, "What prices will be required to induce producers to offer various quantities of apples?"

Price per Pound	Quantity Supplied per Week
$5	60
4	50
3	35
2	20
1	5

TABLE 7-2   An Individual Producer's Hypothetical Supply of Apples

It can be seen clearly in Table 7-2 that there is a direct relationship between price and quantity supplied. As the price rises, so does the quantity supplied; as the price falls, so does the quantity supplied. The law of supply works because producers are willing to provide more of a given product at a high price than they are at a lower price. For the producer, a higher price is an incentive to produce more.

The relationship between price and quantity supplied can be explained on the basis of substitutability. For example, when resources and productive techniques are readily adaptable to producing a variety of products, a farmer will shift his or her resources from other commodities to apples, for example, if the price of that product is rising. This occurs simply because the farmer will earn more money. Realistically, switching from producing one very different product may be quite complex and expensive, but such shifting does occur among different producers.

The concept of supply is graphically presented in Figure 7-4 utilizing the single producer's data from Table 7-2, represented by S1S1. The supply curve slopes upward to the left. Figure 7-5 shows the same single producer's data along with data from hundreds of other hypothetical apple producers to create a *market* supply curve instead of an *individual* supply curve.

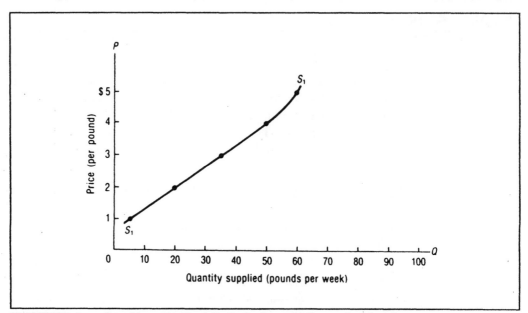

FIGURE 7-4   One Hypothetical Seller's Supply Curve for Apples

Several Non-Price Determinants of Supply Exist

The non-price determinants of supply include (1) techniques of production, (2) prices of resources, (3) prices of other goods, (4) expectations of future prices, (5) number of sellers in the market, and (6) taxes and subsidies. A change in any determinant will cause the supply curve to shift to the right or the left. As illustrated in Figure 7-5, a shift to the right, from *S1S1*, to *S2S2*, represents an increase in supply; a shift to the left, from *S1S1* to *S3S3*, designates a decrease in supply. A change in supply is involved when the entire supply curve shifts. Supply curves are also predicated on the economist's ceteris paribus assumption.

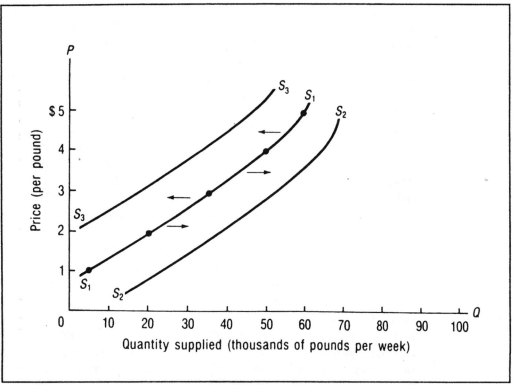

FIGURE 7-5   Supply Curve for Many Sellers of Apples

Market Equilibrium is the Ideal Where Price Meets Supply

When the concepts of supply and demand are brought together, you can visualize how the interaction of consumer buying decisions and producer selling decisions determine the price of a product and the quality that is bought and sold in the market. Table 7-3 shows the market supply and demand for apples assuming a competitive market.

Total Quantity Supplied per Week (pounds)	Price per Pound	Total Quantity Demanded per Week (pounds)	Surplus (+) or Shortage (-) (pounds)
60,000	$5	10,000	+50,000
50,000	$4	20,000	+30,000
35,000	$3	35,000	0
20,000	$2	55,000	-35,000
5,000	$1	89,000	-84,000

TABLE 7-3   Hypothetical Market Supply of and Demand for Apples

The question to be answered is, "At which price might apples sell in this market?" At a price of $1 per pound, the price of apples is so low that consumer demand is very high.

But, the same $1 price is too low to encourage farmers from putting their resources into apple production. The price of $1 cannot persist as the market price because competition among buyers will bid the price up. At a price of $2 per pound, the supply shortage has been reduced but not eliminated. At the other extreme, a price of $5 per pound results in consumers willing to take only 10,000 pounds of the large supply of 60,000 pounds. Thus, the high price encourages farmers to produce apples but discourages consumers from buying (creating an unwanted surplus). At a price of $4 per pound a surplus still exists, and competition among sellers should continue to bid down the price of apples.

Finally, at a price of $3 per pound, and only at this price, does the quantity of apples farmers are willing to produce and able to supply to the market equal the amount of apples consumers are willing to buy. There is neither a shortage nor a surplus at this **equilibrium price** where the price between buyers and sellers is in balance. Differences between supply and demand intentions of sellers and consumers will prompt price changes that will bring their plans together.

A graphic presentation results in the same conclusion, as shown in Figure 7-6. The intersection of the downward-sloping demand curve *DD* and the upward-sloping supply curve *SS* indicates the equilibrium price and quantity, in this instance $3 per pound and 35,000 pounds. A shortage of apples would occur at below-equilibrium prices. For example, apples priced at $2 would create a 35,000-pound shortage, drive prices up, and in so doing increase the quantity supplied and reduce the quantity demanded until equilibrium is reached. Further, apples priced at $4 per pound would create a 30,000-pound surplus, and in so doing push prices down and thereby increase the quantity demanded and reduce the quantity supplied until equilibrium is reached. At the equilibrium price, there is no burdensome surplus for sellers and no shortages for the consumers.

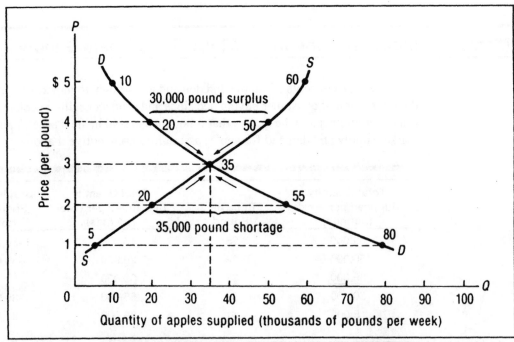

FIGURE 7-6   **Equilibrium Price and Quantity for Apples As Determined by Market Demand and Supply**

When Supply and Demand Does Not Work

Under competitive conditions, the number of possible relationships between supply and demand is enormous. For example, demand may increase while supply remains constant, or vice versa. Perhaps demand will increase while supply decreases, or vice versa. Or perhaps demand and supply will increase, but demand will increase more than supply.

In the real world it is extremely difficult, if not impossible, to construct actual demand and supply curves for various goods in the market. Yet we can still reach useful conclusions about what such curves would look like in competitive markets if we construct them. When prices are not at the point of equilibrium, economists study particular markets in an attempt to ascertain why the laws of supply and demand are being violated. The answer lies in the economist's assumption about "other things being equal" because this is rarely the case.

Farm Prices Often are Not Set by Supply and Demand

If a seller, such as a farmer, wants to set the price different than the market price established by the free forces of competitive supply and demand, the market will have to be rigged or the forces of supply and demand will have to be changed. This is precisely what happens in three instances: (1) when government sets a *parity price* for an agricultural commodity that is higher than the market price, (2) when government sets price ceilings, and (3) when business firms illegally conspire to fix prices that are higher than the market price.

Instability in farm prices occurs, in part, because of short-run business fluctuations, wide variations in foreign demand, natural hazards (such as weather), and the pressure of competition in making adjustments to changing market conditions. Demand for farm products is both price and income inelastic. In an effort to guarantee consistent supplies of the product for consumers, as well as keep farmers in business, government sets prices on many commodities. These are known as **price supports** because government establishes prices that are higher than the equilibrium prices. A **parity price** of a farm commodity is a standard for measuring the purchasing power of that commodity in relation to prices of other goods and services during a definite base period. Since a high guaranteed parity price would result in excessive commodity surpluses (and additional tax dollars going to pay for storage costs), the government parity prices are generally accompanied by production limitations.[1]

Price Ceilings are Occasionally Imposed by Government

Price ceilings are government-established prices that are lower than equilibrium prices. They upset the rationing function of prices by causing product and resource shortages. Government then typically introduces some sort of bureaucratic rationing system for products at the controlled prices. Using the argument of equity, a number of prices in the American economy are set by government instead of letting market forces prevail, such as agricultural price supports, the minimum wage, and rent controls found in some communities.

---

[1] The Office of Management and Budget and the Joint Committee on Taxation estimate that total farm subsidies from the federal government annually are $30 billion.

Price-Fixing Eliminates the Competitive Forces of Supply and Demand

Instead of having prices set by the forces of supply and demand, some business firms conspire to set high prices. They do this by (1) shrinking supply or (2) controlling the price. They can enjoy the excess profits until an alternative product develops or the government successfully accuses them of collusion in interfering with the free competitive forces of demand and supply. A federal or state court then finds them guilty of illegal **price fixing**. See the box on page 262 for a list of "Top Ten Corporate Price-Fixers."

Income and Substitution Effects

The discussion so far has suggested that there is an inverse relationship between price and quantity demanded. One complementary explanation suggests that consumers are both able and willing to buy more of the product. The **income effect** suggests that a consumer will buy more of a product, as well as other products, as the price declines in relation to the consumer's income. For example, if you usually buy 1 pound of fish each week at $4 per pound and it declines to $3 per pound, you now have $1 available for buying more fish or another commodity. A decline in price increases the real income of the consumer.

This explanation is incomplete, however, because of the **substitution effect**. This complementary explanation of demand suggests that a lower price for a product increases the relative attractiveness of that product and makes consumers want to buy more of it. In the fish example, as the price drops, the prices of other products remain unchanged, which makes the price of fish even more attractive. Consequently, the lower price will induce the consumer to substitute fish for some of the now less attractive items in the food budget. At the lower price, fish may be substituted for steak, veal, or chicken. The income and substitution effects combine to help make consumers willing and able to buy more of a specific good at a low price than at a higher price.

Opportunity Cost

An **opportunity cost** is the most valuable alternative that must be sacrificed to satisfy a want; it is the thing that we must do without when we decide upon a particular allocation of resources. For example, the opportunity cost of buying a $16 compact disk might be an evening at the movie theater with a friend. Therefore, giving up the movies—the cost of the best alternative—is the opportunity cost involved when you choose to buy the CD. Note that most opportunity-cost decisions are in situations where once you choose an alternative, you cannot select the others.

Knowing the opportunity cost of alternatives allows you to place a value on the resource. Consumers use the principle of opportunity cost either consciously or unconsciously in their decision making. When understood and used consciously, the concept of opportunity costs helps people prioritize their decisions because they must make choices based on the best value that will provide maximum satisfaction among alternative opportunities.

Opportunity costs often involve money amounts, as well as psychic benefits, and these both should be considered carefully in decision making. Further, most opportunity costs involve personal tastes and preferences that are difficult to quantify. However, properly valuing the costs and benefits of alternatives is a key step in rational decision making.

Some opportunity costs may have larger costs than you might think. For example, by paying $10,000 for a motor vehicle, first you lose the dollars paid, then you lose the alternative use for those dollars, and finally you lose the value of another $10,000 (probably $14,000 before taxes) that must be earned to take the place of the dollar paid. People often refer to **tradeoffs** when discussing opportunity costs because analyzing the opportunities involves trading one thing for another. In a world of scarcity, a tradeoff involves sacrificing one resource for another.

DID YOU KNOW?
Going to College Has Opportunity Costs

If four years of college tuition and related expenses amount to $40,000, that is not the total cost of going to school. If you could have obtained a job paying $12 an hour and worked 52 weeks a year for 40 hours a week, you would have earned $99,840 ($12 x 40 x 52 x 4 years). Thus, in this example the total real cost of going to college is $139,840.

Marginal Cost

It often is difficult for consumers to maximize their self-interest in marketplace transactions. Recognizing this, most consumers try to optimize their preferences. **Optimizing** is making something, such as a buying decision, as good or as effective as possible. The concept of marginal cost makes some consumer economics decisions more effective.

Utility is the ability of a good or service to satisfy a human want. Utility also is a subjective notion because the utility of a specific product may vary widely from person to person. As a result, utility is not susceptible to precise quantitative measurement. **Marginal cost** is the additional cost of something compared to the additional value received. Sometimes making consumer decisions is difficult enough without having to consider too many variables. The marginal cost concept reminds us to compare only important variables.

For example, two new automobiles are available on a dealership lot in Chicago, Illinois, where Scott Marshall is trying to make a decision. Both cars are the same make and model. One with a sticker price of $13,100 has a moderate number of options. The other with a sticker price of $14,800 has numerous options. It is unnecessary for Scott to consider all the options when comparing both vehicles. The concept of marginal cost says to compare the additional cost, $1,700 in this instance ($14,800 - $13,100), with the cost of the additional options. Scott must only decide if all the additional options are worth $1,700.

AN ECONOMIC FOCUS ON...The Propensity to Consume*

The consumption expenditure of a household is determined mainly by its level of disposable income. It means that consumption expenditure depends on disposable income, so that we can predict how much consumption will be associated with a given level of income.

The relationship between consumption expenditure and income is known as the **consumption function**, or the **propensity to consume**, a term that is associated with the British economist John Maynard Keynes. A consumption function for a hypothetical household is illustrated by the schedule in the first two columns of Table 7-4. The difference between income and consumption is saving, shown in column 3.

The consumption and saving data are graphed in Figure 7-7. Disposable income is measured on the horizontal axis and consumption expenditure on the vertical axis. The 45-degree line is a guideline which indicates that any point on the line is equidistant from the two axes. This means that if a household consumption expenditure lies on this line, it is then equal to the household's income (i.e. the household spends all of its income on consumption).

The consumption function is drawn as a straight line, C, which represents the data in columns 1 and 2 of the table. The intersection of this line with the 45-degree line is the household's **break-even point**, or often called the **point of zero saving** where consumption is exactly equal to income. This point is assumed to occur when disposable income is $200.

To the right of the break-even point the household is consuming less than its income. The difference, saving, is represented by the vertical distance between the consumption line and the 45-degree line. To the left of the break-even point the household is consuming more than its income. The difference, dissaving, is attained by the household either by going into debt or by dipping into past savings.

Given the data in columns 1 and 2, we can calculate two important measures of the relationship of income and consumption. One measure is the **average propensity to consume (APC)**. It is the ratio of consumption to income. It denotes how a household divides its income between consumption and saving. For example, at an income level of $400, the household will spend 80 cents of each dollar or a total of $320, and it will save 20 cents of each dollar or a total of $80. In other words, it will spend 80% of its income, and save 20%. Note that since consumption plus saving equal **income**, then the average propensity to consume (APC), and the **average propensity to save (APS)**, (defined as the ratio of saving to income), must always total 1 at any income level. Columns 4 and 5 in Table 7-4 show the derived APC's and APS's. Graphically, the APC at any point on line C, is measured as the slope of a line from the origin to that point.

The second important measure of the relationship of consumption and income is the **marginal propensity to consume (MPC)**. It indicates the percentage of each additional dollar of disposable income that will be consumed. An MPC of 0.60, as shown in column 6 in Table 7-4, means that 60% of any increase in income will be spent on consumption. The formula for calculating MPC therefore can be represented by:

$$MPC = \frac{\text{change in consumption}}{\text{change in income}}$$

The fraction of each additional dollar of income that does not go into consumption will go into saving and is defined as the **marginal propensity to save (MPS)**. The MPS's corresponding to the changes in income are shown in the last column of Table 7-4. The sum of MPC and MPS must always add to 1. Graphically, the MPC at any point on line C is measured as the slope of line C. Note, however, if the relationship between income and consumption is represented by a curve rather than a straight line, then the MPC is measured as the slope of a line that is tangent to the point on the curve.

The **consumption function** shown in Figure 7-7 is characterized by a declining APC and a constant MPC. Figure 7-8 shows some other types of conceivable consumption functions. In Figure 7-8, function (1) has a constant MPC that is less than one, and a constant APC. Function (2) has a steadily rising MPC, however it is still less than 1 within the limits shown. The APC falls from T at point A to 1 at point B and thereafter continues to decline until point C, when APC and MPC are equal. Beyond C, MPC exceeds APC, and APC rises. Function (3) has an MPC which declines from a magnitude in excess of 1 to 1 at point d, and thereafter to lower magnitudes. The APC is always higher, declining to 1 at point E, and thereafter continuing to fall. Function (4) has a constant MPC of 1, and APC of less than 1, which rises from zero at point F and approaches 1.

The relationship between marginal and average propensities in general are characterized by the following rules: (1) if marginal is constant and equal to average, average is similarly constant; (2) if marginal is less than average, average is declining; (3) if marginal is greater than average, average is rising; (4) if marginal is rising or declining and at some point equals average, average at that point has reached a maximum or minimum.

It is important to conclude that at any given level of income, the APC relates consumption to income, whereas the MPC relates a **change** in consumption to a change in income. The marginal approach is invaluable in examining consumer behavior toward change.

*Mohamed Abdel-Ghany, Professor, The University of Alabama

Table 7-4. Hypothetical Consumption Function

Disposable Income	Consumption	Saving	APC	APS	MPC	MPS
100	140	-40	1.40	-.40		
200	200	0	1.00	.00	.6	.4
300	260	40	.87	.13	.6	.4
400	320	80	.80	.20	.6	.4
500	380	120	.76	.24	.6	.4

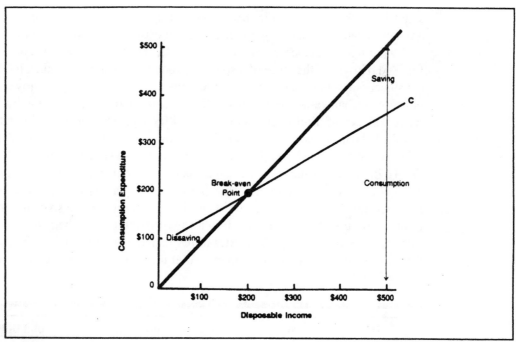

FIGURE 7-7

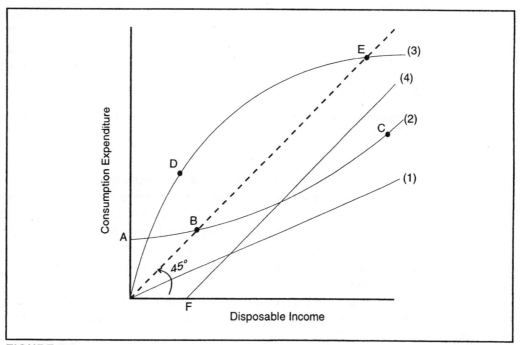

FIGURE 7-8

Diminishing Marginal Utility

Marginal utility refers to the extra utility, or satisfaction, that a consumer obtains from one additional unit of a specific product or service. You might receive a certain amount of satisfaction from eating a piece of candy (utility), and you can obtain a slightly different amount of satisfaction (marginal utility) from eating a second piece of candy.

Although consumer wants are insatiable, wants for specific commodities can be fulfilled. However, the more of a specific product a consumer obtains, the less anxious the consumer is to obtain more units of the same product. You might enjoy eating one bag of popcorn at a ball game, but the desire for a second is less intense; for a third or fourth, very weak. The **law of diminishing marginal utility** suggests that specific consumer wants can be fulfilled with succeeding fewer units of a commodity. Thus, a consumer's marginal utility will decline as he or she acquires additional units of a specific product.

To illustrate, assume that we can measure utility or satisfaction with units called **utils**. Table 7-5 illustrates the relationship between the quantity of a product, such as bags of popcorn, and the accompanying utility derived from each successive unit. It is assumed that diminishing marginal utility sets in with the first number of bags of popcorn purchased. Each successive unit yields less extra utility than the previous one as the consumer's desire for popcorn gets closer to fulfillment. Total utility can be found by totaling the marginal utility figures.

Units of Popcorn	Marginal Utility (utils)	Total Utility (utils)
1	10	10
2	8	18
3	7	25
4	6	31
5	5	36
6	4	40
7	3	43

TABLE 7-5   The Law of Diminishing Marginal Utility (Applied to Popcorn)

The law of diminishing marginal utility suggests that the demand curve for a specific product is downward sloping. If the successive units of a product provide smaller and smaller amounts of marginal, or extra, utility, the consumer will buy additional units of a product only if its price falls. A consumer might buy more popcorn if the price drops from $4 to $3 or even $2 per bag, but because of diminishing marginal utility, he or she will choose not to buy more at this price because giving up more money for popcorn means giving up other goods, which are alternative ways of getting utility. Sellers recognize that because of the principle of diminishing marginal utility, they must lower the price on a product in order to induce consumers to purchase large quantities of the product.

AN ECONOMIC FOCUS ON...Indifference Curve and Budget Line Analysis*

The roots of the **indifference curve analysis**, also known as the **ordinal utility theory**, can be traced back to the work of the Italian economist Vilfredo Pareto.[1] The economists Eugene Slutsky[2], John Hicks, R.G.D. Allen[3], and Harold Hotelling[4] have contributed to the development of the theory that was formalized by John Hicks.

Indifference curve analysis replaced the **marginal utility theory** by assuming that utility is ordinally measurable, rather than cardinally measurable. In other words, the consumer is assumed to be able to order or rank on a scale of preferences all alternative sets of consumption possibilities rather than be required to assign numbers known as "utils" to measure utility.

Therefore, for any two combinations (or bundles) A and B of goods, a consumer either prefers A to B, B to A, or is indifferent between them. The consumer's preferences also are assumed to be consistent and transitive. If A is preferred to B and B to C, then A is preferred to C.

The consumer's preferences are assumed to express a diminishing **marginal rate of substitution**. It is the rate at which an individual is willing to give up one good in exchange for another good, while maintaining the same level of satisfaction. Finally, it is assumed that more of a good is preferred to less.

Figure 7-9 is an indifference map showing the preference of a consumer for two goods, let us assume oranges and apples. The quantities of the goods are measured along the two axes. Any point on the map represents a specific combination of oranges and apples. The consumer is assumed to be able to rank all of these combinations, indicating with respect to any pair of combinations whether he/she prefers one to the other, or is indifferent.

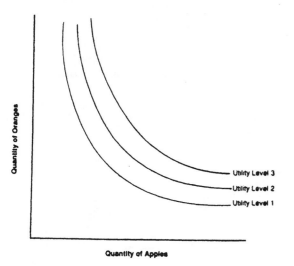

FIGURE 7-9

Any one **indifference curve** shows combinations of oranges and apples yielding the same level of utility to the consumer, while higher or lower levels of utility are represented by indifference curves lying farther from or closer to the origin, respectively.

Indifference curves have three characteristics which result from the assumptions made earlier. First, indifference curves are concave from above with a downward slope from the assumption of diminishing rate of marginal substitution.

The second characteristic is that indifference curves cannot intersect (from transitivity and more preferred to less). This characteristic is illustrated in Figure 7-10. In this graph (1) and (2) are indifference curves, and the points A, B, and C represent three different combinations of oranges and apples. C must obviously be preferred to B because it contains more oranges as well as more apples. C and A are equivalent because they lie on the same indifference curve (2). Similarly, A and B are indifferent, since they lie on indifference curve (1). Since C is indifferent to A and A is indifferent to B, therefore C must be indifferent to B (due to the transitivity assumption). However, as previously mentioned, C is preferred to B because it contains more of oranges as well as apples. Hence, we can conclude that indifference curves cannot possibly intersect.

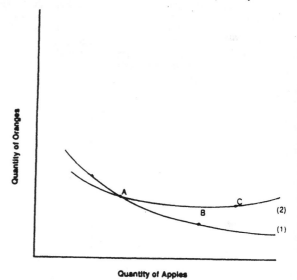

FIGURE 7-10

The third characteristics of indifference curves is that they pass everywhere in the commodity space. For example, an infinite number of indifference curves lie between any two of the indifference curves shown in Figure 7-9.

So far we have presented a picture of the consumer's preferences only. His/her indifference map shows what he/she is willing to do with respect to different combinations of oranges and apples. What the consumer is able to do depends upon the consumer's income and the prices of oranges and apples.

The **budget line** (it may also be called the **opportunity line**) describes the possibilities open to the consumer, given his/her money income and the prices of oranges and apples. We can represent the budget line on an indifference map. Suppose that the consumer budget is $10 (the amount to be spent on oranges and apples), the price of oranges is $2 per pound, and the price of apples is $1 per pound.

(continued)

If the consumer should spend all of the $10 on oranges, he/she would buy 5 pounds of it. Similarly, he/she could purchase 10 pounds of apples if he/she were to spend all of the $10 on apples. The budget line is the straight line connecting these two points. It is shown on Figure 7-11 as line YX. It represents all combinations of oranges and apples that the consumer's budget will allow him/her to purchase.

The slope of the budget line YX is OY/OX. Where OY is the amount of oranges the consumer could purchase with the entire $10. Likewise, OX is the amount of apples the consumer could purchase with the entire $10. Since OY equals the budget/price of oranges, and OX equals the budget/price of apples, then the slope of the budget line equals:

(the budget/price of oranges)/(the budget/price of apples) =
price of apples/price of oranges
which is the rate of relative prices.

Given the consumer's indifference map and his/her budget line, satisfaction is maximized at the point at which the budget line is tangent to an indifference curve. This point is represented by point A in Figure 7-11. It implies the purchase of quantity X_1 of apples and Y_1 of oranges. Note that the combination A is on the highest indifference curve that the consumer's budget line will allow him/her to reach and it is the only combination available to him/her on that indifference curve.

Combinations such as B or C are on a lower indifference curve and as such will not be chosen. Even though combination D is on a higher indifference curve, it lies above the budget line and therefore is unattainable.

At the point of tangency A, the slope of the budget line (Px/Py) is equal to the slope of the indifference curve at that point (marginal rate of substitution of y for x). Thus, the consumer in our example maximizes satisfaction when his/her purchase of oranges and apples is such that the rate at which he/she is willing to give up oranges for apples is just equal to the ratio of the price of apples to the price of oranges.

[1]Pareto, Vilfredo (1906). Manuel D'Economic Politique.

[2]Slutsky, E. (1915). Sulla Teoria del Bilancio del Consumatore. *Giornale deli Economist*, LT, 1-16.

[3]Hick, J., & Allen, R.G.D. (1934). A Reconsideration of the Theory of Value. *Economica*, XIV, 52-76, 196-219.

[4]Hotelling, H. (1935, January). Demand Functions with Limited Budgets. *Econometrica*, 66-78.

*Mohamed Abdel-Ghany, Professor, The University of Alabama

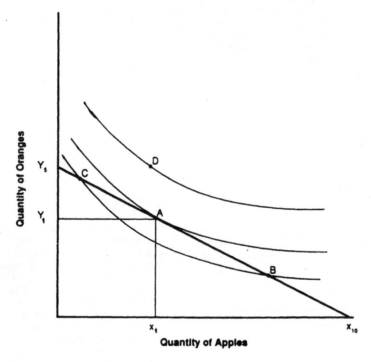

FIGURE 7-11

Review and Summary of Key Terms and Concepts

1. What is a **market economy** and what role does **economic voting** play?

2. Distinguish between **demand** in a general sense and **demand** from the perspective of an economist.

3. Explain and give an example why a **demand curve** slopes downward and to the right.

4. Give 5 examples of products and services that are said to be relatively **elastic**; give 5 more examples which are **inelastic**.

5. Distinguish between **supply** in a general sense and **supply** from the perspective of an economist and then define the **law of supply**.

6. Explain the concept of **equilibrium price** and give three examples from everyday living.

7. Summarize why **farm prices** are unstable and what many governments do in attempting to resolve the instability, and in your response be sure to define **price supports** and **parity price**.

8. Distinguish between **price fixing** and **price ceilings**.

9. What does the **substitution effect** have to do with the **law of demand**?

10. Distinguish between the terms **marginal utility** and **the law of diminishing marginal utility**.

11. What are **opportunity costs** and why are they important to consumers?

12. Distinguish between the **life cycle hypothesis** and the **permanent income hypothesis**.

Useful Resources for Consumers

National Council on Economic Education
1140 Avenue of the Americas
New York, NY 10036
800-338-1192
www.economicsamerica.org

CIA World Fact Book
www.odci.gov/cia/publications/factbook/index.html

EconData
www.econdata.net

Economagic
www.economagic.com

Economics America
www.economicsamerica.org/

National Association for Business Economics
www.nabe.com/

Resources for Economists on the Internet
www.rfe.org

"What Do You Think" Questions

1. Try to envision the United States exactly as it is minus **property rights** for individuals and describe some ways in which our economic system would be different.

2. There literally are thousands of **markets** for consumers looking to purchase lunch in a restaurant. Think about the concept of **competition** in the immediate geographic area where you live and make two lists: (A) factors that enhance competition, and (B) factors that detract from competition.

3. The laws of **supply** and **demand** work well in an economic system when, in the words of the economists, "**others things are equal**." The world of reality, however, offers many exceptions because of **non-price determinants of demand**. Briefly describe 5 situations where these laws do not function effectively.

4. List examples from everyday life where the **substitution effect** negates the **income effect** in the areas of food, entertainment, and transportation.

**Appendix Issue 7-A
The Life Cycle and Permanent Income Hypotheses***

Economists offer two related explanations for human consumptions behavior. The life cycle hypothesis (LCH) and the permanent income hypothesis (PIH) are the two most useful models to understand the savings and spending behaviors of consumers. Even though the two models differ in definitions and in depicting consumer savings behavior, they have essentially similar promises and conclusions. Both models, under the utility framework, view consumers as being rational and informed. Thus, consumers will wisely arrange their whole resources over the life cycle and maintain a certain level of consumption. The essence is that humans consume based upon their idea of what their long-run or permanent income is expected to be. To maintain a steady rate of consumption, consumers save little when current income is low; savings is higher when current income is higher.

Life Cycle Hypothesis

The **life cycle hypothesis** was proposed by Franco Modigliani and his colleagues during the 1950s. According to this model, as a consumer you will arrange your life resources in such a way that you would like to enjoy the same level of consumption before and after your retirement. In order to do this, you have to save some money for your retirement while you are working instead of spending all you earn. When you reach your retirement age, you begin to **dissave** (spending more than earning). If you know how long your life expectancy is going to be, you could figure out how much you should save to keep your level of living unchanged after you stop earning. Since your savings will increase when you start working and decrease when you stop

working, the amount of your savings can be depicted as a hump-shaped line along with your age.

Using a simple formula, you can figure out how much you should save when you know how many years you are going to work and how long you are going to live after retirement. If R = retirement years, W = working years, C = consumption level, Y = annual income, and S = Y - C = annual savings, we have: RC = WS = W(Y-C). It means that the total savings from working should equal the total expenses needed for retirement.

For example, if you have a job with an annual salary of $50,000, and you know you will work for 30 years and live a retired life for 20 years, you can determine that your consumption level must be $30,000. That means if you still want to lead a life at the same level of living after retirement, you have to save $20,000 annually when working. In this example, there are several assumptions: the interest rate is zero; your annual income will remain the same; there is no change in your family compositions so that the consumption level is unchanged all your life; and you are not going to give money to your children or other people when you die. If necessary, you may relax some of these assumptions and re-estimate your consumption and savings levels.

Permanent Income Hypothesis

In a seminal book published in 1957, Milton Friedman proposed the **permanent income hypothesis**. This model has the similar conclusions as that of the life cycle hypothesis, but uses some different terms. PIH suggests that consumer income can be categorized as permanent income, current income, and transitory income. If your annual income is **current income**, then the average (there are several ways of figuring it out) of your annual incomes over your earning years is your **permanent income**. The difference between the current income and the permanent income is **transitory income**.

PIH posits that consumers always save and consume a fixed fraction of their permanent income, and save total transitory income. Thus, total savings consists of the sum of a fixed fraction of permanent income and all transitory income. It implies that consumers will leave a large amount of money to their children or other people when they die, which is the major difference between PIH and LCH.

For instance, if you have a job with an annual salary of $50,000 over your earning years, your permanent income will be the same as your current income, $50,000, and your transitory income will be zero. If your saving rate is 20%, you will spend $40,000 and save $10,000 every year. In another case, if you earn $40,000 in the first year, $50,000 in the second year, and $60,000 in the third year, your permanent income is $50,000, and your transitory incomes will be $10,000, 0, and $10,000, respectively. You will still spend $40,000 each year and save the remaining. For example, in the first year, you will save nothing. In the third year, you will save 20% permanent income, and all transitory income. Then, the total savings are $2,000. Here we do not consider retirement years and income from household assets. If these two variables are accounted, the permanent income will be adjusted, but the principle will be the same.

Shortcomings of Models

LCH and PIH are superior to the Keynesian absolute income hypothesis because they can explain why the American long-term saving rate remains almost the same while income has increased sharply and some other macro economic phenomena. However, many empirical studies show that these models cannot satisfactorily explain consumer saving behavior, especially when microeconomic data are used. The fundamental shortcoming of these two models is that they are based on the assumption that consumers are rational and fully informed. Neither is true in the real world.

Many revisions have been proposed, and among them is a **behavioral version of life-cycle hypothesis (BLH)**. BLH, proposed by Hersh Shefrin and Richard Thaler, acknowledges the limitations of consumers. Basically, the hypothesis holds three assumptions. First, consumers lack self-control, and they look for external instruments to help them to save enough money for retirement needs. Second, consumers have mental accounts in their minds, and they treat these mental accounts differently in terms of saving and consumption. Specifically, these accounts are current income account, asset account, and future income account. Consumers tend to spend all their current income account, but spend nearly nothing from their future income account. The tendency of spending their asset account is somewhere in between the previous two. Third, consumers frame their incomes according to these income sources, which means they have different consumption and saving patterns when incomes come from dissimilar sources.

They are more likely to save income from uncertain sources, such as bonuses, premiums, gifts, or other windfalls, and more likely to spend income from regular sources, such as salaries. BLH seems to take into account some key limitations of human beings, and it addresses behavioral characteristics of consumer savings. Proponents of BLH claim that their hypothesis is a more general one and LCH is a special case of BLH. Since this model is somewhat new, the testing of its validity is just in its beginning stage.

*Jing-jian Xiao, Associate Professor, University of Rhode Island

Chapter 8

Consumers in the Global Marketplace

OBJECTIVES

After reading this chapter, you should be able to:

1. Summarize the major world economic problems.

2. Explain the key economic concepts important to trade among nations.

3. Understand the net benefits of and barriers to free trade.

4. Appreciate the role of the United States in globalization, including identification of its inequities and net benefits.

5. Realize that regional trade agreements and the World Trade Organization are the rule-making entities of global trade.

6. Appreciate the need for the efforts of the international consumer movement to positively impact individuals and families living around the world.

Global integration has occurred on a massive scale in the last thirty years. It has been fostered by cheap and better communications and the development of worldwide markets for trade and finance. Because of the increasing interdependence among national economies, the world is a single economic marketplace. Of vital importance to the consumer interest is how each country's government deals with the economic issues and how world organizations choose to organize trade and deal with environmental concerns. The international consumer movement watches these events with a keen interest, participating in many of them.

This chapter focuses on how to pursue the consumer interest in the global marketplace. It begins by examining some of the world's fundamental economic problems, such as pollution, overpopulation and income inequality. Next is an exploration of four economic concepts that are key to understanding global trade. This is followed by a review of the net benefits of and barriers to free trade. An overview of globalization and the role the United States plays are discussed as well as the inequities and benefits of globalization. This includes an understanding of some of the economic problems and challenges facing the United States as it tries to compete in a global economy, such as low savings and big deficits. This is followed by a review of regional trade agreements and the World Trade Organization. The chapter closes with a review of the role of the international consumer movement, including a look at the dark side of marketing to developing countries.

World Economic Problems

The central economic problem facing all societies is the **scarcity** of limited resources to satisfy the unlimited needs and wants of humans. There never are enough resources to go around for everyone. In a given year, the **resources** available to produce goods (primarily labor, capital and technology) cannot be greatly increased and the technology available for production is subject to a limited amount of improvement.

People around the world look increasingly to government to solve their problems. Thus it is the task of politicians to deal with scarce resources in an attempt to resolve the fundamental **world economic problems** facing their countries. These economic problems include adequate food, clothing, shelter, medical care, and education for the people. Unfortunately, people often expect more of their politicians and their governments than they are able to deliver.

Economic progress is the solution to resolving such problems. **Progress** is steady improvement and movement toward a goal as a society or civilization. Education is at the heart of such progress. Each country moves forward at its own rate of growth, and some countries have benefitted more from economic progress than others. The decisions about how to create material well-being, where the benefits and costs are distributed, and how to weigh economic growth against other societal values are made in each country by government, businesses and consumers. **Sustainable development** is key to balanced progress. The United Nations defines this as "development that meets the needs of the present without compromising the ability of future generations to meet their own needs."

Countries moving toward more **advanced stages of economic development** enjoy many benefits of economic progress. Examples are high levels of living, shorter work weeks, less physically strenuous labor, longer life spans, more productive lives, excellent recreational facilities and choices, access to higher education, new technology, modern medicine, conveniences, high-quality products, and automation. The **industrialized countries of the world**, so-called **first-world countries**, such as the United States, United Kingdom, France, and Italy, have benefitted most from economic progress. **First-world countries** are often called **developed countries** as they are affluent, market-based economies.

Second-world countries are the centrally-planned economies of the communist and some former-communist nations of the world that have limited trade and interdependence with other countries. Compared to the first-world countries, second-world countries have **little economic development** and a much lower quality of life.

Third-world countries are underdeveloped or developing countries with little economic wealth and their economies rely substantial on agriculture and/or mining. Third-world countries are also called **developing countries** or **less developed countries (LDCs)**, and they are disadvantaged in such areas as health care, literacy, employment skills, and life expectancy. These countries are located primarily in South and East Asia, Africa, the Middle East, and Latin America. Of this population, 25 percent live in China and 20 percent live in India. Of the world's 6.2 billion people, **4.9 billion live in third-world countries**, 0.4 billion live in Eastern Europe and the former Soviet Union, and 0.9 billion live in industrialized nations.

The world's countries are also characterized by classifying them as the **north (the developed)** and the **south (the developing)**, implying that a nation's economic wealth is associated with the hemisphere in which it is located. Perhaps the most accurate way to describe countries is by their gross national product (GNP) and per capita income (see www.worldbank.org/data/), and that is how the World Bank makes its distinctions.

Eight fundamental economic problems exist: (1) population growth that strains resources, (2) damaging pollution, (3) crime, corruption and anarchy, (4) income inequality, (5) persistent poverty, (6) excessive military spending, (7) growing external debt, and (8) market reforms.

Economic Problem: Excessive Population Growth

The world faces a difficult challenge in **trying to provide food**, clothing, and medical care for its people. It took from the origin of mankind until 1960 for the world population to reach 3 billion. It took 17 years to grow from 3 to 5 billion, and only 12 more years for the world population to increase from 5 to 6 billion.

People younger than 15 make up **more than one-third of the population in 74 developing countries**. More than half are younger than age 20 and 45 percent of Africans are under age 15. (In the United States, approximately **28 percent** of the population is under age 20.) These young people will be entering their reproductive years in this generation. The world's growing population and accompanying overcrowding cause severe environmental degradation (deforestation and soil erosion), put extreme pressure on land and water resources (water depletion), and produce people with little expectation of good health, education, or employment.

With world population today at 6.2 billion, the United Nations projects that by 2010 **another billion** people will be added for a total of 7.2 billion. It is projected to be nine billion by 2050, a 50 percent increase from today. The world's population is growing at a rate of 90 million a year, 7.5 million a month, 1.7 million a week, 245,000 a day, 10,000 an hour, or 170 a minute—and 97 percent are born in developing countries. The World Bank predicts that two-thirds of the additional billions of people will live in countries where the average person earns **less than $2 a day**. Such numbers will place an enormous strain on political leaders, economic resources and the environment. The result will be increased planetary overcrowding.

A variety of efforts is being undertaken in most societies to control population growth in an effort to preserve the quality of life for future generations. One proposed worldwide economic goal is **zero population growth**. This suggests that for every child born and for every immigrant who enters a country, an equal number dies or leaves the country. A worldwide **fertility rate of about 2.11** would accomplish that goal. (The .11 allows for the deaths of children.) Ready access to family-planning services and increased educational opportunities combined with strong political leadership help lower birth rates and reduce the strain on economic resources. As an extreme example, China has a 1.2 billion population, and its official policy of "one couple, one child" includes heavy-handed measures ranging from forced abortions to expensive fines.

Just the **opposite problem** exists in almost all of Europe where the fertility rates range from **a low 1.2** in Spain and 1.3 in Italy to 1.7 in Sweden and the United Kingdom. Those aging societies lack a young labor force to earn, spend and pay taxes to support their elders' social benefits, and this is expected to cause labor shortages that will threaten economic growth. The fertility rate in the United States is 2.548, and the U.S. is the only major developed country with **a sustainable population**.

Population in many developing countries has been greatly affected by the **AIDS** virus, with more than 30 percent of adults in seven southern Africa countries infected. Thirty-eight million adults and children are living with HIV/AIDS. Sixty-eight million are expected to die by 2020. This means that part of an entire generation of people in their twenties and thirties will die and be unavailable to work and contribute to economic growth and prosperity in their countries. For example, life expectancy in Zambia **is now 33 years**, down from 65 only a dozen years ago.

Economic Problem: Damaging Pollution

Governments around the world have difficulty **raising taxes to pay for cleanup expenses** for damage to air, water, and land that often occurs with industrial progress and aggravated by excessive population growth. One in five people on earth does not have access to safe drinking water, and more people die every year from unsafe water than from all forms of violence, including war. People also pay for pollution with forfeited health and well-being. Conserving and replacing remaining natural resources are costly priorities of every nation in the world. In the United States, for example, taxes are collected and paid out of the government's Super Fund to pay for some of the nation's worst pollution cleanup sites.

Economic Problem: Crime, Corruption and Anarchy

The **lawlessness and tyranny** currently seen in many of the poorer regions of the world are illustrative of what our planet is likely to resemble in the not-too-distant future. Slums and shanty towns are proliferating into sprawling villages with surging numbers of young people who have no job opportunities and little hope for a better life. Many turn to crime. Unsafe streets—particularly at night—are teeming with young people committing unprovoked crimes in cities around the world. This occurs in countries like South Africa, Liberia and Somalia as well as Iraq, Pakistan and Brazil. Continuing refugee migration to urban areas contributes to a growing crisis of resource scarcity.

Distinctions **between crime and war** are becoming blurred. For many, says Robert Kaplan, war is a "step up economically, not down." In many countries, the initial motivations for war are largely replaced with conflicts over minerals, land, farm produce and tax revenues. Warring factions, says a U.N. report, engage "in **criminal activities** including theft, embezzlement, diversions of public funds, undervaluation of goods, smuggling, false invoicing, nonpayment of taxes, kickbacks to public officials, and bribery." Extortion by law-enforcement and immigration officials also prevails in many capital cities. An inept and corrupt political and business class practicing destructive behaviors results in reduced economic growth, impotent courts and law enforcement institutions, weak banks, inept regulators, closed markets, and meager foreign reserves. Think of Columbia. Places with **declining resources**—like Nigeria, Brazil, Yugoslavia and Indonesia—are becoming ungovernable as nation states. Language, ethnicity, history, and religion are more likely to define civilizations in the future, rather than today's political borders. Transparency International (www.transparency.org/) ranks countries on the level of corruption.

ECONOMIC INSIGHT:
Capital Flight Hurts Developing Countries

Affluent business people in developing countries often have access to illicit systems to exchange local-country money for hard currencies. **Capital flight** occurs when wealthy citizens of one country smuggle their cash to another country that is more likely to be a safe haven for the funds. Their money is safe from runaway inflation and a poor net investment return, from steep taxes on business profits and from government overthrows where capital can be expropriated. The amounts on deposit in the United States, Switzerland and France are staggering. Mexico, for example, owes over $100 billion in foreign debt yet its citizens have **nearly that amount on deposit in foreign banks**. Capital flight seriously damages the economies of those countries because once the funds are shipped abroad, that capital is not available to lend and utilize for local economic development.

Economic Problem: Income Inequality

Three-fourths of the world's population live in developing countries where **per capita income** is far less than in developed countries. In the U.S., per capita income exceeds **$29,000**. It is $4,300 in Mexico, $1,200 in the Philippines, $750 in China, $350 in Kenya, and $100 in Ethiopia.

Trying to live on such low incomes is difficult, as one might imagine. Realize, too, that incomes are not distributed evenly in societies. The degree of **income inequality** varies widely among countries. The bottom 90 percent of the world's population live in developing countries, and they account for only 20 percent of the world's income. The richest 10 percent reside in developed countries and they account for 80 percent of total income. The **Lorenz curve** is a widely used measure of income inequality across nations (see www.wikipedia.org/wiki/Lorenz_curve).

Economic Problem: Persistent Poverty

Poverty is the state of being poor where one lacks the means of providing material needs or comforts. Much of the world's population is denied the basic rewards of affluence: getting a job, learning to read, and living longer. **One quarter of the world's population lives in poverty**. Some 1.2 billion have no access to drinkable water and 2 billion live without electricity. According to the World Bank, 1.4 billion people live on less than $1 a day.

Two-thirds of the world's population goe to **sleep hungry** at night. Millions of people in the world die of malnutrition and hunger-related diseases every year; 40,000 die every day. Infectious and parasitic diseases are the leading cause of deaths in developing countries (42% of the total), but hardly anyone dies of such problems in developed countries (1%).

India's Nobel economist, Amata Sen, reports that, "in the terrible history of famines in the world, no substantial famine **has ever occurred** in any independent and democratic country with a relatively free press."

Poverty is also a cost of economic development because often it is caused by the **inequitable distribution of the benefits of change**. Governments around the globe are faced with deciding how their societies will attempt to lessen the discomfort of poverty by redistributing income. This is increasingly difficult to do in a world where the population is getting older. Over the past 30 years, the average life span has risen from 50 to 63.

Economic Problem: Excessive Military Spending

Military spending by third-world countries amounts to about $30 billion annually.[1] A report by the United Nations Development Programme observed that many of the world's poorest countries **spend more on military** than other items. For example, Angola, Chad, Pakistan, Peru, Syria, Uganda, and Congo spend half as much on education *and* health as on military. If such countries would cut back military spending by perhaps half, that amount would be available for **economic development**. This could increase the production and management of material wealth of a country or state through **investments** in such things as education, infrastructure, and agriculture.

Economic Problem: Growing External Debt

The industrialized countries have made **enormous loans** to the developing countries in the past, expecting that the principal would be repaid along with regular interest charges. Many loans were made to oil-exporting nations that had been earning great profits because of oil-price increases. The beginnings of the international debt crisis occurred when Mexico stated 20 years ago that it was no longer able to repay its debt obligations to foreign creditors. In the years since, about two dozen countries made similar pronouncements. Their **debt service**, amounts required to repay principal and interest, on more than $1.5 trillion owed had simply become too overwhelming. Countries like Argentina, Brazil, Chile, Mexico, Nigeria, and the Philippines accumulated debt equal to **25 to 90 percent** of their gross domestic products. Their debt service today is 20 to 45 percent of the value of exports from these countries.[2]

The size of an economy is a large factor in a country's ability, or inability, to handle its debt. Uganda, a country where one child in five dies before reaching age 5, is illustrative. The Ugandan government spends **$3 per person** on health care and **$17 per person** on debt repayments.

International debt problems for individual countries occur for **several reasons**:

1. large **budget deficits** fueled by too much government spending;

2. too **few taxes** on citizens;

3. too much money spent on consumer goods rather than **savings and investments**;

---

[1] Annual expenditures in the United States for the Department of Defense is $400 billion and rising; it is $10 billion in Russia.

[2] Debt equals about 9 percent of the U.S. gross domestic product and as a result, the United States requires a continuous inflow of foreign lending and investment to offset its passion for spending on imports.

4. closed economies and **heavily subsided industries** that protect local businesses from international competition, quality goods, and lower prices;

5. high **inflation** exacerbated by printing more and more paper currency;[3]

6. loans made with **variable interest rates** that rise and fall with inflation;

7. sluggish worldwide **economic growth**;

8. growing difficulties in earning **hard currencies** to use for repayments (e.g., legal tenders that are willingly accepted in international trade, such as dollars, pounds, yens, Deutsche marks); and

9. political leadership **unwilling** to recognize and act upon solutions in a timely manner.

Answers to the growing external debt problem are still being sought in an effort to avoid financial ruin for both creditors and debtors. The last 20 years have seen a lot of **debt relief** (or **debt restructuring**). Here governments obtain agreements from lenders to develop new repayment terms that typically extend the loan and permit a grace period when repayments for interest and/or principal are not required. The years ahead will continue to see rising international debts.

ECONOMIC INSIGHT:
Developing Countries Make Good Trading Partners

For over 50 years most of the industrialized countries have **helped developing countries** improve the lives of their people. Once the world leader in aid to developing nations, the U.S. now **ranks fourth** in dollars spent on such aid ($7.3 billion) and last among donor nations in the percentage of economic output spent on aid (0.1% of gross domestic product). Over the last 20 years, infant mortality rates in the developing countries have been cut in half, life expectancy has increased more than 10 years, 1 billion people have clean water who previously did not, and average real incomes have doubled. Developing countries make good trading partners too, buying approximately $200 billion in U.S. goods. This trade supports **three million American jobs**.

Economic Problem: Market Reforms

Numerous countries are strapped with huge international debts and they are creating government and business reforms both to strengthen their economies and meet their financial obligations. The most **common reform** in many developing countries is to shift their economic systems **away from socialism and toward market-oriented capitalism**. The policies of the **International Monetary Fund**, an organization that makes short-term loans to countries in economic crisis, strongly supports such transitions.

There is a worldwide trend toward countries adopting U.S. style **market reforms**. This requires private property rights, free markets, free flow of resources, shrinking state payrolls, and privatizing inefficient government-run industries. **Privatization** is the selling of government-owned businesses to private citizens. Countries moving in this direction must

---

[3] **Hyperinflation** is an extremely high rate of inflation (over 100%) in an economy which undermines both business and political confidence. A loaf of bread in Germany cost $1 billion marks in 1921.

permit prices to rise on basic items (e.g., food, clothing, rent, fuel) cut subsidies (e.g., transportation, telecommunications, housing, bread), strengthen banking systems, allow unprofitable enterprises to fail and go bankrupt, and allow profitable companies and their shareholders to keep a larger share of their profits. These efforts usually result in increased government spending on education and health care, which reduces poverty rates.

Some of the **societal costs** of market reforms are terribly difficult for many to accept. These include decreased government spending, massive layoffs of government workers and armed forces, less government intervention in the economy, relaxed health and safety standards, longer working hours for lower incomes, high inflation, and the absence of a social safety net to take care of the disabled, aged and unemployed. One of the major criticisms of market reforms is that **it benefits too few people**. Crime often rises, and this contributes to discontent as well. It sometimes takes a generation for the people to feel that their lives are better.

Key Economic Concepts in Global Trade

The purpose of trade is to import; exports are the price a country pays for the imports. There are four economic concepts that are essential to understanding global trade.

Pareto Efficiency: Economic Trade is a "Win-Win" Situation

Economic trade across international boundaries is **a necessity** because no one country has everything it needs or wants. One country wants something that can be produced with relative ease in another country. Many people **falsely assume** that international trade is a **zero-sum game** where the wealth of all traders is simply redistributed because the gain of each winner is the other's loss.

In reality, trade is a win-win situation and well-informed people around the world support expanding international trade. If both parties in an economic trade did not intend on gaining, they would not engage in a voluntary exchange. International trade is based upon the concept of **Pareto efficiency** (or **Pareto optimality**) where both sides to a condition cannot be made better off without reducing the advantage of the other. Thus, each party in the context **must be satisfied**. Countries experience mutual benefits and gains from trade.

Economies of Scale

At the heart of economic trade is the economic concept of **economies of scale** where the cost per unit decreases as the quantity of production increases and all resources are variable. Thus, lower average costs of production occur as the volume of production increases. It is uneconomical to produce 100 aircraft, 1,000 television sets or 5,000 automobiles, but quite economical to produce many thousands or hundreds of thousands. The task for each country is to **find customers at home** and elsewhere for all those products.

Absolute Advantage

Countries **specialize** in making certain goods because of varying combinations of resources and skills. Hence the high-tech countries of the United States and Japan are well equipped to produce automobiles and China and Mexico are efficient producers of patio chairs, shoes and power tools. An **absolute advantage** occurs when a country has a monopolistic position or if it produces an item at the lowest cost. Absolute advantage is determined by comparing the true costs of producing particular goods in different countries, including the number of hours of labor required and the wages paid for that labor.

Comparative Advantage

Note that while one country such as the United States is extremely efficient in terms of hours of labor, absolute advantage is not the critical factor in deciding whether or not to trade. Some countries have an absolute advantage for several products while another country may have no absolute advantages, yet **trading opportunities exist** because each should seek its comparative advantage. A country has a **comparative advantage** in a good or service if it can supply such with a smaller sacrifice of alternative goods and services than can the rest of the trading world. In international trade it pays a country to trade when it specializes in producing a specific product more efficiently than any others. Moreover, countries should trade **what they are good at producing**.

To illustrate this point consider this example. A successful president of an accounting firm may possess excellent typing skills, perhaps even better than his or her administrative assistant. Since the assistant may be incapable of managing a large firm, he or she would run the business poorly. Thus, the president has an absolute advantage in both typing and managing. However, the president's time—the comparative advantage—is best spent managing the accounting firm. The administrative assistant has a comparative advantage in typing, since he or she would be ineffectively running the business. Therefore, the whole business runs quite efficiently because each works in accordance with his or her comparative advantage.

International trade among countries is based on the principle of comparative advantage. Each country has **a comparative advantage in producing some products** and they should specialize accordingly. The U.S. Department of Commerce estimates that every $1 billion in exports creates more than 19,000 jobs in the United States.

AN ECONOMIC FOCUS: The Consumer Interest in International Trade

It has become a truism that consumers now operate in a global marketplace. From the viewpoint of a citizen of the United States, we not only import a tremendous quantity of goods from countries like Japan, Germany, and China; but "All-American" companies like Gillette, Colgate, IBM, Coca-Cola, Digital Equipment, Dow Chemical, Xerox, and Caterpillar receive more than **half of their sales revenue** from overseas markets. Because of the growing importance of imports and exports in global economics, it is important for consumers and their representatives to understand where the interests of consumers lie in discussions of free trade and trade restrictions.

The consumer movement, especially in the United States but also elsewhere, has historically attempted to steer clear of involvement in the debate over free trade and protectionism. Because organized labor typically opposes **free trade** (to save American jobs), consumer activists have been caught between two conflicting forces: the **consumer interest** in lower prices brought about through free trade, and the consumer interest in having strong political allies, in this case organized labor. The consumer movement's low profile on the free trade debate was sustainable when trade issues themselves were thought of as relatively unimportant, technical issues. Today, however, the prominence of trade issues has **forced the consumer movement to define the consumer interest** vis-a-vis trade issues and reconcile that interest with those of other groups in society including, but not confined to, organized labor. In particular, the consumer movement has found itself drawn into discussions about the North American Free Trade Agreement (NAFTA) and the World Trade Organization (WTO).

The cornerstone of the argument in favor of free trade is the theory of **comparative advantage**. The theory, first put into formal terms by economist David Ricardo in 1817, is often misunderstood as merely an argument about the benefits of specialization. It takes no great genius to argue that if farmers in the United States are especially productive when growing potatoes and Mexican farmers are especially productive when growing tomatoes, the two nations should specialize and engage in trade. But what if it were true (which it isn't) that U.S. workers are more productive with respect to every good and service than Mexican workers? Would it make sense for the United States to trade with Mexico at all? The theory of comparative advantage explains why it would.

To simplify matters, imagine a world composed of only the United States and Mexico and producing only two goods--beer and tortilla chips. Imagine further that it takes a U.S. worker one minute to produce a six-pack of beer and two minutes to produce a bag of tortilla chips, while it takes a Mexican worker three minutes to produce a six-pack of beer and four minutes to produce a bag of tortilla chips. Note that U.S. workers are more productive than Mexican workers on both counts.

The key to understanding the theory of comparative advantage is to **realize that a country trades *with itself* every time it decides to produce one good rather than another**. In our example, every time the United States devotes a minute of worker time to producing tortilla chips, it is giving up two six-packs of beer. Thus, the United States should be willing to trade beer for tortilla chips if it can give up less than two minutes of worker time for each six-pack it exports. Conversely, Mexico gives up 1.33 six-packs of beer every time it produces a bag of chips; Mexico will gladly trade chips for beer if it can get more than 1.33 six-packs for a bag of chips.

Suppose someone proposes an exchange rate of 1.5 six-packs of beer for one bag of chips. Will the United States want to deal? Yes, because it costs the U.S. twice as much in worker time (i.e., two six-packs of foregone beer production) to produce chips as to produce beer. Will Mexico want to trade under these terms? Yes again because one bag of chips will only yield 1.33 six-packs in Mexico but 1.5 six-packs in international trade.

Note that the theory of comparative advantage implies an improvement in the **standard of living** for all parties involved. Referring back to our example, U.S. workers have to work, in the absence of trade, for three minutes to buy a six-pack of beer and a bag of chips. With trade, they need only work 2.5 minutes. Similarly, the effort necessary for Mexican workers to afford the same purchase declines from 7 minutes to 6.6 minutes. These differences may seem small, but aggregate them over more workers and more time and you realize the potential benefits of free trade. All of a sudden, the "dismal science" of economics yields **a win-win situation**.

Despite the impressive lineage and logic of the theory of comparative advantage, there are many parties who view it as too narrow or insensitive to the power differences that exist among trading parties. Consumerists like Ralph Nader have objected to free trade agreements on the grounds that strict consumer protection standards can be **challenged as "barriers to trade."** If the United States, for example, wants strict limits on pesticide residues on food, this may be challenged by foreign governments as a form of protectionism if American farmers use fewer pesticides than foreign producers. To choose a recent actual example, an American standard requiring tuna to be harvested with minimal threat to dolphins (who become ensnared in tuna nets) was attacked by Mexico and declared an unfair trade barrier under the rules of WTO. Positions can be reversed, too, as when Thailand's ban on cigarette advertising was attacked by American cigarette manufacturers on the basis that the ban restricted their ability to compete and therefore constituted a barrier to trade.

After years of quiescence, consumer activists have been drawn into the debate over free trade and protectionism. Until recently, most consumerists willing to take a public position on international trade issues have downplayed the benefits of free trade and emphasized its potential threats to consumer, environmental, and worker protection standards. While Ralph Nader is against free trade, **Consumers Union**, perhaps the most powerful organization in the U.S. consumer movement, supports it.

*Robert N. Mayer, Professor, University of Utah

Globalization and the United States

Globalization is the international, sophisticated, open, and free flowing movement of economic trade in capital, goods, services, people, information, and ideas, along with applications of technology. Globalization is already a **fact of life** as it has been evolving for thousands of years.

Thirty years ago economic trade comprised **9 percent** of the gross domestic product of the United States and now it is **24 percent** of the economy's output. Globalization has encouraged an explosion of wealth and technology. Foreigners now own 7 percent of U.S. stocks, 20 percent of corporate bonds and 35 percent of federal treasury issues.

The *Foreign Policy* magazine Globalization Index ranks the U.S. 12ᵗʰ among the 50 most globalized countries on such factors as foreign trade, Internet use, international telephone traffic, and number of international visitors. Singapore ranks first. The more globalized countries tend to have **more income equality** within their borders than less globalized countries.

Being the largest economy in the world, the United States remains a dominant player in global economics. World trade is $13 trillion today, compared to $7 trillion a decade ago. **More than half** of all international trade occurs between **industrialized countries**: Australia, Canada, Japan, New Zealand, United States and all the Western European countries. The leading products being traded around the globe are petroleum (the U.S. imports 53 percent of its oil consumption, and this will rise to 65 to 70 percent by the year 2025), motor vehicles, and machinery. The U.S. is a major trading partner for a number of countries. **Canada is the U.S.'s best trading partner and Mexico is second**. The U.S.'s worst trade deficits are with Japan and China. Trade comprises about 30 percent of U.S. economic output, compared to only 9 percent in 1960. Still, the U.S. economy produces 90 percent of what it consumes.

While the U.S. remains the world's largest exporter, the slower-growing economies in Europe and Asia, especially in Japan, make it **difficult for the U.S. to sell goods abroad.** Europe's **"structural economic slump"** continues to some extent because its high payroll taxes and tight employment regulations raise labor costs. Such policies deter the start of new businesses and threaten marginal businesses. The challenge is compounded by the enormous amount of **excess capacity** around the globe to produce most products. The excess has been estimated at 30 percent, and that factor remains at the core of persistently high unemployment figures for a number of industrialized countries.

Criticisms of Globalization

In today's global society, employment is shifted around the world to **where labor is cheapest**, all other things being equal. As a result, some sectors of the U.S. economy have been hurt with layoffs and factory closings. This happens in foreign countries, too.

Among the **objections to globalization** is that there is a gap between traditional political thinking based on the nation-state. Critics argue that international organizations like the World Bank, International Monetary Fund, and World Trade Organization intrude into national sovereignty. Critics demand that within these organizations much greater emphasis needs to be given "to protect the rights of governments, including state and local governments; establish appropriate levels of protection for health, safety, and the environment; and protect the rights of consumers to make informed decisions based on how products are made."[4] A threat to consumer protection occurs when standards within international agreements, such as for food safety, **are reduced** to the lowest common denominator. Critics also accurately argue that international organizations often are undemocratic and secretive.

Critics of globalization—including organizations of workers, environmentalists, and farmers—argue that it has **many failures**. These include a growing gap between the "haves" and the "have nots," dangerous and unhealthy working environments that are the norm, and illegal **sweatshops** (shops or factories where employees work long hours for low wages under terrible working conditions). For information, see the union perspective at www.uniteunion.org and www.americanapparel.org as well as the views of the U.S. Department of Labor (www.dol.gov). Other failures, say the critics, are the use of child labor and **forced labor** (prisoners or slaves), workers denied basic rights to organize and strike, **environmental degradation** (tearing down forests, over-fishing, rapid depletion of minerals, and poisoning of land by agrochemicals), rural communities being bypassed and/or dramatically changed by "progress," and too much influence of corporate power over the political process.

Another part of the **fear of globalization** is the growing dominance of American culture and values. These are personified by movies, syndicated television shows, magazines, fast food, Internet communications in English only, and American slang. Developing countries in particular are experiencing inevitable political unease, says former Secretary of State, Henry Kissinger, because they feel they are "at the mercy of forces neither the individuals nor the government can influence any longer."

Globalization is not the evil force claimed by protesters who desire to improve the environment, union members out to protect jobs, consumer advocates asking for a voice in proceedings, and radicals who believe big corporations are evil by nature. They seem **well-intentioned but uninformed**, observes Mortimer B. Zuckerman, Editor-in-Chief of *U.S. News & World Report*.[5]

ECONOMIC INSIGHT:
The U.S. Exports "Its Values" Around the World

America exports its **values** primarily through music, Hollywood films, old television reruns, magazines, theme parks, and advertisements. Such exports provide a substantial balance of payment surplus for the United States. Respect for copyright protection around the globe is essential to the success of this type of international trade.

Critics argue that **American images control the whole world**. They claim that the cultural identity of nations and of individuals is at risk. Some countries, France and Canada in particular, have established barriers, ostensibly to keep some of the American culture out. These include restrictions on who can own media and regulations that a certain percentage of films be domestically produced.

Benefits of Globalization

Globalization means a period of **growing economic interdependence among nations**, and it has had tremendous net benefits for the world's peoples. While American and foreign

---

[4] Consumers have stake in trade policy, (2000, April). *CFA News* (Consumer Federation of America), 2.
[5] Zuckerman, M.B. (2000, July 3). A bit of straight talk. *U.S. News & World Report*, 60

businesses are profiting by selling goods to other countries, more jobs are created thus helping keep unemployment low. Increased trade has sharply raised living standards over the past 50 years for citizens of Japan, South Korea, China, and Singapore. Similar benefits are reaching many more countries (e.g., Mexico, Poland, South Africa, and Brazil) that are now enjoying increased levels of living as a result. Consumers everywhere are **big winners** because they get greater choices and lower prices. Other long-term benefits from globalization are rising wages, better working conditions, and increased protection for the environment. While improvements may not occur immediately, history shows that they definitely do over time. Massive changes in world society have happened over the past fifty years and further changes will be brought about by globalization.

The Future of Trade and Globalization

Leaders are challenged to reconcile the interests of individual countries with the global economy, how to encourage economic growth with little inflation, and how to help former bureaucratically controlled command economic systems become capitalistic market-driven economies without causing hyperinflation and political turmoil. Leaders also need to listen to the voices of critics, hear them, and "work aggressively to correct the glaring inequities of today," says David Gergen, *U.S. News & World Report.*

A challenge for the U.S. is to stimulate the global economy, but it is complicated by the large trade surpluses of Pacific Rim countries. A nation's **balance of trade** is the total value of its imports less its exports. Because of excessive imports, the U.S. has an enormous and growing trade deficit; more imports than exports. Twenty-five years ago, the U.S. was the world's largest creditor with other countries owing $270 billion; today the **U.S. is the world's largest debtor** as it owes more than $1.5 trillion.

Such deficits are the function of the **gap** between how much Americans save and invest. It is not a reflection of the quality of products made in the U.S. The trade deficit is a mirror image of the gap between domestic savings and investments because countries have to sell more goods and services to the U.S. than they buy to generate the extra cash to lend to America.

A **long-term solution** to these challenges is to take actions to turn this country's priorities around to better focus on increasing productive investments, not consumption. **Investment** is spending intended to promote future production by adding to the stock of capital goods, such as equipment, machinery and technology. Examples of **social investments** include investments in work skills and education, infrastructure, and research and development. Investment, not consumption, is the key economic catalyst for economic growth.

The United States' 50-year emphasis on **consumer consumption** (spend, lend, borrow, and speculate) may be difficult to turn around toward a focus on investment. Private consumption in the U.S. accounts for **87 percent** of GDP compared with 72 percent for Germany and 66 percent for Japan. Strong incentives to save and invest do not exist in the United States. The current system penalizes savings and investments with income taxes on interest, dividends and corporate income.

Free Trade

Economist Adam Smith wrote in 1776 that, "If a foreign country can supply us with a commodity cheaper than we ourselves can make it, better buy it from them with some part of the produce of our own industry, employed in a way in which we have some advantage."

Trade policy **should be about protecting consumer interests** by preserving their access to the world's supply of goods and services at the lowest possible prices.

The interest of consumers around the world is centered in low prices, good quality and lots of choices, and these factors are enhanced through the reduction of trade restraints. Import barriers that protect business or labor interests *within a particular country* **punish consumers** with higher prices *within* that country.

Free trade (more accurately called **trade expansion**) is considered free or open when goods and services can move into markets without restrictions and prices are determined by supply and demand. When goods are traded between two countries without taxes, it is described as **duty free trade**. The idea of freely traded goods across international borders is appealing because it improves the quality of life, at the lowest possible cost, by allowing goods and services to come from anywhere in the world. However, the political realities of each nation result in them placing restrictions on international trade. Many countries have explicit or implicit forms of **industrial policy aimed at protecting** certain businesses, farmers, and labor groups. As a result, trade disputes occur between and among countries.

The Benefits of Free Trade

It is well established that economic growth is essential for improving the well-being of people. The ultimate purpose of free trade is **to import more**, and this means more consumer consumption. Free trade does not create more jobs; instead, it creates *better* jobs. And, those higher paying jobs allow the workers to acquire goods and services to live well. Free trade means greater exports, faster economic growth, and better jobs for each trading partner. Exporting firms in the U.S. pay 10 percent more than other businesses in wages and benefits. Increased trade provides the economies of the global community with a healthier, well-nourished, well-educated and better-skilled labor force. Communities of such able people are the best foundation for future economic growth.

If free trade were allowed to operate among all nations, the principles of comparative advantage would cause economic resources within each country to be shifted to the production of goods for which comparative advantages existed. Benefits of free trade would include **lower prices** for consumers, greater choices of goods, increased worldwide employment, and efficient allocation of international resources. Also, one of the benefits of free trade is a sure way to promote democracy.

Some Barriers to Free Trade

In spite of the benefits of free trade, each national government is generally much more interested in the **well-being of its own citizens** rather than the people of the world. This is especially true in economic trade. Therefore, for a host of political (mostly profit-protecting) reasons, nations erect barriers to free trade where motivations are grounded in ignorance, cynicism and cowardice. Foremost among the barriers is **corruption**. Immoral and dishonest politicians and business persons pervert free trade. A number of countries, including many Asian countries, practice **crony capitalism** where governments prop up certain businesses considered key to their economies, and political reelections, with special favors, including overlooking the companies keeping two, or even three, sets of accounting books to make them seem profitable. Less obvious a barrier is corruption of a country's political system to protect certain companies and industries. Political campaign contributions from such groups are just like bribes because they are, in effect, protection money. (See Chapters 4, 9 and 18 for numerous examples of criminal corporate behavior in the United States.)

Free trade requires **transparency** in both government procurement, rather than bribery in big construction contracts and sweetheart deals to exclude imports, and in decision-making and dispute-settlement procedures. Outside observers should be able to view and understand transactions. What is most needed is consumer confidence in the processes of **setting standards and resolving trade disputes**. The American National Standards Institute (ANSI), a private nonprofit organization, furthers voluntary standards and certification activities as a means of advancing the national economy; benefitting the public health, safety and environment; and facilitating trade and commerce. It communicates U.S. interests to international organizations, such as the International Standards Organization (ISO).

Most **barriers to free trade** are legal restrictions on imported goods in the form of tariffs, quotas, embargoes, **health and safety standards** (including, whether a genuine fear or not, genetically engineered foods), foreign-exchange controls, and/or dumping. For example, barriers to the Japanese market add as much as 40 percent to the price of U.S. imports sold there and 30 percent to cars sold in France. Levi's jeans that sell for $38 in the U.S. sell for more than $65 in Britain and Sweden.

A **tariff** (or **import duty**) is an **international sales tax** on imported and exported goods (even though no similar tax is applied to identical goods produced domestically), and it is designed to make imported goods more expensive to the domestic consumers. Many developing countries rely upon tariffs as an important source of revenue. Average tariffs in the **U.S. are 2.8 percent**, although there are higher tariffs on imported orange juice (40%), brooms (42%) and flashlights (25%). Tariffs average 19 percent for the Philippines and 12 percent for Brazil. Fewer products will be imported if they must be sold at a higher price, thus giving an advantage to producers with zero tariffs.

A **quota** (or an **import quota**) is a government limit on the quantity (often a proportional share or maximum amount) of a certain good that can be legally imported into a particular country during a given time period. An **embargo** (or a **trade embargo**) is an effort to bring a complete halt to trading for a particular product. While tariffs and quotas are designed to protect economic markets, embargoes are imposed for political reasons. **Health and safety standards** serve to guard the public health by requiring that certain products meet specific standards, and these are sometimes used to keep foreign competitors out of domestic markets.

Foreign-exchange controls are restrictions on amounts of foreign currencies that can be legally purchased or sold. When importers are restricted from obtaining foreign currency, they are limited from using that currency to purchase goods to import. A **currency devaluation** is a purposeful decrease in the value of a nation's currency relative to the values of currencies of other countries. This increases the costs of imported goods and decreases the cost of domestically produced goods for foreign purchasers. **Buy-domestic policy** is a procurement procedure requiring that governments purchase only from local producers. It is the sometimes popular "Buy American" slogan made into law in the U.S. and abroad. Many countries have these policies covering their own locally produced goods; so do many U.S. states. **Subsidies** are government payments in the form of cash, tax reductions, low-interest loans, low-cost insurance, government-industry partnership, and/or government-sponsored research, to encourage exports. Subsidies, a permanent fixture of government around the world, amount to more than $500 billion among all countries.[6]

---

[6] According to the Worldwatch Institute, local, state and federal governments in the U.S. pay $120 billion a year in road and driving costs, in addition to gasoline, vehicle and highway taxes. This amounts to 70 cents for every gallon of gasoline or diesel fuel sold. Are these subsidies or simply infrastructure?

AN ECONOMIC FOCUS ON... How the Supply of and Demand for Labor Affect Wage Rates in Developing Countries*

Many American-owned firms have established labor-intensive manufacturing facilities in developing countries, such as Mexico. Fifteen years ago, over half of Mexico's 400 largest industries were foreign owned. Today, General Motors is one of Mexico's largest employers.

The **low cost of labor** is one of the major reasons for U.S. firms moving manufacturing facilities to developing countries. Such foreign ventures by U.S. firms emerged in the 1960s and continues today. U.S. tax and foreign policies encourage U.S. firms to invest in Mexico and other developing countries in order (1) to provide people in those countries with employment and (2) to give the American firms the advantages of lower wage rates. The U.S. firms **offer developing countries key factors of production** such as capital, technology and managerial skills. That allows the utilization of an existing labor force that is relatively abundant and is underemployed and/or unemployed.

Basic labor economics explain how supply of and demand for labor affect wage rates in developing countries. The concept of **supply explains the lack of suitable employees in the United States** when examining the behavior of both workers and potential workers in the U.S. For purposes of illustration, assume that U.S. workers have decided to work in a specific occupation and that all jobs in that particular occupation are quite similar, thus comparable. In choosing an employer, these employees then only need to consider the wages that various employers are offering. As a result, relevant U.S. firms would offer competitive wages. No firm would offer a wage higher than competing firms because it would be paying more than necessary to attract a suitable number and quality of employees. If the U.S. firm pays less than competitive wages, as is the case for those U.S. companies inclined to move to Mexico, potential employees will seek employment with the firm paying higher wages. This then leaves the lower-paying U.S. firm without a sufficient supply of labor. A firm may attract desired employees at a lower than average pay only if it offered non-comparable jobs, i.e., with more pleasant working conditions, longer paid vacations, etc. This is simply not the case for the firms that have found it advantageous to move their operations to Mexico.

The availability of potential employees in Mexico stems from the depressed economic conditions of that country. Because the labor force in Mexico is largely underemployed or unemployed, the number of entrants to the Mexican labor force has and is expected to continue to greatly exceed departures. Therefore, the number of potential employees is actually greater than the number of jobs available. Due to such an **oversupply of labor**, employers can offer a minimal wage and still attract the quality and number of employees desired. For example, in a recent year, the average hourly compensation for workers in the United States was over $14 while it was less than $2.50 in Mexico. Such lower wages easily offset the slightly lower productivity rates of the U.S. manufacturing firms located in Mexico. At such low labor costs, U.S. employers in Mexico are willing to employ more workers than they would in the United States, thus becoming almost as productive as similar firms in the United States. Such savings in wages also allows employers to pay to transport their products back to the U.S. and to other markets around the world while still offering them for sale at competitive prices.

Companies in the United States are increasingly establishing operations in Mexico and other developing countries **to reduce costs and improve their competitive edge** in pricing in the global market. The low cost of labor is incentive enough to encourage many such ventures.[1]

---

[1]Rather than moving abroad, some U.S. manufacturing facilities (particularly women's garment manufacturers) employ **sweatshop labor** within the borders of the United States, factories that pay less than the minimum wage, ignore federal wage and safety standards, and require 60-hour workweeks.

*Tamra Minor, Assistant to the Vice President, The Ohio State University

Dumping is the practice of selling goods in foreign countries for less than the price charged domestically, or for less than the price of production. Countries dump goods to damage foreign competition, to drive rival firms out of a foreign market, to secure a foothold in a particular foreign market, to preserve jobs at home, and sometimes to earn foreign currency, especially hard currency. Once a complaint has been filed with the U.S. Department of Commerce, the government must follow strict guidelines to determine whether dumping occurred and if domestic firms have been injured. If so, addition taxes will be levied. Recently, U.S. steelmakers have complained that Japanese and Brazilian steel exporters were dumping.

The Results of Protectionism

Those who favor restrictions on international trade to **reduce foreign competition** against domestic goods and services believe in **protectionism**. A classic example of a trade barrier is the 1920 Jones Act that requires trade between domestic ports within the United States must be via U.S.-owned ships that were built in the U.S., fly the U.S. flag, and employ only U.S. workers. That boosts shipping costs, so **consumers pay higher prices**.

Protectionists argue for trade restrictions to protect the health of consumers (from supposedly dangerous or unhealthy goods), to defend new or weak industries, to safeguard national security (perhaps by keeping certain technology out of the hands of potential enemies), to improve a nation's balance of payments, and to retaliate against another country's trade restrictions. Protectionism can reach the point of a **trade war** where a state of conflict is carried on between nations as each attempts to retaliate against the other's barriers to international trade.

The world learned during the 1930s that the Great Depression was partially due to the **protectionists' attitudes** of the United States and its trading partners during those years. The Smoot-Hawley Tariff Act of 1930 placed U.S. import tariffs on thousands of products, averaging 60 percent, ostensibly to "raise the incomes of U.S. workers." The nations of the world retaliated with their own tariffs and within four years world trade dropped 70 percent. Incomes and prices dropped similarly. In 1934, the Reciprocal Trade Agreements Act became law which raised tariffs, commencing the decline in trade. Beginning in 1947, the General Agreement on Trade and Tariffs (GATT) began the effort toward free trade among nations. Today, tariffs on imports **average about 5 percent**.

The Institute for International Economics (IIE) reports that barriers to imports **cost American consumers $70 billion a year**, or about $1,000 for the average family. The IIE authors calculate that of the $70 billion, $16 billion goes to the federal government in tariff revenue and $43 billion goes to producers and shareholders in 21 U.S. industries (who can boost their share of the American market and raise prices without serious competition). Four billion goes to 190,000 U.S. blue-collar workers, who get to keep their jobs because of protectionism. Perhaps most shocking is the cost to consumers in higher prices—it amounts to $170,000 a year for each job saved; five times the annual pay of those workers.

U.S. Industrial Policy of Managed Trade

The U.S. has an explicit **industrial policy**. Here the government plays a growing role in coordinating a strategic plan of policies aimed at protecting and developing selected domestic industries. An industrial policy redirects the **invisible hand** of the free competitive market by having the visible hand of government give a push to particular economic activities. It does this by asking strategically sophisticated competitors to pursue government and business-established national industrial goals. The **claim** is that government must help direct the nation's industrial policy because one cannot trust the future to the invisible hand of the competitive market.

For example, the U.S. pays $3 billion for a research program on hydrogen-powered cars. In Europe, the Airbus consortium, which with massive financial infusions from four European governments (Great Britain, France, Germany and Spain) over the past decade, has captured one-third of the world market for large commercial jets. Another example is Japan's Ministry of Industry and Trade (MITI) that has vigorously pursued an industrial policy for **more than 30 years**.

One part of this international economic trade policy already implicitly practiced among a number of countries (and in some places explicitly) is called **managed trade** (or **results-based trade**). This is an open use of government policy to intervene in the market and **arrange country-to-country deals** for precise splits of import markets. The result is tacit government agreements on acceptable levels of trade surpluses. For example, Japan would be permitted to sell X number of vehicles in the United States when the U.S. is permitted to sell Y pounds of rice in Japan.

The worst type of industrial policy **subsidizes failing industries** and companies in an effort to preserve employment. The next worst is for government to spend too much money on ventures with little potential payoffs. One clear risk is from massive price increases from so-called protected industries. Because of inflated prices, managed trade is against the consumer interest; however, such trade *may* be in the public interest of the United States (as well as other countries).

ECONOMIC INSIGHT:
Cartels Overcharge Consumers

A **cartel** is a group of firms that formally agree to coordinate their production and pricing decisions in a manner that maximizes joint profits. This is done by controlling and limiting production as well as fixing prices. Cartels are illegal in the United States because they in effect act as a monopoly.

Over twenty years ago, the **Organization of Petroleum Exporting Countries (OPEC)** cartel shocked the world with the first of two sharp increases in oil prices. The second shock saw OPEC raise prices eightfold. The once powerful 12-country cartel still exists but it is no longer able to keep all of its members in line. Every time OPEC sets quotas individual countries quietly violate the agreement by going ahead and producing and charging what they please. To increase their incomes, individual countries find they can increase sales of oil, surreptitiously cheating, while simultaneously watching all their cartel friends voluntarily restrain supply.

As a result, world oil production is rising and prices generally remain competitive, in part because a number of oil-producing countries do not belong to OPEC. A cartel must firmly control supply to manipulate prices. International cartels also exist in coffee and diamonds.

Regional Trade Agreements and the World Trade Organization

The threat of economic stagnation serves to motivate countries to negotiate trade agreements with other countries resulting in a number of regional trade agreements. A **regional trade agreement** is an effort by an economic community of countries to greatly reduce tariffs to encourage economic trade among the members' nations. In effect, they represent a series of tradeoffs among trading partners **seeking to expand markets**. There are more than 130 trade agreements in the world.

An **economic community** is an organization of nations formed to promote free trade among themselves and to create common economic policies. Names of regional trade agreements include the European Union (EU), Latin American Free Trade Association (LAFTA), Southern Africa Development Community, Asia-Pacific Economic Cooperation (APEC), and the North American Free Trade Agreement (NAFTA). The U.S. wants to expand NAFTA into an operational 34-nation Free Trade Area of the Americas (FTAA) from Arctic to the Antarctic (excluding Cuba) to provide increased trade for the 900 million consumers in the hemisphere. Mideast governments from Muslim nations are pushing for trade pacts with the United States.

A commonality among developing countries is an extremely **low gross domestic product**. As a result, second and third-world countries generally visualize economic development as a way to improve the well-being of their peoples. Thus, they usually seek **equitable trade relations** with other countries so as to enable the poorer countries to develop over time the capacity to compete on a more equal basis in international markets. Key in such trade agreements is to not undermine the achievement of domestic self-reliance in the production of food. Trade agreements recognize **equitable** trade arrangements.

North American Free Trade Agreement

The **North American Free Trade Agreement (NAFTA)** went into effect in 1994. It establishes a framework for reducing trade barriers and increasing business investment throughout North America—the U.S., Canada and Mexico. NAFTA is working. One of the biggest benefits has been to commit Mexico, which **had been a closed economy** only a few years earlier, to free trade and participation in the international community. Mexico now purchases more U.S. products than any other nation except Canada and Japan. The U.S. Department of Labor reports that in the first five years 210,000 workers suffered NAFTA-related job losses. This figure is less that the average number of new jobs created every month in the United States.

European Union

The **European Union (EU)** is a group of nearly 25 European countries that have as its stated objective the removal of trade barriers and administrative restrictions to the free movement of goods, services, people and money within the community. This loose confederation is a market equivalent to that of the United States, although the total population involved is larger, 450 million. The pan-European approach promotes low inflation, lower cross-border prices and an economic growth rate in Europe in excess of 3 percent. The **euro** is the official currency of the EU.

The EU, headquartered in Brussels, is **in the process** of removing customs, tariffs, and non-tariff barriers among the major European countries with the aim of creating a "single market" for the purchase and sale of goods and services. Full economic unification of the member nations of the EU and elimination of all trade barriers are occurring slowly. Harmonization of rules and regulations will clearly facilitate free circulation of goods and services among the European nations. The EU's Commissioner for Competition works with the U.S. Federal Trade Commission on issues involving mergers and monopoly power between and among countries. Decisions will be community-wide rather than national and will be made through the European Parliament, a supranational body serving as a weak central government.

DID YOU KNOW?
Consumer Protections Threatened by Trade Agreements

A threat to consumer protection occurs when standards within international agreements are reduced to the lowest common denominator. **Codex**, which stands for the **Codex Alimentarius Commission of the United Nations**, is the international organization designated by the World Trade Organization to set food safety standards. Codex standards **may be challenged as trade barriers**, and such complaints are brought to the WTO for adjudication to determine where a standard is scientifically justified or constitutes an illegal trade barrier.

Consumers worldwide are served when international harmonization elevates health and safety standards. For example, Codex has issued guidelines to sanction inspection systems by company employees rather than government officials. In addition, Codex permits food additives not approved by the Food and Drug Administration and levels of lead in fruit juices, milk and other foods not permitted in the United States. "These standards will carry a presumption of validity in trade disputes, and it may just be a matter of time before the U.S. government must decide whether to **accept imports of these products or face trade sanctions**," says Bruce Silverglade of the Center for Science in the Public Interest.

The World Trade Organization

All trade around the globe today is overseen by the worldwide organization called the **World Trade Organization (WTO)**. The WTO is the legal institutional foundation of the multilateral trading system, and its mission is to **advance trade liberalization** (by eliminating quotas on manufactured goods and other barriers) and to mediate international trade complaints. The WTO, which began as a treaty, is headquartered in Geneva, Switzerland. WTO member countries represent more than 90 percent of world trade, although WTO rules oversee less than 8 percent of the value of world trade.

The WTO aims to lower world tariffs; cut agricultural and steel subsidies; protect copyrights, patents and other intellectual properties; and open previously closed markets. The impact of lowering tariffs is predicted to **add $200 billion** to world trade over the next decade. The United States recently submitted a proposal to the WTO to eliminate all taxes on industrial and consumer goods imported to the U.S. by 2015, which would eliminate $18 billion in taxes that America pays each year.

It also referees global commerce by attempting to **settle disagreements** among the 128 countries using WTO rules. The WTO has the power to settle disputes on international trade by enforcing rules, but it encourages parties to reach solutions on their own. When a panel issues a final ruling determining that a country has violated WTO rules, it is binding. The offender is supposed to correct its behavior or pay damages, although negotiation over the terms of the sanctions is permitted. The WTO has no independent enforcement power other than expressing approval of retaliatory actions taken by the "injured" nation. In effect, the WTO sets the rules for trade wars.

The U.S. is the **biggest user** of the dispute-settlement process and it has been a victor in more than 80 percent of the cases. Recent U.S. wins have been against Japan for unfair liquor taxes, Pakistan on pharmaceutical copyrights, Turkey for high taxes on movies, and Canada for restricting American magazines. The European Union continues to ban U.S. beef treated with hormones, but the WTO, in ruling that the hormones are harmless, has slapped $117 million in punitive tariffs on EU exports. The European ban on U.S. genetically-modified foods, primarily corn and soybeans, was upheld by the European Union; the U.S. may take the case to the World Court.

The International Consumer Movement

Citizens around the globe are concerned about how economic development and international trade policies affect consumers. People want to know how to obtain protection against products harmful to health and the environment, how to deal with health and safety problems, how to be part of the decisions that are made in corporate board rooms that affect well-being, and how to reduce disparities in income and consumption among consumers. "National boundaries, says consumer advocate Rhoda Kartpatkin, must not be permitted to become artificial limits to the moral obligations of producers and sellers."

The world needs **sustainable consumption**, which is defined by the United Nations as "that which meets the needs of present and future generations for goods and services in ways that are economically, socially and environmentally sustainable." Sustainable consumption should occur in land use, transportation, energy, and housing. Karpatkin observes that "Decent consuming goes hand in hard with earning a decent standard of living. Decent earning should be part of a consumer ethic."

Consumers International

Consumers International (CI) was established in 1960 by Colston Warne (who also founded *Consumer Reports* magazine) with leaders from the United States, the United Kingdom, Australia, the Netherlands, and Belgium. It was originally called the International Organization of Consumers Unions. CI was created by relatively affluent societies primarily to promote cooperation in the fields of testing and information from independent organizations. Today, CI strives "to promote a fairer society through defending the rights of all consumers, including poor, marginalized and disadvantaged people." CI supports its member organizations, expands the consumer movement, and represents consumers' interests on the international level.

To accomplish these ends, CI encourages **initiatives** in areas of the world **where the consumer movement is relatively new**. Consumers International "stimulates research and action on international issues such as pharmaceuticals, pesticides, tobacco, and baby foods . . . it facilitates comparative testing of consumer goods and services and advocates the consumer case at international forums and elsewhere."

Consumers International is a Strong Voice for Consumers

CI is a growing and forceful voice on international consumer issues representing **220 large and small consumer associations** in more than 100 countries in every stage of economic development and on every continent in the world. CI is headquartered in London. It has regional offices for Asia and the Pacific in Penang, Malaysia, one for Latin America and the Caribbean in Santiago, Chile, and one for Africa in Harare, Zimbabwe. CI acts as an information source and clearinghouse with a number of regular publications, including *World Consumer.*

Consumers in Developing Countries are at Risk to the "Dark Side" of Marketing*

Consumers in developing countries, particularly the **urban and rural poor**, usually have very limited discretionary income and little formal education, yet they are often subject to sophisticated sales pressures. Consumers in poorer countries have an exceptionally high degree of **ris**k to be faced when trying to make prudent consumer decisions. The risk arises from a lack of standards, predatory practices of certain sellers, food adulteration, etc. Information is scarce and therefore extremely valuable. Can you imagine the buyer-seller relationship between limited-literacy consumers in developing countries with no background in efficient buying trying to make knowledgeable purchase decisions for processed foods, beauty aids, and over-the-counter drugs?

The global market offers many opportunities for some of the **worst aspects of capitalism**: profiteering, selling of unsafe products, and a disregard of any generally accepted standard of consumer protection. Such selling is often from the industrialized countries (the **north**) to consumers in the developing countries (the **south**). The results of some of the marketing of products to consumers in developing countries include misinformation about the products, endangerment of consumers, unnecessary injuries and deaths, suffering, neglect, exploitation, cynicism, distrust, and fear.

Following are some illustrations of the **dark side of marketing** to consumers in developing countries: the export of banned or restricted agricultural pesticides and chemicals (polycholorinated biphenyls or PCB's, DDT, aldrin, dieldrin, and paraquat) and other outlawed products; shipping abroad nuclear, toxic and medical wastes; mislabeling (birth control pills); selling ineffective drugs; not identifying and labeling the known side effects of prescription drugs; selling dangerous pharmaceuticals (thalidomide for tension and clioquinol for diarrhea); testing dangerous technologies (Depo-Provera for birth control); exploitively marketing inappropriate breast-milk substitutes; permitting unsafe manufacturing facilities (Bhopal); and selling unsafe products (asbestos).

Why do such things happen? The slogan **"buyer beware"** remains the rule in the developing world, and there are few, if any, consumer protection agencies to prevent these difficulties or to help consumers seek redress. In developing countries, the government infrastructure that provides for consumer protection is often ineffective and/or inattentive to consumer problems. Also, a framework of self-regulatory market institutions often does not exist.

What can be done? Economists argue that the important point is to arrange affairs so that the producer, and ultimately the consumer, bear the full cost of producing any good or service. If this is not done, the hazards show up as acid rain or as shiploads of toxic waste cruising the seas in search of ill-informed victims in **a country without effective standards**.

Small improvements are being made to reduce the export of **toxic wastes and dangerous pharmaceuticals**. Consumer leaders from 42 African countries met in 1996 and issued the Harare Guidelines asking for each of their countries to support the **U.N. Guidelines for Consumer Protection**. It is not clear, however, that the poorest countries can provide the minimal resources since a **World Health Organization (WHO)** study found that only 5 of 11 developing countries had fully functioning pharmaceutical testing labs capable of detecting hazardous products.

The waste of money on useless or **dangerous products** has a direct effect on health and well-being. It seems doubly tragic to waste scarce foreign exchange on such products when effective—and sometimes low-cost—alternatives are available.

Realize that environmentally preferred choices often **cost a little more** than traditional products; thus, consumers must confront the same short-run, long-range choices that society faces. When products are eventually priced to reflect the full costs of production—including environmental degradation—almost all environmentally damaging products will be priced higher than those that are environmentally friendly. The purchases made by consumers can either add to environmental degradation or become part of the several solutions being used by society as a whole.

The idea is for consumers to "think globally and act locally." Those who are concerned about issues like inappropriate global marketing of infant milk formula, unsafe pharmaceutical products, banned pesticides, and toxic wastes perhaps ought not be called just consumer advocates or environmentalists because they are acting in the role of concerned planetary citizens. People, said consumer advocate Esther Peterson, are enlarging their definition of the consumer interest to include **responsible and involved citizenship** focusing on ethical concerns about a "fair, safe, and healthy world."

*Robert R. Kerton, Professor of Economics, University of Waterloo, Ontario, Canada.

Consumers International Seeks Social Justice and Fairness

The broad aim of Consumers International is to promote social justice and fairness in the marketplace. The international consumer movement is based on the belief that people everywhere have basic rights. **Eight world consumer rights** have been identified by CI : basic needs, safety, information, choice, representation, redress, consumer education, and a healthy environment. March 15 is celebrated throughout the world as **Consumer Rights Day**.

The right to basic needs includes food, housing, and health care. CI also focuses on improper marketing practices and the worldwide trade in hazardous products. One of CI's goals is "to cause so much concern that anti-consumer marketing practices will be corrected by the sellers or regulated by the appropriate international bodies and national governments."

United Nations Guidelines on Consumer Protection

The international consumer movement works to bring **more rational consumer protection standards** into existence around the world. The *United Nations Guidelines on Consumer Protection* were passed by the General Assembly in 1985. The guidelines serve as a rallying cry for consumer organizations in countries with weak consumer protection and a guide for governments that want to enact suitable legislation.

The guidelines are based on the following tenets that are **already well accepted in the industrialized nations**: "Products should be safe and not of inferior quality to that which they purport to be; that restrictive business practices that negatively affect consumers' economic interests should be regulated; that consumers are entitled to the information required to make rational choices and to the kind of consumer education necessary to that end; and that there should be effective and speedy redress procedures for legitimate complaints." The UN guidelines are designed to give protection against fraudulent, deceptive, unfair, and dangerous goods.

Implementation of these measures and principles must be assessed in view of the **conditions prevailing in each country,** because as suggested by the United Nations Economic and Social Council Secretariat, "The primary responsibility for consumer protection rests with each state." Therefore, each government must adopt its own consumer protection policies.

Esther Peterson once commented on the necessity for effective international consumer protection: "It takes time. It comes piece by piece, slowly, painfully, and only after excruciating battles among our own politicians and economic interests, and often only after consumer tragedies of great sadness." Also, "consumerism must seek to bring the issues to the forefront—to **bring about solutions** that not only will prevent old tragedies from recurring but new ones from developing." Peterson said that society needs a greater supply of new "professionals who will move our efforts forward—professionals who will contribute to our efforts for what I like to call a 'better, safer, happier world.'"

AN ECONOMIC FOCUS: China's Consumer Movement*

China started its economic reform and open-door economic policies in the late 1970s. Since then the **market economy has been growing** and the Chinese people are becoming consumers in a real sense. Because of the economic growth and Western lifestyle exposure, Chinese people's expectation for consumption has risen rapidly along with the increase of their incomes. They are facing more choices of consumer goods and services. However, their consumer knowledge is not growing as fast as their income and expectations. They are confused, embarrassed, and even cheated in the marketplace. Many consumer problems now exist and have drawn public attention.

Because too many consumer problems and a number of serious tragedies would hurt the stability of the society and the continuation of economic and political reform, a consumer movement led by the government has been launched, particularly in communities where **open-door economic policies** exist. These are Chinese government policies that permit and encourage a certain amount of free enterprise.

The **government is the initiator**, promoter, and implementor of several consumer protection campaigns. One major effort by government to protect consumers is to create a nationwide network of consumer protection. In the early 1980s, China's first government consumer protection agency was founded near Beijing and soon another was founded near Hong Kong.

The China Consumer Association, a national government consumer protection organization, was founded three months later in Beijing. By 1988, the China Consumer Associa-

tion had 1,170 county and city branches including the two that were founded before the national headquarters. These provincial and city consumer agencies have similar functions as those of state and local consumer agencies in the U.S. But there is no American counterpart to match the China Consumer Association as it is a national government consumer protection agency. The China Consumer Association is a member of Consumers International.

The **China Consumer Association** and its branches have the following characteristics. First, the staff members come directly from other government regulatory agencies. For instance, the staff members of the national headquarters are from China National Administration of Industry and Commerce that regulates advertising and trademarks, China Commodity Inspection Bureau that regulates the quality of imported goods, and China Standards Bureau that has authority to issue consumer goods standards. Second, the agencies always invite high-ranking officials as their honorary presidents, an efficient way to request operational funds and get things done effectively. Third, the agencies often have well-known experts or scholars to be their advisors, and these advisors serve on a voluntary basis. Fourth, the operational funds are provided by government at corresponding levels, even though the funds are usually inadequate. Fifth, complaint-handling and random market inspections are the major functions of these agencies.

China's consumer movement is still in its early stage. Even today, no private organization of active consumers exits.

*Jing-jian Xiao, Professor, University of Rhode Island

Review and Summary of Key Terms and Concepts

1. Briefly discuss the idea of **progress** in the context of economic growth of societies.

2. Distinguish among the terms **first-world** and **developing countries**.

3. Give some examples of how the **population growth** strains economic resources.

4. Why are **persistent poverty** and **excessive military spending** considered world economic problems?

5. Provide an overview of the problem of **growing international debt** in the context of equitable trade relations between the developing countries and the industrialized countries.

6.   Explain the idea of international trade not being a **zero-sum game**, but in an environment of **Pareto efficiency**. In your response, be sure to explain the concept of **comparative advantage**.

7.   What do the concepts of **economies of scale** and **absolute advantage** have to do with a country's international trade?

8.   Briefly describe the idea of **globalization**, what it is, why some people are concerned about it and where it is going.

9.   Summarize the **consumer interest** in international trade.

10. Explain why the U.S. **saves** less than it invests.

11. What are the pluses and minuses of **free trade**?

12. Choose among the following terms and explain two: **tariff, quota, embargo, foreign-exchange controls, currency devaluation, buy-domestic policy, subsidies** and **dumping**.

13. Summarize how the supply and demand for labor affects wage rates in developing countries.

14. What are the results of **protectionism**?

15. Explain the idea of **managed trade**.

16. What is required for a **cartel** to operate successfully.

17. What are **regional trade agreements** and list what participating nations hope to accomplish by joining them.

18. Describe what **WTO** is trying to accomplish.

19. Summarize the major concerns of the **international consumer movement**.

20. List some examples of the **dark side of marketing** to consumers in developing countries.

21. In a general way, what are the **United Nations Guidelines on Consumer Protection** trying to accomplish?

Useful Resources for Consumers

Activists and progressives directory
www.macronet.org/groups.html

Cato Institute Center for Trade Policy Studies
www.freetrade.org/

Consumer's Choice Council
www.consumerscouncil.org

Consumers International
www.consumersinternational.org

European consumer voice in standardization
www.anec.org

Free Trade Area of the Americas
www.ftaa-alca.org/alca_e.asp

Global Trade Watch
www.citizen.org/pctrade/tradehome.html

International Economics Study Center
www.internationalecon.com/

International Standards Organization
www.iso.org

Institute for Global Communications
www.igc.org

Groups active in environmental monitoring
www.gsf.de/unep/contents.html

MultiNational Monitor
www.essential.org/monitor/index.htm

North American Free Trade
Area Secretariat
www.nafta-sec-alena.org/

Public Citizen
www.publiccitizen.org

One World On-Line Supersite
www.oneworld.org/index.html

Transparency International
www.transparency.org/

Union of Needletrades,
Industrial and Textile
Employees
www.uniteunion.org

United Nations
www.unitednations.org

United Nations Commission
on International Trade Law
www.uncitral.org/

United Nations Development
Programme
www.undp.org/

United Nations Environment
Programme
www.unep.org/

United Nations Industrial
Development Organization
www.unido.org/

United Nations Population
Fund
www.unfpa.org/

United Nations Office on
Drugs and Crime
www.unodc.org/odccp/index.
html

World Bank
www.web.worldbank.org

Yahoo list of public interest
groups
dir.yahoo.com/business_and_
economy/
organizations/

"What Do You Think" Questions

1. The terms **first-world countries** and **third-world countries** are relative to each other. Given that relativity will always exist, what responsibilities do you think the **industrial societies** should have toward the **developing countries**?

2. If you could wave a magic wand for one day, which one of the five **fundamental world problems** would you eliminate on earth? Explain why.

3. Are you optimistic or pessimistic about the future of the United States as a **leading world economy**. Explain why.

4. The organized **consumer movement of China** is represented almost solely by government. This is a different approach than that followed by the United States. Which approach is better, and why?

5. Should consumers **support free trade**? Why or why not?

Chapter 9

Government Regulation of Economic Interests

OBJECTIVES

After reading this chapter, you should be able to

1. Comprehend how businesses operate and attend to their social responsibilities.

2. Appreciate that self-regulation is essential to good business practices.

3. Explain why governments regulate economic and social interests.

4. Realize that the effects of little or no competition are economic fraud.

5. Recognize that government has many powers to promote fair competition.

The economic role of business in the United States today is twofold: to seek profits and to do so in a socially responsible manner. Profits must be earned and this is accomplished primarily by businesses that regulate their own behaviors. While there are many successful efforts in self-regulation, government also regulates business interests. It does this with a view toward promoting the public interest. The common good is to keep the marketplace functioning well to serve the interests of both businesses and consumers. Since consumers cannot be armed adequately to protect themselves against corporate crime, the law enforcement agencies acting on behalf of the public should protect them. Government is involved in economic matters through its efforts to promote fair competition in the marketplace, and it does this through its antitrust and consumer protection laws.

This chapter begins with a review of how businesses operate and attend to their social responsibilities. Next we review the self-regulatory role of business in society because this is fundamental to a successful consumer-oriented marketplace. Vital to one's perceptions about government is an understanding of the several reasons why governments regulate economic and social interests. **Regulations** are enactments and applications of principles, rules, laws, and adjudicative actions to control or govern behavior. Consumers support government regulation because they realize economic fraud is the result of little or no competition. The chapter concludes with an examination of the many powers that government has to promote fair competition.

The Economic Role of Business in Society

It is natural to think of **producers** as growers of wheat or apples or manufacturers of automobiles, television sets and computers. Other businesses produce services, such as restaurants, beauty shops, and insurance companies. All are producers in an economic sense because they create goods and services, and we commonly refer to all as **businesses**.

Why Businesses Operate as They Do

The primary purpose of a business is the maximization of profits to increase the wealth of owners. **Profit** is the difference between revenue and cost. Any profits earned by a business become the property of its owners. In reality, profit rewards success. An **entrepreneur** is one who organizes, owns, operates, and assumes the risks for a business venture. In order to earn profits, entrepreneurs start businesses to provide a supply of goods and services to meet demands of consumers and perhaps other businesses. Businesses often focus on maximizing short-term profits, but they must **constantly reinvest** to remain competitive and stay in business for the long term.

To be **successful** in our market economy, businesses must (1) specialize in providing a limited number of goods and services, (2) be aware of consumer demand, (3) apply the productive resources of labor, land, money, tools, and equipment to the production of goods and services, and (4) be free to apply those resources to meet the consumer demand.

The **desire to increase profits** leads a firm to shift from one combination of factors of production to another, to cut costs, and to improve services. If a business does poorly, becomes insolvent and is unable to pay its financial obligations, it may seek **bankruptcy**. Here the company requests protection from creditors in a bankruptcy court where the assets and liabilities are then administered for the benefit of its creditors. Sometimes a business is able to realign its affairs to become profitable again. Should the bankruptcy court-guided effort fail, the firm may be sold or closed, and if the latter, the company's remaining assets are distributed among its creditors.

Social Responsibilities of Business

Following two decades of debate and agitation during the early part of the 20th century, throughout "the rise and fall of Populist, Progressive, and Socialist parties, and innumerable strikes and lockouts, **a corporate-liberal consensus** had finally been achieved. It was now the accepted wisdom—in the board rooms and in Washington—that the role of government was not to supercede or control the corporation, but to legalize and legitimize it by regulating its excesses."[1] Thus, the government's role for one hundred years has been to force large corporations that cheat the public "to behave, play fair, and stop buying politicians."

As a result, businesses today **participate in the values**, ideas, and beliefs of American society in general. Now businesses generally pursue the profit motive in a socially responsible and ethical manner. **Ethics** in this context are societal standards of right and wrong behavior. Ethics involves societal perspectives on right and wrong, as well as one's personal views. In business, ethics forms the foundation for what kind of organization is operated. It is hoped that these include values like fairness, balance, candor, and decency. **Society suffers** when businesses do not exercise self-restraint and good judgment.

Responsibility to the larger community is part of the ethical behavior of business. Poor business ethics derives only short-term profits, while over the longer term, such skimping on quality or service hurts the organization. **Good ethics** result in good business. **Corporate social responsibility** means exhibiting moral and ethical values when making business decisions and actions, especially in the areas of economics, law, and philanthropy. Consumers today are increasingly **demanding that corporations behave more responsibly** and demonstrate genuine concerns about integrity, safety, health, quality of work, and treatment of people. Among the issues are environmental pollution, dumping of hazardous wastes, offensive television programming, testing on animals, hazardous products, and fair treatment of gays and lesbians in the workplace. A growing number of consumers consider these issues in their personal definitions of quality. Business must no longer just perform successfully in the marketplace; it must demonstrate socially responsible behavior.

Self-Regulation is Essential to Good Business Practices

In an effort to avoid government regulation as well as to promote good business practices, businesses increasingly have utilized **self-regulation**. This is a willingness of businesses to regulate themselves in a socially responsible manner by privately creating and publicizing codes of good practices. A popular form of self-regulation is to set **standards** for products and services in an industry, publish them, and then enforce them.

Effective self-regulation requires an awareness of a problem, recognition of its seriousness, and requisite motivation to take action. For example, the furniture industry established flammability standards for upholstery fabrics to greatly reduce fires caused by smokers, which had been a serious problem. The mattress industry also voluntarily

---

[1] D. Nasaw (2000), *The Chief: The Life of William Randolph Hearst*, p. 330.

established similar standards. The television broadcaster NBC receives 50,000 commercial submissions every year, and their self-regulatory efforts result in 25 percent of those ads being challenged for substantiation; another10 percent are challenged and require revisions of some kind.

The concept of self-regulation **assumes the need for regulation**. Just the threat of legislation in itself often brings changes in self-regulation that benefit consumers. While there is a legitimate role for self-regulation, government, not business, is responsible for law enforcement. The concept of self-regulation raises the question of what the government ought to do versus what business or industry ought to do. Still, if government were not a factor, business would want strong and visible self-regulation to nurture the public's confidence in industry. Business prefers being guided by private self-regulatory groups instead of being directed by the federal government or the laws of 50 different states.

Purposes of Self-Regulation

Self-regulation demonstrates the **ability of business to respond to the needs of consumers** without government intervention. Self-regulation also seeks to correct abuses by certain businesses in the marketplace, and industries that are strongly self-regulated generally are successful in maintaining a good image and avoiding strict government regulations. Speed, informality, and modest cost are important benefits of a self-regulatory system. Consumers gain from self-regulation by having increased confidence in the marketplace and by saving tax dollars that might otherwise be expended by government regulatory agencies.

The purposes of self-regulation also are **self-serving**. Douglas Blanke, director of consumer policy for the Minnesota Attorney General's Office, states that self-regulation's bad image is due, in part, from **occupational** (and **professional**) **licensing boards** that generally are protective of their self-interests. These boards are government-sanctioned entities that are exempt from antitrust laws. They are created to set standards for and promote each occupation or profession. As examples, self-serving physicians insist that other professionals not be permitted to prescribe drugs; opticians and optometrists get laws passed to keep their profits high; plumbers get rules passed to keep others out of their business; and lawyers protect their own. Blanke argues that self-regulation should take an affirmative role to instill confidence in an industry. To illustrate, in a settlement reached by the Minnesota state Attorney General with a new-car dealer, the dealer contributed to a Better Business Bureau account that was used to create guidelines for auto advertising and to fund a monitoring effort to police future ads.

The interest of the business community in self-regulation is commendable and **crucial** to the effective operation of the American economy. Government would find it impossible to regulate businesses without the existing positive climate of self-regulation throughout the business community. This accountability function helps ensure quality in the marketplace.

Examples of Self-Regulation

Some form of self-regulation is in effect in **almost all industries**. Following are five illustrations of the kinds of self-regulation in the United States.

Chambers of Commerce

In almost every community in America there is a **Chamber of Commerce**. The primary task of each local Chamber of Commerce is to **promote economic activity** in its geographic area because a growing economy creates employment opportunities and raises the tax base so local government can provide more and better quality services to its citizens. Chambers of Commerce usually engage in efforts to support ethical business operations, consequently reducing fraudulent business practices.

Better Business Bureaus

Another example of self-regulation is the **Better Business Bureau (BBB)** and most large communities have one. This is the oldest and most well-known business self-regulatory organization. Obviously, business cannot thrive in a market where many businesses practice deception. Thus, the BBB **promotes ethical standards** by vigorously supporting good businesses and publicizing the names of businesses that do not comply with their standards. The BBB raises funds by selling memberships to ethical businesses that support these standards and they publicize fraudulent schemes occurring in their area.

The nation's 140 BBBs collect information and maintain files on businesses in their communities, identifying businesses that have unsatisfactory complaint records. While not all businesses are members of the BBB, those that are must **agree to uphold ethical standards** or they are forced to forego membership. While BBBs cannot order refunds or put companies out of business, they do mediate disputes and warn consumers to stay away from companies with poor reputations.

Standards-Setting Organizations

There are more than **400 standards-setting organizations** in the United States, such as trade associations, professional and technical organizations, testing laboratories, and laboratories concerned exclusively with standards. The ASTM (formerly known as the American Society for Testing and Materials) and the American National Standards Institute deal exclusively in developing standards for industry for materials, products, systems, and services. Trade associations such as the Aerospace Industries Association, the American Petroleum Institute, and the Electronic Industries Association also write standards. For example, the American Gas Association directs the development of standards for gas-related residential and industrial products that help producers manufacture better products. Voluntary standards are set by professional and technical associations like the American Society of Mechanical Engineers and the Society of Automotive Engineers. Testing laboratories such as Underwriters Laboratories (UL) also establish voluntary uniform and quality standards to provide some perceived **benefits to product users**.

Advertising Self-Regulation

The American Association of Advertising Agencies has established and published **ethical standards** for its trade association members. As a result, individual companies usually adopt parallel guidelines for their advertisements. The industry enforces its advertising standards through its self-regulatory National Advertising Review Board (NARB), that is made up of people from the advertising industry and the public.

Operationally, the NARB works alongside the National Advertising Division (NAD) of the Council of Better Business Bureaus. The NAD professional staff investigates more than 150 complaints annually about possible breaches of truth and accuracy in national advertising. Its task is to determine the truth of the claims in question.

The NAD **initiates investigations**, determines the issues, collects and evaluates data, and negotiates settlements. Typically the advertiser is asked for **advertising substantiation**. This is a request that an advertiser verify and give substance to the objective claims about its products to show that it has a reasonable basis for those claims. Should the NAD find an absence of adequate documentation it requests that the advertiser modify or change the claims; it cannot order changes. If a resolution cannot be reached, appeals can be made to a five-member panel of the NARB. Cases are kept confidential until resolved, and no fines are imposed. In a typical year about 70 percent of the advertising challenges are brought by competing advertisers, 20 percent are initiated by NAD staff, and 10 percent are brought by local Better Business Bureaus, consumers, and other sources. The NARB's **Children's Advertising Review Unit** receives about 50 inquiries every year.

Should the company still **refuse to change** the advertising, the refusal is publicized by the NARB and the case information is forwarded to the appropriate government regulatory agency for action, typically the Federal Trade Commission. Critics complain that by the time the NAD gets around to making decisions on a deceptive ad, it has probably been replaced. Almost 100 percent of all advertisers have cooperated with these self-regulatory efforts.

Other Trade Associations

Thousands of **trade associations** exist that represent the interests of particular occupations or industries. While each is interested in promoting and protecting its own special interest, as it should, many trade associations also are **effective supporters of self-regulation** that benefits consumers.

Why Governments Regulate

In free societies **governments exist to carry out the will of the people**. The fundamental purposes of government are to control individual action, safeguard individual and national rights, and promote the general welfare in accordance with the principles decreed to be legitimate. At its most fundamental level, the existence of government is necessary to provide **net community benefits**. This is done by protecting property rights, permitting commerce, and setting an appropriate economic framework for markets to operate. Government's central dilemma is to persuade people to forego or limit anticipated private gain on behalf of more general realizable gains to themselves and to the general welfare. Governments are responsible for **taking care of all the problems** that the marketplace leaves behind and undone; those are the most difficult to resolve.

To **govern** means to choose. Therefore, the act of **governing** is, in part, budgeting. This includes making decisions about how much to spend and on what. When government regulates, society itself is making decisions to promote certain public or community-interest goals. The debate about the role of government in society is largely not about more government versus less government; rather it is about what kind of government.

ECONOMIC INSIGHT:
Why Government Takes on So Many Jobs

Economist William J. Baumol of New York University has postulated that while **productivity** has increased in most parts of the manufacturing economy over the years, it has deteriorated in some labor-intensive services because such occupations "require a high level of personal input." Such endeavors as health care, education, legal services, child care, and restaurant and repair services **take time and people**. It is nearly i**mpossible to generate substantive productivity increases** because many processes simply cannot be hurried.

Because of this "cost disease of personal services," prices rise faster than the costs of other goods and services in the economy that can and do become more productive, assuming, of course, that such service providers are paid incomes at today's contemporary level of living. When afflicted services are vital to society, they migrate to or get dumped on the public sector. This is called **Baumol's disease** or **cost disease**.

Additional examples include police and fire protection, postal services, sanitation services, welfare, and the performing arts. Without subsidization from the public treasury, such services would disappear. The continuation of these services **causes the costs of government to rise**.

Most of the high-tech aspects of what Baumol calls the **"stagnant services"** are not labor-saving devices and they do not lower expenses; rather they increase costs. This stagnancy in productivity—inherent to many jobs in the public sector—is a significant factor in the rising cost of government services. But most taxpayers do not understand the principle. Instead, many simply illogically argue to "cut excessive government spending." Baumol's prediction for the future is that by the year 2040, "health care and education will consume **more than 60 percent** of the American gross domestic product."

Governments institute regulations in the economy to **serve particular social goals**, priorities, and public-policy purposes. **Public policy** refers to governmental plans and actions affecting a large segment of the citizenry that are taken to promote the general public interest.

There are **two categories** of government regulation. **Economic regulation** prescribes prices and output levels for natural monopolies as well as a number of other industries. Economic regulation often has been undertaken because the **industry requested it**. Government agencies concerned with economic regulation include Department of Commerce, Interstate Commerce Commission, U.S. Department of Agriculture, Federal Communications Commission, and Securities and Exchange Commission.

Social regulation is concerned with the conditions under which goods and services are produced and the impact of the goods on the public. It focuses on performance standards, workplace health and safety, and consumer issues of product safety, health, environment, employment fairness, and a variety of non-economic issues that apply across several industries. Social regulations often have been **forced on industries** by legislators responding to consumers or other non-industry groups. Government agencies that are concerned with social regulation include the Occupational Safety and Health Administration (OSHA), Consumer Product Safety Commission (CPSC), Food and Drug Administration (FDA), and Environmental Protection Agency (EPA).

When government regulates markets, it is saying that market forces are **inadequate to fully realize certain goals**. Government intervenes with regulations when marketplace forces do not promote the common good and where market failures occur. This also conveys the message that the American capitalistic marketplace generally succeeds.

Some people have the misperception that it is the government that creates jobs. It is more accurate to state that government spending—putting money in the hands of government agencies, consumers and businesses for them to spend **creates demand**.

Businesses that offer goods and services to meet such demands then create jobs while in pursuit of profits.

Government Attempts to Create External Benefits

Many people expect their governments to regulate protection against health and safety threats and against environmental dangers. However, free economic markets provide **little incentive** for companies not to pollute the environment. Just the opposite motivation occurs because polluters do not have to pay anyone for the privilege of dirtying the water or air. Thus, we have a basic **rationale for environmental regulations**.

CONSUMER UPDATE:
Some Things that Government Does Right!

Contrary to the rhetorical rage against so-called **"big, bloated, unaccountable government"** by conservative politicians and social commentators, surveys show the great majority of people believe that **government has been successful** in promoting space exploration, providing for the national defense, keeping the nation at peace, growing the economy, protecting the environment, supporting medical research, providing health care for seniors, protecting consumers and employees, protecting individual rights, and preventing race and sex discrimination. Here are some things that government has **done right**:

- U.S. government expenditures when compared to business spending is the lowest in the industrialized world.
- U.S. tax burden is the lowest among all industrialized countries.
- Federal workforce is the smallest in thirty years, 1.8 million; state and local governments employ 5 million workers, including 2 million teachers.
- Poverty rate today is 20 percent less than thirty years ago.
- Poverty rate among the elderly dropped from 30 to 12 percent in thirty years.
- Seniors have access to health care through Medicare and Medicaid.
- Older Americans have the highest life expectancy than seniors anywhere.
- Federal work-study and loan programs helped millions attend college who could not otherwise go.
- Requirements reduced air pollution by a quarter while the U.S. economy expanded by more than 85 percent and the population grew by 28 percent.
- Government programs have helped 40 million Americans buy homes.
- U.S. Food and Drug Administration has the best record internationally for preventing unsafe drugs from reaching consumers.
- Rebuilt Europe after World War II.
- Expanded right to vote and equal access in public accommodations.
- Reduced workplace discrimination.
- Forty years of U.S. spending won the Cold War.

In a perfectly competitive market, all costs associated with a transaction between a buyer and a seller would be **captured in the selling price**. However, in the real and imperfect world, external issues (**externalities**) arise from market imperfections and require government action. Both positive and negative externalities exist that result from the selfish interests of businesses. **External costs** are those costs passed on to the community as a result of market transactions. For example, a company that emits fumes into the air is creating negative externalities from its operations. As output rises, the firm is able to pass some of its costs of operating onto the community in the form of emissions into the atmosphere that lower the quality of community life. Since there is no economic incentive for the firm to stop passing along these costs, it is in the public interest for government to take action. Clean air, therefore, becomes a **public good**, and government intervenes in the form of a tax or a fine on the company to compensate the community. On other occasions, government might force the company to employ costly technology to reduce the air pollution or it might order an outright ban of the practice.

External benefits are those gains captured as a result of private transactions and **passed on to the community**. The likelihood of external benefits often provides the major justification for government rather than private action. For example, local shipping companies would never be sufficiently inclined to pay for erecting and maintaining a lighthouse to warn of a treacherous shoal on a body of water because their costs would outweigh their benefits. In addition, international shipping companies would simply enjoy the advantage of being **free-riders**. This market-failure situation can be remedied by government intervention to create external benefits. Government could put a tax on all the ships, tax goods being carried by ships, arrange an international authority to build lighthouses, or use some other method. Shippers would benefit from a lighthouse by having greater reliability of shipping and reduced insurance rates, while the community might enjoy more land use as well as additional employment opportunities. Only a public authority has the power to create such external benefits.

ECONOMIC INSIGHT:
The Costs of Government Regulation are Paid by Consumers

The federal government's Office of Management and Budget reports that the cost of approximately 5,000 health, safety, and environmental regulations yielded **net benefits** of between $32 billion and $1,621 trillion annually. Costs to the economy were $174 billion to $234 billion.

To help keep regulatory agencies in check, the U.S. government's General Accounting Office is now charged with determining if regulatory agencies are doing a good job of **estimating costs and benefits of regulations**. Consumer advocates worry that deliberate Congressional under-funding of regulatory agencies may stop the latter from issuing new health and safety regulations.

Business pay the **initial costs** of regulations. Other parties, such as labor groups, environmentalists and consumers, want the benefits because they are the beneficiaries. Experts agree that it is difficult to calculate the benefits of regulations, such as for a pesticide regulation or an air-bag deactivation rule. Cost estimates are difficult to predict correctly, too, because the numbers change drastically after implementation as business often finds less expensive ways to meet the regulations.

The reality is that 100 percent of the costs of regulations incurred by businesses are, of course, **passed on to consumers** and other taxpayers through the prices of the regulated industry's products and services. Surveys consistently show that over 90 percent of consumers agree that government regulation, especially on health, safety and environmental issues, should not be reduced or eliminated.

---
[1]Skrzycki, C. (2000, February 4).OMB's cost analysis questioned. *The Washington Post*, E1.

Governments Encourage or Discourage Certain Behaviors

In pursuit of the public interest, governments attempt to **encourage or discourage** certain private behaviors in two ways: First, because they can tax and spend, government can **divert production resources** such as money, away from use in the private sector of the economy to the public sector to encourage certain behaviors. The existence of free public schools encourages more education, for example. Government spending on highway construction programs is another illustration. Second, government can **intervene directly** into the free market by establishing rules and regulations that restrict the market in some attempt to enhance the public good. For example, having building codes helps assure safe housing and increases the marketability of such dwellings.

When is it Desirable for Government to Control the Market?

There are **two instances** when it is desirable for government to step in and control the market rather than protect and promote competition. The first occurs when events have substantial **negative externalities**, or **spillover costs** that affect other parts of the economy. Automobiles, for example, operate properly and get good mileage even when they are polluting. As a result, government intervenes in the marketplace by requiring pollution-control devices. The second instance where it is desirable for government to control some aspect of the market occurs with **natural monopolies**. When a government has determined that it may be more efficient to have one capital-intensive firm supply a product or service rather than several competing firms, it allows such natural monopolies to operate under exclusive government franchises. Public utilities are **natural monopolies** in the United States. These are private industries offering services whose prices are set with the approval or direction of a public service commission acting on behalf of government.

Utility Companies are Regulated by Government

One of overarching conceptual **beliefs** in the United States is that competition should control markets. In the instance of utilities, however, the **economies of scale** in businesses like electricity and water argue that it would be foolishly expensive for government to encourage competition that would waste economic resources. Who would want to have two or even three transmission systems with sets of wires going down alleyways and running into every home for the same purpose? Instead, government allows natural monopolies to exist in utilities. There are about 180 major electric utility companies in the United States.

To protect the public **interest in the benefits of competition**—good quality, fair prices, and dependable supply—the government creates regulatory agencies to carefully monitor the utilities' businesses. A **public utility** is a private business organization subject to government regulation that provides an essential service or commodity to the public, such as water, electricity, transportation, and communications. When only one company provides the utility service, government correctly expects great economies of scale in production, since fixed costs generally do not vary with output. The idea is to **pass these economies on** to utility customers.

Public Utility Commissions Regulate Utility Companies

When the government allows a natural monopoly to exist, it sets up a **public utility commission (PUC)** to help ensure that prices are fair and that services are adequate. A PUC is an organized government agency whose primary task is to oversee the economic affairs of utility companies. In these regulated industries, government usually allows privately owned monopolies to operate subject to a **fair and reasonable rate-of-return regulation** in which **rates (prices)** historically have been based on a company recovering its expenses, as well as an established, allowable, but not guaranteed profit margin. Instead of strict rate-of-return stipulations, governments increasingly are regulating utilities by permitting

price caps that set ceilings on prices charged to customers and give companies the opportunity to earn more than a specified rate of return. The additional earnings are subject to sharing provisions so that customers and companies share in any efficiency gains. Government monitors both the financial performance of the companies and the quality of the service they provide. Moving to more **incentive-based** forms of regulation limits price increases without restricting earnings while simultaneously promoting the availability of competitive alternatives.

In rate hearings, government regulators are in the **conflicted position** of trying to fix low rates for users (consumers, businesses, and other governments) while judging the adequacy of the rates to provide a fair return to utility company investors. Setting prices for the services of public utilities is a complex process. It often calls for a determination of the value of the assets owned by the utility company, the nature and amount of operating costs, establishment of a level of rates, and the identification of the public interest. This is why most states have established **consumer counsels**, sometimes called **state utility consumer advocates**, to adequately represent the consumer viewpoint in the decision-making process before public utility commissions. About 150 of these consumer counsels belong to the National Association of State Utility Consumer Advocates.

Deregulation of Companies

The **pressure for deregulation** comes from large users of the product, such as manufacturers in the case of electricity and hotels in the case of cable televison. Large users can bargain with the deregulated providers for good prices and service, but consumers and small businesses cannot. The promise of deregulation is more competitors selling a greater variety of products and services at lower prices. **Deregulation** means that the public should rely primarily on competition and market forces to regulate the economy and the business firms within it, especially the firms that are natural monopolies and those providing essential services. Deregulation removes or reduces the regulatory authority and active ties of government that formerly provided oversight of the industry and, in particular, ensured that both **supply and price were fair**. When regulated prices go away there are no incentives for companies to increase supply because greater supply reduces prices and profits.

Techniques to deregulate include: (1) identifying and publicizing burdensome and inefficient laws and regulations, (2) amending or repealing laws and regulations, (3) **privatizing**, which involves relinquishing government control and turning responsibilities over to business, (4) imposing **sunset laws** that provide for required periodic review and sometimes termination of laws and agencies unless their existence can be justified, (5) abandoning traditional rate regulation, and (6) permitting new competition.

Consumer advocates have several concerns regarding deregulation; for example the **electrical power industry**. They worry that if larger-use customers get price reductions (projected between 10 and 20 percent), will the power companies raise the rates (or not pass on cost reductions) to smaller users, such as consumers in geographic areas that currently have low rates. This is exactly what has happened in the United Kingdom over the past decade. Another concern is that the coal-fired plants in the mid-west that produce electricity the cheapest (5 to 7 cents per kilowatt hour) could increase their output at the expense of increased air pollution. Will **universal service** continue to be provided to rural consumers at affordable subsidized rates, because historically such costs have been shared by all? Will consumers or investors pay for **stranded costs**; investments that the companies made under regulation and cannot be recovered, such as nuclear plants? Also, who will profit from the sale of the previously publically-owned assets, like an electrical power plant?

AN ECONOMIC FOCUS ON...Large-Scale Production and Price Regulation*

Industries such as electric power, gas, water, railroading, local street transportation, cable television, and telephone and telegraph communication are characterized by **substantial economies of scale**. The high level of investment in capital facilities (such as power generators, railroad tracks and terminals, gas transmission lines) means that **average total costs will decline** over a wide range of output. Therefore, one large firm would be able to produce a given quantity at a lower cost than several small competing firms.

So consumers must rely on an essential service of a monopolist, which, without regulation might charge unreasonable prices. Legislatures have therefore established state and federal regulatory commissions **to control prices** of such services in return for protecting these firms from competition by granting them franchises to operate.

Due to the economies of scale, the market demand curve, also known as the **average revenue (AR)** curve, cuts marginal cost curve at a point to the left of the marginal-cost-average-total-cost intersection as depicted in Figure 9-1. The unregulated firm (monopolist) would produce the quantity Q_m and charge consumers the price P_m. Because in this situation the price exceeds average total cost, the monopolist realizes a substantial economic profit that contributes to income inequality in the society. The price also exceeds marginal cost, indicating a substantial under allocation of resources to this service.

The quantity and the price that would prevail under perfect competition, where the marginal cost equals price (average revenue) is represented by Q_c

and P_c in Figure 9-1. But charging this price would lead to losses for the firm since marginal cost is below average total cost.

The price that the commission would permit the firm to charge consumers is P_r. This price allows the firm to cover costs including the opportunity cost of capital (normal profits). The firm will produce the quantity Q_r at this price.

It is clear that price regulation can simultaneously reduce price, increase quantity, and reduce the economic profits of monopolies. However, government **traditional price regulation falls short** of being a satisfactory substitute for competition because it allows for inefficiencies to exist. If a firm is allowed to charge a price that is below the profit-maximizing one, it would be in its best interest to exaggerate its reported cost, if it can. There is also a chance that an inefficient management can allow costs to creep up higher than necessary, and then request the commission to grant higher rates. If higher rates are granted, then the firm will be able to earn the normal return on these unnecessary costs.

It can be concluded then, if price to the consumer is to be fair, not only should profits of the regulated monopolies be reasonable but **operating costs should be held at a minimum**. It is the public responsibility of commissions to only allow necessary and legitimate costs.

*Mohamed Abdel-Ghany, Professor, The University of Alabama

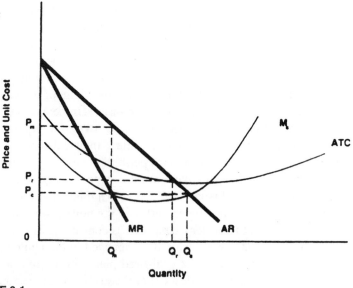

FIGURE 9-1

Deregulation **fails** when regulators lack the resources to fulfill their legal mandates, lack the money to enforce rules or conduct inspections, are very interested in maintaining cozy relationships with the industries they regulate, and when they are ordered by the legislature to reverse some of their longstanding policies that protect the public interest.

Common **failures** of deregulation are a lack of good information to help consumers make decisions (think cell phones, long-distance telephone rates and airlines), no legal rights for consumers to obtain redress with appropriate penalties (think airline rights), and no controls on rising prices (think cable television). Deregulation also fails when the legislature does not re-regulate when it is obvious that consumers and small businesses are getting screwed (think about the $10+ billion fleecing of California taxpayers and electric utility customers). Without government serving as a backstop consumers and small businesses are vulnerable to being victimized by deregulated businesses.

ECONOMIC INSIGHT:
The Historical Culture of U.S. Government Regulation

The separation of the powers of government is at the heart of the United States Constitution through its three branches: executive, legislative, and judicial. Each branch of government serves as a countervailing power against the others. The **executive branch** consists of the President, the White House staff, several executive agencies (such as the Office of Management and Budget, the U.S. Trade Representative, and the Council on Economic Advisors), and members of the Cabinet who represent such departments as Treasury, Justice, Agriculture, Commerce, and Health and Human Resources. The **judicial branch** consists of the legal tribunals of the United States, which include the U.S. Supreme Court, the U.S. Court of International Trade, the U.S. Tax Court, the U.S. Courts of Appeals, and the U.S. District Courts. The **legislative branch** consists of the U.S. Senate and the U.S. House of Representatives.

The President has a **check on Congress** through the veto power. Congress checks the executive and judicial branches in its "power of the purse," right to confirm appointments, and impeachment. Each house of Congress checks the other in that both houses must consent to legislation. Congress also performs an oversight function as it reviews the efforts of regulatory agencies. Both the President and Congress are subject to the **power of the federal courts**.

Because the United States is **a nation of laws**, governments in America cannot act without appropriate legal authority. Therefore, the power to govern is derived from a constitution, statutory laws passed by the legislature, regulations issued by administrative agencies, and decisions made by the courts. When laws and regulations are violated, government can investigate and prosecute. Depending on the statutes violated, penalties can be either civil or criminal, and in some instances both.

Civil law as distinguished from civil law is the body of law that deals with the rights of private citizens, such as consumers and businesspersons. To prove liability in a civil lawsuit requires a "preponderance of evidence." In civil cases where the government is involved, government generally seeks to remedy the wrong, and in many instances, government asks the courts to fine the individual or company involved. **Criminal law** deals with crime and punishment. Proof in criminal actions requires "proof beyond a reasonable doubt," and violators are subject to imprisonment by government. Judicial court decisions, or **doctrines** are important authoritative sources for interpretations of statutes.

In criminal situations, a judge can order the defendant to jail. In civil situations, a judge can order the defendant to perform certain tasks or refrain from doing certain things. A judge also can order civil **compensatory damages**, which are monetary amounts assessed against a defendant to make up, offset, or reimburse the financial costs (e.g., labor, out-of-pocket expenses, medical costs) alleged by the plaintiff. **Punitive damages**, which are monetary amounts assessed against a defendant with the intent to inflict punishment for wrongdoing, may also be ordered.

Almost all regulatory agencies were **originally created to protect consumers**, although over time some became so powerful that they over-regulated supplies and prices. The history of **regulatory deregulation** shows that consumers have benefitted from new competition in commercial aviation, railroad and trucking industries. Deregulation has been less successful in the area of natural monopolies, such as natural gas pipelines and electricity markets. While deregulation has resulted in long-distance prices being cut in half, competition among the local telephone companies has been a failure.

The Effects of Little or No Competition are Economic Fraud

One of government's primary tasks began with its involvement in economic matters in order to promote fair competition and ensure public well-being and safety. Overall **economic well-being** is the level of living of individuals and families or the public.

An unregulated economic marketplace discriminates against both the public and the honest businesses, notes consumer advocate Carol Tucker Foreman. **When competitors agree** to fix prices, rig bids, limit output, allocate customers by dividing business among them, or make other anti-competitive arrangements that provide no benefits to consumers, **economic fraud** occurs. These are some examples of **price-fixing**. It occurs when competing companies attempt to interfere with market forces of supply and/or prices so they might profiteer. Instead of competition holding down prices, in these instances prices are illegally fixed to increase the profits of participating firms. The prices that result when competitors band together in these ways are artificially high. This happens because the businesses are **falsely holding themselves out as competitors** despite their quiet agreement not to compete. Less competition also means fewer product choices for consumers.

Anti-competitive practices that might be unlawful if undertaken by private business are immune from attack if they are **performed by government**. For example, all the county government commissioners can get together in a geographic area and agree to fix identical prices for camping fees, but movie theater owners cannot. Also, governments sometimes enter into contracts with businesses that result in extremely high, noncompetitive prices. For example, you cannot buy a fairly priced meal at most large airports because local governments often get a piece of the sale of every meal.

Government Sometimes Prohibits Competition

Government controls the marketplace for old-fashioned historical and political reasons.

Agricultural Marketing Orders and Cooperatives

A **cartel** is a combination of independent firms formed to regulate production, pricing, and marketing of goods by controlling and limiting production in an effort to maintain or increase prices and profits. A cartel agreement is aimed solely at eliminating competition. The federal government's program of **agricultural marketing orders** permits grower's cartels to restrict supplies to keep profits high for the sellers. In effect, these are cartels.

In the U.S., these federally sanctioned cartels are operated through **agricultural cooperatives** that are permitted to legally conspire to fix prices and/or supply. Many products are affected, such as oranges, apples, peanut butter, and milk. The powerful agriculture lobby was successful in getting Congress to pass a law prohibiting the Federal Trade Commission from even studying agriculture marketing orders. The Capper-Volstead Act restricts FTC's efforts to bring antitrust challenges in the farming industry.

ECONOMIC INSIGHT:
Top Ten Corporate Price-Fixers

Companies who commit economic frauds, that are largely hidden from the public eye, steal billions every year. Many are instances of **price-fixing** where competing sellers interfere with market forces to control prices and/or supply. Many of the world's largest companies have been caught by the Federal Trade Commission, the Antitrust Division of the Attorney General's Office, and/or various state Attorneys General for fixing prices, trying to eliminate competition and other deceptive practices. It is important to note that in these **"settlements"** with government, there is almost never any finding of wrongdoing on the part of the corporation, and the company officers do not admit to breaking any law. Of the hundreds of big corporations caught every year doing dishonest deeds, here is a short list of big corporations that cheated millions of consumers:

10. **Universal Music, Sony Music, Warner Music, Bertelsmann's BMG Music** and **EMI Group** agreed with legal action from 50 states to pay a $68 million fine and distribute $76 million in CDs to public and non-profit groups because they cheated consumers by fixing CD prices high for five years. Some 3.5 million class-action claimants got $12.60 each.

9. **California Association of Realtors** were found by appeals court to have "swindled real estate agents out of millions of dollars" by fixing prices on regional Multiple Listing Service (MLS) services.

8. **Gemstar-TV Guide** paid the federal government $6 million to settle allegations that the two companies fixed prices before they merged.

7. **Nine West Group** paid $34 million to settle charges that it engaged in resale price-fixing with certain retailers that fixed retail prices for their shoes and restricted promotion periods.

6. **Hoffma- La Roche**, the ringleader according to the European Commission, paid a $750 million fine for fixing prices on vitamins for a decade, along with seven other manufacturers.

5. **Nintendo** was fined $100 million by the European Commission for trying to rig the computer game market.

4. **Household International** paid $484 million in a settlement with state attorneys general for alleged abusive and deceptive practices on sub-prime home loans that targeted seniors and minorities. The average refund was $1,500.

3. **First Alliance Mortgage**, accused by federal and state governments of deceiving poor and elderly homeowners into taking out loans with large hidden fees, paid $60 million to 18,000 of its customers. The average refund was $3,000.

2. **Exxon** was ordered to pay $500 million to 10,000 gas station owners who were overcharged for gasoline for 12 years.

1. **Hasbro** settled with 44 state attorneys general who claimed that **Toys R Us** pressured its suppliers not to ship Mr. Potato Head and Barbie dolls to warehouse distributors.

ECONOMIC INSIGHT:
A Dozen Ways Big Business Gets Government to Help Them Overcharge Consumers

American business executives often say that they prefer an economic environment that is left to operate freely, without government intervention. In reality, **businesses prefer some government regulation** instead of having to face competition, where it might be difficult to make a profit or even remain in business. **Internet businesses**, that are quite efficient, for example, face attacks by states passing laws to protect traditional business interests.

Under the facade of protecting consumers from fly-by-night companies, businesses persuade governments to set up **barriers to the low-cost sellers** to protect themselves against competitors. Examples of anti-consumer state laws are:

- Every state prohibits car manufacturers from selling vehicles directly to consumers, thus adding an overcharge of at least $1,500 for each car.

- Arizona restricts the **purchase and financing** of new motor vehicles solely to car dealers.

- Car buyers can purchase virtually **identical vehicles** from Canadian dealers for 1 to 40 percent less than those priced at U.S.-based dealers. Buyers use part of their savings to purchase private new-car warranties. Automakers are punishing Canadian dealers and lobbying to get laws passed to block imports from Canada.

- Texas consumers are prohibited from using online services to **compare prices** among local new car dealers after paying an up-front fee.

- Maryland and 14 other states forbid **gasoline sellers** from charging less than the average wholesale price in the area.

- Wisconsin **law requires a markup** of nine percent on gasoline, so consumers in that state cannot get discounts at Sam's Clubs, KMart and BJ's Wholesale Club.

- Florida discourages **vehicle warranty repair** competition by limiting such repairs and maintenance solely to dealers.

- Hospitals can **block new medical facilities** from doing business in a relevant marketing area.

- Fifteen states prohibit the sale of replacement **contact lenses** from a retail business other than one operated by a physician, an optometrist, or an optician.

- Georgia requires contact lens-buyers and sellers to **meet face-to-face**; thus online purchases are prohibited. In contrast, many other states permit consumers to purchase contact lens from supermarkets, drugstores and mail-order outlets.

- California requires Internet-based real estate sellers, like Buyowner.com, to have a **physical office** in the state (an unnecessary expense for online companies).

- Half the states bar direct shipment of **wine sales** across state lines, and buying wine online is a felony in some states.

The **overcharges** that consumers are forced to pay (perhaps is should be called **"protection money"**?) from these laws amount to at least $25 billion annually. The federal government is asleep at the switch on these anti-competitive laws, even though they are required under the **Commerce Clause** of the U.S. Constitution to stop states from restricting interstate business (commerce across state lines). As former Senator Warren Magnusson once observed, "All each industry seeks is a fair advantage over its rivals."

Profit Protections for Farmers and Ranchers

The nation's farming and ranching industries remain **heavily subsidized** by government. Tax dollars ($200 billion over ten years, or $1,800 per household) are being paid to farmers for producing more goods, such as corn, wheat, corn, and soybeans, than its customers can buy. U.S. policy stimulates surpluses which the taxpayers pay to buy and store. **Two-thirds of subsidies go to ten percent** of the farmers and ranchers. European Union countries provide similar subsidies. This flies in the face of free-trade rhetoric. Discussions at the World Trade Organization over the next few years are expected to eventually lead to the end of these subsidies, and that will open markets for developing countries. (See the farm subsidy statistics of the Environmental Working Group at www.ewg.org.)

Milk is the only product in America that overcharges consumers based on where the cows are milked. The nation's milk pricing system pays dairy farmers a price differential based on their distance from Eau Claire, Wisconsin. As a result, consumers pay a hidden tax in the form of higher prices to all of the dairy farmers throughout the United States.

Sugar producers, also known as **Big Sugar**, enjoy $2 billion annually of profit protection from the government as the latter both buys up surpluses and uses import quotas to seal off the U.S. market from competitors. Eighty-five percent of U.S. sugar must be produced domestically. Even Haiti cannot break the trade barrier of the most sugar-addicted nation in the world to sell its single competitive product. Sadly, since sugar in the U.S. is **two to three times the world price**, Kraft Foods closed a Life Savers plant in Holland, Michigan with 600 manufacturing workers and moved it to Quebec to save $10 million annually. Branch Confections wiped out 1,100 jobs in Chicago for the same reason. Big Sugar also convinced the Florida legislature to postpone a requirement to reduce the runoff from sugar plantations into the Everglades.

Government's "Too-big-to-fail" Doctrine

Enshrined in status quo thinking is government's **"too-big-to-fail"** doctrine. This is the notion that government (e.g., Treasury, Federal Reserve Board, Congress, and state governments) should intervene to protect and/or save a corporation or industry in economic trouble if its collapse would cause a shock or significant harm to the economy. In years past, the government has passed specific laws and made favorable loans to mutual funds (Long-Term Capital Management), auto manufacturers (Chrysler), airlines ($15 billion), the commercial real estate industry, junk bonds, leveraged takeovers, loans to developing countries, and the entire savings and loan industry ($500 billion). Questions of cost and the appropriateness of such social policy are **rarely debated seriously** in the public arena. Consumers and taxpayers pay the bills for such bailouts.

Exemptions from Antitrust Laws

Circumstances and reasons are always unique, but Congress and the courts have exempted a **number of businesses** from antitrust laws. Examples include natural monopolies, fishing organizations, agricultural cooperatives, labor unions, export trade associations, insurance companies (regulated by the states only), newspaper joint operating arrangements, professional baseball,[2] and the joint export activities of American companies. Other industries have partial exemptions: banking, communications, learned professions, natural gas transmission, professional sports, securities and commodity exchanges, airlines, railroads, and shipping. Former Senator Howard H. Metzenbaum says that the U.S. Congress is **not antitrust oriented** for three reasons: (1) members are tainted by money received from political action committees (PACs), (2) powerful business lobbies are against strengthening antitrust laws, and (3) consumers have not strongly indicated that they want more competition and better prices.

Protection for the Insurance Industry

The influential **insurance industry** got the McCarran-Ferguson Act passed that prohibits regulation by the federal government. Therefore, states regulate the industry and they do so weakly because they are underfunded, understaffed, and **overly influenced** by those they seek to monitor and supervise. The insurance industry got another law passed that prohibits the federal government from even studying the topic of insurance. The powerful special interests are afraid of what might be discovered. As a result, consumers pay for overpriced insurance.

Government Gets Businesses to Sign Consent Agreements

To stop price-fixing as well as any other unfair or deceptive trade practice, the appropriate government agency conducts an investigation. In the area of antitrust, for example, if an investigation shows that a violation exists, the Federal Trade Commission files a lawsuit against the alleged offender(s) and seeks a trial. The FTC frequently settles the case out of court with a **consent agreement** (also called a **consent decree**). This is a negotiated agreement between the respondents and the government. The business agrees that it will refrain from engaging in the particular practice to which the commission objects and promises not to do something like that in the future. When a business signs a consent agreement, it is not an admission of prior wrongdoing. Sometimes a consent agreement includes a **cease and desist order**, a legal order from a court prohibiting some specific activity.

Should the alleged improper practice be observed by the FTC **in the future**, the government has an easy time demonstrating violation of the consent decree. Here the firm will be found in contempt of court and fined. **Contempt of court** occurs when a person or firm violates an order of the court or refuses to perform as ordered by a judge. In effect, cease and desist orders define unfair and deceptive trade practices with the specificity of each individual case.

The majority of antitrust cases are **initiated by the federal government** and are settled in out-of-court agreements between the parties. Judges must approve of all settlements, and in each case a consent decree is filed with the court indicating that the firm agrees to its terms. In a small number of instances, one firm sues another for an antitrust violation, as was the case when Pennzoil sued Texaco and was awarded $6 billion in damages.

---

[2] Baseball's antitrust exemption comes from a Supreme Court decision in 1922 that baseball did not engage in interstate commerce. Since this clearly is a false assertion, the U.S. Congress eventually may overturn the exemption with a new law.

Government Laws Against Illegal Business Practices

Antitrust policy is justified on the basis that the government should enhance the competitive environment to protect and preserve a **"level playing field"** on which firms may compete. Free and open competition benefits consumers by ensuring low prices, innovations, and improved products. In a freely competitive market, each competing business tries to attract customers by cutting prices and/or increasing the quality of its product or service. Antitrust laws **should be most strongly supported** by the business community.

The reality of the world is that pure or perfect competition does not exist. We have an imperfectly competitive marketplace. Economies of scale and technology give the advantage to the largest and most efficient firms. American society wants competition because **we value it as an ideal**. We need government to be a watchdog because the average consumer would not recognize an antitrust violation even after falling over it.

We **worry** when only a few firms dominate an industry, because they might set higher prices than would exist if things were more competitive. We also do not want any natural or artificial **barriers to entry** into a business or industry because those who restrict entry are likely to unfairly control prices.

The public view of **big business** is not positive. People have been suspicious since the trusts and monopolies of the late 19th century. A **monopoly** (or **pure monopoly**) means that there is a single seller of a good or service for which there are no close substitutes. When a monopoly exists, the firm purposefully restricts output and increases prices. The prices are higher than they would be if competition were present in the marketplace. However, **bigness**, as measured by size, number, quantity, magnitude, or extent, does not necessarily mean power to monopolize supply and prices. Such power depends upon the position of the firm in the market in which it operates.

Antitrust Laws

The federal government promotes fair competition with its **antitrust laws**. These are statutes concerned with government regulation of virtually any anti-competitive business practices involving **abuse of economic power**. The word **trust** comes from a business practice in the 1890s in which several companies combined their assets into a common legal ownership and then attempted to minimize or eliminate competition.

The antitrust laws are aimed at preserving industrial market organization and **maintaining firm conduct in the public interest**. The goal is to prevent giant corporations from acting unfairly to dominate smaller rivals, as well as to prevent attempts to fix prices, carve up markets, or commit other anti-competitive acts.

All fifty states have their own **state antitrust laws** to combat marketplace abuses and protect competitors, small businesses, farmers, and consumers. Antitrust lawsuits can be brought by the U.S. Department of Justice, the Federal Trade Commission, Federal Communications Commission, state attorneys general, and private persons and companies. **Parens patriae** is a legal concept permitted under this law that allows a state attorney general to bring civil actions in federal court on behalf of the people of his or her state to secure monetary relief for price-fixing and anti-competitive business practices.

Section 1 of the Sherman Antitrust Act, passed in 1890, "outlaws every contract, combination..., or conspiracy, in restraint of trade" and the U.S. Supreme Court decided that the Act only prohibits contracts and efforts that **restrain trade unreasonably**. The courts decide what is unreasonable.

Monopolistic power in the American economy today refers to the **extent of a firm's control** over the supply of the good that is produced by the industry of which it is a part. This means that the business has the power to raise prices above competitive levels by altering supply and/or prices. Monopolies may arise from a number of sources, such as economies of scale, restrictions on entry into certain industries, control of raw materials, or exclusive patent or copyright ownership. When a monopoly exists, the forces of **supply and demand cannot determine production and price**.

Unreasonable Methods of Monopolizing Behavior

Section 2 of the Sherman Act makes it unlawful for a firm "to monopolize or attempt to monopolize" trade or commerce. Being a monopoly is not illegal and neither is legitimately trying to achieve a monopoly. It is okay for sellers to grow and dominate the market as a consequence of a superior product, business acumen, or historical accident. What is **illegal is to try to monopolize through unreasonable methods** and the anti-competitive effects must be demonstrated.

Illegal Business Practices

Following are a number of business **practices that are illegal** because they unreasonably exclude firms from the market or significantly impair their ability to compete:

1. **Horizontal price-fixing**–Occurs when competitors make direct agreements about the quantity of goods that will be produced, offered for sale, or bought, or they divide up the available market by assigning one another certain exclusive territories or certain customers.

2. **Vertical price-fixing**–An expressed or implied agreement between a supplier and a retailer that obligates the retailer to resell a product at a minimum price dictated by the manufacturer. Manufacturers can lawfully state a **manufacturer's suggested retail price (MSRP)** but not coerce the retailer into agreeing to it. To avoid conflict with manufacturers, some retailers choose to place advertisements stating, "Call for best price." The law allows a manufacturer to establish a sales policy that prohibits retailers from pricing merchandise below the MSRP and to terminate dealers that do not honor that policy, thus cutting off supplies of the product to the retailer.[3] These are known as **retail price maintenance agreements**.

3. **Agreements on price or price-related matters**–Any restraints on prices and credit terms are illegal since these are the principal ways that firms compete.

4. **Agreements to restrict output**–A reduced supply of goods drives up prices.

---

[3] The **Consumer Goods Pricing Act** of 1975 specifically prohibits the use of retail price maintenance agreements between manufacturers and sellers in interstate commerce, and it was upheld by the U.S. Supreme Court. Today, a number of manufacturers (mostly of cameras, electronics, and appliances), along with the support of conservative Republicans, are **trying to stop price competition** at the retail level by getting the U.S. Congress to pass a law that would re-establish manufacturer's minimum prices and **prohibit retailers (primarily discount stores and Internet sellers) from marketing products below those prices**. Wal-Mart is leading the effort to block passage of an anti-discounting law because that would reduce incentives for retailers to invest in new low-cost ways to sell products.

5. **Agreements to restrain other business practices**–Arrangements that limit competition, such as when competitors limit showroom hours, are unlawful

6. **Agreements to restrict advertising**–If restraints lack business justification and have anti-competitive effects, such as depriving consumers of important information, they are unlawful.

7. **Tie-in agreements (reciprocal dealing agreements)**–Occur when the sale of one product (the *tying* product)is conditional based on the customer purchasing a second product (the *tied* product) from the seller that the customer may not want or can buy elsewhere at a lower price.

8. **Boycotts**–Agreements among two or more competitors to refuse to deal with another person or business, or to deal with others only on certain terms and conditions, or to coerce suppliers or customers not to deal with one of their competitors.

9. **Interlocking directorships**–Occur in large competing corporations when one person serves as a director of two or more corporations (other than banks or common carriers who are exempt) that eliminate competition.

10. **Joint ventures**–Occur when the combined efforts of two or more businesses to accomplish a lawful objective, such as joint research and development projects, restrains competition to the extent that the benefits of the venture to society are **offset by the cost of the restraints to trade**. (Some joint ventures, especially for overseas sales, are permitted by special laws passed by Congress.)

Economic Concentration

Firms often merge because to be profitable they need to **control or lower costs** in a competitive environment where they cannot raise prices. Examples of industries that are experiencing such price and cost pressures include airlines, pharmacies, oil services, cosmetics, disk drives, and office products.

Despite the American cultural belief in and support of competition, the antitrust laws have been **unsuccessful in stopping the trend** toward economic concentration in industry. Monopolies and oligopolies are deemed illegal under the Sherman Antitrust Act only when they **unreasonably restrain trade.** The government pursues anti-competitive corporate behaviors, not anti-concentration events. The days are gone, says Robert Pitofsky, chairman of the Federal Trade Commission, when government's antitrust laws were charged with promoting the "mythic virtues of smallness." Rather than being anti-bigness, today's antitrust efforts are aimed at **pro-efficiency**. The federal government **approves about 4,000** mergers every year, all based upon the premise of greater efficiency. Thus, says Pitofsky, the "efficiencies from a merger should weigh on the antitrust scales in favor of merging parties."

An **oligopoly** is a market condition in which the bulk of production is accounted for by the output of a few dominant firms with the effect that the actions of any one firm will materially affect price and hence have a measurable impact on competitors. Because of the limited number of firms, each firm must consider the reaction of rivals in matters relating to output and price. Price competition in oligopolistic industries is often minimal, such as among the six national airlines that control more than 90 percent of the market. If they are not competing in your city, you are very likely paying excessively high prices. Government deregulation of the airline industry has created a large number of "local" monopolies, particularly for passengers who originate or terminate flights at "hub airports" in the nation's

50 largest markets. A study by the U.S. General Accounting Office concluded that "Flyers pay **22 percent more** to fly out of U.S. airports with little competition."

In order to determine the **degree of monopoly power** in certain markets, concentration ratios are used. A **concentration ratio** is the percentage of industry sales produced by the four leading firms in that industry. One can suspect a substantial degree of monopoly power when the four-firm concentration ratio reaches 70 percent. Table 9-1 provides an indication of the concentration in production in selected industries. From the data it is clear that the common market structure in a substantial portion of the American market for selected goods and services can be characterized as **imperfect competition**. Much of the American economy **is dominated** by concentrated corporate power.

TABLE 9-1   Economic Concentration in Selected Industries

Industry	Percent of Industry			
	Four Largest Firms	Eight Largest Firms	Twenty Largest Firms	Fifty Largest Firms
Book Publishing	23	38	62	77
Mobile Homes	35	50	70	88
Cigarettes	39	57	80	98
Carpets and Rugs	40	53	76	91
Small Arms	43	66	89	96
Creamery Butter	49	78	98	100
Meat Packing Plants	50	66	79	88
Cutlery	56	69	87	98
Flour and Other Grain Mill Products	56	68	83	95
Distilled Liquor, Except Brandy	62	82	97	100
Lawn and Garden Equipment	62	79	98	99
Roasted Coffee	66	75	89	96
Aircraft	79	93	99	99+
Household Refrigerators and Freezers	82	98	100	100
Hard Surface Floor Coverings	83	99	100	100
Motor Vehicles and Car Bodies	84	91	99	99
Greeting Cards	84	88	95	99
Cereal Breakfast Foods	85	98	99+	100
Electric Lamps	86	94	98	99+
Chewing and Smoking Tobacco	87	98	99+	100
Vegetable Oil Mills	89	97	99	100
Malt Beverages	90	98	100	100

Source: *1992 Census of Manufacturers: Concentration Ratios in Manufacturing* (Washington, D.C.: U.S. Department of Commerce, Bureau of the Census), 1997. These data remain the latest available. Full data available at www.census.gov/mp/www/pub/mfg/msmfg04f.html.

Under **monopolistic competition**, a number of firms produce similar, but differentiated goods and such limited product differentiation usually gives each firm some degree of control over prices. This is the situation with coffee growers. Pricing under noncompetitive situations is likely to be higher than it would be under conditions of pure competition.

Large Mergers

Section 7 of the **Clayton Act**, passed in 1914, prohibits mergers and acquisitions where the effect "may be substantially to lessen competition, or to tend to create a monopoly." Determining exactly whether or not a merger will have a monopoly effect requires **an evaluation of the economic market**. A **merger** is the acquisition of one company by another resulting in a union of two or more commercial interests or corporations. Most mergers occur for reasons such as ridding a company of inept management, improving efficiency, meeting changes in market demand, responding to foreign competition, and taking advantage of tax laws. A **horizontal merger** results from bringing under one control a number of companies engaged in the sale of the same or similar products. Mergers among firms competing in the same product and geographic markets have traditionally been subject to the most thorough government scrutiny because they result in an increase in concentration in a relevant market.

A **vertical merger** results from bringing under one control a number of companies that had, or could have had, a supplier-customer relationship, because they may have previously engaged in different steps in manufacturing or marketing a product. These mergers are also examined and occasionally challenged by government. A **conglomerate merger** results from bringing under one control a number of companies belonging to quite unrelated industries. In effect, conglomerates integrate across industries. They occur when two firms merge that are not in direct competition with each other because they compete in different product or geographic markets. Such mergers are rarely challenged except when certain factors exist, such as potentials for reciprocity, for eliminating potential competition, and for giving the acquired firm an unfair advantage over its competitors.

Generally, the government's judgment is that a restraint of trade occurring through a merger **must be undue *and* unreasonable** before it is challenged. Mere **bigness** is not proof of a violation. Thus, corporations with hundreds of thousands of employees, millions of stockholders, and billions of dollars in assets and annual sales are not automatically deemed illegal. The potential for the exercise and abuse of market power multiplies as an increasingly higher proportion of sales becomes concentrated in the hands of a smaller number of sellers. The FTC uses the **Herfindahl Index** as a measure of concentration; the degree to which a few firms control the output and pricing decisions in a market. The index is used to test whether a merger will reduce competitiveness in a particular market.

Section 7A of the Clayton Act, passed in 1976, called the **Hart-Scott-Rodino Act** requires the **prior notification** of large mergers to both the FTC and the Justice Department. It provides that all persons and businesses considering a merger of significant size (one party to the transaction has assets or net sales of $100 million or more and the other has assets or net sales of $10 million or more) are required to notify the Antitrust Division of the Justice Department as well as the Federal Trade Commission. The law establishes a waiting period before certain acquisitions or tender offers may be consummated. After careful economic analysis, the government may challenge any merger that is likely to substantially lessen competition and increase prices to consumers. The Clayton Act is a statute with only civil penalties, although private plaintiffs can sue for treble damages or injunctive relief.

Unfair Methods, Acts and Deceptive Practices

Congress passed the Federal Trade Commission Act in 1914 to create the Federal Trade Commission (FTC). It is a bipartisan commission of five presidential appointees confirmed by the Senate for staggered terms. The FTC has investigatory powers to **"prevent" unfair methods, acts, and practices** that lessen competition in interstate commerce, and it rules on mergers and acquisitions. The FTC was originally designed to be a continuous, aggressive and effective organization that studies and prevents the practices that lead to monopolies.

Realizing the limits of the FTC's effectiveness, in 1938 Congress passed the Wheeler-Lea amendment to add to the FTC's powers a **"ban" on unfair or deceptive practices**. This required the FTC to turn its attention to unfair and deceptive practices that disadvantaged honest competitors and harmed consumers. The law provides that the prohibitions can be interpreted and enforced through administrative proceedings by the FTC, subject to review by the courts. As amended more recently, **Section 5** of the act uses sweeping language that empowers the FTC to "prevent unfair methods of competition and unfair or deceptive acts or practices *in or affecting* commerce." This section allows the FTC to prohibit existing, incipient, and potential practices. "**Unfairness** would be found if an act or practice causes injury that is (1) substantial, (2) not outweighed by countervailing benefits to consumers or competition, and (3) not reasonably avoidable by the injured consumers."

Price Discrimination

The 1936 Robinson-Patman Act prohibits **price discrimination that lessens competition among wholesalers or retailers** and harms consumers. It is illegal for companies engaged in interstate commerce to grant allowances, services, discounts, or facilities for the same commodities to large firms, such as chain stores, without granting similar discounts to smaller independent stores when the selling costs do not vary between the two. Robinson-Patman does permit selling at different prices when it costs the manufacturer less, on a per-unit basis, to deal with large volume customers. A discriminatory price also **may be lawful** when it is charged in good faith to meet (not beat) an equally low price of a competitor. The law is commonly referred to as the **chain store act**.

Price discrimination also has been used as a predatory tactic. **Predatory pricing** is below-cost pricing designed to **drive out smaller firms** that cannot compete at those prices. The low prices offered by large retailers typically reflect their buying power as well as low overhead costs and other efficiencies, not predatory pricing. The antitrust laws encourage competition that leads to low prices; thus the government only examines firms' actions when they lead to higher prices.

ECONOMIC INSIGHT:
Antitrust Tools to Promote Fair Competition

Government uses four primary antitrust tools to promote fair competition.

1. **Empowered individuals**. Section 4 of the Clayton Act gives private individuals the **right to enforce** the antitrust provisions of the Sherman Antitrust Act and the Clayton Act. Persons injured may recover treble damages plus costs and attorney's fees from the defendants. The damages can include lost profits and increased costs of doing business resulting from the violation, and this amount is then **tripled** before being assessed. It is not unusual for one company that alleges illegal economic harm from a competitor to ask the government to conduct an investigation.

2. **Prevent mergers**. Government can prevent mergers that would have a negative effect on competition using the same powers employed to break up large firms.

3. **Break up large firms**. When a firm becomes so large that it dominates an entire industry, it might be forced to divide into several smaller corporations in order to create more competition. Government uses three types of orders in these situations: (a) **divestiture**, which requires a defendant to sell the stock or assets of acquired companies; (b) **divorcement**, which requires a defendant to sever a relationship by ridding itself of a functional level of operations (such as an oil refinery being forced to sell its competitive retail outlets), refrain from particular conduct in the future, and cancel existing contracts; and (c) **dissolution**, which requires a defendant to liquidate its assets and go out of business.

4. **Legal action against price-fixers.** Government can take legal action to assess civil fines and penalties for price-fixers and, if appropriate, seek redress through criminal punishment, although the latter is extremely rare.

The government has the legal powers to (1) directly enforce **subpoenas (civil investigative demands)**, (2) seek preliminary injunctive relief, and (3) represent itself in civil actions. Violations of various antitrust laws may give rise to both criminal and civil penalties. Individuals may be fined up to $100,000 per violation and/or be imprisoned for up to three years. Corporations may be fined up to $1 million per violation. The FTC enforces over twenty antitrust and consumer laws, including provisions of the Magnusson-Moss Warranty Act, the Wool Products Labeling Act, the Truth in Lending Act, and the Fair Packaging and Labeling Act.

Review and Summary of Key Terms and Concepts

1. Distinguish between **ethics** and **corporate social responsibility**.

2. Briefly discuss the concept **self-regulation** as being essential to good business practices, and include in your explanation a definition of the term **regulations**.

3. What do **standards-setting organizations** do?

4. Briefly describe the process of **advertising self-regulation** and mention the role of advertising substantiation in your response..

5. Summarize why **governments regulate**, being sure to explain **net community benefits**.

6. Explain the concept of **Baumol's Disease**.

7. List five things that **government does right**.

8. Describe the concepts of **external costs** and **external benefits** in explaining why governments regulate economic interests.

9. Distinguish between **rate-of-return regulation** and **price cap regulation**.

10. Explain the existence of **state utility consumer advocates** when **natural monopolies** already have **public utility commissions** to represent the public interest.

11. What are some pluses and minuses of **deregulation**?

13. What can a consumer conclude about **large-scale production and price regulation**?

14. Distinguish between **civil law** and **criminal law**.

15. Distinguish between **compensatory damages** and **punitive damages**.

16. What concerns does the American public have about when **few firms dominate an industry**?

17. Summarize the **effects of little or no competition**.

18. Give two examples of when **government prohibits competition**.

19. How is a **consent agreement** utilized by regulators?

20. How does government go about promoting **fair competition**?

21. Summarize the aims of the **antitrust laws**, being sure to explain the term monopolistic power in your response.

22. Summarize two **illegal business practices** that seem particularly unfair to consumers.

23. Explain why **economic concentration** is a fact of life in American industry and why government attempts to maintain a **level playing field** for businesses.

24. Identify three industries that are **highly concentrated**.

25. Distinguish among **vertical merger, horizontal merger** and **conglomerate merger**.

26. Summarize the concept of **unfair or deceptive acts or practices**.

27. List the four primary **antitrust tools** used by government.

Useful Resources for Consumers

American National Standards Institute
www.ansi.org/

Council of Better Business Bureaus
www.bbb.org/

Environmental Working Group (farm subsidies)
www.ewg.org

Children's Advertising Review Unit
www.caru.org

Energy Information Administration
Department of Energy
www.eia.doe.gov

National Advertising Division Council of the Better Business Bureaus
www.nadreview.org/

National Association of State
Utility Consumer Advocates
www.nasuca.org/

National Association of
Regulatory Utility
Commissioners
www.naruc.org/

U.S. Chamber of Commerce
www.uschamber.com/default

"What Do You Think" Questions

1. Imagine a **market-driven economy** in which businesses did not practice effective **self-regulation**. What would the economic marketplace look like in those circumstances? In your response, be sure to comment on the **role of government**, the **quality of life** for citizens, and the **consumer interest** in good quality and low prices.

2. Creating **external benefits** is a vital function of government. List five examples of external benefits important to you.

3. Examine the list of a number of **things that government does right** and select two that are important to you. Tell why you think it was important for government to expend national resources in those areas.

Chapter 10

Government Regulation of Consumer Interests

OBJECTIVES

After reading this chapter, you should be able to

1. Recognize the important role of special-interest groups in governmental decision making.

2. Explain the process of how governments regulate the marketplace to benefit consumers.

3. Recognize how lawmakers strengthen consumer protection laws or undercut and weaken them.

4. Comprehend the powers of the Federal Trade Commission.

5. Identify how benefit-cost analysis is used by government to help make decisions to protect consumers.

6. Describe several sources of inadequacy in the regulatory process.

A national consensus exists that products should be safe, the environment should be protected and the government should oversee businesses to assure a better economic marketplace. Significant government commitments have occurred over the past forty years to regulate the economic marketplace to benefit consumers. Consumers are now an important special-interest group in American society. In seeking to counterbalance the power of sellers in the marketplace, consumers have regularly sought assistance from government. A myriad of laws and regulations now exists. Understanding the effects of government regulation on the consumers is vital to citizens concerned about protecting their interests.

This chapter begins with an examination of the role of special-interest groups in government regulation. The chapter next examines efforts of how federal, state and local governments regulate the economic marketplace to benefit consumers. Next is an overview of how lawmakers strengthen consumer protection laws or undercut and weaken them. The powers of the Federal Trade Commission, the nation's premier federal consumer protection agency, are also explained. Finally, the benefits and costs of government regulation are analyzed along with a discussion of regulatory inadequacy.

Special-Interest Groups and Government Regulation

A **special-interest group** is a group of persons that **attempts to influence** the statutory, regulatory, economic, and political decisions of government as it appeals for special consideration for its particular concerns. They want to be treated differently than the rest of the people by the government. The members of such groups usually have a common bond, such as occupation, industry, or interest. Often they have a professional staff working in the **state capitals and in Washington**, D.C. to look out for their interests.

Special-interest groups are a **vital ingredient** in the economy because they do have an effect on governmental decision-making. They fund research studies, organize communications from people with similar views on topics, influence decision-makers, and keep their special-interest members alerted to happenings that might affect them. When people complain about special-interest groups being too powerful, they usually are referring to big money buying access to the political process.

Lobbyists Are Important to Effective Government

Lobbyists are people who attempt to influence legislators and regulators to **take a desired action**, typically in favor of a special interest. They try to communicate the special interests of their group to government officials who might make decisions favorable or unfavorable to their constituency, whether it is tobacco, sugar, medicine, banking, or dairy farming. Lobbying is a **useful input** to the decisions made by government, because the people and companies most affected by such decisions provide a clear voice on those effects. Over 35,000 lobbyists are registered with the U.S. Senate, more than 330 for each Senator.

The U.S. Supreme Court in the *Noerr* decision affirmed that two or more persons may associate together for the legitimate purpose of trying to persuade government to take (or not take) particular actions that may be harmful to competitors. Thus, the lobbying actions of trade associations and other groups **are legal** because lobbying is a constitutionally guaranteed process.

It is important for special-interest groups to have their views represented in government decision-making because each has special concerns. After all affected groups have presented their views, elected officials and other government officials must consider **what is best** for all concerned.

Many special-interest groups have lobbyists. Local governments (e.g., counties, townships, cities) often create groups to look out for their interests in the state legislature. Similarly, state governments have lobbyists working in Washington to protect their interests, since the federal government sometimes tries to usurp their rights and impose programs on the states.

The U.S. sugar beet growers are naturally interested in **staying in business**. For this reason, they work to restrict the amount of sugar that can be imported. Lobbyists for the American Medical Association would be interested in stopping any effort to place restrictions on physicians' fees, such as in Medicare or Medicaid programs. Similarly, a regulated telephone company would be interested in encouraging legislation to continue its monopolistic position in the industry, as well as to permit it to compete with other companies in areas where they are presently prohibited by regulatory authorities.

There is nothing bad about the concept of lobbying, although the general public does have a **negative impression** of the process, probably because of the millions of dollars in campaign contributions made by corporations and other large organizations. (Details in Chapter 11.) Satirist P. J. O'Rourke observes that, "When buying and selling are controlled by legislation, the first things to be bought and sold are legislators." Watching politicians raise 100 million a *month* from wealthy individuals adds to their unsavory image. Only when legislators stop having to raise thousands of dollars every day will they be freed from the stigma of corruption.

Consumers Have Lobbying Organizations

Consumers also have lobbying organizations, and the following are some of many that have offices located in Washington. The **National Consumers League (NCL)**, the nation's oldest consumer organization, promotes the interests of consumers and workers and has 2,000 organizational and individual members. The **Consumer Federation of America (CFA)** is a federation of 260 national, state, and local consumer organizations that advances pro-consumer policy before the U.S. Congress, the executive branch, federal regulatory agencies, and the courts. **Consumers Union of the United States** publishes *Consumer Reports*, an informative testing magazine subscribed to by five million consumers, and it lobbies on national and state consumer issues. **U.S. Public Interest Research Group** is a organization of professionals that focuses on issues nationally and at the state level.

Public Voice for Food and Health Policy sponsors a yearly food policy conference with the supermarket industry and lobbies on food and health issues. **Public Citizen** is an organization with 80,000 members that works for consumer justice and citizen empowerment, particularly on consumer and environmental issues. **Congress Watch** is funded by Public Citizen and is the legislative advocacy arm of that organization. **Common Cause** is a nonpartisan organization primarily focused on accountability and reform in public affairs. The **Center for the Study of Responsive Law** is an organization inspired by Ralph Nader that frequently litigates against the federal government on behalf of the consumer interest, and it financially supports a network of public and consumer interest organizations, such as **Bank Watch**.

The **National Coalition for Consumer Education** is a network of individuals interested in promoting consumer education and an awareness of important consumer issues. The **National Institute for Consumer Education** acts as a clearinghouse for consumer education, and it lobbies on the need for consumer education in the schools. **Consumers International** promotes cooperation among consumer organizations around the world in the areas of consumer education, information, protection, research, and testing.

People who **work professionally** in the consumer affairs field include consumer advocates, corporate and government consumer affairs representatives, investigative consumer reporters, and consumer academics. While each has somewhat different goals, they try to represent the interests of consumers as well as their special-interest organizations. With the White House and both houses of Congress controlled by Republicans, consumer advocates are basically being defensive and **trying to hold onto the present consumers' protections**.

Regulations are Negotiated

Most laws and regulations are negotiated with all the parties that have an interest in the outcome. The participants in a regulatory proposal—government regulators, business lobbyists, consumer spokespersons, whomever—often convene in **face-to-face meetings** that are broadly representative of all concerned parties. They typically work with a skilled mediator, who usually is either a neutral government employee or private individual. The parties strive in public meetings to try to develop a compromise satisfactory to all; a consensus. This is sometimes called a **negotiated regulation**, or **neg reg**.

The final agreement often includes promises to **refrain from filing lawsuits** to stop the compromise from becoming reality. Once agreed upon—and this is often a short-term process of a year or two—the proposed rule or regulation is published in the *Federal Register* for comments as per usual procedures. Critics can still go to court should they desire, but most do not because courts tend not to intervene on limited grounds. Also, litigation is costly and time consuming. Negotiated regulations avoid some of the biggest regulatory pitfalls: delay, bickering, politicizing the issue, and impasse.

How Governments Regulate

Consumer protection, according to Sylvia Lane, professor emeritus, University of California at Berkeley, is the **prevention** of physical or economic disadvantage or damage to the buyers and/or users of goods and services for personal or household use. Consumer protection is a public good and can only be brought about in optimal conditions by government actions. Thus, all government consumer protection is **paternalistic**.

Regulation of the marketplace, including many aspects of the consumer interest, is a **fundamental responsibility of government**. General economic and legal policies on regulating the U.S. marketplace are determined by the legislative, executive and judicial decisions of federal, state and local governments. The actual responsibility for carrying out the policies is given to administrative agencies of the executive branch. Each agency then decides which problems within its domain are most important and goes about regulating them.

Administrative Agencies: The "Fourth" Branch of Government

Administrative agencies are governmental bodies other than courts or legislatures that have the legal power to take actions affecting the rights of private individuals and organizations. Administrative agencies are created by enabling legislation specifying the name, composition, and powers of the agency. For example, the U.S. Congress has created both the Federal Trade Commission and the Consumer Product Safety Commission and has delegated certain powers to those agencies. Also, most state and local legislators have created a number of administrative agencies, such as public utility commissions, banking and insurance departments, and weights and measures offices. These agencies act as the **"fourth branch of government"** and as such are subject to providing the basic constitutional guarantees of due process, equal protection, and freedom of speech. The enabling legislation for each agency (such as the 1914 Federal Trade Commission Act) contains **fairly specific guidelines** and standards limiting the exercise of agency discretion.

Legislatures are concerned with **broad solutions** to problems, and they pass laws to accomplish society's goals. Then regulatory power is delegated to administrative agencies because the legislature does not have the high level of expertise nor the amount of time required to deal with the many technical matters. The legislature, be it the U.S. Congress or a state general assembly, performs an **oversight function** by occasionally holding hearings and reviewing the quality of efforts of each agency. Also, it is normal that laws and regulations are sometimes revised and amended as legislators and regulators respond to the various interest groups in society.

Executive (Dependent) and Independent Agencies

More than eighty federal regulatory agencies exist. They are headed either by a single administrator or by a **collegial group**, which is a form of administration where authority is shared among colleagues, often five to seven commissioners.

Most regulatory agencies are considered to be **executive (dependent) agencies**, which means that their power resides within the executive branch of government (e.g., president, governor, mayor, county supervisor). At the federal government level, administrative agencies reside within the Executive Office of the President; at the state level, such agencies reside within the office of the governor. Such a location suggests that the regulatory agency is extremely dependent on the executive branch of government, relying on the executive office for its operational philosophy and budget. Examples at the federal level include the Office of Management and Budget (OMB), Department of Energy (DOE), National Highway Traffic and Safety Administration (NHTSA), and Food and Drug Administration (FDA), and at the state level the state Department of Agriculture. Agency heads are appointed by and **serve at the pleasure of the President**.

Other regulatory agencies are called **independent agencies**. These are politically autonomous agencies that are **basically self-governing**. When the laws were passed to create them, it was thought that independence from the executive branch of government was important. They are accountable directly to the legislature and are somewhat free from the influence, guidance, and control of the executive branch of government. Although the leadership positions of independent agencies at the federal level are appointed by the President, typically the terms are arranged in alternating and overlapping time periods so that one President cannot appoint an entire board. The terms of office are usually five to seven years. Administrators must be approved by Congress, and no more than a simple majority may be from **one political party**.

Independent agencies are open to **some executive influence** because members of the chief executive's staff frequently attempt to persuade administrators to adopt the President's position on key matters. Examples of independent agencies include the Consumer Product Safety Commission, Federal Trade Commission, Board of Governors of the Federal Reserve System, U.S. Postal Service, and Securities and Exchange Commission, and at the state level the public utility commission.

Powers of Regulatory Agencies

Each regulatory agency exists and operates according to the enabling **legal mandate** of a specific statutory law. The agency administers the particular **powers** given under the statute that created the agency, as well as any authorities provided in other statutes. For example, the Federal Trade Commission administers the Federal Trade Commission Act, the Magnuson-Moss Warranty Act, and several other laws.

Regulatory agencies generally have one, two, or three broad discretionary powers: investigative, quasi-legislative, and quasi-judicial powers.

Investigative Power

Investigative power means the legal ability to **gain information** about private practices and activities that will permit detection and prosecution of regulatory violations. The two most important and most intrusive investigatory powers are subpoenas and search and seizure orders. **Subpoenas** are legal orders that can compel unwilling witnesses to appear and testify at agency hearings and can compel the production of most types of documentary evidence, such as office memoranda and accounting records. **Search and seizure orders** are legal orders that permit lawful entry of private property, such as a home, an office, or a factory, in an attempt to gather information. For example, both the Internal Revenue Service and Food and Drug Administration have the legal authority to seek the truth about fraudulent claims, perhaps on tax deductions or prescription drug testing.

Quasi-legislative Power: Rulemaking Authority

Quasi-legislative power means the authority to **make rules and regulations** to carry out an agency's primary legal mandates. A **rule** is defined by the federal Administrative Procedure Act (APA) as "an agency statement of general or particular applicability and future effect designed to complement, interpret, or prescribe law or policy." Agency actions must be taken in accordance with the constraints of the APA, passed in 1946 in an attempt to standardize federal agency procedures. All federal agency rules, whether they are procedural, interpretative, or legislative, are compiled and published in the *Code of Federal Regulations*. Similar standards and guidelines exist in all states.

A **trade regulation rule** (also **trade rule** or **regulation**) is a legally written **declaration that has the force and effect of law** covering entire industries throughout the country that defines with greater specificity the acts and practices that the agency considers appropriate. For example, in its concern about unfair or deceptive practices, the Federal Trade Commission has a regulation requiring that all gasoline retailers post octane ratings on gas pumps. Thus, an agency with quasi-legislative powers acts like a legislative body. Using such powers granted by the Congress, the regulatory agency can regulate business practices. For example, the National Highway Traffic and Safety Administration (NHTSA) operates under its original legal mandate of 1966, and since then it has issued more than 130 safety rules and regulations for vehicles. Some results of NHTSA regulations include the requirements that automobile windshields be made of safety glass and that vehicles have a third brake light in the rear window.

Informal Rulemaking

Rules can sometimes be written by agencies based on their **interpretation of existing statutory law**. Rule-making by various agencies can be done informally or formally by administrative agencies, depending on their enabling legislation. **Informal rule-making** involves publication of the proposed regulation in the *Federal Register* of a **"Notice of Proposed Rule-Making"** which provides reasons for the action, as well as a time and place for proceedings to be held by the agency. This is followed by a comment period, during which interested parties can submit their views, and then by publication of the final rule in the *Federal Register*. Occasionally, *all* proposed federal regulations are put into a compendium called *Unified Agenda of Federal Regulations*, published in the *Federal Register*.

Formal Rulemaking

After an investigation, the FTC staff may find evidence of unfair or deceptive practices in an entire industry and recommend that the Commission begin a **formal rulemaking proceeding**. If the recommendation is accepted, a "Notice of Proposed Rulemaking" is published in the *Federal Register* stating the time and place of the hearings, the issues to be considered, and instructions to groups or individuals who want to participate. Throughout the rulemaking proceeding the public will have **opportunities to attend the hearings and file written comments**. The Commission will consider these comments along with the entire rulemaking record—the hearing testimony, the staff reports, and the presiding officer's report—before deciding whether to accept, reject, or modify the proposed rule.

This is sometimes called **on-the-record rule-making** for two reasons: (1) because the process provides procedures designed to afford interested parties greater opportunities to make their views known than that afforded by informal rule-making, and (2) the Commission's final rule must be **based upon the information contained in the record**. Formal rule-making has the appearances of a trial, and it is not unusual for a case to drag on for five or 10 years before a rule becomes effective. Rules may be challenged in the courts.

Quasi-Judicial Power

Quasi-judicial (or **adjudicatory**) **power** is the authority of a regulatory agency to **bring charges and prosecute** if it suspects that its laws, rules, or regulations have been violated, and to hear civil and criminal cases for legal and equitable relief. The agency can render a judicial decision on such matters as well. Most regulatory agencies have quasi-judicial powers because they are needed to prosecute violators.

The administrative adjudicatory process normally **begins with a complaint** filed by the agency against a respondent, typically a business. The respondent is entitled to a formal hearing before the agency at which the respondent may be cross-examined, may be represented by legal counsel, may confront and cross-examine witnesses, and may present evidence of his or her own. No juries are used in administrative proceedings, and the case is usually heard by an agency employee called an **administrative law judge** who legally is charged with the responsibility to be impartial and act in an independent manner during all proceedings. Administrative law judges are usually separated organizationally from an agency's investigative and prosecutorial functions. After hearing the evidence, the administrative law **judge renders a decision** stating his or her findings of fact and conclusions of law and imposes whatever penalty is deemed appropriate within the parameters established by enabling legislation (such as a fine or a cease and desist order). Appeals are reviewed by the top administrator or commissioners of the administrative agency.

Violators of most consumer protection laws, rules, or regulations may suffer **one or two penalties**: civil penalties (fines) and/or court-ordered redress for economic injuries. Forms of redress include recission or reformation of contracts, refund of money, return of property, or the payment of compensatory damages. Few consumer protection statutes call for criminal sanctions.

Agencies With All the Powers

Agencies with both quasi-judicial and quasi-legislative power have the authorities of **all three branches of government**. Such an agency can write its own regulations that have the force and effect of law. They can investigate problems and possible violations of the agency's legal statutes and regulations, bring charges against, and prosecute alleged violators, and adjudicate individual cases by conducting a hearing where an administrative law judge decides on the guilt or innocence of the person or company involved, as well as assess damages and criminal penalties. These agencies also serve as an "appeals court," because a losing defendant can appeal a judgment to the agency's commissioners or administrator. If that judgment is still negative, the case may be appealed outside the regulatory framework directly to the appropriate U.S. District Court or U.S. Court of Appeals or state court. The loser generally has the **right to judicial review**. Examples of agencies with the powers of all three branches of government include the Federal Trade Commission and the Consumer Product Safety Commission.

DID YOU KNOW?
Consumers Sometimes Lack "Standing" to Sue

The U.S. Supreme Court's *Illinois Brick Company* decision prohibits consumers from suing price fixers in federal court **unless they are *directly* affected**. Thus, only the direct purchaser, such as the middleman or wholesaler, affected by a manufacturer's price-fixing can sue. The U.S. Supreme Court has upheld *state* antitrust laws allowing those indirectly injured by illegal price-fixing, such as consumers, to sue for damages in state courts. Thus, affected parties may or may not have a right to participate in a legal situation. It depends upon their **standing to sue**, that is, whether or not in the view of the court they are an aggrieved party whose interests have been substantially affected.

State and Local Government Consumer Protection

While numerous consumer protection regulations are crucial responsibilities of the federal government, important regulatory powers and obligations are **accepted by state and local governments**. Each of the nation's 50 states has its own constitution based on democratic principles that are consistent with the U.S. Constitution and guide the governance of citizens. Many powers are reserved to the states, such as traffic safety, weights and measures, regulation of utility rates, inspection of meat plants and restaurants, regulation of consumer sales and contracts, and licensing and registration of a number of trades and professions. Each state constitution also gives it inherent police powers to regulate for the health, safety, welfare, and morals of its citizens, and this is the source of many state and local consumer protection laws and regulations.

State enforcement of laws and regulations s**upplements that at the federal level**, and since states are closer to consumer problems, they often provide fairly effective consumer protection. At the state level the attorney general is the chief legal officer, and that person often oversees the state Office of Consumer Affairs to enforce consumer protection statutes and regulations.

All states have similar types of laws governing business and consumer transactions. One group of statutes is called the **Uniform Commercial Code (UCC)**, and it regulates most legal contracts. All states also have a set of statutes designed **to prevent unfair and deceptive sales practices** applicable to consumer transactions. The latter laws are similar to the federal statutes enforced by the Federal Trade Commission that prohibit "unfair competition and unfair or deceptive acts or practices."

Most state laws empower a state agency, usually the **attorney general's office**, to enforce provisions of the statute by conducting investigations, commencing actions for civil penalties, and seeking **injunctions**. An injunction is a judicial order that commands, directs, orders, or prohibits a person or firm from doing a certain act or specific course of action. After a hearing on the issues, for example, a judge could issue an injunction that prohibits a seller from making certain sales or advertising claims.

States Follow One of Four Legal Approaches

State consumer protection laws follow one of four approaches. First, the strongest and most common statute is a **"little FTC act"** modeled on the **Uniform Trade Practices and Consumer Protection Law**. Such laws broadly prohibit unfair methods of competition and unfair or deceptive acts or practices, and generally empower both the attorney general and individual consumers with the right to sue violators. Second, most other state statutes are modeled after the **Uniform Deceptive Trade Practices Act**, that more narrowly prohibits 11 specific deceptive trade practices and forbids "any other conduct that similarly creates a likelihood of confusion or misunderstanding." This act typically does not give special powers to the attorney general and limits consumer remedies to injunctions.

Third, several states have **consumer fraud acts** that focus on consumer issues to prohibit deceptive or unconscionable acts or practices and frauds, but do not prohibit unfair competition. Fourth, a few states have a **uniform consumer sales practices act** that applies only to consumer transactions to prohibit deceptive and unconscionable practices. In most states the consumer protection statute specifies that the court look to Federal Trade Commission cases and regulations for guidance in interpreting the state statutes.

Unconscionability

Common law in all states provides for the legal concept of protecting consumers against unconscionable acts and practices. **Unconscionability** is a legal doctrine having to do with unscrupulousness under which the court may invalidate an agreement, or a portion of it, if it is **so one-sided as to be unreasonable**. Perhaps the seller took advantage of the consumer's ignorance, inability to read, inability to read English, physical infirmity or some recent personal crisis (i.e., death in the family, accident). The term unconscionability implies that the consumer believed that he or she had no choice in the buying situation that resulted with the purchasing terms being so one-sided that they unreasonably favored the seller. Examples of unconscionability might include highly inflated prices, unfair contractual terms, horribly high interest charges, and some rent-to-own contracts. For example, a Connecticut court voided a contract where a consumer agreed under a "rent-to-own" contract to pay $1268 for a television set that sold at retail for $499.

State Attorneys General and Consumer Problems

Numerous **state attorneys general** have been aggressive in their efforts to advance the interests of consumers and protect their citizens. For example, more than 40 states passed "lemon laws" to protect buyers of new vehicles that cannot be repaired satisfactorily.[1] Also, when the Federal Trade Commission did not take action, the Texas attorney general sued Kraft for misleading advertising of Cheese Whiz because Kraft called it "real cheese." Several states, including California and New York, sued McDonald's for falsely advertising the high-caloric Chicken McNuggets as a "lean meal." The informal coordinating mechanism for state enforcement authorities is the **National Association of Attorneys General (NAAG)**.

Office of Consumer Affairs

In the area of consumer protection, each state typically has a state **office of consumer affairs (OCA)** in the executive branch, located either in the attorney general's office or in the governor's office, to handle inquiries and complaints about possible violations of state laws. Most OCAs have a telephone hotline to receive complaints. The most common complaints to OCAs usually involve home improvements and car sales there. Complaints include used vehicle sales, home construction, vehicle repairs, new vehicle sales, telemarketing, landlord/tenant, mail fraud, appliance sales/repair and mail order. Complaints about big-ticket items such as computers, electronics, appliances, and furniture have been increasing.

In addition to a central Office of Consumer Affairs in the capital city, many states also have a network of **OCAs located throughout the state**. At the local level a number of individual cities and counties have their own OCA units that respond to violations of local statutes and regulations, as well as state laws. Most OCAs have the legal authority to investigate complaints and subpoena records and testimony.

---

[1] Conservative Republicans are attempting to pass a federal lemon law that would weaken today's strong state statutes. See Chapter 11.

Weights and Measures Offices

Many consumer purchases are sold by weight and measures like volume, length, and count. In fact, government regulation of weights and measures was probably the **first form of consumer protection** many hundreds of years ago. **Weights and measures offices** work to protect consumers, businesses, and manufacturers from deceptive and unfair practices. They are generally located in state agriculture departments and consumer protection agencies. Each state has a weights and measures laboratory and staff to check the accuracy of equipment used in the marketplace, such as for gasoline, propane gas, and grocery store scanners. A **seal**, a device to prove authenticity, is usually put on the equipment to attest to the correctness of the accuracy, legal weight, quality or another standard.

Consumer Watchdogs on Public Boards

Most states have representatives from the public who serve on various regulatory boards and commissions, such as the insurance, banking, and utility commissions. These are often called **public members** or **consumer watchdogs**. Such representatives are charged with presenting the consumer's voice on these industry-dominated boards and commissions.

How Lawmakers Strengthen Consumer Protection Laws or Undercut and Weaken Them

Many powers are reserved in the U.S. Constitution for the federal government, including national defense, coining money, regulating commerce with foreign nations, maintaining uniform laws on bankruptcies, and establishing post offices. Because the U.S. Constitution establishes a **separation of powers doctrine**, the states are responsible for other interests, such as education. In the area of commerce or trade the responsibilities of regulation also are divided.

The **commerce clause** of the Constitution provides the power for Congress to pass consumer protection laws, since it authorizes the federal government to regulate *interstate* commerce and prohibits states from passing laws that **seriously hamper** interstate or foreign trade. As a result, the federal government traditionally steps in to regulate **interstate commerce** (trade across state boundaries) rather than **intrastate commerce** (trade within state boundaries). In today's enormous and complex marketplace, sales of most goods go across state lines and affect interstate commerce. Consequently, many activities that are purely intrastate can be regulated to some extent by the federal government, particularly when such trade has a *substantial effect* on interstate commerce.

The **supremacy clause** of the Constitution makes federal law the law of the land unless Congress says otherwise. Thus, federal laws are supreme over conflicting state enactments. This ensures that when Congress does pass legislation or regulatory agencies make rules, such legislation and rules preempt or supersede conflicting state laws. This renders the states powerless to act except in ways directly mandated by the federal government. This is also called the doctrine of **preemption**. Consequently, the federal government has the major role in determining how consumer protection responsibilities are divided between the federal and state governments. In so doing, the federal government generally maintains a cooperative attitude with the states as it seeks to set minimum national consumer protection standards. Federal administrative agencies have the same power.

If Congress does not have legislation in a particular area or field of regulation, then states are free to pass laws, assuming that they do not **unduly burden interstate commerce**. Courts generally are **reluctant to strike down state and local consumer protection laws** and regulations that serve a legitimate state purpose and protect the consumer unless the burdens on interstate commerce are excessive. At the same time, the commerce clause ostensibly discourages states from passing more stringent laws than the federal government. However many states have very strong laws on privacy, minority rights, and some areas of consumer protection, such as vehicle lemon laws. For the past twenty years, state Attorneys General have been more aggressive than the federal government in protecting the interests of consumers.

"Republican leaders in Congress," says New York Attorney General Eliot Spitzer, "have **systematically undercut state efforts** to enforce the law and protect consumers.[2] They are leading the effort in government regulation toward **devolution**, the shifting of power to state and local governments, and **deregulation**, releasing companies from government regulations which lower prices and improve services. This new **federalist policy** of Republican conservatives professes to return power to the states, but in reality it has substantially weakened consumer protection. Spitzer continues "They are out to shackle the hands of those of us who are out there fighting for consumers, equity, and enforcement."

A popular tactic of Republican conservatives who oppose consumer protection efforts is to pass a carefully worded federal law with **weak standards**, because it would preempt any stronger state or local laws. Other widely used techniques to reduce consumer protection are to **cut the budgets** of federal consumer protection agencies and to specifically prohibit the federal government from performing certain tasks, such as conducting a study on the insurance industry. Critics of the agenda of Republican conservatives argue that such transfers of powers to the states will also weaken civil rights, health policy, environmental safeguards, and today's **social safety net** for the poor, elderly and disabled.

Liberals and moderates are challenged to better explain the benefits of public interest regulation so they can again become the majority power in Congress and do more to protect consumers from getting ripped off.

Federal Trade Commission Powers

The **Federal Trade Commission (FTC)** is the foremost federal consumer protection agency designed to **keep the American marketplace free and fair**. It is responsible for preventing deceptive practices, false advertising, and unfair competition in the marketplace. It administers laws and regulations governing advertising, credit transactions, product warranties, and packaging and labeling. The U.S. Supreme Court has broadened the power of the FTC by allowing it to regulate anti-competitive practices that are not covered specifically in the various antitrust statutes. The FTC can **write regulations** intended to carry out the meaning of the Federal Trade Commission Act, and it can assess civil penalties.

---

[2] *CFA News* (March-April 2003), Consumer Federation of America, p. 2

Founded in 1914, it has a budget of $176 million and a staff of 1,100 to carry out its statutory duties. The FTC is directed by five commissioners appointed by the President for 7-year terms. Terms of office are staggered. Although the FTC does not investigate and take action to resolve individual complaints, it investigates and prosecutes when it receives a **large number of complaints** and/or suspects that substantial harm is occurring.

The FTC has a wide **array of legal devices** for ensuring compliance with statutes it administers. It seeks to ensure voluntary compliance whenever possible through **advisory opinions** (official FTC responses to inquiries by private parties), **industry guides** (FTC interpretations of the laws it administers), and **trade regulation rules** (www.ftc.gov/ftc/trr.htm). The FTC's Office of Consumer Protection oversees the majority of the FTC's efforts (www.ftc.gov/ftc/consumer.htm).

Quasi-Judicial Powers

When the FTC suspects a law or regulation has been violated, the agency has the **quasi-judicial power** to investigate, prosecute, and make a determination on the matter in an adjudicative proceeding before an FTC administrative law judge. Should an initial investigation show promise, a formal investigation is launched. Should the business not be willing to surrender any needed records, the FTC can use its subpoena power to require the respondent to surrender any needed records. The subpoena is a key investigative tool of the judiciary.

If the investigation of a business shows that a violation exists, the FTC frequently settles the case with a **consent agreement**. When a business signs the agreement, it is not an admission of wrongdoing. Rather it is **a promise** by the firm and an agreement between the firm and the FTC that the firm will not do something specific in the future. Consent agreements always describe the practices that must not occur. Should the illegal practice continue in the future, the FTC has an easy time demonstrating violation of the consent agreement, in which case the firm will be found in contempt of court and fined.

Consent agreements **can be very powerful tools** in ensuring a fair marketplace. In some instances, the agreement might require the business to refund money to consumers or rescind or change contracts. Before consent agreements are final, however, the terms of the proposed agreement are published in the public record for comment by any interested party for 60 days. The final order, modified if needed, is then issued by the FTC. Settling cases with consent agreements **saves the FTC the time and effort** of having to fully prosecute cases. It also gets questionable practices stopped rather quickly. When a case is not settled with a voluntary consent agreement, a **formal complaint of violation** is issued by the FTC. In effect, the FTC prosecutes the case. A **hearing** is held before an administrative law judge who works for the FTC. Testimony and other evidence are presented in this court of law, and the judge hands down a decision that either the complaint be dismissed or that a formal cease and desist order be entered and then enforced with a consent decree.

The initial decision of an administrative law judge **can be appealed** to the five FTC commissioners, who can sustain, reverse, or amend the decision. The case can be further appealed through our federal court system to the U.S. Court of Appeals and, if necessary, to the U.S. Supreme Court. Once the decision is made to utilize the regular judicial system, the case may continue for many years.

In instances of **false advertising**, the FTC judge often determines that a specific consent decree be ordered, such as one demanding an affirmative disclosure, corrective advertising, or a multiple-product order. **Affirmative disclosure orders** require firms to do something in the future, such as provide additional disclosures of specific key facts in future ads when they include the particular claims that were found to be deceptive. For example, the FTC required that the makers of Geritol disclose that the product "will be of no benefit" for a great majority of persons who suffer from tiredness whenever they run ads making such claims about tiredness symptoms. Affirmative disclosures are designed to help consumers form accurate perceptions about product characteristics and values, as well as health and safety risks. Since affirmative disclosure orders come into effect only when future advertising claims involve previous claims that were found to be deceptive, such orders are of little value when the advertiser simply omits the previous claims. Thus, Geritol can claim to cure "iron deficiency anemia" without having to disclose anything else.

As a result, some advertisers are forced by the FTC to run **corrective advertising**. This is a remedial concept requiring advertisers to spend a certain amount of money buying advertising to correct false impressions created by past advertisements. Thus, corrective advertising disclaims previous false advertising claims. Before corrective advertisements can be run, the FTC must approve them. The intent of corrective advertising is to deprive the business of the gains obtained by unfair methods and to deter false advertising in the future.

Multiple-product orders are formal FTC consent decrees that require future advertising about all the products sold by a firm, not just the product that was falsely advertised, carry affirmative or corrective statements. This rarely-used power is designed to deter firms that have a history of false advertising from doing so in the future, particularly those who sell a multitude of products and a variety of product lines.

Quasi-Legislative Powers

The FTC's primary method to deter unfair and deceptive practices is to go after businesses on a **case-by-case basis**, much like the police going after criminals one at a time. While necessary, this process has little impact on whole industries.

The FTC also can **issue trade regulations** to prevent unfair and deceptive practices that cover entire industries. Thus, the FTC has **quasi-legislative powers**. For example, instead of trying to prosecute each funeral home that uses deceptive labeling practices one at a time, the FTC issued its "funeral rule." This regulation was designed to stop unscrupulous funeral directors who misrepresented state and local legal requirements regarding embalming, and overcharged for products and services. Handicapped by grief, consumers often made poor decisions in the absence of adequate information. The regulation requires funeral directors to provide information about prices and services over the telephone and, if requested, in writing to those who request such. Thus, consumers can now easily compare casket prices and funeral services when arranging a funeral.

Republican conservatives (see Chapter 11), however, **do not like government trade regulations**, and as a result Congress passed a law to restrict the FTC's authority to issue trade regulations in the area of advertising based on the concept of unfairness. Therefore, in instances of unfair advertising, the FTC can only attack through its adjudicative process one case at a time.

Benefits and Costs of Government Regulation

Laws and regulations to help consumers typically are concerned with **(1) protecting consumers from the health and safety aspects of products** that are difficult to correctly evaluate, such as prescription drugs, toy safety, wholesale meat, deceptive advertising, automobile bumpers, crib safety, and food additives, **(2) protecting consumers from unfair treatment**, such as having the opportunity for equal credit, avoiding harassment for unpaid debts, having access to basic banking services for the economically disadvantaged, being assisted with warranty complaints, being overcharge via price-fixing, and having access to small claims courts, and **(3) promoting the availability of more adequate information** to consumers to help them make comparisons, such as fair packaging and labeling of food products, gasohol labeling, nutritional labeling, and costs of credit.

The **positive impacts** of consumer protection laws and regulations include reduced suffering, the protection of lives, more parity, better choices, increased physical well-being, and economic savings. The magnitude of these benefits needs to be estimated and carefully assessed. The idea of benefit-cost analysis evolved from attempts to measure the efficiency of public policy initiatives.

Benefit-Cost Analysis is a Tool

Consumers appear to be **indifferent** toward the large sums of money government spends to protect health and safety, even though these costs are paid through higher prices. Traditionally, the approach taken in government regulation was simple: government issued executive orders and passed laws and regulations when leaders *thought* important problems existed that could be alleviated or resolved by issuing rules and/or spending money. Governments passed **broad and substantive legislation** in many key areas of consumer protection, including food, drugs, clothing, cosmetics, medical devices, credit, automobiles, warranties, housing, investments, and product safety. Sometimes the laws created private remedies for consumers.

Four difficulties arose from this approach to regulation. First, government typically spent increasing amounts of money on the problems every year. Second, no one was sure how effective the laws and regulations really were. Third, regulations were designed to place the burdens of compliance primarily upon companies while minimizing responsibilities of consumers. Fourth, the negative aspects of the regulation were usually overlooked, including the costs of achieving the regulatory goal, because of the presumed good the regulations were doing. Only in recent years has concern about **unfunded mandates** (regulatory costs imposed on lower levels of government) become an issue.

Benefit-cost analysis (or **cost-benefit analysis**) is a technique of comparing the costs and benefits of risk reduction **when one chooses** a decision, policy, or action that yields the highest net benefit, given limited time and money. The **net benefit** is the total of all the benefits of a course of action less all the costs. **Most federal regulatory agencies are required** by various executive orders of previous presidents to apply cost-benefit formulas during formal rulemaking. Reasons include a belief that in some instances government had intruded too much into private affairs and a growing belief by Republican conservatives that business was **over-regulated**.

Every year a bill is proposed that would disallow a regulation if the projected social and dollar costs of a law or regulation were projected to exceed its benefits. This is simply a thinly veiled **threat to reduce the power of government**. Fortunately, the U.S. Supreme Court has ruled against such laws.

Benefit-cost regulation is an **imprecise science** that requires many assumptions about applying dollar costs to certain events. On the cost side of the equation, for example, how much does it truly cost to put safety belts in all automobiles? Does one have to consider the expenses of engineering, as well as the use of buildings and land? What about the alternative costs if the engineering efforts were used elsewhere by the manufacturers? On the benefit side, how much is a saved life worth? (In the federal government's benefit-cost analysis, a human life is worth about $2.6 million.) Is a child's life worth more than a parent's? What about the benefits of a reduction in serious injuries? Government agencies and special-interest groups have economists, mathematicians, and other specialists conducting benefit-cost research studies to **help make their judgments** about various regulatory proposals.

The President's **Office of Management and Budget (OMB)** has **centralized control over the regulatory processes** of the federal government because OMB must be notified of all regulatory policies, goals, and objectives, as well as of all significant regulatory actions underway or planned. Before OMB will approve a regulation, the proposing agency must demonstrate that the societal benefits outweigh the costs of the proposal.

Perhaps not surprisingly, measuring risks and determining the acceptability of risks are **normative political efforts**. Government must carefully review the methodology and biases in such studies (including its own) and use that information, as well as other factors in decision-making. Benefit-cost analysis **should be just one of many tools** utilized by government in making decisions about the value of consumer protection proposals, or defending or strengthening current efforts. It is a vital tool that can help regulators decide which problems to attack with their limited resources, assist in choosing priorities, and provide guidance in rulemaking.

Specification and Performance Standards

Many government regulations on behalf of consumers have to do with **establishing product standards**. Government has options as to the type of standard to utilize. For example, assume that the federal government is considering strengthening its standard for automobile bumpers. The proposal might be to require bumpers to withstand impacts of up to 5 miles an hour rather than the current 2½ miles per hour.

One factor in the decision is whether government will issue specification standards or performance standards. **Specification** (or **design**) **standards** are quantitative and qualitative measures of comparison that specify technically and **precisely how something will function** when it is attained by manufacturers and other sellers. For example, the bumper could be required to be made of a prescribed size and quantity of specific metals and plastic materials of certain grades and weights and be attached to the automobile chassis with particular sized bolts. **Performance standards** are quantitative and qualitative measures of comparison that **specify the criteria in terms of outputs** of objectively measured units, such as content, strength, and other performance characteristics. For example, the bumper could be required to suffer no more than a 20-degree indentation in a 5 mile per hour frontal impact with a stationary barrier. Sellers tend to prefer performance standards over specification standards because they are less restrictive and they encourage competitive and efficient designs to reach the same goals.

A question faced by government is whether the regulation will be absolute or conditional. An **absolute standard** is not limited by restrictions or exceptions and thus has a **single level of acceptability**. For example, any automobiles failing to meet the bumper standard could be labeled unsafe and could not be sold. A **conditional standard** is a qualified statement allowing for contingencies when certain conditions exist regarding the user of the product or its application. For example, if 85 percent of a sample of automobile bumpers pass the 5 mile per hour test, all bumpers from that manufacturer are presumed to have met the standard.

Another question facing government regulators is whether particular standards be **voluntary or required**. Trade associations can only set voluntary standards. Government has a great number of guidelines for voluntary standards, as well as mandatory standards. When government relies too heavily on voluntary standards, critics suggest that there is a tendency for business to go into "slow motion."

Sources of Regulatory Inadequacy

Regulations are intrusions into the private marketplace; they are disruptive. Yet government must establish rules and regulations to **meet the demands of both consumers and sellers** for a better and safer marketplace. This is part of the price we pay for a civilized society. We all want good regulations too.

However, there are several factors that result in **regulatory inadequacy**. We must realize that when a legislative body writes a law addressing a consumer problem, it purposefully keeps the language **broad** to allow flexibility in resolving the problem. Implementation of the law is then delegated to a regulatory agency that often must write specific regulations interpreting the legal mandate.

As a result, often the laws and regulations themselves are **inadequately written** to properly address the problems. This sometimes results when business takes rigid positions and opposes constraining regulations, while opposing groups, usually environmentalists and consumers, take equally extreme and adversarial views. It also occurs when opponents who cannot block a legislative or regulatory proposal try during the process **to weaken** those that are likely to become official public policy. The consensus that is usually required to get a proposal approved often requires compromises from all sides, and this has seriously weakened many consumer protection laws and regulations.

The political and legal processes are also quite **responsive to appeals** from special-interest groups desiring to delay implementation of regulations. Another difficulty is that consumers may not trust the regulatory agency to actually protect their interests when administered by conservatives.

The legislature to some extent maintains **an oversight function**, since it requires government agency administrators to speak at congressional hearings to review progress in implementing regulatory laws. Crucial to good regulatory performance is constant pressure from Congress and the public.

Since legislators and regulators are humans, they cannot foresee all the possible effects of proposed laws and regulations. Government decision-makers might be bright and dedicated, but they cannot anticipate everything, and as a consequence, many regulations **are amended** not long after they are written.

The **abilities and prejudices** of the bureaucratic leaders administering an agency are always a factor in regulatory successes and failures. Some leaders have considerable expertise in the areas they regulate; some are appointees possessing only management skills. Most regulators are subject to political influences. Some have **divided loyalties** because they desire employment, or re-employment, in the industry they regulate after completing government service.

Most government agencies have **fragmented responsibilities** because they enforce a number of executive orders, laws, and regulations, often sharing responsibility with other agencies. There also is a tendency among regulators to remain rigid in their beliefs and to continue doing what they always have done rather than consider new approaches to resolving consumer problems.

Some government agencies are headed by a **single administrator** who may therefore lack access to alternative views and information in decision-making. Other agencies are headed by a **collegial group**, which is a form of administration where authority is shared among colleagues. A criticism of the collegial approach is that it is often too slow in making decisions. Finally, another source of regulatory inadequacy is that government has **limited resources**. It can spend only so much time and money to address consumer problems.

Review and Summary of Key Terms and Concepts

1. What do the terms **special-interest groups** and **lobbying** mean, and why are they vital to effective government?

2. List three **consumer lobbying organizations** and identify the focus of their lobbying efforts.

3. Define **neg-reg (negotiated regulation)** and give two benefits of the process.

4. Define **consumer protection**.

5. What is meant by the **commerce clause** of the U.S. Constitution?

6. Distinguish between **interstate** and **intrastate commerce**.

7. Explain how the **supremacy clause** of the U.S. Constitution can be used to increase consumer protection.

8. How does a legislature perform its **oversight function**?

9. How are **administrative agencies** involved in the regulatory process?

10. Distinguish between **executive agencies** and **independent agencies**.

11. Distinguish between the regulatory **investigative powers** of **subpoenas** and **search and seizure orders**.

12. Explain what **quasi-legislative power** means. In your response, explain the term **trade regulation rule**.

13. Distinguish between **formal rule-making** and **informal rule-making**.

14. Explain what **quasi-judicial** power means. In your response, comment upon the fact that some regulatory agencies have the powers of all three branches of government.

15. What is meant by having the **standing to sue**?

16. Distinguish between the **Uniform Commercial Code** and **consumer protection statutes**.

17. Summarize the essence of the popular legal approach to providing state consumer protection, the **little FTC act**.

18. What is meant by the term **unconscionability**?

19. Summarize the role of **state attorneys general** in consumer protection.

20. Distinguish between the efforts of state **offices of consumer affairs** and **weights and measures**.

21. Compare and contrast the FTC's powers of **affirmative disclosure orders** and **corrective advertising**.

22. Explain the idea behind **benefit-cost analysis**, including **net benefit**.

23. Distinguish between **specification standards** and **performance standards**.

24. Distinguish between **absolute standards** and **conditional standards**.

25. List three sources of **regulatory inadequacy**.

Useful Resources for Consumers

Center for the Study of Responsive Law
www.csrl.org

Center for Responsive Politics
www.opensecrets.org/

Common Cause
www.commoncause.org

Congress Watch
www.citizen.org/congress/

Consumer Federation of America
www.consumerfed.org

Consumers International
www.consumersinternational.org

Consumers Union of the United States
www.consumersunion.org

Federal Elections Commission
www.fec.gov

Food and Drug Administration
www.fda.gov

Health Research Group
www.publiccitizen.org/hrg

National Consumers League
www.nclnet.org/

National Institute for Consumer Education
www.consumer-education.jp/nice/eng/

Political Money Line
www.tray.com/fecinfo

Public Citizen
www.publiccitizen.org/

Public Voice for Food and Health Policy
www.publicvoicedc.com

U.S. Public Interest Research Group
www.pirg.org/

"What Do You Think" Questions

1. If the nation did not have **special-interest groups** lobbying legislators and regulators, who would represent the interests of business? Of consumers? Of other governments? Briefly describe that kind of society.

2. Considering all the problems and challenges facing consumers, select one area of interest and describe a proposed federal statute to protect consumers that, using the **supremacy clause**, would improve the quality of life.

3.   Should **independent agencies** be required to yield to the direction of the executive branch of government? Cite examples in your discussion of why or why not.

4.   Realizing that it is fairly easy to come up with the "right answer" when performing a **benefit-cost analysis**, choose a consumer problem you would like to see remedied and assign made-up prices to variables on both the benefit and cost sides so that the answer comes out in favor of a proposal to protect consumers.

Part Four:

INFORMATION PROCESSING

Chapter 11

Policymaking and Consumer Issues

OBJECTIVES

After reading this chapter, you should be able to

1. Illustrate how policymaking occurs within a system of issue networks.

2. Understand how government resolves public policy disputes.

3. Describe how one's economic ideology and political beliefs affect an understanding of consumer issues.

4. Identify the types of consumer protection proposals which would receive the most support.

5. Comprehend how to analyze and resolve consumer issues.

Many of the headlines and stories in newspapers, magazines, and television magazines, such as *60 Minutes*, *20/20*, and *Dateline NBC*, focus on consumer issues, and that interest is what constitutes the remainder of this book. This chapter provides an introduction to the breadth of current concerns involved in the consumer interest, with more details on the issues presented in subsequent chapters. Crucial to being able to effectively analyze issues is to have a well-informed citizenry–that's you!–with the skills to participate in the public policy decision making process.

This chapter begins with a description of how policymaking occurs in the United States, and how this is influenced by money, power and the status quo. It continues with an overview of how government goes about resolving public interest disputes. Next we examine economic ideology and political beliefs as they affect one's understanding of consumer issues. This requires an appreciation of the terms conservatism and liberalism as well as the perspectives of the Republican and Democratic political parties. As a consumer one needs to understand his or her own personal perceptions when interpreting consumer issues. In this way an individual has a rather expansive understanding of why others might be opposed to his or her position and how he or she might be successful in promoting acceptance of proposals on specific consumer issues. An added benefit of knowledge about oneself, is that people enjoy associating with others who share the similar perspectives. An analysis of which consumer protection proposals are likely to receive support and which will be opposed is then presented. The chapter concludes with an examination of how to analyze and resolve consumer issues. One appendix is included at the end of the chapter on Proposed Consumer Protection Laws.

Policymaking in the United States

Policymaking in the United States is characterized not by warring ideologies of conservatives versus liberals or Republicans against Democrats, but rather by **coalitions of people and organizations** interested in the issues. The politics of public policy-making, including consumer protection proposals, are usually the politics of **moderation and accommodation** rather than prolonged and strained battles between groups with opposing views.

Power Clusters

Public policy in the United States is made within a system of power clusters. The term **power clusters** was coined by Daniel M. Ogden, Jr., who argues that a number of participants are involved in most policy shaping. Power clusters are **small circles of semi-autonomous participants** interested in broad, interrelated subject fields such as agriculture, in which the government plays an active role. These circles operate independently of all other clusters to identify policy issues, shape policy alternatives, propose new legislation, and implement policy. Each power cluster includes government administrative agencies, legislative committees, special-interest groups, professionals, volunteers, and an attentive public. Some people call power clusters **issue networks**, where there are a large number of participants with variable degrees of commitment or dependence on others in their environment. Issue networks do not dominate a program, since no one group controls the politics and issues. Moreover, power clusters and issue networks are **communications networks** established by the participants in each field of public policy.

Power clusters exist in **all categories** of domestic and foreign policy, such as defense, education, natural resources, communications, transportation, justice and law enforcement, urban affairs, health, welfare, commerce, banking, finance, and consumerism. Many clusters have sub-clusters that deal with more specific subjects. For example, the natural resources power cluster has sub-clusters concerned with water, air, forests, minerals, recreation, and energy policies. Each cluster has a large contingent of active special-interest professionals who work in business, academic settings, public interest organizations, private consulting firms, law firms, and in professional and trade associations.

Attentive Public and Latent Public

An **attentive public** is one that **pays attention** to one area of public policy, usually because they earn a living in the area and want to advance both economically and socially. The attentive public group reads, listens, has opinions, and talks selectively about the issues of the power cluster. Such a group can easily be aroused over a major controversy and may get actively involved in an organized interest group.

A **latent public** also exists. This group has interests that are affected by a specific power cluster but generally perceives that policies, if changed, would not affect them adversely. Individuals are usually active in only one power cluster throughout their lives. A **major switch in policy** that may adversely affect the latent public can stimulate them to interfere in the power cluster's decision-making to protect their own interests. For example, citizens not normally aroused by consumer interest concerns wrote letters, attended public meetings, and put great pressure on the federal government to improve government oversight after E.coli food poisoning scares. The latent public also becomes aroused when a **NIMBY** (not in my back yard) event occurs, such as closing a school, opening a recycling plant, or re-zoning a residential area for business.

The latent public is **difficult to keep aroused**, however. A weakness of the latent American public, especially on consumer issues, is that their attention span is about three days. Author Richard Condon argues that television permits the public to be entertained by politics instead of participating in it. The media finds it difficult to stay focused on any one public policy issue for more than a week.

After years of continuing declines of public **trust in government**, Americans' **faith has improved** since the terrorist attacks of September 11, 2001. Forty years ago 71 percent trusted the government to do what is right "just about always" or "most of the time." That percentage was only 42 percent in 2000, and it is now 64 percent, reports the University of Michigan National Election Study. In a turnabout, a recent Pew Research Center reports that about half the members of Congress report that they did not trust their constituents' knowledge of issues.

How Public Policy is Shaped

Public policy is shaped by **interaction among the affected parties**: (1) the identified executive government agencies, (2) the legislative committees, and (3) the organized special-interest groups. The three parties are sometimes collectively called the iron triangle because they are the most active participants in making public policy.

Many different people provide inputs to public policy, so decisions that reconcile policy goals and judgments are the **product of multiple interactions** among people in the public and private sectors. Policy decisions, therefore, are a result of intense interactions by those parties who will be most affected by actions. **Changes go on continuously**.

All clusters are **bipartisan or nonpartisan** because they are organized to shape policy, not win elections. Issues that concern political parties are broader, inter-cluster topics such as talks on spending programs that may affect the outcome of elections. Partisanship does not focus on policy-making; rather it focuses on office-seeking and office-holding. Research suggests that only about 40 percent of the roll call votes in Congress are identifiably partisan. The political parties average about **60 percent loyalty** from their members on partisan votes.

Power Cluster Behavior

Power clusters exhibit **five patterns of behavior** that shape the policymaking process: (1) they maintain close personal and institutional ties, (2) key participants, driven by their need to be effective, are active participants in the power cluster, (3) power cluster participants try to work out differences among themselves to reach acceptable policy agreements before bills are sent to the legislature, (4) each cluster usually has deep-seated and well-established internal, often philosophical, conflicts among competing interests, and (5) each power cluster, although it is an informal communications network, develops its own internal power structure.

The power cluster system has evolved naturally in the United States because of the concept of **separation of powers**. At the federal level, the members of Congress are quite independent. In addition, government is open to participation by organized groups in the policy-making process. Power clusters ensure that policy-making **retains continuity and stability**, without disruption through changes in political power. Because they are decentralized, power clusters can resist presidential and gubernatorial direction; they are **accountable to no one** because they are informal networks.

The power clusters also promote **professionalism and efficiency**. Each power cluster retains ties to the nation's universities, which can provide a constant source of new professional recruits for its functions in society. Successful leaders must understand the power cluster system and know how to work with it.

Money, Power and the Status Quo

The **status quo** is the existing condition or state of affairs. The status quo in society **already has the power**, money, advantage, and influence—and they want to keep it! The status quo **vigorously defends its vested interests**, especially when it is under question. The status quo feels threatened by the exposure of facts. The status quo prefers society to remain ignorant because this shelters them. Those with money and power do not want change because it is threatening, unless of course, it further advantages themselves. The status quo is **often against the interest of consumers** because sellers want to remain powerful at the expense of consumers.

Money is the mortar that binds politicians together to keep the status quo exactly as it is. Campaigning for political office is very costly, particularly since it takes expensive television advertising to reach voters. Contributors are breaking records pouring more and more money into political campaigns. Most contributors avoid breaking the law, but succeed in **sidestepping the regulations** or find holes in the rules. Contributors offer their support to assure **access to politicians** when needed on key issues.

Do Big Corporations Own American Politics?

"Yes" is the short answer to the question "Do big corporations own American politics?" **Special-interest lobbying**, as noted in Chapter 10, and campaign contributions are cornerstone freedoms in the American society. Bribery, of course, must not be tolerated. Our **campaign laws** are designed to accommodate the rights of special-interests as well as prevent unequivocal corruption. Money makes our political systems function, and big business and wealthy contributors have a **much bigger say** in public policy than ordinary citizens like "Jessica," "Jose" and "Jack" who earn $40,000 annually.

An important part of a special interest's influence may be to help finance campaign costs. **Political action committees (PACs)** are lobbying organizations that collect funds to support particular candidates. Millions of dollars are then given to candidates who, when elected, may remember the source of their campaign funds. Campaign contributions do **"buy access"** to the politicians. Spending time and money getting to know legislators is important to lobbyists so they will have access when the time comes to earnestly talk about an issue. Businesses and business political action committees enjoy a certain degree of power over politicians, primarily through their money, expertise, and control of information.

Congress continues to **find it difficult to tighten the laws** governing how campaign money is raised and spent on elections. Re-election rates remain well above 90 percent. While personal contributions to PACs are limited in amount, currently $10,000 to a candidate, corporations and wealthy individuals may make *unlimited* donations to soft-money political action committees.

Soft money is that donated by corporations, unions and individuals. It cannot be given to political parties. Soft money is **free of contribution limits**, but must be disclosed by the recipients. Soft money is used for voter registration and television advertising that serve as campaign advertising. Soft-money PACs are not supposed to have any "consultations" with a particular political campaign. Over the past ten years, corporations have doled out more than $1 billion in soft-money contributions.

Soft money is what is behind **issue-advocacy groups**. They are very important key players in the political process because they purchase paid advertising, especially on television, with soft money contributions. Funded by wealthy donors who control the **issue advertising** message (praise or attack), the people putting up the money are **not required to identify themselves**. Campaign regulations require that these ads may not call directly for the election or defeat of a particular person or issue. However, "somehow" the advertising still communicates the prohibited message. This also is called **"independent advertising."** Many special interest groups advertise to persuade public opinion. Pro-Republican groups outspend Democratic groups by a ratio of 3 to 1.

PAC Support for Democrats and Republicans

Democratic PAC support comes from **teachers, state and municipal employees, unions**, including the International Brotherhood of Teamsters, AFL-CIO, United Auto Workers, and United Steelworkers of America, as well as the Association of Trial Lawyers, plus issue groups like Planned Parenthood, NAACP, AARP, and Sierra Club.

Republican support comes primarily **from business**, with money from businesses such as Joseph E. Seagram, Philip Morris, Walt Disney, National Association of Realtors, and American Medical Association, plus issue groups like the National Rifle Association and the National Right to Life. Republican PAC support comes from tobacco, energy, physicians, chambers of commerce, automobile manufacturers, beer, liquor, restaurants, oil, utilities, insurance, banks, pharmaceuticals, telecommunications, Christian groups, airlines and airline manufacturers, and real estate. Big spenders, like the insurance industry, donate $200,000 to *each* lawmaker a year. In the last election, the pharmaceutical industry spent $260 million on political influence. **Business groups outspend labor by a ratio of over 10 to 1.** For information on money in politics, see www.publiccitizen.org, www.fec.gov, www.opensecrets.org, and www.tray.com/fecinfo.

How Government Helps Resolve Public Policy Disputes

Public interest decision-making occurs in the real world in what might be described as a **political society** where those making the decisions on behalf of the public interest may interpret that interest with **a bit of human bias**.

Government's Political Biases

One common partiality in the United States is a bias toward **supporting competition**. Another is a bias toward serving business more than consumers or the general public; this is often called a **free market bias**. Other historical biases include keeping government control and decision-making **close to the people at the local level**, preferring to regulate at the state level instead of the federal level, and resolving consumer problems with solutions that **optimize individual choice**. The tradition is to prefer non-governmental self-regulatory efforts of businesses to address consumer problems. Another heritage is to seek **voluntary solutions** rather than mandatory.

Government Makes Public Policy Decisions

Government, unfortunately, **frequently falls short** of effectively promoting the public interest when it tries to do so. For example, policymakers often listen too carefully to the business side of an issue and give them an advantage over the views of unions, consumers, environmentalists, or civil rights activists. In addition, government's politicians often protect the interests of workers (keeping jobs in America) rather than protect the concerns of consumers (low prices on imported goods). Politicians sometimes yield to the views of wealthy special-interest groups that make financial contributions to their elections, rather than consider the ideas of less affluent consumer organizations. Thus, for a variety of reasons, governments may make policy determinations that favors the interest of business on one issue and a decision that favors organized labor, environmentalists or consumers on another.

It is challenging for a bureaucrat in a regulatory agency **to responsibly carry out the public interest** while being legally responsible to protect conflicting interests. One of the major challenges faced by agency leaders is to correctly identify the consumer interest while carrying out their public interest decision-making. It is important to ascertain the **true desires/interests** of unions, retirees, poor people, and businesses (both large and small). For example, those working at the U.S. Department of Agriculture have difficulty reconciling the conflicting goals of consumers (good nutrition) and producers (sell more beef), particularly when business interests are pressed upon them **much more frequently** than the interests of consumers. The ratio of business-to-consumer contacts with executives of regulatory agencies is typically **40 to 1**; forty hours of listening to the business perspective for every one hour with a consumer advocate.

Government Resolves Public Interest Disputes

Public interest disputes are often about optimizing collective or **widely shared benefits** for the community as a whole. Citizens pursue various public interest concerns when they demand accountability from their elected representatives, fairer taxes, a cleaner and safer environment, sustained economic growth, protection of endangered species of animals and plants, reduction of outside financial influences on legislators, and more consideration for the economically disadvantaged in society.

Public issues almost always involve the government and its effort to regulate the good of the people. Most could be called citizenship issues. Resolution of many of these problems and issues by government generally costs substantial sums of money which are paid by the nation's taxpayers. **Public interest concerns** include providing access for citizens to certain goods and services, such as basic health care via the Medicaid program for low-income people, minimum societal standards of food safety, pollution emission standards on vehicles, and protecting America's borders from danger. Public interest issues often arise because of real or perceived **market failures** or the threat of market failures in which community values have a decisive impact.

Interest conflicts often arise between and among different groups, and decisions made in the public interest are often difficult and full of controversy. While government may try to persuade competing interests to a particular position, government has both the authority and responsibility to make **final determinations** on public interest issues. In effect, when government makes decisions it arbitrates from the perspective of the public interest. Eventually, the **public interest is what government supports**, however imperfect.

In pursuit of the public interest, government should **attend to the needs of all** appropriate groups and try to reconcile them. Ultimately, the public good of the people should be protected solely by government. Those who should always represent the public interest (and not special interests) include members of the U.S. Congress and the state legislatures, elected local government officials, and the numerous government regulators and bureaucrats serving in the legislative, executive and judicial branches of government. See the National Institute for Money in State Politics at www.followthemoney.org/.

Economic Ideology and Political Beliefs

An **issue** is a public or social concern that, because of its salience or the degree of its impact, **attracts the attention and interest** of many people, organizations and public policymakers for discussion, debate, or dispute. Most, but not all consumer protection issues and proposals are controversial. The major reason for the controversy is that the American people **differ in their perceptions of economic reality**. They do not agree on how the economy really works or how its performance might be improved. When several people look at the American marketplace, each may see different things. One's perception of truth about the competitiveness of the market, the role of consumers, and how consumer problems can best be remedied is dependent on one's economic ideology.

An **economic ideology** is a set of beliefs and attitudes about the American economic marketplace **and the proper roles** of business, government, and consumers in that market. Briefly put, an **ideology** is a simplified picture of the world, a coherent perspective that justifies personal decisions and actions. People pick and choose for ideological reasons which problems and issues to confront, and which to ignore. **Beliefs** are mental acceptances of or convictions about the truth or actuality of something. Being in the eye of the beholder, **beliefs can be true or false**.

The attitudes Americans have toward consumer protection proposals vary because of their economic ideologies and their political perspectives. To get a consumer protection proposal successfully accepted first requires an understanding of the economic belief systems of all parties involved in decision-making. One's perceptions of economic reality often reveal **motivations for or against** various proposals.

Stephen Brobeck, executive director of the Consumer Federation of America, says "one key to working with consumer advocates is to identify **mutual or complementary interests**. For any corporation that is committed not merely to short-term profitability but to long-term growth, this common ground exists. Business and consumer groups share many of the same objectives—products that work and that consumers want, informed buyers who understand the value of these products, and a means of redress when things go wrong."

It is helpful **to know the likely views and arguments** of supporters and opponents of a particular proposal. The more knowledgeable one is about the views of another, the more likely it is that effective dialogue can occur between them. The sponsor of a consumer protection proposal must look for possible areas of agreement for specific aspects of the concept among supporters and opponents. Then the sponsor builds support for the idea among affected groups, compromises with opponents where necessary, and shapes a final proposal that the majority can support. Consumer protection efforts are subject to a variety of forces, including conflicting political interests, opposing ideas, economic recession, budget constraints, and the economic ideology of the political administration in power.

There are **three predominant economic belief systems** in America: (1) neoclassical, (2) managerial, and (3) reformist.[1] Each has its own set of beliefs about the structure of our economy, about how the companies in the United States behave, and about the effects of that behavior on consumers. In addition, each ideology includes beliefs about the best ways to remedy consumer problems and whether certain things are in fact consumer concerns. People tend to hold one set of rather consistent economic beliefs; however, on any given issue people are apt to blend ideologies. The perspectives of people **evolve** and often change over time. Table 11-1 summarizes the basic views of the three economic belief systems.[2]

---

[1] The essence of this discussion has evolved from four sources: Christner, A. M. (1989), Protecting consumers with pre-purchase information: Four economic ideological views, *Proceedings of the American Council on Consumer Interests* (University of Missouri), 268-275; Herrmann, R. O. (1977, September-October), Relating economic ideologies to consumer protection: A suggested unit in consumer education, *Business Education World*, 13-15; Mayer, R. N. (1989), *The Consumer Movement: Guardians of the Marketplace* (Wayne Publishers); and Monsen, J. R., Jr. (1963), *Modern American Capitalism: Ideologies and Issues* (Houghton Mifflin).

[2] A fourth economic ideology exists but is not discussed here. Professor Ann Christner describes the **radical reformist** position as one that believes "the market system is inherently flawed and should be replaced by a more equitable mechanism."

TABLE 11-1   Three Primary Economic Belief Systems

	Reformist	Managerial	Neoclassical
How competitive is our economy?	Dominated by monopolies and oligopolies	Highly competitive, even though it is dominated by large firms	Highly competitive
How do firms compete with each other?	Advertising, minor differences in product design, and services	Prices, product features, advertising, services	Prices
What keeps the behavior of individual firms in line?	Nothing except firm's desire for security and stable growth	Competition of other firms for customers, managers' sense of responsibility to workers, shareholders, consumers	Competition of other firms for customers
How are consumers characterized?	Consumers are relatively powerless; their wants and needs are manipulated by advertising and other techniques and they buy goods of questionable value	Decisions are usually rational, but due to laziness, apathy, or ignorance, consumers do not always make the best decisions	Shoppers are intelligent; all choices are rational, made in the consumer's self-interest, and have satisfactory results
What is the role of consumers in the economy?	They are important buyers in the marketplace whose decisions are manipulated by advertising and other techniques	They are a big influence in the economy, and their buying decisions can be manipulated by advertising	They guide the market by casting their "dollar votes' for products and services they prefer
What kinds of problems do consumers have?	A variety of problems arising from unchecked corporate power: excessive prices, unsafe products, difficulty in obtaining redress	Misleading advertising, difficulties in obtaining redress	Fraud and deception, unsafe products
How can these consumer problems best be remedied?	Government regulation	Business self-regulation, improved systems of complaint handling	Legal action by individual consumer affected
What should be the role of government in regulating the economy?	Antitrust action and strengthened government regulation	Removing barriers to competition, maintaining a high level of economic activity	Minimal, so as not to interfere with competition

The Neoclassical Belief System

The **neoclassical belief system** holds that our economy is basically a free enterprise competitive system that favors market mechanisms to achieve society's goals. Neoclassicists see the market as not controlled by monopolies and oligopolies but governed by a large number of firms vigorously competing based primarily on price. Competitors will watch each other, and if one firm slips up, the judicial system is there to reprimand the offender. Antitrust laws and regulatory agencies are necessary, but basically **business should regulate itself**. Neoclassicists also want to look carefully at the costs and benefits of any proposals to regulate.

The neoclassicists believe that the **role of consumers** is that of intelligent shoppers who are aware of their choices and who are basically immune to manipulation by advertising and other forms of persuasion. Consumers are already informed when they act in their self-interest by casting their targeted "dollar votes" for the products and services they really need. Their power over the marketplace is called **consumer sovereignty**, because the consumer ultimately decides which products and services society will produce and consume.

The neoclassicist believes that there are **few consumer problems other than frauds**, deceptions, and unsafe products. It is assumed that consumers seek and process only as much information as they desire or are able to handle. Losses from poor choices are assumed to be minimal. The way to resolve these consumer problems is through **individual lawsuits** by those affected. Government controls and regulations are considered ineffective, unwanted, and an interference with the free competitive marketplace. Neoclassicists would prefer that informed buyers gather and use information for personal buying decisions because this encourages price competition and quality products. Individual rights and **freedom of choice** are paramount in weighing the costs and benefits of any proposal to resolve consumer problems.

Neoclassicists would oppose consumer supported government proposals to grade the quality of produce with a simple A-B-C-D system and to mark food items with a price. Mandatory information **disclosure laws would be considered unnecessary**. This is so because the neoclassicist believes that the self-correcting forces of the marketplace will offer such devices or information when the public dollars demand it. Neoclassicists suggest that the additional costs of mandatory programs represent a hidden tax on products so labeled. Advocates of the neoclassical belief system include Nobel Prize-winning economist Milton Friedman, Washington University economics professor Murray Weidenbaum, former President Ronald Reagan, and a number of **conservative business persons and politicians**.

The Managerial Belief System

The **managerial belief system** emphasizes the key role of the **professional manager** in today's corporations, and it holds that the best protection for consumers comes from corporate competition and the corporate manager's sense of responsibility. Crucial to this system of thinking is the belief that corporate managers serve responsibly (almost as trustees) and in the interest of workers, shareholders, and consumers. The corporate manager is presumed to **possess a high degree of social conscience** that helps protect consumers.

While managerialists recognize that the economy is dominated by large corporations, they believe that competition is based on many **things other than price**. Of great importance is the recognition that advertising does affect consumers by stimulating demand, which in turn ensures a high level of overall economic activity.

Managerialists see the primary role of government as helping to maintain a **high level of economic growth**. They recognize that some government actions are needed to protect consumers; thus they are against misleading advertising. Managerialists would not support proposed government regulations to require national no-fault auto insurance or to strengthen automobile bumper standards, but they would rely on the judgment of corporate managers to determine if and when consumers really wanted these types of remedies for consumer problems. Business should be self-regulatory and government should work toward removing barriers to competition. Some of the biggest supporters of the managerial belief system are the magazines ***Fortune* and *Forbes* along with the newspaper *The Wall Street Journal*.**

The Reformist Belief System

The **reformist belief system** has its roots in the progressive tradition of the 1890s and the liberal reform movement of the 1960s. Proponents are interested in progressive and gradual changes, rather than radical changes in political and social situations. The economy is perceived as being **dominated by monopolies and shared monopolies**. Corporations work with little competition to serve their own ends–profits for the shareholders, security, and continued growth. Economist John Kenneth Galbraith has elaborated on this reformist belief system and has labeled such corporations as the **planning system** that exercises great control over consumers and governments. The remainder of the economy is viewed by Galbraith in much the same way as the neoclassicists; he calls the remaining small firms that are quite competitive the **market system**. Reformists are concerned about the fairness of the marketplace, particularly as the market affects **vulnerable consumers**, such as the elderly, children, and the undereducated. Reformists are also concerned with the market's imperfections, and they seek to fix the flaws in the system.

Reformists do not view consumers as the dominant force in the economy, since **advertising effectively shapes their values** and beliefs to accommodate the needs of the planning system. Consumer problems arise from **unchecked corporate power**. These problems include excessive prices, unsafe products, and difficulty in seeking redress. Reformists want to **force businesses** to use objective advertising information instead of subjective persuasions. They want government intervention to standardize and simplify information formats for products and services, to prevent misleading information, and to set standards for a number of products and services. These standards would reduce the need for consumers to judge safety and effectiveness for many buying decisions.

Supporters of the reformist perspective include the **Consumer Federation of America, Consumers Union**, and the National Consumers League. Consumer advocate **Ralph Nader's** perception of the economy is based on this belief system. Many of the proposals to resolve consumer problems that are suggested by his and other consumer organizations come from the reformist belief system. Nader and his followers prescribe **stronger antitrust actions** and strict government regulation of corporate activities in order to discourage irresponsible actions (such as pollution), encourage responsible actions (such as making safer products), and provide much **more access to information** so that consumers can act more intelligently in the marketplace. Reformists want government-funded comparative consumer information made available with no commercial influence, perhaps to be dispensed through computer vending machines in shopping malls. Reformists suggest that consumers need government protection because of the complexities in the marketplace.

Political Belief Systems

The economic belief systems of consumers are affected by their political beliefs and their ideology. In the broadest sense, a **political ideology** is a person's set of **attitudes and beliefs** about freedom, equality, humankind, and the desired role of government. A person's political ideology also refers to their **view of the world**, an image of the relationship of people to their government and how power is used in society. Surveys show that less than a third of Americans have anything more than a rudimentary understanding of what it means to be politically conservative or liberal. Only half of all adults know which party controls Congress.

Conservatism

Two broad and hazy perspectives dominate political thinking in the United States: conservatism and liberalism.[3] The political spectrum is described as conservative-liberal, right-left, and capitalist-socialist. Supporters of **conservatism** believe in **limited government**—except in national defense—and have faith in encouraging personal achievement. The U.S. conservative movement has long been rooted in **opposition**—to many things. They do not believe in drastic change. The two cardinal beliefs of conservatives are private-property rights and free enterprise. Conservatives embrace self-help, empowerment, free economic markets, and, except for abortion rights and a number of other moral issues, decentralized individual choice.

Conservatives generally **distrust government** and want it out of the way. However, as writer James K. Glassman notes, "conservatives do not object to government coercion or arbitrary power as long as it is used for the right purposes." Glassman observes that conservatives believe that if they, being decent men, run government, they are "entitled to force the values they hold on other people." "Good government" says conservative Bill Bennett, "is good when it serves *our* purposes."

Conservatives place great faith in the **private sector** of the economy rather than relying on government, supporting the old Jeffersonian belief that "government governs best when it governs least." Conservatives believe that it is the job of private enterprise, **not government**, to create rising living standards, provide access to health care, and offer ways out of poverty. "The solution, or even parts of it, can never, ever come from government," writes E. J. Dionne, Jr. Conservatives believe that people should accept as "natural" whatever the capitalistic market offers. "Citizen service" says talk show host Rush Limbaugh, "is a repudiation of the principles upon which this country is based. We are all here **for ourselves**."

Conservatives believe that government action, if taken at all, should be taken at the **lowest possible level**, preferring local and state decisions to action by the federal government. Conservatives want to protect the status quo—most yearn for yesterday when things were better. By its very nature, conservatism cannot offer fundamental alternatives to the current directions in society other than to slow down undesirable developments. Historically, conservatives have seldom favored civil rights and affirmative action programs, suggesting instead that people should be encouraged to be more tolerant and helpful to others. Being believers in the market economy, conservatives support tenant ownership of

---

[3] Two other ideologies supported by significant but small portions of the American population are socialism and libertarianism. **Socialism** seeks public ownership of the means of production, public jobs for all who want to work, and increased taxes on the wealthy. **Libertarianism** cherishes individual liberty, and preaches opposition to government and an end to just about all its programs.

public housing, choice in schooling, and making welfare recipients work. Conservatives believe individuals should be more responsible for themselves and people should work harder to make things better. (See www.conservatism.com/.)

Liberalism

Liberalism is not a dirty word, as many conservative Republican politicians would have everyone believe. In fact, liberals are historically the **most mainstream** of republican governments (lower case "r") around the world. The word "liberal" is translated from Greek as **"a free man"** as opposed to a slave. It implies freedom of thought, freedom from conventional beliefs, and the right of others to think differently than oneself. (See www.turnleft.com.) Hundreds of years ago, the popular phrase "liberal democracy" was coined. Liberal ideals are embodied in **all the constitutions** of the world's democracies. These include the rule of law, separation of powers, personal and economic freedom, and secular government. Early in the 20th century in the U.S., liberals were known as progressives. America, in fact, remains a liberal country.

Liberals believe that democratic governments are fundamentally **important in the solution** of a nation's collective problems. Liberalism involves a belief that government should be used to bring about justice and equality of opportunity. They believe that government can help liberate people. Liberals, writes Mark Shields, believe that "the government can be the national instrument of democracy, capable of promoting economic and social justice."

Liberals wish to **preserve the rights** of individuals. While liberals want to retain private property rights and support free enterprise, they also are willing to **have government intervene** to correct the defects in the capitalistic market-oriented economic system. Liberals realize that a market economy has tremendous advantages for the nation, but that capitalism needs rules and regulations. Liberals believe that individuals need some security against the risks of life in the economic turmoil of a capitalistic society. Therefore, they fight for the interests of those who work for a living.

Liberals believe that **government is the most effective way** to improve society. Liberals figure that government programs are needed even though they sometimes cause a loss of liberties. They believe, writes Mark Shields, that "government's highest purpose is to strengthen the capacities of individuals to achieve self-reliance and nurture the country's rich network of civic organizations that are independent of both the state and the marketplace." They support government efforts to aid the poor and help the unemployed.

Liberals are concerned with improving the adequacy of health care, eliminating unsafe products, and improving access to education and affordable housing. As a result, liberals are often viewed as being compassionate. Liberals **challenge the status quo and change it**—they want a better world and they use government to make it better. Historically, liberals have supported civil rights, women's rights, gay and lesbian rights, affirmative action programs, progressive taxation, the right to unionize, and regulatory efforts that protect the environment and the health and safety of workers and consumers.

Congressman James Leach of Iowa says that liberals are accused of seeking **freedom from personal responsibility** by transferring inconvenient family and social problems to state bureaucracies. At the same time, modern-day conservatives are criticized for seeking freedom from government (and seeking deregulation) **without accepting personal responsibility for social imperatives**. *U.S. News & World Report* observes that "The left wants more private solutions and responsibility and **neither side sees much virtue in the other's arguments**."

Political Party Beliefs

Research from the Center for Political Studies at the University of Michigan shows that voters in the most recent national election described themselves **politically** in the following ways: liberal or tend towards **liberal, 14 percent**; moderate, 28 percent; conservative and tend towards **conservative, 36 percent**; and don't know or no preference, 22 percent. The political party interests are: **Democrat, 47 percent**; **Republican, 42 percent**; independent, 10 percent, and apolitical, 1 percent.

Most of the people in the Republican party are somewhat conservative and most of those in the Democratic party are more liberal. There are some liberal Republicans and conservative Democrats as well. People's politics are a reflection of who they are, **what they value**, and what they hope for the future.

The Higher Education Research Council notes that the number of **college freshmen** calling themselves politically liberal is at the highest level in 20 years, 28 percent. The number calling themselves conservative, 20 percent, continues to decline. Most remain middle-of-the-road, 52 percent. **One-third** of students report that **"keeping up to date with political affairs"** is "very important" or an "essential" life goal. (It was 60 percent a generation ago.) Those who say they "discuss politics" is 16 percent. Today, 42 percent want to "develop a meaningful philosophy of life." (This compares to 80 percent a generation ago.) There is a sense of optimism among today's freshmen as 27 percent believe that an "individual can have an effect on the course of events."

Data from the Consumer Federation of America reveals how members of Congress voted on consumer issues. The **pro-consumer voting record** was just **26 percent** among House **Republicans** and 21 percent among Senate Republicans. Pro-consumer voting among **Democrats** was **79 percent** in the House and 81 percent in the Senate. Republicans are consistently pro-business and anti-consumer in their voting.

The Republican party argues that concentration of **power in the national government should be avoided** in most instances because state and local governments that are closer to the people, should be assigned the first tasks of governing. Conversely, the Democratic party holds that a **strong national government** is needed to deal with today's complex problems that are often too costly for state and local governments to undertake. Democrats desire federal regulations for consistency throughout the country and to ensure an expanding level of economic activity. Republicans believe that unfettered free enterprise is the force needed for economic growth, and it should be regulated as little as possible; Democrats are less trusting of business.

CONSUMER UPDATE:
Humorist P. J. O'Rourke on Democrats and Republicans

P. J. O'Rourke writes in *Parliament of Whores*, that, "Democrats are also the party of government activism, the party that says government can make you richer, smarter, taller, and get the chickenweed out of your lawn. Republicans are the party that says government doesn't work, and then they get elected and prove it."

Republicans are **against federal control** of anything, except on concerns that fit their moral values. They want prayer in schools; tuition vouchers for private schools, religious education in public schools; assisted suicide banned; abortion banned; birth control banned, including RU-486; stem-cell research obtained from fetuses banned; and creationism taught in the schools, rather than evolution. Democrats are more open-minded, and choose not to force moral values on others. On consumer issues, **Republicans** are **against class action lawsuits**; preferring to require that complaints go to arbitration (see Chapter 18) instead of into the court system. Republicans favor putting a maximum dollar cap on lawsuits, such as $100,000. Republicans are against corporations; weakening or eliminating federal consumer protections and they prefer that each of the 50 states pass their own consumer protection laws. **Democrats strongly support consumer issues**.

What are Your Economic and Political Belief Systems?

1. **My *economic ideology* can best be described as:**
    Reformist   Managerialist   Neoclassist

2. ***Two* of the characteristics of the economic ideology in which I believe that I like are:**
    A.
    B.

3. **My *political ideology* can best be described as:**
    Liberalism   Conservatism

4. ***Two* of the characteristics of the political ideology (liberalism or conservatism) that I like are:**
    A.
    B.

5. ***Two* of the characteristics of the political party (Democrat or Republican) that I like are:**
    A.
    B.

6. **What two issues important to you should the President and Congress be dealing with?**

Republican and Democratic politicians in the United States, instead of working together across ideologies to resolve real problems says one politician, too often "slip from discourse about honest differences, which is healthy, into dishonest demonization." They may choose to frame their arguments from the more **narrow or trivial partisan perspectives of party ideology** rather than developing a principled argument on the issues. This promotes polarization of the electorate and endless arguments over **"value issues"** on such topics as family values, feminism, bilingualism, work, neighborhood, virtue, religion, children, crime, welfare, abortion, quotas, and the death penalty. **This turns politics into phony moralizing**–"I'm a *better person* than you are because I...."

Many voters want **real solutions** to the basic problems of society, not "entertaining debates" on value issues. Real problems include dealing with stagnant incomes, vanishing health insurance, unaffordable child care, aging parents, unemployed offspring, crumbling infrastructure, unavailable housing, inadequate education, the growing gap between rich and poor, financial assistance for the working poor, failed drug policy, campaign reform, and making both home ownership and a college education more available.

Voter turnout among young adults is **only 36 percent**, according to a poll by the Harvard Institute of Politics. If more voted, they could easily swing a close election to one candidate or another.

Writer Reinhold Niebhur once observed that the temper and integrity with which the political fight is waged are more important for the health of our American society than the outcome of any issue. Congressman Philip R. Sharp reminds us that "Congress is not a convent; it is not a tea party. It is the public arena where **we battle over ideals and scrap over funding**; where we champion just causes and represent regional interests. It is not always pretty or pleasant. It is this system of representation that best assures that the people will control our government."

CONSUMER UPDATE:
Communitarian: A Political Ideology *Between* Conservatism and Liberalism

The term **communitarian** identifies a political movement in American society that is a moderate ideology somewhere between conservatism and liberalism, particularly on individual rights and responsibilities. It strongly **supports the teaching of values and shared moral principles** in schools. At its heart, a communitarian believes that there is much more to being a human than the simple pursuit of narrow self-interest. Life requires a **civil society**, and preserving the freedoms that Americans enjoy should require the cooperative efforts of many.

George Washington University's Professor Amitai Etzioni founded the movement on the belief that the cultural shift to excessive individualism, the quest for personal gratification, and excessive consumerism have been hurting families and the society. Etzioni's *The Spirit of Community* is a manifesto for the cause.

Communitarians believe that **people are each other's keepers**. Communitarians offer a blueprint for a **collective society** rather than simply a return to individual responsibility. Supporters argue that the political debate should focus less on entitlements and rights and more on obligations and responsibilities.

Some of the **beliefs of communitarians** include: taking driver's licenses away from students who drop out of school, kicking people out of housing projects when caught with guns or drugs, applying anti-loitering ordinances to get drug dealers off the streets, having spot tests to identify drunken drivers, requiring voluntary national service, placing time-limits on welfare payments to single mothers, guaranteeing child-support payments, reforming divorce laws to protect children's interests, providing fringe benefits to part-time workers, eliminating the tax penalty for married couples, and requiring public funding of campaigns.

Support for Consumer Protection Proposals

Recognize that each individual consumer has but **a small economic stake** in each consumer protection proposal. For example, an improved unit-pricing food label might only save each consumer a dollar or two per year. However, the consumer interest concerns of value for money and equity for all consumers can soon mobilize considerable forces of volunteers. Most consumers realize that as individuals they do not have the expertise, time, or willingness to deal with sellers on a one-to-one basis to obtain value for money and equity. Therefore, they join consumer organizations to help them financially and **support consumer protection proposals** put forth by consumer advocates and public interest organizations.

Support for consumer protection proposals varies given the diverse opinions held by the American people who perceive reality according to one of the three dominant economic belief systems. The **widest support** would likely go to proposals that would optimize consumer choice by improving the opportunity to effectively exercise individual responsibility, such as nutritional labeling and health warnings. Support for making product information available is strong provided that the effort is low in cost, reaches many consumers, comes primarily from business, and involves a minimum of government involvement. Information by itself encourages competition and more and better products; that is a goal valued by all three belief systems.

Antitrust proposals would receive the **least support**. Despite their belief in competitive markets, the neoclassicists would fear any kind of government intrusion and oppose even limited interventions to increase competition. Ralph Nader would favor antitrust enforcement. Those of the managerial belief system would oppose antitrust efforts if they would reduce the effectiveness of the corporate manager. Proposals for safety-related concerns would receive mixed support. Reformists support efforts to reduce safety hazards, but those holding to the managerial and the neoclassicist belief systems would not agree with extensive government involvement, preferring first to rely on industry self-regulation.

Consumer advocates usually have a **reformist viewpoint**. They prefer laws and regulations at the federal level to be effective **nationally**, rather than passing laws one state at a time. Businesspeople typically have a neoclassical or managerial viewpoint, and they often prefer to be regulated at the state level since they usually get more flexibility there. Consumer advocates are often **biased against big corporations**, believing that when businesses aggressively pursue profit maximization, the consumer viewpoint often becomes lost. While this is true, reality also shows that businesses pursue many policies that are either neutral or beneficial to consumers. Consumer advocates defend the use of **class action lawsuits** and **punitive damages** to penalize corporate misbehavior. Businesses object to such powers because they believe them to be too costly. (See Chapter 3 for more information.) Consumer advocates are effective at pointing out how to save consumers money in the marketplace; how to prevent thousands of product-related deaths, injuries, and illnesses through health and safety regulations; and how to help ensure fairness in the marketplace through various interventions and disclosure requirements. Neoclassicists and managerialists are usually strong supporters of deregulation. They are also effective at pointing out that the costs of many consumer policy proposals far outweigh any potential benefits.

Analyzing and Resolving Consumer Issues

The process of analyzing and **resolving consumer issues** involves constructive thinking, purposeful analytic thinking, preparation of alternative solutions, government action in the resolution of alternatives, and finally, the discovery of mutually satisfactory solutions.

Constructive Thinking

Constructive thinking is necessary in the resolution of consumer issues. If conditions are ideal, the parties to a civilized argument or discussion in a democratic environment **understand what questions they are arguing about**, possess some relevant facts, accept facts demonstrated by others, and recognize a point where they should gather more facts.

They would **disagree about** (1) which facts are the most important, (2) the significance of each fact, and/or (3) how the facts are related to one another.

When resolving consumer issues, it must be realistically recognized that **some parties to an argument are uninformed**, of dull mentality, or under the influence of a strong emotional bias. In such instances, persuasion to an acceptable resolution is more difficult and sometimes impossible. Thus, a crucial **first step** in successfully resolving consumer issues is to attempt to understand the emotional beliefs and attitudes, economic and political belief systems, and logic of the persons who hold opposing views. In this manner one can begin to determine ways of thinking-feeling and translate the emotive-evaluative statements made by others. Willing people can then take appropriate steps toward resolving their differences. Persuasion depends primarily upon finding common values. To persuade someone to a viewpoint, one must **link the new viewpoint** with another value or argument shared by both.

Purposeful Analytical Thinking

Analytical thinking (or analysis) is an attempt to clarify and simplify a problem or issue using discipline and direction. The purpose of analytical thinking is to determine precisely what a proposition means. A **proposition** is a plan, scheme, or proposal to resolve a problem or issue. Analytical thinking does not tell upon which side truth rests, rather it identifies the questions fundamental to the eventual resolution of a problem or issue.

Analytical thinking requires **a description of the status quo**. This could include the nature of the alleged problem or issue and its seriousness, as well as a review of existing relevant laws and regulations. Analysis also requires recognition of what is causing the problem or issue to be discussed. What is the origin and history of the proposition? What is the current controversy that makes this an issue? Why is this issue or problem critical at this time? Realistic interpretations of the causes are important because these may reveal appropriate lines for successful argument later.

Analytical thinking reveals that those groups involved in consumer issues tend to **try to protect or maximize their own personal interests** or what they think is the public interest. Groups try to protect their interests and advance only those policies that they think will benefit society or themselves. Purposeful analytical thinking requires that one constantly ask how much each group or its program will gain or lose from government action or inaction and how much time and effort each group should expend lobbying on the issue. Disagreements often surround concerns about choice, fairness, safety, competitive markets, right to information, benefit-cost analysis, and assigning responsibility for action.

The **early stage** of how the problem or issue is originally shaped may be as critical to later success as the later stage of what groups to involve in the formulation of the policy. Similar careful attention must be given to the stages of policy adoption, policy implementation, and policy evaluation. At all stages it is vital to frame the debate of an issue in the proper (and most favorable) terms. Business might want to say, "How clean and wholesome do you want your chicken?" and "How much are you prepared to spend?" Meanwhile, consumers should try to keep the focus on "Do you want clean and wholesome chicken or unsafe chicken?"

Participants in support of consumer protection proposals must **clarify their goals** or objectives and rank them. They should then list all possible solutions while investigating the likelihood of achieving each. After considering each alternative, they should then choose an approach that will achieve the consequences most closely matching their goals.

Preparing Alternative Solutions

Each side to a debate is interested in maximizing its position and will **compromise only when necessary**. Typically, there is an initial difference of opinion on what the outcome or resolution should be and one group, supporters of the status quo, has more power than the other. Thus, the mind-set begins with the stronger group demanding their position on the issue which means the weaker group has an uphill battle. The task then becomes one of reaching resolution without the stronger party compelling a solution that imposes a loss on the other because the weaker party will break off negotiations in such circumstances.

In order for **an acceptable resolution** to be reached between private parties, both must benefit. What is necessary for resolution between private parties is that the benefits of agreement equal or exceed the costs of not agreeing. When there are only private parties involved in resolving an issue, the **three resolution choices** are (1) compromise, (2) one side wins while the other side loses, or (3) deadlock. While the first alternative, compromise, may be desirable, the likelihood of the other two alternatives is greater.

Since parties involved in resolving issues often vary in strength, they may never reach a compromise because the **stronger one either defeats the weaker or a compromise is forced** by the stronger with more benefits going to the stronger. For example, strong business lobbies often defeat proposals by consumer groups for effective and easily understandable grade labeling on food products, such as an A, B, C, D system. Accordingly, many consumer issues remain unresolved between business and consumer groups because of the likelihood of sub-optimal resolution alternatives. In fact, these can be described as **market-failure situations**.

Government Action in Creating Solutions

Public issues are different from private issues. Government gets involved in the resolution of numerous consumer problems and issues for **two reasons**: (1) because it desires to ensure outcomes that will protect the public interest, and (2) because it often perceives that government can improve the outcome of many resolutions. Moreover, government intervenes in the generation of alternative solutions for many consumer problems and issues on the justification that there will be **net public benefits**. When government is involved in resolving consumer problems and issues, it must induce others—consumers, laborers, businesses, and other nations—to forego or limit anticipated private gain and instead accept realistic gains to themselves and to society in general.

A rational strategy for both business and consumer interest groups is to analyze **how to get government support and deny it to others**. When government refuses to become seriously involved in resolving a consumer issue, the private parties are left to try to reach a compromise situation, realizing that a good compromise might not ever be reached.

The **extent and degree of government involvement** depends on the particulars of each issue and the values of the public (e.g., consumers, manufacturers, retailers, labor) about what would constitute a reasonable, just, and equitable compromise alternative. Government can ensure outcomes that will protect the public interest, not just serve the interests of consumers over business, for example, and at the same time improve the quality of the compromise. Thus, active government involvement in the resolution of consumer issues has the potential to **improve the efficiency of market forces**.

> **CONSUMER UPDATE: How to Successfully
> Move a Consumer Issue Forward***
>
> The goal in working on consumer issues is to **improve the lives of consumers**. You have to be there during the legislative, regulatory, and policy making discussions or someone else will make decisions in your absence. Their views may well be different from yours. To be successful, advocates of the consumer interest should **set idealistic goals**, and push for genuine progress toward the goals.
>
> Advocates of the consumer interest should: (1) **adopt effective tactics** (or stand by and get marginalized in the process), (2) **use appropriate rhetoric** (because inappropriate statements and negative personalizations will dissuade today's opponents from supporting your position on the next issue), (3) **avoid attributing bad motives to your opponents** (for the same reasons), and (4) **put your issue into the context of the popular issues of the day**, such as the proposal "helps reduce health care costs" or "helps increase productivity." The overall key to influencing government while you are working on the issue is to develop and offer a well-reasoned analysis of how government and the other participants can successfully make progress.
>
> *Mark Silbergeld, Director, Consumers Union Washington Office

Lobbying the Government Decision-making Process

Attempting to **influence the outcome** of a legislative or regulatory decision is a time-honored tradition in all societies. In a representative democracy, lobbying is a constitutional right of every citizen. Lobbying is the **most fundamental way** a person can exercise his or her constitutional right to speak out and petition government. A lobbyist's job is to educate public policy decision-makers about an issue and obtain commitments to support one position or another. Lobbyists who receive compensation to influence legislation generally must register with the legislature being lobbied; citizens who simply try to influence the process usually need not register.

Lobbying can take the form of **personal contact** with legislators and their staffs (no more than 30 minutes at a time), mobilization of large numbers of organized citizens, "grassroots" support from a particular constituency, coalitions of groups, involvement of public officials, support of affected private individuals and groups, arousing the public, and fractionalizing and manipulating the opponents. Multiple approaches are common.

The Legislative Process

The **political culture and procedures** of each of the 50 state legislatures and the U.S. Congress vary, and successful lobbying requires knowledge of the processes. Legislatures typically meet once or twice a year. Legislators are elected by the people in the district where they live, and part of a legislator's responsibilities is to accurately reflect the views of those citizens. Most of the work of legislatures is done through their committees, and the **committee chairs** are powerful members of the legislature.

Procedurally, after a bill has been introduced by a member of the legislature, often by an influential legislator, it is assigned to a committee where consideration of the proposal begins as a subcommittee or a committee hears its merits. Testimony may or may not be considered. Knowledge of the **relative power and biases** of each member of the committee is crucial to the lobbying process to get the bill successfully reported out of committee.

The bill then **may or may not be debated** by the whole house. Amendments may or may not be offered (or even permitted) at this point. Many legislatures then require a second reading and then a third reading to put the bill to a final vote. When a bill passes the first house, it goes on to the second house (if one exists). Here the proposal goes through the same process all over again. Amendments made in the second house must also be approved by the first house before the bill goes to the governor (or the president at the federal level). Differences are generally worked out by a conference committee, composed of powerful legislators, and substantial changes are often made at this point. The governor (or the president at the national level) affects the political process by signing or vetoing the bill. A legislature usually needs a two-thirds vote to override the veto and make the bill law.

Know Your Lawmakers

A **mountain of public information** is available about each legislator. Getting to know where a legislator is "coming from" is vital to the lobbying process because each legislator inevitably votes in his or her enlightened self-interest. Each person's political and economic ideologies can be surmised by reviewing factors such as a legislator's voting record, political party affiliation, employment history, financial interests, business dealings, campaign contributors, and a socio-economic description of the district being represented. Remember that a legislator's position on any single issue will be motivated by a mixture of objectives, some internal and some external, but almost always by the interest in being re-elected. Often the most important factor for a legislator in determining how to vote is knowledge of how his or her constituents feel about it. When talking with your legislator, personalize the issue. Emphasize how it affects the lives of your family and friends.

Know Your Issue

The **quality of the arguments put forth in support of and against a proposal** have much to do with legislative success or failure. Try to emphasize solutions that will not cost the government money. Virtually all the pro and con arguments surrounding a proposal must be considered carefully. Key sources of information for a lobbyist include the staff of legislators and committees, regulatory agencies, and trade associations. Remember that legislators always need solid, rational reasons to support a particular position. A good lobbyist needs to know the arguments of opponents quite well so such points can be honestly, accurately, and objectively projected, and then refuted and downplayed when appropriate. Legislators are generally in need of background information about issues. If you become the expert and have the most information to offer, leaders will rely upon you as a resource.

Recognize that it is far **easier to defeat a proposal** than to carefully shepherd it to success because there are so many opportunities for opponents to have access to the political process and thwart the efforts of others. The measure of success to corporate lobbyists, the monied interests, is how many times the legislative process was sidetracked. At the national level, over 6,000 bills are introduced every year and most are defeated; well over 90 percent of all bills never pass.

Successful lobbying requires being **ready to adapt, negotiate and compromise**. Few good proposals pass the first time around, and an effort requiring **5 to 10 years** for a bill to pass is typical. Thus, commitment to an issue over a long time is vital to success.

Resolution Through Cooperation

Communication and cooperation move debates of consumer issues toward negotiated resolutions, not confrontation. Smart corporate executives know that it is to their advantage to intervene early in the issue-resolution process so that mutual interests with others can be identified and dealt with appropriately. Increasingly, corporations, unions and consumers are working together in resolving consumer issues. Cooperation requires **building relationships** among consumer advocates, academics, government personnel, and business persons. The process demands some degree of trust and understanding between those on opposing sides of issues. It requires creative collaboration where people seek to build respect for each other instead of identifying winners and losers. To succeed, each should look for a resolution that all parties can agree to and promote that option.

The **evolution of a consumer issue** is as follows: (1) problem identified by joint fact-finding committee; (2) opinion leaders discuss, research, and hold meetings to define problem; (3) hearings held and opinion leaders meet to bridge differences that have emerged; (4) affected parties meet to negotiate a solution; and (5) differences narrowed and mutually satisfactory solutions found.

The participants who cooperatively come together to try to resolve consumer issues may have divergent views at the outset, but they must be **willing to listen to other perspectives**. The intent should be to discover ways to work together so that all parties are sitting together facing the problem instead of facing each other. This requires clarifying areas of disagreement in non-argumentative ways and initially looking for areas of agreement, no matter how small. This approach develops inclusive relationships that are built on trust. The result is thinking together to resolve problems and issues.

Public recognition of positive work should go to the politicians because they have a stake in the issue. Politicians also need to feel psychologically committed. Genuine success is judged on how the **economic welfare of consumers has been improved**.

Review and Summary of Key Terms and Concepts

1. Summarize the concept of **power clusters** and tell what they do.
2. Explain the differences between the **attentive public and the latent public**.
3. Offer some generalizations about money and the **status quo** and the power of **money in politics**.
4. How do **political action committees** influence elections, and in your response explain **issue advertising**.
5. What are some of government's **political biases**?
6. Give an example (not from the book) of a **public interest dispute**, and tell how they are resolved.
7. Why do people view **issues** differently, and in your response explain the term **economic ideology**.
8. Summarize some key aspects of the **neoclassical belief system**, and include in your response how that perspective views the kinds of **problems facing consumers**.

9. Name two primary differences between the **managerial** and the **neoclassical belief systems**.

10. Briefly summarize the **reformist belief system**, being sure to explain the **planning system** and the **market system**.

11. Compare and contrast three of the beliefs of the major political ideologies: **conservatism** and **liberalism**.

12. Distinguish between the two major political parties: **Republican and Democrat**.

13. Summarize the beliefs of **communitarianism**.

14. Which types of **consumer protection proposals** would receive the most support? The least support?

15. Distinguish between **constructive thinking** and **analytical thinking**.

16. Offer some guidelines on **moving a consumer** issue forward.

17. Explain why government gets into policy debates about **public issues**.

18. List some guidelines on **how to lobby** the legislature.

Useful Resources for Consumers

Consumer Action
www.consumer-action.org/

Capitol Advantage (source for all elected officials)
www.congress.org/congressor
g/home/

First Gov for Consumers
www.consumer.gov/

Consumer World (a mega Internet site)
www.consumerworld.org

Consumer Action
www.consumer-action.org/

Consumer Federation of America
www.consumerfed.org

Democratic National Committee
www.democrats.org/

National Consumers League
www.ncl.org

National Institute on Money in State Politics
www.followthemoney.org/

Public Citizen Congress Watch
www.publiccitizen.org

Republican National Committee
www.rnc.org/

"What Do You Think" Questions

1. From your experience, what do you think is a powerful **power cluster** in the United States? Identify ten organizations and key people in that **issue network**. Think from perspectives of local, state and national.

2. What is your **economic belief system**? Looking at Table 11-1, identify two characteristics of that belief system that you really agree with, and explain why you hold those views.

3. Describe yourself as a **liberal** or a **conservative** (a middle-of-the-road choice is not available in this exercise). Then identify the three most important characteristics of that political ideology that you really agree with, and explain why you hold those views.

> ## Appendix Issue 11-A:
> ## Proposed Consumer Protection Laws

The significant proposed consumer protection legislation and regulations are shown in Table 11A-l below. One could easily analyze which measures have the support or opposition of persons holding the different economic belief systems.

Year Passed	Law or Regulation	Major Provisions
Proposed	Consumer Protection Against Price-fixing Act	To reverse Supreme Court antitrust law rulings and strictly prohibit vertical price-fixing, especially to stop manufacturers from ordering discount stores to not sell below certain prices
Proposed	Retail Competition Enforcement Act	To promote price competition and make price-fixing less burdensome to prove
Proposed	Airline Competition Enhancement Act	To give the FTC authority to oversee the airline industry to encourage competition
Proposed	Financial Consumer Associations Act	To permit federally-chartered membership organizations to inject a consumer perspective into aspects of financial decisions made by government policy makers
Proposed	Product Liability Reform Act	Anti-consumer effort to put restrictions on punitive damages in lawsuits, such as $250,000
Proposed	Class Action Fairness Act	To move such lawsuits from state courts to the federal level where businesses win more often
Proposed	Public Participation Act	To provide funds to reimburse costs and expenses of persons testifying before regulatory agencies, such as consumers and owners of small businesses
Proposed	Product Liability Reform Act	To decrease the protections offered by strong state product liability laws in existence in most states by limiting the ability of consumers to sue for damages—an anti-consumer bill
Proposed	National Lemon Act	To decrease the protections offered by strong state lemon laws in existence in all states
Proposed	National No-fault Automobile Insurance Act	To set minimum standards for a comprehensive automobile insurance program in which an accident victim's personal injury expenses are paid by his or her own insurance company, regardless of who is at fault
Proposed	Reform of McCarran-Ferguson Act	To repeal the antitrust exemption granted the insurance industry under the McCarran-Ferguson Act and substitute federal regulation

TABLE 11A-1   Proposed Consumer Protection Legislation and Regulations

Chapter 12

Decision-making

OBJECTIVES

After reading this chapter, you should be able to

1. Explain why consumer decision-making is difficult.

2. Understand a model of consumer choice.

3. Appreciate why consumers are often pro-environment.

4. Recognize types of truth in advertising, including marketing to children.

T oday's consumers can be described (to borrow a phrase) as "harried consumers." They are overwhelmed with choices, challenged with new technologies, and flooded with information, much of which is very good and quite useful. Also, we live in a time when crass commercialism and private materialism have become society's dominant value system; perhaps even its ideology. **Commercialism**, says Michael Jacobson in *Marketing Madness*, is "the ubiquitous product marketing that leads to a preoccupation with individual consumption to the detriment of oneself and society." Consumers today have a weak understanding of sellers' persuasive marketing techniques and thus fall prey to many bad deals and rip-offs. Consumers also frequently fail to prioritize among their many needs and wants, and as a result, they often fail to make rational buying decisions.

This chapter begins by identifying many reasons why decision-making is difficult for today's consumers; even more so than 20 or 30 years ago. It then presents an economist's model of consumer choice that focuses on two decision-making components that interact to determine optimal consumer purchase decisions. Following is a discussion on why most consumers are pro-environment. The chapter concludes with an analysis of the various types of truth in advertising (yes, some ads are truthful!), as well as a look at advertising directed to children.

Reasons Why Decision-making is Difficult

Consumption decisions are more difficult than they were 20 or 30 years ago. A typical **consumer decision** occurs as a consumer selects from among alternatives or preferences a good or service in a marketplace transaction. Consumers generally try to make good decisions. To do so, each decision is made according to the consumer's values and attitudes in the context of the availability and price of choices at the time.

Economists use the term **rational self-interest** to describe how people make choices. At the individual level, most consumer decisions are undertaken egoistically in a reasonable effort to maximize utility. **Utility** is each person's subjective measure of something's usefulness. The utility of a good or service is its ability to satisfy a human want. While utility is the ability to satisfy, the actual satisfaction occurs only when goods having utility are used, which destroys some of their ability to satisfy further. A reduction of utility presumably increases human welfare.

Consumers Search for Value

Total customer value, says P. H. Kotler, "is the bundle of benefits customers expect from a given product or service. Consumers search for value in their purchasing decisions. Erick de Gier, Research Director for *Consumentenbond* in the Netherlands, suggests that the **determinants of total customer value** are product value, service value, image value, monetary price, time cost, energy cost, and psychic cost. These are the factors that contribute to or detract from consumer satisfaction.

Consumer dissatisfaction in marketplace transactions **occurs** for a number of reasons, suggests Swedish professor Sloveig Wikstrom: (1) when the number of products increases, the likelihood of unsuccessful transactions increases, (2) when the growing complexity of goods and services makes assessment more difficult, (3) when the number of varieties can become almost overwhelming, (4) when consumers are overconfident that the government is protecting them, (5) when people are busier and have less time, (6) and when increased education and advertising raise consumers' expectations.

Consumers also become frustrated, annoyed, and even dissatisfied when the products and services they purchase **do not perform as anticipated** and fail to meet their reasonable expectations about the standard **signals of quality**: performance, durability, safety, and quality in general. **Buyer's remorse** is the term given to a consumer's mistaken expectations about a product, and it occurs when buyers regret their purchases.

Numbers and Complexities of Products

The **processes of searching and decision-making** have become more **complicated** because of the proliferation and diversity of products, technological advances, product complexity, and changes in retail markets, including the Internet. An information overload problem exists for consumers buying services in long-distance telecommunications, banking and credit. Consumer markets today are larger and more complex than ever before, resulting in an enormous number of products from which to choose. More than **2,500 new products** are introduced every year, and even though 90 percent survive less than three years, this still creates a crowded marketplace. For example, there are more than 600 models of new vehicles in the marketplace. It is a sign of a healthy, democratic, capitalistic society to have a great number of products and services to choose from, but such diversity simultaneously provides confusion for consumers.

Consumers also are bombarded with volumes of **technical information that are difficult to process**. Without the **advice of experts** to guide them, consumers today have difficulty in even understanding which product attributes contribute to quality, desirability, safety, and good performance. Therefore, consumers increasingly rely on the informed judgments of others, particularly product-rating magazines, to help them in decision-making. The most reliable information source is *Consumer Reports* (www.consumerreports.org). Consumer Reports buys the products they test from retail stores just like people do. Then CR puts the products through extensive testing, and they report the findings, both good and bad. Over the years, CR has seriously criticized many name brand products and successfully weathered all lawsuits. Many other sources of product information exist, although they are not as objective. Other websites that provide product information are www.CNET.com, www.Epionions.com, www.ConsumerReview.com, www.mysimon.com, and www.dealtime.com, www.Productopia.com.

The many challenges of effective choice-making force most consumers to **optimize their preferences** rather than deciding on the very best product and seller. They do this by **ranking choices from the best to worst**. Final selection then is based on the optimal choice for the individual or family. **Optimizing** is making something as good or as effective as possible.

CONSUMER UPDATE:
Buy Textbooks on the Internet

Even though you might get a better deal **online**, the textbooks you want are not always there. See www.allbookstores.com, www.campusi.com, www.barnesandnoble.com/textbooks, www.amazon.com, www.studentmarket.com, collegebooksdirect.com, www.half.com, and www.efollet.com.

Consumers Follow Rules of Thumb

In decision-making, many consumers react to marketplace complexities by following **rules of thumb**. These are useful principles that have wide application but are not intended to be strictly accurate. Consumers use various rules of thumb to **reduce search costs**. Professor Brenda Cude, University of Georgia, offers some examples of rules of thumb about quality that many consumers use: "buy brand-name goods" (actually a poor predictor), "use seals of approval" (sometimes helpful), "buy top-of-the-line merchandise" (better quality, but one also gets unnecessary product features), and "buy high-priced goods" (true for some goods, but false for others). A rule of thumb about price is that "larger sizes are better buys," however, this is often invalid.

Irrational Marketplace Decisions

Humans have "inherent **information processing limits** and inabilities to estimate probabilities accurately," says Professor Norman Silber, Hofstra University. It seems that human cognitive limitations sometimes affect decision-making negatively. Silber explains that consumers often do not maximize their best interests because irrationality "may be reasonable where the decision-making task is overwhelming." One explanation for the behavior is that the greater the stress and the perceived risk in a decision-making situation, the more frustrated and anxious some consumers become. Here many consumers **act "reasonably" by not searching for information**.

Much human behavior is irrational, including consumer decision-making. All people must accept their personal limits as humans and move on. The emotional, non-logical, instinctive side of human nature is probably the normal way of doing things; analytical effort in decision-making often is not the dominant manner when thinking, feeling, and acting. This is why much advertising is emotional rather than rational. People make many illogical decisions.

Style Over Substance

It can be argued that today's consumers are **only interested in buying style**. Author Stuart Ewen observes that in packaging, furnishings, dress, and architecture, style has replaced substance. He states that, "**style** is the symbolic leap away from the constraints of mere subsistence." Sellers recognize that consumers are deeply interested in buying style and image more than reality. Ewen suggests that this is not all bad, but that it encourages consumers to buy images rather than substantive value. This is one reason why advertising is often not aimed at what the product or service will do, but rather at illusions, such as sex appeal, wealth, prestige, and beauty.

Author Lewis H. Lapman argues that, "we are a nation of dreamers captivated by the power of metaphor..." and "material acquisitions matter much less than the states of being that they supposedly announce and contain. It isn't the thing itself that's important but **what the thing represents**...Products bestow health, long life, status, sexual prowess, intelligence, national security, happiness and peace of mind; all the blessings that devout Christians expect from the hand of God...The collections of goods and services testify not only to social status but also to an individual's worth as a human being."

Consumers Ignore the Discount Rate

The **discount rate** is a measure of the value of a dollar today compared to one received some time in the future. In spite of the simplicity of mathematically applying the impact of inflation and interest earned (perhaps 56 percent combined) to the choices and deriving the correct answer, many people set unreasonably high discount rates for choices they face. They often set **irrationally high rates** that never could be actually earned. Consumers often make the wrong value-for-money decision even when they discount the choices by 20, 30 or even 100 percent.

Decision-making is tough enough without having to consider the effects over the long term. However, consumers waste money when the time value of money is ignored. The correct consumer finance decision is, when possible, to **spend a little more up** front to save a lot more money in the future. For example, **energy efficiency labels** adorn many large appliances and show consumers which brands operate more efficiently. To illustrate, visualize product A selling for $600 that costs $25 to operate annually, and product B selling for $500 that costs $75 to operate annually. The better choice is simple: pay $100 extra for product A and recoup the $100 from lower operating costs in just a few years. Unfortunately, many consumers consistently make the wrong choice, both in terms of value for money and disutility for the community at large. Why? One of the reasons appears to be an **inability** of many people to accept the wisdom of discount rates, even when it is explained to them.

Payoffs from Information Processing

Many people do not comparison shop, even for expensive purchases, because they assume that the marginal benefits of comparison shopping will not exceed the marginal costs. Research on the topic of information search suggests that **searching lowers the price** paid by consumers up to a point, but after that, searching becomes unproductive.

When the search and decision-making processes of consumers are effective, the choices are made with relatively small expenditures of time, effort, and money. **Poor consumer search** and decision-making means that consumers spend more, in both money and time, yet satisfy fewer requirements. Snider concludes that the availability of perfect information that would enable cost-effective decisions to be made, would save consumers **20 percent** or permit selections that gave 20 percent more value. Cornell professor emeritus E. Scott Maynes calls such positive results **consumer payoffs**; "gains obtained through effective purchasing via lower prices, better quality, or both." Individual consumers who are able and willing to seek the lower price/higher quality deals actually do pay less than others. Winning the lower prices may take time, effort and energy, but for many it's worth it—better prices and/or better quality.

Price Discrimination is Good for Informed Consumers

Sellers are **willing to deal**. **Price discrimination**, says Cornell professor emeritus Scott Maynes, occurs when "a single seller charges different customers different prices for the same product." Examples include discounts on motels for senior citizens, weekday (or evening only) supermarket specials, frequent-flyer clubs, rebates, free delivery services, upgrades of a product or service, and cents-off coupons. Here the seller discriminates against one type of buyer in favor of another with the goal to charge each consumer the highest price that each is willing to pay. As a result, only **savvy consumers** pay a low or fair price.

The uninformed pay more. Therefore, smart consumers in the marketplace have to shop diligently. Other consumers just pay more!

DID YOU KNOW?
Frequent-Buyer Loyalty Programs

"Earn miles while you drive, fly, sleep, shop, eat, talk, breathe..." "Use our credit card and get a rebate of 1 to 5 percent." "Use our telephone service and get 4,000 free air miles!" "Earn air miles at our hotel.""Shop at our mall and get 2 percent off at selected stores." "Accrue 700 shopping points at our store to earn a $25 gift certificate." "Join our retail book club and get up to 10 percent off on all purchases." "Purchase $15 in fast food and earn a free video rental." "Swipe your card to get the lowest grocery store specials."

These offers are examples of **price discrimination** in general, and **frequent-buyer (or loyalty) programs** in particular. They are intended to develop customer loyalty to the seller. Loyalty programs in supermarket and drug store chains usually are free, and they are very popular.

These sellers collect massive amounts of **private information** on the buying habits of consumers. For some, giving up private information is worth getting weekly discounts advertised on certain goods and extra discount coupons in the mail. Others resent giving away person information to get the lowest prices. Some people give out **bogus information** (made up name and address) when filling out the application. When tied to use of a credit card, consumers need to compare the genuine value of each price/quality offer along with the costs required to participate, such as an annual fee and a certain interest rate on a credit card.

Decision-making Time Is Limited

Adding to our burden of rational decision-making is that most Americans have limited time because they are **very busy people**. Lifestyles for many Americans are busier than they were a generation ago, particularly for those who have only a little time left at the end of a long working day. The growing numbers of dual-earner households, especially those with children, often lament their hurried lifestyles. Partly as a result, products and services that use time more efficiently generally sell well.

✳Author James H. Snider calculated that the average American spends **nine percent** of his or her non-working, non-sleeping time **gathering information for consumer decision-making**. That includes time spent watching television advertising, and Snider calculates that it amounts to four hours of time for every $100 spent. He estimates that poorly informed decision-making results in consumer confusion and frustration that adds 20 percent to the cost of every purchasing decision people make. *Your Money or Your Life* reports that on average, shopping consumes six hours a week. Also, three out of four purchases are unplanned.

Searching and Comparison Shopping

The U.S. consumer seems to follow the mottos of "Shop until you drop" and "Work, spend, work, spend." Still, not all people spend hours and hours looking for product information. Some **hate to shop**. Many people have a long work commute so they have less time to shop. As a result, many consumers do not compare, but instead say, "I want that," and quickly act on their emotions. Others, after shopping for 1 or 2 hours in a mall, get stressed, exhausted, and even annoyed because they are worn out after concentrating so hard when searching and making comparisons and choices. Thus, people limit their searches for information.

Subjective expected utility (SEU) theory submits that a consumer's decision to engage in a specific behavior is dependent on the marginal rewards and costs that are expected from the behavior. Thus, the **more you think you will benefit** from comparison shopping (i.e., getting a good buy, increasing the purchasing power of one's income, enjoying the tax-free savings), the more likely you are to devote scarce time and energy to such tasks.

KEY TOPIC IN CONSUMER ECONOMICS:
Advertising Dollars Censor Consumer Access to Information

The power of **advertising dollars** is increasingly coming into conflict with a vital interest of consumers' right to information, specifically access to unbiased useful buying information. What is watched on television and read in newspapers are often **censored** by advertisers. This occurs when the **media is pressured by advertisers** not report or to tailor certain stories or topics. Censorship also happens when broadcasters and newspaper editors are afraid to upset a large advertiser so they avoid doing certain investigative stories and/or tone down deserved criticisms.

Since automobile advertisements make up 20 to 40 percent of the revenue of a local newspaper or television station, auto dealerships can put quick financial pressure on those media owners to do as they say. **Advertiser boycott incidents** have occurred at WLWT-TV in Cincinnati, at WCCO-TV in Minneapolis and at the *Birmingham News.*

San Jose Mercury News reporter Mark Schwanhausser wrote "A Car Buyer's Guide to Sanity" that motivated a trade group representing area new-car dealers to start an advertising boycott of the *San Jose Mercury News.* Fourteen months and over $1 million of lost advertising dollars later, the Federal Trade Commission forced the dealers to settle charges of **illegal restraint of competition**. The chairman of the FTC commented that, "Advertising is a key source of price and other information and when competitors band together to restrict it, consumers lose."

Because of the fear of advertising boycotts, articles on "how to buy" and "how to bargain" for vehicles are **rarely found** in some local markets. Stories on car-dealer trickery (i.e., odometer rollbacks, bait and switch) seldom reach the public in local markets, and when they are published, local dealer names are not identified. Some newspapers also have refused to run ads for discount auto-buying services, so as not to offend local auto dealers, their largest source of advertising revenue.

Good Buys and Best Buys

An alternative shopping model exists for some consumers. The Carsky-Dickenson-Smith model demonstrates that **price becomes the dominant force in decision-making**. The **consumer's goals** are to develop a sense for an acceptable level of quality or performance and to establish **trigger prices** for when a product might be a **"good buy."** Consumers regularly monitor (**search**) the shopping environment maintaining familiarity with product variants and prices for a set of acceptable brands, while eliminating unsatisfactory brands and products. When a seller substantially lowers the price on an acceptable product, that action may trigger a purchase. This system eliminates the need to comparison shop in the traditional sense, taking a purposeful effort to compare models, product features, sellers, warranties and prices to obtain a **"best buy."**

Sellers are using the related **compromise effect** to increase sales of more profitable products. They are bringing out items at extremely high prices so consumers can feel good about rejecting those products and **buying something more moderately priced** that still is expensive. The high reference point makes consumers buy at a higher price.

AN ECONOMIC FOCUS ON...
Information Search in the Buying Process*

Information is a necessary ingredient in a consumer's buying process. Sometimes consumers seem to know where to buy and what to buy without any information search, especially when making repeated purchases. The reasons are twofold: (1) they may already know the information they need, or (2) they do not think an external search is worth doing. The first reason indicates the consumer's internal search and the second displays the results of cost-benefit analysis of information search.

Information needs in the buying process can be categorized as **price-related** and **quality-related**. If quality is given, consumers tend to search for the lowest price in the market. However, consumers often terminate the search before they find the best buy because their search is limited by their money, time, energy, and/or psychic resources. Consumers will stop the search when they perceive that the **marginal search cost** exceeds the **marginal benefit**. If a consumer wants to buy a used car, he or she may visit several car dealers, examine regional auto pricing guides known as *Yellow Book* or *Blue Book*, or read a newspaper's classified sections. These actions are examples of external information search and involve money costs (books and newspapers, transportation expenses), and time and energy costs (visiting and talking with dealers, reading books and newspapers). The consumer may have to deal with dealer's tricks and persuasion, which involves psychic costs. The buyer may omit some of these actions to make the purchase decision sooner. The extent to which external information is searched depends on the buyer's perception that how much money to spend, how much time to take, how hard to search, and how assertive to be are worth the benefit of the search.

Businesses with **price advantages** have an incentive to provide price information for consumers, particularly when the sponsor's prices are contrasted with their competitor's prices. Consumers can use this information to reduce search costs.

The situation becomes more complicated for consumers when product qualities vary. Due to the diversity of quality and asymmetry of information, poor quality products are encouraged to stay in the market and quality products tend to be pushed out of the market. **Adverse selection** occurs in many markets because a lack of information about unobserved qualities are then mis-valued.

Let's consider the used car purchase again. In the market, used car sellers want to sell their cars. Some of these cars are good, called "plums," and some others are bad, called "lemons." Sellers usually have better knowledge of their own cars than buyers, and this situation is called **asymmetric information**. Each plum is worth, say $2,000, and each lemon, $1,000. Because consumers cannot distinguish between plums and lemons, they would like to pay only an expected value of these used cars, say $1,500 when the numbers of plums and lemons are the same. This situation will encourage lemon sellers to sell cars, and discourage plum sellers. If a seller sells both plums and lemons, (s)he tends to cheat consumers by claiming lemon cars as plum cars. Thus, because of asymmetric information and diverse qualities, consumers tend to lose in marketplace transactions. The market then becomes dominated by crummy cars offered at low prices.

Quality cheating is limited by some market mechanisms. If the business believes its short-run profit from cheating will negatively affect its long-term profit, the business may choose to be honest with consumers. To be more competitive and profitable, producers of quality products tend to signal their quality features to consumers.

Quality signals have several forms. (1) **Warranty.** Producers of quality products would like to provide warranties for consumers to enhance consumer's confidence in these products. Producers of poor quality products cannot afford to do this. (2) **Advertisements of quality characteristics.** Sponsors of puffery ads cannot last forever since the dishonest quality claims can be detected after product purchases, and negative word-of-mouth and publicity will spread among consumers. (3) **Reputation.** Sellers with a good reputation tend not to cheat since its cost is too high compared to the benefit of cheating. Sellers with a good reputation can charge consumers premium prices because of their reputation. If sellers with a good reputation cheat and are disovered, they will lose their profits from premium prices. Signals from quality product producers and sellers give consumer hints in effectively searching for information and making smart purchase decisions.

The consumer information environment also can be improved by **government regulations** that increase benefits or decrease the **costs of information search.** Government can play an important role in helping consumers get access to useful information. A strict system pushes producers to offer sufficient information on appropriate use of products and to decrease the probability of accidents and tragedies. Regulations on fraudulent and deceptive marketing behavior will suppress the occurrence of questionable quality claims and misleading advertising. Government sometimes sets minimum quality standards and this gives consumers confidence in product quality. Requiring understandable information on packaging and labeling decreases consumer's comprehension and computation costs.

Third parties, such as consumer groups, independent testing organizations, media institutions, and schools also may be helpful in the consumer information search process. Efforts by third parties may **decrease consumers' compiling costs**, perhaps by offering price comparisons of retail stores and quality indexes of movies or restaurants. Third parties may decrease a consumer's comprehension costs by offering **straightforward and understandable information** and/or educational programs for complex products or services. Such efforts may decrease a consumer's computation costs by figuring out and presenting healthy nutritional quotients, monthly payments of a long-term mortgage loan, or the annuity amount after retirement. Third parties may also increase the benefit of a consumer's use of information by providing new information that consumers are unaware of, by reminding consumers of some existing information, or by altering consumer's attitudes about some existing information.

*Jing-jian Xiao, Professor, University of Rhode Island

> **KEY TOPIC IN CONSUMER ECONOMICS:**
> **Poor Consumers are Disadvantaged in the Marketplace**
>
> Economically **poor** consumers **do pay more** in the marketplace. Many factors cause disadvantaged consumers to do more poorly than the remainder of society in the economic marketplace. Sporadic income causes some to buy more than they can afford and to use credit, even for essentials like food. Poor people are less likely to read newspapers and generally do not seek much product information. They often take on too much debt. They sometimes spend **70 percent of take-home pay on necessities**; many spend half their income on housing costs alone. Most poor people do not save. Insurance is usually not purchased in amounts needed for adequate protection. The geographic markets in which they shop do not enhance efficient choices. Some merchants to the poor use **exploitative selling techniques**, and some sellers discriminate on the basis of race, ethnicity or appearance. Both urban and rural poor have a restricted shopping area because the **availability of transportation** to better shopping areas and the time to get there are often limited.

Lifestyles, Values and Decision-making

Our **values and goals** also get mixed into the choice-making equation along with our personal lifestyles, particular customs and ceremonies, and how much money we are willing to spend. A **lifestyle** is a way of life or style of living that reflects the attitudes and values of an individual or group. It is typically reflected by the sum of the spending decisions made by a consumer. One's lifestyle is often measured by a person's activities, interests, and opinions. When people shop, they **confront their values** by simultaneously facing and deciding on environmental questions ("Will the disposal of this product be harmful to the environment?"), health and safety questions ("Does this food have dangerous properties?"), and social responsibility questions ("Has the manufacturer been a socially-responsible employer in developing countries?").

More and more consumers are telling U.S. sellers that while they seek low prices in marketplace transactions, their personal definitions of quality include **fair treatment of labor**. Sellers in the United States are increasingly avoiding foreign suppliers that have been cited for poor or non-existent health, safety and environmental standards. Collectively, these additional buying criteria can be described as being **politically correct**.

Geistfeld Model of Consumer Choice[1]

This section provides a model of consumer choice that helps explain the factors that determine optimal consumer purchase decisions. It also is known as the **Geistfeld Model of Consumer Choice**. An **optimal consumer purchase decision** is a personal judgment about a purchase of a good or service that is the most favorable or desirable at the time the decision is made.

Economics is a helpful tool to understand the problems encountered by consumers when making purchase decisions. The simple model developed here focuses on **two decision-**

---

[1] This section was written by Loren V. Geistfeld, Professor, The Ohio State University.

making components that interact to determine optimal consumer purchase decisions: (1) **indifference curves** that reflect the **amount of satisfaction consumers receive** from a purchase decision, and (2) the **budget constraint** that reflects the reality that consumers **make optimal purchase decisions** in a world of limited resources. These factors come together through a process in which consumers attempt to make optimal purchases that maximize their satisfaction subject to income and the prices of goods and services. This is followed by a discussion of the information needs of consumers.

Indifference Curves

An **indifference curve** is comprised of combinations of goods and services providing **a constant level of satisfaction** to a consumer. An indifference curve is shown on an **indifference map** which is that portion in the positive quadrant of a graph that indicates the consumer's preferences among all combinations of goods and services. The **farther an indifference curve** is from the origin of the graph, the more the combinations of goods along that curve are preferred. An indifference map shows only what a consumer is willing to buy; it does not show what one is able to purchase. A single indifference curve represents a consumer's **willingness to trade** one good for another such that satisfaction is constant. In other words, a consumer finds equally satisfactory all combinations of goods along a particular indifference curve. In Figure 12-1 the consumer is indifferent between the apple-banana combinations described by A, B, C and D. This happens because the consumer receives the same amount of satisfaction from each of these combinations making it impossible for the consumer to say that one is better than another. There are several indifference curves in Figure 12-1. As you move up and to the right, **each curve denotes a higher level of satisfaction**.

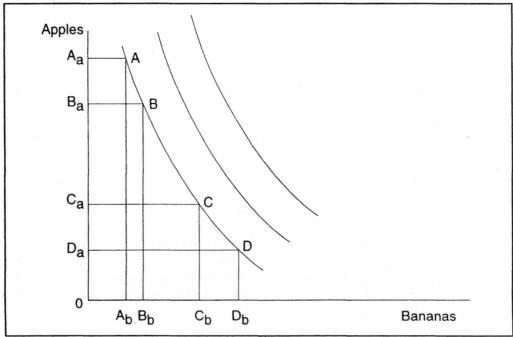

FIGURE 12-1

The "saucer" shape of the indifference curves has important implications. With "saucer shaped" indifference curves, movement along a curve indicates a consumer is **less willing to substitute** one good for another. This is why indifference curves reflect personal trade-off or the *willingness* to trade. The technical term for this phenomenon is **diminishing marginal rate of substitution**. This means that if you start with a bundle, a combination of apples and bananas, where you have many apples and few bananas, you are willing to give up a large number of apples to get a few more bananas. Bundle A in Figure 12-1 illustrates the situation in which a consumer starts with many apples and few bananas. If the consumer is to be enticed to move to bundle B, a large number of apples (A_a - B_a) is given up for a few more bananas (B_b - A_b). A consumer starting with bundle C reflecting few apples and many bananas moves to bundle D. By design the number of apples given up in the A-B move is the same as the number of apples given up in the C-D move. In the C-D move the consumer gives up (C_a - D_a) apples while gaining (D_b - C_b) bananas which is greater than the additional number of bananas needed to hold satisfaction constant in the A-B move. The **reason** for the difference is that in the A-B move the consumer has so many apples that they are boring to eat, while bananas are few in number making them interesting to eat. The consumer is willing to swap many boring apples for a few interesting bananas. The C-D move is one in which bananas are boring because a consumer has many of them, while apples are fun to eat since a consumer has few of them. In this situation a consumer needs a large bunch of boring bananas to compensate for giving up a few interesting apples. Remember that **satisfaction is constant** through all of these substitutions.

Budget Constraint

The **budget constraint** describes the relationship between the amount of money one can (or is willing to) spend and the prices of items to be purchased. What one can spend *constrains* or limits what can be purchased. For example, if you go to a store with $10 in your pocket, you are *constrained* to spend no more than $10 while in the store.

When consumers are constrained as to how much they can spend, the prices of goods and services reflect a consumer's **ability to trade** one good for another. Suppose you have $1 to spend on candy and gum costs $0.25 while candy bars cost $0.50. If the entire $1 is spent on gum, you can buy four packages. The only way you can buy a candy bar is to *trade* two packages of gum for one candy bar. The fact that you need to trade two packages of gum for one candy bar is determined by the prices of gum and candy bars and the desire to spend $1 on candy.

A **budget line** is a line on an indifference map showing **all the combinations** of goods that can be purchased with a certain level of income. It reflects the reality that consumers' income levels or budgets limit the amounts they can purchase. Putting the budget line on an indifference map indicates the single combination of goods that the consumer is both willing and able to buy. In Figure 12-2, the straight budget line (ab) represents the budget constraint or the combinations of apples and bananas, given their respective prices, that are available to a consumer when spending everything on apples and bananas. Point "a", which is on the vertical axis, represents the number of apples that a consumer can buy if everything is spent to buy apples, while "b", which is on the horizontal axis, represents the number of bananas that a consumer can buy if everything is spent on bananas. Moving along the budget constraint from F to G illustrates the **ability to trade** apples for bananas. The prices of apples and bananas are such that if (F_a - G_a) apples are given up, (G_b - F_b) bananas can be purchased.

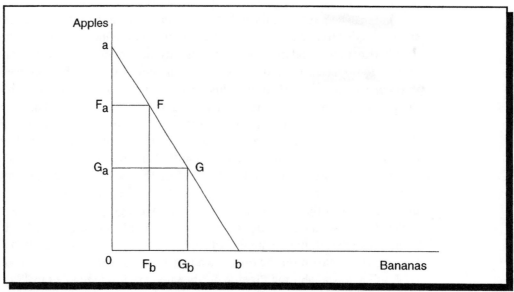

FIGURE 12-2

Maximizing Satisfaction

Maximizing satisfaction from a purchase involves a consumer's ability to trade (budget constraint) and willingness to trade (indifference curve). The **optimal** (or satisfaction maximizing) purchase is where the ability to trade and the willingness to trade are the same. Willingness to trade is also called **personal trade-off**, and ability to trade is also called **market trade-off**.

A way to understand why satisfaction is maximized when ability and willingness to trade are the same is to examine what happens when they are not the same. In Figure 12-3 if a consumer starts with bundle R and gives up $(R_a - S_a)$ apples, what happens with respect to willingness to trade and ability to trade? Bundle S is on the same indifference curve as bundle R indicating satisfaction is constant between the two bundles. This suggests the consumer is willing to trade $(R_a - S_a)$ apples for $(S_b - R_b)$ bananas since satisfaction is constant. However, what happens with respect to the ability to trade? If the consumer sells $(R_a - S_a)$ apples, sufficient money is made available to purchase $(T_b - R_b)$ additional bananas. $(T_b - R_b)$ is greater than the number of bananas needed to keep the level of satisfaction constant by $(T_b - S_b)$ bananas. Since the ability to trade apples for bananas allows the consumer to get more bananas than is needed to hold satisfaction constant, the level of satisfaction can be increased by acquiring a different bundle than reflected by bundle R. In essence, **willingness to trade** moves the consumer to bundle S but **ability to trade** allows a move to bundle T. Since willingness and ability to trade are not the same, the consumer can realize a greater level of satisfaction by going from bundle R to bundle T which is associated with a higher indifference curve.

Purchasing With Inadequate Information

Before discussing specific consumer information needs, it is important to illustrate the result of making **a purchase decision with faulty information**. This is done by using the consumer choice model described above. Suppose a consumer has a misperception concerning

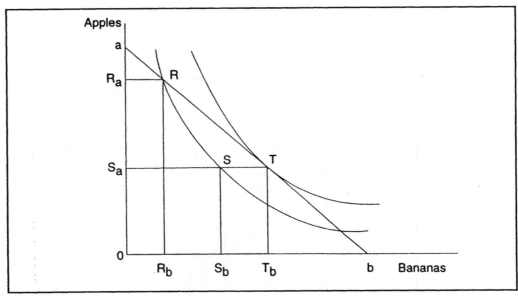

FIGURE 12-3

the price of a good. This results in a perceived budget constraint that is different from the actual budget constraint. If a consumer *perceives* the price of bananas to be such that the line ab_2 is perceived to be the budget constraint (Figure 12-4), the consumer will believe that W_a apples and W_b bananas will maximize satisfaction. However, the *actual* price of bananas is higher than the *perceived* price. This results in the actual budget constraint being the line ab_1. **Maximizing satisfaction** with respect to the actual budget constraint results in a different bundle of apples and bananas than when the consumer attempts to maximize satisfaction with respect to the perceived budget constraint. To illustrate the problem of **incorrect perception** (inaccurate information), assume the consumer first buys apples and then bananas. The consumer purchases what is believed to be the optimal number of apples, W_a. Given this number of apples, the consumer will start purchasing bananas with the intention of getting W_b. However, once the consumer has purchased V_b bananas all available income has been spent. In other words, the consumer ends up with bundle V rather than bundle W. The consumer thought that indifference curve I was the maximum level of satisfaction, but indifference curve II is the level of satisfaction actually realized. If the consumer had been responding to the actual (or correct) price for bananas, satisfaction would have been maximized at bundle X. In this instance the consumer suffers a loss in satisfaction due to ignorance. This is reflected by the difference in satisfaction levels between indifference curve II where the consumer actually ended up and indifference curve III where the consumer would have been with correct price information.

Consumers Need Two Types of Information

The above discussion suggests consumers need two types of information to maximize satisfaction. The first type of information relates to the **accurate perception** of the budget constraint. The second information type relates to accurate perception of one's indifference curves.

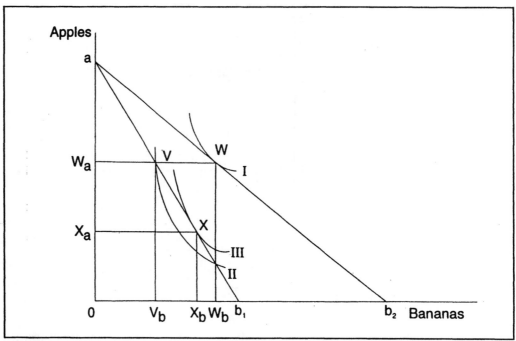

FIGURE 12-4

First Need—Budget Constraint Information

There are two types of **budget constraint information**: income and prices. Consumers **who overestimate income** will attempt to attain a level of satisfaction that is impossible to reach. When consumers underestimate income, they will not purchase enough of a good resulting in a lower than optimal level of satisfaction. Income information problems are most likely to arise for consumers who are self-employed, seasonal workers, or on commissions. These consumers face a situation in which the amount and flow of income can be quite variable making it difficult to know what it actually is. In general, income information is the least serious of consumer information problems.

Price ignorance arises when prices of goods vary across sellers and over time making it impossible for consumers to always know all prices. At a given point in time different sellers may charge different prices for the same good or service. Over different points in time prices may change suggesting today's price information may have no bearing on prices tomorrow.

Why do prices vary from **one seller to another**? One reason is that different sellers face **different costs**. A seller who purchases a good at a lower price than other sellers or who has a more efficient operation, can sell at a lower price than a seller not facing these conditions. A second reason is that sellers use **different pricing schemes**. This means that the methods used by sellers to determine selling price are not the same across all sellers. Price variability is also affected by sellers providing services beyond the actual good purchased. Sellers provide service contracts, extended guarantees, "free" credit, "free" delivery, "free" installation, "free" alterations, etc. As more of these **seller services** are provided, selling price will tend to increase.

As noted earlier, prices also vary **over time**. One example is *seasonal variation* in prices. Seasonal price variation is not uniform across all sellers and is most effective where the seller has a **"captive market."** Consider what happens in resort areas between the off-season and the on-season.

The **exit and entry of sellers** also causes price variability. A high price seller may leave the market and be replaced by a low price seller. This makes one's sense of price range out of date.

"Full price" can be used to illustrate the price information problem. There are two conceptualizations of full price. The first is **full price as item price plus search costs**. This approach recognizes that time and effort spent on information search is not "free." There are several types of search costs that should be recognized, writes Cornell professor emeritus Scott Maynes in *Decision-making for Consumers*: (A) **direct money costs** are those out-of-pocket expenses directly associated with the search activity; (B) **direct non-money costs** are costs directly associated with a search that do not cost actual dollars; **Indirect money costs** reflect dollars one gives up because of engaging in search; and (D) **indirect non-money costs** reflect what one gives up other than money because of engaging in search. The inclusion of search costs makes price less obvious since search costs vary across individuals and the various elements of search are not always easily recognized.

The second conceptualization is **full price as item price plus use costs**. This is often used with appliances or automobiles. This approach takes operating costs, maintenance costs and depreciation into consideration making the price of a good more than just what is paid to the retailer when it is purchased. Use costs can vary greatly across models. This gives rise to a situation in which an item with a high "store price" may have a relatively low "full price" since its use costs are low.

Second Need—Indifference Curve Information

An important aspect of indifference curve related information is that a consumer must be aware of needs or wants. If a consumer is unaware of needs or wants, purchase decisions do not reflect what is "truly" desired by a consumer.

Society considers some individuals to be **incapable of determining "true" needs and wants**. Children are not allowed to eat only candy. Speeders receive tickets even though they have a "need" to drive fast. Burglars are punished even though they "need" something inside of a home.

"True" preferences can be distorted. One form of distortion arises when consumers make purchase decisions based on the perceived responses of other consumers. Three such distortions are: the bandwagon effect, the snob effect, and the Veblen effect (see chapter 4 in H. Leibenstein's *Beyond Economic Man*). The **bandwagon effect** reflects social conformity or social emulation. It arises when consumers *purchase a good or service because others are purchasing it*. The **snob effect** is a social rejection effect. It arises when a consumer *refuses to purchase a good or service because other consumers have purchased it*. The **conspicuous consumption effect**, which is often called the **Veblen effect**, arises when consumers *purchase a good or service because it bears a high price and purchase visibly demonstrates a consumer's ability to purchase an expensive item*. An element common to these effects is that the consumer responds to the reactions and responses of others. This creates a situation in which purchase decisions may be made in response to something other than one's "true" preferences.

Even in those situations where consumers clearly perceive "true" needs and wants, consumers need much information to make informed decisions. To begin, consumers must be aware of all products or services that meet a particular need or want, observes Cornell professor emeritus Scott Maynes. To achieve this two questions need to be answered. First, what product set meets the need or want in question? Is the relevant set composed of subcompact automobiles or luxury automobiles? Both are not included since they fulfill quite different functions. Second, what brand/model combinations make up the desired product set? Is the set composed of Taurus and Integra models or is a Continental Mark VIII also included? Clearly the product set does not include the Continental product since the Taurus and Integra are included. Lack of awareness of a total product set may give rise to a **sub-optimal decision**—the consumer purchases an Escort when a Neon would have better met his or her needs.

Once the product set has been identified, a consumer must assess the extent to which each particular brand/model combinations meet specific needs. This is essentially a question of **assessing quality**. First, what product characteristics meet the specific need? Second, how important is each characteristic to meeting the need? Third, to what extent does a brand/model possess the desired characteristics?

Information is not equally available on all goods and services, observes professor David B. Eastwood, University of Tennessee, Knoxville. **Experience goods** are those for which characteristic information is not available until after the good has been purchased and used. **Search goods** are those for which information on characteristics is available prior to using the good. **Credence goods** are goods where a consumer is unable to assess quality even after use. This usually applies to services requiring a high level of expertise. Many goods involve elements related to all three information types—consumers can look-up EPA gas mileage rating for an automobile (search), they may learn through use that actual gas mileage is quite different from the EPA rating (experience), and when the car breaks down and needs to be repaired, they often do not know whether the $900 transmission was needed as long as the problem ceases to exist (credence).

A Concluding Comment on Consumer Choice

This section provided a framework to help understand the **importance of being an informed consumer**. Uninformed consumers make optimal purchase decisions through luck. Informed consumers make optimal purchase decisions through careful planning and decision-making. However, the amount and complexity of information needed to make fully-informed decisions can be overwhelming. Consumer education and consumer policy provide an environment conducive to reducing consumer ignorance. However, even in a "friendly" environment consumers must search for information to facilitate optimal purchase decision-making.

Consumers Often are Pro-environment

Environmental problems facing consumers around the world today include: (1) climatic changes that may result from the possible depletion of the ozone layer, (2) exhaustion of world resources, such as fossil fuels and certain species of plants and animals, (3) safe disposal of garbage and hazardous wastes, (4) water waste, inadequacy, and contamination, (5) impact of acid rain on lakes and forests, (6) storage and disposal of radioactive waste, (7) presence of toxic residues in food, and (8) smog over urban areas. These problems represent areas of concern that growing numbers of consumers consider when making decisions in marketplace transactions.

A **pro-environmental consumer** takes into consideration the environmental impact of his or her decisions in marketplace transactions. **Eight out of ten Americans** today call themselves environmentalists and report that they consider environmental factors in their purchasing decisions. Examples of pro-environmental consumer decisions include: refusing to purchase plastic styrofoam cups and plates, disposable diapers, products in non-recyclable packaging, and non-rechargeable batteries—that is, refusing unless recycling depositories are nearby. (See www.obviously.com/recycle/.)

CONSUMER UPDATE:
On the Difference Between an Environmentalist
and a Consumer Advocate

Environmentalists do not care who gets to fish for halibut in the Alaskan Gulf, the owners of large fishing boats or small ones; they simply want to reduce overfishing to protect the species. **Consumer advocates** want ample supplies of quality fish at low prices (for themselves and others). Therefore, consumer advocates do not want the big boaters to put the small boaters out of business because they know that reduced competition will quickly reduce the quantity of fish available and push up prices. In this particular case, as in many others, people are both environmentalists and consumer advocates.

Consumers are concerned about which companies treat them fairly and **which companies treat the environment fairly**. Consumers today still seek their self-interest in efficiency and getting their money's worth. More than half of all consumers report in surveys that they also have expanded their definition of "quality" to include considering how their decisions impact the environment. Many consumers refuse to buy certain products, and they occasionally boycott products and sellers based on environmental reasons. **Four out of five consumers are willing to pay more** when products meet standards of quality on issues of safety, healthiness, and the environment. A challenge for consumers is to obtain sufficient information to be able to judge how their decisions will affect particular environmental problems.

Green Labeling

Businesses, **motivated by conscience and competition**, have responded to the consumer's clamor for recycled facial tissue, toilet paper, unbleached coffee filters and reusable canvas grocery bags. Part of the response has been **green labeling**, an attempt to provide guidelines to shoppers indicating how environmentally friendly a product is. Such labeling is voluntary. Many sellers' labels and advertising use green terminology, such as "CFC Free," "ozone friendly," "biodegradable," "compostable," and "recyclable."

Some products also carry the independent "seal of approval" of an environmentally conscious organization, such as **Green Seal**; their label is a blue globe emblazoned with a green check. The Center for Auto Safety has a **Green Cars Rating System** to provide information about cars. The FTC levies fines against sellers who make unsubstantiated or misleading environmental claims.

Key considerations in marketplace transactions include consuming resources in short supply, using resources efficiently, and considering the effects on environmental degradation. To address these concerns there are **four guiding questions** for pro-environmental consumers: (1) Does it reduce waste? (2) Are the containers and products reusable? (3) Are the products and packaging recyclable? and (4) Do the available choices make you want to respond (positively or negatively) to products in the marketplace? Citizen-consumers who cast their dollar votes for environmentally friendly products are telling the marketplace to do more.

CONSUMER UPDATE:
Coalition for Environmentally Responsible Economies

The **Coalition of Environmentally Responsible Economies (CERES)** (pronounced seer-eez) is a U.S.-led coalition of environmental, investor and advocacy groups working together for a sustainable future. It promotes corporate environmental responsibility beyond that established in law on a world-wide basis. Over the long run, investors can help ensure that corporate ecological and public-health disasters are minimal and that technologies and systems to stop environmental degradation are developed. CERES (www.ceres.org/) encourages the idea of **environmental auditing**; corporations reviewing their activities to determine how well they measure up to a set of standards. Over 50 corporations have signed on to the principles since CERES's **Valdez Principles** (named after the oil leak disaster) were created.

Free Riders and Pollution[2]

To an economist, pollution has its roots in a specific set of circumstances often referred to as market failure. **Market failure** occurs when the competitive marketplace fails to provide a maximization of utility for consumers as a whole commensurate with the ability of firms to make a fair rate of return. In general, market failure entails either the underproduction of public goods or the overproduction of public bads.

Public Goods

A **public good** (or **public service**) is one that has attributes or benefits of shared consumption and non-exclusion. Examples include clean air, ample supplies of water, state recreation parks, radio and television broadcasts, police protection, and national defense. **Shared consumption** means that one person's use does not lessen the satisfaction another person can derive from that same good. **Non-exclusion** means that it is difficult or impossible to exclude anyone from gaining satisfaction from the good. Non-exclusion also implies that it is not possible to extract a direct payment from individuals receiving satisfaction from the benefits.

The **benefits from public goods** are often referred to as **positive externalities** and any person outside the transaction who receives them is a **free rider**. For example, your neighbor might wish to put up a sodium-vapor light in his yard for safety. This would be a private transaction between your neighbor and the light provider. Yet you will benefit if the light can't be restricted from shining on to your property. Nor could the neighbor charge you for the light you receive because you can simply refuse to pay. Of course, neighbors could band together to provide safety lighting services and share the cost. However, there is a natural incentive to free ride, especially if the free riders suspect that the light will be put up even if they fail to participate. The impact of free riders may be such that those willing to pay would fail to raise enough money to provide the street light even though the benefits to all far outweigh the costs to all. That is why local governments are often in the street light

---

[2] This section was written by Raymond E. Forgue, Associate Professor, University of Kentucky.

business. Governments have the power to provide the service and **spread the cost** via taxes over the entire group receiving the benefits.

Public Bads

Public bads operate in a similar but opposite way. A **public bad** is any product or service for which persons outside a private marketplace transaction are **harmed by the transaction**, cannot reasonably avoid the harm, and have difficulty forcing those causing it to reimburse them for the harm caused. The harm is often referred to as a **negative externality**. However, the person receiving the harm is not the free rider. Instead, the free rider is the person who receives the benefits from the transaction. In essence, some of the costs of providing the benefits are placed on the party(ies) outside the transaction.

Pollution is a good example of a **public bad**. Let's say your neighbor decides to open a landfill on his property and then sells landfill services to individuals who wish to dispose of garbage. As his neighbor, you might suffer negative effects from this transaction between your neighbor and his customers. Your air might be fouled with noxious odors or the water in the area might be contaminated from runoff from the landfill.

Pollution is basically a situation where **someone outside a transaction** bears some of the costs of the transaction. Competitive pressures will keep firms looking for ways to cut costs, and pollution is certainly a way to cut costs (by shifting them to someone else). So who is the free rider here? Your first response might be to point to the polluter, or in our example, the neighbor with the landfill. Obviously, they are causing the pollution. But it is their **customers who are receiving the benefits** of the landfill by having a place to dump their garbage. Where does their responsibility lie? Should they not pay the full cost of the benefits they receive?

Ways of Controlling Negative Externalities[3]

There are **five ways** to decrease the intensity of negative externalities such as pollution:

1. **Put a cost on the party responsible for causing the externalities.** With a pollution tax, polluters must pay a tax that (ideally) is commensurate with the harm caused by the pollution. The tax should be passed on to the customers of the polluter since (ideally) the price of a product should fully cover costs of production.

2. **Write a law to expand property rights.** Here the expanded property rights would be for those folks who live down wind, down stream, and next door to a pollution source. The expanded property rights would allow them to assert (possibly through a lawsuit) that they are being harmed, and force some type of reimbursement. The threat of paying reimbursements would provide an incentive for polluters to clean up their act.

3. **Create a law to restrict the behavior causing the negative externality.** This could be enforced by existing federal and state pollution control authorities.

4. **Create a market to reduce the externality.** Government presently has some laws that give value to "low polluting production facilities." These **pollution-permit rights** may be sold to high polluting companies.

---

[3] Some of these ideas are from both Raymond E. Forgue and Jing-jian Xiao, Professor, University of Rhode Island.

5. **Transfer the social costs of the externality into private costs.** Some laws exist that require the costs of pollution damages from one firm are spread to other companies in the business.

In all these scenarios, the costs of pollution taxes and actions taken to avoid lawsuits would be **passed on to the customers of polluters**. The irony in all this is that we all are the customers. We use landfills. We buy products made in a polluting way. We also are the victims of pollution.

For years businesses have been saying that pollution controls will add to the price of products and services, and economists have agreed. Such a statement should not be viewed solely as a polluter's attempt to avoid reduced profits. It is a statement of reality. People who buy products and services made in a polluting way are free riders receiving the benefits and **not paying the full costs of production**—production that is harmful to those external to the marketplace transaction.

CONSUMER UPDATE:
Global Warming and the Asian Brown Cloud

The earth has warmed about **2 degrees** in the last five centuries, and this **global warming** probably has occurred because of industrial pollution. The **greenhouse effect** is the sequence of events where heat energy from the sun is trapped in the earth's atmosphere by ozone, water vapor, and carbon dioxide. The increased production of manmade pollution gases, especially carbon dioxide from the burning of coal, oil, and natural gas, traps solar heat in the lower ozone atmosphere. This acts like **panes of glass in a greenhouse**, preventing it from escaping back into space, and that raises the temperature of the earth. The decade of the 1990s was the warmest on the planet in the past 1,200 years. Three scientists won the Nobel Prize in chemistry for research confirming the threat that human activity poses to the stratospheric ozone layer.

Part of the cause of global warming is the use of **chlorofluorocarbons (CFCs)**, which are synthetic chemical substances used as refrigerants, plastic foamers (such as in foam cushions, insulation, cups, and egg cartons), and computer-chip solvents. Human activities are the cause of the growing hole in the earth's protective **ozone layer** over Antarctica, and this increases the risk of skin cancer.

Industrialized countries consume as much as **90 percent** of the world's ozone-depleting substances. The George W. Bush Administration rejected the **Marrakech rules** negotiated by 165 countries to implement the 1997 Kyoto Protocol to limit carbon emissions or cut them below 1990 levels. Bush declared that "We have no interest in implementing the treaty." Filling a void created by inaction in Washington, the nation's leading state in the fight against pollution, California, has a new law that gives the Air Resources Board the power to set "economically feasible" emissions standards aimed at curbing the maximum amount of greenhouse gases beginning in 2009. This also means that hundreds of thousands of electric-powered **zero-emission vehicles** may be sold in California.

Confounding this effort is the **Asian Brown Cloud** that is a **two-mile thick blanket** of sulfates, soot, organic compounds, dust, fly ash, and other materials hanging over thousands of miles of India, Bangladesh, and southeast Asia, including parts of China. The dark cloud absorbs sunlight and doubles the rate it warms the atmosphere above while cooling the area below. The Asian Brown Cloud is also changing the weather in the world.

Advertising Truth to Consumers

Advertising is the action of attracting **public attention** to a product or business, especially to proclaim its qualities or advantages. Advertisements are units of persuasion. The purpose of advertising is to familiarize consumers with particular products and services. Advertising pays for all the expenses of commercial television and accounts for more than 70 percent of newspaper revenues. **Twenty percent** of all air time on commercial television consists of advertising.

More than **$1,100 per person** is spent each year by sellers advertising products and services in the United States. For example, Chrysler Corporation spends $300 on advertising for each vehicle sold, while Volkswagen spends $700. Research indicates that a family that watches television an average of 6 hours a day will see about 500 advertisements a week and 25,000 commercials a year; the average high school graduate has spent 12,000 hours in classrooms and watched 20,000 hours of television. The New Mexico Media Literacy Project (www.nmmlp.org/) helps consumers learn how to evaluate advertising.

CONSUMER UPDATE:
Products With the Largest Advertising Expenses

Data from the Federal Trade Commission collected almost twenty years ago (no updates are available) reveals that eight industries spend **more than ten percent** of each sale's dollar for **advertising**: proprietary **drugs, 20%**; perfumes, cosmetics, and other toilet preparations, 15%; flavoring extracts and syrups, 14%; cutlery, 13%; cereal breakfast foods, 11%; pet foods, 11%; distilled liquor, 11%; and periodicals, 10%. **Total selling expenses** other than advertising expenses are substantial for many consumer products: **photocopying equipment, 53%**; proprietary drugs, 36%; bread, cake, and related products, 32%; perfumes, cosmetics and other toilet preparations, 31%; flavoring extracts and syrups, 28%; bottled and canned soft drinks, 26%; typewriters and office machines, 25%; ophthalmic goods, 24%; hosiery, 24%; and calculating and accounting machines, 24%.

At its best, advertising provides **useful and reliable buying information** to consumers to assist in their decision-making. At its worst, advertising distorts the decision-making process by manipulating consumers, appealing to their emotions and creating imagery without substance, and sometimes providing false or misleading information that causes confusion and encourages consumers to make poor choices. (Chapter 4 details how government regulates unfair and deceptive practices in advertising.)

Types of Truth in Advertising

There are **four types** of truth in advertising: (1) literal truth, (2) true impression, (3) discernible exaggeration, and (4) false impression, observes advertising expert Stephen Greyser.

1. **Literal truth advertising** is that which can be objectively supported by the facts. If an electric shaver claims to "cut closer than a blade," isn't it logical for consumers to expect that the manufacturer would have ample test results available to the public

evidencing this fact? Many consumers say they like literal truth advertisements because they provide useful information.

2. **True impression advertising** is that which is literally true but which **creates a false impression**. A Tylenol headache remedy advertisement may claim that the product "contains twice as much pain reliever" and it actually may contain double the standard amount of the analgesic, but this does not mean that the product will be twice as effective. An Ultrabrite toothpaste commercial claims that the product cleans teeth while also creating the false impression that usage will improve one's sex appeal.

   An **endorsement** (or **testimonial**) is any advertising message that consumers are likely to believe **reflects the opinions**, beliefs, findings, or experience of a party other than the sponsoring advertiser. This includes verbal statements, demonstrations, or depictions of the name, signature, likeness, or other identifying personal characteristics of an individual or the name or seal of an organization.

   Endorsements in media are a form of true impression advertising. They leave the sometimes **false impression** that the endorser (usually a famous athlete or movie star) actually compared many products before recommending one, that use of the product gave the endorser the ability or skills that he or she possesses, and that the endorser is not receiving money to promote the product. While such statements may be literally true, they are intended by the advertiser to create very strong and positive impressions that may be false.

   The **FTC advertising guidelines** require that endorsements always reflect the honest opinions, findings, beliefs, or experiences of the endorser; that the endorser continues to subscribe to the views presented; and that, if asked, the advertiser can substantiate the endorsement. When payment or promise of compensation might materially affect the credibility of the endorsement, that **connection must be disclosed**.

   Comparative claim advertising also leaves false impressions whereby the advertiser sometimes **unfairly compares** product features with those of competing brands. A Ford automobile advertisement claiming "a luxurious interior like the Mercedes-Benz" and "a smoother ride than a Porsche" may invite the false impression that the automobile provides all the features of the Mercedes or Porsche rather than the selected few. A similar false impression occurs when Coca-Cola claims "that 2 million families that drink Pepsi switched to Diet Coke last year" because the ad fails to mention that Coke lost the same number of drinkers to its competitors.

3. **Discernible exaggeration advertising** is that which is so far from the literal truth that **no consumer is going to be deceived**. Advertising statements such as "The finest money can buy" and "The best product on the market today" are seen by consumers as obvious exaggerations. Similarly, a television advertisement that shows a washing machine that grows to ten feet in height obviously is exaggerating, yet the manufacturer may succeed in communicating by exaggeration that this product is bigger and better than the competition.

4. **False impression advertising** is that which either deliberately or unintentionally creates a false impression in the mind of the consumer. A classic example is the Wonder Bread advertisement that years ago suggested that by eating their nutritious bread a child could "grow bigger and stronger during the 'Wonder Years'—ages 1 through 12—the years that your child grows to ninety percent of his adult height." The federal government charged that this commercial was giving the **misleading**

and false impression that Wonder Bread was nutritionally unique when compared to other breads. False impression advertising is the *only* **type considered illegal** by government.

Corrective advertising is **remedial** in concept and it is meant to take away the unfair advantage that an advertiser may have gained by running unfair advertisements. Only a few companies have been ordered by the FTC to run corrective advertising: (1) **Profile Bread**—had to run new ads explaining that the reason why Profile Bread has fewer calories is because it was *sliced thinner*; (2) **Listerine**—ran ads saying that "contrary to prior advertising, Listerine will not help prevent colds or sore throats or lessen their severity"; (3)

Exxon—ran 15-second television spots saying that "Consumers can save money if they understand that most cars won't run longer, faster, cleaner or better on 'premium' gasoline."

The Center for the Study of Commercialism has asked the Federal Trade Commission to require film makers to tell patrons when movies contain paid **"product placements,"** such as having an actor on screen drink a Coke instead of a Pepsi. Their reasoning is that consumers are being advertised to without being told. A coalition of consumer groups gives the **"Lemon Awards"** for the "most misleading, unfair and irresponsible" advertising campaigns of the past year.

ISSUE FOR DEBATE:
Top Ten Corporations Caught Lying in False Advertising

Virtually no company ever pleads guilty to criminal charges, admits to liability for misdeeds or denies these types of allegations in a court of law. Instead, they simply "agree to a settlement" with the government.

10. **Rexall**—Agreed to give back $12 million to consumers to settle charges that its weight-loss drug, Cellasene, did not work as advertised.

9. **Laser Vision Institute** and **LasikPlus**.—Barred from claiming that consumers will never have to wear glasses or contacts or claim that the surgery is safer than wearing glasses or contacts.

8. **Hasbro**—"G.I. Joe" cannot hover and fly.

7. **Apple Computer**—Misrepresented that an upgrade was available to consumers at the time that they purchased a certain computer; also broke a promise to provide free technical support to customers.

6. **Exxon**—Agreed to pay for advertising campaign to inform consumers that regular gasoline, not high octane, is the right fuel for most cars, contrary to Exxon's previous advertising.

5. **Toyota Motor Sales USA** and **Volkswagen of America**—Ended practices of omitting or burying key cost information in small and at times unreadable print in their lease advertisements, and are prohibited from misrepresenting the total amount due at lease signing.

4. **New Balance Athletic Shoes**—Misrepresented that all of their athletic footwear is made in the United States when a substantial amount is made wholly abroad

3. **Gateway**—False statements in advertising refund policy and its on-site warranty service.

2. **Mrs. Fields Cookies**—Advertisements touting a cookie line as "low fat" were false and misleading for two of the cookies in the line.

1. **Cancer Treatment Centers of America** – Made false and unsubstantiated claims in advertising and promoting their cancer treatments.

Advertising Directed at Children

According to a report by the House Committee on Energy and Commerce, children today spend more time watching television than they do in school. The average youngster watches **26 to 40 hours of television per week** or as estimated 30,000 to 40,000 commercials a year. A large proportion of the advertisements is for expensive toys, candy, highly-sugared cereals and soft drinks, fast food of little nutritional value, and expensive clothing. Teenagers see an estimated 100,000 alcohol advertisements before they reach drinking age. Teenagers spend about $6,000 annually on all the products and services they purchase most of which appeared in advertisements.

Marketing to Children

Children tend to be trusting, and they are **inclined to believe** what adults say is true. Lacking the maturity of an adult, children are easy targets for marketers. Child advocates argue that this segment of consumers is the most vulnerable and helpless and advertising aimed at them is inherently unfair.

Child advocates argue that: (1) children **lack the maturity and knowledge** needed to understand and evaluate television advertising, (2) many have difficulty distinguishing between programming and commercials, especially product-based programs and cartoons, (3) **subtle merchandising** continues which is the not-so-obvious toys and foods written into the plots of animated shows, (4) children have difficulty discerning ads from programming when a **program-length show** also advertises toys featured as a character in the show, and (5) advertisers should be held to a higher standard when advertising to children. (See www.aaf.org/.) The National Assessment of Educational Progress calls television advertising directed to children "a diet calculated to reduce minds and bodies to mush."

Advertising to Captive Schoolchildren

Many school districts have exclusive **multi-million dollar contracts** with sellers of soft drinks, sneakers and telecommunications to advertise in gyms, stadiums, school buses and atop schools' roofs. These deals **limit student choice** and require the schools to say only nice things about the seller.

Channel One is an innovative but controversial program from Whittle Communications that **gives telecommunications equipment** to school districts in exchange for permission to air 10 minutes of news and 2 minutes of commercials a day in the middle and high schools. That amounts to the equivalent of six full days during the school year watching Channel One. About 12,000 of the nation's 30,000 middle and high schools receive Channel One. Elementary schoolchildren today are more familiar with the Budweiser frogs than Tony the Tiger.

Research has found that advertising to children **promotes violence**, advocates anti-intellectualism, encourages food choices of little or no nutritional value, contributes to obesity and high cholesterol levels, hinders the development of moral and ethical values in children, and stimulates excessive materialism. It also **fosters family conflicts** as children increasingly demand advertised goods, and promotes a distorted and surreal view of life portrayed on television suggesting that human problems can be solved by buying the advertised products. As a result, many people believe quite strongly that schools should be a haven from commercialism. *Consumer Reports* calls such in-school commercialism "a perversion of education."

Commercial-free television programming for children is designed to impart **knowledge, values and ethics**. About twenty television cable companies have a non-profit venture, *Cable in the Classroom*, that provides schools with free educational programming and study materials. Participants include Arts & Entertainment, Black Entertainment Television, and C-Span. The Public Broadcasting Service (PBS) has offered children's television programming for many years. Federal spending for **public television broadcasting** (the channel without traditional commercial advertising) in the **United States is $1 per person**, $17 in Japan, $32 in Canada, and **$38 in Great Britain**.

Review and Summary of Key Terms and Concepts

1.   Distinguish between **total customer value** and **consumer dissatisfaction**.

2.   List four reasons why **consumer decisions** are difficult to make.

3.   Summarize the mistake consumers often make with the **discount rate**.

4.   Discuss the idea of **consumer payoffs**.

5.   Give some examples of **price discrimination**, and explain why it exists.

6.   Summarize the problem of **censorship with advertising dollars**.

7.   How do **lifestyles** and **values** sometimes affect consumer **decision-making**?

8.   Explain the concept of **adverse selection** in the context of information search.

9.   Give three **signals of quality** that occur in the buying process.

10. Summarize how **indifference curves** work, being certain to define **willingness to trade**.

11. What is meant by **budget constraint**, especially in the context of a **budget line**?

12. What is meant by **maximizing satisfaction**?

13. What two kinds of **information needs** are necessary for consumer choice?

14. Distinguish between the **snob effect** and **conspicuous consumption**.

15. Distinguish among **experience goods, search goods and credence goods**.

16. What does it mean to be a **pro-environmental consumer**?

17. Explain the idea of **public goods** and give some examples.

18. What is a **free rider**, and what does government try to do about it?

19. List two ways to **control negative externalities**.

20. Distinguish between **literal truth** and **true impression advertising**.

21. List some of the problems that child advocates see with **advertising aimed at children**.

Useful Resources for Consumers

Accuracy in Media
www.aim.org/

American Council for an
Energy-Efficient Country
www.aceee.org/

Alliance to Save Energy
www.ase.org/

Eco-Labels (Consumers Union)
www.eco-labels.org/home.cfm

MagNet (environmental issues)
www.betterworld.com/index.htm

Better Business Bureau Online
www.bbbonline.org

Cnet Networks (buyng info)
www.cnet.com

Coalition for Environmentally
Responsible Economies
www.ceres.org/

Consumer Information
Center
www.gsa.gov/staff/pa/cic/cic
.htm

Consumer Review Com
(buying info)
www.ConsumerReview.com

Deal Time (buying info)
www.dealtime.com

Don't Buy It: Get Media
Smart
www.pbskids.org/dontbuyit/

Environmental Defense
Fund
www.edf.org/

First Gov for Consumers
www.consumer.gov/

Forum for Citizens'
Television and Media (links
to sites)
www.mlpj.org/linkor-e.html

Friends of the Earth
www.foe.org/

Greenpeace, U.S.A.
www.greenpeace.org/

Home Energy Saver
(calculate energy use)
homeenergysaver.lbl.gov/

My Simon (buying info)
www.mysimon.com

New Mexico Media Literacy
Project
www.nmmlp.org/

Product Topia
www.Productopia.com

Roar (buying)
www.Epionions.com

South Coast (California) Air
Quality Management District
www.cleanairchoices.org/

"What Do You Think" Questions

1. Do you think that **poor consumers** really pay more in the economic marketplace? Give examples to support your opinion.

2. Do you think Americans **value style over substance**? In your response, provide examples of style over substance.

3. **Evaluate an advertisement** that is objectionable to you. Tell what was misleading, confusing, ridiculous, disgusting, or otherwise objectionable about the message.

4. From your experience, describe examples of advertisements that offer **literal truth, true impression** and **discernible exaggeration**.

Chapter 13

The Planned Buying Process

OBJECTIVES

After reading this chapter, you should be able to

1. Recognize that consumers buy by habit and impulse and consume in a conspicuous manner

2. Appreciate using the process of planned buying for important purchases.

3. Recognize key sources of buying information.

4. Understand how to define the buying problem and identify needs and wants.

5. Explain how to identify alternatives, compare choices and negotiate.

6. Summarize how to select the best alternative and accept and evaluate your action.

Consumers consider **many factors** when choosing a product, such as price, durability and safety. In vehicle buying, the focus of this chapter, consumers today are conditioned to wait for rebates, discounts, and sales. This is confirmed by a *Worth* magazine survey reporting that about half of us are "always looking for a bargain." To get a really good deal, especially on expensive purchases, consumers need to follow a careful buying process called planned buying.

Planned buying involves defining a purchasing problem, identifying personal needs and wants in the context of personal values and goals, identifying alternatives, comparing choices, negotiating, selecting the best alternative, and accepting and evaluating the action. Planned buying is a learned skill and takes time and effort to perform. The expectation is that after reading this chapter, you will understand enough from this modeling process to learn to effectively comparison shop for expensive goods. Each of these areas is explained in this chapter. Following a description of the general buying behaviors of consumers, this chapter provides an illustration of planned buying using the example of purchasing an automobile.

General Buying Behaviors of Consumers

Consumers typically use one or more of three buying behaviors: habit buying, impulse buying, and conspicuous consumption.

Habit Buying

A **habit** is a constant, almost **unconscious inclination** to perform an act, acquired through its frequent repetition. Many purchases are made on the basis of habit, including purchases associated with for customs and ceremonies. People get into the habit of buying a certain product, perhaps one brand of chewing gum or one particular make of automobile, or shopping at a certain store, or eating in the same restaurant, or always paying the same amount on their outstanding credit-card balance. These become programmed decisions of established routines and commitments. Habits are helpful in the sense that they allow or permit time for other decision making that may require considerable time and thought. Followed blindly, however, habits keep consumers from comparing and considering other alternatives.

Impulse Buying

Impulse buying is unplanned, spur-of-the-moment buying of unnecessary products and services. Usually the consumer is already in the seller's place of business where he or she sees something he or she likes, and he or she **just buys it**. Merchants exploit impulse-buying behavior by displaying inexpensive items near the checkout counter and developing special signs and displays to encourage spending.

Impulse buying is **sometimes a good idea**, particularly if a desired item is on sale or the consumer sees something that may have been forgotten before. For example, people often buy on impulse when they are shopping in grocery stores as they see and purchase items that are not on their shopping lists. Others buy on impulse what they see advertised on home shopping television programs. **Home shopping** is a method of enabling consumers to purchase goods and services by means of an electronic device, such as a television screen and key pad, telephone, or home computer. The act of buying something on impulse that may break one's budget also **often makes some people feel good**. This happens to a lot of people when they shop on the Internet. Overdoing impulse buying, particularly with the help of **credit cards**, can lead to serious financial difficulties. Asking yourself "Why am I buying this?" and "Can I afford this?" helps curb impulse spending, as does making a shopping list and keeping to it.

KEY CONSUMER ECONOMIC INSIGHT:
The Shopping Scene

The shopping scene today is **marvelous**. Consumers can surf the Internet, scan paper and Web catalogues, visit department stores and speciality retailers, spend time at outlet malls, watch home shopping television shows, buy on the telephone, and go to warehouse clubs, like Costco, BJs and Sam's Club. Consumers also can shop at **"category killer stores,"** like Circuit City, Lowe's and CompUSA, that have enormous product choices as well as low prices.

By doing your homework–obtaining product information–you **gain valuable product knowledge** and can determine the best value for your needs. For many products, shoppers should check models and prices online before going to visit stores. Once you know what is a fair price you can buy with confidence. Some retailers provide convenient in-store kiosks for customers. You can shop on Internet auction sites, too.

Conspicuous Consumption

Conspicuous consumption is a person's desire to consume goods and services **more for their ability to impress** others and demonstrate social status than for their intrinsic value. The economist Thorstein Veblen coined the term conspicuous consumption to illustrate the transitory pleasure that some types of consumption provided. He suggested that one's happiness with a particular good or service was greatly determined by the number and quality of goods had by others. It seems that one's imagination attributes greater value to objects when they belong to someone else. If you have more than your neighbor, you are happy; if not, you are unhappy. Conspicuous consumption is **fed by emulation and the media** so consumers want to **replace old goods** before they wear out and buy new things whether they are needed or not. This is satisfying for many people, but in many cases buying what other people have gives people far less pleasure than anticipated.

For example, Jerry Springer of Chicago, Illinois had been driving his automobile for a few years when one day his next door neighbor brought home a brand-new car. Jerry went over to visit and enviously admired the shiny paint and beautiful interior. By the next day, Jerry's view of his old reliable vehicle had begun to change, and within two weeks he had purchased a new car that was even more expensive than the one his neighbor bought.

Many Americans, probably **more than half** of us, practice conspicuous consumption and feel envious when they believe they do not measure up in areas that are self-defining—those areas that are important to how they view themselves as people. For many, not measuring up to some standard of material things (such as big homes, living in a prestigious development, fancy cars, stylish clothes, jewelry, etc.) threatens their self-worth. New York psychiatrist Theodore Issac Rubin says that for many Americans, money and its symbols "have become a basis of self-acceptance."

This type of buying behavior leads people to buy things in an effort to try to **"keep up with the Joneses"** or "the Bill Gates' family." Conspicuous consumption sometimes leads to **overspending** as individuals and families spend to demonstrate their self-worth to themselves and to society. The bad news about conspicuous consumption is that just when you pull even with the Joneses, **they spurt ahead**—so the cycle continues. Such chronic envy can lead to false thoughts of perceived character shortcomings where people tell themselves that they are "failures" and "not good enough to live the good life." Left unresolved, such envy can lead to anxiety and depression. Conspicuous consumption **never ends**, unless one's personal values are confronted and changed.

Conspicuous consumers who are **trying to change** can begin with working on self-bolstering by thinking about their good qualities, selectively ignoring some of the things they are lusting after, and improving their feelings of self-reliance by not getting angry about the perceived unfairness of life. Some individuals practice *inconspicuous consumption* by purchasing relatively inexpensive things, such as driving old vehicles and often wearing old sneakers. Both conspicuous and inconspicuous consumers can be happy in their purchase decisions if they understand the value judgments they are making. People with a high regard for individuality generally are not conspicuous consumers. Stanley Lebergott argues in *Pursuing Happiness: American Consumers in the Twentieth Century* that Americans **work in order to consume** because consumption expands the experience of life; in other words, it helps create human happiness.

ISSUE FOR DEBATE:
Americans Should Reject Materialism

In American society many people define themselves with what they own. Their **self-esteem** is tied to material dependency. American society has evolved to where **materialism** has become an ethic. This is the doctrine that physical well-being and worldly possessions constitute the greatest good and highest value in life. Materialism involves the need for instant gratification and occasional compulsive spending. Here consumers twist personal wants into needs and buy products and services on credit, even if they cannot afford the monthly payments.

Planned Buying for Important Purchases

Planned buying is a rational decision making process of buying goods and services where one analytically determines which alternative is a priority by examining the marginal costs and benefits involved. Typically, these purchase decisions involve an **extensive external information search**. Consumers who make planned, rational buying decisions reduce the uncertainty and risk associated with purchases.

Bad marketplace decisions, says The Ohio State University's professor Sherman Hanna, are made for **three reasons**: (1) lack of information, (2) inability to process information, and (3) lack of time to gather or process information. Planned buying allows consumers to make good decisions.

Consumer Behavior authors J. F. Engel and R. D. Blackwell observe that the planned buying process occurs most often with **high-involvement goods**, which are those whose characteristics include high purchase cost, high ongoing operation and maintenance costs, and technological complexity. G. L. Stigler argues in the *Journal of Political Economy* that the optimal amount of search for consumers to undertake is that for which the **marginal benefits of a search are equal to the marginal costs**. Since the benefits depend, in part, on the cost of the good to be purchased, the higher the cost of the good, the higher the potential savings from search behavior. University of Rhode Island professor Anne M. Christner observes that people should consider a rational approach to buying and **rely on the advice of trusted experts** when shopping for complicated goods such as vehicles and computers, and intangible services, such as insurance and investments.

The basic decision-making model of planned buying includes **several steps** that are discussed below.

1. **Define the problem.** Clearly identify the problem. What are you trying to accomplish? For example, if you think you want to buy an automobile, the first clarifying question is "Why?" Do you simply want basic transportation to get you back and forth to work, or do you need something more comfortable and dependable for long trips? Understanding the main issues in making the decision helps you clearly define the problem in terms of your personal values.

2. **Identify your needs and wants.** The task is to establish priorities between your needs and wants. To do so, most people ask, "Will this fit my budget?" After that, the following question is usually, "How much can I get for my money?" Basically, this step involves determining whether you can satisfy all your needs, as well as all your wants, or satisfy all your needs but only some of your wants.

3. **Identify the possible alternatives.** With most planned buying decisions, you already have some background information on the product alternatives, usually gained from experience, perhaps from friends, from the media, or from previous visits to sellers. The task is to collect information and learn about the topic. You especially need information on the criteria or product characteristics that are important in evaluating a product or service. When you are spending a substantial amount of money, it is wise to obtain ample information to increase the likelihood of making a good decision. It may be appropriate in your pre-shopping research to spend time on the Internet, go to a library and visit some stores to collect information.

4. **Compare the choices.** It is important to examine each alternative. **Evaluation** is the activity of identifying alternative solutions to a problem and determining the relative merits of each. The evaluation effort may be an informal ordering of information done mentally, and such a process is sufficient for most purchases.

    To evaluate, you must select proper **criteria** that become the basis for comparing preference alternatives. You must decide which evaluative criteria or product characteristics are important to you. For example, perhaps you are considering the purchase of a room air-conditioner and *Consumer Reports* (www.consumerreports.org) magazine downgrades one particular model because it does not dehumidify the air as well as other models. If you live in Denver or Phoenix, where it is dry, that factor is of little or no importance; if you live in Houston, it may be of great importance.

    Examples of criteria often considered important in planned buying are safety, convenience, performance, price, privacy, design, styling, dependability, durability, warranty, operating costs, efficiency, economy, time use, ecological impact, health, materials, service, brand, store image, location, availability of credit, repair services, delivery, and maintenance. Sometimes color is important too.

    In this step you are really **comparison shopping**. This is the process of collecting and comparing information on products and services, including library and field data on price, brand, warranty, financing, and other services offered by retailers, to find what you think is the best buy. A **best buy** is a product or service that, in your opinion, represents acceptable quality at a fair or low price. The **quality** of an item, such as a product, brand, seller, or combination of these factors, says Cornell University Professor Scott Maynes, consists of "the extent to which the specimen provides the service characteristics that the individual consumer desires."

During this step you are trying to compare the alternatives based on **your evaluative criteria**, and this may include product features, warranties, service contracts, and financing options. This step requires that you become knowledgeable on the topic.

To effectively comparison shop, you also must decide **which criteria are more important** than others in satisfying your physical and psychological needs. Often people place a great deal of weight on one criterion, and this makes decision-making easier. Still, there are no hard and fast rules, because consumers use numerous methods to evaluate preferences. When you choose a best buy for yourself, the choice is subjective and personal. When you make the choice of a particular level of quality, you do so because you anticipate that you will be satisfied with your selection.

5. **Negotiate.** The process of conferring with a seller in order to come to terms and reach an agreement on price, as well as other aspects of the deal is **negotiating**. Many consumers are hesitant and uncomfortable about **bargaining** or **haggling** when buying appliances, electronic goods, and vehicles, but sellers expect to bargain on price. With inexpensive products, little if any negotiating occurs. Much negotiating goes on for more expensive products and services. Here there will be offers and counteroffers until there is agreement on the final terms.

DID YOU KNOW?
Life Expectancy of Consumer Products

Product	Years
Compactor	10
Dishwasher	12
Disposal	10
Dryer	14
Freezer	16
Microwave oven	8
Range	18
Refrigerator	14
Washer	12
Electric dryer	14
Gas dryer	13
Color TV set	8
Stereo receiver	8
Toaster	8
Camcorder	7
CD player	7
Personal computer	6

*Sources: *Appliance Magazine*, U.S. Department of Energy, and National Association of Home Builders.

6. **Select the best alternative.** The task is to decide which product or service is best for you given your needs and wants. This step allows you to rank the preferences for choice. A **consumer decision** is the mental process of selecting the most desirable alternative from among the choices available. If a person logically decides on the basis of known facts, it becomes a rational, correct, and normal consumer decision at the time of the purchase. It can be argued that a consumer could change his or her mind later, as new facts become available, but at the time of the decision, the consumer's determination was rational.

    A decision also **could be unreasonable**. It is determined by how the decision was made, not whether it is correct or not. **Four conditions** may exist that allow consumers to make incorrect purchase decisions: (1) the decision may be based on incorrect assumptions; (2) the facts upon which the decision is based may be insufficient; (3) the facts may be incorrect; and (4) the consumer's judgment may not be sound. Nevertheless, even some decisions made rationally may be incorrect due to gaps in what the consumer knows.

7. **Accept and evaluate your action.** The rational consumer reflects on important decisions after a period of weeks or months. The intent is not to check the results of the decision to be sure, to doubt the decision, or to be irritated that a few dollars might have been saved by doing something else. Rather, the task is to **reaffirm the wisdom** of utilizing the process that resulted in your decision and to use any valuable recollections in future decision-making opportunities.

Sources of Buying Information for Consumers

Consumers have a **variety of sources** of buying information. Useful information may come from past buying experiences, as well as friends and relatives. A barrage of information is available through advertising, but most of it is biased and aimed at persuading you to spend your money.

Consumers need **sufficient buying information** to help them make effective decisions. They need to acquire information up to the point where the marginal costs of finding additional useful, usually objective, information does not outweigh the marginal benefits of collecting it. **Objective information** is knowledge that is presented in a factual or objective manner and is accurate, complete, understandable, and up to date. Consumers need **two types of objective information**: (1) information to determine what evaluative criteria others believe are important when making a selection, and (2) how much importance they personally should give to each criterion.

Consumer Reports Magazine

Consumers Union publishes *Consumer Reports* (CR) magazine. It is the single most sought after source for **objective and reliable buying data**. *Consumer Reports* accepts no commercial advertising, accepts no free samples from manufacturers for testing, and uses anonymous shoppers to purchase samples from retail stores. CR is responsible only to its subscribers and members. CR conducts extensive comparative testing of products and publishes the findings. *Consumer Reports* often goes to court to prevent the use of its test ratings in advertisements. CR also releases summaries of its results for use on radio and television. CR tests all kinds of consumer products, such as irons, televisions, air-conditioners, automobiles, air fresheners, frozen TV dinners, and computers.

Consumer Reports tries to **do what average consumers would do** when evaluating products. First, CR **establishes the evaluative criteria** used in rating each product along with an explanation of their importance. For example, if CR is testing irons it is of some importance to have temperature settings that are accurate and easy to read, as well as settings to permit proper ironing of wash-and-wear fabrics, cottons, and wools. Second, CR puts a **certain weight** on each of the evaluative criteria considered. For example, the accuracy of the temperature readings may be of less importance than how well the iron performs.

Consumer Reports classifies products into three categories: **acceptable, conditionally acceptable, and not acceptable**. Products in each category are listed in the magazine in descending order of estimated overall quality. Consumers generally only want to purchase items that are rated acceptable because the other two ratings are quite negative. Products are rated not acceptable when there is some type of safety hazard, such as an automobile turning over too easily during road testing. The conditionally acceptable rating is used when products have a problem but it can be overcome with special precautions or a simple modification. Sometimes *Consumer Reports* finds a product in the acceptable category that is clearly superior to the others tested and it is **"check-rated"** as a **best buy** with an appropriate marking. Armed with this type of buying information, consumers can apply their own weights to evaluative criteria, narrow their choices, and shop in their local marketplace to examine products, compare price and other factors, and make their decisions.

Subscribers to *Consumer Reports* are **extremely satisfied** with the buying information provided because the publication has one of the highest renewal rates in the industry. *Consumer Reports* magazine also conducts research on consumer and public interest issues, such as water safety, life insurance, health food advertising, and small claims courts. Consumers Union has a 12-step online guide to buying a car from a dealership, tips on financing and pricing, and what to consider when servicing and maintaining a car after the sale. See www.consumerreports.org/content/Special/Virtualdealer/opener.html.

Other Sources

Special interest magazines on topics like skiing, photography, boating, personal finance, golf, and automobiles are popular. Examples of consumer-oriented magazines are *Kiplinger's Personal Finance Magazine, Money, Consumer Digest, Better Homes and Gardens, Car and Driver, High Fidelity, Personal Computing, Automobile Mechanics, Golf Digest,* and *Stereo Review*. Some of these publications provide up to date, easy-to-understand and useful information, even though there are **serious limitations** about the objectivity and reliability of the information.

The **Internet** has fundamentally changed buying for consumers, including for vehicles. Instead of shopping in a dealer showroom, consumers can compare, price, finance, purchase, and have the vehicle of their choice delivered to the home or office. The Internet provides loads of useful information, including the seller's cost of every make and model. Using the Internet enhances consumers' ability to search, shop and find information.

Safety seals are certifications of approval by independent testing organizations given to products that meet their **minimum standards of safety and performance**. If the organization sets high standards, its seals serve as useful guides for consumers. Five popular safety seals are Underwriters Laboratories (UL), the American Standards Association (ASA), the American Gas Association (AGA), the National Association of Furniturers Seal of Integrity (NAFSI), and the Association of Home Appliance Manufacturers (AHAM). As an aside, consumers should realize that the UL seal applies only to the electrical part of the appliance to which it is attached, usually the cord.

Magazine seals, such as *Good Housekeeping* and *Parents*, are certifications of approval given to products and services that, in the judgment of the organization, meet whatever standards the organization has established. These magazines do limited testing and give approval to any product that **advertises in its pages**.

Better Business Bureaus (BBBs) provide helpful information **about sellers**, not products. The BBB tells callers the number of years they have maintained files on a seller; whether or not they have received recent complaints about the firm, and the nature of those complaints; whether or not the seller has responded to any complaints forwarded by the BBB, and the disposition of those complaints; recent government actions against the firms; and information about any questionable advertising and selling practices used by the sellers. Some BBBs offer online information about sellers.

Point-of-purchase information is practical or technical knowledge printed on the package or product label or displayed nearby that discloses, instructs, or warns consumers about products for sale. It is readily available information designed to help the consumer make a decision. Various laws usually require that consumer product labels provide the brand name; the generic or common name; the name and address of the manufacturer, packer, or distributor; and the quantity of the contents. Most labels provide more than the minimum amount of information. For example, food products usually list the ingredients as well as instructions on use. **Energy efficiency labels** are found on refrigerators, freezers, and air-conditioners. "**Energy Star**" is the label give by the government to appliances and products that exceed the present federal energy standards. Department of Energy regulations mandate a 35 percent increase in clothes-washer efficiency by 2007. **Product warranties** are available for review in retail stores.

ECONOMIC INSIGHT:
Judging Quality with Brand Names, Store Brands and Generic Brands

Consumers judge quality in many ways, and one useful technique is the brand name on the product or service. **Manufacturers' brands** (also known as **brand names**) are products and services that have a trademark or distinctive name identifying the manufacturer or dealer and are heavily advertised. Nationally advertised products such as Coke, McDonalds, Jordache, and IBM are brand names. These products are usually labeled "made by...." While the name is not a guarantee of quality, the company has already invested considerable sums of money into its **reputation** and has an interest in maintaining that image with products and services of a consistent grade of quality. Two additional pluses for brand name products are that they **may offer the best product warranties** and be repaired at the largest number of authorized facilities.

Store brands (also known as **private brands**) are products and services sold only by a particular retailer, chain, or dealer and are labeled accordingly. Products such as Sears Kenmore appliances are well-known quality products sold to the public. Most store-brand products are manufactured by someone other than the seller and are made to the seller's **specifications**; thus labels usually read "made for..." or "distributed by...." Store brands often offer good quality at reasonable costs because the reputation of the seller is well known and because advertising costs are lower than for manufacturers' brands.

Generic brands are **lower-quality products** sold without a well-known brand name on the label (although most generic products do have names) and sold at substantial savings compared to manufacturers' brand and store-brand products. The name of the manufacturer, packer, or distributor is on the package. Generic-brand products, such as cola drinks, grape jelly, canned fruits, paper towels, cosmetics, and cigarettes, are commonly sold in grocery stores. The lower prices are due to the usually lower quality (but still for many very suitable), less expensive ingredients, simpler packaging, limited number of sizes, and little or no advertising costs.

Defining the Problem in the Context of Your Needs and Wants

Planned buying begins by clearly **identifying the problem**. What do you want to buy? Why? What are you trying to accomplish? To illustrate, assume that Bonnie Sidwell of Ypsilanti, Michigan is interested in buying an automobile. Bonnie started a new job about ten miles from her home and requires very dependable transportation for the daily 20-mile drive. Good public transportation is not available, and car pooling will not be an option because her work hours are somewhat variable. Bonnie has been driving her mother's old car that now must be returned so her younger sister can have it. Bonnie would like a new automobile instead of another used one because she anticipates using it for long drives to the mountains when she goes camping during vacations and long weekends, although an almost new car would be okay. She wants something that is large enough to hold her camping equipment but that gets good gas mileage. Bonnie has about $4,700 in savings that she could use for a down payment, so she must finance the remainder of the purchase, as do 70 percent of new car buyers. Bonnie expects to keep the new car about as long as the average consumer, **over eight years**.

Next in the process of planned buying is to **establish priorities** in the context of your values and goals. Questions to ask: "Will this fit my budget?" and "How much can I get for my money?" Here you determine whether you can get all your needs and wants satisfied with a particular purchase or whether you can have all your needs satisfied but only some of your wants.

Can Bonnie Afford to Buy an Automobile?

With only $2,700 as a down payment, Bonnie wonders **whether or not she can finance** an automobile purchase given her limited budget. She makes a salary of $36,380, but after withholding for federal and state income taxes, Social Security taxes, saving in her employer's retirement plan, health and life insurance premiums, and union dues, she takes home $27,000, or $2,250 per month. First, she telephoned her insurance agent to find that the automobile insurance premium for a not-very-expensive new car would be about $900 annually, or $75 a month instead of her current payment of $350 annually.

Even though most of her take-home pay of $2,250 is committed, Bonnie came up with $345 in **possible cutbacks**. This included the needed $75 a month for higher auto insurance premiums and a reduction in her saving for retirement in her employer's 401(k) retirement plan (discussed in Chapter 18). Cutting retirement savings is never a smart decision since that is typically one's only retirement account. But Bonnie figures she will get a good raise and bonus next year, and then she can again contribute a substantial amount to her retirement fund. She also was able to drop the private life insurance policy she purchased last year, since her new employer provides life insurance as an employee benefit.

Bonnie really did not like all the choices she had made in her budgeted expenses. She figured that by making the various cutbacks she could budget $270 ($345 – $75 for auto insurance) a month for car payments. After thinking it over some more, Bonnie decided to cut back only $80, rather than $100, a month on savings because she needed to save that amount to pay for a camping vacation next summer. Thus, Bonnie determined that she would have $250 ($270 – $20) **available each month** to spend on financing an automobile.

How Much Automobile Can Bonnie Get for Her Money?

Among the **600 makes and models** of vehicles available in the market today, Bonnie likes Geos, Nissans, Fords, and Hondas. After thinking about the probable costs of these cars, she figured that she could decide to fulfill her needs by purchasing an inexpensive new Nissan or Ford. Or, she could fulfill her needs *and* her wants by buying a used Honda or Geo. Her **alternatives** are to make more cutbacks in her budget, to work overtime, to get a part-time job, or to buy a less expensive or used vehicle.

Bonnie made a **list of her needs and wants** to help clarify her priorities in this decision-making process. Her worksheet is shown in Figure 13-1. Bonnie found, to her surprise, that there were several features she did not consider as needs and her wants were not as numerous as she had thought.

Needs	Automobile Feature	Wants	Don't Care
✓	Power steering		
	Tinted windows	✓	
	Automatic windows	✓	
✓	Automatic transmission		
	Leather seats		✓
✓	AM-FM Radio		
	Cassette player	✓	
	Super sound system		✓
	Telescope and tilt steering wheel		✓
	Automatic light dimmer		✓
	Air conditioning	✓	
✓	Whitewall tires		
	Four-wheel drive		✓

FIGURE 13-1   Wants and Needs Worksheet (for Bonnie Sidwell)

Bonnie telephoned her **credit union** for more information. She wanted to know how much car she could expect to get with her $4,700 down payment money and a maximum of $250 a month. Since interest rates to finance automobiles were about 10 percent at both lenders, they provided the following information: $12,000 would cost $255 for five years, $304 for four years and $387 for three years, and $14,000 would cost $298 for five years, $355 for four years, and $452 for three years. These numbers meant that Bonnie could not buy an automobile for more than $16,700 ($12,000 in borrowed funds plus her $4,700 in savings).

Used Car Prices

Next, Bonnie visited the local lenders and asked to look at their books that showed the values of used automobiles. Her credit union showed her a copy of the *Kelley Blue Book* (www.Kbb.com/) as well as the *NADA Book* (National Automobile Dealers Association at www.nada.com). These are reports published by independent organizations that show the average wholesale and retail prices for various automobiles, depending on the condition of the vehicle, mileage, options, and other factors. After reviewing similar information on the Web, including www.edmunds.com, www.Carclub.com and Microsoft's www.autos.msn.com/, Bonnie determined that she could afford either a 4- or 5-year-old expensive car with lots of options or a 2-year-old less expensive model, because most of them had prices less than $16,000. Her other option was to buy an inexpensive new car with fewer desired options.

Identifying Possible Alternatives

The third step in planned buying is to **collect information and learn** about the topic. With most planned-buying decisions, you already have some background information on the topic, usually gained from experience, perhaps obtained from friends, the media, or previous visits to sellers. However, you need more, including information on the product characteristics that are important in evaluating a product or service, particularly when you are spending a substantial sum. These represent the criteria you will use to evaluate different factors. Thus, it is appropriate in your pre-shopping research to search the Internet, perhaps visit the library, and certainly visit some retailers to collect information.

Many dealers tell shoppers that it's "company policy" that they run a mandatory **credit check** before they will allow a test drive, and that they must check your credit even though you intend on getting financing elsewhere. **Don't believe it!** When you turn on your heel to leave the showroom, the seller will quickly tell you that you can be an exception. When the seller does a credit check (an examination of your credit history requires your written permission), they gain enough information about you that will allow them to charge you a higher price than you otherwise could have negotiated. Don't give them your social security number either. Show your license but do not allow them to copy it.

Over the next few weeks, Bonnie went **window shopping** for both new and used automobiles. This is the process of conducting pre-shopping research to gather information about products and services that might be purchased at a later time. Since Bonnie told her friends and coworkers that she was interested in buying a car, they gave her advice on models to avoid, as well as which ones they liked, and why. Bonnie went to the library for information and she visited some automobile dealers, where she asked a lot of questions and took notes. (The average **age of used automobiles** in the U.S. is **eight years**; one in four cars is at least **12 years old**.) Most dealers gave her informational brochures from the manufacturers. She took several new and used automobiles for test drives and gained a lot from the experiences. One model, for example, was uncomfortable to ride in because the driver's seat just could not be properly adjusted to fit her body.

KEY TOPIC IN CONSUMER ECONOMICS:
Dealer Ploys to Get You to Pay More Money[1]

When a dealer uses these ploys, simply say "I'm not going to pay that!" Then if necessary, get up and walk out. Either go to another dealer or buy your car online.

1. **Small print in the contract** - You take the car home after being told that you qualify for a low-interest loan, only to be telephoned a week later saying, "You didn't qualify after all." **Result:** Your trade-in car has already been sold and you must pay a higher interest rate because the small print in the contract reads "Subject to financing approval.".

2. **False credit score** - Dealer lies about your credit score telling you that is lower than it really is so you will not qualify for a low-interest loan. **Result:** You pay more.

3. **How much can you afford to pay a month?** - Answering this gives the salesperson enough information to jiggle the price and the interest rate on a car he or she will recommend rather than negotiate price on the car you want. **Result:** You pay more.

4. **Add-on fees** - Even though you have agreed on price, at the last minute lots of fees show up on the pre-printed contract. Things like "dealer preparation," "documentation," "advertising fee," "protection for paint and fabric," "rust proofing," "extended warranty," "pinstriping," "security," "additional dealer markup," or a certain "options package." **Result:** Unless you fight to cross out these charges, you will buy overpriced items you do not want.

5. **No payments for one year** - Zero down, zero interest and zero payments for a year means that in one year you will owe all those monthly payments at one time and you will have to refinance what is owed. **Result:** You cannot refinance at a low rate because you will owe much more than the value of the car.

---

[1]For more dealer ploys, see *Tricks of the Trade* in the April 2003 issue of *Consumer Reports*.

Shrewdly, Bonnie did not carry her checkbook with her so that she might not weaken to sales pressure and be persuaded to buy before she completed her efforts. Also, she had heard about **push money** (or **spiff**) and did not want to fall victim to such pressure. This is a special cash incentive, not a regular commission, offered to salespersons by the manufacturer, dealer, or business owner to sell particular products, usually because that merchandise is selling slowly or because the profit is especially large. Push money motivates salespersons to sell one product over another, and the consumer generally never realizes why the product features of one item are discussed so heavily over another. Navy financial expert Dean Brassington reminds shoppers that, "At the sales lot, you're going against a pro who sells more cars in a month than most people buy in a lifetime."

KEY TOPIC IN CONSUMER ECONOMICS:
Auto Safety Ratings and Repair Cost Estimates

National Highway Traffic Safety Administration (NHTSA) requires that safety information be **listed on new-car sales stickers**. The figures are the results of the government's safety tests for frontal crashes. Five stars are given for the safest rating; one star for the lowest (www.nhtsa.gov). The Insurance Information Institute makes available the **driver death rate** for vehicles. Also, NHTSA has prepared booklets that contain information that rate vehicles based on their repair-cost histories and the likely **impact on collision insurance**. Regulations require new-car dealers to make the information available to shoppers.

In the library, Bonnie found some excellent publications with information on automobiles. The annual **April issue** of *Consumer Reports* is devoted solely to the buying of new and used automobiles, and it includes articles on how to negotiate the best price. An example of the type of useful Ratings published by *Consumer Reports* (for cell phones in this instance) is given in Figure 13-2. *Consumer Reports* articles include details on the methodology of the testing project, as well as criteria for the Ratings. For used cars, the *Consumer Reports Used Cars Buying Guide Issue* includes comparative information and Ratings. Also, you may call the Consumer Reports Used Car Price Service at 800-258-1169. Other consumer-related publications on automobiles include *Car and Driver, Motor Trend, Road & Track Magazine*, and *Edmund's New Car Prices*. *Kiplinger's Personal Finance Magazine* has a useful annual buying guide issue. Check out Jack Gillis' annual *The Ultimate Car Book* that includes **crash worthiness information**.

Comparing Choices

It is important to examine the choices. In this step you are really **comparison shopping**. This is the process of collecting and comparing information on products and services, including library and field data on price, brand, warranty, financing, leasing, and other services offered by sellers, to find **what you think is the best buy**. A **best buy** is a product or service that, in your opinion, represents acceptable quality at a fair or low price for that level of quality. During this step you are trying to compare the alternatives based on the evaluative criteria you are using, and this may include product features, warranties, service contracts, and financing options. To do this you also must decide which criteria are more important than others.

The **search for information was extremely beneficial** for Bonnie. By talking to friends, going to the library, and returning to visit some of the automobile dealers, she learned a lot about what models and features to avoid and why, as well as about what was important to her. She also learned about dealer service and reputation, warranties, rebates, and financing options offered by the sellers.

Rebates are refunds occasionally available on new cars and other products offered as an incentive by the manufacturer and sometimes the dealer to encourage sale of particular models. They are a deduction from an amount to be paid or the return of part of an amount given in payment. Rebates may result in a lower net price for a specific vehicle. However, making the best decision is often confusing and difficult because rebates are often offered in conjunction with special option packages and various low-interest and other financing and leasing alternatives. **Option packages** are automobile manufacturer incentive packages that offer popular, and sometimes less popular options at a lower price than normal, in an effort to get buyers to spend money on extras. Sometimes you must choose either the rebate on an in-stock or unpopular vehicle or the reduced-rate financing.

Secret Warranties Exist

Manufacturers are required by law to tell consumers if a vehicle defect affects safety or emissions. Manufacturers also offer a number of **secret warranties** on vehicles. This is a list of defects that car manufacturers will fix for free or at reduced cost when persistent problems develop beyond the traditional warranty time period. The people who find out about secret warranty programs are aggressive, persistent and/or lucky consumers who complain to dealers. Only four states have Secret Warranty Disclosure Laws (CA, CN, VA, WS) that require auto manufacturers to notify consumers of post-warranty adjustment programs within 90 days of adopting an adjustment program. Manufacturers also are required to reimburse consumers who have previously obtained repairs on their own.

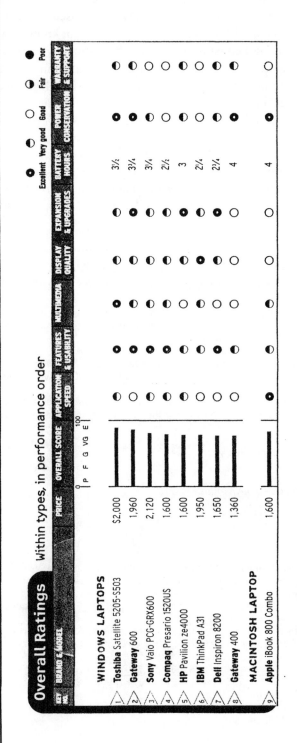

Overall Ratings Within types, in performance order

Legend: Excellent ● Very good ◐ Good ○ Fair ◑ Poor ●

KEY NO.	BRAND & MODEL	PRICE	BATTERY HOURS
	WINDOWS LAPTOPS		
1	**Toshiba** Satellite 5205-S503	$2,000	3½
2	**Gateway** 600	1,960	3¾
3	**Sony** Vaio PCG-GRX600	2,120	3¾
4	**Compaq** Presario 1520US	1,600	2½
5	**HP** Pavilion ze4000	1,600	3
6	**IBM** ThinkPad A31	1,950	2¼
7	**Dell** Inspiron 8200	1,650	2¼
8	**Gateway** 400	1,360	4
	MACINTOSH LAPTOP		
9	**Apple** iBook 800 Combo	1,600	4

(Additional rated attributes shown in the figure: Overall Score, Application Speed, Features & Usability, Multimedia, Display Quality, Expansion & Upgrades, Power Conservation, Warranty & Support.)

The tests behind the Ratings

Overall score includes speed, ease of use, multimedia performance, display, features, and battery life. **Application speed** tracks how the computer compared with a benchmark (a 1-GHz Pentium III laptop for Windows machines; a 466-MHz *iBook* for the Macintosh). **Features & usability** covers the pointing device, other controls, and useful features. **Multimedia** assesses sound quality and the display of still and moving images. **Display quality** includes our judgments of brightness, contrast, uniformity, color accuracy, viewing angle, and glare. **Expansion & upgrades** includes the potential for and ease of expanding a computer's capabilities and upgrading its performance. **Battery hours** shows, to the nearest quarter-hour, how long the battery lasted in our continuous-use test. **Power conservation** reflects the versatility and ease of using battery-saving options. **Warranty & support** summarizes warranty provisions and the availability of technical support, but not its quality. **Price** is approximate retail, with a combo DVD/CD-RW drive, and doesn't include shipping.

Most models have: 1.8- to 2.0-GHz Pentium 4 (Windows models). 256 MB RAM, upgradable to 512 MB or more. 30-GB hard drive. 15-inch active-matrix LCD screen with 1,024x768-pixel resolution. 32 MB of video RAM. Modular bay that can hold a diskette drive, CD drive, or second battery. DVD/CD-RW combo drive in a modular bay. 56 kbps v.92 modem. 10/100 Mbps Ethernet adapter and place for optional internal wireless-network adapter. Two USB-1 ports, FireWire port, parallel printer port, serial data port. Two Type II PC-card slots. Connections for external monitor, keyboard, mouse. Video output for TV. Works application suite and programs for personal finance, virus protection, and CD writing.

FIGURE 13-2   Consumer Reports Ratings for Laptop Computers

The **vehicle problems** under secret warranties are not the subject of formal recalls. Examples of defects are problems with engine stalling, transmission, head gaskets, cracked cylinder head, engine knocks, coolant leaks, power windows, rust, peeling paint, and tires. Secret warranties offered by automobile manufacturers are disclosed in a **technical service bulletin (TSB)** sent to dealers and other repair people to let them know how to address a specific problem. The **dealers, not consumers, are notified,** and they offer to make repairs at their discretion. About 500 secret warranties are in effect at any point in time, reports the Center for Auto Safety. Manufacturers call these efforts **goodwill adjustments**.

As part of previous legal settlements, both Ford and General Motors must make some bulletins available to the public. (Concerned vehicle owners can telephone Ford at 800-241-FORD and General Motors at 800-551-4123.) Secret warranties are tracked by the National Highway Traffic Safety Administration (www.nhtsa.gov), as does *Nuts & Bolts* (800-888-0091). Check the website for the Center for Auto Safety (www.autosafety.org) for details on secret warranties. The Center's newsletter *Lemon Times* is mailed to all members for $20 annually. It is estimated that auto manufacturers spend between $500 and $900 annually per vehicle for secret warranty repairs.

KEY TOPIC IN CONSUMER ECONOMICS:
Take the Cash Rebate or a Low-Interest Loan?

When purchasing a vehicle, you may be faced with having to compare an offer of a low interest rate or a cash rebate. The comparison may seem even more difficult when you arrange your own financing. Here is **how to find the better deal**.

Suppose an auto dealer offers 4.79 percent financing for 3 years with a $906 finance charge, or you can receive a $1,500 rebate if you pay cash or arrange your own financing. Assume that the price of the vehicle before the rebate is $14,000, that you can make a $2,000 down payment, and that you can get a 9.5 percent loan on your own.

To compare the two offers fairly, you must add the opportunity-cost value of the rebate to the finance charge of the dealer financing. Then compare the **annual percentage rate** for each using Formula 13.1 where

Y = number of payment periods in 1 *year*
F = *finance* charge in dollars
D = *debt* (amount borrowed)
P = total number of scheduled *payments*

$$APR = \frac{Y(95P + 9)F}{12(P(P + 1)(4D + F)}$$

Steps to follow:
1. Determine the dollar amount of the rebate ($1,500 in this example).
2. Add it to the finance charge (dollar cost of credit) for the dealer financing ($906 in this example).
3. Use the following APR formula to calculate an adjusted APR for the dealer financing (12.9 percent in this example).
4. Compare the result (12.9 percent in this example) to the APR that you arranged on your own (9.5 percent in this example). The lower of the two is the better deal.

$$APR = \frac{12[(95 \times 36) + 9](\$906 + \$1,500)}{(12 \times 36)(36 + 1)[(4 \times \$12,000) + (\$906 + \$1,500)]} \quad \textbf{(Formula 13.1)}$$
$$= \frac{56,184}{444,000}$$
$$= 12.9 \text{ percent}$$

The financing arranged on your own is more attractive. In fact, any loan you arrange that carries an APR lower than 12.9 percent compares favorably with the dealer-arranged financing in this example.

ECONOMIC INSIGHT:
Weak Automobile Bumpers

Public Citizen reports that low-speed accidents account for over $4 billion in costs per year that largely could be avoided **if cars had 5-mile-per-hour bumpers**. A five-mile an hour impact, such as backing a car into a parking lot lamppost, typically causes damage amounting to **$1,000 to $4,000** because the bumper gives away resulting in damage to the vehicle. The auto manufacturers pressured Congress to persuade the National Highway Traffic Safety Administration to kill the federal vehicle standards for car bumpers in the interest of reducing manufacturing costs and increasing gas mileage. The former standard required that cars be equipped with bumpers that prevented all damage to any exterior part of the automobile and the bumper itself in collisions up to 5 miles per hour into a wall or 10 miles per hour into another car. Both insurance companies and consumers want stronger bumpers.

DID YOU KNOW?
How Much Does It Cost to Drive?

According to the American Automobile Association (AAA), those who drive 15,000 miles will pay an average **50.2 cents per mile**. That includes $5,764 in ownership costs and $1,770 in operating costs.

OWNERSHIP COSTS

Insurance	
Comprehensive ($250 deductible)	$ 173
Collision ($500 deductible)	357
Bodily injury and property damage	
($100,000, $300,000, $50,000)	484
License, registration and taxes	201
Depreciation (15,000 miles)	3,721
Financing charge (20% down; loan	
@8.59%/4 years)	828
Total Ownership Costs	**$5,764**

OPERATING COSTS

Gas and oil (5.9 cents per mile)	$ 885
Maintenance (4.1 cents per mile)	615
Tires (1.8 cents per mile)	270
Total Operating Costs	**$1,770**
COST PER MILE	**50.2 cents**

Source: American Automobile Association.

Service Contracts and Extended Warranties are Bad Deals

A **service contract** is an agreement between the buyer of a product and the contract seller to provide free repairs on defective or malfunctioning products for some specified time period. They are also called an **extended warranty** or a **maintenance agreement**. The agreement is separate from and not part of the basis of a sale of products and services. The seller could be a dealer, manufacturer, or independent insurance company to whom the buyer has paid a fee. These contracts typically do not pay for routine maintenance. The cost of a service contract is paid either in a lump sum or in monthly payments. Service contracts are a form of insurance and are marketed in much the same manner.

About one-third of the buyers purchase a service contract and nearly two-thirds buy contracts for consumer electronics purchases even though it makes **no economic sense** to insure against risks that can, if necessary, be paid for out of current income or savings. Eighty percent of service contracts go unused. Part of the reason is that service contracts often duplicate a product's warranty coverage, and the latter pays first. Service contracts do not offer the same legal rights as warranties.

Based on massive amounts of repair information, the sellers of service contracts can determine with great precision how many repairs each product will need in the future. Reliable products are not likely to need repair during the warranty period. For example, Component Guard, a large service-contract company, states that only **7 percent** of the 45 million VCRs need servicing in the first year of ownership, when they are still under warranty! If the company goes out of business, your contract may be worthless; the service contract industry has a reputation for companies going bankrupt.

Service contracts are **very profitable** contracts sold to consumers by dealers. Court documents uncovered by the *Wall Street Journal* revealed that a Nissan automobile extended service contract cost the consumer $795. Of that amount, $131 goes for insurance coverage that actually pays for repairs, Nissan gets $60, the warranty company gets $38, and $11 goes for membership in an automobile club. The remaining $555 goes to the dealer. William Sliney, president of the Service Contract Industry Council, reports that profit margins for dealers are fantastic. For every $100 service contract sold, the store keeps $80 to $96. Retailers often make more money selling service contracts than they make selling the products themselves. Service contracts are so profitable that sellers hire telemarketing firms to phone consumers soon before the manufacturer's warranty is up to suggest that an extended service contract be purchased.

Consumers **who might benefit** by purchasing a service contract are people who purchase a three or a four-year-old-used vehicle that has lots of electronic components because expensive things can go bad. If you are the kind of person who seems to have a "cloud of bad luck" following you in life, a service contract might be an excellent purchase.

Leasing is a Good Choice for Some Consumers

Leasing is a contract granting use of property during a specified period in exchange for specified rent. Car leasing is popular as an alternative to financing as **one-third** of new-vehicle customers lease. People are increasingly swayed toward leasing because of smaller down payments, lower monthly payment, and not having to deal with getting rid of an old vehicle. With a lease you are, in effect, renting the vehicle for 3, 4, 5, or more years with the title remaining with the lease grantor.

The down payment is usually small, less than $500. Sometimes there is no down payment. Your monthly payments are based on the price of the vehicle minus its projected resale value at the end of the time period (known as the **residual value**). That figure is divided by the number of months in the contract. Monthly lease payments are lower than monthly loan repayments for equivalent time periods. The reason is that with a lease you are not paying for the vehicle's entire cost, because at the end of the lease the consumer does not own the car. The lease payment covers the car's **depreciation** (the reduction in the car's value), financing of that amount, sales tax, dealer expenses, and profit. Sometimes automobile insurance and a service contract are also included in the monthly payment.

You can obtain an open-end lease or a closed-end lease. An **open-end lease** is a leasing arrangement in which the consumer **must pay any difference** between the projected resale value of the car and its true market value at the end of the lease period. With all leases, you are expected to return the car in good shape and have averaged less than 15,000 miles a year. Otherwise, extra costs may be assessed.

In contrast, at the completion of a closed-end lease, the consumer walks away free and clear. A **closed-end lease** is a leasing arrangement in which there is no charge if the true market value of the leased vehicle is lower than the projected resale value at the end of the lease period. The monthly payment for a closed-end lease (the industry standard) is higher than that for an open-end lease. With either of these lease arrangements you may purchase the car for its resale value at the end of the leasing period.

Consumers with no money for a down payment and those who plan on keeping the vehicle for four years or less should consider leasing. The downside is that you might have **never-ending lease payments**. If you sell a car sooner than four years, you might not get out of it what you owe; in that instance you are **upside-down**, owing more than the vehicle is worth. You can buy horribly overpriced insurance from a dealer that in the event of an accident or theft resulting in a total loss, pays for the "gap" between the market value of your car and what you owe. People who should consider leasing are those who do not want to tie up an amount for a down payment and those who do not like putting their money into depreciating assets, such as cars.

The government's Consumer Leasing Act (see Chapter 5) has a number of weaknesses. Consumer advocates want a government requirement that the dealer provide an example of the costs at the end of the first year to illustrate the "substantial additional charges" that are imposed because of **early termination**. When consumers trade their cars in for newer models or have a serious accident their leases terminate. More than 30 percent of leases terminate early.

Another flaw in the law is that dealers are not required to disclose the interest rate charged. Logic tells you that you must be "paying interest," but the government lets the leasing companies pretend that they do not. To determine an approximate interest rate, begin with the **capitalized cost**. This is the leasing equivalent of the selling price. Negotiate this first before monthly payments are discussed. The **money factor** is the interest charge, or the difference between the capitalized cost and the residual value. A salesperson might talk about the money factor, such as 3.33, and imply that the figure is a low interest rate. The truth can be found by multiplying the money factor, .00333 in this example (see how the decimal point moved) by 24 (it's always 24 regardless of the number of years in a lease), and in this example the annual percentage rate is approximately 8 percent.

Financing Options

When comparison shopping for a car with the knowledge that you are going to finance the purchase, you may have the **opportunity to choose** between seller financing and borrowing from a conventional lender, such as a bank or credit union. Sometimes seller financing is offered by the automobile manufacturers through their dealers. It may be possible to take advantage of a special low (or zero) interest rate when you use such **seller financing**. You may have a higher monthly payment because of restrictions on the time period of the loan, since special rates are usually only available for financing over one, two or three years. Most low-interest specials run concurrently with some type of rebate plan for people who pay cash or arrange their own financing. You might be able to get a low interest-rate loan through your bank or credit union.

For low interest-rate loans on vehicles, go to www.Bankrate.com, www.LendingTree.com, and www.hsh.com. To figure a **loan versus rebate** and perform **buy/lease calculations**, see www.cornerstonecu.org/ccu_online/calculator/loan_rebate.htm, www.intellichoice.com, www.leasesource.com, www.carwizard.com, and www.kiplinger.com/spending/cars.

With a **balloon automobile loan**, the buyer takes title to the car, and the last monthly payment is equal to the projected resale value of the vehicle at the end of the loan period. This has the effect of lowering the other monthly payments in order to make them more competitive with the amount of each month's lease payments. When the final balloon payment is due, you have **three options**: (1) pay the balloon payment and keep the car, (2) return the car to the lender, or (3) sell the car and pay the balloon payment with the proceeds.

Establishing Priorities

To assist her in decision-making, Bonnie constructed **a chart** to prioritize her choices in terms of her values, as shown in Table 13-1. She first listed several criteria that were really important to her, such as price and dependability, and then she ranked them.

Bonnie's Criteria	Bonnie's Ranking
Low price	1
Dependability	2
Safety	3
Comfort	4
Warranty	5
Design	6
Fuel economy	7
Performance	8
Service department reputation	9
Seller financing	10

TABLE 13-1   Bonnie's Priorities on What Is Important to Her

Bonnie skipped leasing because she simply wanted to own her car, not lease it. She plans on telephoning both her bank and credit union, as well as check the Web to find out about their financing options. She also thought about extended warranties and concluded that they were a **waste of money**. She figures that since the vehicle has a warranty, any problems that occur will occur during the manufacturer's warranty period of three years and be covered. Should she have problems later on, she can take the product back for repair without a service contract and simply pay for anything herself.

Bonnie easily found safety information in *Consumer Reports*, the National Highway Traffic Safety Administration, and the Center for Auto Safety. She also searched for fuel-efficient and clean motor vehicles on the **Green Vehicle Guide** website of the Environmental Protection Agency. (www.epa.gov/emissweb/).

Bonnie's **comparison-shopping efforts** resulted in her locating two good used cars and three new automobiles. In comparing the choices, she focused on what factors were important to her. As shown in Table 13-1, Bonnie decided that price, dependability, safety, and comfort were the four most important factors. All the cars were affordable, since they were priced below $16,000, so Bonnie reflected on dependability and safety. Although she really liked the used cars she test drove, Bonnie finally decided to eliminate them from her alternatives because she believed that a new car would be more dependable. So after much thinking, she narrowed her choices to the three new automobiles.

To help in her decision-making, Bonnie made another chart to rate each of the cars on her four most important criteria (see Table 13-2). This process quickly helped Bonnie eliminate the number three car; she thought that either of the two cars would provide excellent transportation and comfort. Now Bonnie thought she was **ready to negotiate** for the better deal between the two cars.

Criteria	Car 1	Car 2	Car 3
Price	A	A	A
Dependability*	A -	B +	B
Safety*	B +	A	A
Comfort	A	A	B

*Bonnie's impressions gained from *Consumer Reports* ratings of same model car for previous years.

TABLE 13-2 Bonnie's Final Ratings Based on Her Criteria

Negotiating

Much negotiating goes on for expensive products and services. Here there are offers and counteroffers until there is agreement on the final terms.

The Goal of Negotiation

To succeed in a negotiation, it is important to maintain **a posture of being knowledgeable and having control**. The salesperson will try to convince you to buy on his or her terms. Chances are that the salesperson will tell you during the bargaining process that the price you are offering amounts to "stealing the car." Don't believe it, because no one ever, ever, ever buys underpriced cars from a dealer. You must be prepared to say "No," and buy elsewhere if the terms are not satisfactory. Otherwise, the advantage will be the seller's. The best strategy when shopping for a car is to be willing *not* to buy one from that dealer that day.

The **lowest price** a consumer can hope to expect to pay for a new automobile is **$150 to $200 over the dealer's cost**. The best bargaining philosophy is to negotiate upward from the dealer's cost of the product, not to negotiate downward from any sticker prices. The task for the consumer is to correctly figure out how much the dealer paid for the vehicle, and confidently make an appropriate offer. Since the dealer wants to sell at a higher price than $150 over cost whenever possible, the dealer is likely to first argue that a shopper's cost figures are wrong, and then reject any offer close to that amount, unless he or she is convinced the consumer will go elsewhere to make the purchase.

Price information is available on the **Internet**. Before you negotiate with a dealer, you can equip any new vehicle with options (www.carsdirect.com and www.CarOrder.com). Other sites provide details on pricing (www.consumerreports.org, www.money.com/carbuyer, www.kbb.com, and www.edmunds.com). **Ownership costs** also can be estimated (www.intellichoice.com). See www.dealernet.com to locate 7,000 dealers nationwide.

State laws **prevent the direct sale** of automobiles to consumers over the Internet. They also restrict the location of dealerships and prevent competition on warranty service. These anti-consumer laws cost consumers $25 billion a year, reports the Consumer Federation of America.

Nevertheless, use of the **Internet** has put consumers in an informed position when negotiating price. According to CNW Marketing/Research, the **average discounts** off the sticker price on vehicles are as follows: budget, 15 percent; mid-size, 13 percent; luxury, 13 percent; sport, 19 percent; full-size pickup; 8 percent, compact SUV, 10 percent; and full-size SUV, 8 percent.

Negotiating Price

Bonnie knew that research shows **women consistently pay more** for the same vehicle as men. To avoid that discrimination, Bonnie started the process of negotiation by first ascertaining the invoice price. The **invoice price** (or **dealer's cost**) is what the dealership pays before manufacturer discounts and other rebates). It is higher than the actual price finally paid by the dealer because the dealer later receives rebates, allowances, discounts, and incentive awards from the manufacturer. The invoice price does include the manufacturer's delivery charges.

The **base price** or **base cost** is the cost of the car without options, but including standard equipment, factory warranty, and freight. This information is printed on the sticker price. The **sticker price**, or the automobile **manufacturer's suggested retail price (MSRP)**, includes the base cost, certain manufacturer-installed options on the vehicle, and the manufacturer's transportation charges. Federal regulations require that the sticker price be on a label affixed to the car window of newly manufactured vehicles.

KEY TOPIC IN CONSUMER ECONOMICS:
False Auto Price Advertising

State laws often require that any **invoice price** cited in an advertisement be made available by the dealer for **customer inspection**. States typically prohibit dealer ads for vehicles containing the words *at cost, below cost, invoice price, wholesale, factory sale,* and *dealer rebates.* False price advertising also occurs when a used car dealer illegally promotes a vehicle as **"executive driven,"** implying that it might have been driven by a top executive when, in some cases, the vehicle was bought at auction or from a rental company. In some states, advertising a used vehicle for $100 over cost violates the law when there are additional charges to the consumer, such as preparation, destination, and document fees. In spite of state laws, advertised new vehicle prices do not accurately reflect truth because **dealerships are given rebates** by manufacturers after vehicles are sold.

Holdback, or **dealer holdback**, is a percentage of either the MSRP or invoice price of a new vehicle paid to the dealer by the manufacturer typically to assist with the dealer's financing of the vehicle. Because of holdback, dealers can advertise a car at $1 over invoice and still make a good profit. Holdback is different from the rebates that go to the customer or the dealer. Knowing this should guide you to making a lower offer than the invoice price. Many websites (see www.edmunds.com) have holdback information.

While visiting automobile dealers earlier, Bonnie also learned that the sticker price of new cars is apparently just the beginning price, since some dealers affix *another sticker* of their own to the MSRP—the **dealer sticker price**. This pricing information is euphemistically called the **adjusted market value (AMV)** or **additional dealer markup (ADM)**. This is a popular technique of raising the dealer's profit margin on new cars by adding a substantial charge to the sticker price. Also, dealers like to pad the sticker price by adding in such things as "pre-delivery inspection," "dealer preparation," "undercoating," rust proofing," and "protective finish." Today's cars come with rust-resistant construction that makes after-market undercoating unnecessary and paint sealants that don't need expensive special waxing. You can apply fabric treatments in 10 minutes yourself with a $10 can of Scotch Guard. "Forget about this stuff," says www.Edmonds.com.

Some automobile dealers also charge extra ostensibly to pay for advertising costs billed to the dealer by the manufacturer. This is called **national dealer advertising (NDA)** and it is another bogus fee to increase dealer profit. Also watch out for an inflated **destination charge**, typically $300 to $700. This should be the cost of shipping the vehicle from the final assembly point to the dealer, but it may include other expenses the seller wants to pass on to the buyer. This figure is often contained in the ADM.

The MSRP or sticker price includes an ample markup for the dealer to make a handsome profit. A dealer must maintain a reasonable profit margin on vehicles sold or go out of business, and most are doing well. **Profit margin** (or **margin**) is the difference between the net cost of a product obtained from a manufacturer and the dealer's price to the consumer.

To illustrate, the sticker price for one of Bonnie's alternatives was $16,144, and next to it was attached a smaller "price summary" with the following additional figures: $350 for dealer preparation, $300 for undercoating, $400 for ADM, and $600 for NDA for a subtotal of $1650 for a grand total of $17,794.

Markup for dealers varies among vehicles, options, and special manufacturer incentives. Experts agree that in general, dealer markup ranges from 10 to 35 percent of the base price of the car. Markups on small vehicles are $2,000 to $3,000, $4,500 to $6,000 on mid-sized, and $12,000 on full-size. Markups on options range from 20 to 100 percent. One of the vehicles Bonnie was considering had a total price of $17,900, and after checking one source (www.edmunds.com), Bonnie determined that the dealer probably paid $15,956 for it.

Dealer incentives are cash, perhaps $200 to $300, offered by manufacturers to dealers for selling certain models during a specific time period. These are usually models that are not selling well. **Rebates** are also sometimes offered to consumers by manufacturers as incentives to encourage them to purchase certain makes and models that are not selling well. Consumers appreciate rebates and low interest rates. Sometimes a dealer will argue that the cost for a particular rebate is being shared by both the manufacturer and the dealer, and if that is actually the case, the dealer's true cost must include his or her part of the rebate. Look for a **factory-direct rebate** that comes straight from the manufacturer, not one involving the dealer. Rebates typically only apply to cars in stock, so if the car you want is not on the lot, you are out of luck. If a dealer incentive is being offered, be sure to **negotiate for a portion of it**. (See www.edmunds.com for the latest dealer incentives.)

In the illustration with Bonnie, the dealer with the $17,900 has an additional dealer markup (ADM) of $1,650 within the $17,900, so there is lots of room for Bonnie to discuss pricing. Each of the ADM items should be questioned, and **every figure is negotiable**. For example, ADM and dealer preparation are simply pure-profit figures for the dealer. *Consumer Reports* "recommends against accepting any items on a separate dealer sticker. If the dealer will not sell the car without these added charges, we suggest you shop elsewhere for the best price."

Haggle, Use One-Price Shopping or a Buying Service

Haggling is bargaining, dickering, and arguing in an attempt to come to terms. Haggling over auto prices and options has long been an American tradition, and more than two-thirds of consumers haggle over price. Confronted with poor sales, a number of dealers are converting to **one-price shopping**. Here prices are supposed to be nonnegotiable and fair, with no haggling allowed. How much a consumer gains depends upon how much one is willing to pay to eliminate haggling with sales personnel. In reality, however, consumers can negotiate. A CNW Marketing study of one-price shopping car dealerships found that "if you asked for a discount, you got it." CNW Marketing concludes that it appears that one-price auto dealers set a price about **two or three percent higher** than the average negotiated price at traditional dealerships. Consumers who want to pay the lowest price possible should avoid one-price shopping.

You can also purchase a new vehicle with the help of a buying service or professional shopper on the Internet. A **buying service** is a no-fee organization that arranges discount purchases for buyers of new cars who are referred to nearby participating automobile dealers who have agreed to charge specific discount prices. After you sign up, a local dealer will call offering a no-haggle price, often within 4 percent of the invoice price. The buying service earns its income by collecting a finder's fee from the dealer. See www.autovantage.com, www.autobytel.com (both owned by the same company), www.CarOrder.com, www.carpoint. msn.com, www.carsdirect.com, www.autoweb.com, www.Netscape.com, and www.Green Light.com. Dealers sell on the Internet, too (see www.usautosales.com). Membership clubs also have buying services (see www.aaa.com and www.costcoauto.com.)

Professional shoppers, for a fee ($165 to $450) based on the sticker price, will find the best available price from a nearby dealer and finalize the sale. Alternatively, for a lower fee, they will obtain price quotes so you can finalize the deal. See www.Carsdirect.com, www.Driveoff.com, www.autoadvisor.com (800-326-1976), www.carbargains.com (800-475-7283), and www.carsource1.com (800-517-2277). Consumers who love to haggle can get slightly lower prices than what buying services and professional shoppers offer, although many believe it is not worth the hassle.

Selecting, Accepting and Evaluating

The selection task is to decide which product or service is best for you given your needs and wants. It is easy to give in when you have **"new car fever"** and accept a good-sounding deal being offered in a dealer's showroom. This may not be the best place to make a decision because of pressures to buy that may be applied by the seller, and/or by your own desire to get the process over with. It is better to **wait until you get home** to make the decision. There you can retrace the steps in the buying process, making sure that your decision is based on good information and a good understanding of your needs and wants. Then you can return to the dealer's showroom and sign the necessary papers. In short, the wise consumer waits, thinks, compares, reflects, and then decides.

To put that car in front of her home, Bonnie needs to be concerned about **selecting the better** of her two remaining alternatives. Her final two choices evaluated similarly, so Bonnie's decision was based primarily on price, as shown in Table 13-3. The dealer for car one originally wanted $17,794 for everything. The dealer for car two wanted $18,480, which included $15,410 for the car, $1,300 for the same options, and $1,770 for additional dealer markup. The dealer for car one did not want to negotiate the base price of the car, but he was willing to come down on the options and ADM. The dealer for car two did drop his price on the car a little, and he came down some on the options and ADM. The unwillingness of the dealer selling car one to negotiate very much made Bonnie's decision easier, so she chose car two. The car fit her needs and wants, and the final price was $16,590 which she thought was a fair price, since she figured the dealer probably paid the manufacturer $15,956.

Car and Options	Price Quoted	Final Price
Car 1 base price	$ 15,100	$15,100
Options	1,044	800
ADM	1,650	300
TOTAL	$17,794	$16,200
Car 2 base price	15,410	14,800
Options	1,300	1,050
ADM	1,770	740
TOTAL	$18,480	$16,590

TABLE 13-3   Bonnie's Final Selection

Bonnie thought she had adequate information to make a good decision, so she made it. Bonnie also had to pay $438 in sales taxes and $75 for license tags. Thus, the grand total was $17,103. Bonnie made her down payment of $4,700 and financed the balance of $12,403 ($17,103 - $4,700) at a 10 percent interest rate for five years through her credit union with a monthly payment of $264, just $14 more than what she had budgeted.

The rational consumer often **reflects on important decisions** after a period of weeks or months. The intent is not to doubt the decision, or be irritated that a few dollars might have been saved by doing something else. Rather, the task is to reaffirm the wisdom of utilizing the process that resulted in the decision and to use any valuable recollections in future decision-making opportunities. Over the next few months, Bonnie seemed to recognize every car on the road that was the same model as hers. She liked her car and enjoyed it. Occasionally, she saw dealer advertisements for the same model with a price of a hundred dollars or so less than the amount she paid, but it did not bother her in the least. She has learned in her planned shopping venture that dealers can lower their prices on three things: base cost (what is advertised), options and ADM. She knew she did well in negotiating and paid a **fair price** for the automobile.

KEY TOPIC IN CONSUMER ECONOMICS:
Tips on Buying a Used Vehicle

You can purchase a good used car because so many people today lease vehicles and then turn them back to sellers. There are millions of essentially perfect used vehicles available. To **check reliability and prices**, see *Consumer Reports* Used Car Price Service. To track a vehicle's history, including discrepancies in mileage statements, whether the vehicle has been wrecked, salvaged, damaged by flood or bought back by a manufacturer under a state lemon law, you might consider paying $20 by telephone (800-346-3846) or $12.50 via the **Internet** (www.carfaxreport.com). National no-haggle used-vehicle superstore chains have an average profit of only $300 per vehicle. See www.CarsDirect.com, www.AutoConnect.com, www.CarMax, and www.Driver'sMartWorldwide, and their vehicles typically come with warranties.

Bonnie was confidently looking forward to making other expensive purchases, such as some exercise equipment and a compact disc music system, so she could put to practice some of the experience she gained from going through the steps of planned buying in buying her car. Bonnie especially enjoyed collecting information and establishing her own criteria with which to compare products. Moreover, Bonnie discovered in this planned buying endeavor that not only did she learn a lot, but she also **enjoys her automobile more** because of the experience.

Review and Summary of Key Terms and Concepts

1. Distinguish between **habit buying** and **impulse buying**, and give a reason why habit buying is sometimes useful to consumers.

2. Explain the idea of **conspicuous consumption** and give an example.

3. What is **planned buying**?

4. What are the three reasons why consumers make **bad decisions**?

5. What do the terms **comparison shopping**, **best buy**, and **quality** mean in the context of planned buying?

6. *Consumer Reports* magazine is known for its objectivity. Give some reasons why that is true.

7. Summarize the value of **safety seals** and **seals of approval** to consumers.

8. Distinguish among: **brand names**, **store brands**, and **generic brands**.

9. What do publications like the **Kelley Blue Book** and **NADA Book** contain that is helpful for used automobile shoppers?

10. Why is **window shopping** important for the auto shopper, and how does a **credit check** fit into the picture?

11. Explain **push money** and why it might result in consumers buying the wrong products.

12. What is **comparison shopping**, and what is a **best buy**?

13. What are **rebates**, and why do sellers use them?

14. What are **secret warranties**, and how do they work?

15. Explain the idea behind **service contracts**, from the perspectives of both the seller and the consumer.

16. Make up a mathematical example that demonstrates Formula 13.1, taking the vehicle manufacturer's **cash rebate** or a **low-interest deal**.

17. Distinguish between an **open-end** and a **closed-end lease**.

18. Explain how a **balloon automobile loan** operates, and how is that similar to being **upside down** financially.

19. Distinguish between the **invoice price** and the **dealer sticker price**.

20. What is **dealer holdback** and how can the consumer use this information to his or her advantage?

21. Explain why **one-price shopping** is a good idea for some, but not all consumers.

22. What is the essence of the idea to **accept and evaluate** the decision?

Useful Resources for Consumers

Autobytel
www.autobytel.com

AutoWeb
www.autoweb.com

Center for Auto Safety
www.autosafety.org/

Consumer Reports (new cars)
www.ConsumerReports.org/carprices/new6

Environmental Protection Agency
Green Vehicle Guide
www.epa.gov/emissweb/

First Gov for Consumers
www.consumer.gov/

High Point Convention & Visitors Bureau
www.highpoint.org/

Twenty miles of sellers and 37 furniture galleries carrying 600 lines of furniture. Brochures and maps are available to where two-thirds of the furniture in the U.S. is manufactured; shipping is inexpensive. Check the status of the company with the North Carolina Attorney General's Office of Consumer Protection 919-733-7741

Kelley Blue Book
www.kbb.com/

Mark Eskeldson
Automobile consumer advocate
www.carinfo.com/

NADA Book (National Automobile Dealers Association)
www.nada.org

National Highway Traffic Safety Administration Owner-reported problems and database of Manufacturer Service Bulletins
www.nhtsa.dot.gov/ and www.nhtsa.dot.gov/nsa/nsa search.shtml

"What Do You Think" Questions

1. From your life experiences, list two **best buys**. Explain why each of those purchases was a best buy.

2. **Secret warranties** give one class of consumers, the aggressive complainers, an advantage over other consumers. Do you think that manufacturers should be permitted to offer such policy adjustments? Why or why not? Also, do you think that laws should be passed to require secret warranty disclosures to all consumers? Why or why not?

3. When **choosing priorities** such as Bonnie did in her car buying process, how would you rate the several factors that she used (dependability, safety, etc.) if you were purchasing an automobile? Rank them on a one-to-ten scale. Explain why you listed your top two factors as most important.

Part Five:

CONSUMER ECONOMIC ISSUES

Chapter 14

Food Issues

OBJECTIVES

After reading this chapter, you should be able to

1. Recognize good eating habits.

2. Differentiate among food regulatory agencies.

3. Identify some anti-competitive practices in the food industry.

4. Recognize several questionable and confusing food selling practices.

The average U.S. household spends only 10.9 percent of earnings for food, thanks to tremendous efficiencies in food production. This compares with 17.7 percent in Germany and 33.2 percent in Mexico. Americans also like to eat. The population of the U.S. is the fattest in world history. Sixty-one percent of adults are **overweight**, defined as 10 to 30 pounds over a healthy weight for their gender, height and frame. Twenty-seven percent are **obese**, defined as 30 or more pounds overweight Of the 50 million Americans who are obese, 17 million, almost one-third, have diagnosed diabetes. Obesity and diabetes are twin epidemics. A study by the RAND Institute found that being overweight "causes more chronic health problems than smoking, heavy drinking and being poor." At any point in time, almost half of adult women and one-quarter of adult men are attempting to lose weight.

This chapter is aimed at helping you better understand the food issues affecting consumers and how you can deal with them. It begins by examining factors associated with good eating habits. Next it describes the agencies and laws that protect food consumers in the United States. The topic of assessing food risks is followed by a description of some anti-competitive practices in the food industry and an overview of some questionable food-selling practices.

American Eating Habits

A **nutrient** is something that **promotes growth** or development. Most people do not know much about proper eating habits and/or simply do not care. As a result, the American population will not live as long as should be expected. Advertising causes part of these problems and, as a result, consumers have difficulty getting what they need and want when they go food shopping.

For many of us, breakfast is a **nutritional flop**. About 20 percent of us do not eat any breakfast at all. Many of those who do eat breakfast enjoy cereal with milk. Numerous consumers have fallen prey to misleading advertising claims of cereal manufacturers. A breakfast composed of cereal may provide some useful nutritional benefits (such as the calcium in the milk); however, the great majority of breakfast cereals offer little in the way of nutrition. The main ingredient in breakfast cereal often is sugar. Other breakfast meals such as bacon, eggs, toast, and orange juice, may appear to be nutritionally superior, but they contain too many calories, additives, and fats. Hurried mothers, fathers, and children often skip meals, especially breakfast. Research shows that after going all night without food, a good breakfast provides the necessary fuel for people to **operate effectively** during the morning hours.

Many children learn **poor eating habits in schools** because many school-lunch programs use too much food high in fat. Critics argue that the National School Lunch Program that feeds 25 million children daily in 95,000 schools, encourages unhealthy eating of too many fats. A USDA study found that the average amount of fat in a week of the nation's school lunches is 38 percent instead of the **recommended 30 percent**.

The adults also are **eating too much**. Americans today eat 140 pounds more of food per year than they did a decade earlier. Over the years food portion sizes have increased, and consumers usually eat what's on their plate. Scarfing down a supersize Extra Value Meal, which includes a Quarter Pounder With Cheese, supersize fries, and a supersize drink, amounts to 1,550 calories. The American food slogan today is "Supersize it!"

KEY TOPIC IN CONSUMER ECONOMICS:
Why Learn About Food and Health?

Some question why consumer educators and health advocates insist upon educating people about food and health. There are two reasons. First, you need to know enough to make **informed choices** in personal decision-making. Second, you may wish to participate in changing **public policy** in food and health.

In the area of public policy, for example, the Center for Science in the Public Interest (CSPI) is calling for a change in this nation's public health policies. They are encouraging government to help persuade consumers to adopt **good nutrition practices to help prevent diet-related diseases** such as heart disease, diabetes, stroke, and cancer. CSPI wants the government to: (1) promote information that helps people eat healthy diets, including low-fat and vegetarian diets, (2) have the U.S. Surgeon General publish an annual report on nutrition, (3) motivate broadcasters to promote good nutrition for children, and (4) require that medical facilities serve lower-fat, lower-salt meals.

Government is demonstrating a growing interest in the **obesity epidemic** because a recent study confirmed that 10 percent of all health care spending can be attributed to excessive weight. That is the same amount attributed to smoking. A *Baltimore Sun* editorial noted that "Overeating can be as dangerous as booze and cigarettes, and it has an impact on us all."

Calorie Intake and Weight

Your body's primary job is to keep your heart and other vital organs operating. Necessary tasks include keeping you breathing, maintaining normal body temperature, giving you the strength to get out of bed in the morning and get through a normal day, and seeing to it that you have enough extra power to cope with any hard physical or mental stresses. All these **tasks require energy**, which you get from foods that contain calories. A **calorie** is a measure of the energy, or heat, produced by consuming food.

Since nearly everything we eat contains some calories, most of us are able to perform our daily chores. Foods give the **energy** the body needs throughout the day, and even during the night when we are sleeping. Different foods have various amounts of calories, or energy value. Sweet, greasy, or concentrated foods often have high calorie counts, while watery, bulky, or coarse foods usually have lower ones.

The number of calories a person needs each day differs with sex, height, weight, age, individual metabolism and physical activity. Any calories not used are stored in the body as fat. As a rule, if you consume fewer calories of food than you burn, you lose weight. Each decrease in consumption of about 3,500 calories should cause a **weight loss of one pound**. The only long-term way to lose weight is through a combination of calorie reduction *and* **physical exercise**. Many consumers are so physically inactive that their bodies do not utilize all the food energy in their diets.

You can determine your **body mass index (BMI)**, a measure of weight in relation to height, by using Table 14-1. Anyone with a BMI of 25 or over is considered **overweight**. Those with a BMI of 30 or more are considered **obese**, or roughly 30 pounds over a healthy weight.

TABLE 14-1   Ideal Weight Guidelines Using the Body Mass Index

To use the table, find the appropriate height in the left-hand column. Move across the row to the given weight. The number at the top of the column is the BMI for that height and weight. A BMI of 25 or over is considered overweight and a BMI of 30 or more is considered obese.

BMI (kg/m²)	19	20	21	22	23	24	25	26	27	28	29	30	35	40
Height (in.)	Weight (lb.)													
58	91	96	100	105	110	115	119	124	129	134	138	143	167	191
59	94	99	104	109	114	119	124	128	133	138	143	148	173	198
60	97	102	107	112	118	123	128	133	138	143	148	153	179	204
61	100	106	111	116	122	127	132	137	143	148	153	158	185	211
62	104	109	115	120	126	131	136	142	147	153	158	164	191	218
63	107	113	118	124	130	135	141	146	152	158	163	169	197	225
64	110	116	122	128	134	140	145	151	157	163	169	174	204	232
65	114	120	126	132	138	144	150	156	162	168	174	180	210	240
66	118	124	130	136	142	148	155	161	167	173	179	186	216	247
67	121	127	134	140	146	153	159	166	172	178	185	191	223	255
68	125	131	138	144	151	158	164	171	177	184	190	197	230	262
69	128	135	142	149	155	162	169	176	182	189	196	203	236	270
70	132	139	146	153	160	167	174	181	188	195	202	207	243	278
71	136	143	150	157	165	172	179	186	193	200	208	215	250	286
72	140	147	154	162	169	177	184	191	199	206	213	221	258	294
73	144	151	159	166	174	182	189	197	204	212	219	227	265	302
74	148	155	163	171	179	186	194	202	210	218	225	233	272	311
75	152	160	168	176	184	192	200	208	216	224	232	240	279	319
76	156	164	172	180	189	197	205	213	221	230	238	246	287	328

*Source: United States Centers for Disease Control and Prevention, National Center for Health Statistics.

The Poor Quality of American Diets

Obvious signs of nutritional deficiency are not apparent in the American public. This is probably because most diets, no matter how poor, still provide enough of the needed nutrients to prevent deficiency diseases.

CONSUMER UPDATE:
Advertising Food to Kids on Television

Various national surveys show that young children have a **high level of nutritional awareness**. But like their parents, the so-called **knowledge is often not used** when making food choices. **Why?** (1) High-fat and high-sodium school lunches, and family meals that often do not meet standards for healthy eating; (2) Restaurant food contains 22 percent more fat than food consumed at home; (3) Packaging that entices children to purchase foods of little nutritional value; and (4) Excessive television watching that uses fewer calories than lying in bed and reduces opportunities for physical activities. According to the Institute for Medicine "the average U.S. child sees **10,000 food commercials on TV a year**, 95% for sugar and fat-laden products." As a result, children eat a lot of **junk food**, those with high sugar, high fat, and low nutritional value.

Obesity is now the number one health problem among children in the United Kingdom as well as in the United States, where the quiet epidemic means 1 in 5 children is overweight. One-third of vegetables eaten by kids are potato chips and french fries cooked in the least healthy way possible. Soaking potatoes in hot oil can raise levels of artery-clogging fats and contribute to a sugar overload. Fries made using hydrogenated vegetable oils contain unhealthy **trans-fatty acids** that increase the risk of heart disease, high cholesterol and diabetes. Trans fat has been nicknamed **"phantom fat"** because the FDA does not require it to be listed on food labels. The FDA does recommend that "Intake of trans fats should be as low as possible."

Critics, remembering the decades of lying and stalling by the tobacco industry (see Chapter 16), are calling for changes in food policy. **Public debates** are needed on (1) prohibiting all food advertising directed at children, (2) removing sweet drinks and snack foods from schools, (3) ending food company sponsorship of scholastic and athletic activities, and (4) requiring fast-food restaurants to put nutrient information on food packages and on large charts on walls inside the restaurants.

Scientific Evidence Links Diet to Disease

The effects of **poor dietary habits** vary from few noticeable effects to severe difficulties. Health problems from **malnutrition** (poor nutrition often because of an insufficient or poorly balanced diet) include poor health, obesity, mental stress, physical deficiencies, and increased susceptibility to diseases. After tracking caloric intake for more than 30 years, the United States Department of Agriculture (USDA) reports that Americans are consuming **more food per capita** than ever before. The U.S. Surgeon General has reported that five of the top ten causes of death are substantially linked to diet. Obesity contributes to a number of serious health disorders, including hypertension, diabetes, gallstones, osteoarthritis (because the excess weight puts added pressure on the joints), adult-onset diabetes, and heart disease. Arteries are either assaulted by animal-based cholesterol or protected by fruits, vegetables and grains. **One in four men** in the United States dies of a heart attack or a stroke before age 65. To calculate your heart attack risk, see www.cholesterol.usatoday.com.

Cancer also is linked to diet. A sixteen-year-long research study published in *The New England Journal of Medicine* found that extra weight contributes to "about **20 percent of all cancer deaths** in women and 14 percent of those in men." Foods high in fat increase cancer risk, while those high in fiber content appear to reduce risk. **Fibrous foods** include whole grains, cereals, vegetables, and fruits.

Many people are eating themselves to early deaths. People who are overweight by 10 to 30 pounds at age forty"are likely to die at least **three years sooner** than those who are slim," according a recent Framingham study. Obese men lose an average of 5.8 years of life and obese women lose 7.1 years.

Good Nutrition and Good Health

Good health is a primary factor in our happiness and our ability to work productively. Good nutrition is part of **preventive medicine**; it helps maintain healthy bodies and protects them against chronic diseases. Consumers who regularly eat wisely and consume healthier snacks can expect to enjoy vitality, energy and a higher quality of life. Those who maintain proper weight and avoid tobacco not only live longer, but have fewer years of sickness and dependency upon others. The *New England Journal of Medicine* observed that "Of those people who follow prudent health habits, the majority will reach their ninth decade in good health and then die after, at most, a relatively brief period of illness."

KEY TOPIC IN CONSUMER ECONOMICS:
The Poor Pay More for Food

Despite the extensive network of federal programs for the poor, the **majority** of beneficiaries remain in poverty, unable to afford an adequate diet. That includes the ten percent of all Americans who receive food stamps. The poor have more **restricted access** to food stores than the non-poor because most are not within walking distance of a supermarket. The poor have more **limited choices** because they often frequent small stores, sometimes called **bodegas**, that are tiny grocery shops that don't stock fresh meat or fish, and sell unrefrigerated eggs and lettuce. The few number of supermarkets in poor areas are cramped, usually offering only one-third the physical space available in supermarkets in middle-class neighborhoods.

For these reasons, the poor are forced to **pay higher prices** for food. A study of food prices in impoverished inner-city neighborhoods in New York City by the Community Resource Center found that poor people spent **13 to 25 percent more** on groceries than their suburban counterparts. A 20-city study commissioned by Public Voice for Food and Health Policy found that small corner stores were charging as much as 40 percent more than larger supermarkets.

The Importance of Low-Fat Eating to Good Health

Low-fat eating is **important** to good health. The U.S. Surgeon General's Report on Nutrition and Health observes that "there can no longer be any doubt about the link between diet and disease." It cites saturated fat and dietary cholesterol as the "most pervasive villains in the American diet." Of the 2.1 million Americans who die every year, diet was associated with the cause of death in at least two-thirds of them. The report concludes that "If you do not smoke or drink excessively, your choice of diet can influence your long-term health prospects more than any other action you might take." The Department of Health and Human Services and many public-health experts report that diet-related diseases kill more than 300,000 Americans annually. The number refers to deaths caused by poor diet and inactivity, not fatness.

Fats are necessary in the diet, but too much can cause problems. For most Americans, approximately 40 percent of the daily caloric intake is from fat. Current recommendations are to **limit fat to 30 percent**, or less, of total caloric intake. Only one in five Americans consumes the recommended amount of fat.

The body handles fat in **three ways**: (1) burns it up to produce energy, (2) stores it in tissues, or (3) deposits it in the form of cholesterol along the walls of the arteries (the blood vessels that carry oxygen and food throughout the body). **Cholesterol** is a fat-like substance produced by all animals, including humans, that serves as a building block of cells, vitamins, and hormones. It is a waxy substance in the blood that does not mix with water, but excessive amounts can accumulate in one's arteries. High cholesterol levels cause hardened, narrow arteries that pinch off blood circulation and eventually cause a heart attack or stroke.

CONSUMER UPDATE:
Unhealthy Theater Popcorn

The Center for Science in the Public Interest reports that if **cooked in coconut oil** (a saturated fat that has been shown to raise blood cholesterol levels), a medium container of buttered popcorn has 71 grams of fat—more than a day's worth of artery-clogging fat! Popcorn with canola oil is not very healthy either, in spite of those misleading signs in movie theaters that state "Now Popping With Canola Oil. Low in Saturated Fats. No Cholesterol." What those theaters are *really* cooking in have lots of partially **hydrogenated fats**, a source of trans-fatty acids, and are still 100% fat. Consumers who want healthy popcorn eat air-popped popcorn; ask the theater for some. **Air-popped popcorn** is almost a "free-food," something people can eat lots of without taking in very many calories.

The total amount of saturated fat that one consumes has a great effect on raising blood cholesterol levels. **Saturated fats** are those that are solid at room temperature, such as butter, beef fat, and coconut and palm oils (found in some baked goods and coffee creamers). Other foods include high-fat dairy products, fatty meats, the skin and fat of poultry, lard, palm oil, and coconut oil. Saturated fat tends to increase the blood level of the **"bad" LDL cholesterol**. The predominant source of fat in the typical woman's diet is salad dressing; for men it is hamburger.

It is important for good long-term health to **cut down on fat intake**. The phrase "cut down" does not say cut out. Proper eating habits and drugs can improve cholesterol levels. Consumers can control the amount of cholesterol and fats they eat.

The aim for those interested in good health should be to reduce fat consumption to **30 percent or less**, which is about a 25 percent reduction for most people. Interest in healthy diets has increased the number of vegetarians in the United States to 12 million, and about 15 percent of college students are **vegetarians**. A survey of teenagers found the 35 percent of the girls and 18 percent of the boys thought that being veggie was "in." A more health conscious population has increased its consumption of fruits and vegetables, although the eating healthy trend seems to have peaked. Only **one in ten new products makes a health claim**, compared to five in ten only a few years ago. While some restaurants are adding delicious low-fat items to their menus, many restaurant foods are very high in fat. Some foods with the most calories per serving reports the Center for Science in the Public Interest, are cheese fries with ranch dressing (3,010 calories), fried whole onion with dipping sauce

(2,130), orange beef (1,770), large movie theater popcorn (1,640), Cheesecake Factory Carrot Cake (1,560), and fettuccine Alfredo (1,480 calories).

ISSUE FOR DEBATE:
Food Health Claims Should Be Better Regulated

Food products and labeling are regulated by the U.S. Department of Agriculture and the Food and Drug Administration. Under a less stringent set of rules the Federal Trade Commission oversees **advertising of food products**. The FTC polices advertising primarily on a case-by-case basis after a problem has been discovered, rather than by issuing rules that would eliminate problems throughout an industry.

The FDA and FTC say that food products may make **health claims** even if the benefits have **not yet been conclusively proven**. The government says that it wants to "help get more nutrition information to consumers" as long as the claims are backed with "the weight of the scientific evidence." One result is consumer confusion and deception. (Dietary supplement health claims are examined in Chapter 15.)

Healthy Eating is Not Difficult[1]

We have heard that "We are what we eat." What we eat **influences our quality of life** both now and as we age. The science of nutrition is a relatively young one, and knowledge is growing rapidly regarding the effect our food choices can have on our health. Many questions remain for nutrition scientists to answer, but one link between diet and health has been proven indisputably, and that is the association between excess consumption of dietary fat and certain diseases. On a short-term basis, eating too much fat can make you **feel sluggish** and contribute to a weight gain; future effects can be more serious, such as the development of heart disease, diabetes, and some cancers.

Healthy **low-fat meals** can be purchased or prepared with **little disruption** to one's lifestyle. For example, try substituting less saturated oils, such as olive and canola for butter or shortening in cooking, and use margarine that is softer or more liquid and thus less saturated as a spread and also for cooking. Removing excess fats when preparing food is not difficult, and often results in a tastier meal. For example, allowing homemade spaghetti sauce or soup to cool overnight in the refrigerator enables much of the fat which rises to the surface to be easily removed.

Other ways to reduce fat intake include using **reduced-fat salad dressing**, enjoying a bagel instead of a glazed donut, trimming fat from beef, choosing lean meats, eating no more than six ounces of meat per day, consuming poultry without its skin, drinking skim milk, buying tuna canned in water, and snacking on fruits, popcorn without butter, and pretzels. When eating out, try grilled chicken or fish, lean roast beef, vegetables atop a mound of steamed (not fried) rice, and pasta with a tomato-based sauce.

A few **small changes in diet** can add up to big changes in health. Books with low-fat menus and recipes can be found in stores everywhere. Many reduced-fat and fat-free products are on the market; however, these products are not calorie-free and can still contribute to weight gain. Excess body weight in itself can contribute to health problems. Food is meant to be enjoyed, and the addition of a limited amount of fats to a meal can make food more palatable. The line between watching what you eat and becoming "fat phobic"—going to extremes avoiding fats—can be a fine one.

---

[1] This section was written by Lucy S. Garman, M.S., R.D.

Nutritional Labeling and Education Act

Passage of the Nutritional Labeling and Education Act (NLEA) is an attempt by government to **help consumers eat better**. Research shows that NLEA already has helped 89 percent of Americans to improve their understanding of nutrition and dietary intake. The food labeling requirements are designed both to inform and educate consumers by offering consumers detailed information in the food label so that they will take an active and responsible role in protecting their health by being better able to compare food products and plan healthy diets. NLEA requires nutrition labeling for most foods (except meat and poultry) and authorizes the use of nutrient content claims and suitable FDA-approved health claims. More than 300,000 products are affected. NLEA is jointly administered by the Food and Drug Administration and the U.S. Department of Agriculture. Highlights include:

- Nutritional labeling for almost all foods.

- Information on the amount per serving of saturated fat, cholesterol, dietary fiber, and other nutrients.

- Nutrient reference values, expressed as Percent of Daily Value, that can help consumers see how a food fits into an overall daily diet.

- Uniform definitions for terms that describe a food's nutrient content, such as "light," "low fat," "fat-free" and "high fiber."

- Claims about the relationship between a nutrient and a disease (such as fat and cancer) are regulated.

- Serving sizes are standardized in both common household and metric measures.

- Total percentage of juice in juice drinks must be declared.

- Nutrition information on many raw foods may be provided on a voluntary basis.

Exceptions to NLEA include restaurant foods and ready-to-eat foods, among others. Packages with less than 12 square inches available for labeling are also exempt, but they must provide an address or telephone number where such information may be obtained.

Food labels are headed with the title "**Nutrition Facts**." Mandatory components include: total calories, calories from fat, total fat, saturated fat, cholesterol, sodium, total carbohydrate, dietary fiber, sugars, protein, vitamin A, vitamin C, calcium, and iron. The order in which these nutrients appear reflects the priority of current dietary guidelines. Numerous other components may be listed voluntarily. However, if a nutritional claim is made about the optional components, or if a food is fortified or enriched with them, nutritional information about these components becomes mandatory. A sample label that meets the regulations is shown in Figure 14-2.

NLEA requires **Daily Values (DVs) on food labels** which are a set of dietary references that apply to fat, saturated fat, cholesterol, carbohydrate, protein, fiber, sodium and potassium. DVs serve as a basis for the percent of the Daily Value of each nutrient for a serving that the food provides. They are reference values to help consumers gain a perspective on what their overall dietary intake ought to be. The need for each nutrient varies according to age, gender and physical size. The DV labeling information is based upon a **2,000 calorie diet**.

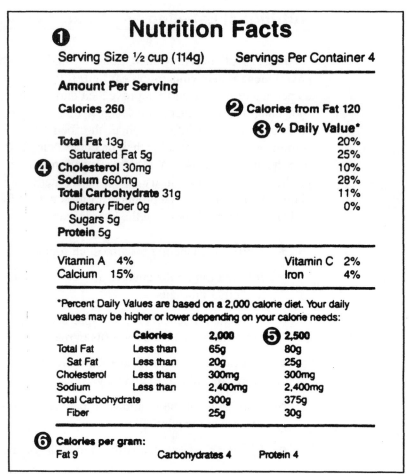

<table>
<tr><td colspan="2">

1. Shows standardized descriptions of serving sizes

2. Translates fats into calories

3. Shows how much of one day's recommended allotment of a nutrient one serving will provide based on a 2000-calorie diet

4. Lists nutrients that are most important to health

5. Shows daily values for 2000 and 2500 calorie diets.

6. Tells the number of calories per gram of fat carbohydrates, and protein

</td></tr>
</table>

FIGURE 14-2   Sample Food Label

Definitions are now available for such terms as free, low, lean, extra lean, high, good source, reduced, less, light, more, fresh, and healthy. NELA also requires that many FDA-certified color additives be labeled to help people with allergies avoid them. NELA supersedes many of the older regulatory provisions pertaining to nutritional labeling, diet-food labeling, standardized food identities, and the Fair Packaging and Labeling Act.

Research shows that about 60 percent of consumers almost always **read nutrition labels**. Consumers now can tell by glancing at a food label when there is a large amount of fat in a processed food, such as in breakfast cereals. Quaker 100% Natural Cereal, for example, has 6 grams of fat, meaning that 54 percent of the total 140 calories in a serving (before milk is added) come from fat. The FDA says consumers can be guided by the "5-20" rule: a product that has 5 percent or less of the "daily value" of fat can be considered a "low-fat food," while any single food that supplies 20 percent or more of one's daily value should be considered "high fat." The upper limit for most men probably should be **65 grams of fat per day, although 50 would be a better number**; the maximum for women should be lower.

Dietary Reference Intakes (DRIs) are new terms that offer a more complete picture of nutritional health needs that show what most people need to help them maintain health via **adequate intake (AI)** and what constitutes levels of nutrients that are too high via the tolerable **upper intake level (UL)**.

USDA's Food Guide Pyramid

The U.S. Department of Agriculture has published a Food Guide Pyramid to support its latest dietary guidelines. This is an effort to help Americans **make trade-offs** in their food choices and develop healthier diets. As illustrated in Figure 14-2, the pyramid shows what and how much people should eat from each food group. The emphasis is on consuming different proportions of food categories rather than specific foods themselves. It is one's entire diet that is important. Variety, moderation, and proportions are keys to healthy eating. You may use a government web site (www.usda.gov/cnpp) to enter what you ate during the day and receive a score based on how well your diet matches up with the government's dietary guidelines.

The USDA's Food Guide Pyramid is not without **its critics**. Some have pointed out the USDA's close association with the meat and dairy industries, and the Pyramid's emphasis on those foods, as well as the Pyramid's failure to distinguish among refined, less healthy carbohydrates, and those containing whole grains. Dr. Walter Willett, professor of epidemiology at Harvard School of Public Health and professor of medicine at Harvard Medical School has created his own pyramid. It emphasizes whole grains, vegetables and plant oils (corn, safflower, olive, canola), with fair amounts of fruits, nuts, and legumes, but only 0-2 servings of fish, poultry or eggs per day. Only 1-2 dairy servings are recommended per day or a calcium supplement, and very limited amounts of red meat, refined starches, and animal fats. His pyramid also recommends drinking alcohol in moderation, unless you have a reason not to.

Other food guide pyramids have been recommended. Two popular ones are the Mediterranean Food Guide Pyramid and a Vegetarian Food Guide Pyramid (see www-org.usm.edu/~nfs167/chap1.htm for comparisons). Each person is unique, and should adapt health recommendations to his or her individual habits and cultural influences. One size does not necessarily fit all.

Agencies and Laws that Protect Food Consumers

Since 1906 when the first federal food and drug law was enacted, the government has had an **important role** in helping consumers. Many laws and regulations protect consumers. Food safety and inspection are divided among a dozen agencies and departments, including the Department of Agriculture, the Food and Drug Administration, the Environmental Protection Agency.

U.S. Department of Agriculture

The U.S. Department of Agriculture enforces laws and regulations concerning **meat and poultry products**, including the Meat Inspection Act (1906), Wholesome Meat Act (1967), Wholesome Poultry Products Act (1968), and Nutrition Labeling and Education Act (1990). The Meat Inspection Act prohibits the sale of any processed meat product if the labeling is false or misleading, or if any inferiority has been concealed in any manner. The USDA's **Food Safety and Inspection Service (FSIS)** inspects meat and poultry for sanitation, accurate labeling, and correct use of chemical additives. Products that pass inspection are given appropriate **USDA inspection marks**. Those which fail are either reprocessed to

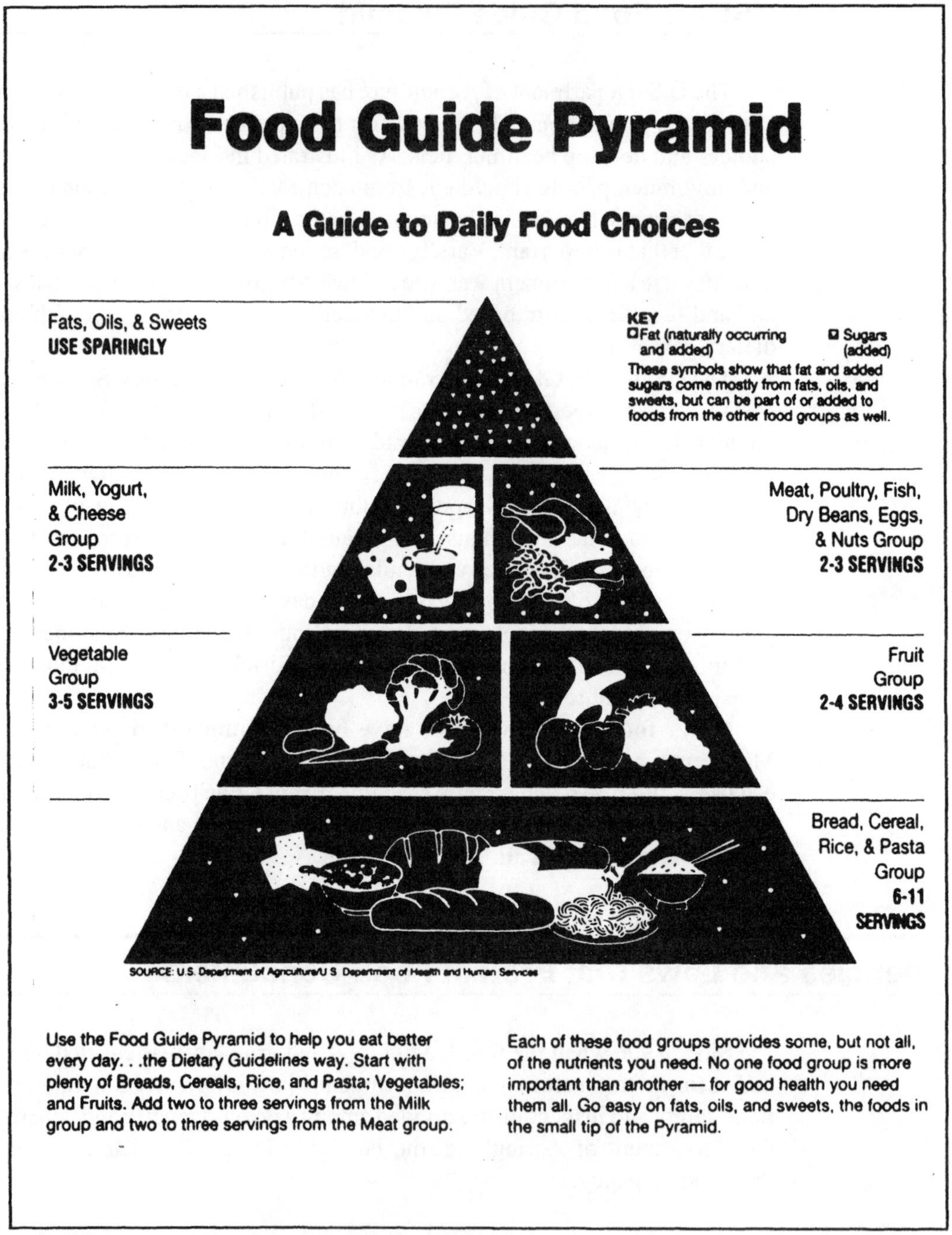

Food Guide Pyramid

A Guide to Daily Food Choices

Fats, Oils, & Sweets
USE SPARINGLY

KEY
☐ Fat (naturally occurring   ☐ Sugars
and added)   (added)
These symbols show that fat and added sugars come mostly from fats, oils, and sweets, but can be part of or added to foods from the other food groups as well.

Milk, Yogurt,
& Cheese
Group
2-3 SERVINGS

Meat, Poultry, Fish,
Dry Beans, Eggs,
& Nuts Group
2-3 SERVINGS

Vegetable
Group
3-5 SERVINGS

Fruit
Group
2-4 SERVINGS

Bread, Cereal,
Rice, & Pasta
Group
**6-11
SERVINGS**

SOURCE: U.S. Department of Agriculture/U S Department of Health and Human Services

Use the Food Guide Pyramid to help you eat better every day. . .the Dietary Guidelines way. Start with plenty of Breads, Cereals, Rice, and Pasta; Vegetables; and Fruits. Add two to three servings from the Milk group and two to three servings from the Meat group.

Each of these food groups provides some, but not all, of the nutrients you need. No one food group is more important than another — for good health you need them all. Go easy on fats, oils, and sweets, the foods in the small tip of the Pyramid.

FIGURE 14-3   USDA Food Guide Pyramid

satisfy inspection standards or are destroyed. In addition, the USDA monitors the nation's 6,400 slaughterhouses and processing plants for sanitation, contamination, disease-causing bacteria and signs of pesticide residues as well as tests for microbes at the end of the food processing. Curiously, neither the USDA nor the Food and Drug Administration has the authority to order a **recall** and they rely on voluntary cooperation from industry.

The USDA has a new system of **bacteria identification** in meat, poultry and seafood products known as **Hazard Analysis and Critical Control Points (HACCP)**. A critical control point could be a steam pasteurization unit that treats cattle carcasses in a slaughterhouse or a set of temperature controls in a food processing plant. HACCP has greatly reduced food poisoning in the United States. To reduce **food-borne illnesses**, USDA requires that **"safe-handling instructions"** for consumers be attached to all raw meat products.

The USDA has a **voluntary grading service** that provides buyers with consistent standards of quality. The department has established grade standards for meat, poultry, dairy products, eggs, fruit, and vegetables. Grading is voluntary and not related to safety.

The USDA has an inherent **conflict of interest** because it is responsible for increasing the demand for beef, pork, eggs, and dairy products (that may contain high amounts of fat) while also being responsible for informing and educating the public about proper nutrition. In one year the USDA spent $21 million for nutrition education and $60 million promoting agricultural products through the USDA's government-sponsored trade associations: Cattlemen's Beef Promotion and Research Board, National Pork Board, Egg Board, and the National Dairy Promotion and Research Board.

CONSUMER UPDATE:
How Good is Food Safety in the United States?

Food purchased in the United States is the **safest in the world**. Through the years, the government has allowed the meat industry to become more self-regulating, with the result that the number of **food-borne illnesses** has continued to decrease even though the number of government inspections has declined. Critics, however, warn that inspection programs are still inadequate in detecting bacterial contamination.

Contamination of the food supply can occur at any stage of production, distribution and preparation. The Center for Disease Control and Prevention estimates that more than 80 million food-borne illnesses occur every year, primarily from **salmonella, listeria, campylobacter, E. coli**, and other organisms in foods like hotdogs, lunch meats, hamburger patties, apple juice, fresh produce and fruit contaminated by these invisible but deadly microbes. These result in fever, vomiting, and diarrhea. Every day about 200,000 consumers are sickened by food-borne disease, 900 are hospitalized, and 14 die. That's over **5,000 deaths annually**. Infection with the virulent E. coli bacteria (20,000 sickened annually) may mean death (800 annually), so it is wise (especially for meat eaters) to pay attention to the advice to properly handle and adequately cook food. Proper cooking kills most bacteria that cause food-borne illness.

Concerns also exist about **"mad cow" disease**, one type of transmissible spongiform encephalopathy disease once found in the British, European and Canadian beef industries, that is caused from turning unsalable remains of animals, including ground spinal cords and bones, into high-protein mash used in animal feed. It causes Creutzfeldt-Jakob Disease that results in deterioration of the nervous system. A USDA study found two out of 300 samples had evidence of spinal cord in meat packing plants that use a technology called **advanced meat recovery (AMR)**, a system that debones meat using hydraulic pressure. The FDA has banned feeding animals such ruminants and prohibits beef imports from certain countries.

Food and Drug Administration

The FDA is responsible for ensuring the **purity and safety** of the nation's food supply (other than meat and poultry products that are regulated by the USDA). They also oversee the safety of drugs, cosmetics, medical devices, and the truthful, informative labeling of such products so that they are safe for human use. The FDA regulates veterinary products, such as pet food, cattle feed, animal drugs, and radiological devices, such as microwaves, tanning booths, and television sets. It shares regulation of pesticides with the **Environmental Protection Agency (EPA)**. The FDA has broad control over the safety, purity, and wholesomeness of processed foods. Also, the FDA regulates prescription and over-the-counter drugs.

When the FDA discovers unsanitary, unsafe, adulterated, or mislabeled products that cause deaths, injuries, or adverse reactions, they **conduct an investigation**. The FDA says that a food is **adulterated** if it bears or contains any poisonous or deleterious substance which may render it injurious to health. A product is **misbranded** if its labeling is false or misleading, if it is offered for sale under the name of another food, and/or if it is an imitation of another food, unless its label bears the word imitation.

ISSUE FOR DEBATE:
Genetically Engineered Food Products Should be Labeled as Such

Biotechnology is an important part of the solution to world poverty. It can produce hardier, disease-resistant, pest-resistant, and vitamin-fortified crops; all in a carefully regulated environment. Farmers who use **genetically modified (GM)** products reduce reliance on costly pesticides. Research is underway that will deliver medicines and edible vaccines through common foods. A few **cloned cows**, made from exact genetic copies, are producing milk and the offspring of cloned cows and pigs could be in the supermarket soon. **Transgenics** are animals, plants or even bacteria that have had genes from something else inserted into their genetic makeup to speed growth, confer disease resistance, produce drugs, or do other useful things for humans. A transgenic salmon is expected to be approved for sale.

Political developments in the area of biotechnology are causing governments to think more about **genetically engineered foods** such as potatoes that ward off pests coming to the marketplace. The FDA approved a genetically engineered hormone that increases milk productivity of cows (**BGH**, also known as **recombinant bovine somatotropin ([rBST]**). The milk is not required to be labeled any differently than traditional milk.

The FDA position is that food products created through DNA technology will raise **no new or unique safety issues**. The FDA does **not require pre-market approval** of such products or require that foods enhanced by genetic engineering be labeled as such. New nutrients and ingredients are treated the same as a sweetener or preservative. Moreover, the federal government **does not presume a lack of safety** for biotechnology food products.

U.S. manufacturers of genetically enhanced food say that **labeling will put them out of business**, which is what happened to one company in Great Britain. They argue that consumers are not informed enough to understand that such labeled products are not harmful and, in many ways, are superior. Most consumers would be likely to avoid products labeled "Genetically Enhanced" and prefer products labeled "Not Genetically Enhanced."

Much of the corn (found in juice, soda, frozen pizza and spaghetti sauce), soy (in tuna, crackers, cookies and salad dressing), and cotton (in nut and soup) grown in the U.S. is genetically engineered. Therefore, ingesting food made from genetically engineered crops is **inevitable** for most Americans. These modified foods produce larger harvests and are less vulnerable to disease and drought.

Genetically modified crops are creating **trade confrontations** between the U.S. and the European Union (see chapter 8) because the EU banned importing and growing genetically altered crops. Most European consumers choose to not consume genetically engineered foods, in part, because they shop in very small food stores and at open-air produce markets and those sellers refuse to stock foods that don't sell. Many Europeans call genetically engineered food "**Frankenfoods**," although their anxieties about personal health risks are largely bogus. The White House calls these European policies "unscientific, Luddite and immoral." For an informed view of all sides of these issues, see the Pew Initiative for Food and Biotechnology (www.pewagbiotech.org/).

After investigating, the FDA can use one of **four authorities**: (1) suggest a **voluntary recall**, which is a firm's removal or correction of a marketed product when that product violates the laws enforced by the FDA; (2) **seizure**, which is forcibly taking into custody goods deemed in violation of a law (and such goods are usually destroyed); (3) an **injunction**, which is a legal order of the court enjoining, restraining, or prohibiting a party from a specific course of action to prevent an unfair business practice, such as stopping offending articles from being sold in interstate commerce; and (4) **prosecution**, which is charging the company and its officials with violations of applicable civil and criminal statutes. Consumers often ignore information on government warnings and recalls, and they get sick or die as a result.

Most illnesses that occur from seafood are **preventable**. The FDA currently inspects the nation's 3,800 seafood processors about once **every four years**. The Food and Drug Administration requires seafood processors to implement a quality control program following the HACCP guidelines. HACCP uses microbiology detection techniques combined with production standards to identify, monitor, and avoid contamination. Standards exist on such things as the maximum time fish may remain on a loading dock, the temperature of the room where filleting occurs, and the adequacy of pasteurization processes. Processors and importers are required to keep detailed records on every step of handling seafood.

Food Additives

A **food additive** is a substance **directly or indirectly** added in small amounts to foods during processing, production, or packaging to improve, strengthen, or otherwise alter it. Food additives are used to maintain or improve nutritional quality, to preserve freshness, to reduce food waste, to enhance the attractiveness of foods, and to provide essential aids in processing and preparing foods. Some additives are vitamins and minerals that perhaps are needed in a person's diet, or they may be added back to a food because they have been removed in processing. Other substances are added to make the food look or taste better. For example, Simplesse is an additive used as a fat substitute in such products as ice cream and salad dressing. Olean (the brand name for Olestra), another fake fat, is controversial because of its possible side effects of "abdominal cramping and loose stools" as well as a tendency to inhibit the absorption of some vitamins and nutrients.

Antibiotics are used to treat disease outbreaks in pigs, poultry and cattle, and in low doses to make the animals grow faster. This usage contributes to people becoming **resistant to antibiotics** through the consumption of treated animals. Additives, including pesticides, are widely used because society is willing to accept their risks in return for a high quality, inexpensive, and physically attractive food supply. Food additives found to be unsafe can be banned by the FDA in various foods, drugs, and cosmetics, by the USDA in meat and poultry, or, in some cases, by the Environmental Protection Agency (EPA).

Food irradiation (or **radiation ionization**) uses gamma or electron ionizing radiation to destroy bacteria and other pathogens that can cause spoilage and disease. It is the **only known method** to eliminate deadly E. coli bacteria in raw meat, and it can significantly reduce levels of other pathogens, including listeria, salmonella, and campylobacter. The process sterilizes such foods as herbs, cereal grains, fresh fruits, and vegetables, and extends their shelf life. Chicken, turkey, game hens, beef, animal feed, and pet treats have been approved for irradiation by the USDA and 30 other countries. Consumer organizations support food irradiation. Labels on **irradiated products** must have the international symbol of irradiation, known as a **radura**, on the label along with a statement that they were treated. Congress authorized irradiation of ground beef served in schools, although disclosure appears on the label in tiny print that euphemistically notes the food was "pasteurized."

There have been **no studies showing any radiation effects** whatsoever; food does not become "radioactive" because the effects are not long-lasting. Irradiation used by processors provides consumers an added measure of protection. A poll by CBS found that three-quarters of the public would not eat irradiated food; thus a lot of people are ignorant about the facts.

Almost all of these same people probably have and use a microwave at home which does not cause food to become "radioactive."

Intentional and Incidental Additives

Controversy about the hundreds of food additives being used in processed foods led to the passage of the **Food Additives Amendment** in 1958. The law requires **proof of the safety** of any new chemical additive before it can be marketed. A core principle of the law is the requirement that additives be evaluated on the basis of their safety without any consideration of their benefits.

There are nearly **3,000 food additives** that are classified as **intentional additives**; that is, those substances which are purposefully and directly put into foods. Over 90 percent of intentional food additives are common flavoring substances or herbs and spices, such as salt, pepper, sugar, corn syrup, and citric acid. **Incidental** (or **unavoidable**) **additives** are substances that become part of the food product unintentionally and indirectly. Two potent carcinogens that are incidental additives are mercury in fish and aflatoxin in some corn and peanuts. Pesticide residues may remain on farm products and substances may migrate from the packing material into a food.

Contaminants classified as **unavoidable** include such things as hairs, feathers, worms, rodent excreta, urine, rat hairs, bacteria, insect larva, insect fragments, decomposed matter, molds, decomposition, dirt, sand, rocks, and sticks and stones. For example, the maximum filth allowance for chocolate is "150 insect fragments and 4 rat hairs per half pound." Canned and frozen blackberries and raspberries are allowed "an average of 10 insects and insect larvae per pound." Peanut butter allowances permit an "average of 225 insect fragments or 9 rodent hairs per pound."

Incidental additives are regulated by FDA through **action levels** (or **threshold levels**), which are government-set standards for the maximum unavoidable contamination of perhaps 10,000 additives. Action levels are informal standards not issued through regulations, and they have no binding effect. They are merely guidelines. The occurrence of incidental additives should be lowered by good harvesting, storing, and manufacturing practices.

FDA regulations under the 1960 Color Additive Amendments **set limits** on the amounts of **color** that can be used in foods, drugs, and cosmetics. No color can be used to conceal any inferiority of a product, since this might deceive consumers. A number of food colors were banned under this law. Today, Red No. 3 and Yellow No. 5 remain controversial food colors that are still undergoing testing.

The GRAS List

The Food Additives Amendment also established the **generally recognized as safe (GRAS)** list. This is a government-approved list of more than **600 substances** that have been used for years and are considered safe by experts in the field as long as they are used as they were originally intended and with good manufacturing practices. Products on the GRAS list do not meet the FDA's clearance standards for safety as required for all legally defined food additives, but they are **still considered safe for use in foods**. The substances on the GRAS list range from salt and sugar to monosodium glutamate (MSG). This grand fathering clause allows provisional listing of established substances and empowers the head of the FDA to extend the listing.

Sulfites in Foods

Sulfites are a group of sulfur-based chemicals on the GRAS list that have been used for years as food additives. A **sulfite** is a **preservative** or antioxidant that reduces food spoilage by bacteria. It also reduces food discoloration during preparation, storage, or distribution. With sulfites, such food products as potatoes, mushrooms, and shrimp appear whiter and lettuce will not wilt or brown as quickly. This valuable additive also causes severe health risks such as hives and shock in certain individuals, including about 100,000 asthmatics and others with allergies. Sulfites have been implicated in at least a dozen deaths. The FDA has banned sulfites from raw fruits and vegetables, except potatoes.

FDA rules require that if a packaged food has more than 10 parts per million of sulfites, it **must identify the sulfite on the label**. Examples include sulfur dioxide, sodium sulfite, sodium and potassium bisulfite, and sodium and potassium metabisulfite. The regulation requires that prescription drugs containing sulfites provide a warning statement to that effect. Alcoholic beverages containing sulfites, mainly wines, must indicate such on the label.

The Food and Drug Administration requires that **restaurant menu items** for which **health claims** are made must meet the same standards as labeled packaged foods on grocery store items. "Low fat," for example, must contain 3 or fewer grams of fat per serving. Comprehensive testing is not required; rather standardized recipes must be followed that are designed to meet the health claim.

Pesticides in Foods

The Miller Pesticide Chemicals Amendment of 1954 provides the legal authority to establish specific **maximum amounts of pesticide residues** that are allowed to remain on agricultural products. A **pesticide** is a chemical used to kill pests, especially insects and weeds, to prevent damage and destruction of agricultural crops. Since being created in 1972, the Environmental Protection Agency (EPA) has had primary authority over pesticides. The EPA and the USDA have jointly established enforceable residue **tolerance levels** based on the toxicity of each pesticide (even though not all have been tested by the EPA).

Tolerance levels are the maximum legally allowed pesticide residues on foods for more than 600 chemicals, including **470 pesticides** used on 10,000 foods. Of these, 73 are known carcinogens that cause tumors in laboratory animals that were fed large dosages for extended periods of time. Many more pesticides have not been thoroughly tested for carcinogens or other chronic health effects. A National Academy of Science report concluded that infants and children are particularly susceptible to health risks from pesticide residues.

The EPA is generally bound by law to **balance the health costs of pesticides against their benefits** to the food supply. The USDA tests pesticides itself or delegates the job to other nationally recognized groups and decides on a safe level for human consumption. Both the USDA and FDA monitor inspections of harvested crops by regularly examining such things as samples of soil, silt, runoff water, fish, and plant life. This law is one reason why the chemical **DDT**, which causes reproductive problems, is no longer allowed to be used to spray agricultural products. DDT is still used in 25 developing countries primarily as a means of controlling malaria where it is sprayed in small amounts inside homes to repel mosquitoes that carry the parasite which causes malaria which kills 2.5 million people annually.

The EPA is responsible for setting **pesticide residue limits** on raw foods. The standard for public health is to ensure an adequate, wholesome, and economical food supply. Once a carcinogenic substance is found, the EPA sets the legal residue level 100 times lower to allow an extra margin of safety.

Sweeteners

The regulations on sweeteners provide a **safety standard** that require a "reasonable certainty of **no harm**." This means that the consumption of a treated food product will not result in a greater than 1-in-a million chance of getting cancer from a lifetime of exposure. Thus, the marginal benefits of use are expected to outweigh the costs. Saccharin, long used in Sweet & Low, was recently removed from the government's official list of carcinogens. The FDA considers the sweeteners aspartame (Nutrasweet and Equal), neotame, sunett, and sucralose as considered safe for most people.

Food Preservatives

Food preservatives are a number of natural substances and chemical additives that tend to preserve or are capable of preserving food products. For example, sodium nitrite inhibits the growth of poisonous botulism bacteria in bacon, hot dogs, and luncheon meat, and it also adds a specific flavor to these foods. When combined with secondary amines in the body through normal digestive processes, the nitrites produce something called **nitrosamines**, that are carcinogenic. The FDA has insisted on **lowering the amount of nitrites** allowed in food products even though nitrites are not carcinogenic by themselves and it is continuing to run tests on nitrites.

Organic Food Labeling

A single set of national standards for labeling food **organic** became law in 2002. There are three levels of organic labeling. For a product to be labeled **"100% organic"** it must contain only organic ingredients. In addition, the product must be certified by the U.S. Department of Agriculture that it is free of synthetic pesticides and fertilizers, antibiotics, genetic engineering, irradiation, sewage sludge or artificial ingredients. Products labeled "organic" must contain ingredients that are at least 95 percent organic. Those labeled **"Made with organic ingredients"** must be at least 70 percent organic. The USDA points out that it makes "no claim that organically produced food is safer or more nutritious than conventionally produced food."

Research Conducted on Animals

Regulatory decisions are based on **human tests** when such data exist, but often such information is not available. Evidence on carcinogens often comes from animal testing that is widely used and accepted by the scientific community. Small animals, such as rats and mice are commonly used to find out if certain substances cause cancer. Research has determined that all substances found to **cause cancer in animals in laboratory experiments also cause cancer in humans**. Thus, **animal research** is critical to assessing the safety of many products. However, animal testing also is not without controversy.

In laboratory experiments, **large doses** of substances must be used because evidence shows conclusively that as the size of the dose increases, so does the number of animals that get cancer. If a testing dose is too high, research animals may die of poisoning, but not cancer.

Since humans metabolize substances more slowly than these animals, some substances **persist much longer** in the human body. No level of small exposure to a carcinogen, such as asbestos, has ever been shown to be safe. In addition, since humans are exposed to a number of different carcinogens, exposure to one may add to the risk associated with others. The overwhelming **consensus is that science must rely** on animal tests to make prudent public-policy decisions even though science does not yet have definitive answers to the health questions that environmentalists and consumer advocates are asking.

Research and a Risk-Free Society

The government continues to make efforts to **reduce risks** to humans, but a risk-free society is impossible to obtain. Besides, such a society, if possible, would be intolerably expensive. Accordingly, government is forced by various laws and regulations to weigh dangers to health against economic costs.

R. David Pittle, Technical Director for *Consumer Reports*, reminds us that **most substances do not cause cancer, no matter how high the dose**. Of the many thousands of substances in use such as food additives, pesticides, and chemicals, only a relatively small number have been shown to cause cancer. However, when millions of consumers are exposed to small doses of carcinogenic chemicals, the risk of an increase in cancer cases rises sharply because of the **cumulative effects**. Human cancer may not manifest itself for many years after the exposure. Thus, it is prudent and ethical for the government to continue to take appropriate actions to protect the public from environmental pollutants, pesticides, and food additives.

However, says University of Wisconsin's (Madison) professor Robin Douthitt, simply providing information about risks such as pesticides and biotechnology products "is not the solution to this complex problem. As much attention must be paid to consumer perception of risk as to scientific variables. Ignoring consumer concerns, or worse yet, labeling them as irrational and discounting them, is guaranteed to create hostility and will **ultimately stand in the way of successful product acceptance**." It is in the interests of both sellers and consumers to have strong regulatory powers to ensure consumer confidence in delegating risk assessment to the regulators.

Anti-Competitive Practices in the Food Industry

Like some other segments of the American economy, the food industry does not offer consumers the benefits of a fully competitive marketplace. Examples follow.

Agreements that Squeeze Out Competitors

In the U.S. the soft-drink business is a $50 billion a year industry. Consumers drink about **50 gallons of soda** per person each year. Coca-Cola Company and Pepsico have taken steps to increase their profits and reduce choices for American consumers through special **calendar marketing agreements**. These are contracts where, in exchange for payments or rebates from the local soft-drink bottling companies, the food supermarkets agree to feature only one brand of soft drink for **certain weeks during the year**. These agreements result in extensive advertising, the best in-store displays, and often the lowest prices. Since a soft-drink bottler can profit with extremely low prices only when a considerable sales volume exists, with calendar marketing agreements Coke and Pepsi can lower prices while off-brands cannot. Coke bottlers get an agreement for 26 weeks and Pepsi bottlers get an agreement for the other 26 weeks. The result is that supermarkets then cannot display or advertise other brands for 52 weeks, and that's a whole year. Sometimes Coke and Pepsi skip a few weeks during January and February, when soft-drink sales are lower.

Also, **allocation** (or **slotting**) **agreements** exist where supermarkets and food manufacturers sign contracts to allocate shelf space in exchange for fees ranging from a few hundred dollars to $25,000 per item per store per year. Agreements sometimes call for **premium placement** on eye-level or end-of-aisle displays. Fees are common for beverages, snacks, and frozen foods. Small manufacturers cannot afford "pay to stay" fees. McCormick & Company settled charges with the FTC that they illegally gave favorable prices to supermarkets that provided better allocation spaces. Wal-Mart, once again a top competitor, says is does not charge such fees. The question remains "When will state attorneys general and the Federal Trade Commission put a stop to these decades old marketing practices that raise prices and **limit consumer access** to innovative products?"

Agricultural Marketing Orders

The federal government's system of **agricultural marketing orders** permits grower cartels to **restrict supplies to keep profits high** for the sellers. Agricultural cooperatives operate under the authority of the Federal Cooperative Act of 1923. That makes them exempt from antitrust laws, and they have a great deal of political power because the marketing order program permits sellers to legally conspire to fix prices and control supplies. For example, rules prevent the sale of undersized fruit on the open market, even though the fruit might taste great and could be readily consumed by most people or distributed to low-income consumers. Also, 90 percent of **cheese prices are fixed** by the National Cheese Exchange, a group that includes Kraft, Borden, General Foods and Land O'Lakes. And half to three-quarters of all milk prices are fixed.

The Federal Trade Commission is prohibited by law from **ever studying agricultural marketing orders**. The Capper-Volstead Act restricts the FTC's efforts to bring antitrust challenges in the farming industry. The special interests are afraid of what might be discovered. Such government-controlled practices are not designed to provide consumers with low prices, yet the status quo has continued for more than 60 years.

Economic Concentration in the Meat Packing Industry

Four companies control about three-fourths of the meat packing industry (IBP, ConAgra, Cargill, and National Beef). Critics complain that the big companies can drive the little ones out of business. This is accomplished by big companies (especially those that operate non-union plants) paying farmers too much for cattle and purposely selling meat too cheaply. **Predatory pricing** eliminates competition. In the short run, it is good for consumers to have lower prices. In the long run, as competition disappears, consumers will have to pay whatever prices the producers determine.

Questionable and Confusing Food Selling Practices

There are a number of selling practices that are questionable and confusing. As a result, many **consumers waste money**. Efforts at self-regulation have not resolved these situations.

Vendor Hush-Hush Payments. Under-the-table payments from food (and other) product suppliers to grocers and retailers are common. These hush-hush transactions, called **vendor payments**, are in exchange for promoting certain products or selling a set quantity of a product. While the payments are legal, two problems occur. First, consumers are in the dark about the seller's motives. They have no reason to believe that a retailer receives a kickback for promoting one product over another. Second, the legal payments are absolutely enormous and they rarely are disclosed in the grocers' or retailers' financial statements. Albertsons, Kroger and Safeway receive more money from vendor payments annually than they get from selling groceries. Best Buy got three-quarters of a billion dollars from vender payments last year.

Privacy at the Checkout Counter. Billions of pieces of information are collected by the supermarket industry on consumer purchases. Now when you charge your groceries with a bank credit card or with an automated teller machine (ATM) card, you can wonder if the stores are combining your grocery purchasing information with personal information about you (including your credit file) and selling it. The answer is probably "Yes." Privacy in the supermarket is given up for consumers who shop in stores that use a **checkout coupon system**. This is a small device that is part of the cash register system at the checkout counter that prints instant coupons to stimulate future purchases based upon the food items just purchased. When you purchase hamburgers, for example, it might print out a coupon for catsup. When you buy snack chips, it might give you a coupon for bean dip. Some systems give automatic discounts without clipping coupons. A grassroots anti-card group Consumers Against Supermarket Privacy Invasion and Numbering has a website (www.nocards.org) focused on this issue. **Frequent-buyer loyalty programs** (discussed in Chapter 12) collect similar amounts of personal information on shoppers. (See Chapters 3 and 5 for more on privacy, including laws.)

Price Manipulation. Some stores try to draw consumers in by advertising specials while **raising the prices for other items**. In some stores, selected prices are raised between 5 and 7 p.m. (to catch workers shopping on the way home) and then lowered. Although reliable research evidence is not available, critics allege that some stores raise their prices when customers' welfare checks are scheduled to arrive.

Scanning Errors. A study of 294 retailers by federal and state governments reports that consumers were charged errors 5 percent of the time. About half the 17,000 purchases were overcharges and half were undercharges.

Cents-Off Food Coupons. More than three-quarters of the shoppers redeem coupons for an average of 17 coupons per month. Cents-off food coupons are marketing devices designed to encourage purchase of specific products by having a redeemable value printed on the face of the coupon, averaging 50 cents. While coupon redeemers save money, critics charge that coupons are wasteful, expensive, and time consuming. Each year more than 300 billion coupons are printed (1,200 for every man, woman and child in the United States), **redeemed (only 2 percent)**, stored by retailers who charge sellers eight cents each, and processed.

Games, Sweepstakes, and Trading Stamps. It has been calculated that games, sweepstakes, and trading stamps cost the consumer from ½ cent to 3 ½ cents for every dollar spent at the grocery store. When they work such promotional devices are good marketing techniques for the stores. If sales increase proportionately, costs are covered by the increased profits. All shoppers pay for ineffective promotions by paying higher prices.

Packaging Costs. The cost of packaging adds greatly to grocery prices, amounting to about 8.5 percent of the food dollar. Manufacturers use color and interesting packaging to catch the eye of the grocery shopper.

Food Products that Shrink. Food manufacturers are constantly reducing their product's content, weight or volume without lowering prices. The result of the trickery is that consumers pay more for an equal or lesser amount of the product. Marketers know how to slice the bologna thin and shrink the size of a container of yogurt. Products that have been downsized include Cheer detergent, Starbucks and Brim coffees, Dreyer's and Edy's Grand ice cream, Dannon yogurt, StarKist tuna fish, Knorr soup, Lipton instant tea, and Kellogg NutriGrain.

Shortweighting and **slackfilling**. **Shortweighting** is giving less weight of a product contained in a package than the label indicates. This is against the law. **Slackfilling** is leaving nonfunctional empty space in a container to give the impression that there is a lot more of the product in a package than is really there. This happens.

Absence of Prices on Food Products. On more than 95 percent of all food products there is a **bar code** or **universal product code (UPC)** that is a grid of lines, bars, and numbers representing a 10-digit number. The UPC is used in the company's perpetual stock-control program system. This speeds up checkout procedures and reduces pricing errors, but many consumers want prices marked on each product. Some consumers have difficulty remembering prices of goods they purchase week to week, and they also are challenged when trying to compare prices within the store. For example, once you have bought a can of corn for 79 cents, will you remember the price when you get to the freezer section to compare it with the price of frozen corn? Or compare in the fresh produce section? Bar codes are soon to be replaced by a system of **smart cards embedded** into every product.

Absence of Unit Prices. **Unit pricing** is the cost calculation for a small unit of measure, such as an ounce or a pound, used to compare the costs of a product in different-sized packages. It is provided to consumers by most grocery stores as information on a shelf-tag along with the price of the product. For example, a six-pack of 12-ounce Coke priced at $1.79 may have a unit price of 2.49 cents per ounce, while a 2-quart bottle of Coke priced at $1.19 may have a unit price of 1.86 cents per ounce. With today's computers, there is **no excuse** for grocery stores not making unit-price information available to help consumers make price comparisons. Be alert to the fact that unit prices are not always lowest for products with the greatest quantity. Frequently the medium-sized grocery items have the lowest unit prices. Some states and cities legally require that unit prices be posted in grocery stores.

Absence of Open Dating. **Open dating** is a system of ensuring quality and freshness by placing a date on perishable products that indicates either when the product should be sold or when it should be consumed. Alternative dates include the **pack date** (when the product was manufactured or packaged, but this information usually is of little value to consumers), the **pull date** (the last day the product should be sold by the store), the **expiration date** (the last date the product should be used by the consumer), and the **quality assurance date** (the last date when the product will be at its peak of condition, such as "for maximum enjoyment, use before March 15, 2003"). Some food manufacturers have new color-changing tags that turn from gray to black as food freshness diminishes. Studies show that sellers save money when open dating is used because losses are lower. Some states and cities require grocery stores to use open dating of perishable products, such as milk, cheese, and eggs. Consumers buy lots of old merchandise thinking it to be fresh.

Illusionary Net Weights. Canned and frozen foods present special labeling problems for consumers. The **net weight** is the requirement that food products indicate the weight of the contents, exclusive of the container. The net weight typically represents a combination of both the food and the packaging liquids or syrups. This makes it impossible to compare, for example, many canned food products with frozen-food counterparts. Mushrooms and olives are exceptions, since they must list their drained weight on the labels, which is the weight of the food after the liquid is drained. Drained weights represent the best weight comparison method for consumers, yet most canned and frozen foods are not labeled in this informative manner. And food processors are now required to disclose the water content of raw meat and poultry products as well as explain in the labeling why it is in there.

Food Products that Deceive. Procter & Gamble has been accused of trying to deceive the public that its *Sunny Delight* drink is mostly fruit juice. P&G advertises it as a "real fruit beverage" and it is sold in the refrigerated section next to real orange juice. A consumer group survey found that after viewing a label, 65 percent of kids and half of parents thought that Sunny Delight was made mostly from real fruit juice. The fact is that it contains only 5 percent juice!

Illusionary Grade Labeling. The federal government has a series of grade labels that give the impression of ensuring some level of quality, but this is not the case. Labeling of beef, eggs, poultry, fruits, and the like is voluntary, and more than half the time the grades are not put on the final food products. Sometimes the grades are illusionary as well. For example, less than one-half of the nation's beef is graded according to the USDA's voluntary system of grading for eating-quality or palatability. In addition the USDA grades emphasize maturity and marbling. These are the flecks of fat within lean muscle that contribute to juiciness and tenderness of meat.

Confusing Grade Labels. Grade labels are helpful to wholesalers, processors, and retailers because the system helps these buyers get the products they want. Consumers like the idea of product grading, but the current approach leaves much to be desired. Consider, for example, the USDA grades for fruits and vegetables, since they are probably the easiest to comprehend. The top grade for apples in all states but Washington is "U.S. Extra Fancy" and the second grade is "U.S. Fancy." In Washington state, it is "Washington Extra Fancy" and then "Washington Fancy." "U.S. Fancy" is the top grade for corn, grapefruit, and oranges, but it is "U.S. Extra No. 1" for lima beans and "U.S. No. 1" for turnips. Why can't government decide on a simple scale such as "A, B, C, D, F" or "1, 2, 3, 4, 5," assuming that consumers would understand that "A" and "1" would be the highest? Also, why can't such systems be mandatory instead of voluntary for fruits and vegetables, beef, poultry, eggs, cheeses, canned fruits, and other food products?

Review and Summary of Key Terms and Concepts

1. Summarize the **obesity** problem in the United States.

2. Characterize the **eating habits** of Americans.

3. Why should people learn about **food** and **health**?

4. Why do children eat so many **junk foods**?

5. Summarize the relationship between **disease** and **diet**.

6. Why do some poor Americans **pay more** for food than middle-income people?

7. Describe the importance of **low-fat eating** to good health.

8. Cite three examples of how it is not difficult to eat **healthy**.

9. List two things that the **Nutrition Labeling and Education Act** aims to accomplish.

10. What are **daily values (DVs)**?

11. Summarize the essence of the USDA's **Food Guide Pyramid**.

12. Briefly explain the **HACCP system.**

13. Comment on the **safety** of the U.S. food supply.

14. Distinguish between a **voluntary recall** and **seizure**.

15. Define the following terms: **adulterated** and **misbranded.**

16. Summarize the argument about labeling **genetically engineered foods**.

17. Define **food additive**, and give an example of an **intentional** additive and an **incidental** additive.

18. What is the **generally recognized as safe list (GRAS)**?

19. What are **tolerance levels** of pesticides?.

20. Summarize the difficulty of **assessing risks** in society.

21. Distinguish between **calendar marketing agreements** and **agricultural marketing orders**.

22. Choose two **questionable and confusing food selling practices** that negatively affect consumers, and explain each.

Useful Resources for Consumers

California Food Policy Advocates
www.cfpa.net/

Center for Science in the Public Interest
www.cspinet.org/

Environmental Protection Agency
www.epa.gov/

First Gov for Consumers
www.consumer.gov/

Food Policy Institute at Consumer Federation of America
www.consumerfed.org/backpage/fpi.htm

Food Research and Action Center
www.frac.org/

Food Safety (Government)
www.foodsafety.gov/

People for the Ethical Treatment of Animals (PETA)
www.peta-online.org

Pew Initiative for Food and Biotechnology
www.pewagbiotech.org/

Privacy Foundation Organization
www.privacyfoundation.org

Privacy Rights Clearinghouse
www.privacyrights.org

U.S. Department of Agriculture
www.usda.gov

U.S. Food and Drug Administration
www.fda.gov

USDA's Meat and Poultry Hotline
www.usda.gov/fsis/

"What Do You Think" Questions

1. Look at Figure 14-2, and, after reviewing the detail of the Nutrition Labeling and Education Act, write two paragraphs summarizing what the law is expected to accomplish.

2. From your life experiences, which three questionable food selling practices have you seen? Describe the circumstances of those situations, and what you did about them at the time.

3. What do you think the government ought to do about the number of anti-competitive practices in the food industry? Why?

Chapter 15

Health Care Issues

OBJECTIVES

After reading this chapter, you should be able to

1. Recognize the challenges of purchasing health care services.

2. List guidelines on how to purchase health care services.

3. Summarize the failings of the U.S. health care system and how to fix it.

4. Explain the relative values of prescription and over-the-counter drugs.

5. Comprehend how smoking and alcohol endanger individuals and society.

U nquestionably, your health is your most important asset. Americans today are leading healthier lives than years ago and they are living longer. Consumers are increasingly conscious of health care and are showing growing interest in the concepts of preventive care, wellness and self-care. At the same time our expectations keep rising for good professional health care. Consumers need reliable information on the price and quality of health care so they can evaluate and compare health products and services and make the best decisions for themselves.

This chapter begins with a review of the challenges of purchasing health care services, one of the most complicated and confusing areas of consumer consumption. Following are guidelines on how to purchase services. The next section examines why the U.S. health care system does not work well and offers suggested public policies to improve it. Following is a discussion on the positive and negative aspects of prescription and over-the-counter drugs, including dietary supplements. The chapter closes with an examination of the negative effects of tobacco and alcohol on individuals and society.

The Challenges of Purchasing Health Care Services

Consumer health deals with the decisions consumers make regarding the purchase and use of available health products and services. Sometimes decisions must be made in a hurry because of emergency situations. Health information is often **confusing and complex** because scientific evidence is technical and not always clear to unsophisticated consumers. This causes many transactions to be based on presumed confidence in sellers instead of proven competence. Another difficulty lies in the fact that many health problems are private and personal, resulting in a human tendency not to want to discuss such matters.

Buying health services is difficult for **four reasons**: (1) there are so many providers of similar health services (even though there may be few actual choices), (2) price information is not standardized and sometimes is difficult to obtain, (3) it is hard to determine reliability, and (4) redress mechanisms are inefficient.

When consumers experience problems with health care services they have to use **nontraditional forms of redress**, such as complaining to a county medical board or hospital self-regulatory organization. This results in many complaints, especially small ones, never being resolved while a number of big grievances, such as medical errors and malpractice, are settled with lawsuits.

Medical errors happen every day. Everyone has heard about the doctor who amputated the wrong leg, performed a double mastectomy due to a mixup in biopsy results and implanted a heart and lungs of the wrong blood type. According to the Institute of Medicine, nearly 4 percent of all hospitalizations involve medical errors and between 44,000 and 98,000 people die annually because of these mistakes. When a mistake is made there is no legal requirement to disclose that information to the patient. **Medical secrecy goes on** and on because care givers are fearful that they will be punished.

The National Practitioner Data Bank (www.npdb-hipdb.com/) is a taxpayer-funded 10-year-old computerized **database about malpractice payments** totaling $25 billion and disciplinary actions against 135,000 of the nation's 650,000 physicians. One of every six doctors in the country has a record in the data bank. Ninety percent of disciplinary actions are for **serious offences** (e.g., substandard care, criminal conviction, substance abuse, sex-related offenses, mis-prescribing of drugs, providing false information to the state board, loss of hospital privileges, insurance fraud). However, current law makes the data

unavailable for inspection by consumers. It is unconscionable that patients do not have a right to know about physicians before seeking his or her care.

Only two state governments (GA, NC) **require pharmacies** to report deadly or serious mistakes in dispensing prescription drugs, and no state requires hospitals to report mistakes that cause serious injury or death to patients. Throughout the health care field there is a longtime tradition of keeping consumers uninformed.

Untrained medical swindlers and unscrupulous individuals without adequate training, **quacks**, exist in the medical field. Quacks typically warn of the dangers of conventional treatments, use testimonials, promote secret cures, and claim persecution by the established medical community. (See the National Council Against Health Fraud [www.ncahf.org] and the FDA website [www.fda.gov/opacom/backgrounders/tophealt.html].)

DID YOU KNOW? Life Expectancies in Years

Women

Japan	82.5
France	81.3
Switzerland	81.3
Netherlands	80.5
Sweden	80.4
United States	78.6

Men

Japan	76.2
France	74.3
Switzerland	74.2
Netherlands	74.1
Sweden	73.8
United States	71.6

Source: World Health Organization

Guidelines on How to Purchase Services

Nearly half of all consumer expenditures are for services as opposed to products. A **service** is work or an action performed at the request of a consumer. In every instance, what consumers are buying from service providers is performance. It is **difficult for consumers to learn enough** about each of these individual services (and dozens of others) and then recall meaningful evaluative comments when necessary. Some guidelines on how to purchase services are offered here, as suggested by Barbara Heinzerling (University of Akron) and Anita B. Metzen (University of Missouri).

1. **Learn about the service area of interest.** It is foolish for consumers to remain ignorant about a service area when considering spending $20 or $2,000, and perhaps

enduring health risks in the process. Consumers need to systematically seek and use relevant facts and other information about a service area when it is going to be needed. A good place to start is the **Internet**.

2. **Check for registration, certification, and licensure.** There are more than 1,500 state boards and commissions that license or register professions and occupations. **Registration** is the formal recording of names suggesting that a person in a particular profession or occupation is qualified to perform certain tasks because he or she meets minimum established standards. Registration may be through a voluntary membership association or through state and local governments. Government registration generally requires only that a person inform the agency that they wish to practice the profession. Registered occupations are rarely restricted to any significant extent. Television and automobile repair shops are examples of registered occupations.

    Certification is a formal confirmation that something is true, accurate, or genuine, especially as in having met a particular standard. Certification of occupations asserts positive assurances about the qualification of those people to perform certain tasks. It usually includes a document testifying to the facts or truth of something. People often receive certificates when they complete a course of study not leading to a diploma. Both private organizations and government regulatory agencies offer certification that examines the credentials of individuals wanting to practice an occupation and/or gives them an examination. Examples include accountants, nurses, nutritionists, financial counselors, and physical therapists. However, anyone who wants to can practice these occupations without certification. Consumers can purchase services from certified practitioners or from those who generally charge lower prices and are not certified.

    Licensure is an official recording of names by a state board, commission, or other government agency that provides legal permission or authorization to do a specific thing, such as practice a particular profession or occupation. The applicant either presents appropriate credentials or takes an examination. This is the **most restrictive form of occupational regulation**, and non-licensed people may not practice these occupations. Examples include physicians, lawyers, cosmetologists, barbers, and dry cleaners. Be aware that **grandfather** provisions also exist in occupational regulation. This practice permits current, usually older practitioners to be registered, certified, or licensed without being examined for competence.

3. **Identify consumer problems unique to the service area.** When learning about a service area, determine the problems that are unique to purchasing those services. For example, when comparison shopping for a physician to perform cosmetic surgery, consumers should learn about the dangers of anesthesia, alternative surgical techniques being utilized, and the types of postoperative swelling problems that typically occur. Asking the physician about consumer problems is helpful, but it is not enough. Responsible consumers seek out and utilize a variety of sources to identify problems unique to a service area.

4. **Determine if a service provider has conflicting interests.** Ask if the health care provider also is an insurer or if the health care provider has an ownership interest in related products and services.

5. **Inquire about complaint procedures.** Consumers thinking about purchasing in a service area should find out the levels and channels appropriate for complaining

should it become necessary. Service providers themselves should be happy to discuss complaint procedures in their profession or occupation, although some are overly sensitive to the topic. While learning about complaint procedures, consumers can also learn about problems unique to each service and what standards are met in the profession or occupation.

6. **Develop a short list of criteria that are most important to you.** Comparing performance in service areas is difficult. To help in the selection process consumers are advised to list and rank two or three criteria they feel are most important. Then base a service selection decision primarily on those factors.

DID YOU KNOW?
Questions to Ask Your Health Care Provider

To stand up for your rights here are some **questions you might want to ask** your health care provider:

1. What are your **quality-of-care indicators** or **report cards** that grade hospitals, health plans, doctors and other medical professionals, as well as provide complete price information? (For useful information, see www.myhealthfinder.com, www.healthgrades.com, www.checkbook.com, www.jcaho.org, and www.ncqa.org).
2. How are providers compensated, and are financial incentives offered to physicians contingent on how much care is withheld (i.e., discouraging them from referring patients to specialists)?
3. What out-of-network care is provided?
4. What conditions and notification requirements are serious enough to warrant hospitalization?
5. How does the plan decide which services or treatments will be covered?
6. How does the plan decide whether a proposed treatment is investigational or experimental and therefore subject to rejection?
7. Are there limits on how much a covered person can spend on prescription drugs annually or limits on particular drugs, and how much are the co-payments?
8. Does the plan cover expensive medical equipment such as wheelchairs?
9. Does the plan cover oral surgery or cosmetic surgery?
10. How are complaints and appeals handled? (See www.patientadvocacy.org.)

The Bruised and Broken U.S. Health Care System

Capitalism is the reason why the United States has the **most advanced healthcare** in the world. However, the system is in a state of great disrepair, and the national government has been unable to seriously address its problems. These are: (1) rapidly **escalating medical costs**; (2) **uninsured consumers**; (3) **rising premiums** for those who are insured; (4) **young people** paying far more than their fair share in health insurance premiums; and (5) **inferior hospitals and doctors** not being forced out of business. To complicate matters, the health insurance system minimizes the costs of treating people with illnesses, avoids insuring people with serious and potentially serious health problems, and purposefully delays and rips off consumers who are due insurance reimbursements.

Highest Health Costs in the World

Health care consumes **one of every seven dollars** of the nation's goods and services. Total health care spending 20 years ago was $250 billion; now it is more than $1 trillion. Health care is a major expense of governments, employers, and consumers. Today Americans spend more than 16 percent of the nation's gross domestic product on health care. No other industrialized country spends more than 10 percent; Canada, France, and Germany are less than 9 percent, while Japan and Britain are less than 7 percent. Twenty cents of every dollar of federal spending in the U.S. is for health care, and the costs continue to rise every year.

Per capita spending on health care is **$5,000 in the U.S.**, $2,100 in Canada, $2,000 in Germany and France, $1,600 in Japan, and $1,400 in Great Britain, reports the Organization for Economic Cooperation and Development. For people in the U.S. with jobs that have health benefits, the costs are often split between employers and employees. The average employer/employee monthly premium for a health policy for a family is about **$550** and 22 percent is paid by the employer. Similar health care coverage not sold through employers cost double or triple. Out-of-pocket expenditures on health care raise prices even higher.

The Insured and the Uninsured

About 85 percent of Americans, 185 million, have health coverage under an employment-based program. **Fifteen percent, 40 million**, are without health insurance, and 86 percent of them are employed. The **uninsured** are the poor, near-poor, working poor, and many middle-income consumers. They are left to their own devices, or to chance or charity. Millions also are without health coverage during some part of the year because they lost their health insurance through unemployment or could not afford the premiums.

People **lack health coverage** because (1) it is not offered by their employers, (2) they cannot afford to pay high health insurance premiums, or (3) they have been dropped by their insurers because of certain illnesses or because of old age. One-third of the uninsured live in households with more than $50,000 in annual income.

The uninsured are **ripped off** almost every time they purchase health services. One dirty little secret of the insurance companies is that they pay discounted prices to health care providers but they charge full price to the uninsured. An insurance company might pay $300 to a hospital to perform a $1,300 health procedure on an insured person but they charge an **uninsured person the full $1,300**. The uninsured pay more, lots more. Not surprisingly, unpaid medical bills are a major reason why people seek credit counseling and bankruptcy.

Uninsured people actually do get a certain amount of medical care, but primarily through **hospital emergency rooms**. It is a myth that emergency services for the uninsured are free. The physicians must be paid as well as the cost for supplies. Those who are insured are paying those bills through higher medical care premiums. This is an example of **cost-shifting**. Health care providers raise premiums an extra 25 to 30 percent to cover the cost of care to the uninsured—and those costs are among the highest of all since most care for the uninsured is provided in emergency rooms. Since they don't have family physicians, they keep going to emergency rooms! The **top reasons** 100 million patients give for **emergency room visits** are in descending order: stomach pain and cramps, chest pain, fever, headaches, cuts on the upper body, shortness of breath, coughing, back problems, throat problems, and vomiting. The number one diagnosis by emergency room physicians is ear infection.

Young People Overpay

Our **young people**— because they generally are **quite healthy**—pay what is in effect a hidden tax to care for the uninsured. Bureau of Labor Statistics data reveal that spending on health care by age group is: people under age 25: 2%; age 25-34: 4%; age 35-44: 5%; age 45-54: 5%; age 55-64: 7%; age 65-74: 11%; and age 75+ 16%. Three quarters of Americans, mostly the young, pay less than $500 in out-of-pocket expenses a year for medical care. *Health Affairs* revealed that "The healthiest 50 percent of Americans account for only 3 percent of annual health costs...and the sickest 10 percent account for 72 percent of costs."

One day the younger generation will **wake up and rebel** upon discovering that (1) 20, 25 or 30 percent of wealth spent on health care in America is going to status-quo profiteers; (2) 90 percent of the money will be spent on behalf of recipients over age 60; (3) 40 million Americans without health insurance continue to overtax the economics of the health care system; (4) the 20 percent of everyone's federal and state income taxes that currently go for public health programs, such as **Medicare** (for 35 million elderly), **Medicaid** (covering 40 million poor people), and the **Veterans' Administration hospitals** (covering 14 million) is not enough; and (5) medical care for the 2.1 million **felons** in jails and prisons who receive treatment guaranteed by the Supreme Court is more costly as the prison population ages. To pay for medical programs, including a **prescription benefit** for Medicare recipients, older Americans will probably vote to increase taxes on those who are employed, the younger generation.

Why Health Care Reform Always Fails

Every president of the United States for sixty years, since Franklin Roosevelt—both Democrats and Republicans (except President George W. Bush)—has proposed major health care reform for the nation. **All have failed** to get the support of the U.S. Congress.

Numerous incentives exist for the special-interest groups to **protect the status quo** of health care and of course, it's all about money. The system is **full of profit-motivated distortions**. The major interest groups involved are doctors, hospitals, insurance companies, drug companies, big and small businesses, employer groups, consumers, and labor unions. Those providing care want society to spend more, not less, on health care. Those paying the bills want to keep costs down. Employers—who receive tax subsidies to provide workers with health care—have dealt with the rising cost problem by transferring most of the increases in health premiums to employees and reducing coverage for active workers, those retiring early, and workers already retired.

Bruce Bodaken, CEO of Blue Shield of California, says that "The current system and its underlying economics are unsustainable." Keeping the U.S. health care system in the private sector, unlike *all* the other 21 industrialized countries in the world (including South Africa and Spain) will keep the U.S. system costing **twice as much as it should** while serving only three-quarters of the population. Hawaii, an exceptional state in many ways, has had **universal health coverage** for all residents for more than 20 years.

Reform is Difficult

There are **four ways to reduce health-care costs**: (1) **Cut costs**, such as payments to hospitals, doctors and other providers; (2) **Reduce access**, perhaps by cutting back on unnecessary surgeries, tests, procedures, wasteful practices, medical errors, and fraud; (3) **Deliver services efficiently**, including preventive care, and (4) **Require workers to pay** higher premiums, co-payments and deductibles for reduced benefits. All of these ideas have been tried over the past twenty years, but none has succeeded.

Reform may require that **consumers become healthier**. Factors that drive up health costs are personal indulgences in unhealthy behaviors—that are avoidable—such as smoking, being overweight, alcohol and drug abuse, driving without seat belts, and unsafe sex. These are **lifestyle risk factors**. The U.S. Public Health Service says that "Approximately 50 percent of the deaths in people under 75 are due to personal behaviors that can be modified." Reform here requires a long-term social marketing campaign to persuade people to change their behaviors. It also will require a **preventive care** medical philosophy where consumers are encouraged to visit their physicians more frequently so that early detection and treatment of illnesses can occur. Incentives might help. For example, doctors could be paid yearly bonuses for each patient whose health improves.

Reform also will require effective **cost containment**. This means that some medical procedures will be considered optional, such as infertility services, traumatic brain injuries, acute cirrhosis of liver transplants, and some types of cosmetic surgeries. This is a form of **rationing**, a system that prioritizes the types of medical services covered. Rationing already exists in today's health care system, because only those who are insured get the services.

Access to care may need to be constrained by **managed care**. This refers to health care organizations, such as **health maintenance organizations (HMOs)** and **preferred provider organizations (PPOs)**, that control costs by controlling access. This is accomplished largely by coordinating care through a primary-care generalist and by carefully assessing the necessity for health care. Managed care companies closely monitor how physicians treat specific illnesses; insist upon appropriate, rather than expensive medical care; limit referrals to costly specialists; and require preauthorization for hospital care. More than 90 percent of people who have insurance are already being served by managed care.

CONSUMER UPDATE:
Medical Privacy Protections

Privacy is important to patients. The **Health Insurance Portability and Accountability Act of 1996 (HIPAA)** is a privacy law. It provides important protections and rights for millions of working Americans and their families who have preexisting medical conditions or might suffer discrimination in health coverage based on a factor that relates to an individual's health. Regulations issued in 2003 under HIPAA by the Department of Health and Human Services provide for the first time that:

- Patients have a right to get a copy of their medical records, examine it for accuracy, and request corrections;

- Doctors and hospitals are prohibited from giving out patient information to third parties for marketing purposes (such as for drug advertising) unless the patient specifically agrees;

- Employers are prohibited from examining an employee's medical records without the worker's written permission; and

- Patients may prohibit hospitals from giving information about their condition to reporters, clergy, friends, and family.

Also, consumers may obtain a **free copy** of their medical files from the **Medical Information Bureau (MIB)** (www.mib.com). MIB keeps records of consumers with serious medical conditions, poor driving records and other factors than may affect longevity. The information is primarily used by life insurance companies to screen out those applying for policies.

Reform Proposals

The nation's health care system is broken, and **even business leaders** are saying that doing nothing is no longer an option. There is a crisis of the uninsured as well as rising costs. Proposals for reform are being discussed once again. Some of the alternatives are:

1. **Single-payer universal system**—A government-run, universal care health system, like Medicare, where virtually all health products and services are covered, including surgery, hospitalization, physical therapy, prescription drugs, well-care, vision, and long-term care.

2. **Kennedy universal plan**—Require all employers to provide health insurance for employees and their dependents and subsidies would be provided for workers in small companies. Co-payments would be based on a person's ability to pay. Proposed by Senator Edward Kennedy.

3. **Gephardt universal plan**—Require all employers to provide health insurance and employers that currently offer insurance would receive a tax credit while other employers would get a much larger credit. Workers would pay part of their premiums, and subsidies would be provided for non-working people. Proposed by Representative Richard Gephardt.

4. **Breaux universal plan**—Require all Americans to obtain private health insurance and those without employer-provided coverage could purchase coverage at group rates. Subsidies would be available to the poor. Proposed by Senator John Breaux.

5. **California universal plan**—Require all employers to purchase coverage or contribute toward an employee health care benefit. Subsidies help the poor. Proposed by California Blue Cross CEO Bruce Bodaken.

6. **Dean uninsured plan**—Cover uninsured people up to age 25 by putting them in the Medicaid program. Proposed by former Vermont governor Howard Dean.

7. **Tax-credit plan**—Use tax credits to help uninsured pay for health insurance premiums. Proposed by a number of Republicans.

8. **Worker-directed plan**—Employers would set up **health-care savings accounts** for employees giving each an annual allowance, perhaps $2,500 for a family, to spend on medical expenses. Once those funds are gone, workers must pay their own bills until they meet an annual deductible after which a traditional plan pays for perhaps 80 percent of catastrophic medical expenses. Unspent funds could be used the following year.

Medical Malpractice Damages

About thirty years ago, California legislators placed a **cap** or a maximum amount on the **pain-and-suffering damages**, also known as **punitive damages**, that patients can sue for in instances of medical malpractice. This limits the rights of injured patients to seek full recovery in the courts. Today about half the states have similar caps and Congress may pass a national cap. Not subject to caps are **compensatory damages**, also known as **economic damages**. These are damages **awarded plaintiffs** for lost wages, medical bills, other tangible losses, such

The Medical Care Market Has Characteristics That Make It Difficult to Reform*

The unique nature of the medical care market is recognized by health economists because a **basic principle of economic theory—supply and demand—historically has not worked in health care.** In most commodity markets, prices tend to fall as supply increases as some high-cost firms will be forced out of business. The excess supply of medical professionals, hospital beds, and high-tech equipment, however, tends to keep charges and fees high.

Economic theory also assumes an independence between demand and supply. In the medical care market, however, the demand can be created by providers. Studies have found that physicians can boost consumer demand for their services.

The **distinctive characteristics** of the medical care market—including an almost insatiable demand—are as follows:

1. **The demand for medical services has considerable uncertainty.** It is possible to predict the rate of illness for a population based on past experiences and scientific data, but, except for hereditary diseases, illness is not predictable for an individual.

2. **Consumers think they have a "right" to good health care, including the newest medical technologies.**

3. **Third-party control over payment is unique in the medical care market.** Until recent years, insurance companies simply paid charges from providers without questioning the cost or the quality.

4. **Financing mechanisms, such as health care coverage as insurance, provide enormous ability to buy medical care.** These include Medicare and Medicaid (federal programs for the elderly and poor, respectively), and private health insurance. Since insurance lowers the out-of-pocket cost for medical care to individual consumers, this may result in a moral hazard where consumers utilize more medical services than if they had to pay the entire price themselves.

5. **An aging population consumes four times as much health care as the rest of the population.** Young adults utilize perhaps 10 percent of health care expenditures annually, which is far less than older adults.

6. **Prices are kept high because entry to the medical profession is restricted.** There are three entry barriers in the physician's market: graduation from an approved medical school, licensure, and continual training.

7. **Physicians keep prices high by restricting price competition because they rarely cut prices.**

8. **Uncertainty in product quality is a serious problem in purchasing medical care products.** Consumers in the medical care market tend to be poorly informed about the products. Many consumers are not able to evaluate the quality of services because of its scientific language and complexity. Thus, the information and knowledge gap between providers and consumers in the medical care market leads to poor decision-making on the part of consumers.

9. **Consumers are not engaged in reforming the health care system.** Consumers are not asking questions or the right questions. Most are not seeking new sources of information, such as on the Internet, and they are not participating in the reform discussions.

10. **Health care has positive external benefits.** Externalities occur when actions of one individual in a market affect the welfare of others. In the case of communicable disease, for example, the provision of a preventive or curative care to an individual yields a benefit beyond the prevention or cures of the illness itself. When a sizable proportion of a population is immunized to a disease, the risk of infection for other people is reduced. The impact of a broken chain of infection on the health of the general population is manifold: the number of infected people will be fewer, public health care expenditures on the disease will be saved, and community well-being will be improved.

These unique characteristics distinguish the medical care markets from other commodity markets. Its complexity and uniqueness have contributed to the current national health care crisis. Many aspects of the health care market need change to better serve consumers and society.

*Gong-Soog Hong, Professor, Utah State University

as a lifetime of payments for medical care to someone paralyzed. The argument is that most lawsuits are frivolous and jury awards are too high. The solution proposed by some is **tort reform**, placing caps on punitive damages. Examples are the damages for the value of "a father's presence in his children's lives" and "a wife's companionship."

The fact is that the number of paid medical **claims per doctor has not changed in twenty years**. While some doctors spend only **3.2 percent** of their revenues on malpractice insurance, specialists in obstetrics, neurology and some surgical fields pay much more. The causes for high premiums are high numbers of medical errors, occasional physician negligence and inadequate doctor discipline, as well as low profits in the insurance industry brought about by poor investment returns. A study by Public Citizen showed that 6 percent of physicians were responsible for 51 percent of the medical malpractice cases.

A Harvard University study found that only **one in eight victims** of medical negligence ever files a claim. According to the Physicians Insurers Association of America, 61 percent of lawsuits are dismissed or dropped (these patients do not get a dime), 32 percent are settled with an average payout of $300,000 and 7 percent go to trial. Of those lawsuits, patients win only one-fifth of the time, and the average payout is $500,000. One in twelve paid claims is for $1 million or more.

Placing caps on lawsuits is **against the consumer interest** and it has two unfortunate consequences. First, the sum of $250,000 is totally inadequate for what many harmed patients deserve. Second, caps in effect force many victims to not sue for lack of evidence. People who have difficulty proving economic losses in income and medical expenses include many seniors, low-income workers, at-home mothers, and parents of infants. When a newborn dies because of medical negligence, the parents can sue for only $250,000, no matter how grievous the medical mistakes, and even if the doctors had previous similar complaints against them. Thus, says former California governor Jerry Brown, caps put "negligent or incompetent physicians outside the reach of judicial accountability."

The answer to the so-called litigation crisis is not caps. The **solution is twofold**. First, reform the medical system to focus on patient safety to reduce errors and negligence. Second, reform insurance so competent physicians do not pay the same premiums as incompetent doctors.

CONSUMER UPDATE:
Toxic Shock Syndrome

Seventy-five years ago a cardboard tube of compressed cotton with a little string inside became the first **tampon**, a woman's hygiene product. Twenty-five years ago Proctor & Gamble developed a super-absorbent tampon, *Rely*. That product began the surge in cases of **Toxic Shock Syndrome (TSS)**, an infection caused by a virulent penicillin resistant bacteria that poisons the bloodstream. TSS causes high fevers, chills, rashes, vomiting, diarrhea, drops in blood pressure, and in some instances death. Tampon absorbency ratings are now standardized.

The Centers for Disease Control reports that the incidence is 1 to 2 cases per 100,000 women between 15 and 44 years of age. Wearing a tampon for too long a time is a major factor in TSS, and 5 percent of cases are fatal.

Prescription and Over-the-counter Drugs

A key element of the health care industry is the purchase of medicines. The **Food and Drug Administration (FDA)** is responsible for ensuring the **safety and effectiveness** of both prescription and over-the-counter drugs. Its authorities include the Food, Drug and Cosmetic Act of 1938, and the Kefauver-Harris Drug Amendments of 1962. The FDA regulates more than **4,000 drugs** and several thousand medical devices. As a regulatory agency, the FDA is limited in what it can do to safeguard the public good. While the FDA can seize misbranded or adulterated products, it cannot order a recall of products. Instead it must negotiate with sellers.

What are Drugs?

A **drug** is defined by the FDA as a product intended to affect the structure or function of the human body or to treat, prevent, or ameliorate a disease. Drugs must: (1) be tested for safety and effectiveness before being marketed, (2) be labeled with its purpose, directions for use, warnings, active ingredients, and expiration date, (3) be made by a registered manufacturer who must be responsible to the FDA, and (4) meet established standards for purity, quality, potency, and dissolvability.

The ethical drug industry sells both prescription and over-the-counter drugs. A **prescription** is a written instruction usually from a physician for the preparation and administration of a drug or, in some states, products such as insulin syringes. **Prescription drugs** are prepared and/or sold by **registered pharmacists** who are persons trained in pharmacy and registered with a state government to sell such products. Prescription drugs are sold to consumers by pharmacists in retail drug stores and through mail-order facilities; the latter making up more than 15 percent of the total U.S. prescription drug market, primarily because of lower prices. **Over-the-counter drugs (OTC)** are less powerful medicines capable of being sold legally without a prescription in places such as supermarkets, discount stores, pharmacies, airports, convenience stores, and vending machines.

Perhaps **only 10 to 50 percent** of a drug's active ingredients is used by the body. The rest is excreted. Many drugs do not work for 30 to 60 percent of those who take them, and many consumers might be better off taking another drug. In some cases drugs actually hurt users. All drugs have **side effects**, undesirable secondary effects of a drug or therapy. Some are the result of bad interactions between different drugs while others are simply bad reactions or side effects to a particular drug. The FDA estimates that millions of people have harmful reactions to prescription drugs. The number of people who die each year from **adverse drug reactions** is about 160,000. These mishaps are the fourth leading cause of death in the U.S. Millions more have negative reactions to OTC drugs.

Pre-market Review of Prescription Drugs

The FDA has the most rigorous **pre-market review** and clearance of prescription drugs in the world. It is designed to ensure the safety and efficacy of drugs for human use. Prescription drug products **may not be sold** until approved by the FDA as safe and effective, and that must be proven by substantial evidence conducted in well-controlled clinical investigations. American pre-testing drug policy is aimed at (1) preventing injuries and deaths, and (2) preventing people from using medications that will do them no good when they could be using approved drugs that might help. The FDA philosophy is to prevent the marketing of unsafe drugs rather than removing such products from the market after they have been found to be unsafe.

When a new drug is created the manufacturer obtains a **patent**, which is a grant by the government assuring the inventor of the sole right to make, use, and sell the product for a certain time period, usually 20 years. Several clinical tests follow. The manufacturer conducts animal tests and later human tests, and submits the results to the FDA along with the results of all other studies associated with the drug, including tests run by other companies and in other countries. The FDA **reviews clinical tests** by others, but does not conduct them.

When the FDA, with the help of its scientific advisory committees, is **convinced of the safety** of a new drug, the drug is approved. The FDA cautiously makes its decision by balancing the scientific and social benefits and risks of a drug.

If a drug on the market is later deemed to have serious side-effects or is questionable in its effectiveness (e.g., 24 deaths from Posicor, 52 liver failures linked to Rezulin), FDA procedures call for the drug company to provide further information, during which time the manufacturer is still allowed to market the product. If the drug is still deemed questionable, the FDA **begins withdrawal procedures**. Prescription drugs recently removed from the market under FDA pressure include Zomax and Nomifensine. On rare occasions the FDA puts strong safeguards in place to protect the health of patients using a newly approved drug. For example, RU-486–mifepristone, the abortion pill–requires a woman to make three visits to a doctor or clinic.

The FDA has a system of **user fees** imposed on drug companies that has helped improve product approval times. Funds are used to hire more government reviewers to examine safety and effectiveness data submitted to the FDA. The Congressionally mandated expedited process permits **faster evaluation** of the 50 to 100 new drugs every year. For example, the FDA's new drug application pre-market process that formerly averaged six to seven years (and could go up to twelve years) now is down to an average of 21 months. This speeds the availability of treatments to ailing patients (e.g., suffering from cancer, heart disease and AIDS). New procedures also give consumers greater access to experimental treatments before they are formally approved for widespread use.

Consumer advocates are **alarmed with the faster process**. They remember that it was the conservative FDA that kept the sedative **thalidomide** off the United States' market in the late 1950s that eventually led to 20,000 severely deformed and crippled babies born around the world. Today, thalidomide shows promise for treating cancer, AIDS, rheumatoid arthritis, multiple sclerosis, leprosy, and some forms of blindness. Thalidomide is generally considered to be a safe drug; however, it should never be used by pregnant women. Consumer advocates say there is no argument about quickly approving life saving drugs, but the FDA is under pressure to move fast on all kinds of less important drugs.

A drug approved by the FDA for one use is not necessarily safe or effective for other uses. Once a drug is on sale a physician generally **may prescribe it in any dosage and for any purpose** whether or not that purpose has been scientifically evaluated. This is **off-label usage**. Some examples: (1) Retin-A, approved for severe acne has not been approved for facial wrinkles; (2) collagen cannot be promoted to enlarge the lips; and (3) silicone cannot be used in injectable form. Many patients who have used drugs inappropriately have suffered.

Prescription Drugs Cost Lots More in the United States

All industrialized countries in the world **except the United States** either pay for prescription drugs for consumers or have some form of price regulations on prescription drugs. Drug companies are charging American consumers much more than what they charge in Europe for many of the same prescriptions. According to studies by the U.S. General Accounting Office for the Senate Special Committee on Aging, in Great Britain, of 77 frequently prescribed drugs, **66 cost more in the U.S.** and 47 cost more than twice as much. Canadians pay only 62 percent as much as U.S. consumers for the same drugs. Canada's review board tries to ensure that drug prices "are not excessive."

Profits from prescription drugs are used to **finance research** that benefits everyone. U.S. Drug companies spend more on marketing and advertising ($14 billion) than on research and development ($11.3 billion). Drug prices rise every year in excess of the rate of inflation in the economy, and they make up 20 percent of the total cost of health care expenses of many employers. The ethical drug industry has grown because of innovative basic research and effective marketing.

Three-quarters of prescriptions are **subsidized by employers** while employees make a co-payment of $10 to $40. Typically, neither consumers nor their physicians are fully aware of the high prices of prescription drugs. The only people who pay the full list price out-of-pocket are those who do not have insurance. Many of those consumers are purchasing prescription drugs on the Internet from Canadian-based pharmacies with prices that are discounted 30 to 60 percent from U.S. prices.

Generic Drugs

A **generic drug** is a copycat version of an expensive brand name prescription drug that has come to the market because the brand name product's **patent protection expired**. When a new drug is patented, it is given a generic name that usually is descriptive of its chemical composition. In addition, the manufacturer sells the drug under its brand name. The brand name of a drug is typically something shorter, easier to pronounce, uncomplicated for physicians to remember, and more marketable. For example, Lomotil is the trade name for a popular drug used to help control diarrhea. It is also sold by other manufacturers under the generic name diphenoxylate hydrochloride with atropine sulfate.

All manufacturers must comply with the FDA's **Good Manufacturing Practices** (GMP) and follow their **Standard Operating Procedures**. Any company, including the original maker, that meets the manufacturing standards of the FDA can make generics. Such drugs must meet similar standards for strength, purity, effectiveness, and safety.

To gain approval for a generic drug firms are required to submit test data to show that a **sample batch is equivalent** to the brand name drug being copied. The FDA approves a generic product to be therapeutically equivalent when it has a **bioavailability**, the rate and extent that a drug is absorbed, of no more than plus or minus 20 percent; the average difference is only 3.5 percent. The maker of the generic drug does not have to carry out clinical studies to establish safety and efficacy other than conducting a single human study with 20 to 24 people to ensure that the generic and the brand name drug are absorbed into the bloodstream at about the same rate.

The FDA has concluded that today's 2,000+ generic drugs **are therapeutically equivalent** to brand name drugs of the same strength and dosage form. Details are listed in the *United States Pharmacopeia (USP)*, a book published by a nonprofit organization of the same name that sets minimum quality standards that must be met by all drugs marketed in the United States. Drugs that do not meet the standards are subject to seizure by the FDA.

Generic drugs account for **47 percent** of all prescriptions, although about 75 percent of all drugs have a generic equivalent. Contrasted with brand name drugs, generic drugs generally cost about one-half to one-third the price of brand name drugs. These discounts, which average 30 percent but are as much as 90 percent, occur because the generic manufacturers do not have the heavy marketing costs associated with the brand name. Most experts agree with pharmacologist Joe Graedon, author of the *People's Pharmacy*, that overall, generic drugs are safe and effective and represent an extraordinary price savings. It still pays to comparison shop for prescription drugs because prices vary widely. Generally, suburban discount drug stores have the lowest prices, while other sellers may charge 10, 30, or even 200 percent more for the same prescription; generic or brand name.

Problems and Dangers of OTC Drugs

Self-medication with over-the-counter drugs is an important part of our health care system. Sixty percent of all medications sold are non-prescription. Thousands of prescription drugs are sold in the United States and more than 400 use ingredients and dosages that were available only by prescription 15 years ago.

Americans treat **60 to 90 percent** of their own ailments with OTC products. Resulting consumer problems include mis-diagnoses, side effects, drug interactions, overuse, overdose and failure to get professional care when symptoms persist. Another problem is the lack of **efficacy** of many over-the-counter drugs. This is the power or capacity to produce a desired effect. The 1962 Kefauver-Harris Drug Amendment states that all drugs must be proven safe and effective before being marketed, and most are effective. However, people get the idea from advertising that over-the-counter drugs are going to cure their problems. The fact is that over-the-counter drugs (and many prescription drugs too) can only relieve symptoms.

According to labeling requirements of the FDA, all over-the-counter drug products must **label products in a consistent manner**. Labels must show the active ingredients in medications and make the known risks clearer. Labels also must reduce the illegible glob of tiny print that makes hunting for information difficult by using a font size no smaller than "six points high." This is about half the size of the typical textbook font size of eleven or twelve points. More than 170,000 hospitalizations occur annually because of the misuse of OTC drugs.

The federal **Anti-Tampering Act** provides penalties for anyone who tampers with foods, drugs, cosmetics, or the labeling of such containers. Consumers should report any problems with cosmetics to the seller, manufacturer, and the Food and Drug Administration. (No child under age five has died in the past 15 years from poisoning by accidental ingestion of aspirin.)

The **Poison Prevention Packaging Act** ordered child-resistant packaging on aspirin, vitamins, and a number of other over-the-counter and prescription drugs. FDA regulations require that of a sample group of children, 85 percent must not be able to open the container in five minutes. At the same time, at least 90 percent of the adults must be able to open it. Accidental poisonings have dropped about 50 percent, and there have been no deaths of children ingesting drugs from child-resistant packaging for 15 years.

Aspirin and Similar Pain Relievers

Analgesics are pain-relievers available without a prescription. All nonprescription analgesics **relieve pain**, but they cannot cure its underlying cause. Analgesics relieve headaches and provide temporarily relief from minor arthritic or rheumatic pain, pain of menstrual cramps, toothache, muscular aches and pains, backache, and the aches and pains of colds or flu. Not all analgesics work on the same health problems.

Aspirin is the most common over-the-counter analgesic drug sold in the United States. Each year consumers take 30 billion aspirin tablets with a total weight of 45 million pounds. **Aspirin** is defined in the *United States Pharmacopeia* as acetylsalicylic acid because that is its active ingredient. Aspirin, which is not patented, comes in many different forms such as plain, buffered, effervescent tablets or powders, or is contained in other analgesics, antacids, antihistamines, and decongestants. Aspirin is a powerful wonder drug used in tablet form since 1899 for fevers, headaches, and arthritis pain. Aspirin reduces pain, inflammation, and fever. No one knows the exact mechanism by which aspirin works, but it does.

Findings published in the *New England Journal of Medicine* based on a nationwide study of more than 22,000 physicians confirms that for healthy men over the age of 50, small quantities of **aspirin can reduce the risk of heart attacks** by nearly half. Aspirin's ability to keep blood platelets from sticking together may be useful in reducing heart attacks. Low doses of aspirin also thin the blood; therefore it may increase the chances of a stroke caused by bleeding in the brain. Since taking aspirin as a preventive is definitely not a do-it-yourself project, interested consumers should visit their personal physician for appropriate advice.

The Main OTC Pain Relievers

Some consumers **buy the wrong OTC products** to relieve pain. It helps to understand what each product does. All OTC drugs have potential serious side effects, and those that are more potent and effective have more associated side effects. For example, the FDA requires warning labels on OTC pain relievers to inform chronic alcohol drinkers (three or more a day) that they may be at increased risk of kidney and liver damage or stomach bleeding from use of these products.

Independent research shows that, except for inflammation control where aspirin products are superior, all other products **work equally well** as pain relievers. Thus, you can choose to spend perhaps one cent to cure a headache with an aspirin tablet or 25 cents to cure the same headache with another product. For unknown reasons, people may respond better to one drug instead of another.

Aspirin is acetylsalicylic acid, and it is sold by nearly 400 companies. Common brand names include Bayer, Empirin, St. Joseph, Ecotrin (coated to dissolve in the intestine, instead of the stomach), Anacin (with caffeine), and Excedrin (with caffeine and acetaminophen [see below]). It reduces pain and fever and lessens stiffness or swelling.

Ibuprofen is sold under the brand names Advil, Motrin I-B, Nuprin, Aleve (longer lasting), and Medipren. It relieves pain and reduces fever and inflamation. People who are allergic to aspirin generally are allergic to ibuprofen.

Acetaminophen is sold under many brand names including Tylenol, Aspirin-Free Anacin, Tempra, Midol and Pamprin, and it is sometimes described as an aspirin substitute. Since acetaminophen is a non-aspirin product it totally lacks an ability to reduce inflammation. It is used for pain and fever. Acetaminophen overdoses cause approximately 100 deaths from acute liver failure and 15,000 emergency room visits annually. Thirty percent of people waiting for liver transplants are from acetaminophen related causes.

CONSUMER UPDATE:
Advertising Drugs: Illegal, Unethical or Both

Nearly half the population relies on **advertising** as their **primary source of information** about over-the-counter drugs, and increasingly they rely upon advertising for prescription drug information. The FDA complains that drug **advertising often overstates** the benefits, understates the risks and falsely suggests that one drug is superior to another. Drug advertising is saturated with puffery claims and statements that are true, but leave false impressions. More than **500** prescription drug advertisements have been found by the FDA to violate federal laws and regulations since 1997. The FDA has filed over 90 complaints for **false and misleading claims** about **claritin, flonase, celebrex, allegra, pravachol, zyrtec,** and medicines to help people lose weight and stop smoking. They mislead consumers into thinking a medication is better or safer than it really is.

Direct-to-consumer advertising of prescription drugs gives consumers more information and choice about the drugs they take, and it increases their awareness of untreated disorders. Prescription drug ads must describe what the drug does as long as they also mention the drug's major side effects and tell where to get more information. The result of this advertising is that doctors are partially cut out of the process because consumers go to physicians to demand certain drugs that they have seen on television or the evening news. Not all doctors can say "No" to their patients. Media coverage of new drugs can be characterized too often like a cheering squad rather than the normal role of skeptics. Direct-to-consumer advertising drives up costs and leads people to pop pills they do not need.

The **Federal Trade Commission regulates the advertising** of prescription and over-the-counter drugs, supplements, and medical devices, while the Food and Drug Administration regulates the labeling of those products. Both the FTC and FDA have guidelines for **health claims**. The FDA says a company may make health claims on labels only when significant "scientific evidence" supports the position.

The Federal Trade Commission is much **more lenient** than the FDA in what it allows food and drug companies to advertise when promoting products. The FTC's standard for over-the-counter advertising is that companies must have **a reasonable basis** for believing there is a connection between a product and prevention of a certain disease. As long as the claim can be backed up by studies, OTC sellers are free to declare the benefits of their products without disclosing possible dangers. Therefore, new and controversial scientific findings are often used to make health claims in advertising. The Federal Trade Commission has been ineffective in stopping advertising that exaggerates the need for health products or promises more results than people should realistically expect.

Bayer was found by an FTC judge to be neither qualitatively nor therapeutically superior to **any other aspirin products**, despite its ads to the contrary. The Federal Trade Commission found that Bayer aspirin is "one of a number of high-quality 5-grain aspirin brands available to consumers." Such misleading ads must work because an FTC study found that **40 percent** of consumers still believe Bayer's advertising that it is the most effective aspirin. The FTC ordered the manufacturers of all the top-selling pain relievers to stop their false advertising. The conclusion of non-industry-sponsored scientific studies about aspirin and other pain relievers is that two 5-grain aspirin tablets are just as good as anything else in dealing with pain, fever, and inflammation.

Dietary Supplements: Lies and Dangers

Thanks to a Republican Congress, the days of snake-oil selling in the 1800's era of **"buyer beware" are back in fashion** in the 21ˢᵗ century. **Dietary supplements** are vitamins, minerals, amino acids, herbal remedies and exotic therapies touted to improve health and longevity. They are classified as foods, thus they are neither drugs nor over-the-counter drugs, and they are subject to very **limited governmental oversight**.

The Food and Drug Administration has **meager powers** to regulate dietary supplements because of the 1994 Dietary Supplement Health and Education Act. Supplement companies may market new products without prior FDA approval as long as they do not claim to prevent, treat, or cure a disease, which is what prescription drugs may claim. Dietary supplement manufacturers, however, are permitted to make claims about how their products affect the "structure or function" of the human body. So saying "Promotes healthy heart function" is an allowed health claim, while "Fights heart disease" is not permitted even though both statements relate to the same condition.

Dietary supplement companies are **aggressively advertising** to children and their parents with the promise of "natural"remedies and "healthy alternatives" to prescription or OTC drugs. The result is that Americans are **fooled and cheated** every day because–in the name of free choice–the law permits false advertising. And consumers report that television is their "leading source of health information."

The FDA **cannot act swiftly** to pull adulterated or tainted products off the market. Instead, the FDA must file a lawsuit in federal court and build a case that may take years to show that a supplement presents "significant or unreasonable risk of illness or injury." This generally cannot be shown until people are hurt or dead. The burden of proof for food supplements is *on the FDA*, a backward and ineffective form of regulation. The FDA does not even have the power to find out if the product in the container is what's stated on the label, thus consumers have no idea whether these products are pure, effective or safe.

In 2003 the FDA commenced rulemaking for **quality control purposes**. If finalized, supplement sellers, just like food sellers, will be required to follow **Good Manufacturing Practices (GMP)**. Here the FDA requires that the products be made in sanitary conditions, the ingredients be tested for purity, consistency and strength, and the labels list the amount and dose of ingredients.

Nearly **100 foods** that contain herbal medicines are **advertising false health claims**. These so-called **functional foods** are food products that claim to have added ingredients to provide an extra nutritional boost in spite of the fact that there exists zero scientific evidence that they work. The food companies advertise health claims but do not repeat the claims on the product labeling. Another way food companies are getting around the law is to have their food product reclassified as a dietary supplement because these products are largely exempt from regulation. When solid research evidence does exist, as was the case with two margarine products, Benecol and Take Control, the FDA examines the studies and, when approved, the claim is permitted in labeling. In this case the products are allowed to make the health claim that the products can lower harmful cholesterol and reduces the risk of heart disease.

Another **legal loophole** for the supplement industry is that they are permitted to produce and distribute point-of-sale articles on the health value of supplements (without review by the FDA) that are packed with untruths. Sellers also are supposed to provide articles with contrary views. Unbelievably, the law permits nutritional claims other than those previously established for foods, provided a disclaimer is included saying "This statement has not been evaluated by the FDA."

The FDA has the authority to require prior approval to put health claims on labels and prohibit wild health claims, such as "cures cancer." Producers of supplements must submit proof of "significant scientific agreement" among "qualified experts" to support a **health claim** touting the relationship between a substance and a disease or health-related condition before it can be on a label. FDA approvals have been given to calcium as it "may help prevent osteoporosis" and folic acid that "may help prevent birth defects."

While food stores cannot claim the substances prevent or cure disease (without proof to the FDA), they do make **cryptic and indirect statements** that "imply" values never proved. Rigorous research does not exist on supplements, even for widely used products like vitamin C, St. John's Wort, and Gingko Biloba. Supplements also lack consistency among products from manufacturer to manufacturer.

This loose regulatory authority **opens the door wide for misrepresentation and fraud**. Consumer critics call this the "Orin Hatch Please-Lie-to-Consumers Act" because Senator Hatch was the sponsor of the legislation that opened all the loopholes. The failure of Congress and the FDA to act against functional foods, says Bruce Silverglade of the Center for Science in the Public Interest, "is threatening to undermine the whole Food and Drug Administration Act." He says "These products blur the distinctions between foods and drugs." Some **herbal extracts** act more like drugs than nutrients and may be dangerous.

The FDA has no legal option other than to monitor the supplement industry by **relying on reports of adverse reactions**. Problems arise with dietary supplements because most have serious side-effects. L-tryptophan was banned after being linked to 27 deaths. GHB, gamma hydroxy butyrate, has caused 57 serious poisoning cases. The "natural high" promoted by Herbal Ecstacy that contains the stimulant ephedrine, has been linked to 15 deaths. Ephedra/ephedrine alkaloids (a stimulant, weight-loss product known as *ma-huang*) have been linked to 25 deaths. Amino acid supplement pills, such as tyrosine, when ingested in large quantities, cause unexpected and unwanted effects. When so many untested herbal extracts are on the market, it is no wonder that dietary supplements make up **40 percent of all complaints to the FDA**.

If you eat a **balanced diet**, you probably do not need to spend money on dietary supplements. The National Research Council recommends dietary allowances for each of 13 nutrients and few, if any people need more than the U.S. Recommended Dietary Allowances (RDAs) by consuming dietary supplements. Most people can get along just fine with less. A *Money* magazine study concluded that "More than 90 percent of the products sold by health stores...were of questionable value," and that consumers "waste money following most health store recommendations."

The debate about the curing power of **magnets** is similar to the supplements story. The reason why federal regulators have not acted to stop the unsupported health claims of magnet sellers (e.g., cures back pain, menstrual pain, arthritis) is because the business is not a priority. Given its limited budget, the FDA prefers to go after companies whose products cause harm.

Smoking and Health

Smoking in the U.S. is **down 42 percent** over the past twenty years, although 50 million Americans or 24 percent of the adult population still smokes. Ninety-nine percent of U.S. smokers started before age 21, and the average age of first use of cigarettes is 14. Most teens who try cigarettes get hooked within weeks of starting. Of teenagers who try smoking cigarettes, 70 percent become habitual smokers by age 18. People continue to smoke because of addiction, or ignorance or both.

Eighty percent of smokers say they have **tried to quit**, and 70 percent say they want to quit; 40 percent will try to quit in any given year. Nicotine is a drug and tobacco products are drug delivery dispenser devices and as a result, only 3 percent of smoking adults succeeds in quitting every year. Nicotine patch and gum products are useful in helping consumers quit smoking, but it is very difficult to quit. In calling for an aggressive advertising campaign to help people give up cigarettes, the Royal College of Physicians in the United Kingdom reported that addiction to tobacco smoke is second to no other addiction, including heroin or cocaine.

Ugly Health Links of Smoking

Smoking is the **chief cause of lung cancer** and has been specifically linked with other cancers, heart disease, stroke, and such respiratory diseases as pneumonia, chronic bronchitis, asthma, emphysema, and various lung disorders. Smoking during pregnancy (13 percent admit they do) increases the frequency of low-birthweight infants, premature births, lung disorders in newborns, mental retardation, and sudden infant death syndrome (SIDS). Women who smoke during pregnancy pass potent carcinogens to the babies developing in their wombs. Smoking has been closely linked with depression, hearing loss, asthma induction, bronchitis, pneumonia, periodontal disease, cataracts and leukemia. Smoking accelerates irreversible hardening of the arteries and raises the skin cancer incidence rate by 50 percent. Smoking triples the likelihood of premature facial wrinkling. It causes impotence at a rate twice as high as non-smokers, including men in their twenties.

Smoking and Death

The Centers for Disease Control reports that in the United States about 2.1 million people die each year and at least 442,000 of those deaths (about **20 percent**) are directly attributable to smoking. The U.S. Surgeon General reports that in the last fifty years 10 million Americans have died of smoking-related causes.

Worldwide "**sixty million deaths** have been caused by smoking since the 1950s" reports the World Health Organization (WHO) in *Mortality From Smoking in Developed Countries.* Four million deaths annually are attributable to smoking, says WHO, and this will rise to 10 million a year by 2020 because smoking in developing countries, especially among women, continues to be attractive to young people. There are 1.2 billion smokers worldwide, and **half will die prematurely** from smoking-related diseases.

"Smoking is like no other hazard" says WHO. "It will kill **one in two** smokers eventually." Lifetime smokers have a 50 percent chance of dying from tobacco. Cigarettes are the only product in the world that if used as designed and promoted will ultimately kill you. Kurt Vonnegut, author of 19 novels, once observed that smoking was the "only respectable form of suicide."

The American Medical Association (AMA) reports that the likelihood of contracting lung cancer is **17 times higher** for people who smoke than for nonsmokers. One-third of all smokers will die of lung cancer, reports the AMA, and four out of 10 will be women "because women who smoke like men will die like men." This year alone, 170,000 cases of lung cancer will be diagnosed in the U.S. and 157,000 people will die.

The **life expectancy** of smokers, reports the U.S. Centers for Disease Control and Prevention, is **five years less** than non-smokers. A study in the *Archives of Internal Medicine* shows that quitting smoking extends an average male smoker's life 2.6 to 4.4 years, and the average female smoker's life 2.6 to 3.7 years. The earlier one quits smoking the greater the benefits, and older smokers who quit also gain. The Surgeon General reports that half of the excess risk of heart disease disappears within the first year of quitting smoking. See www.mskcc.org/predictiontools/lungcancer to calculate the risk of lung cancer.

Secondhand Smoke Kills 40,000+ Every Year

Studies of nonsmokers show that they are being harmed by the smoke of others in buses, trains, subways, planes, offices, restaurants, and other public places. **Secondhand smoke** is a mixture of the smoke given off by the burning end of a cigarette, pipe or cigar and the smoke exhaled from the lungs of smokers. It kills **40,000+** Americans every year, report the U.S. Surgeon General and the Environmental Protection Agency.

Passive smoking is breathing secondhand smoke. A Centers for Disease Control and Prevention study showed that secondhand smoke invades the lungs of about 88 percent of America's non-smokers. Secondhand smoke greatly increases the likelihood of respiratory illnesses in children, and it is the third leading preventable cause of death; active smoking and alcohol use are first and second. The *Journal of Cancer* reports that women who live with smokers absorb five to six times more tobacco-specific cancer-causing chemicals than those who live with non-smokers. Secondhand tobacco smoke increases the risk of lung cancer by **20 percent**.

ISSUE FOR DEBATE:
Government Should Encourage Americans to Have Better Diets and Do Less Smoking and Drinking

Top 10 Official Causes of Death		Top 9 Underlying Causes of Death	
Heart Disease	725,000	Tobacco	434,000
Cancer	539,000	Diet/inactivity	300,000
Stroke	158,000	Alcohol	100,000
Drug-caused deaths	106,000	Certain infections	90,000
Chronic lung disease	114,000	Toxic agents	60,000
Pneumonia & influenza	94,000	Firearms	35,000
Diabetes	65,000	Sexual behavior	30,000
Suicide	29,000	Motor vehicles	25,000
Kidney	26,000	Illegal drugs	20,000
Liver disease	25,000		

Conclusion: Nearly half of the 2.148 million deaths annually could have been prevented through behavioral changes such as stopping smoking, eating healthier food, exercising more, avoiding alcohol and practicing safe sex.

Source: National Center for Health Statistics and *Journal of the American Medical Association*

Tobacco Executives Told the Worst Lies in History

Virtually everyone has "known" for a hundred years that smoking has some health risks (it's logical!) and people "knew" that smoking was probably addictive; well, addictive for some people maybe. The American society further **deluded itself** by believing the constant claims by the tobacco industry that "There still isn't a shred of substantial evidence to link cigarette smoking and cancer of the lung directly."

It is against the **consumer fraud statutes** for companies to tell lies (see Chapter 5). These laws require companies that make and sell products to provide consumers with honest and accurate information. For government to successfully prosecute violators requires evidence.

The truth was **finally revealed** in the 1990s as plaintiffs' lawyers and several state attorneys general pried tobacco-stained fingers off boxes of hidden files. The contents of 37 tons of internal tobacco company documents (e.g., research, reports, memos) proved beyond a shadow of a doubt that they lied about everything. A 1953 document hidden by R. J. Reynolds, for example, concluded that "Studies of clinical data tend to confirm the relationship between heavy and prolonged tobacco smoking and incidence of cancer of the lung." The tobacco executives lied to the public, the Congress, and probably their spouses. The reality was that since the 1950s, the executives running the tobacco companies knew that cigarettes were addictive and caused vascular and other diseases, but they kept the knowledge secret so they could continue making money.

The movie *The Insider* told the story well as tobacco giant Brown & Williamson's Jeffrey Wigand turned **whistleblower**, showing the tobacco executives to have been liars, corrupters of children, manipulators of science, and promoters of nefarious tactics "in hopes of spreading their cancer-causing products to new generations of teenagers." Those executives told the worst lies in history as their coverup efforts "traded sixty million deaths worldwide for corporate profits." Finally, on October 13, 1999, the tobacco industry admitted the truth when the Phillip Morris website stated for the **first time ever** that "Yes, smoking is harmful to health and smoking is addictive." Phillip Morris changed its corporate name to Altria Group.

In 1998, the four largest tobacco companies that supply 90 percent of Americans' cigarettes signed a **landmark legal settlement**. They agreed to compensate 46 states $246 billion over 25 years in return for exemption from state claims for the many years of smoking-related health care expenses the states paid to care for their citizens. The other four states settled separately for $40 billion. The Centers for Disease Control and Prevention reports that for each of the 22 billion packs of cigarettes sold in the U.S., $3.45 is spent on medical care related to smoking.

The Future

"Think of the cigarette pack as a storage container for a day's supply of nicotine...Think of the cigarette as a dispenser for a dose unit of nicotine," says a Philip Morris internal research strategy paper. The tobacco executives know that it is **difficult** for addicted smokers to quit. Even so, smoking remains a choice. People can choose to ignore the warnings and accept the risk of harming themselves or quit.

However, the ill-effects of smoking—to smokers and nonsmokers alike—are **no longer ignored by society**. States and municipal governments and countries overseas are instituting smoking bans in workplaces, restaurants, bars, pubs, sports arenas, nightclubs, bingo halls, and even taxis.

The United Kingdom has announced a **total ban on tobacco advertising**, and a phased-in regulation prohibiting tobacco companies from sponsoring national and global sporting events. The European Union is requiring cigarette sellers to reduce the harmful ingredients in tobacco products, and a new United Nations treaty is being designed to combat tobacco use globally by making it difficult to promote cigarette use.

Following a U.S. Supreme Court decision restraining its powers to regulate tobacco, the FDA continues to **wait for the U.S. Congress** to write a law establishing which agency will regulate the tobacco industry.

Politicians in almost all the **state legislatures** demonstrated little interest in trying to achieve the public health goal of preventing smoking. Most states are spending their tobacco money on highway construction, tax cuts and other projects. The states have spent **only 8 percent** of the settlement money on anti-smoking campaigns. The most effective anti-smoking group is the American Legacy Foundation, which was created by the National Association of Attorneys General. Its "Truth" campaign is funded by the tobacco industry settlement (www.thetruth.com/).

A cynical tobacco executive once stated that "We need a half-million new smokers a year just to stay in business." To pay billions of dollars in compensation to states and to pay millions to a growing number of consumer plaintiffs suing tobacco companies, the industry has to **recruit more than 3,000 new smokers every day** to replace the 2,000 who quit and 1,100 who die. The tobacco industry calls these kids "replacement smokers."

Big Tobacco spends $23 million a day promoting tobacco and to pay those costs the industry has raised prices. This shifts the financial burden of the settlement to current and future smokers, thus permitting the companies and shareholders to avoid any genuine penalty.

The tobacco companies are still flourishing financially. Big Tobacco's spending on advertising and promotion jumped 22 percent to $8.3 billion the first year after the tobacco settlement; last year they spent $11 billion on advertising. Most spending was on retail store displays, gift items, discounts, and print advertising.

The reality now is that the **states are partners of the tobacco industry**. The states cannot be too tough regulating and reducing smoking or they put at risk their $246 billion 25-year revenue stream from the tobacco companies. States have **drastically cut spending on anti-smoking efforts**, and the Truth campaign in particular. Many observers agree with *Orlando Sentinel's* Mike Thomas who has written that "It's interesting to note that it's always the Republicans who try to kill anti-smoking efforts–after getting the bulk of tobacco contributions." The Florida legislature under the leadership of Governor Jeb Bush cut the "Truth" campaign funding from $70 million to $1 million. In contrast, California's "Truth" advertising fully funded by a 25-cent-per-pack tax on cigarettes has cut adult smoking to 17 percent, the second-lowest in the nation behind Utah's 13 percent. California's youth smoking rate is the lowest in the nation at 6 percent. It is a lamentable situation that today most state governments are in bed with Big Tobacco supporting their need to find new smokers and they will be for twenty more years.

Unless **prevented by governments worldwide**, U.S. tobacco companies will continue to find many new smokers in overseas markets as smoking there has grown 250 percent in the past decade. R. J. Reynolds and Philip Morris sell two-thirds of their cigarettes in other countries. Advertising is very effective overseas as the smoking rate is 78 percent in both the Philippines and Vietnam, 75 percent in Indonesia and China, 75 percent in Russia, and 63 percent in Japan.

In closing, **smoking is terrible** in so many ways. If you are a smoker and remain so some weeks after reading the above facts and statistics you are allowing your nicotine addiction to run your life rather than using your brain to make an easy intelligent decision. If you are a non-smoker, try to persuade others to quit.

ISSUE FOR DEBATE:
Raise Cigarette Taxes to Discourage Consumption

Taxes paid by cigarette smokers pay for **only a fraction** of the increased health costs caused by smoking. American smokers pay an average price of nearly $3 per pack in many states; it's $7 in New York. Canadians pay more than $5 a pack. Over 25 percent of the price is for taxes. Norway has the highest average price pack, $9, of which 77 percent is taxes.

As **cigarette taxes go up, smoking consumption goes down**. Studies show that cigarette consumption drops by about 6.5 percent with each 10 percent price increase. Oregon raised cigarette taxes to 78 cents a pack and consumption dropped 20 percent in two years; the extra money went toward smoking prevention and education programs. The number of Oregon high school seniors who smoke has dropped to 24 percent.

Many in the United States believe that cigarette taxes ought to go up from the present average of 38 cents per pack to at least $3 or $4 to push the price per pack to $8 to $10. The American Society of Oncologists is urging an immediate $2-a-pack-increase in taxes.

Alcohol and Health

Among the general population, **40 percent report that they never drink** and more than 80 percent say they never drink and drive. College students are different; more than 80 percent drink regularly. College students report alcohol consumption as the prime means of getting high. Half of all college freshmen get smashed during their first week on campus. A U.S. Department of Education survey of 58,000 college students revealed that about one-third of the male and female students drink primarily to get drunk; nearly half of the college students under age 21 reported binge drinking in the past two weeks. Most drinkers are unaware that taking aspirin before drinking significantly increases the concentration of alcohol in the blood.

Columbia University's Center on Addiction and Substance Abuse revealed that 20 percent of college students **abandoned safe-sex practices** after drinking. Sixty percent of college women with sexually transmitted diseases were drunk when they became infected.

Alcoholic beverages contain intoxicating compounds. Many people assume that alcohol makes them funny, brave, more sociable, sexier, or better in some other ways. While these statements are being debated by individuals personally and by professional researchers, it is well known that alcohol use **leads to arrests**, injuries, vandalism, and drunk-driving deaths.

Alcohol advertising is **aimed at children**, too. The **distilled spirits industry** (hard liquor) has dropped its decades-old voluntary ban against broadcast advertising. Taking a cue from the tobacco industry, some liquor ads have cuddly little animals to sell the product—"aimed at adults, of course," says the industry. About one-third of *Spin* magazine's readership is under age 18, and half are under age 21, yet booze ads fill the pages.

More elementary school children are more familiar with Budweiser's frogs and lizards than they are with Kellogg's Tony the Tiger. Sweet drinks containing alcohol, such as Hooper's Hootch and a number of **alcopops** (lemonades, colas, and orange flavored drinks containing alcohol) are blatantly marketed at young teenagers. Liquor manufacturers deny such allegations. Alcohol is the most frequently portrayed food or beverage on prime-time television and young people are exposed to approximately **2,000 alcohol advertisements per year**.

Alcohol contains a number of chemicals, some of which cause long-lasting **birth defects** from fetal alcohol syndrome. Even one drink a day may hurt a fetus. Two drinks a week during pregnancy have been shown to increase the chances of a miscarriage. Alcohol is the most common known cause of mental retardation, and it only occurs when pregnant women drink alcohol.

KEY TOPIC IN CONSUMER ECONOMICS:
Why Do Some People Persist in Harming Their Health?

People process information differently about risks and **make rationalizations**. Many people reason that catastrophic events such as airplane crashes, will happen to others, not to them. Such a deduction about catastrophic events is probably correct from a statistical point of view because comparatively speaking, very few people die in accidents.

The odds are **extremely low** that the average American will die: from being struck by lightning (1:million), in a commercial airplane (1:7 million), in a private airplane (1:2 million in a small plane), in a flood (1:40,000), in a tornado, 1:30,000; from murder (1:10,000), in an accident not in a vehicle (1:20,000), and in an auto accident (1:8,000). The odds of catching the AIDS virus from a blood transfusion is 1:500,000.

People are **inclined to make similar rationalizations** about such perils as radon, dioxin, pesticides, certain chemicals and colors added to foods, radiation, smoking, and alcohol. There is a human tendency to believe they are immune from such dangers. The thinking goes "Oh, the odds are certainly against any of that stuff hurting me." Such thinking is false! This is an example of where human logic falls apart. People have a tendency to personalize the odds of something happening to them even when the reality of evidence shows otherwise.

Such thoughts are simply **rationalizations**. This is the theory that the exercise of **personal reasoning**, rather than the acceptance of empirical evidence provides the only valid basis for action or belief. Many people rationalize about health and safety risks. It occurs, in part, because: (1) people do not want to think about death and danger, (2) the odds of many calamities and dangers are unknown to consumers, (3) people often fail to add their behavior patterns to the factor of chance, and (4) most of us are incapable of making mathematically-correct risk assessments.

Because of such rationalizations many people smoke cigarettes, eat fatty foods, avoid regular exercise, sun bathe all summer long, choose not to wear seat belts, drink excessively, and sometimes drive too fast, all the time **falsely assuming** that the "odds are with them." Such people often believe they are making informed decisions, but they are not. Consumers need to make more informed decisions about what to eat, what behaviors to avoid, and where to live, work and play.

Too much alcohol is not healthy. Alcohol is blamed for more than **108,000 deaths annually**, including more than **17,000 alcohol-related traffic deaths**. There are **10 million alcohol-related accidents** and two million arrests for public drunkenness reported each year. Nearly half of all accidental deaths, suicides, and homicides are alcohol-related, and one-third of all drowning victims were intoxicated at the time of death. Other alcohol related problems are cirrhosis of the liver, pancreas difficulties, cancer, hypertension, depression, and suicide. Alcohol kills three times as many people in the U.S. as all other drugs combined. An estimated **40 percent** of people in the United States will be in an alcohol-related automobile crash **during their lifetimes**. Drinking hurts young people more than adults, and the American Medical Association supports a ban on alcohol advertising on broadcast television before 10:00 p.m.

Alcohol also has some detectable **health benefits**. Studies have found that moderate consumption of alcohol (as few as one drink every other day) benefits healthy adults of all age groups, but primarily for men over age 50. It helps increase HDLs (the good cholesterol) and reduces blood clots that can trigger a heart attack. Researchers have also determined that pigments known as polyphenols found in red wine "inhibit the production of a peptide that contributes to hardening of the arteries."

Consumers know more about the **contents** of the cat and dog food for their pets than the alcoholic beverages they drink. Congress has been unable to pass a law requiring that consumers be informed about the composition of the alcoholic products they consume.

The National Public Services Research Center, a nonprofit research institute, regularly calculates the annual social cost of how Americans live their lives. Of all abused substances tobacco takes a **$94 billion** toll on health care costs. That amounts to **$350** per person per year. The alcohol-related costs to society (including medical care, lost wages, and lost hours of work) total $128 billion. That is the equivalent, says the Center, of 50 cents per drink consumed annually.

Review and Summary of Key Terms and Concepts

1. Why are **buying health services** so challenging?

2. Describe two **guidelines on how to purchase services**.

3. Distinguish among: **registration, certification** and **licensure**.

4. Cite some facts suggesting that the U.S. **health system** does not serve consumers well.

5. Explain how Americans with insurance are already paying the health care costs for those who are **uninsured**.

6. List some factors that lead to the failure of proposals for **health care reform**?

7. What are the effects of putting **caps on punitive damages** for medical malpractice?

8. List three of the unique aspects of the **medical care market** that make it difficult to reform.

9. What is **managed care** and how does it reduce health care costs?

10. What is the role of the **primary care physician**?

11. Distinguish between **prescription** and **over-the-counter (OTC)** drugs.

12. Summarize how the U.S. does a **pre-market review** of prescription drugs.

13. What is a **generic drug**, and what does the term **bioavailability** have to do with generic drugs?

14. What are some of the **problems and dangers** of over-the-counter drugs?

15. What are some of the pluses and minuses of **aspirin**?

16. Summarize some of the difficulties in **drug advertising**.

17. What are some of the difficulties consumers have with **dietary supplements**?

18. Describe some relationships among the top ten **official causes of death** and the top nine **underlying causes of death**.

19. Cite some facts and arguments against **tobacco smoking**.

20. Offer some pluses and minuses of **alcohol consumption**.

21. Why do some people persist in **harming their health**?

Useful Resources for Consumers

Action on Smoking and Health
www.ash.org/

American Academy of Family Physicians (patient information site)
www.familydoctor.org

American Association of Retired Persons
www.aarp.org

American Association of Health Plans
www.aahp.org/

American Medical Association
www.ama-assn.org/ama/pub/category/3457.html

Buying Medicines and Medical Products Online (Food and Drug Administration)
www.fda.gov/oc/buyonline/default.htm

Cancer clinical trials
www.emergingmed.com

Centers for Disease Control and Prevention
www.cdc.gov

Center for Patient Advocacy
www.patientadvocacy.org

Families USA
www.familiesusa.org

First Gov for Consumers
www.consumer.gov/

Food and Drug Administration
www.fda.gov/cder/consumerinfo

Health Research Group
www.citizen.org/hrg/

Memorial Sloan-Kettering Cancer Center
Lung Cancer Rick Assessment Tool
www.mskcc.org/predictiontools/lungcancer

Medline Plus Health Information
www.nlm.nih.gov/medlineplus/

National Cancer Institute
www.cancernet.nci.nih.gov

National Center for Health Statistics
www.cdc.gov/nchs/

National Council Against Health Fraud
www.ncahf.org

National Institutes of Health
www.nih.gov

National Library of Medicine
www.nlm.nih.gov/medlineplus

Quackwatch
www.quackwatch.com

U.S. Department of Health and Human Resources
www.os.dhhs.gov

"What Do You Think" Questions

1. Select one of the **guidelines on how to purchase services** that you believe is especially difficult for consumers to follow. Offer suggestions to government and the health care profession on how to improve the situation.

2. If you were the benevolent "dictator" of the United States and supported **health care reform**, list some possible actions you would take.

3. What additional actions do you think government should take to discourage young people from **smoking**?

4. What are your views on why some people persist in **harming their health**?

Chapter 16

Product Safety Issues

OBJECTIVES

After reading this chapter, you should be able to

1. Comprehend that many products cause injuries and deaths.

2. Appreciate how governments make benefit-cost decisions in product safety.

3. Recognize the role of the Consumer Product Safety Commission.

4. Describe how the National Highway Traffic Safety Administration reduces deaths, injuries, and property losses.

5. Realize that criticisms of product safety laws are unwarranted.

6. Recognize that product liability lawsuits are powerful weapons of consumers.

Some consumer products have **built-in hazards**, such as knives that cut, motor vehicles that crash, matches that burn, and skateboards that tip allowing riders to get hurt when falling. Other consumer products have hazards that are not so apparent, perhaps hidden. For example, it is almost impossible for consumers to know that their motor vehicle brakes or steering are defectively manufactured. Small children have difficulty recognizing the hazardous nature of playing with matches, drinking bottles of home-use pesticides, or riding on an all-terrain vehicle. The result of product dangers such as these is a considerable number of injuries and deaths.

This chapter begins by examining the topics of product safety and effectiveness and the causal factors in injuries. The concept of benefit-cost analysis also is examined since it is fundamental to government involvement in product safety regulation. Next the chapter focuses on the role of two major federal agencies involved in product safety: the Consumer Product Safety Commission (CPSC) and the National Highway Traffic Safety Administration (NHTSA). Following a summary of criticisms of product safety efforts, the chapter concludes with an examination of why product liability lawsuits are so vital to the consumer interest.

Product Safety and Effectiveness

"Blame the customer" was the traditional defense of businesses that manufactured and sold harmful products. Fifty years ago "blame the driver" was what the auto manufacturers said. Until recently, cigarette manufacturers claimed that addiction and commercials were not the problem, rather it was "smoker behavior." Most consumer product manufacturers have changed from the then prevalent 1960s perspective that "**customer misuse** caused the injuries and death, not the products" to "yes, we should try to make safer products."

Today consumers, government, and industry strongly support the **self-regulatory efforts** of product manufacturers as they go to considerable efforts to design, develop, and sell safe products. Sellers want increased sales and profits, not lawsuits and bad publicity. Still the competitive marketplace has not been a very effective mechanism for providing the degree of safety that American society demands because millions of injuries and thousands of deaths occur each year.

A **constant tension** exists between safety advocates and product manufacturers, with the government acting as **referee**. As a result, a number of federal laws and regulations have been passed to help protect consumers from unsafe products. Many government agencies are involved in product safety, such as the Consumer Product Safety Commission, Food and Drug Administration, Environmental Protection Agency, and National Highway Traffic Safety Administration.

Republican conservative **critics** of efforts to regulate product safety argue that: (1) regulations limit the freedom of people to make individual choices by themselves when government mandates some product designs and bans particular products from the marketplace, (2) standards and recalls increase the cost of all products, and (3) regulatory efforts lead to a government that is bigger, more expensive and more restrictive.

However, **most people agree** that whenever innocent consumers, especially children are being killed or injured, it is the responsibility of the government to intervene to protect the public health. While federally mandated safety standards cost manufacturers millions of dollars, they save lives and reduce injuries. **SAFE Circle** (www.saferam.org), a voluntary group of businesses, promotes and publicizes good product safety practices, educates business about safety, encourages companies to adopt forward-looking safety practices, and recognizes outstanding corporate safety behavior.

Many Products Cause Injuries

Each year about 60 million, or **one in four** Americans are injured or killed. Research by *The Washington Post* found that this includes 143,000 deaths, 2.3 million hospitalizations, and 54 million less severe injuries. The associated causes of death include motor vehicle crashes, 41,800; firearms, 32,000 (39 percent are homicides); falls, 13,000; poisonings, 6,000; drownings, 6,000; fires and burns, 4,000; and **consumer products, 29,000**. Half of the injuries are caused by consumer products commonly found around the home, such as bicycles, toys, lawn mowers, household chemicals, furniture, appliances, and power tools. The injuries often require medical treatment and/or absence from work. The total cost is estimated at $42 billion a year.

The child's world of reality is filled with too many **sharp edges** (instead of rounded ones), objects that are breakable, and some toxic materials. It seems that nothing is "childproof." **Accidents** are the **leading killers of children**. More children die of preventable injuries each year than from all childhood diseases combined. Each year nearly **8,000 children under age 15 die** of accidents associated with consumer products; another 50,000 are permanently disabled. Today's complex technology certainly poses threats to the physical security of Americans, both children and adults.

DID YOU KNOW?
Toy Safety Recommendations for Gift Givers

There 30+ toy-related deaths annually and more than half are from **choking**. Another 160,000 are treated in hospital emergency rooms. The Child Safety Act banned toys that contain small parts for children under age 3 and ordered choke-hazard warnings for those between 3 and 6. However, gift purchasers should never assume that the toys they find on store shelves are safe, even though the great majority are.

Be skeptical of prepackaged toys unless a sample is available to examine. Gift givers should **avoid buying a toy with small parts** that can be pulled off and ingested. Refrain from buying anything with small parts (including balls), such as anything less than 1 1/4 inches in diameter or smaller than a child's fist. Avoid items with a long cord, chain, string or elastic band, as it could encircle a child's neck. Products with sharp edges and points should be avoided. Consumers should vigorously shake a toy before purchasing it, because if it comes apart, lacerations are likely to occur with use. Age labeling on toys is not designed for a child's mental age, but for his or her chronological age.

Causal Factors in Injuries

Product safety supporters are primarily concerned about: (1) reducing the **incidence** of injuries by preventing them from occurring in the first place, and (2) reducing the **severity** of injuries when they do occur.

A number of factors must be examined **before government can attempt to regulate** improved product safety. Foremost is the need for **adequate information**. Reliable systems of epidemiologic information need to be in place to provide useful and meaningful data regarding deaths and injuries.

Casual factors also need to be clearly identified. People often "blame the product" for an injury, and sometimes poor product design *is* the cause of injuries that result through normal product use. Some products have defects that occur during the manufacturing processes. A product designed with no safety flaws **in normal use may result in injury** if it is damaged or used beyond some safe product life. Other factors include new scientific information about dangers from materials previously thought safe, accidental contamination, tampering, unforeseen misuse of products, and/or failure to meet safety standards.

CONSUMER UPDATE:
Top Ten Sellers of Unsafe Products

10. **General Motors**—2.3 million C/K pickups, model years 1973 through 1987, are still on the road despite the fact that they are rolling firebombs because the 5-foot gasoline tank is mounted on the outside of the truck's frame. So far, 800 deaths and thousands of disfigured fire victims have been reported.

9. **Ford**—The Environmental Working Group (which has internal memos) says Ford lied about safety in the Bronco II in two investigations of the National Highway Traffic Safety Administration.

8. **Wal-Mart Stores** and subsidiary **Icon Health and Fitness**—Were sued by the Department of Justice for failing to report serious safety hazards associated with home exercise equipment. Many of the incidents occurred at Wal-Mart stores while customers were trying out the equipment. This is the first time that the government has sued a retailer in federal court for failing to report product-related injuries.

7. **Customer Company** paid $225,000 to settle allegations that it knowingly sold disposable cigarette lighters that failed to meet government requirements for child resistance.

6. **Federated Department Stores (Bloomingdale's, Macy's)**—Paid $850,000 civil penalty to settle charges that it knowingly sold loose-fitting, 100 percent untreated cotton flammable garments as children's sleepwear.

5. **High Star Toys**—Over four years and on 12 occasions the company imported 19 different toys that failed to comply with The CPSC's small parts regulation; fined $45,000.

4. **Glitter and Spice Enterprises**—Stopped the sale of and recalled chiffon skirts and blouses that failed flammability standards for clothing. Six months later they were caught selling these unsafe products. Fined $10,000 and two owners placed on three years of probation.

3. **Tensor, Inc.**—Paid $125,000 civil penalty for failing to report defects in a timely manner with its 500-watt halogen light bulbs used in torchiere lamps, in spite of receiving over 250 complaints of the bulbs in these lamps shattering, resulting in at least six burn injuries and 35 fires.

2. **Fisher-Price**—Paid $1.1 million to settle charges that it failed to report serious safety defects with its "Power Wheels" ride-on toy vehicles that presented fire hazards and failed to stop. The firm kept consumer complaints secret until The CPSC investigated.

1. **Cosco and Safety 1st** — Over seven years repeatedly withheld information about deadly flaws in 2.4 million of their cribs, strollers, highchairs, baby bath seats, and car seat carriers; instead blaming misuse as 300 babies got hurt and two died; $1.75 million fine was the largest in CPSC history against a children's product manufacturer.

The CPSC requires **child-resistant packaging** on more than 30 types of household cleaners and medicines. More than 800 children's lives have been saved from accidental poisoning from aspirin and other drugs over the past 30 years. The added cost for child-resistant products, says the CPSC, is between half a cent and two cents.

Even though **user behavior** is often the proximate cause of accidents associated with consumer products rather than the product, injuries often occur when a product that is safe to use is misused. Environmental factors also may be involved, such as weather or darkness. For example, when a child is riding his or her bicycle home at dusk, it is difficult to see small pebbles and potholes in the road that may "cause" an accident.

Incorrect age use is another causal factor. Children often get injured or die when driving an adult-styled product, such as an **all-terrain vehicle (ATV)** that has oversized tires and handlebars. Over the past 20 years ATVs have been responsible for 1,200 deaths of children under age 16 and 400,000 injuries. Although kids under age 16 make up only 14 percent of ATV drivers, they represent 36 percent of the fatalities and 40 percent of the injuries. The CPSC reports that injuries have doubled in the past four years, partly because of bigger and faster ATVs. It's a simple problem to figure out. These powerful machines can roll over quite easily. Consumer advocates want states to consider mandatory licensing and required safety classes and helmet use. Also, safety advocates have filed a petition with the Consumer Product Safety Commission (CPSC) requesting that it prohibit the sale of adult-sized four-wheel ATVs for use by children under age 16.

Another causal factor may be the **psychological** or **physical condition** of the consumer. For example, a man who is physically and mentally tired from a long workday and who is also in a hurry so he can go out for supper, may not be in the safest condition at 7 o'clock in the evening to mow his lawn.

Product manufacturers sometimes say that **human behavioral** and **environmental conditions** are beyond their responsibility in terms of product safety design because it is impossible to figure all the ways consumers can use or abuse products. They also argue that reliable product safety data suggest that less than half the injuries associated with consumer products result primarily because of the product itself. Most consumer **misuse is foreseeable** or easy to anticipate; however, some hazards seem almost impossible to deal with, such as when children choke and die as a result of ingesting pieces of uninflated balloons. Consumer advocates argue that it is futile to rely solely on trying to modify consumer behavior when increased government regulation of product safety features can quickly reduce injuries. It has been estimated that perhaps 20 percent of all product injuries could be prevented if the manufacturers sold better-designed products.

Benefit-Cost Analysis and Safety

Failure to use rational principles in **decision-making** means that some consumers will suffer needless injuries and deaths. Thus governments and businesses try to use rational principles in making safety decisions so society can save lives and reduce injuries for a given level of spending on safety. **Benefit-cost analysis** (or **cost-benefit analysis**) is an approach to policy recommendation that permits analysts to compare and advocate policies by quantifying all their total monetary costs and benefits, including various intangibles that are not easily measured. The economically rational policy recommendation, therefore, is to choose actions that maximize social welfare by yielding the highest net benefits given limited time and money. A **net benefit** is the total of all the benefits of a course of action less all the costs.

For example, if the costs of a proposal (such as adding design and material changes) add up to $1.00 per product and the benefits (such as reduced injuries and fewer deaths) are expected to amount to $1.10 per incident, the proposal passes the test. In effect, the opportunity costs of an investment are calculated on the basis of what net benefits might be gained. Since it is impossible to pin down precisely *all* the marginal benefits associated with proposed changes (such as how to measure risk or the value of nature), it is extremely **unwise to make final policy decisions based solely on quantitative benefit-cost analyses**.

When calculating cost-benefit analyses the Environmental Protection Agency sometimes assigns a value of $3.7 million for a **human life**. They use a figure of $2.3 million for people older than age 70.

Another example is a corporation that fixes faulty designs in future products, but does not want to correct **old problems**, preferring instead to fight lawsuits because the cost is frequently less than that of recalls. This is an application of benefit-cost analysis. A **recall** is a request by a manufacturer of a product specified as defective for its return to the seller for necessary repair, exchange, adjustment, or refund. Recalls can be performed voluntarily by a business or when ordered by a government agency.

The Consumer Product Safety Commission by a 2-to-1 vote denied a petition to require that all children's products come with postage-free **registration cards** to help notify purchasers when a product is determined to be dangerous. A Consumer Federation of America-sponsored website, www.SafeChild.net, has a free, noncommercial e-mail notification service for major child-safety product recalls. Their **Toy Recall Database** lets users conduct a search of 350 major recalls during the past decade. Also, Safety Alerts (www.safetyalerts.com/) lists all types of recalls.

How Much Risk is Acceptable?

How society answers the question "How much risk is acceptable in consumer products?" reveals a lot about how the economic resources of the country are going to be spent. Years ago the National Commission on Product Safety made observations about the reasonableness of product hazards. They reported that **reasonable risks** occur "when consumers understand that risks exist, can appraise their probability and severity, know how to cope with them, and voluntarily accept them and get the benefits that could not be obtained in less risky ways." The commission report observed that **unreasonable risks** occur "when consumers do not know that they exist; or when, though aware of them, **consumers are unable to estimate their frequency and severity**; or when consumers **do not know how to cope with them**, and hence are likely to incur harm unnecessarily; or when risk is unnecessary in that it could be reduced or eliminated at a cost in money or in the performance of the product that consumers would willingly incur if they knew the facts and were given the choice."

DID YOU KNOW?
General Motors' Price on Fire Deaths Used to be $2.40

A 27-year old cost-benefit analysis conducted by a young engineer, Edward Ivey, at General Motors was called the **Ivey Report**, in which the author determined that the cost would be about $2.40 per vehicle to prevent post-collision fuel-fed fires. It has never been determined if GM knowingly chose to continue to produce cars that could explode in crashes.

The question is whether or not consumers **can make rational decisions** regarding safety. Factors to consider are how well known is the risk, if all user groups (i.e., children, elderly, and other adults) understand the risks, and the likelihood of abnormal uses of the product. Compounding the difficulty of risk determination is the fact that consumers must **make risk decisions many times every da**y, and that lessens their appreciation of each individual risk. Most consumers do not have the ability to accurately estimate their exposures to risk and the expected value of losses associated with product choices.

Another difficulty regarding unreasonable risks occurs when government attempts to decide **how much risk** is acceptable for each particular product. Government does this with the realization that any action taken will infringe upon the free choice of people to make personal decisions about their welfare. Advocates of minimal marketplace intervention suggest that consumers should be given choices between safer, more expensive products and cheaper, less safe products. Government intervention also places the burden of future risk evaluation on government, rather than on consumers.

Measuring Risk for Public-Policy Decisions

An important aspect of public-policy decision-making is to assess the **magnitude of the risk**. One must first know the perils and hazards associated with a product. Then it is possible to define the degree and nature of the risk of injury that a proposed rule is designed to eliminate. Once the risk is defined, it may be possible to predict how effective a standard will be in reducing injuries and deaths and improving public health and safety.

Consider the hypothetical example in Table 16-1. Chain saws have a much higher level of risk than electric power drills and may be a more likely candidate for government regulation. One of the biggest difficulties in trying to objectively measure the magnitude of risk is establishing and **assigning values** for both injuries and deaths with injury-severity numbers and dollars.

Product	Probability of Injury	Injury Severity	Market Size	Level of Risk
Electric power drills	0.001	1	5 million	5,000
Chain saws	0.10	5	1 million	50,000

TABLE 16-1   Hypothetical Measurement of the Magnitude of Risk

Factors to Consider in Making Product Safety Decisions

Government uses **several factors** when considering whether or not to make a public-policy decision to regulate product safety:

1. There must be a known hazard.

2. There has to be some probability that the hazard causes injuries or deaths.

3. The magnitude of the loss must be such that the problem warrants attention.

4. There must be one or more preferably inexpensive alternatives to reduce the incidence and severity of losses.

5. The benefits must seem to outweigh the costs of implementing a safety regulation.

6. An industry group must fail to either establish voluntary product safety standards or take other self-regulatory steps to address the hazard.

7. There must be a political willingness to take action to regulate.

CONSUMER UPDATE:
Responsibilities of Consumers in Product Safety

Consumers have the responsibility to:

- Examine merchandise for safety features before buying.
- Question sellers about the safety attributes of products before purchase.
- Complete and return postage-paid registration cards on purchases so you can be notified in case of a recall.
- Carefully read product labels and literature, and heed warning labels.
- Read and follow care and use instructions carefully.
- Use products as intended and with reasonable caution and care.
- Assume personal responsibility for normal precautions when using a product.
- Inform retailers, manufacturers, trade organizations, and government agencies when a product does not perform safely.
- Identify possible defects and report them to the proper government authorities.
- Respond to recalls.

The Consumer Product Safety Commission

At the time the Consumer Product Safety Commission (CPSC) was created, unsafe products were abundant and widely distributed. Self-regulation was not working very well. Consumer groups were actively involved throughout the 1960s in publicizing product safety shortcomings until Congress finally got into the act to **preempt weak and nonexistent state laws**. Until creation of the CPSC, government had taken a **piecemeal approach** to product safety, attacking problems in response to individual tragedies and public outcries. The CPSC was formally established in 1973 to protect consumers against unreasonable risks of injuries associated with consumer products. The **serious risks** are amputation, electrocution, burns, asphyxiation, cancer and death.

Creation of the CPSC was a major step forward as it established for the first time an agency dedicated to ensuring that consumers are protected from unreasonable product risks. The responsibilities for a number of existing fragmented product safety efforts were **centralized** and a reasonably comprehensive approach to product safety evolved. The main goal of the commission is to provide for a safer public market of consumer goods.

The CPSC is a five-member **independent** regulatory agency. Its members are appointed by the President for 7-year terms and approved by the U.S. Senate. One commissioner serves as chair. The CPSC has a staff of 500 and an annual budget of $50 million; that amounts to 45 cents per year per household. The CPSC's budget is less than 2 percent of the $3.5 billion of the Environmental Protection Agency and less than 5 percent of the Food and Drug Administration's $1 billion.

The commission regulates only products **sold in the United States**. Some examples are bicycles, chain saws, toys, coffee makers, television antennas, baby cribs, and stereos. The CPSC regulates through standard-setting, product bans, refunds, and recalls. Few products are not under its control. Other federal agencies have developed special expertise with certain products and have legal jurisdiction over them, such as motor vehicles, bullets, fireworks, food, drugs, cosmetics, medical devices, alcohol, tobacco, aircraft, boats, and pesticides. Despite the fact that firearms kill twice as many people as all household products combined, there is no federal agency responsible for ensuring that defectively designed guns are not sold. Firearms are **exempt** from oversight by the CPSC.

CPSC Legal Mandates and Responsibilities

The CPSC has **two key legal authorities**: the Consumer Products Safety Act and the Federal Hazardous Substances Act. It also enforces the Flammable Fabrics Act, the Child Protection Act, the Poison Prevention Packaging Act, the Refrigerator Safety Act, and the Child Safety Protection Act. The broad responsibilities of The CPSC are:

- To gather and disseminate information related to product injuries;

- To protect the public against unreasonable risks of injury associated with consumer products used in and around the home, in schools, and in recreation areas;

- To promote the use of uniform safety standards;

- To help consumers evaluate the comparative safety of products;

- To require manufacturers of CPSC-regulated products to conduct a testing program to ensure that their products are safe and meet appropriate safety standards; and

- To promote research and investigation into the causes and the prevention of product-related deaths, injuries, and illnesses.

The CPSC works with industry to develop **voluntary safety standards**, those adopted by industry organizations. The Consumer Product Safety Act (CSPA) requires the agency to defer to voluntary standards instead of promulgating mandatory standards where there is a voluntary standard that adequately addresses a product safety problem and there is substantial compliance with that standard.

The CPSC **issues and enforces** mandatory safety standards, bans unsafe products, encourages and/or orders recalls and repairs of unsafe products, conducts research on potential product hazards, and conducts information and education programs. The CPSC has a toll-free hotline (800-638-2772) to receive reports about potentially hazardous consumer products and provide safety information to the public about product recalls.

A number of hazardous products **are found every year**, observes David Pittle, Technical Director at *Consumer Reports* and former chairman of the Product Safety Commission. Examples are swing sets with ladders with wrung spacings far too close together (too easy to lead to strangulation for a child playing on them); a prominent swing that could flip over backwards; and food blenders that presented shock hazards when they were wet.

CPSC Authorities and Powers

The Consumer Product Safety Commission has several authorities and powers:

1. **It has the authority to set mandatory product safety standards for consumer products** under Section 7 of the Consumer Products Safety Act. Standards may set forth requirements as to product performance, composition, content, construction, finish, packaging, and design. Products may also be required to carry warnings or instructions. Standards that have the force of law must be reasonably necessary to prevent or reduce an unreasonable risk of injury associated with such products. The

CPSC standards typically preempt state or local product safety standards when it is in the public interest to do so.

2. **It can ban a product after taking court action to declare it an imminent or substantial hazard.** The CPSC can do this when it determines that there is no feasible standard that will protect the public from unreasonable risk of injury. An **imminent hazard** is a product that presents an impending and unreasonable risk of death, serious illness, or severe personal injury. An imminent hazard presents the highest risk to the public. For example, several years ago one particular brand of a mechanic's trouble light was declared an imminent hazard because its poor design allowed people to easily become electrocuted. The lights were withdrawn from the market and recalled from consumers who had purchased them.

   A **substantial hazard** is a product that fails to comply with applicable consumer product safety rules and creates a substantial risk of injury to the public. Substantial hazards also include product defects which because of the pattern of the defect, the number of defective products distributed in commerce, the severity of the risk, or otherwise creates a substantial risk of injury to the public. Products found to be substantial hazards under Section 15 of the CPSA are usually one item in a manufacturer's product line, such as a defective electric lamp. Here The CPSC can initiate action to ban the product from the marketplace. Upon approval by a U.S. District Court, hazardous products are then **banned**, which means that the product can no longer be sold. **Banning** is an official decree of prohibition by a federal court issued when no feasible safety standard would adequately protect the public.

   Most products that are banned are removed from the market under **Section 8** of the CPSA because they present an unreasonable risk of injury to the public by failing to meet known standards and regulations. Examples of banned products include: flammable imported rayon scarves, unstable refuse bins that fall on people, flammable contact adhesives used on floor tiles, paints containing leads, patching compounds containing asbestos, and lawn darts (a game similar to horse-shoes). The values of these products in the market were far outweighed by the number of serious accidents and deaths.

3. **It can issue administrative recall orders of products found to present a substantial hazard to compel repair, replacement or refunds.** After a hearing, The CPSC can compel manufacturers to recall a hazardous product, refund its purchase price, repair or modify it to proper safety standards, or replace it with a comparable item that meets appropriate safety standards. The CPSC can suggest a voluntary recall to a manufacturer or order a mandatory one, but most recalls are voluntary. Recalls and repairs are ordered for products that fail to comply with mandatory standards or that present substantial hazards or imminent hazards to consumers. This approach is called **managing by exception**, since most consumer products are safe. When a product is recalled, the manufacturer must make efforts to notify buyers that a safety defect has been discovered, often by mail or with radio and television announcements and advertisements.

   Examples of products that have been recalled are: Power Wheels that caught on fire, toy basketball hoops that strangled children, Flying Warriers plastic that broke and caused eye injury, Felix the Cat Roller Fun Balls that had seams that separated and presented a choking hazard, hair dryers that expelled asbestos, paint strippers that were too powerful, baby cribs that caused strangulation of infants (see www.Dannyfoundation.org), toys with parts that were swallowed by small children because they failed an established regulation, and smoke detectors that failed to operate in the presence of smoke. The CPSC makes about 200 to 300 product recalls each year, although the consumers **return less than 20 percent** of recalled products.

4.   **If necessary, The CPSC can file a legal request in federal court to have goods recalled and/or seized that do not comply with a regulation.**

5.   **The CPSC can impose both civil and criminal penalties.** Civil fines for CPSA violations are $2,000 for each offence and up to $500,000 for multiple infractions. People who knowingly and willfully violate the laws are subject to one year in prison.

6.   **Manufacturers can be fined for failing to notify The CPSC within 24 hours after realizing that they have a hazardous product.** Section 15 of the Consumer Product Safety Act requires that manufacturers notify The CPSC if they become aware that any product either fails to comply with appropriate product safety rules and standards or contains a defect that could create a substantial hazard to consumers. Failure to report can subject a company to fines of up to $1.25 million. Half of the most serious product hazards are discovered by CPSC investigators, instead of being reported by the companies as required by law. Companies that were recently fined include Black & Decker (toaster fires, $575,000), Baby's Dream Cribs (fingertip amputations, $200,000), Hasbro (skull fractures from infant carriers, $400,000), and Cosco (strangulation from toddler bed guardrails, $725,000). Children's product manufacturers too often knowingly sell unsafe products, including six infant deaths in Playskool portable cribs and 14 infant deaths in Graco's Convert-a-Cradle.

  After repeated violations of **section 15**, two companies, Cosco and Safety 1st (owned by Dorel Industries of Montreal), again **did not tell** the CPSC about hundreds of injuries and two deaths, this time from collapsing strollers, baby-trapping cribs, and Options 5 highchair. They repeatedly kept quiet and hid potentially deadly flaws in their products, and blamed consumer misuse as babies got hurt and died. The slap-on-the-wrists $1.3 million penalty was CSPC's highest, but no criminal charges were filed even though Cosco failed to notify The CPSC about thousands of complaint reports over the past seven years regarding other dangerous products they manufactured. Cosco allegedly sold the recalled beds in Mexico.

  From this case, manufacturers everywhere should know that the Congress and CSPC are **not serious enough** about product safety. Other companies will interpret the $1.3 million fine as simply another cost of doing business, as it was equal to a cup of Starbucks coffee for the billion-dollar company. Congress needs to give CSPC more authority and a much larger budget. Also, if the CPSC does not enforce its rules and orders, individual consumers can sue in a U.S. District Court to make it happen.

CPSC Injury Data-Collection System

  To help determine the **nature and scope of injuries** from consumer products, The CPSC has a national data-collection system known as the **National Electronic Injury Surveillance System (NEISS** which is pronounced "nice"). NEISS is the backbone of the commission's injury reporting system. NEISS collects data from death certificates and interviews with nurses, physicians, and injury victims from 101 statistically-representative hospital emergency rooms located across the country. This permits The CPSC to calculate national injury estimates by associated product.

  Approximately **38 percent of all injuries** are treated in **hospital emergency rooms**, 41 percent are treated in doctors' offices, 18 percent are treated at home, and 3 percent become inpatient cases. Participating hospitals classify injuries according to about 15,000 consumer products. NEISS excludes mishaps linked to vehicles, foods, drugs, cosmetics, pesticides, or the workplace because other agencies handle those. The information from hospitals is processed by The CPSC and extrapolated into national statistics. NEISS projections can then help identify those products most often related to injuries.

Sports, with basketball and football leading the list, account for **one-third** of the 12 million emergency room visits every year. Other products that are associated with injuries most frequently reported by hospital emergency rooms are in descending order: stairs, ramps, landings, floors, beds and mattresses, tables, glass doors, windows, panels, playground equipment, bathroom structure and fixtures, and cans and containers. Consumer products that are frequently involved in injuries or which can cause severe injuries are usually considered priority items for regulation.

CPSC Rulemaking Procedures

The CPSC has rules to establish performance, design, composition, packaging and construction standards for a number of products. **Examples** of products with mandatory safety standards are bicycles, matchbooks,; cigarette lighters (deaths have dropped from 250 to 125 annually), walk-behind lawn power mowers, residential garage door openers, baby cribs, baby rattles, child-resistant packaging, swimming pool slides, power lawn mowers, chain saws, home-use pesticides, and cellulose insulation. The CPSC rules require fire-risk hang tags and permanent labels on snug-fitting sleepwear made of cotton or cotton blends as well as flammability labels on general wearing apparel, furniture, mattresses, carpeting, and rugs. The CPSC issues safety standards in an effort to reduce injuries and save lives. For example, think about how much easier it is to see a bicycle on the street at night because of the **mandatory safety reflectors**.

CPSC Rulemaking Authority

The CPSC can **promulgate regulations** under authorities granted from the Consumer Product Safety Act. It also can issue regulations under authorities granted from the Federal Hazardous Substances Act and the Flammable Fabrics Act, although these can only be used for toys or other articles intended for use by children that present electrical, mechanical, or thermal hazards. In rulemaking, The CPSC **must follow the standard government rulemaking procedures** under the guidelines of the federal Administrative Procedures Act. It takes a minimum of about 18 months for The CPSC to issue informal regulations and three or four years using formal rulemaking procedures.

Any interested person, including a consumer or consumer organization, may **petition** The CPSC to commence a proceeding for the issuance, amendment, or revocation of a consumer product safety rule as described in the APA. CPSA uses performance standards whenever possible, rather than specific design standards. Thus consumers, industry, and government may play a vital role in the development of a trade regulation.

The CPSC can participate in some **voluntary standards** proceeding as a nonvoting member. The CPSC is required to try to get industry to develop reasonable voluntary safety standards whenever possible. Accordingly, many well-qualified industry groups have been intimately involved in the rulemaking process. Examples include the Underwriters' Laboratories (UL), the American Society for Testing and Materials (ASTM), and the American National Standards Institute (ANSI). Although voluntary standards can be implemented more quickly than mandatory standards, critics allege that the standard-setting bodies often fail to make the process more open to government and consumer groups.

Rulemaking to develop a standard is a **very technical**, complex and expensive process that requires the cooperative efforts of manufacturers and sellers. In general, hearings must be held to allow citizens to make inputs to the process. Often state and federal governments rely on voluntary standards because they lack the expertise and resources to develop their own. When writing standards, particularly mandatory standards, it is common to have an official record in a rulemaking procedure amount to thousands of pages, including research data, testimony and comments.

Certain Factors Must be Considered in CPSC Rulemaking

Before any product safety standard can be promulgated, the laws require that **several factors** be considered: (1) the incidence and severity of injuries or illnesses associated with a product, (2) the nature of the risk of injuries that will be reduced or eliminated, (3) the expected support from the public given their attitude toward the proposed rule, (4) the effect of the proposed rule on the public's need for the product, and (5) the effect of the proposed rule on competition and manufacturing. The CPSC is required to use **benefit-cost analysis** in the decision-making process.

Needed Consumer Product Safety Regulations

Many product safety areas are ripe for government regulatory actions, such as requiring warning labels and more informative product labels, issuing mandatory safety standards, banning products, demanding recalls, and establishing procedures to notify consumers about recalls. Government may or may not take action to regulate. Some examples are:

- **Baby bath seats** (80 infant deaths);

- **Bunk beds** (200 deaths and 35,000 injuries in 8 years);

- **Ordinary rubber balloons** (259 deaths in 20 years);

- **Bicycle helmets** (300 deaths and 50,000 head injuries annually);

- **Unstable TV stands** (28 deaths in 8 years);

- **Tight-fitting pajamas** for infants;

- **Unstable soda machines** (37 deaths and 113 injuries in 8 years);

- **Swimming pool covers** that trap and drown (26 deaths);

- **Baby cribs** with slats that fall out of side rails (12 deaths);

- **Portable bed rails** (14 deaths);

- **Accordion-style baby gates** (8 deaths);

- **Child-resistant mouthwash bottles** (3 deaths);

- **Small balls and toys** (186 choking deaths in 11 years);

- **Empty 5-gallon buckets** (1 child dies every nine days in a few inches of water);

- **Hand-held hair dryers** that electrocute about 20 people each year, usually when the dryers are dropped into the bathtub with the switch in the incorrectly presumed-safe "off position";

- **Baby walkers** (29,000 emergency room visits annually);

- **Space heaters** (the old-style oil and gas heaters asphyxiate victims and all types burn children, and they cause 21,000 house fires and 300 deaths annually);

- **Halogen lamps** have bulbs that warm to 970 degrees and sometimes set fire to curtains, bedding material and ceilings (30 fires and 2 deaths annually);

- **Infant car seat/carriers** (460 injuries);

- **All-terrain vehicles (ATVs)** (1,200 deaths and 400,000 injuries) and

- **Public playgrounds** (200,000 injuries from falls annually).

The National Highway Traffic Safety Administration

The National Highway Traffic Safety Administration (NHTSA) is an administrative unit in the Department of Transportation created in 1966. The NHTSA's single administrator is appointed by the President.

NHTSA Legal Mandates and Authorities

The NHTSA enforces the National Traffic and Motor Vehicle Safety Act, Highway Safety Act, Motor Vehicle Information and Cost Savings Act, Intermodal Surface Transportation Act, and the TREAD Act of 2000 (Transportation Recall Enhancement, Accountability and Documentation Act). The NHTSA was established to reduce highway deaths, injuries, and property losses caused by motor vehicle accidents. The NHTSA establishes and enforces minimum safety and performance standards for motor vehicles and related equipment called the **Federal Motor Vehicle Safety Standards (FMVSS)**. The NHTSA's budget is $350 million and it has 700 employees. Since the NHTSA was established, it is estimated that **1.2 million lives have been saved** and many millions of injuries avoided.

Traffic deaths in the U.S. rose last year to 42,850 for the first time in more than a decade, due in part to rising alcohol-related deaths (17,970), motorcycle deaths (3,276) and non-use of seatbelts (59 percent of deaths). Two-thirds of deaths are passengers. The annual 6.8 million vehicle crashes result in 4 million people sent to emergency rooms, 400,000 hospitalizations and half of those with permanent disabilities. More than a quarter of accidents are caused by people who are distracted by other activities, such as talking on a cell phone or eating. If every state strictly enforced **seat-belt laws**, deaths would drop by 7,000 each year. Seatbelt usage is 75 percent nationally.

Motor vehicle crashes are the **leading killers** of Americans under the age of 35 and the leading cause of head injuries, epilepsy, quadriplegia, paraplegia, and facial injuries. People are now surviving vehicle accidents that a few years ago would have been fatal. A result is rising medical costs for crash survivors with serious injuries.

Even though twice as many miles are driven annually compared to 25 years ago, the fatality rate in cars has dropped from 5.7 deaths per 100 million vehicles to a 1.8 rate, **a 70-year low**. That is a difference of between 50,000 and perhaps 130,000 deaths that would have occurred without government motor vehicle safety laws. Why has this occurred? Ralph Nader's answer is: "Regulations."

Fatality rates per 100,000 deaths by **age group** are: age 16 (35); 17 - 19 (25); 20 and older (11). Drivers age 15 to 20 make up 7 percent of the population but account for 15 percent of the fatalities. Males account for 76 percent of fatalities and females 24 percent. The Department of Transportation says that 61 percent of those who died in vehicle accidents were not wearing seat belts, and 60 percent of them would have survived had they buckled up.

DID YOU KNOW?
Vehicle Death Rates

When yesteryear's heavier cars averaged 14 miles per gallon (mpg), the death rate per 10,000 was **3.5**. The **death rate** in today's 28 mpg much lighter vehicles is 2.1. The Insurance Institute for Highway Safety and the Center for Auto Safety say that automobiles can be downsized without trading off safety.

The odds of dying in a vehicle crash today are **1 in 8,000**. The death rates per 10,000 registered vehicles by the size of autos are: very small, 2.9; small, 2.1; small mid-size, 2.1; medium mid-size, 1.4; large, 1.1; very large, 0.7. (See www.highwaysafety.org/.) The incidence of severe injuries and death increases as the length of the wheelbase decreases because both size and weight are factors. The laws of physics dictate that, everything else being equal, the **larger the vehicle the safer the occupants**.

Of all motor vehicle deaths, the proportion of fatally injured drivers with high blood **alcohol concentrations** (0.10 percent or more) remains at 38 percent. Among fatally injured male drivers, 44 percent had blood alcohol levels above 0.10 percent compared to 22 percent of women.

The NHTSA has jurisdiction over **all types of motor vehicles** such as automobiles, trucks, buses, recreational vehicles, motorcycles, and mopeds. It handles complaints about the safety of motor vehicles and failures of associated vehicle equipment and accessories. The NHTSA conducts investigations looking for safety-related defects and equipment failures that cause safety problems. The NHTSA has rulemaking authority. It also enforces laws and regulations requiring recalls and associated remedies for motor vehicles and vehicle equipment, and it is empowered to force manufacturers to recall and repair unsafe vehicles. There are about **300 recalls every year**

CONSUMER UPDATE:
Bridgestone-Firestone Tires/Ford Explorer SUV Tire Blowouts
Scandal Shows that NHTSA Needs More Powers to Police the Market

The Bridgestone/Firestone/Ford tire scandal took **203 lives**, was implicated in 250 serious injuries, and it caught flatfooted the government's National Highway Traffic Safety Administration (NHTSA). The **tire blowouts** due to tire separations occurred mostly in Ford Explorers, and 6.5 million tires were recalled. History buffs may remember that Firestone had the same scandal in 1978, with blowouts due to failing the *same* 30-year old tire performance tests. That time Firestone was forced to recall 14.5 million tires...." There is no question that the company knew they had a problem [for several years]," says Joan Claybrook of Public Citizen (and former head of the NHTSA), "but they **kept it quiet**."

The Bridgestone/Firestone scandal demonstrated that The NHTSA has weak powers and, as a result, the federal agency cannot do a very good job policing the economic marketplace. It has no power, like the CPSC does, to require manufacturers to report to the NHTSA when companies are sued about an alleged safety defect or repeated complaints about a possible defect. The NHTSA can fine companies $1,100 per violation, but for a total of no more than $925,000–hardly a threat for companies with billions of dollars in annual sales. Public Citizen's Joan Claybrook recommends that Congress give **new powers** to the NHTSA including "an increase in civil penalties for failure to recall a defective vehicle or part or withholding information from the agency; add criminal penalties for reckless endangerment and knowing and willful refusal to recall a defective vehicle or part or for withholding information that results in deaths and injuries; require reporting of warranty and lawsuit information to give the government an early warning of a problem; and require that manufacturers report recalls in foreign countries to the NHTSA."

NHTSA Mandates

The NHTSA is legally required to perform several mandates:

- Investigate safety defects in motor vehicles.

- Establish and enforce federal motor vehicle safety standards.

- Promote the use of safety belts, child safety belts, and air bags.

- Help states and communities reduce the threat of drunk drivers.

- Investigate odometer fraud.

- Establish and enforce vehicle anti-theft regulations.

- Set and enforce fuel economy standards.

- Conduct research on driver behavior and traffic safety.

- Provide the public with information on motor vehicle safety topics.

NHTSA Recalls

The NHTSA has the authority to **order recalls** whenever substantial numbers of a safety-related defect are observed that present an unreasonable risk of accident or injury. Examples of recalls include ignition switches that could cause fires, unsafe seat belts, rear hatch latch popping open, defective steering mechanisms, failure of pins to hold seats in place, motor vehicle tire treads separating, gasoline tanks that explode in rear-end collisions, transmissions jumping from the park gear into reverse in unattended vehicles, and sudden acceleration of cars while in gear. The **success rate** for NHTSA recalls in a recent five-year period was 68 percent of all vehicles, 51 percent of equipment problems, and 28 percent for difficulties with tires. The NHTSA estimates that nearly one-third of the more than 31 million vehicles recalled in the past 30 years are rolling around unfixed.

When NHTSA suspects a safety-related defect, a **preliminary low-level safety investigation** is conducted. This informal inquiry asks manufacturers to provide information about an alleged problem. The NHTSA then conducts an engineering analysis of the safety consequences. Most often such investigations are dropped for lack of persuasive evidence. Should an analysis be negative, the manufacturer may be sent a **recall request letter** that asks the company to conduct a voluntary recall in an effort to get a defective product off the market quickly. About half such requests result in voluntary recalls, since manufacturers often contest NHTSA's findings. Most recalls supervised by the agency are initiated voluntarily by the manufacturers, not in response to government defect investigations. Court-ordered recalls are rare.

If the manufacturer **declines to recall** and the evidence points to a safety-related defect, the NHTSA opens a **formal defect investigation**. This serious investigation may take two months or two years. After the investigation is complete, the NHTSA makes its initial defect determination. It then holds a public meeting at which the public and the manufacturers present their views. The agency later makes a final decision on the matter. When a problem is judged to be serious, the NHTSA orders a recall of the product, and requires that the manufacturer remedy the difficulty.

The NHTSA can make recalls in **three situations**: (1) when specific safety defects are discovered, (2) when a manufacturer fails to comply with a Federal Motor Vehicle Safety Standards, and (3) when safety problems are observed that are common to a number of similar vehicles.

After a product is manufactured, the NHTSA has **eight years** to take action to recall vehicles and vehicle equipment and three years for tires before the agency's legal authority expires. Owners of recalled vehicles must be notified by first-class mail of any safety defects. Defective vehicles that are recalled under government order must be repaired by an authorized dealer for free. Manufacturer's policies vary when there is a voluntary recall even though the manufacturers pay the dealers to make the repairs.

CONSUMER UPDATE:
Vehicle Rollover Risk Ratings

In collisions between SUVs and cars, the occupant of the car is four times as likely to die as the occupant in the SUV. And this is one of the reasons why many consumers purchase SUVs. However an SUV offers false security.

Light trucks—a term that includes sport-utility vehicle, pickups, minivans, and some vans—account for half of the vehicles on the road today. These vehicles tend to **roll over, flip, or spin out of control** more easily than automobiles. For example, the Tracker has the highest driver death rate of any vehicle; 3.2 deaths per 10,000 registered vehicles. Real-world experience shows that these types of vehicle are inherently more dangerous than traditionally styled passenger cars. Some sport utility vehicles are nearly 20 times more likely than cars to experience a fatal rollover. Of the 10,000 drivers and passengers killed in rollover crashes annually, two-thirds die in sport utility vehicles. The NHTSA says "Almost invariably, occupants who are unbelted do not survive a rollover."

After 30 years of consideration, the National Highway Traffic Safety Administration now requires that window stickers on new cars and trucks include a **rollover rating system** for all passenger vehicles and light trucks to indicate how likely the vehicle is to turn over in a single-vehicle accident. Vehicles get one to five stars with five being the highest. **One star means a 40 percent or greater risk of rollover and five stars means a risk of less than 10 percent.** The top NHTSA administrator, Jeffrey Runge, said about the SUV rollover data he would not drive those that scored the lowest "if they were the last vehicles on earth."

Consumer advocates are not satisfied with the rollover standard. They want a **dynamic**, real-world standard, rather than a static test, to determine how vehicles do when maneuvering to avoid an accident. The rollover data found in *Consumer Reports* magazine is based on emergency-handling. Their rating system judged the Isuzu Trooper as "unacceptable." *Consumer Reports* won the **SLAPP lawsuit** (Strategic Litigation Against Public Participation) brought by Isuzu. SLAPP lawsuits are brought by businesses or industry groups to stop citizens and public interest groups from petitioning and speaking on public issues, and it takes deep financial pockets to fight back. The NHTSA has issued a new regulation that requires over-padding of pillars, side rails, roofs, and the frames around windshields, doors, and windows.

Safety advocates also want the NHTSA to require **stability-control** devices on trucks and SUVs. These are used in Europe and cost about $500 per vehicle. So far they have reduced single-car accidents by one-third and reduced deaths by 15 percent.

It is possible that a vehicle may be one of the 20 million that has some **unrepaired safety defect**. The NHTSA can provide these data to consumers, as well as information on safety defect investigations and new car crash test results. You can get a report on a motor vehicle and find out if it is part of a recall by calling the NHTSA's toll-free hotline (800-424-9393) and giving them the make, model, year, and **vehicle identification number (VIN)**. The VIN number is the numeral indicating a specific vehicle made by a manufacturer. It is visible on the dashboard when you look through the front windshield on the driver's side. Only the manufacturers' computers can tell if the defects in any particular recalled vehicle have been repaired.

The NHTSA also can assist callers who are having difficulty obtaining repair work for an existing safety recall. Manufacturers are **obligated to repair** recalled vehicles no matter how old the cars or who owns them.[1] The NHTSA also accepts complaints about safety problems in motor vehicles, tires, and vehicle equipment; copies of complaints are forwarded to the manufacturers.

NHTSA Vehicle Crashing and Testing

The NHTSA has a **New Car Assessment Program** for **crashworthiness** to determine a vehicle's overall ability to protect seat-belted front-seat drivers and passengers. To simulate a head-on crash, the NHTSA tows vehicles at 35 miles per hour into a stationary barrier and measures the impact on dummies' heads, chests, and thighbones; more than 80 percent of all crashes occur at speeds less than 35 miles per hour. Large cars are better at absorbing energy and maintaining structural integrity than small vehicles because they have more body to take the crush of the impact.

The NHTSA annually reports the results of 100+ crash safety tests it conducts by make and model. (See www.nhtsa.dot.gov/NCAP/Cars.cfm.) NHTSA's 5-star rating system summarizes the results. A 5-star rating means that there is a 10 percent or less chance of serious injury from an accident that requires immediate hospitalization and possible loss of life. At the other end of the scale, a 1-star rating means there is a 46 percent or greater chance of injury in a crash.

NHTSA Safety Standards

Over **100 Federal Motor Vehicle Safety Standards** are in effect on motor vehicles. Examples include: rear center-mounted brake signals, shatterproof windshields, collapsible steering columns, energy-absorbing bumpers, headrest restraints on the front seats, padded dashboards, non-protruding interior appliances, collapsible arm rests, seat-belt warning systems, inside-trunk latch release, over-the shoulder and lap seat belts, and front-seat air bags. The NHTSA is currently phasing in improved tire labels and loading information as well as a tire-pressure monitoring system that alerts the driver to possible problems.

ISSUE FOR DEBATE:
The U.S. Should Require Daytime Running Lights on Vehicles

For several years Canada has required all new vehicles to have **daytime running lights** as a safety feature. These automatically keep the vehicle's high-beam headlights on at a reduced brightness. This is a safety feature designed to make cars more visible to pedestrians and other drivers during daytime hours. The NHTSA *permits* daytime running lights on vehicles, but does not require them. General Motors has asked the NHTSA to mandate running lights.

Air Bag Safety

Seat belts provide protection for vehicle passengers. The chances of being killed in an accident are almost **25 times greater** if one is thrown from the vehicle. The National Public Service Research Institute (NPSRI) calculates that the cost for people injured in accidents

---

[1] However, there is no law requiring consumer notification on most of the 240 medical devices that are implanted into people, such as artificial knees and breast implants.

who fail to buckle their seat belts is $12 billion. Thus, says the NPSRI, every adult who regularly uses his or her safety belt pays $110 a year to cover the nonusers.

A **passive restraint system** is an automatic safety device that requires no special effort from the protected vehicle passenger to operate in the event of an accident. Air bags and automatic seat belts both are illustrations of passive restraint systems. Air bags inflate in a crash to cushion the heads of drivers and front-seat passengers. Thus, passengers are usually restrained from hitting the steering wheel, steering column, dashboard instrument panel, side doors, and windshield. Air bags give passengers a one-in-eight chance of increased survival in a crash.

Air bag safety is a growing concern. The downside of air bags is that while the devices have saved 5,415 lives since they were required in 1991, 158 people have died (60 percent were children) from the force of the deploying air bags. Nearly all those killed were either unbelted or improperly belted; some were leaning too close to the bag housing. The NHTSA estimates that half would have survived if they had used seat belts. **Air-bag cutoff switches** are permitted, although fewer than 3000 have been installed at customers' requests. The bag offers good protection against fatal head and upper-body injuries; however, leg and foot injuries are causing long hospital stays and big medical bills for those who once would have died in such crashes.

The NHTSA recently issued **air bag rules** favored by automakers and opposed by consumer groups that will be fully implemented in 2006. The standard will protect occupants, particularly women and children, in a 25-mile per hour crash. Consumer groups wanted a 30-mile per hour standard, arguing that the new standard will do little to protect those in high-speed crashes. Consumers need to understand that air bags provide only limited protection in collisions, and maximum protection is obtained by using both safety belts and air bags.

ISSUE FOR DEBATE:
Motorcycle Safety Helmets Should be Mandatory

Laws requiring motorcycle riders to wear protective helmets existed in almost **all states 25 years ago**. In the name of giving motorcycle riders the freedom to chose, conservative Republicans in most states have weakened or repealed almost all the laws. The result: Over 2,600 deaths motorcycle deaths year. The Insurance Institute for Highway Safety and the Highway Loss Date Institute report that "repeals were associated with about 40 percent more cyclist deaths compared with the years the laws were in effect." A Department of Transportation report found that **67 percent of motorcyclists in accidents would not have suffered brain damage** had they been wearing a helmet. (See www.cordis.lu/cost-transport/src/cost-327.htm.) The National Public Service Research Institute calculates that the injury cost to the public due to non-use of helmets is $375 million a year, or about 40 cents per motorcycle mile. Some are calling for mandatory helmet laws in all states.

Needed Vehicle Safety Regulations

Many vehicle safety areas are ripe for government regulatory action. **The NHTSA should require**:

- **Rollover warning labels** for trucks and SUVs that turn over easily;
- **Stability-control** devices on trucks and SUVs (now used in Europe; $500) that reduce single-car accidents by one-third.

- **Truck trailers to glow in the dark** with red-and-white reflective sheeting on the sides and rear of the vehicles;
- **Improved bumpers** to withstand a 5-mile per hour impact;
- More **compatible bumper heights** for passenger vehicles and light trucks;
- **Side-impact air bags** for the head (5,000 deaths annually);
- Safer **child seat restraints**;
- Shoulder backseat lap-belts for **children's booster seats**;
- **Third-row seat protection** from rear-end collisions (22 percent of all crashes are rear-end);
- Standards for the glaringly **bright high-intensity-discharge (HID) headlights**;
- **Glare standards** for indirect sources, such as bright metal surfaces in vehicle interiors;
- Friendlier **front-end designs** to reduce pedestrian deaths;
- Better **head restraints** and seatbacks to reduce whiplash;
- Effectiveness standards to improve the returns for **recalls**;
- Standards for **seat belts** to more adequately be adjusted for comfort and safety;
- **Direct** (rather than indirect) **tire-pressure alert system**; and
- Child **safety-seat ratings**.

ISSUE FOR DEBATE:
SUVs Should be Efficient or Taxed, Just Like Automobiles

For over 25 years the federal government has had a **gas guzzler tax** to encourage manufacturers to make more fuel-efficient cars so the nation can conserve oil, improve gas mileage, and help cut pollution as required in the Clean Air Act. Regulations in 1975 required vehicle manufacturers to achieve certain **fuel-efficiency standards** that forced the gas-guzzling dinosaurs of the road (most got 10 to 14 miles per gallon) to disappear from the market. Theses standards are known as the **corporate average fleet economy (CAFE)**.

The CAFÉ requirements permit a single manufacturer to sell cars that get **mileage higher and lower** than the numbers above as long as the average meets the standard; currently 27.5 miles per gallon. Autos sold that get worse than the average mileage standard are required to pay a tax anywhere from $1,000 to $7,700 per vehicle. Light trucks were exempt from the 1978 standard since at that time they made up only about one-fifth of sales, and they were considered "heavy work" vehicles.

Today's definition of **light trucks** includes minivans, full-size vans, pickup trucks, and sport utility vehicles, and they make up over half of new-car and truck sales. SUVs emit twice as much carbon dioxide as passengers cars, and they create a growing demand for imported oil. Ford Motor Co. chairman acknowledged in a *New York Times* interview that "SUVs contribute to global warming and endanger other motorists." The government has finally issued CAFÉ standards for light trucks. For those sold in 2007, it is 22.2 miles per gallon.

Criticisms of Government Product Safety Efforts

The are several criticisms of government regulatory effects in the area of product safety. For example, a good recall often results in no more than 30 to 35 percent of the defectively dangerous products being returned. It is often **10 percent or lower**. Recalls are unsuccessful because they are expensive, it is difficult to track down consumers (fewer than 10 percent of purchasers fill out warranty-registration cards), consumers often ignore recall notices or misinterpret that the perceived danger of a defective product is low. Part of the problem is that **people are bombarded with warning labels** on household products, signs in restaurants and bars cautioning that certain products may cause cancer or birth defects, and recall notices from manufacturers.

Time delays are immense. Getting an effective regulation into effect can take two or even twenty years. When the government wants a recall, negotiations over what constitutes a proper repair of a dangerous product can go on for months while companies benefit from the delay because they have fewer products to repair.

Critics say that government relies too much on the **voluntary efforts** of manufacturers and sellers. Writing product standards is a complex task requiring the inputs of many specialists in an effort to reach consensus that occurs through the process of compromise, and it may not lead to a good standard. In addition, voluntary standards are usually weaker than mandatory standards imposed by the government.

There have been **very few mandatory standards** written by the CSPC and the NHTSA. The agencies focus so much on voluntary safety standards that there is no realistic threat that mandatory rules will be adopted if businesses cannot agree on their own guidelines. Lacking a willingness to exercise regulatory authority, agencies no longer have a threat, a "big stick," to motivate manufacturers and sellers to exhibit a serious interest in product safety. The reason government established the CSPC and the NHTSA in the first place and gave them the authority to issue mandatory regulations was because voluntary efforts by industry failed.

Critics suggest that some agencies are **politicized** so much that they have lost some of their potential effectiveness. Internal battles and political infighting hamper the work of regulators. Too much time is wasted arguing with other administration officials and congressional committees. In addition, agencies often lack enough independence to candidly speak their views in public because they first have to submit their budget requests for approval to the Office of Management and Budget in the executive branch.

Another difficulty is an inclination **not to prosecute**. The Justice Department sometimes does not prosecute violations of product and motor vehicle safety laws and regulations, contrary to the desires of the product safety administrators. Since the NHTSA is part of the Department of Transportation, its lawsuits must be brought by the Justice Department. As an independent agency The CPSC retains latitude to prosecute its own cases, although its tendency is to negotiate solutions rather than go to court.

Budget cutbacks have greatly reduced the effectiveness of government to regulate product safety. The budgets at the CPSC and the NHTSA are less than half what they were twenty years ago.

Product Liability Lawsuits—A Powerful Weapon of Consumers—Under Assault by Conservatives

One of the consumer's most **fundamental rights is to remedy a wrong**. A **tort** is a wrongful act resulting in injury to a person or property, for which the injured party may seek compensation. Our current product liability system compensates consumers for injuries, deters corporate conduct that creates unsafe products, and discloses outrageous corporate practices. Consumers in America are supposed to have their problems listened to, and if necessary, to have their day in court. Vital to the consumer right of remedy is being able to file a lawsuit to recover damages for injuries from defective products.

Contrary to the false allegations of business trade groups, **consumers rarely sue** sellers. A Rand Corporation research study found that only 1 in 50 persons hurt by products away from the workplace make a claim for compensation.

Product liability lawsuits are generally filed on a **contingency basis** where the attorney's fee is zero unless the consumer-plaintiff wins (about half the time) or they reach an out-of-court settlement (about 95 percent of all cases). For attorneys money is the motivation in a contingency lawsuit because they typically collect one-third of the amount of any win or settlement. Of course, attorneys get nothing if they lose. If an attorney will not accept a case on a contingency basis, the alternative is to pay $100 to $300 an hour for legal and investigative fees for the many months and years it takes to get a case to court. It is through the slow discovery process in product liability lawsuits that unscrupulous and criminal corporate behavior is found.

The **contingency fee** in a product liability lawsuit is the **poor consumers's only tool** to obtain equity and redress at the courtroom door. Otherwise, consumers would have no voice to represent them in cases where companies sell them toxic, hazardous, or mislabeled products that injure and kill. Without the contingency fee system, the economics of bringing most product liability cases would be prohibitive. The vast majority of product liability cases, including class-action lawsuits, would never be filed without a sufficiently motivated legal staff. Consumer-plaintiffs in product liability lawsuits typically win **compensatory damages** that are assessed to cover a plaintiff's medical bills, lost wages, and pain and suffering. Plaintiffs also usually win coverage of attorney's fees.

Punitive Damages Penalize Only the Worst Behavior

Punitive damages typically occur in product liability cases and medical malpractice lawsuits. Punitive damages are awarded by a judge or jury in very few cases. **Punitive damages**, which may be assessed in addition to compensatory awards, are those that inflict or aim to **inflict punishment** against people and companies to deter future actions. In order for punitive damages to be awarded a high standard must be met. Punitive damages are awarded only when the defendant has been proven guilty of gross negligence or willful disregard of the consequences. The awarding of punitive damages is fundamental to protecting the consumer interest in obtaining equity for other consumers.

Over the past 25 years, only 355 product liability cases involved the awarding of punitive damages, reports Suffolk University's Michael Rustad. That is an average of only **14 cases per year** nationwide. However, because they usually involve popular consumer goods, they attract disproportionate attention from consumers, regulators, and reform-minded critics. Tort court filings account for only 9 percent of the 14 million civil cases filed annually, and just 4 of that 9 percent are product liability lawsuits. The Rand Corporation found in a survey that large courts find punitive awards in only **2.6 percent** of product-liability cases, and most of those are in cases dealing with economic losses causes by stockbrokers and other financial institutions.

Data from the National Association of Insurance Commissioners show that less than one half of product liability lawsuit litigants receives **any compensation**. The average winning claim over the past decade was $13,200; the winning plaintiff **averaged $8,600** and the plaintiff's attorney averaged $4600. The "prize winning awards" that receive all the media attention averaged less than $500,000 over the past decade, according to Jury Verdict Research. The cost of "all product liability settlements and verdicts, insured, and uninsured, totaled $4.1 billion in a recent year," says Consumer Federation of America.

Punitive damage awards put firms **on notice** to improve their behaviors. In addition, punitive damages often lead to product recalls, redesigns, and warnings about product dangers. Competitors that make similar products also are put on notice to similarly improve their product designs. Thus, some form of **equity** is achieved for all consumers. The Supreme Court has upheld the concept of punitive damages, saying that "any punitive damages awarding more than 10 times the actual damages for the injury sustained [compensatory damages] should be presumed excessive,"[2] and a 4-1 ratio of punitive to compensatory is not meant to be "binding," but should be "instructive." Furthermore, juries may not consider any out-of-state misbehavior when weighing the gravity of the defendant's actions.

DID YOU KNOW?
Silicone Breast Implant Lawsuit

The sixteen-year long **class-action lawsuit** against manufacturers of silicone breast implants that allegedly caused problems such as autoimmune diseases and hardened breasts may have concluded. Plaintiffs in the **Dow Corning** lawsuit have offered a settlement providing $3.2 billion to be used to compensate the more than 112,000 women who received the devices over the past 25 years. The fund is designed to provide medical monitoring and surgical costs. Claimants who want their implants removed will get $5,000 for the surgery or $20,000 if their implants rupture.

The National Academy of Sciences issued a report concluding that silicone breast implants do not cause serious diseases such as cancer, lupus, or other chronic disorders. This finding is consistent with a series of other reports that concluded there is no reason to believe that breast implants have damaged the health of millions of women. But Dow Corning does make mistakes in failing to test their products adequately.

Risk problems did come from the tissue around the implants, implant ruptures and infections. **Nothing conclusive** was found regarding the immune system. Thus, no real answers exist on the dangers of silicone implants. The FDA declared a moratorium on silicone breast implants years ago, except for reconstructive surgery as part of a clinical study. In 2000 the FDA approved the use of saline breast implants although they have "relatively high complication and failure rates," including a **20 to 40 percent chance** that the 130,000 women who have implants each year will need another operation within three years.

Today's Product Liability Laws Protect Consumers

Product liability is generally a matter of **state law** and variations exist throughout the country. Some lawsuits are brought as a breach of warranty under contract law. Most product liability cases are brought to court under the concepts of negligence or strict tort liability. The legal doctrine of **strict liability** provides that plaintiffs only have to show that a defective product was the cause of their injury. Thirty years ago plaintiffs had to convince juries that the product manufacturer's employees had acted in a negligent manner, an extremely difficult standard.

Strict liability was cited in the 1963 *Greenman v. Yuba Power Products* case which chose to examine the product itself rather than the conduct of the manufacturer's employees. The Yuba decision held that a manufacturer is strictly liable in tort when an article it places in the market, knowing that it is to be used without inspection for defects, **proves to have a defect** that causes injury to a human being." And the purpose of such liability is to insure that the cost of injuries resulting from defective products is borne by the manufacturers that put such products in the marketplace rather than the injured persons who are **powerless to protect**

---

[2] Punitive damages go on the chopping block (April 8, 2003), Joan Biskupic, *USA Today*.

themselves." Thus, the strict liability theory allows plaintiffs to collect damages without having the burden of proving actual negligence. The emergence of the concept of strict liability has made it easier for consumers to prove and collect damages from a manufacturer.

Because of strict liability, manufacturers today have little choice except to **make safer products**. Absolute safety is impossible, so manufacturers will continue to test their products and purchase sufficient liability insurance. The price of every consumer product includes an amount to cover liability insurance premiums, just as there are amounts to provide for salaries of executives and profits for shareholders. Society has become more conscious of the need to demand safe products and to penalize those manufacturers who refuse or are unable to sell safe goods.

CONSUMER UPDATE:
Top Ten Product Liability Lawsuits

Examples of liability lawsuits where the defendant companies lost or settled out of court with either the government or plaintiff-consumers include:

10. **Breast implants** that leaked silicone gel;

9. **General Motors 1983-87 full-size pickup trucks** had gas tanks mounted outside the frame that so far have claimed over 300 lives in crashes that became gasoline infernos);

8. **Suzuki Samurai** vehicle rollovers in sharp turns;

7. **Medtronic heart pacemakers** that failed;

6. **General Electric Coffeematic Brew** that started fires because it turned itself on, but not off;

5. **Asbestos overexposure** in the workplace resulted in 600,000 cancer related lawsuits;

4. **Cigarette manufacturers** whose products killed 60 million people worldwide;

3. **Bridgestone/Firestone-Ford Explorer** rollover tire scandal;

2. **Dalkon Shield** intrauterine birth control device left 400,000 women sterile and 112,000 injured; and

1. **Child bedframes and cribs** (never recalled) that continue to strangle infants and kids.

These cases often involve hundreds of thousands, and sometimes millions of wronged consumers. Other examples include defective cars that were not crashworthy enough; football helmets that did not have enough resistance to shock to prevent head and neck injuries; children's sleepwear that did not have sufficient flame retardancy; recliner chairs that did not prevent children from strangling as they became trapped between the seat and the leg rest; and side effects of a prescription drug that caused a birth deformity.

Criticism of Product Liability Lawsuits is Unwarranted

One occasionally accurate criticism of the threat of product liability lawsuits has been the delay of some, but not many **innovations**. For example, spa pool manufacturers decided against installing an alarm system to alert parents when children get into the pool because they feared lawsuits if the alarm worked. Consumer advocates argue that the smartest manufacturers find ways to make better and safer products than their competitors.

Critics of tort liability argue that the system **creates too many uncertainties** about manufacturers' liabilities and the size of damage awards. The notorious cases of McDonald's coffee (where a woman was awarded $2.7 million after spilling hot coffee on herself) and

BMW (where the purchaser of a new car was awarded $6 million after discovering that part of the vehicle had been surreptitiously repainted by the seller) are exceptions rather than the rule. In almost all of these cases, judges reduce the award, although the media never seem to get that corrected message to the people. In the cases just cited, the BMW award was reduced to $50,000 and the overly hot coffee award against McDonald's was reduced to $600,000, as the 65-year old plaintiff had to undergo seven skin graft operations. In another case, two plaintiffs whose six children burned in a vehicle fire were awarded $5 billion from General Motors; within weeks it was reduced to $1 billion, and on appeal the amount likely will be **reduced again** by another judge.

Juries have awarded enormous punitive damages in the recent cases against the tobacco and gun industries, and the damage awards have been reduced on appeal. Legal experts say that "jurors are ready to believe that they are the public avengers. Because the governor won't do it and the state legislature won't do it, the jurors are the only ones who will do it." More and more consumers—the public—are angry that serious societal problems are not getting resolved, and this is translated into jury verdicts.

Business critics want the system changed so sellers could reduce their **insurance and litigation costs**, perhaps by an estimated 5 percent. Business has been pushing for 20 years for a **weak federal liability law** that would preempt stronger state laws. Often conservative politicians listen to the concerns of business rather than the interests of consumers, and over 30 states have passed laws that put **caps** on punitive damages. Leading the battle against consumers is the Product Liability Coordinating Committee, a coalition of 700,000 businesses. It is dominated by Union Carbide, Ford Motor Company, and a number of motor vehicle, drug, chemical, and insurance companies. A win for consumers occurred when the Ohio Supreme Court struck down a law that curtailed the ability of consumers to sue for damages. The issue of caps on punitive damages is discussed in Chapter 15 in the context of medical malpractice lawsuits.

Conservatives, most Republicans, President Bush, and the business community seeks to pass a law to put national caps on lawsuits that would override state laws. Further, they want to place caps on punitive damages in *all* civil cases, eliminate strict liability, give immunity for bio-material suppliers, provide immunity for older defective products (those over 15 years), place restrictions on **joint and several liability** (when one liable firm is insolvent, the other wrongdoers must cover the cost), and impose a negligence standard for injuries caused by design defects or failure to warn. They want to eliminate so-called trivial lawsuits by eliminating punitive damage awards in cases in which safety devices do not pose risks of serious injury. They want plaintiffs to be restricted to collecting no more than $250,000 in punitive damages. Conservatives also propose a **loser pays** provision that would require the losing party to pay the winner's legal fees. Such an **anti-consumer provision** would effectively end this important type of consumer protection litigation as most consumers would not be willing to accept such financial risk.

Such a federal law would **preempt stronger state laws** that better protect consumers and they would allow manufacturers to make shoddy goods. Instead of focusing on making safer products, manufacturers could simply budget certain amounts for future civil penalties as a minor cost of doing business. These business-sponsored tort reform proposals would tilt the playing field against consumers. The total dollars spent on legal cases in both product liability and medical malpractice amount to only $7 billion—a pittance says Consumer Federation of America.

Consumer organizations, labor groups, and trial lawyers adamantly support the **continuation of product liability lawsuits to obtain just compensation**. These advocates see product liability lawsuits as the single most important threat to keep sellers in line, and they are correct. If liability were abolished or limited, the poorest manufacturers would have no incentive to avoid making defective products. Such sellers would be free riders if they are not required to pay compensation.

It is not unrealistic to figure that as sellers step away from paying legitimate claims to wronged consumers, business will ask government to bear the cost of such claims. This country has a long history of socializing the costs of business by making taxpayers pay the bills. "After all," would be the argument "if the NHTSA approved the bumper shouldn't the government have to pay the damages?" Any efforts to restrict in any way the right to sue in product liability cases are anti-consumer and threaten the **single most important weapon of consumers** to improve the economic marketplace.

ISSUE FOR DEBATE:
Sealed Court Records by Greedy Corporations Should be Prohibited by Law

In defending itself against scores of wrongful-death lawsuits filed by victims of fiery car crashes in pickup trucks and side-mounted gasoline tanks, **General Motors Corporation** succeeded for over twenty years in suppressing controversial documents in 200 lawsuits in state courts across the country by obtaining **protective orders** from judges and settling many cases out-of-court that prohibit participants from revealing details of a case. As part of the settlement of these cases, GM has obtained **confidentiality agreements** that prohibit opposing lawyers from disclosing details, thus creating in effect a **secret settlement**.

On the request of numerous defendant companies, judges have issued sealing orders that **remove entire lawsuit files from the public record**. Sometimes courts have allowed the records to be **destroyed**. This keeps health, environmental, medical malpractice,and safety concerns out of the public spotlight and forces other litigants to try to uncover the same information again and again, at appreciable expense.

This tactic, designed to keep sensitive information out of the public record, also has been used by many companies involved in product safety lawsuits. Such protective orders have sealed information for the manufacturers of accutane, cigarettes, dangerous playground equipment, grain elevators, defective heart valves, **Agent Orange**, unsafe all-terrain vehicles (ATVs), breast implants, and butane lighters. **Dow Corning** kept the records of a **silicone breast implant secret for eight years**. **Bridgestone/Firestone** kept its lawsuits under wraps for **nine years** while203 people rode to their deaths on their tires. Corporate greed and secrecy are the themes of the award-winning movie, *Erin Brockovich*, starring Julia Roberts.

Such secrecy undermines the **right to know** of all Americans. It keeps vital information hidden from the public. Arthur H, Bryant, director of the Trial Lawyers for Public Justice, says that "By making sure that nobody knows about injuries that are caused, manufacturers can influence the state of scientific knowledge by controlling access to the data on which scientific opinions are based."

Seven states have passed laws that **encourage judges to permit disclosure** of internal company documents that detail health and safety problems to lawyers with similar lawsuits. In such states lawyers can share confidential documents obtained from companies under protective orders with other attorneys. Thus, attorneys with similar cases will not have to litigate the same issues. If an objection is raised, a hearing is held and a judge may impose restrictions if necessary. Although the law does not permit attorneys to share the information with the public, it increases the chances that safety information will reach government safety regulators and be aired at trial.

Courageous judges in Florida, New York, New Jersey, and Texas **have refused to keep such court records secret**. They have ordered the release of sealed records ruling that "labeling corporate negligence a 'trade secret' hides vital facts from the public" and that authorities "may have access to anything under seal that may be helpful and beneficial for the protection of public health." The New Jersey Supreme Court concluded that there is a profound public interest when matters of health, safety, and consumer fraud are involved" and therefore "there must be careful scrutiny prior to sealing records and documents filed with a court in a high public-interest case." Still, today most states seal records.

Wisconsin Senator Herb Kohl has proposed in Congress a "Sunshine in Litigation Act" to ban legal confidentiality agreements in cases involving dangerous products, unsavory business practices, and public hazards. Conservative Republicans in Congress are trying to pass legislation to permit secrecy in court records.

Review and Summary of Key Terms and Concepts

1. Offer a few statistics on **product injuries** affecting adults and children.

2. Give two examples of **causal factors** in injuries.

3. Explain the idea of **benefit-cost analysis**.

4. Discuss the problem of **how much risk is acceptable**.

5. Give an example (different from the one in the book) of **measuring the magnitude of risk**.

6. List three **factors** that government must consider in making product safety decisions.

7. Identify two **legal mandates** of CSPC.

8. Distinguish between an **imminent hazard** and a **substantial hazard**.

9. What is **Section 15** and how does it work to promote product safety?

10. What is the **NEISS** system?

11. Name two consumer products that **need regulation**, and offer guesses as to why they are needed.

12. Cite some **statistics** that indicate the efforts of the National Highway Traffic Safety Administration are needed.

13. Summarize the information about **vehicle death rates**.

14. What happened in the **Bridgestone-Firestone Ford Explorer** scandal?

15. Briefly outline the **NHTSA's recall process**.

16. Comment on the usefulness of **vehicle rollover risk ratings**.

17. Define **passive restraint system** and identify some concerns about air bag safety.

18. Name two vehicle safety problems that **need regulation** and offer guesses as to why they are needed.

19. Give two **criticisms about product safety efforts**.

20. Explain why attorneys collect **contingency fees** from consumers who win product liability lawsuits.

21. Distinguish between **compensatory** and **punitive damages**.

22. Explain the legal doctrine of **strict liability**.

23. What are **secret settlements** why do they exist and why are they against the consumer interest?

24. What are some of the actions conservatives want to do to limit **product liability lawsuits**?

Useful Resources for Consumers

Advocates for Highway and
Auto Safety
www.saferoads.org/

ALLDATA (on automobiles)
www.alldata.com/index.html

American Automobile
Manufacturers Association
www.amma.com/

Center for Auto Safety
www.autosafety.org

Child Safe (recall notification)
www.SafeChild.net

Consumer Product Safety
Commission
www.cpsc.gov

Consumer World
www.consumerworld.org

Crash Test
www.crashtest.com

First Gov for Consumers
www.consumer.gov/

Insurance Institute for
Highway Safety
Highway Loss Data Institute
www.carsafety.org

Insurance Information
Institute
www.iii.org

Safety Forum
www.safetyforum.com/

Mothers Against Drunk
Driving
www.madd.org

National Highway Traffic and
Safety Administration
888-DASH-2-DOT (888-
32742368)
www.nhtsa.org

Recall notices and complaints—
www.nhtsa.dot.gov

Safety Alerts
www.safetyalerts.com/

Safer America for Everyone
www.saferam.org

U.S. Consumer Product Safety
Commission
www.cpsc.gov/

U.S. Department of
Transportation-Auto Recall
News
www.dot.gov/affairs/nhtsain.htm

"What Do You Think" Questions

1. Look over the list of **products that need safety regulations** and the list of **needed vehicle safety regulations** and select two from each list that you agree might be serious problems. Recommend whether to ban each product or redesign each in some ways. If appropriate, give some suggestions for redesign and appropriate labeling.

2. Offer your views on whether judges should be allowed to order the **release of court records** on safety issues.

3. Should **motorcycle safety helmets** be mandatory? Why or why not?

4. The concept of **punitive damages** is the key factor in why businesses are trying to restrict product liability lawsuits. Describe your views on punitive damages as a method to improve product safety in the marketplace.

Chapter 17

Banking, Credit and Housing Issues

OBJECTIVES

After reading this chapter, you should be able to

1. Examine a number of consumer problems and issues in the area of banking.

2. Review several consumer problems and issues in credit.

3. Recognize some consumer problems and issues in housing.

B anking, credit, and housing are areas of spending vital to consumer life today. Getting banking services for a fair price is a challenge for most of us, and it is extremely difficult for economically disadvantaged consumers. In banking, credit, and housing, many consumers face unfair and illegal discrimination. The banking industry seems to invest new ways to rip-off consumers every month. Lenders too, seem to find ways to purposefully confuse consumers so they can assess rip-off charges and hidden fees as well as high interest rates. In housing buyers face the problems of high prices, predatory lending and kickback fees. Many of these financial practices are unethical and some are illegal.

This chapter focuses upon problems and issues of consumers in banking, credit and housing transactions. It begins by examining rising bank fees, truth-in-savings, deregulation, basic banking, and the unbanked. Next, it summarizes and provides an overview of the problems and issues in credit, including aggressive credit-card solicitations, late fees, penalty interest rates, overcharges, FICO credit scores, card blocking, paying only the "low minimum monthly payment, mistakes in credit files, and alternatives for getting out of debt. The chapter concludes with an examination of consumer problems and issues in the area of housing: high prices, predatory lending, discrimination, and the lack of transparency in housing transactions.

Banking Problems and Issues

There are a number of consumer problems and issues in the world of banking. Several are examined below.

Rising Bank Fees

According to research by the U.S. Public Interest Research Group, consumers could **save at least $75 per year** by banking at a **small bank** or **credit union** instead of a big bank. The average annual fees for maintaining a regular checking account at 300 large banks amounted to $266! However, the costs were only $191 at small community banks and just $101 at credit unions. Banks hide fee increases by charging a la carte for services that once were standard with checking accounts. Banks profit handsomely by paying less than half of a percent in interest on checking accounts, or the trifling sum of $9 a year on a $2,500 balance.

Consumers prefer to withdraw their money from an **ATM (automated teller machine)**, and most banks impose **ATM surcharges that average $155 a year per household**. Consumers are paying fees just to use their own money! And ATM charges have been rising 10 to 20 percent every year. There are three possible types of ATM fees: (1) A charge by one's own bank to use its machines, typically 50 cents to $1; (2) A fee if you access your bank from an ATM owned by another bank, $1 to $2; and (3) a special surcharge for non-customers, often $2 or $3. Thus when using a bank other than your normal one, you pay twice for the same transaction! The fee may be as much as $10 on a cruise ship or in a casino. Some states have banned or restricted charging another bank's customers to use an ATM; however, Congress has refused to take any action to help keep fees down.

Ugly Fees and Penalties for Bouncing Checks

The typical bank charge for a **bounced check is $25 to $30** while the real cost the bank incurs is about $3. Bankrate.com (www.bankrate.com) reports that the minimum balance requirement to avoid high fees is $2,600. If your balance slips below that amount, you are subject to a monthly charge that averages $11. Banks also charge **inactivity fees** on accounts with little or no transactions, and the fees are so high (sometimes $10 a month) that they could wipe out a small balance in an account within one or two years.

For a $2 mathematics mistake in a checking account that results in a consumer writing a **bad check** (also called a **bounced check**), or one written with **non-sufficient funds (NSF)** in the account, the banking industry puts one on a **blacklist**. Almost all banks in the U.S. consult Chex-Systems, a list of seven million people for "account abuse," writing bad checks and deliberate fraud. It does not matter to Chex-Systems if later the overdraft was paid. Most banks and credit unions will not open a new account for five years for people on the blacklist. Indeed, the cost for forgetting to subtract items from one's check register can be brutal. You can get a copy of your Chex-Systems report at www.chexhelp.com.

Overdraft Protection Fees

Older consumers may recall that for decades banks have offered an **overdraft line of credit** to customers who maintained big balances or had a savings account. Consumers who would otherwise bounce a check paid perhaps an annual interest rate of 20 percent on the automatic bank loan to cover the value of the overdrawn check(s). That might amount to a few dollars per check. Few banks still offer this service.

Seizing on an opportunity to profit, banks today are selling **overdraft protection services**. This new "bounce protection" program lets checking account holders avoid paying bounced-check fees to retailers for a flat fee of up to $35 for each overdraft. Consumers can choose not to pay such rip-off fees. The Federal Reserve is considering making the **"bounce protection"** fees subject to the Truth-in-Lending regulations. That would require the fees be stated as interest, allowing consumers to comparison shop.

Banks Hate Credit Unions

A **credit union** is a not-for-profit cooperative venture that pools the deposits of member-owners that are then used to invest or lend to other member-owners. Members have some common bond, such as the same employer, church, union, or fraternal association. Persons in one's immediate family are also eligible to join. As non-profits, the revenues earned by credit unions are exempt from income taxes. Since they are not trying to maximize profits for shareholders and pay lavish salaries and bonuses to their executives, as do banks, credit unions **pay high interest rates**, have low loan costs and assess small fees.

Most banks pay such pathetically low interest rates on checking and savings accounts that it almost seems like an illegal conspiracy. **Bank profits** for the last three years have been the highest in history. As a result, more than 82 million smart consumers do their banking at credit unions, a low-cost alternative to banks. Banks hate credit unions, and they are lobbying Congress to pass laws **placing limits** on who can join credit unions and to remove their tax-exempt status. Banks want to eliminate credit union competition in spite of the fact that only about 3 percent of the nation's financial assets are held at credit unions.

Truth in Savings Law

The Truth in Savings Act requires depository institutions to disclose the annual percentage rate on interest-bearing accounts, along with any fees that may be assessed, so that depositors can easily compare various savings options. The **annual percentage yield (APY)** is the total amount of interest that would be received on a $100 deposit, based on the annual rate of simple interest and the frequency of compounding for a 365-day period, expressed as a percentage. The APY must be used in advertising and other disclosures to savers.

Depository institutions are required to calculate interest on the full balance in an account once any minimum balance requirements have been reached. In addition, banks must show the **annual percentage yield earned (APYE)** on periodic statements. While the APY tells what one can expect to earn, the APYE tells what one really did earn. Wise money managers should select the savings option that pays the highest APY and avoid institutions that assess lots of costs and penalties. Comparison shopping could easily earn an extra $10 or $20 a year on a $1,500 savings account balance.

When financial institutions calculate interest on deposits, it is primarily based on four variables: how much money is on deposit, the method of determining the balance, the interest rate applied, and the frequency of compounding, such as annually, semiannually, quarterly, weekly, or daily. The **more frequent** the compounding, the greater the effective return for the saver.

The Savings and Loan Scandal

Deregulation of the savings and loan (S&Ls) and banking industries in the 1980s created opportunities for bad judgments, fraud, mismanagement, and bureaucratic ineptitude, creating the greatest financial fiasco in the history of this country. Columnist George Will observed "Never in history have we had the government spend **$500 *billion*** of the taxpayers' money and not get anything for it." This is, he continued "another instance of no-fault entrepreneurship, wherein **profits are private and losses are socialized**."

The **$500 billion** ($300 billion in bailouts plus $200 billion in interest) amounts to about $5,000 for every adult taxpayer. Sadly, most of the money is gone forever and cannot be recovered. The money was spent, lost in devalued real estate, or stashed in foreign bank accounts. About 3,700 senior executives went to jail for fraudulent activities, and only a modest amount of money has ever been recovered through civil restitution.

The government guarantees every deposit up to $100,000, **regardless of the financial soundness of the institution**. The existence of deposit insurance created what economist Paul Krugman called an "epidemic of **moral hazard**," where institutions, especially those in financial trouble, take on riskier investments only because they are insured. American consumers should be incensed, angry, and outraged that the costs for this fiasco are being paid by them through higher banking fees, reduced interest rates earned on deposits, higher prices on loans, and higher income taxes.

The federal deposit insurance **system remains a root cause** of the industry's problems. The original concept of the insurance system was to protect only individual savings, not institutional investors.

Two vital changes are needed to reform the banking system: risk-based insurance and coinsurance, and both eliminate the custom of placing the full risk on government. The risk is really upon the taxpayers since consumers pay 85 percent of all revenues of the federal government. First, establish a **risk-based insurance** system for bank deposits. Well-run, safe institutions would pay low insurance premiums to the FDIC, while riskier banks and S&Ls would pay higher premiums. Second, restore the power of private market forces to punish unnecessary risk-takers by offering only **coinsurance** on banking deposits. If deposit insurance were limited to only a part of the deposit, perhaps to 80 percent on amounts above $100,000, affected depositors would be compelled to find ways of ensuring that the institutions holding their money had adequate equity, liquidity, and diversification. In this way, big depositors (e.g., businesses, other financial institutions, those with funds deposited in retirement plans, wealthy consumers) would be motivated to assure the safety of the uninsured portion of their deposits. Shaky financial institutions would be forced to purchase **additional private insurance** for the remaining 20 percent of risk or be unable to attract large deposits. Congress has refused to act to lower the insured amount below $100,000 or to establish risk-based premiums.

Deregulation of Banking is Hard on Consumers

Deregulation of the banking industry began in 1999. Changes in laws have removed or reduced the regulatory authority and active ties of the federal government in an effort **to improve efficiency** in the financial services economic marketplace. Banks may compete in their own industry as well as sell insurance, securities, and real estate. Letting well-capitalized banks compete on a head-to-head basis with insurance companies and securities firms should result in lower prices for consumers buying stocks, bonds, mutual funds, and insurance. However, today's deregulated banking industry has consumers working hard to find good deals. In today's banking market:

- Consumers must search harder and longer to find smaller banks and branch offices because many have gone out of business and many have lost their local flavor because of mergers.

- Consumers must deal with explicit pricing services previously offered without charge.

- Consumers must take affirmative actions to protect their privacy from financial services companies that share data with corporate affiliates, other third parties, and telemarketing firms. (See Chapters 3 and 5.)

- Consumers have to shop for good interest rates.

- Consumers are irritated at having to pay $2 to $3 to ask simple questions like "Has my social security check cleared?" or "How much do I have in savings?"

- Low- and moderate-income families and small businesses face less access, fewer choices and higher fees.

The Need for Basic Banking

There are **three fundamental needs in banking**: (1) a safe and accessible place to keep money, (2) a way to obtain cash, and (3) a way to make payments to third parties. However, not all consumers have such vital services available. The concept of **basic banking** (also called **lifeline banking**) is that banking institutions would be required to offer universal access to certain minimal financial services that every consumer must have, regardless of income, in order to function in society. Typically, a basic account is one that: (1) costs $5 or less per month, (2) permits up to ten free checks to be written monthly, (3) has low minimum balance requirements, (4) permits unlimited and free ATM usage, and (5) has a flexible policy on identification requirements (e.g., less than $300). Some states (IL, MA, NJ, NY, and MN) require banks operating within their borders to offer basic banking.

Banks claim that basic banking would **increase their costs** substantially. They would have to add tellers on certain days, have extra cash available, and would run an increased risk of fraud. Critics accuse the banking industry of not wanting low-income consumers in their lobbies mingling with their usual customers. If basic banking services cannot be made available to low-income consumers, millions of consumers are forced to bank under their mattresses and use high-cost alternatives.

Consumer advocates argue that institutions enjoying the privileges and protections provided by the federal bank regulatory systems have an obligation to make essential banking services available to all consumers. The industry replies that banks are not public utilities, and should not be treated like them. Critics observe that any industry that takes a $500 billion bailout like the banks and savings and loan associations did in the 1980s, **should be regulated** like a public utility.

The Unbanked

Millions of adults, especially poor immigrants, blacks, Hispanics, non-English speakers, and many elderly consumers do not have bank accounts, thus they are **unbanked**. Various studies reveal reasons **why** they are unbanked: (1) they do not have enough money to open an account and meet the substantial minimum balance requirements, (2) they lack personal identification (such as a driver's license with a photograph), (3) they lack a credit card (only 73 percent have some type of credit card), (4) they believe they don't write enough checks to make it worthwhile, (5) they lack mathematical and reading skills, (6) the distances are too long between the institution's offices and work or home, (7) they believe banks have high service charges, and (8) they mistrust financial institutions in general.

To increase profits, banks have **closed many branch offices**. This discriminates against consumers living in low- and moderate-income neighborhoods because branch offices are the locations of least profitability. The branch banks that remain typically raise the minimum amount required to open and maintain checking and savings accounts.

A Consumer Federation of America survey reveals that **nine out of 10 banks** are **unwilling to cash checks** for non-depositors. Federal Reserve Board data reveal that only 80 percent of adults have banking accounts. Census data show that 76 percent of families without checking accounts earn less than $20,000 per year. The growing number of consumers without access to the traditional banking system cannot pay their bills with inexpensive checks and are not able to build up a savings fund at a federally insured institution.

A **solution** for the unbanked is increasingly being used throughout the country. Several large banks, including Visa USA, offer unbanked consumers **payroll cards**, also known as **employee debit cards**. Participating employers electronically forward the amount of an employee's take-home pay to a bank account in the name of the worker that he or she can access with ATM card. The card lets a worker get cash from ATM machines and pay for purchases using the card instead of cash. The employee cost is about $5 a month. If the card is a genuine debt card and it is lost, the worker is protected against fraudulent use by the Electronic Funds Transfer Act (see Chapter 5). Alternatively, if it is a stored value card (like college students use in cafeterias) or a "bank account" for the employee set up by the employer there are no federal protections against loss. With the latter accounts, one federal official said, "The poor soul could lose his whole $500 paycheck is he lost the card!"

America Saves (www.americasaves.org) is a nationwide campaign in which a broad coalition of nonprofit, corporate and government groups helps individuals and families who have not saved adequately to "build wealth, not debt." Through information, advice, and encouragement, it assists those who wish to pay down debt, build an emergency fund, save for a home, save for an education, or save for retirement. All adults should have access to the traditional banking system and its many consumer protections.

KEY TOPIC IN CONSUMER ECONOMICS:
The Poor Pay More for All Financial Services

Largely for **cost reasons**, low-income consumers are kept out of most parts of the financial services industry. One in five adults is **unbanked**, and these low-income people have to pay high fees to cash checks because they do not have traditional bank accounts. Consumers without accounts are forced to use the **alternative financial system** that serves the poor through check-cashing outlets, money orders, payday loans, post-dated checks, pawn shops, refund anticipation loans, rent-to-own stores, and rental-purchase agreements.

Over 6,000 neighborhood **check cashing outlets** charge fees from $2 to as high as $30 or $40 to cash a $500 check, even for 100 percent safe government checks! Some firms charge as much as 10 percent of the face value of a check. A study by the Consumer Federation of America found that the household that cashes a $400 check every two weeks and writes four money orders monthly can expect to pay between $150 and $400 annually for these two services. The impact of check cashing on the limited public benefits and meager paychecks of poor families is severe, because charging 2 to 3 percent to cash a welfare check is equivalent to a 2 or 3 percent cut in benefits.

Payday loans occur when a check-cashing business lends money to someone who is short of cash and has difficulty obtaining additional credit from traditional creditors with the requirement that the amount must be repaid in one or two weeks. If the borrower cannot repay the full amount when due, he or she must renew the loan and repay the fee. Fees for a $100 two-week loan ranged from $10 to $35. "Loan sharks don't even make that kind of money," says a Georgia official. Borrowers often pay "for the loan two or three times over," noted a Consumer Federation of America study. CFA found that the national average annual percentage rate for payday loans is 470 percent.

Some lenders accept a post-dated check for the same purpose as payday loans. A **post-dated check** is one written against a consumer's account and dated sometime in the future. The expectation is that the consumer will have sufficient funds in the account at that future point so the check will be honored by the bank. The check-cashing company (the "lender" here) charges triple-digit interest charges to advance funds against a post-dated check. These companies offer credit, even though legally it is not "credit"—at rip-off rates—and such transactions are not illegal in most states. In response to these rip-off charges, some credit unions are encouraging low-income consumers to become members so they can receive short-term loans—at much lower interest rates—when needed.

Pawnshops make small loans in exchange for property, and usually they loan no more than one-half of the value of the property. If the loan is not repaid, the pawnshop keeps the property. Interest rates are as much as 20 percent per month. **Auto title loans** are similar. For example, one's car is worth $2,000 and the owner puts up the car title as collateral for a $900 loan. If the borrower fails to make a payment, perhaps after making ten $100 monthly payments, the car is repossessed. Little or no credit is given for the previous payments. People desperate for cash sometimes use illegal **auto brokers** that sell or sublease that person's car to someone else who is supposed to make the original owner's loan or lease payments. People who are desperate for cash sometimes contact a **sale and lease back** business that buys their property at a low price and then leases it back at a high rental rate. One missed payment and the consumer loses the property.

Credit Problems and Issues

This section examines consumer problems and issues in credit. Topics include aggressive credit-card solicitations, late fees and grace period rip-offs.

Aggressive Credit-Card Solicitations

The number of credit card solicitations is now **five billion** a year. Only 6/10th of 1 percent—one response in every 166 solicitations—accepts the offers. Thus, people receive a credit card solicitation every two weeks. "Congratulations! You have been pre-approved for credit!" Among the credit card issuers Visa has 51 percent of the accounts, MasterCard has 35 percent, Discover, 10 percent, and American Express, 5 percent.

A Gallop survey found that one-quarter of adults do **not have any credit cards**. Of those that do, 33 percent have one or two credit cards and 23 percent have three or four cards. The average household with at least one credit card has an unpaid balance of about $7,000, where a decade ago it was $3,000.

Four out of five college students use credit cards. A recent survey found that freshmen students average $1,500 in credit card debt, sophomores have $1,800, juniors owe $2,700, and seniors owe $3,330 on their credit cards. Someone once observed that "There are only two things you need to get a credit card: A college ID and a pulse." What credit card companies want, says University of Maryland's George Ritzer, "is for students to become addicted—to a lifetime of indebtedness." Visa is pushing its debit-like Visa Buux card to teenagers as young as 13, in an effort says Visa "to start teaching them about financial responsibility."

The major credit reporting organizations, Experian, Equifax, and TransUnion, are capable of creating a computer-generated review of credit files to locate names of people who pass certain tests of credit worthiness. Each company has files on nearly 200 million adults. Oftentimes these **lists are sold** to marketers that wish to offer people credit accounts. This is particularly useful when a branch of a store opens in a new area and management wishes to open new local accounts.

Pre-screening occurs where an application for new credit is mailed to consumers who have a good credit record. Credit very likely will be granted after the consumer mails in the completed application. Sometimes a person's credit history is of such high quality that companies send a **pre-approved** (also called **pre-authorized**) line of credit that can be used almost immediately.

Such marketing techniques seem to **flatter consumers** into falsely thinking that they are "worth" more credit. The thinking goes "I know that I can't afford more credit, but if the bank figures that I can, it must be all right." Many consumers accept a second or third Visa card when they really do not want or need it. (To stop credit card solicitations, see the **"opt out"** discussion in chapter 5.)

Solicitations often go to consumers who are already carrying too much debt. **Crediholics** who cannot resist additional lines of credit soon get into deeper financial difficulties. It is not uncommon to find a person earning $40,000 a year who ran up $60,000 in credit card bills and obtained cash advances from one card to pay another, made occasional late payments, paid large finance charges, and stayed in this situation for years. Creditors love such people since these are their best customers because they provide the highest profits.

One **good result** of credit-card solicitations is that millions of consumers have **easy access** to consumer credit to increase their level of living. The bad news is that many consumers are working hard to repay their creditors, although too few are getting out of debt. Sixty percent of holders of bank-type credit cards say they **"revolve"** their credit card debt, or make regular monthly payments without paying off the full balance. This requires paying more than $1,500 annually in interest and fees, a figure higher than many households spend on electricity, telephone service or vehicle insurance. Monthly repayments for credit card principal and interest take 11 percent or more of take-home pay.

Buying on Credit is a Negative Sale

Buying on credit and making a series of repayments (instead of paying cash) is a "**negative sale**," because after adding up all the charges and fees, credit-card expenditures become the opposite of buying things on sale. The result is as if the lender says "Please repay us slowly so we can mark up your purchases an **additional 18 to 22 percent** annually!" Surveys show that at least 40 percent of credit cardholders do not know how much interest they were charged in the past year for revolving purchases on their bank cards.

Late Fees, Penalty Interest Rates and Overcharges

The income to banks that issue credit cards from late fees has **doubled** in the past seven years. Credit card issuers seem to be in a fee-frenzy competition who can devise the most **unfair fees**. The fees charged today are at absurd levels, and it is simply a case of massive price gouging. About 5 percent of card holders are more than 30 days past due in repaying their credit card debt. A CardWeb study (www.cardweb.com) found that six in ten credit card customers paid a late charge fee last year. Here are some of the ways credit card issuers are increasing revenues at the expense of consumers:

- **Tiered lending** (also called **risk-based pricing**) is the credit industry's idea of price discrimination as the interest rates are higher for borrowers who have less than perfect credit histories, perhaps 28 percent, and lower for low-risk customers, perhaps 18 percent.

- **Pre-approved, low-interest cards** that are misleading because consumers who have less than a pristine credit history do not qualify for the lowest rate and instead they are charged much higher rates;

- **Fixed interest rates** that can change (go up!) with 15 days written notice;

- **Balance transfers** with fat fees hidden in the small print that effectively wipe out your hoped for savings from a lower interest rate;

- **No-fee cards** that turn out to not be the case upon 15 days written notice;

- **Cancellation penalty interest rates** of perhaps 24 percent on a card that originally was at 8 percent put into effect on the unpaid balance when the consumer cancels the account;

- **Shorter grace periods**, the number of days when creditors allow consumers to pay their bill without incurring fees, a decade ago were 30 days and the average is now only 21;

- **Late fees** of $25 or more imposed if the payment has not been received by the creditor by 2:00 p.m. on a specific day;

- **Tiered penalty late fees** that are assessed depending on how much of a balance is owed, such as a $15 late fee for a low-balance customer and a $38 late fee for a big balance customers;

- **Tiered penalty interest rate** of perhaps 24 percent (on top of a late fee) instead of the original interest rate that perhaps was 18 percent;

- **Unadvertised penalty interest rates** that are 5 to 8 percent higher than conventional rates are permanently imposed on cardholders if they are late with as few as one or two payments made to *any other creditor*, and the rates (perhaps 29 percent) apply to any new debt as well as the old debt on the account;

- **Cash advance fees** that begin at 21 percent for the first usage and then quickly rise to 24 percent for later cash advances;

- **Currency exchange fees** of 2 to 4 percent on out-of-USA transactions assessed on top of the already charged exchange rate fee; and

- **Unnecessary and overpriced credit card insurance** (see Chapter 4).

To get **a reduced interest rate on your credit cards**, you simply need to telephone your card issuers and **ask**. A Massachusetts Public Interest Research Group study found that more than half of the consumers who called to complain about high interest rates were successful in reducing the rate by about one-third.

Credit card rates and excessive fees can only be brought down by **competition**, and this will not happen until consumers choose not to use credit from such card issuers. Consumers need to comparison shop for the best deals and interest rates. Smart consumers comparison shop for credit rates and terms. To find credit card issuers that offer deals to meet your needs, check with *Kiplinger's Personal Finance* or *Money* magazine. Credit card offers range from low-interest accounts, no annual fees, cash-back rebates, frequent flyer points, telephone credits, and rebates on cars.

CONSUMER UPDATE:
Top Ten Greedy Credit Card Companies

Among the nation's worst top ten greedy credit card companies are:

10. **Direct Merchants Bank** charges 24 percent on a Gold Mastercard slaps a penalty rate of 32 percent to people who made three late payments within six months or were more than 60 days late on a single bill.

9. **Providian and MBNA** were ordered to pay $300 million to hundreds of thousands of credit card customers who for five years the banks had "misled and deceived in order to increase profits," reports the Office of the Comptroller of the Currency.

8. **Capital One Financial Group** does not receive bills on the weekends and holidays, but it lists those dates on customer bills, and it then charges late fees when bills are, of course, processed late.

7. **Ameritech's Complete Card** which eliminated the **grace period** (the time when no interest is applied).

6. **First Union Bank** and **Advanta** which charge a $25 **cancellation fee** and a $15 **account inactivity fee** that is assessed every six months.

5. **Dozens of card issuers** that have raised their **cash advance fee** to 5 percent ($5 per $100 borrowed with no upper limit).

4. **Associates National Bank** jumps the interest rate to 32.6 percent if the consumer does not pay on time twice in one year.

3. **First Union Bank** charges $38 if the card holder pays one day late.

2. **Dozens of card issuers** who apply a **punitive interest rate** of 25 percent, instead of perhaps 16 percent, after concluding from a peek at your credit file that you no longer meet their "credit standards" that have never been spelled out.

1. **The whole banking industry** that invented **live checks** that are marketed by mail to consumers, and when the real check is cashed (often deposited by elderly consumers) the person gets a 20 to 25 percent, high-interest loan when endorsed and deposited. Thieves love these checks almost as much as the banking industry does.

CONSUMER UPDATE:
Your FICO Credit Score

One's **credit rating** largely determines whether credit is granted. This is an evaluation of a person's previous credit experience. Generally lenders not credit bureaus decide on your credit rating. To help assess potential borrowers, most lenders use a **credit scoring system** that is a statistical measure used to rate credit applicants on the basis of various factors relevant to creditworthiness. Scoring systems help reduce subjectivity in decision-making, avoid discrimination, and improve the likelihood of making correct decisions. Your credit rating also helps the lender decide what interest rate to charge for credit extended.

After years of secrecy, the nation's largest credit scoring firm, Fair, Issac & Co., has been forced by a California law to open the records. A three-digit **FICO score**, on a scale from 300 to 900, predicts how likely one is to repay a loan or to make credit payments on time. Most mortgage lenders use FICO scores which allow them to use **risk-based pricing** for loans; as scores go down interest rates go up. You may obtain your FICO score (or an imitation FICO score) plus your overall credit report for $8 to $12 from www.myfico.com or www.equifax.com.

Other organizations on the web might offer a **better deal**. (See www.eloan.com.) Some states have laws that require free access to FICO scores in particular situations, such as the California requirement that mortgage lenders provide them to home buyers.

About 35 percent of your FICO score is **credit repayment history**, 30 percent is on the amounts owed compared with original loan approved, 15 percent is the length of time one has used credit, 10 percent is if one has been applying for and receiving new loans, and 10 percent is by the mix of one's credit uses. Details are on the Web (www.myfico.com). Once you know your credit score, you can take steps to improve it, perhaps by reducing your loan balances, keeping your outstanding balance at less than 50 percent of the credit limit, paying bills more promptly, and asking lenders as a "goodwill adjustment" to remove some late notices from your report. Increasing a FICO score from 640 to 680 could get one a lower interest rate the next time you need a loan.

FICO scores are used by virtually **all lenders**, including home mortgage lenders and companies financing or leasing vehicles, as well as auto and homeowners'/renters' insurance companies. The latter use the scores to help predict future claims. FICO scores are also examined by landlords and employers.

Inspection of the credit files of the three large credit bureaus (Equifax, Experian and TransUnion) reveals that one's FICO scores range about 50 points from company to company. Sometimes the range is larger because the report contains inaccuracies, omissions, discrepancies, and errors. It is smart to check the contents of your credit file to be certain your FICO score is correct which will increase the likelihood that you are treated fairly by those who have a business interest in examining your credit report. **Rapid rescoring** of your credit file in two or three business days may be possible if you simply need some corrections in your report. You can do this online. Details on your legal rights are provided in Chapter 5.

Paying Only the "Low Minimum Monthly Payment"

Credit card issuers are interested in consumers who **pay their bills on time**, since they profit on each transaction from retailers (1 to 8 percent of each sale). However, creditors relish those who maintain balances. Lenders boost their profits when you pay only the "minimum required monthly payment," often only 2 percent (instead of the years-ago requirement of 5 percent). In addition, you could easily be **in debt forever**.

Guess what happens if you have a Visa or MasterCard credit card balance of $1,000 at 17 percent and you make only the minimum payments of 2 percent? Your repayments would total $2,590 for more than **17 years** and three months. To pay off $2,500 your repayments would be $7,733 and it would take 30 years and three months. These figures *assume that you make no additional charges on the card account again*. Many consumers are ignorant of these facts.

California passed a law requiring credit card bills to carry a **warning notice** cautioning consumers that "Making only the minimum payment will increase the interest you pay and the time it takes to repay your balance." Further, the bills need to detail how much time and interest would be required by making only the minimum payment. The banks have filed suit in federal court to block the law.

DID YOU KNOW?
Bad Credit Boosts Insurance Costs

Your FICO credit score is one of the factors property and casualty companies now use to decide to issue a new policy, to renew it, or to price it. This occurs because insurance companies have determined that credit scores are **good predictors** of the likelihood of future claims. The insurance industry says that people who manage their credit well tend not to drive recklessly or make homeowner's/renter's insurance claims. States that ban the use of credit scores in insurance decision-making raise the premiums for good credit risks.

Grace Period Rip-offs

Three-quarters of cardholders do not know how their grace period works. A **grace period** is the number of days a consumer has before a credit card issuer starts charging interest on new purchases, typically about 21 days. During these days the credit customer receives a free ride by not having to pay finance charges.

Finance charges on credit card accounts are typically calculated by first computing the **average daily balance**. This is the sum of the outstanding balances owed each day during the billing period divided by the number of days in the period. Then the **periodic rate** is applied to that balance. This is the annual percentage rate (APR) divided by the number of billing periods per year, usually 12. For example an annual percentage rate of 18 percent divided by 12 months would equal a periodic rate of 1.5 percent. The **annual percentage rate (APR)** is the total cost of credit to the consumer (including interest and some other charges) expressed as an annual percentage of the amount of credit granted. This is the number that can be used to fairly compare lenders. Unfortunately, credit card issuers have a number of methods to thoroughly confuse consumers. Read on.

To **illustrate**, during a 31-day month a credit card account showed the following: a balance of $120 for 10 days and $70 for 21 days (reflecting a $50 payment). The average daily balance is $86.13 [(10 × $120 = $1,200) + (21 × $70 = $1,470) = $2670; $2,670\31 = $86.13]. Thus on an account with 18 percent APR, a periodic rate of 1.5 percent is multiplied times the average daily balance of $86.13, resulting in a finance charge of $1.29 ($86.13 × 0.015).

There are **two key elements** in determining finance charges on credit cards. First is the number of days in the grace period. Second is whether the balance includes or excludes new purchases.

1. **"Includes new purchases" means no grace period.** The first method of assessing interest is "no grace period with interest calculated on the average daily balance that *includes* new purchases." Here the consumer has no grace period because interest is assessed every day on the balance owed. When a balance is carried forward from a previous month, interest is calculated on the average daily balances **left over from the previous month** and on *every* purchase or cash advance from the exact date of each transaction. This method of assessing credit costs is popular with lenders as it results

in credit cardholders paying a lot of interest. The key phrase to look for in the small print of any credit card agreement is "It *includes* new purchases." Avoid it.

2. **"Excludes new purchases" means with a grace period.** The second method of assessing interest is "full grace period with interest calculated on the average daily balance that *excludes* new purchases." This type of grace period can result in the cardholder (A) never paying interest because they pay the bill in full each month, or (B) paying interest on the previous month's unpaid balance (but not on new purchases) because the consumer sometimes or always chooses to pay less than the full balance owed. Here the cardholder pays interest only on any balance carried forward from the previous month. The consumer gets the benefit of a full grace period because new purchases are *excluded* when figuring the amount of interest owed for the current month. People who pay their credit card balances in full each month will never pay interest and they get an interest-free loan for purchases made. It is also useful for people who do not always pay their bill in full because they get an interest-free loan for purchases made each month. To keep consumers confused and take in more money in interest charges, some credit card companies say that they "exclude new balances" when in reality they **only** do so when the previous month's balance was paid in full by the consumer. The result on such accounts is that when the customer has not paid a bill in full, interest is assessed on all new purchases as they are made, and, of course, interest is charged on the balance carried forward. Sound perplexing? It is.

A promotion that often misleads consumers occurs when the lender offers you a "special grace period" allowing you to **skip one month's credit-card payment**. This usually happens at income tax time or just after the Christmas holidays. If you accept, the lender will not only charge interest on that month's purchases, but will deprive you of the grace period for the following month. And an unpaid balance on one month's bill will automatically result in interest being charged against the next month's purchases, even if the second month's bill is paid within the grace period. Thus, you will be charged interest on all purchases during the two months, and likely from the day you made them. If you carry a balance, you can save a few dollars by mailing your payment as soon as the bill arrives because interest is calculated on a daily basis.

Two-Cycle Method Rip-off

Another method of assessing finance charges on credit cards is the **two-cycle average daily balance method**. It eliminates the grace period on new purchases and *retroactively* eliminates the grace period received for the previous month each time the account carries a balance. The result is often a doubling of the interest charges, a rip-off. This misleading and horribly unfair method permits advertising of one interest rate, perhaps 15 percent, and effectively charging another, more like 30 percent.

Here is an **example** that illustrates how cardholders get legally overcharged. A cardholder makes two purchases of $200 each, one on November 2nd and one on December 2nd. The lender sends out bills on the first of the month and charges an APR of 18 percent, or a periodic rate of 1.5 percent. The cardholder makes no payment on the December bill but pays the January bill in full. Under the favorable method of calculating interest (the average daily balance that excludes new purchases noted above) the cardholder pays $3 in finance charges (.015 × $200 [on the balance from November]); under the least favorable method (the two cycle approach) the cardholder pays $9.00 (.015 × $400 [on the average daily balance from December] + .015 × $200 [on the average daily balance from November]). The result of using the two-cycle average daily balance (including new purchases) method of calculating the interest charges is an **effective rate of interest** of 30 or 40 percent or more! The key phrases to look for in the small print of any credit card agreement are "It *excludes* new purchases" (this is good) and "*two cycle*" method (this is bad).

AN ECONOMIC FOCUS ON...Usury Laws and the Supply and Demand for Consumer Credit*

Adam Smith wrote in 1776 "The man who borrows in order to spend will soon be ruined..."[1] (Smith, 1776, 105).Smith was generally against government interference in the marketplace, but made an exception for the regulation of credit. A **usury law** is a ceiling on the price of credit, usually expressed as a maximum interest rate that can be charged on a particular type of loan or credit card. Usury laws typically are applied to particular types of loans. There has been controversy about usury laws because the effect includes benefiting some consumers who are able to obtain credit at a more reasonable rate, while hurting others, who may be denied credit.

The Supply and Demand for Credit

The price of credit is the interest rate, and can be expressed as:

Interest Rate = Cost of Lender's Funds + Cost of Operation + Risk Premium + Lender's Profit

The cost of the lender's funds will vary with general economic conditions, including the effect of government monetary policies and the anticipation of future inflation. The cost of the lender's operation will depend on many factors, including how difficult it is for the lender to evaluate loan applicants. The **risk premium** is an amount charged to compensate a lender for the likelihood of some failure to repay. It includes the expected loss from borrowers who are late in repaying the loan, or who never repay. The lender's profit will, if the market is competitive, be just sufficient to provide the same rate of return as the next best investment, such as safe government bonds.

Because lenders have other ways to invest their money, there is a supply curve for credit of any particular type, and the higher the interest rate, the more money will be lent (Figure 17-1). There is a demand curve for credit, based on the value different types of consumers place on borrowing money. At the equilibrium point (a) supply equals demand. In the hypothetical example shown in Figure 17-1, the supply and demand for credit for consumers with poor credit records is illustrated. The equilibrium interest rate is 25%. At this level, the amount of money lent might be 50 million dollars. If the government does not allow interest rates for this type of loan to be higher than 10%, the demand for credit might be 80 million dollars (b), but the supply of credit might be 20 million dollars (c). There will be a shortage of credit amounting to 60 million dollars.

(continued)

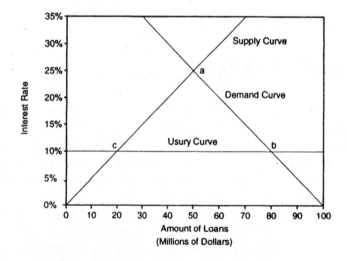

FIGURE 17-1   Supply and Demand for Credit

(continued)

Usury Laws

Usury laws are an interference with the free operation of a market. Based on standard economic theory, usury laws may lead to inefficient allocation of society's scarce resources. Some consumers may see a short-term gain, as the amount they have to pay in finance charges will be reduced. Other consumers will be denied credit, and some consumers will be subject to inconvenience because they cannot obtain a credit card.

Protecting Middle-Income Consumers

Usury laws affect middle-income consumers when they apply for home mortgages and credit cards because rates are set at below-market levels. If inflation is increasing, a low limit on home mortgage interest rates will result in a decrease in loans to home buyers and home builders. A low limit on credit card rates will make it more difficult for consumers to obtain credit cards.

The most common **justification** for applying usury laws in a way to directly benefit middle-income consumers is that competition may be limited. When a pure monopoly exists, there is justification for the government to regulate rates. In consumer credit competition does exist, even if it is not perfect.[2] Increasingly, non-financial corporations are entering the credit card business, so that conditions are right for competition. However, there is evidence that few consumers shop around for credit.[3] When lenders and credit card issuers vigorously compete, advertising of interest rates may reduce the amount of time consumers have to spend shopping for credit.

Such legislation calls for an interest-rate cap on credit-card accounts, which would provide that interest rates on credit cards **could not go higher** than a certain amount. For example, interest charges on credit cards may be prohibited by law from exceeding 15 percent or from being higher than 5 percentage points above the average yield on recently sold U.S. Treasury bills. Six states (Connecticut, Iowa, Kansas, Rhode Island, Virginia, and Washington) have passed some form of credit-card interest rate cap legislation. Most laws peg the interest-rate cap to an economic index, such as the rate on 1-year U.S. Treasury bills, the prime rate, or the federal discount rate.

Defenders of the credit card industry claimed that 15 million individuals would lose cards if national ceilings were imposed.[4] An example of a breakdown of the actual costs of a typical retail credit card seemed to show that even a 21.5% annual interest rate might be reasonable.[5] One justification given for the slowness of decreases in credit card rates in the 1980s was that the cost of funds comprised only 30% of the total cost of credit cards, compared to 90 percent of the cost of mortgage loans.[6]

The Costs of Usury Laws for Middle-Income Consumers

Many studies have found that **usury laws reduce the supply of credit** in states, cause job losses and reduce housing production.[7] Usury laws are apt to hurt young consumers the most, as they tend to need credit to acquire furniture and other durable goods, but have not yet established a good credit record.

Protecting Low-Income Consumers

Usury laws may be designed to help "...the uneducated, the impetuous, and the poor."[8] Research has shown that consumers with low levels of education are much less likely to shop for credit than are more educated consumers. There-fore, competition may be less likely to operate effectively for less educated, lower income consumers than it might for more educated, higher income consumers.

Even if lenders compete vigorously and honestly communicate the relative cost of credit to consumers, some consumers may decide to take on credit at very high interest rates. Consider an annual percentage rate (APR) of over 30%. It is very unlikely that a safe, productive investment would give this high a return. Most people seeking to borrow at a rate that high are **either poorly informed or want to finance spending today**.

A consumer may want to enjoy relatively high consumption today, even if he or she knows that in the future the burden of repayment may reduce their level of living to a very low level.[9] Perhaps usury laws are a reasonable way to protect the consumer from his or her own folly.

Other consumers may feel sure that their incomes will be much higher next year than this year. If a consumer is certain that family income will be much higher next year, borrowing at a very high interest rate may be rational.[10] There may be situations where a consumer would willingly pay very high APRs to finance consumption now. An example is when a family member will return to work next year, but the family has pressing needs now. More research is needed to determine the proportion of families who mistakenly take on credit at high interest rates, versus those who might be acting rationally. It is likely that most consumers who borrow at an APR higher than 30% are acting out of ignorance or irrational optimism.

Conclusions on the Supply and Demand of Credit

Usury laws may protect consumers from making mistakes in obtaining credit, but they also may hurt consumers, especially if the limits are set too low. An APR of 30% for unsecured credit (if inflation is about 5% per year) might be a reasonable compromise, protecting some consumers and only reducing the supply of credit to those with poor credit records. Vigorous consumer information and education efforts and enforcement of disclosure laws, such as Truth-in-Lending, would still be needed, as some consumer borrowing at or below the usury limit might be based on ignorance.

---

[1]Smith, A. (1964; 1776). *The Wealth of Nations* in George W. Wilson (ed.) *Classics of Economic Theory*, 105, Indiana University Press.

[2]Nathan, H.C. (Winter, 1980). Economic Analysis of Usury Laws, *Journal of Bank Research*, 10(4), 209.

[3]Chang, Y.R. & Hanna, S. (1992). Consumer Credit Search Behavior, *Journal of Consumer Studies and Home Economics*, 16, 207-227.

[4]Becker, M. (February, 1988). Credit Card Ceilings: Illusory Gains and real Costs, 76, 42-47.

[5]*Ibid.* 45.

[6]Chaudoin, G.S. (February, 1987). Are Credit Card Interest Rates Too High?, *Illinois Business Review*, 44, 3-6.

[7]Nathan, Economic Analysis.

[8]Avio, K.L. (1972). An Economic Rationale for Statutory Interest Rate Ceilings, *Quarterly Review of Economics and Business*, 13(1), (Spring), 63.

[9]*Ibid*, 61-72.

[10]Chang, Y.R., Fan, X.J. & Hanna, S. (1992). Relative Risk Aversion and Optimal Credit Use with Uncertain Income, *Proceedings of the American Council on Consumer Interests*, 14-22.

*Sherman Hanna, Professor, The Ohio State University

FIGURE 17-1   continued

CONSUMER UPDATE:
Consolidate Student Loans

Median student loan debt for bachelor's degree graduates is **$16,000**. Those who have **government-insured student loan**s might get a lower interest rate and a lower monthly payment by getting a **consolidated loan** where a borrower's loan(s) are paid off and a new consolidation loan is created that usually has a lower interest rate and a smaller monthly payment. The person does not have to put up any collateral or pass a credit check. Loans are granted on one's signature. Most loans range from 10 to 30 years. You **can save** an additional 1/4 of one percent (that little fraction means lots of saved money over time) by agreeing to have loan repayments automatically debited from your financial account. Both the government and private lenders offer such loans, but only the government will consolidate defaulted loans. The 50 largest loan holders are at www.finaid.org. Organizations that will consolidate student loans include:

*Federal Government Direct Consolidation Loans (800-557-7392), www.loanconsolidation.ed.gov.
*Nellie Mae (800-367-8848), www.nelliemae.com
*Sallie Mae (800-695-3317), www.salliemae.com.
*College Funding Services (888-423-7562), www.cfsloans.com
*Education Resources Institute (800-225-8374), www.teri.org

A federal study found that four years after receiving that college diploma, only **16 percent** had paid off their student loans. About half had school debts averaging $10,000. Student loan defaults are about 9 percent, and the government hires private collection agencies to track down those who are not paying back their loans. Also, the IRS takes any refund due such taxpayers.

Card Blocking May Create Penalties

Card blocking (also called **credit-hold** or **debit-hold**) happens when a car-rental agency, hotel, gas station or other merchant puts a hold on your credit or debit card when a charge is authorized before the actual billing amount in known. This is done by merchants to help assure them that if the final charge is higher than expected there will be funds available to pay them. A car rental agency, for example, may put a $300 card block on your credit card for a $200 rental. Gasoline stations automatically block $50 or $60 no matter how much gas you pump. The hold is often **150 percent or more** of the estimated expenditure.

Consumers face problems with card blocking because it **freezes the amount** in their account, consequently **losing the use of those funds** often for two or three days. The payment transaction may be recorded two days later and the block may not be removed for another day. Merchants are not even legally required to tell consumers that they have placed a hold on an account. In the meantime, consumers can easily overdraw their checking accounts which leads to bounced checks or insufficient funds being available through ATM machines. Card blocking also can push consumers over their credit limits. These events create bank fees. "If you are unaware you have several holds on your account," says Jean Ann Fox, director of consumer protection at Consumer Federation of America, "you could be hit with that fee repeatedly."

The Rule of 78s Prepayment Penalty

The **rule of 78s**, sometimes called the **sum-of-the-digits method**, is a commonly used method of calculating rebates of finance charges and the prepayment penalty charged the borrower who pays off an installment loan early. It assumes that you pay more in interest in the beginning of a loan when you have the use of more money and that you pay less and less interest as the debt is reduced.

The rule of 78s method was designed before the days of computers. A loan with this credit clause effectively winds up unfairly **doubling the effective annual percentage rate** for consumers who pay off loans early. In extreme cases, a consumer may even pay more in interest than the principal amount of the loan.

To **illustrate**, suppose on a $500 loan for 12 months $80 in finance charges were scheduled to be paid. If the loan is paid off after only six months, the borrower will not have the interest reduced $40 (half of $80). To calculate the actual reduced interest in dollars, first add together all the numbers between 1 and 12 ($1 + 2 + 3 + 4 + 5 + 6 + 7 + 8 + 9 + 10 + 11 + 12 = 78$). If the loan is paid off after one month, the amount of interest paid is assumed to be 12/78 of the total, with a reduction of 66/78 due the borrower. For a loan paid in full after two months, the amount of interest paid is assumed to be 23/78 of the total (12/78 for month one plus 11/78 for month 2). Note that most of the early repayments go for interest. In this example, after six months, the lender assumes that $58.46 (57/78) has been paid in interest. Thus, the borrower does not get 50 percent of the interest as a reduction for paying the loan off in half the time, but only 27 percent ($21.54/$80). The rule of 78s penalty arises when a consumer pays off a loan early. A common example is trading in a car with an existing auto loan for a newer one.

The Truth in Lending law does not require that lenders disclose this clause in advance. Consumers must **ask for the information** or scan a credit contract to see if it is there. Consumer advocates want to make the rule of 78s illegal.

Mistakes in Credit Files

An estimated **one-third** of all credit files **contain serious errors** that could cause unfair denial of a vehicle loan, a home mortgage, vehicle insurance or a job, reports the U.S. Public Research Group. And those errors result in millions of consumers paying higher interest rates than they should.

Each year about nine million people **ask to see their credit files**. More than three million request to have their files corrected because of invalid or stale information. Credit bureaus are protected against lawsuits for financial damages by consumers who have been wronged (e.g., lost job opportunities, being refused home rentals, rejections for mortgages, automobile loans) when they have made "honest" mistakes. To correct an error or obtain a copy of your credit report, see Chapter 5.

CONSUMER UPDATE:
Bad Credit Records Plague Consumers, Especially African-Americans

A survey of 10,000 consumers by mortgage lender Freddie Mac, a quasi-governmental organization, shows that millions of consumers have bad credit records. The survey defined **bad credit records** as those with delinquent liens, a bankruptcy filling, or a history of late payments.

Nearly half of African-Americans (48 percent) and over a quarter of whites (27 percent) have bad credit records. For whites, the percentage declines as income rises. However, the percentage remains roughly the same for African-Americans in all but the highest income bracket. Freddie Mac suggests that this occurs because fewer African-Americans own their homes (46 percent for African-Americans versus 72 percent for whites) and invest in the stock market, plus job loss is higher among African-Americans.

DID YOU KNOW?
Alternatives for Getting Out of Debt

Here are some suggestions on how to **get out of debt all by yourself**: (1) Track every dollar you spend for one or two months to determine precisely where your money is going; (2) Create a budget to guide your spending and repay all debts; (3) Do not take out additional loans or add to credit card balances; (4) If possible, transfer credit card balances to your lowest interest rate card; (5) Get a credit union loan at a lower rate to pay off your card debt; (6) Pay more than the minimum amount due on credit cards; (7) Pay off the highest interest rate debt first; (8) Do not be late in making any monthly payments; (9) Do not be sucked into zero-percent financing offers that quickly raise rates; (10) Telephone credit card issuers to request lower interest rates; and (11) Contact a credit counseling agency for budget and credit assistance.

Counseling and assistance can be obtained at a non-profit **credit counseling** organization. These companies help people with **unsecured debts**, loans that have no collateral. Examples of unsecured debts are credit and charge card purchases, credit and charge card cash advances, store charges, medical and dental bills, rent, utility bills, health club dues, lawyer bills, union dues, student loans, child support, and alimony. Credit counseling organizations negotiate with creditors to reduce interest rates, eliminate late fees, and re-age the account to bring it up to date. The debtor's monthly repayment amount on a **debt management plan (DMP)** established by a non-profit credit counseling organization is typically reduced by 30 to 40 percent. **Secured debts**, such as on a vehicle or televison, are excluded as lenders typically repossess items for which there is collateral. To become a client, the consumer must agree to cut up credit cards and not open any more accounts. Because of the concessions by creditors, DMP clients can get out of debt in only three or four years rather than 20 or 30 years of paying minimum payments.

The non-profit industry earns its revenue primarily from **voluntary contributions from creditors** who would prefer to provide this indirect financial assistance rather than lose completely which happens when a debtor goes bankrupt. Clients of ethical credit counseling organizations pay a nominal fee to sign up for a debt management plan and make nominal monthly payments, but only if they can afford to do so. Beware of credit counseling firms that charge high up-front fees, such as the entire first month's repayment (often $400 to $800, or more), because they are rip-off companies operating until a state attorney general closes them down.

Either of the two trade associations for the credit counseling industry can put a consumer in contact with a non-profit credit counseling organization: (1) Association of Independent Consumer Credit Counseling Agencies, www.aiccca.org (703-934-6118), and (2) National Foundation for Consumer Credit, www.nfcc.org (800-388-2227).

An alternative for some may be to sign on with a **debt-mediation service** (also called **debt negotiation**). Here the company negotiates with creditors to settle debts for 25 to 60 cents on the dollar. A creditor to whom you owe $5,000, for example, might be offered $2,000 to settle the debt in full. They keeping making offers until creditors say "yes," and it may take a year or more to settle all debts. Of course, most consumers do not have much cash to be able to offer creditors. The debt-mediation service's fee is usually a 25 percent cut of the money saved the consumer. The defaults and markdowns ruin the person's credit record. In addition, the Internal Revenue Service considers the forgiven loans as taxable income. Finally, if one's bills and income are beyond reconciliation, the last alternative is to contact a lawyer to assist in filing for personal bankruptcy.

New Bankruptcy Law

About **1.5 million** people declare personal bankruptcy annually, and that is double the number a decade ago. During the past five years, 5 percent of households have declared personal bankruptcy. That's one in every block of every housing development.

The majority of people declaring personal bankruptcy have experienced some **economic catastrophe** within the previous one or two years. The primary reasons why consumers file for bankruptcy are divorce, job loss and medical bills (even for those with health insurance). The combination of medical bills and heavy consumer debts pushes many into bankruptcy. The median income of a typical bankrupt recently was $26,000, which is about 60 percent of the national median household income of $43,000.

Bankruptcy is a constitutionally guaranteed right that permits people (and businesses) to ask a court to find them officially unable to meet their debts. When the petition is granted, the majority of assets and liabilities of the person are then divided by a trustee and used to repay as much of the unsecured debts as reasonably possible. State and federal laws govern what a debtor can keep: a small **home equity** (the amount by which the value of a home exceeds the debt owed on it [created with the down-payment, rising home prices, and by paying down the mortgage loan balance]) in a home, an inexpensive vehicle, and limited personal property. Seventy percent of debtors choose **Chapter 7**, **straight bankruptcy**, that immediately liquidates debts. The remainder select **Chapter 13**, the **wage earner plan** or **regular income plan**, that is designed to allow repayment of as much of the debt as possible; typically in 36 to 60 months. Only then are the remaining debts discharged. Debts not discharged in bankruptcy include alimony, child support, taxes, and student loans.

A **new bankruptcy law** is expected to pass Congress and become law in 2004. In the bill's present form, new requirements are expected to affect only 10 percent of people seeking bankruptcy. This is the proportion of people who file for bankruptcy that have **incomes greater than their state's median income**, and they would be required to file under Chapter 13. If after the court estimates reasonable living expenses and finds a surplus, those people would be required to repay some of their debts, perhaps 40 to 60 percent on the dollar over three to five years. The new law will require credit counseling for each person seeking bankruptcy and each person will be required to participate in an educational program on money management and credit.

Housing Problems and Issues

Today, a record **67 percent** of families in the United States, or 71 million, own their homes. A home is the largest purchase most people ever make in their lives, and a number of consumer problems and issues exist in the area of housing.

The High Cost of Housing in America

Home ownership is an important **key to affluence**. The easiest way for those with modest incomes to build wealth, says Consumer Federation of America's Stephen Brobeck, is "to buy a home, faithfully make the mortgage payments, and be cautious about borrowing against the accumulating home equity." When home prices are too high for consumers with modest incomes, they are effectively barred from future financial success.

The cost of the average new home sold in the United States is more than **$165,000**. Average prices for single-family dwellings in Orange County, California, are above $500,000, and the median sales price of a home in San Francisco is $550,000. In the least expensive geographic area, Elmira, New York, the median sales price is $75,000.

Census data reveal that 85 percent of households headed by persons under age 25 are renters compared with only 19 percent of those headed by persons aged 55 to 64. **Lower mortgage rates** have helped enormously with housing affordability. For people with an average household income of about $41,000, after making a 20 percent down payment of

$28,000 they could afford a $140,000 home. If interest rates should rise 2 percent, that same income could qualify for only a $105,000 home.

DID YOU KNOW?
Housing Subsidies for the Poor and Some Recent College Graduates

Originally designed for **low-income consumers**, those qualifying for subsidized housing loans also includes college graduates who are earning less than average incomes. Here is how the program works. If the conventional home mortgage rate is 6 percent and requires a $1,200 monthly repayment amount for a home valued at $230,000 with a $200,000 loan, a government subsidy might reduce the interest rate, perhaps to 5 percent. Then the monthly payment for principal and interest would be only $1,074, which is more affordable than $1,200.

One program is the Federal National Mortgage Association (Fannie Mae). It allows borrowers to make a down payment of **as little as $1,000** or three percent of the sales price. Participant's income is not to exceed 60 to 80 percent of the area's median income. For example, in Washington, D.C. the median income is over $64,000. Thus, a person earning $51,000 ($64,000 × .80) qualifies. Since all states have programs to subsidize interest rates for low-income home buyers in certain communities, interested people should contact local housing officials.

The maximum loan amount on the low down-payment housing loans **insured by the Federal Housing Administration (FHA)** is about $180,000 in high-cost areas of the U.S. Since the FHA handles more than 700,000 loans a year, this opens up more higher-priced housing to people who have the income to qualify but do not have the often required 20-percent down payment money to buy a home. The Veterans Administration (VA) has a no-down-payment program. VA-insured loans include members of the military reserves and the national guard who have spent six years on inactive duty. The Federal National Mortgage Association (Fannie Mae) has $1 trillion available for lending.

Reports by the Center on Budget and Policy Priorities (www.cbpp.org) indicate that the growing lack of **affordable housing** has reached a crisis stage for low-income Americans, including many African Americans and Hispanics. Unless and until additional special funds become available, it will continue to be difficult for many people to buy housing in America. A survey of 44 cities by the same organization found that three-quarters of the nation's **poor are paying more** than what the government says is affordable in rent. Fewer than one-third of the urban poor receive rent subsidies.

Predatory Lending

The subprime lending industry makes loans to borrowers with blemished credit histories as well as consumers with good credit ratings. **Subprime loans** are loans at interest rates above conventional. For example, if mortgage rates were 6 percent, a subprime mortgage lender's rate might be 91/2 percent. Also, if the conventional interest rate for a car loan is 12 percent, the subprime rate might be 17 percent.

Predatory lending, a subset of the subprime industry, is the exploitative practice of ripping off consumers by charging excessive amounts of money for credit. It occurs in housing loans, refinanced mortgages, home-equity loans, automobile financing and leasing, consumer installment purchases, and debt consolidation loans. Predatory lending, also called **high-cost lending**, is the abusive practice of charging borrowers excessive loan fees, overpriced and unnecessary insurance policies, large balloon payments, hefty prepayment penalties, and unnecessarily high interest rates. When consumers fail to make the repayments the amount owed is refinanced with even more excessive fees. Eventually, the borrower is unable to pay the larger and larger monthly repayments and the property that secured the loan is lost, either repossessed in the case of vehicles and consumer goods or foreclosed in the case of a home loan.

Homeowners, for example, may be **fast-talked by telemarketers** into borrowing to pay medical bills, to finance home repairs and remodeling, or to pay off credit cards while all the time believing the salesperson's claim that they are getting a **low-cost, low-interest loan**. They are unwittingly talked into doing things that are against their self-interest. This occurs in home financing because borrowers rely on lending professionals to honestly guide them through a complicated process that is not well understood by many consumers in all education and income levels. This occurs in consumer financing because many borrowers are unsophisticated. Unscrupulous slick salespersons are paid a bonus for every overcharge they pack into a consumer's loan. Mainstream mortgage companies Freddie Mac and Fannie Mae estimate that **35 to 50 percent** of borrowers with subprime mortgages would qualify for conventional rates if they knew "what to look for and how to shop for a loan."

Predatory lenders that have signed consent orders with government agencies agreeing not to make predatory loans and to repay millions of dollars to ripped off borrowers include **First Alliance Company, Household Finance,** and **Associates First Capital**. Some states (CA, NC) have strong anti-predatory laws. However, Republican conservatives are attempting to get Congress to pass national legislation with weak consumer protections that would preempt all the current strong state and local laws.

Discrimination in Credit, Housing and Insurance

Discrimination is acting on the basis of bias or intentional prejudice. It is illegal to discriminate in credit financing, as well as in many areas of housing and employment. Various laws prohibit discrimination on the basis of race, color, religion, national origin, gender, sexual orientation, marital status, age, disability, elderliness, or parenthood. As a country, Americans believe in a society in which each person is evaluated on his or her worth, not a community based upon factors that cannot be changed. Still, illegal discrimination goes on.

Home buyers face lending discrimination. A government survey of 9,500 financial institutions shows that home loan denial rates were as follows: Asians, 12.5 percent; Hispanics, 29.5 percent; blacks, 40.5 percent, and Native Americans, 41.4 percent. Mortgage denial rates for most minority applicants according to the Mortgage Bankers Association, were **twice as great** as denial rates for white borrowers (20.6 percent). This finding occurred regardless of income. A Federal Reserve Board study found that black mortgage applicants were rejected for loans at double the rates of whites, regardless of income. A report of the American Bankers Association studying mortgage lending data showed similar disturbing patterns. Mortgage lenders still routinely discriminate.

Renters face discrimination. A study of 25 metropolitan areas by a Department of Housing and Urban Development study found that Hispanics encountered **bias half the time** they tried to rent and more than half the time they attempted to buy a home; blacks faced even higher rates of discrimination. Bias against blacks attempting to rent in affluent Fairfax County, Virginia was found to be 71 percent. After being caught discriminating by the government and fined $28 million, AcuBanc Mortgage Corporation agreed to make $2.1 billion in loans to minorities.

Homeowner's insurance buyers face discrimination. Homeowners insurance is required when a consumer finances a home. **Testers** in Chicago, says the National Fair Housing Alliance, found that Latinos "ran into problems in more than 95 percent of their attempts to obtain insurance." Nationwide, Allstate, American Family, Liberty Mutual, and State Farm have settled federal allegations of discrimination when selling insurance. Nationwide paid $100 million to Housing Opportunities Made Equal (HOME), a fair housing group that alleged the company denied housing insurance to black applicants while approving insurance for whites under similar circumstances. HOME also was awarded $17 million to provide training to Nationwide to ensure that the latter properly serve urban and black neighborhoods across the country. MetLife paid $250 million to settle New York State allegations that it charged black customers higher premiums for less insurance coverage than that provided white customers.

CONSUMER UPDATE
Examples of Discrimination

Sometimes discrimination is subtle and can often be defined by the lack of assistance someone receives. Some examples follow.

- A lender rejected a loan application made by a female applicant with flaws in her credit report but accepted applications by male applicants **with similar flaws**.

- Two minority applicants were told that it would take **several hours** and require the payment of an **application fee** to determine whether or not they qualified for a home loan, while non-minority applicants were given no such requirements.

- Two minority applicants were falsely told that **much more information** was needed before they could receive an indication of how likely they were to qualify, while non-minority applicants were given no such additional requirements.

- Two minority applicants had their housing loan **ratios falsely computed**, while non-minority applicants housing ratios were correctly calculated.

- When a minority couple applied for a loan, upon questioning the lender incorrectly **discouraged them** from applying for a loan, while a non-minority couple with similar background information was not discouraged and the non-minorities also were given tips and hints about how to qualify.

- When a non-minority couple applied for a loan, upon questioning, the lender recommended that the **adverse information** in their credit report be challenged because it was incorrect and the loan was later approved. A minority couple with similar adverse information was simply denied credit without having an opportunity to discuss the report.

- Two minority borrowers inquired about a mortgage loan and were given applications for **fixed-rate loans only** and were **not offered assistance** in completing the applications; later their application was turned down. Two similarly qualified non-minority applicants made an identical inquiry, were given information about adjustable-rate and fixed rate loans, and were given assistance in filling out the application, which the lender later approved.

- A lender's **longtime policy** has been not to extend loans for single family residences for less than $80,000. However, this policy is shown to disproportionately exclude potential minority applicants.

Subprime borrowers face discrimination. Household International paid $484 million in a settlement with state attorneys general for alleged abusive and deceptive practices on sub-prime home loans that targeted seniors and minorities. The average refund was $1,500. First Alliance Mortgage, accused by federal and state governments of deceiving poor and elderly homeowners into taking out loans with large hidden fees, paid $60 million to 18,000 of its customers. The average refund was $3,000.

Blacks and other minorities face discrimination. A life insurance company in Chicago, Unitrin Inc., settled a class action lawsuit about its use of race as a ratings factor in pricing burial life insurance policies. Similarly situated blacks were charged higher premiums than white for many years. A Chicago study revealed that African-Americans and women **pay the highest prices** for new vehicles. Higher prices were routinely quoted to the undercover researchers, and differences ranged from $142 to $875. Federal investigators are currently examining the amount of fees charged to women and minority applicants compared with the fees charged their white counterparts.

DID YOU KNOW?
How to Report Credit Discrimination

If you suspect that you have been discriminated against because of your race, gender or age, telephone any of the following: Housing Discrimination Hotline of the Department of Housing and Urban Development (800-669-9777; www.hud.gov); Justice Department (202-514-4713; www.usdoj.gov/); National Fair Housing Alliance (202-898-1661; www.nationalfairhousing.org/).

Redlining Discriminates

Credit availability is a crucial concern, particularly for low- and moderate income consumers. **Redlining** is refusing to sell a consumer product, such as insurance, in certain neighborhoods or charging such high prices that poor consumers are forced out of certain markets. The term comes from the illegal practice of outlining a geographic area by drawing red lines around disfavored neighborhoods where money would reluctantly be lent or not at all regardless of the creditworthiness of individual loan applicants. Redlining occurs when institutions close their branch offices in poor and middle-income neighborhoods or have policies that reduce access to housing, credit, and homeowner's and automobile insurance. This is discrimination. A number of communities additionally have laws that also prohibit discrimination based on sexual orientation.

Redlining is **prohibited** by federal and state laws. An insurance spokesperson summed up a common industry view by saying that "There really isn't evidence of intentional discrimination against urban residents. What you have are neutral underwriting rules that have a disproportionate impact upon minority, urban residents." A study of 24 million mortgage records by *U.S. News & World Report* reveals that both blatant and subtle forms of redlining continue. Discrimination is destructive, morally repugnant, and against the law. When discrimination occurs, those wronged consumers have no other marketplace choices available at fair or low prices, thus discrimination is against the consumer interest.

CONSUMER UPDATE:
Community Reinvestment Act Ratings

Because of the Community Reinvestment Act (CRA), banks, savings banks, and savings and loan associations are **required to serve all the credit needs of the communities** where they have offices—rich or poor, white or minority—and especially in low- and moderate-income neighborhoods. CRA regulations, described in Chapter 5, require a dialogue between the financial institutions and people in all segments of the communities they serve.

CRA requires that financial institutions play a vital role in revitalizing neighborhoods. The accountability of the banks, savings banks, and savings and loan associations is made clear to the public through posting of regular performance evaluations, **CRA ratings** are used to grade each institution's efforts to serve its community. This rating is based upon proper documentation reviewed by federal inspectors. Interested consumers need only visit a local financial institution to determine its CRA rating and review the institution's CRA public file for a description of efforts. Over $125 billion has been loaned in targeted areas nationwide in the past 20 years.

Appraisers Are Regulated, but Not for Average Consumers

Almost all real estate appraisers are licensed and/or certified. A federal law requires that states enact their own licensing or certification laws. In 21 states appraisers must be licensed; in the other 29 licensed appraisers are only required for deals involving loans with the federal government. However, the federal government largely exempts the need for an appraisal on loans less than $250,000, and that amounts to 80 percent of all loans. Therefore, most properties that consumers purchase are not evaluated by a qualified appraiser. Instead, an **alternative appraisal** called an *evaluation* may be performed, and this person may not be a licensed appraiser. Thus, getting a property appraised is a challenge for many low- and middle--income home buyers.

Mandatory Defect-Disclosure Laws

Many states require sellers to complete a **defect-disclosure form** aimed at detailing what a seller really knows about the condition of a home when selling it. The form requires the seller to complete a detailed, two- to four-page form. Included on the list are such items as the condition of heating and cooling systems, appliances; presence of radon gas, termites, carpenter ants, asbestos, and lead-based paint; noise in the neighborhood; whether or not the well has gone dry; and if the property had ever been involved in a dispute over property-lines. Disclosure forms are not warranties of a home's condition; they are simply lists of defects that could affect a potential buyer's perception of the value of the property. Sellers are urged to be precise in describing flaws, and the liability for undisclosed defects rests with the seller.

The Residential Lead-Based Paint Hazard Reduction Act educates residents about the dangers of **lead paint in older homes**, particularly the 64 million dwellings built before 1978 when lead paint was outlawed. The rules require sellers, landlords, sales agents, and rental agents to provide disclosure forms and pamphlets written by HUD and EPA that tell people how to protect themselves.

Agents Should Disclose to Buyers Whom They Represent

The Federal Trade Commission reports that **three-quarters** of all home buyers **mistakenly believe** that the agent driving them around to see homes and presenting their purchase offers represents *their* interests. While state laws require agents to treat buyers and sellers honestly and fairly, long-standing legal precedent provides that the agents almost always work for the seller, not the buyer. The agent is hired to sell the home for the seller because the seller pays the sales commission. If a potential buyer divulges any confidential information to the agent, such as the price they would be willing to pay if they couldn't get it for less, the agent is legally obligated to pass the information onto the seller. The result: buyers pay too much for housing.

Because of the **confusion** in the minds of so many consumers, a number of states require that home buyers be notified in writing—at the first substantive meeting between the agent and the consumer—who the real estate agent represents. Several states permit buyers' agents to only represent buyers.

Bargaining is Necessary to Reduce Sales Commissions

Tradition provides that real estate agents earn a standard six, or even seven percent commission when selling a home. Sellers pay a **listing agent** (the person who reaches an agreement with a seller to place the home for sale) a commission. This amount is shared with other agents, especially **selling agents** (persons working with potential buyers). Since both agents are paid by the seller, they represent the seller. The great majority of homes are sold using a **multiple-listing service (MLS),** a shared database that lists and describes homes for sale which is available to most agents. Assuming that the seller pays a 6 percent commission upon the sale of a home, the real estate agent who originally listed the property may receive 3 percent and often splits that 50/50 with the owner of the agency. The selling agent may receive the remaining 3 percent and share 40 percent of that amount with the owner of the agency.

The commission is paid regardless of the quality of service received. The commission pays for the earnings of the agent, advertising the property, and office support of the full-service real estate firm. Occasionally, a real estate agent will agree to accept a reduced commission, but consumers have to bargain. No laws require agents to disclose that they **will work for less** than the so-called standard commission rate.

A growing number of realty firms work for flat fees far below the usual six percent commission. One study found that consumers who hired **buyer's brokers**, those who represent only the buyer in a real estate transaction, paid an average of **91 percent** of a home's list price while those using traditional agents paid 96 percent. Buyer's brokers are paid by the hour or a flat fee, often two to three percent of the buyer's target purchase price and require that the homeowner show the home to prospective buyers. Discounters do the advertising, provide advice throughout the process, and handle most or all of the paperwork. Twenty percent of homeowners sell their own homes without the use of a realty agent, and one-third of residential sales are made for less than the standard six percent commission.

Kickback Fees and Up-charges

The Real Estate Settlement Procedures Act (RESPA) attempts to protect consumers from abusive real estate closing practices, especially where kickback fees are given to various service providers. A **kickback fee** is a payment to a person able to influence or control a source of income, often by confidential arrangement or coercion.

A federal appeals court decision allows **up-charging** by title companies and mortgage lenders. This is the practice of marking up the actual prices of credit reports, appraisals and other real estate costs. Related services that a consumer might purchase when buying a home include a loan application, home inspection service, mortgage loan, title insurance, life insurance, and property and casualty insurance. For example, the credit report might cost $15 but the lender might charge you $60. Or the appraisal charge might be $300, but the lender charges you $500.

While a lender may offer "one-stop shopping" which may be convenient, it also can result in seriously **overcharging consumers**. "At most real estate closings," says one expert "consumers are in such a daze that they sign every form you put in front of them." RESPA regulations require written disclosure of any special fees, kickbacks, rebates, or other forms of payment for related services. Consumers also must be told they have the legal right to shop elsewhere for alternatives.

AN ECONOMIC FOCUS ON...The Supply and Demand for Housing

Each housing market is composed of many participants, including builders, landlords, lenders, government regulators, and consumers.[1] Each housing market is local, and each local market is composed of sub-markets: (1) owner-occupied housing of different types and price levels, and (2) rental housing at different rent levels. For simplicity, the following discussion uses the assumption that all housing is rental and identical.

The Supply of Housing

The supply of housing in a private market is determined by the interest of builders in making a profit, and the availability of land, labor, and materials needed to build a housing unit, whatever the actual structure type—single family, townhouse, apartment building, etc. There is rarely any absolute limit on the inputs of land, labor and materials for building housing. Even when the supply of land is limited, builders can build up with multi-level housing. The higher the market price of housing, the more units will be built. If there are not enough workers for building homes, wages will increase and workers will come into the industry. New homebuilding firms will start, with some builders working nights and weekends after their regular jobs.

Credit. The availability of credit is one of the most important limitations on the supply of housing. If the government, especially the Federal Reserve Board in the United States, is trying to control inflation, there may be a decrease in the availability of housing. The supply of housing will be sharply decreased during these times when credit is expensive and difficult to obtain. At other times, the government will try to stimulate the economy and plenty of credit will be available.

The Demand for Housing

The demand for housing is determined by the number of households and the amount of money they want to spend for housing. Obviously, rich consumers can spend more for housing than poor consumers. Families with many children will want different types of housing and different locations than will single persons and childless couples. The demand curve for housing of a particular type and general location is the sum of the quantity each household would want at each price or rent. The demand curve will shift up if incomes increase or if people move into an area. The demand curve will shift down if incomes decrease or if people move out of an area.

Effect of Increase in Demand for Housing. Consider the example of a housing market shown in Figure 17-2. If supply and demand are in balance in the market, the average rent is $250 and there are 50,000 rental units at the intersection of supply and demand (point a). Assume that the demand in the market increases, for instance, because of a sudden increase in population (shown by the change in the demand curve from D to D[1]). The short run supply curve is almost vertical, as shown by S_0. Within the first month after the sudden increase in demand, no new housing units can be built. The supply curve will not be completely vertical, because there may be some vacant units, and some units may be converted from other uses (e.g., commercial space or parts of owner-occupied housing may be rented out). Most of the effect of the increase in demand will be seen in the increase in the rent, shown in the example as an increase from $250 to $355. The number of rental units will increase from 50,000 to 52,000 units.

Short-run Market Response. The change in equilibrium to point b has very little increase in the number of units available and a large increase in rent. A large increase in rent will outrage consumers, but it will also attract builders and landlords because of the opportunity for above average profits. Before new units can come on the market, some consumers will have to "double-up", living with relatives or others, and others will have long commutes to work.

Medium-run Market Response. If there are not excessive limitations on building and renovations, many new rental units will become available. If building can proceed very quickly, within one year the supply curve may have shifted to what is shown by S_1. The new equilibrium point will be point c, which will have a lower rent ($320) and a larger quantity (63,000 units).

Long-run Market Response. After two years, the supply curve will shift to S_2 and the new equilibrium point will be at point d. The rent level will drop to $320 and the quantity will increase to 80,000 units. After five years, it is possible that rents (after general inflation is subtracted) will drop back to the original level ($250). It is even possible that builders will be over-optimistic and overbuild, in which case rents will be driven down below the original level.

Rent Control. Some cities respond to a sudden increase in the demand for housing by passing rent control laws to protect tenants from increases in rents. This effort will inevitably hurt some consumers, as a shortage will continue as long as the rent control is in effect. The ultimate result can be seen in New York City, where the government must spend billions of dollars to build housing for low and moderate households because the private market will not supply it.

Regulations. Regulations such as building codes and zoning restrictions have stated purposes of protecting consumers and of improving the environment of residents. In many cases, however, such regulations also have resulted in higher rents and home prices. Some regulations, such as minimum sizes for building lots, may benefit existing homeowners at the expense of young families and others who would like housing in the area. Even when regulations are at moderate levels, they will tend to shift up the supply curves shown in Figure 17-2, leading to some reduction in the amount of affordable housing for low and moderate income families. If society has a concern for the housing of these families, some type of housing programs or income supplements may be needed.

Conclusion: There Is No Free Lunch

The fundamental truth to consider about housing is that there is no free lunch. Provision of adequate housing for people costs money. The private market can deal efficiently with shifts in demand and supply, and adjust to regulations, but some families will have to pay high fractions of their incomes to obtain housing considered adequate by society. Efforts to improve housing of low and moderate income families will cost money, and ultimately middle and upper income consumers will pay, either through higher prices and rents or by higher taxes.

---

[1]Lindamood, S. & Hanna, S. (1979). *Housing, Society and Consumers: An Introduction* (West Publishing), 132.

*Sherman Hanna, Professor, The Ohio State University

FIGURE 17-2   The Effect of an Increase in Demand (D to D[1]) on the Price and Amount of Rental Housing

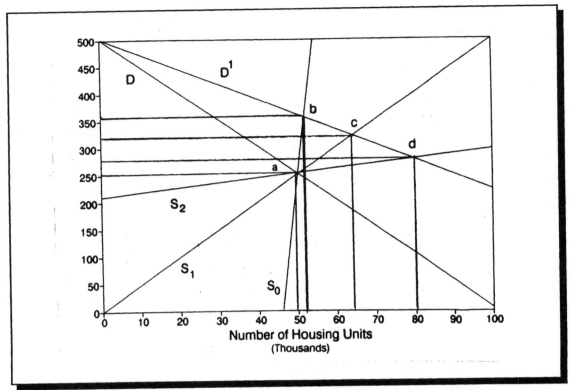

FIGURE 17-2   (continued)

Consumer advocates are worried about anti-competitive practices where firms will be motivated to **steer borrowers** to lenders and other providers in the system that give them the biggest kickbacks, rather than offer the best prices for consumers. As independent service providers are squeezed out of business because of a lack of referrals within the system, future consumers will have fewer choices in a marketplace with no constraints on pricing. Without comparison shopping, consumers are likely to pay too much; perhaps as much as 5 to 10 percent extra.

Escrow Rip-offs

More than three-quarters of all outstanding loans have escrow requirements. **Escrow payments** are monthly prepayments made by a homeowner to a lender to accumulate and later be used to pay the real estate property taxes and homeowner's insurance on the property. The idea is to protect the lender and prevent foreclosure if a homeowner fails to pay taxes and insurance.

Here is how the system works. Should a homeowner expect to owe $1,000 for homeowner's insurance and $2,600 for real estate taxes at the end of a year, he or she will give the lender $300 a month to build up a sufficient amount. These funds go into an escrow account. The bad news is that two out of three homeowners are being taken advantage of by the mortgage lenders. Since savings and loan associations are not legally required to pay interest on escrow accounts, most are **not paying consumers** the billions of dollars in interest income that the financial institutions earn on the deposits. Consumers should earn interest income on such amounts held in escrow or have the amounts temporarily applied to the outstanding balance to reduce interest paid.

Review and Summary of Key Terms and Concepts

1.   Give some examples of rising **bank fees and penalties**.

2.   What is a **negative sale**?

3.   Why does the banking industry want to put **limits on credit unions**?

4.   What does the **Truth in Savings Act** do for consumers?

5.   Give two examples of some **negative impacts of deregulation** of the banking industry on consumers

6.   Provide an overview of the need for **basic banking** and how it is impacted by programs to serve the **unbanked**.

7.   Give some examples of how the **poor pay more** for financial services.

8.   List three of the ways **credit card issuers are increasing revenues** that seem to be the most onerous in your opinion.

9.   Distinguish between **pre-screened** and **pre-approved**.

10. What is **tiered lending**?

11. What is a **FICO score** and why is it important?

12. What does the **grace period** have to do with paying interest?

13. Distinguish between calculating interest charges on the average daily balance **including** and **excluding new purchases**.

14. In a sentence, explain why the **two-cycle average daily balance method** is a rip-off.

15. Summarize how **usury laws** affect the supply and demand for credit for middle-income consumers and low-income consumers.

16. If you regularly pay only the **minimum payment** on credit card balances, what happens if you begin with a balance of $1,000 or $2,000?

17. Explain how the **rule of 78s** penalizes consumers.

18. Offer a few suggestions on **how to get out of debt**.

19. Summarize how a government housing program might be used by a recent **college graduate**.

20. Explain how **predatory lending** works against those with blemished credit histories as well as people with good credit.

21. Give three examples of **discrimination** in credit, housing and insurance.

22. What is a **Community Reinvestment Act rating**?

23. What factors influence creating a greater **supply of housing**?

24. List three factors that determine the **demand for housing**

25. Distinguish between **kickback fees** and **up-charges**.

26. What is a **defect disclosure form**, and why is it used?

27. What are **kickback fees**, and why might these be a problem for consumers?

Useful Resources for Consumers

Association of Independent Consumer Credit Counseling Agencies
(703) 934-6118
www.aiccca.org

Bankrate.com
Auto loans, credit cards, and loans
www.bankrate.com

Cardweb.com
Lists best credit cards
www.cardweb.com

Chex-Systems
www.chexhelp.com.

College financial aid information
www.finaid.org

Countrywide
PITI and calculators
www.countrywide.com

Eloan.com
www.eloan.com

Equifax
800-685-1111
www.equifax.com

Experian
888-397-3742
www.experian. Com

Federal Reserve System
www.federalreserve.gov/

First Gov for Consumers
www.consumer.gov/

Mortgage Bankers Association
Rate, terms, points, rent vs. buy
www.mbaa.org

National Credit Union Administration
www.ncua.gov

National Foundation for Consumer Credit
(800) 388-2227
www.nfcc.org

Office of the Comptroller of the Currency
www.occ.treas.gov

Office of Thrift Supervision
www.access.ots.treas.gov

National Foundation for Credit Counseling
www.nfcc.org

RealEstate.com
www.realestate.com

Realtor.com
www.realtor.com

TransUnion
800-916-8800
www.TransUnion.com

U.S. Department of Housing and Urban Development
800-347-3735 (fraud hotline)
www.hud.gov

"What Do You Think" Questions

1. The **rising prices of banking** affect all consumers, including the poor. What do you think should be done to lower the cost of banking? Consider actions that government, sellers and consumers might take.

2. Tell how you feel about the many methods that **credit card companies** are using to make consumers pay more and more for credit services.

3. What do you think should be done to increase the supply of **affordable housing** in America? Make a short list of your suggestions.

4. List three factors that might make a genuine improvement in reducing **discrimination** in banking, credit and housing.

Chapter 18

Insurance and Investment Issues

OBJECTIVES

After reading this chapter, you should be able to

1. Recognize consumer problems and issues in insurance.

2. Describe consumer problems and issues in investments.

Insurance and investments are important parts of consumer living. Insurance is a necessity, yet most consumers are mystified about how insurance rates are set, they don't know how to compare policies, and people often feel that rates are excessively high. Consumers are right! Insurance is a non-competitive, poorly regulated industry which has successfully fought all attempts at reform. The Internet allows consumers to shop online to save money. The extent of fraud, thievery and lying in Corporate America is frightening. Consumer investors have lost faith in the accounting practices of big corporations. With little choice of where to invest, consumers are faced with biased financial advice, uninsured products being sold in banks, unfair arbitration agreements, and risky retirement plans. Consumers must learn enough about insurance and investments in order to avoid being ripped off and be confident that one's insurance and investments will be there when needed.

This chapter provides an overview of the major consumer problems and issues in the areas of insurance and investments. It begins with the under-regulated insurance industry and it covers some interesting reform proposals. Tips for buying insurance are included. Following is an examination of consumer problems and issues in investments, including the top ten corporations caught lying to investors. The chapter ends with a discussion of the risks to consumers present in today's retirement plans, and it details why timeshares are not investments.

Consumer Problems and Issues in Insurance

This section begins by identifying consumer rights in insurance and a number of consumer problems and issues in insurance. Chapter 4 provides coverage on credit insurance, dread-disease insurance, life insurance scams, and rental car insurance. Health insurance is in Chapter 15.

Consumer Rights in Insurance

Consumers have the **moral right** to affordable insurance and a ratings classification system that is based on relevant, not arbitrary characteristics. Consumers have the legal right to:

- Request **a report** on the types and uses of information collected about you by an insurance company;

- Find out **the reasons** why an insurance company canceled coverage or raised premiums, although medical reasons may be disclosed to your physician rather than to you;

- Correct **misinformation** in the insurance company's files; and

- Receive a free **copy of your credit report** if poor credit information contained in it was used to legitimately turn you down for insurance, credit, housing, or employment.

To assert and protect your moral and legal rights, contact your insurance agent, insurance company, state insurance regulatory agency, and consumer organizations. If you want to **register a complaint**, the National Association of Insurance Commissioners (NAIC) provides links to state insurance commissioners. See www.naic.org.

DID YOU KNOW?
Insurance Company Don'ts

Laws and regulations require that **insurance companies may not**:

1. Refuse, cancel, or not renew your policy for **discriminatory reasons** such as race, gender, age, disability, handicap, and marital status;

2. Refuse coverage because another company turned you down;

3. Offer you higher rates than **originally quoted** when you applied;

4. Charge you a different rate than someone in a similar class unless they have sound reasons;

5. Refuse, cancel, or not renew your homeowner's or renter's policy solely because of location or age of the property;

6. Refuse automobile insurance because you once purchased insurance through the **assigned-risk program**;

7. Cancel your automobile policy after 60 days or more after being in effect, except for your failure to pay premiums or if you provided inaccurate driver's license information on the insurance application; and

8. Cancel (or lapse) a policy at any time without **30 days notice**.

Insurance is a Profitable Industry

The insurance industry is very **profitable**. The story line from insurance companies says they "are losing money and have to raise premiums every year." For example, the property and casualty industry claims that in a recent year they paid out $110 for every $100 brought in through premiums. While this may be technically true, it does not tell the whole story. Insurance companies also earn income by **investing those premiums**. When investment returns are poor, insurers make up the missing revenue by raising premiums. Accounting procedures also allow insurers to project losses, but the losses typically do not turn out to be as big as projected.

Noncompetitive, Poorly Regulated Insurance Industry

The insurance industry is one of the most powerful lobby groups in American history. The industry persuaded Congress in 1943 to pass the McCarran-Ferguson Act that **prohibits the federal government** from regulating insurance. This is in spite of the multi-state nature of the business.

No Federal Regulation

A special commission of the American Bar Association has called for **repeal of the insurance industry's exemption** from federal antitrust laws, the McCarran-Ferguson Act, calling it "inconsistent with the concept of free-market competition." Shifting the responsibility of insurance regulation from states to the federal government would result in lower insurance costs, elimination of discrimination, and greatly improved regulatory oversight. The Federal Trade Commission has joined the Justice Department, state officials, small business representatives, and consumer organizations in supporting repeal of the McCarran-Ferguson Act. Experts say that "the antitrust exemption creates an invitation to **price-fixing** arrangements that stifle product choice and comparison shopping among consumers."

The powerful insurance lobby even got a law passed that prohibits the FTC from **ever conducting research** on the insurance industry. Congress also has not been able to pass a law requiring insurance companies to report annually the geographic areas where they write policies. At the state level fifty states prohibit banks from entry into the automobile insurance market, although they would likely be strong competitors. Joseph M. Belth, professor emeritus at Indiana University, says that "this is an industry in which various forms of deceptive practices flourish, and the state regulators have not done anything about it."

State-approved Price-fixing

State-approved **price-fixing** occurs because insurance companies (automobile, fire, homeowner's, and liability insurers) do not base their rates on their own loss experience and expectations. Instead, they pool their loss information and rely on industry-wide advisory guidelines constructed by rate-making bureaus. The Insurance Services Office (www.iso.com/) creates **average loss figures** based on information obtained from hundreds of insurers' past claims, projected claims, overhead costs, and estimated profit data. Insurers then set their rates above or below the industry guidelines. Consumers who are customers of companies with low expenses can end up paying as much as people who insure with inefficient firms. As a result, prices for equivalent products often span no more than a 25 percent range. If state regulators would outlaw the use of profit and expense data from these averages, it would lead to **more competition** in insurance rates and would lower them from 5 to 15 percent, according to the National Association of Insurance Commissioners.

Price-fixing with Anti-group and Anti-rebate Laws

Can you imagine that when buying a new car the dealer says "Sorry, no rebate for you since the law prohibits it"? Then the dealer says "By the way, our sales people cannot give you a discounted price." Well, that's the situation in auto insurance. **Anti-group laws** are state prohibitions against selling automobile insurance (unlike health or life insurance) in any manner except by one policy at a time. This causes inefficiency and unnecessary costs. Author Andrew Tobias says "Why sell insurance one policy at a time when we require everyone, by law, to have it?"

If states allowed firms to sell group automobile insurance and **let agents offer a discount** by giving up part of their commissions that average 12 to 17 percent of the premium, prices for consumers could drop. Massachusetts and Maryland permit group sales, and policies are **offered through employers**. Discounts range from 5 to 10 percent. Group sales will not succeed until automobile insurance becomes an employee benefit, like health insurance, where employers can deduct the premium costs from their taxes.

The Florida State Supreme Court struck down an **anti-rebate law** that prohibited insurance agents (**the retailers**) from offering discounts to consumers who want to comparison shop and bargain for the lowest price. Agents in Florida may offer a rebate of some of their commissions to customers. In all other states except California, agents are prohibited by law from refunding any portion of a commission to a consumer.

Collusion Between Insurance Companies and Auto Repair Shops

Price-fixing is illegal in all states. However, a **defacto conspiracy** exists between the insurance and auto repair industries, and the result is that premiums for insured drivers are pushed higher and higher.

Here is what happens for insured consumers. When an accident occurs, the involved consumer notifies his or her insurance company. The consumer's insurance agent has a company adjuster look at the vehicle to assess the damages. Then the **adjuster prepares a written estimate** of the damages that the insurance company thinks it should pay for, and that estimate is given to the consumer. The consumer is expected to then go to a particular repair shop to have the repairs made. If the shop finds things that need fixing that were not on the adjuster's estimate, perhaps because the damage was hidden, the shop calls the insurance adjuster, who authorizes an additional necessary amount.

This **appears to satisfy** everyone. The consumer goes away happy that the insurance company paid for the repairs. The insurance company is happy because their own adjusters make fairly competitive estimates. The repair shop likes the fact that they saved time as fewer people come asking them to make estimates.

This cozy arrangement restrains trade because the two industries require insured consumers to patronize only **certain repair shops**, often those associated with new car dealerships. Further, there is no incentive for the repair shop to do the work for a lesser amount because they are always paid an amount that is at least the amount of the insurance company's estimate. Just so you know, consumers who say that the repairs will not be covered by insurance are typically given lower prices.

Poor State Regulation Means High Prices

Prices keep rising for auto insurance, primarily due to smaller investment returns for the industry. According to the Insurance Information Institute, yearly premiums for auto insurance average $855. **Northeastern states** have the highest auto premiums with New Jersey coming in first place at $1,146 per vehicle. Motorists who live in large cities, however, pay 25 to 50 percent more.

State departments of insurance have long been **understaffed** and lacking in legal authority to regulate the insurance industry. The National Association of Insurance Commissioners (NAIC) is the organization of state **insurance regulators**. In recent years, the NAIC has improved collection of uniform financial reporting by insurance companies and has become a stronger voice in the development of uniform policies to better protect consumers.

Retail insurance prices and sales commissions are established by the insurers, who set them high enough to provide a profit to the least efficient agent. That, of course, drives up prices. **Overcharging** occurs. *Money* magazine reports that consumers pay an extra $60 billion a year because of **poor state regulation**. That amounts to the average American spending "an extra $340 a year because the states have failed to regulate this industry." A Congressional study concluded that reform of the auto insurance industry "could save consumers as much as $40 billion a year—a $221 reduction in the average family's premium."

Consumers Go Online to Buy Insurance for Less

Premiums charged for auto insurance vary widely, often **40 percent or more**. You could pay $1,600 for full coverage on a new Dodge Neon ES or perhaps $1,100. In addition, your FICO credit score is added to the rates set by auto insurance companies. Those with a **poor credit score are charged higher** auto insurance premiums, sometimes as high as those with good credit. Insurance companies should be required to adjust your premium when your credit score increases. See Chapter 17 for suggestions on how to improve your credit history. Consumers who do not take the time to comparison shop are likely to pay too much for auto insurance.

State departments of insurance publish rate comparisons on their websites. The highest rated **online research site** for auto insurance is www.insweb.com; others include www. insurance.com,www.insure.com, www.quotesmith.com, and www.quicken.com/insurance. Progressive Insurance Company (www.progressive. com) sells vehicle insurance **by the mile** using its "Autograph" system that uses global-positioning satellites and cellular technology to track where an insured vehicle has been on a monthly basis. Such consumers give up a measure of **privacy** for lower rates.

Reforms for the Auto Insurance Industry

The Insurance Rate Reduction and Reform Act, better known as **Proposition 103**, is an initiative voted into California law in1988. In part, the law reads: "Enormous increases in the cost of insurance have made it both unaffordable and unavailable to millions of Californians. The existing laws inadequately protect consumers and allow insurance companies to charge excessive, unjustified and arbitrary rates." In addition to **price rollbacks**, the law mandated that automobile insurance rates be determined primarily by a driver's safety record and mileage driven. Experts know that automobile insurance rates should be based on factors that genuinely are **related to claims**, such as miles driven, previous accidents, driving violations, and type of vehicle. Factors that have nothing to do with claims are gender, race, marital status, and residence. Yet, in most states the industry continues to use such factors to put drivers into bogus risk classes to price policies.

Andrew Tobias, author of *Auto Insurance Alert!*, observes that "...we have in this country...about the worst [auto insurance] system anyone could possibly devise. It costs us a fortune, yet little of the money we pay makes it through to the people most seriously hurt." The causes of the problem are "huge legal fees and massive fraud" says Tobias. It does not get worse than in Los Angeles where there are 99 bodily injury claims for every 100 accidents. The system rewards drivers for **exaggerating minor or nonexistent injuries** and it rewards their attorneys. Put simply, today's automobile insurance system is obsolete and broken.

One in six adults drives without automobile insurance, and many low-income consumers have no auto insurance because it is extremely expensive, sometimes with annual premiums as high as $4,000 or even $8,000.In some urban areas, **uninsured drivers** number between 50 and 90 percent. A new program in California allows low-income residents in Los Angeles and San Francisco with good driving records to purchase a **"bare-bones" auto insurance policy**. Nationally, not a single state effectively enforces state laws requiring all drivers to have insurance.

About **one-quarter** of accidents **involve uninsured drivers**; however, most other adults falsely believe that low-income drivers of uninsured cars are "high risk" drivers and cause almost all accidents. Three-quarters of adults describe themselves as "excellent drivers."

Thus, they are inclined to believe that the insurance companies know best and the high premiums charged low-income car owners must be correct. This kind of non-thinking explains why most Americans do not understand that the auto insurance industry is a **failing system that must be dramatically reformed**.

No-fault Insurance

Although there are some terrible drivers on the road who are simply dangerous, most at-fault accidents are **random events**. Most consumers live in a "sue-me, sue-you insurance system." When people have accidents they file lawsuits to determine who was at fault and whose insurance company will pay. This is called the **fault system**. The fault system **overcompensates the slightly injured**, under-compensates the gravely hurt, clogs the courts with lawsuits that take years to reach verdicts, and returns to victims only half of the premiums paid in. The rest goes to lawyers and to people who administer the system. A Rand Institute report concluded that victims in an accident of $500 to $1,000 in damages were likely to recover 250 percent of their loss, while those suffering losses of $100,000 or more recovered **an average of 9 percent**. The Insurance Information Institute reports that 11 cents of the traditional premium dollar goes for lawyer fees and another 12 cents goes for pain, suffering, and non-economic damages. The FBI reports that fraudulent "pain and suffering" claims add $200 a year to the average family's auto insurance premium.

A genuine comprehensive **no-fault automobile insurance system** is in effect in three Canadian provinces. Drivers must buy their own insurance to cover their own injuries, and if hurt in an accident they cannot sue anyone else as their claims are paid from their own insurance companies. No-fault in Quebec covers all medical expenses and lifelong wage losses limited to twice the minimum wage. Drivers, passengers, and pedestrians are indemnified regardless of their conduct, even intentional. Uninsured Quebec drivers can collect from no one. Property damage is left to the private insurance companies, and it is compulsory for damage caused to others.

No-fault insurance in the United States is **not widely available**, and is more limited. No-fault allows the consumer to collect directly from his or her insurance company for medical expenses and wage losses resulting from an automobile accident without regard to who was at fault and without making a claim against the other driver (unless that driver was drunk). Under no-fault, the victim must show that any injuries are severe before being allowed to sue another driver. No-fault coverage also pays for injuries to a driver's passengers and pedestrians. In effect, the concept of no-fault is the same as **state worker's compensation programs** as it guarantees that consumers get compensation for injuries and lost wages.

In exchange for guaranteed compensation for injuries and lost wages, injured **drivers give up the right to sue** for damages unless their injuries exceed a **dollar threshold** (actually a test of the severity of the injury), such as $3,000, specified in the no-fault law. Since this will keep lengthy, expensive minor injury cases out of the courts, proponents of no-fault insurance argue that delay in the payment of claims and claims-handling expenses would be greatly reduced, thereby lessening the pressure to increase premiums.

Benefits of No-Fault Insurance

Compared to the traditional fault-based system of auto insurance, there are a number of **benefits of no-fault** insurance as enumerated by University of Virginia's Jeffrey O'Connell:

- No-fault compensates more people (roughly twice as many).

- No-fault provides greater benefits (79 percent more).

- Payments are made more quickly (almost all no-fault payments are made during the first year following injury).

- Drivers get more coverage for their no-fault premium dollar (since administrative costs are reduced).

- As many as two-thirds of the accident-related small claims are kept out of court.

Michigan No-Fault Insurance

Michigan has the **most successful** no-fault law as it requires insurance policies to provide **unlimited medical and rehabilitation benefits**, three years' worth of wage-loss benefits (where an injured person receives 80 percent of gross income up to a maximum, currently $3,500 a month), survivors' benefits, and a $20 daily benefit for replacement services. Michigan does not pay victims for pain and suffering. Lawsuits for damages to vehicles are severely restricted. Lawsuits for personal injury can be brought **only** in cases of "death, serious impairment of body function or permanent serious disfigurement." Instead of 32 percent of consumers' insurance premiums going for court costs and legal fees, as was the case before passage of the Michigan no-fault law, the amount is now six percent. Policyholders can buy collision coverage to pay for damage to their own cars and enough property damage liability coverage to protect them when out of state.

Only **14 states** have some variation of the no-fault concept, though none of these is strictly no-fault because no state forbids lawsuits. Studies have shown that in states with strong no-fault automobile insurance laws, payment delays have been reduced, claims-handling expenses have come down as a proportion of the premiums collected, and premiums, although continuing to rise, have done so at a lower rate than in states without a no-fault system.

However, the results have been mixed because most states just **tacked no-fault coverage onto the existing liability system**. In general, the benefits envisioned after the enactment of no-fault plans have not been **fully realized** because only a few states (such as Michigan, Florida, and New York) have seriously attempted to implement the no-fault concept by **severely restricting lawsuits**. When the threshold is set too low by legislators, consumers are encouraged to sue, thus defeating one key purpose of a no-fault system.

Pay-at-the-Pump No-Fault Insurance

Insurance expert Andrew Tobias has proposed a **pay-at-the-pump no-fault (PPN)** system. The primary source of funds would be from a **less-than-30-cents-a-gallon surcharge**, which would amount to $91 to $141 per vehicle per year. Another charge would be paid annually when consumers registered their cars. Presto! Everyone has generous insurance coverage. Bad drivers would have to pay higher annual registration fees for their cars. PPN would eliminate most sales and underwriting costs, the uninsured motorist problem, and the need for consumers to shop for insurance. Insurers would competitively bid to provide coverage for perhaps 5,000 customers at a time, much as they now do for health insurance. After being involved in an accident you would get your car repaired right away, receive lost income benefits, and have all medical expenses paid because a genuine no-fault system would be established.

PPN "would be good for all drivers except those who now drive uninsured and pay nothing." And that's good. Tobias says that pay-at-the-pump will **cut insurance costs 20 to 40 percent** for most drivers. Good drivers would **not be discriminated against** because of age, gender, or residence. Everyone would pay the same until **some were identified as bad drivers**, and the latter would pay more. Fraudulent bodily injury claims would cease to exist. PPN also would be good for insurance companies that are efficient because they would win even more business than they have now. Prices would be even lower if the state took over the processing of claims, which would eliminate the need for insurance agents and trial lawyers. Supporters of this excellent reform idea are trying to get a proposal made into law in California by getting it passed in a referendum vote. The insurance companies and lawyers have **defeated all efforts** to change the system.

"No Pay, No Play" Insurance

"No pay, no play" limits an uninsured motorist's ability to collect punitive damages (generally pain and suffering) from insured drivers. If a driver did not have insurance ("no pay") and was injured in an accident, his or her **legal rights to sue would be restricted** ("no play"). Fairness is the argument as proponents say anyone who goes on the highways without paying into the liability insurance system ought not to draw benefits from it in the same way that those who comply with the law are able to do. For example, California prohibits uninsured victims from suing for pain and suffering. Louisiana requires uninsured victims to pay the first $10,000 of their bodily injuries and the first $10,000 of their property damages.

Pay-per Mile Auto Insurance[1]

Although forty-eight states make automobile insurance mandatory, **tens of millions of cars still go uninsured.** Why? Because today's **"pay-per-car" insurance system** charges the **highest prices** for cars whose owners reside in low-income neighborhoods where many people, by necessity, must economize. Insurance companies defend the high prices by defaming these people and labeling them **"high-risk" drivers**. (See Table 18.1.) The reality is that the low-income "high-risk" driver is not a driver at all. It is simply a car that drivers are sharing to economize on insurance.

Today, the price of auto insurance covers all the miles you can drive the car. Therefore, the only sure way to save on insurance is to **own fewer cars and drive each more miles** than previously. For example, if a family owns two cars and drives each one 15,000 miles a year, they can cut their premiums in half by selling one car and driving the other car the same 30,000 miles.

Obviously, inconvenience keeps most families from saving this way. But many low-income families have to save by piling more miles on fewer cars, and as a result the average claims per car to insurance companies **increases.** In response, companies jack up prices, which forces more families to economize by illegally taking their less-used cars off policies. Thus, in low-income zip codes, today's system backfires because it **pushes up** both the average miles driven and the resulting cost per insured car, forcing still more cars to go uninsured.

---

[1] This section was written by Patrick Butler, Insurance Project Director, National Organization for Women; Email: info@centspermilenow.org; Web: www.centspermilenow.org.

Official Buyer's Guide for Austin (Travis County), Texas

(Texas Department of Insurance's website is www.tdi.state.tx.us/consumer/auto.html)

Insurance Company	Drivers labeled*	Annual premium per car**
Government Employees	Preferred risk	$320
State Farm Mutual Automobile	Moderate risk	$436
Home State County Mutual	High risk	$714

*Driver records are identical with zero at-fault accidents and no major traffic violations.
**Cars are identically classified in the adult (unisex) driver class, drive-to-work use class and county territory class; premiums are for minimum liability coverage, August 2002.

TABLE 18-1   Official Buyer's Guide for Austin (Travis County), Texas

To address the problem, Texas passed a breakthrough **cents-per-mile choice law**. The law authorizes insurance companies to offer customers a choice between staying with their old premiums or shifting to "pay-per-mile" premiums. Providing this choice is easy for companies to set up. After first assigning a car as usual to a risk class (by territory, car type and use, and driver age), the company offers the customer a choice between staying with, for example, a fixed $600 a year premium or paying the equivalent 4.0¢-a-mile price for the same risk class to buy miles of insurance in advance. At this price, 2,000 miles of insurance costs $80. The number of miles chosen to suit budget and convenience are added to the odometer reading and recorded on the **car's insurance card**. The owner buys more miles in advance when needed. The company has the odometer read annually as well as when the owner changes cars or companies. If the odometer limit is exceeded, the car is uninsured. It's that simple.

The pay-per-mile alternative also eliminates a major enforcement challenge. Today's insurance card shows the policy term dates but not whether **insurance has lapsed** because of nonpayment of an installment premium. Under the pay-per-mile arrangement, checking the odometer reading against the odometer limit on the insurance card shows immediately whether insurance is actually in force. Driving a car, not owning it, is what produces risk for the insurance company. Risk occurs on a mile-by-mile basis, and that's the right way to pay for it.

However, the 2001 Texas law does not require companies to offer the pay-per-mile choice, and so far, **no company** has made this choice available. Failing to do so preserves today's pay-per-car system that inevitably leads to high prices in low-income neighborhoods and many uninsured cars.

Consumers who are angry because cars go uninsured and consumers forced to give up cars to save on insurance have every right to demand that companies offer the pay-per-mile choice. Families are entitled to own as many cars as they need while **paying only for the miles** of insurance protection actually used in driving them. See www.centspermilenow.org for more information.

Beware of Life Insurance Being "Sold" as a Retirement Plan

Some of the largest and historically reputable life insurance companies repeatedly have **lied** to customers—Prudential, Metropolitan Life, Phoenix Home Mutual, and New York Life. Metropolitan Life Insurance Company sold so-called **guaranteed retirement savings plans** to millions of consumers who unknowingly purchased life insurance policies with a savings element known as **cash-value policies**. Typical was the comment from one New York couple: "The agent never once mentioned the word insurance." Instead of making monthly payments to an investment plan, the money went for insurance premiums. Prudential's life insurance agents persuaded seven *million* customers over 14 years to use the built-up cash value of older policies to finance new, more expensive ones. Neither Prudential nor MetLife has revoked the commissions earned by their agents for selling these policies, and not a single employee has ever been charged with a criminal action. MetLife agreed to pay $1.7 billion to policyholders to settle lawsuits.

Tips for Buying Life Insurance

There is **no mathematical advantage** to buying life insurance at an early age. Premiums increase at the **same rate** for everybody regardless of the age at which you start the policy. If you have no dependents, you probably do not need life insurance at all. Life insurance is to protect against **loss of income for dependents**. Do not purchase life insurance from a local agent because they are inclined to **talk you into** purchasing an expensive "permanent" type of life insurance policy that contains a "savings element;" that is an unwise purchase except for the wealthiest and/or sickest people. If you need protection for your dependents, **term insurance** can do the job at the lowest cost.

Most life insurance companies today rate people's health according to several classifications, and the **healthiest consumers** are offered the lowest prices. For those people who are smokers and/or are just not as healthy as others, buying a policy through their **employers** is likely to be cheaper than a policy purchased on the open market. Conversely healthy people get much better prices in the market because lots of unhealthy people are included in the group plans at work, thus the latter's rates are higher. So get on the Internet and scan the databases of insurers.

The best way to judge a **term life insurance policy** (that insures a life and does not have a savings feature) is by the cost each year for each $1,000 of coverage. Careful shopping online can get you a low price policy from a financially solvent company. For example, a 35-year-old healthy male can buy a $500,000 policy with a 20-year level premium that does not rise at all for a really low price of $170. While some websites provide misleading information, the following got high marks in various price comparison studies: www.insweb.com; www.term4sale.com; www.compulife.com; www.quicken.com; and www.quotesmith.com.

Title Insurance for Homes–A Rip-off

Title insurance is a policy that protects the lender's interest in a loan if the title to real estate is later found to be faulty, i.e., have **"defects"** that might involve a legal claim that is not in the public record and about which the buyer is unaware. Consumers who buy homes or refinance mortgages are almost always required to purchase title insurance. Many homeowners also purchase a separate title insurance policy to protect themselves from possible loss. State rating bureaus created with the participation of the title insurance companies themselves, generally set (fix!) prices for title insurance. Since 75 to 90 percent of the average $700 one-time premium typically goes as a kickback commission to the local title company or attorney who arranged the business, as little as $70 goes for the insurance. Industry losses over the years have amounted to 4 or 5 percent of premium income. Such a

single-digit payout-ratio suggests a profiteering industry ripe for government regulation to protect the interests of consumers.

When Insurance Companies Go Broke

All states have a **guaranty program** that attempts to cover losses when an insurance company goes broke and cannot pay claims. Each company licensed to do business in a state is required to contribute to a supervised fund (often 2 percent of premiums) and each company is assessed costs after insolvency occurs. Thus, financially healthy companies are "taxed" to support those that fail. The state fund then pays the claims on the failed carrier, although a delay of one to two years is typical. Each state fund has severe limitations, including caps, on how much it will pay for each claim. These programs are not publicly funded; however, since states typically give companies a credit on their income tax for the premiums, they are **subsidized** with taxpayer money.

State guaranty funds have severe **limitations** on what claims they will pay. Often excluded are Blue Cross/Blue Shield plans, companies that self-insure, and some group-health plans. States often limit the amount claimants may collect, regardless of the loss, and most do not insure guaranteed investment contracts contained in many retirement plans. (This is discussed below.) Smart consumers check *Best's Key Ratings Guide* (www.ambest.com/ratings/) for information on the financial solvency of insurance companies to avoid firms that have shaky finances.

Fifteen to 30 property-casualty insurers fail per year. Historically, the small high-risk companies went broke; now big companies do, too. Most of the insurance company bankruptcies are caused by mismanagement, fraud, excessive price cutting to meet the competition, and unwise diversification into other lines of business. Another factor is the high cost of claims for environmental damage, such as **asbestos removal**, pollution, and chemical spills. Recent insurance company failures include Executive Life Insurance Company, Mutual Security Life, Bankers Life Insurance Company of Richmond, Mutual Benefit Life in New Jersey, and Blue Cross and Blue Shield of West Virginia.

Every year the National Association of Insurance Commissioners (NAIC) identifies sort of a **"watch list"** of the nation's 3,500 insurance companies that may have financial conditions that could impair financial survival. About 150 life/health insurance companies are cited annually for regulatory attention because of similar **concerns about financial solvency**.

CONSUMER UPDATE:
CLUE Reports on Homes

Insurers have invented **"rap sheets"** for homes. Also known as **CLUE reports**, these are records of insurance claims on homes throughout the United States maintained by the Comprehensive Loss Underwriting Exchange (CLUE). Homeowner's insurance companies use the information to deny coverage on certain homes and to deny requests for policy renewal.

The turn-downs and non-renewals occur at terrible times for home buyers. Some **rejections occur at closing**, the very day a prospective buyer is attempting to close the deal to purchase a home. Sometimes the denial occurs a few weeks *after* a home has been purchased. Home mortgage lenders do not allow homes to be uninsured or in the case of calamity, such as a fire, they would lose the collateral for the loan. When faced with a CLUE-based rejection consumers must scramble to find another company to insure the home, often at extremely high prices. Consumers deserve the legal **right to review past claims** on properties for which they are seeking insurance coverage.

Consumer Problems and Issues in Investments

The following describes some major consumer problems in investments. Some investment frauds and rip-offs are examined in Chapter 4.

Investor Rights

A number of self-regulating investment organizations have developed an investor's bill of rights that suggests consumer investors are entitled to:

- **Honesty** in advertising;

- Full and **accurate information** about investments;

- Prior disclosure of **risks**;

- Advance explanation of obligations and costs;

- Time to consider actions;

- Responsible advice that is suitable for particular needs;

- **Ethical** management of funds;

- Complete and **truthful accounting**;

- Easy access to funds and full information on any restrictions; and

- Recourse, if necessary, for dishonesty or unfairness.

Fraud and Thievery in Corporate America

The American society has begun the new millennium discovering that economic thievery and **white-collar crime** have been absolutely rampant in American business for at least a decade. There are tons of evidence revealing systemic problems in a society in which deregulation has gone too far and the **cooking of corporate accounting books** has become endemic. When the accounting numbers are fabricated, consumer investors have no way to accurately judge whether or not a particular company is a good place to invest money.

Hundreds of corporate executives have been and are still being caught for falsifying revenues, restating earnings, deliberately deceiving shareholders, exaggerating claims, taking bribes, giving themselves millions in company loans, lying, stealing money, and committing other criminal acts. **Corporate avarice** has been at an all-time high.

Many of the top **chief-executive officers, CEOs**, in business believe that they are the untouchables who can make their own rules and laws. Part of the problem is the **astronomical salaries** and bonuses paid executives in the top echelons of business are almost unbelievable. For one year of work some executives earn $5 million, or $19 million, $50 million, or more! The former CEO of K-Mart earned $23 million during his two-year term while the company almost closed its doors and many thousands of workers lost their jobs. Ethics seems to be an unknown word to many in business. And any sense of corporate responsibility to society has disappeared.

CONSUMER UPDATE:
Top Ten Corporations Caught Lying to Investors

Almost no companies or their executives ever plead guilty to criminal charges, admit to liability for misdeeds or even deny allegations of misconduct in a court of law. Instead, they simply **"agree to a settlement"** with the government or other plaintiffs. On rare occasion, an executive, a so-called **white-collar criminal**, spends a year or two in a federal penitentiary. The key executives of these companies should be giving depositions and court testimony for many more years in response to over 200 consumer-investor **class action lawsuits** for violating federal securities laws and restating earnings because of "accounting problems." There are so many to choose from such as Qwest, Rite Aid, U.S. Technologies, North American Medical Products, ClearOne Communications, U.S. Technologies, Medical Diagnostic Products, Adelphia Communications, Texon Energy, and Xerox. Tyco's former CEO stole $600 million! The top ten are:

10. **NationsBank**—Paid $6 million for misleading consumers by understating the risks of bond funds it sold to mostly elderly customers who suffered significant losses.

9. **Paine Webber, Merrill Lynch, J.P. Morgan,** and **Salomon Brothers**—Paid a $910 million fine for illegally overcharging investor clients in the Nasdaq stock market.

8. **State Farm**—Paid $200 million for promising false returns to encourage life insurance policyholders to switch to other policies that lost value.

7. **ImClone Systems**—Chief Samual Waksal pleaded guilty to Securities and Exchange Commission criminal charges of insider trading and paid an $800,000 fine.

6. **Quest Communications**—Executives indicted for booking false sales in their accounting records, and the company's stock price dropped from $98 to $3.

5. **Met Life**—Paid $1.7 billion to policyholders for routinely misleading the elderly about life insurance costs for 13 years; also paid a $20 million fine. **Prudential Insurance** paid a $15 million fine for similar actions.

4. **Enron**—Top executives created the largest bankruptcy in American history using fraud, money laundering and conspiricy. Manipulated the natural-gas market and ran an illegal futures exchange. The nation's one-time seventh largest company vaporized $67 billion in investor wealth. **Merrill Lynch** paid a $80 million fine for aiding and abetting the fraudulent schemes that Enron used.

3. **Andersen**—Big Five accounting firm Andersen eventually shut down its business for engaging in wholesale destruction of tons of Enron documents. It is the poster child for accounting fraud in the United States. Company name changed to Accenture.

2. **Merrill Lynch and Citigroup**—Plus eight more Wall Street investment firms agreed to pay a $1.4 billion fine over allegations that its stock analysts misled investors. While Merrill was publicly promoting stocks of companies, at the same time its analysts were internally disparaging the stocks as "crap" and "junk."

1. **WorldCom's**—Top corporate executives lied and schemed (two sets of accounting books!) to make up $11 billion in fraudulent accounting transactions. Investors lost $100 billion. The SEC fined WorldCom $500 million. WorldCom is the worst liar in the world history of business. WorldCom changed its name to **MCI**.

A critic of corporate excesses, Arianna Huffington, author of *Pigs at the Trough*, says that the corporate CEOs, the "pigs," are more than a social crime; they are a direct **threat to our nation's welfare**. These lawbreaking events occur in part because the rewards of business fraud are high and the penalties are low. No one seems accountable. No one apologizes. Greedy and crooked corporate executives will not stop stealing to enrich themselves until they are forced to give back the ill-gotten profits and are jailed. At the same time, corporate donations to politicians keep rising with every election. Big business owns and operates the United States political system, and Huffington writes about the collusion between government and business.

"The orgy of money-grubbing by the corporate cabal has inflicted real, long-lasting pain on a host of deceived Americans," writes Huffington. She calls for changing the status quo to stop this pattern of corruption. The extent of criminal behavior in big business in the United States has given the virtues of **capitalism a bad name** in the rest of the world. This is indeed a **sad time** in the history of business in the United States.

Congress has passed **new laws** to address securities fraud, shareholder fraud and investment fraud. A number of regulatory agencies like the Securities and Exchange Commission have established new regulations. To restore faith in American business practices will require accounting reform, better disclosures and stricter enforcement. The reform efforts must be able to **enforce transparency and honesty**. You probably would not be eager to eat supper at a restaurant that did not have municipal inspections of hygiene and served food that did not pass the scrutiny of the Food and Drug Administration or U.S. Department of Agriculture; it's the same thing with investing in corporations. There has been **no reform** on bloated corporate salaries and Congress has not authorized big increases in budgets for the regulatory agencies that oversee the securities industry.

Most Financial Advisors are Biased

You can **buy financial planning advice** from attorneys, accountants, insurance salespersons and stockbrokers. There are perhaps 500,000 people in America who call themselves financial planners. A **financial planner** is any person who calls himself or herself by that title. Most sell financial products such as insurance and investments. The term financial planner roughly describes a variety of professionals who suggest and/or promise to provide advice to manage a client's financial investments. They work with clients to help them establish and achieve financial needs and objectives.

The SEC says that an **investment advisor**, a more narrow term than a financial planner, is anyone who is paid for giving advice on the purchase or sale of securities to more than 15 people a year. You can find out about the disciplinary history of any brokerage firm and sales representative by contacting the National Association of Securities Dealers (www.nasd.com).

Most financial planners are biased **because they sell something**. The financial advice obtained from a banker, stockbroker, or an insurance salesperson is always slanted toward the transactions and/or products sold by the firm he or she represents. It is in the economic interest of a financial planner working for a brokerage firm to sell you stocks, bonds or some other service from which a commission is earned. In a similar way, the insurance salesperson earns a commission for selling policies and the banker gets a year-end bonus for successfully promoting bank products.

Some financial planners charge a **fee-only**, and they are the only ones who offer **unbiased advice**. They offer their advice for a flat fee or a percentage of your assets. The fee might be $500 and an hourly fee might be $100 to $200 an hour. Sometimes the fee is based on the amount of assets managed and income earned. Fee-only planners do not sell any products themselves. If asked, they refer clients to other providers to purchase investments or insurance products, and kickback commissions and other fees should never occur. Probably fewer than **one in a hundred** planners is a fee-only advisor. The fee-only professional association is the National Association of Personal Financial Advisers (1130 Lake Cook Road, Suite 150, Buffalo Grove, IL 60089; 888-333-6659).

Commission-only financial planners offer their advice on financial topics and receive remuneration only in the form of commissions for products and services sold, such as stocks, mutual funds, insurance, and real estate partnerships. Such a planner might earn a 1 ½ percent commission on stocks purchased or sold and 8 ½ percent on a mutual fund. **Fee-and-commission financial planners** are paid by charging a fee for financial advice in addition to receiving commissions on the direct or indirect sale of products. They are sometimes known as **fee-based financial planners** because they want their identity to be associated with the unbiased fee-only planners.

A Consumer Federation of America study called almost 300 financial planning firms requesting fee-only services and found that **many lied** about how they were paid because one-quarter actually took commissions.

Stockbrokers, accountants, insurance agents and financial planners sometimes push particular choices because they receive **hidden sales incentives** in the form of secret bonuses and commissions. A planner who can win a trip to a resort, jewelry, or a television set by selling you something is a person you want to avoid because he or she may very well be **motivated to "sell" you** an investment that you do not need. Bonuses and prizes are scandalous and abusive selling practices of the so-called legitimate investment industry.

All Bank Investments are *Not* Insured

Treasury securities (notes and bonds) are backed by the "full faith and credit" of the United States, so there is zero risk of loss with these conservative investments. Three organizations insure each person's deposits at banks, savings and loan associations, and credit unions against loss from **fraud or bankruptcy** for up to $100,000. They are, respectively, the Bank Insurance Fund (BIF), Federal Deposit Insurance Commission (FDIC) and National Credit Union Share Insurance Fund (NCUSIF).

However, FDIC (www.fdic.gov) **insurance does not cover investment products sold by banks**, such as mutual funds, stocks, bonds, life insurance policies, and annuities, because they are not deposits. Non-deposit investments are subject to investment risks, including the possible loss of principal, if purchased in the lobby of a bank, savings and loan association, or credit union, or bought in some other way through an FDIC-insured institution.

State banking laws permit these institutions to allow affiliate organizations to operate and sell products **inside the lobby**. Thus, institutions with *"FDIC insured"* signs on all the doors, windows, and tables also are selling certain investments that have zero insurance.

1. **Annuities Are *Not* Insured.** Contracts underwritten by insurance companies that provide for a series of payments to be received at stated intervals for a fixed or variable time period in return for the payment of a premium or premiums are called **annuities**. These investments combine some of the features of mutual funds and insurance. They are issued by insurance companies and sold to consumers, and they have substantial early-withdrawal penalties. Annuities are not insured by the government. Annuities are **bad deals** for 99 percent of investors because sales commissions run 6 to 13 percent compared to perhaps zero to 4 percent for mutual funds and stocks.

2. **Cash-Value Life Insurance Policies Are *Not* Insured.** Policies that are called **cash-value life insurance** pay benefits upon the death of the insured (like all life policies, including term life insurance examined earlier in this chapter). And they

have a savings element (called a **cash value**) that slowly builds up within the policy as long as the insured lives. If desired, the cash value may be **borrowed** by the policyholder, and, of course, any amount not repaid would be withheld from the death benefit. For this "living benefit" the premiums for cash value policies are much higher than for term policies. Cash-value life insurance polices are sometimes called **permanent life insurance** because the time period of coverage under such policies is the entire life of the insured; term policies are for a specific amount of time, such as 1 year or 20 years. Different types of cash-value life insurance policies include: whole-life, ordinary life, adjustable life, universal life, variable life and variable-universal life. Life insurance policies are never insured by the government.

3. **Mutual Funds Are *Not* Insured.** Many banks sell mutual funds. A **mutual fund** is an investment company that combines the funds of investors who have purchased shares of ownership in the investment company and invests that money into a diversified portfolio of securities issued by corporations and/or governments. While many mutual funds perform well as investments, those sold by banks have below-average performance records. Mutual funds are never insured by the government.

   The federal government has a program of **"testers"** who go to banking institutions to find out whether fund salespersons are misleading investors. Studies by the FDIC, SEC and AARP show that more than one out of four banking institutions do not **properly warn consumers** that their investment in a mutual fund is not federally insured, and as many as one-third of bank customers are unaware of any commissions or costs involved. A study by *Consumer Reports* found that two-thirds of banks offered inappropriate investment advice. Critics argue that either banks **must explain more** or government regulation must be implemented to protect investing consumers.

Arbitration Means Giving Up Your Right to Sue

   Arbitration involves presenting a dispute before one or more people who weigh the facts and impose a decision that typically is binding on both parties. Arbitration is touted as being a fast and inexpensive method of resolving disputes, and it is when contrasted to the legal system. Signing a **mandatory arbitration clause** basically gives away your right of appropriate redress, like suing the company or joining a class action lawsuit against them should a service problem arise. If you want to buy a new vehicle today, the first paper you may sign will require you to give up your right to sue the dealer with a **pre-dispute arbitration clause**. There will never be a jury trial because the customer agrees that they will not sue the firm, even in cases of fraud, but instead will submit to arbitration. So, if you want to buy that Hyundai you must sign; otherwise, you must walk away from the deal. Take it, or leave it. Arbitration clauses are also showing up in employment contracts.

   You should **try to avoid** buying from sellers who have such a requirement, although they are tough to avoid. They are found in home sales, retail stores, computer warranties, residential leases, auto dealers, stock brokers, insurance companies, and creditors. Virtually all credit card issuers have sent incomprehensible notices to consumers that inform the customer of a policy change and that you "automatically agree to the terms by charging one more item on your credit card."

   Pre-dispute arbitration clauses establish a set procedure to resolve disputes. First, the dispute is mediated with the seller. Next, the case goes to arbitration. There are no formal rules of evidence, no consistent standards of judgment, little outside oversight of the disposition of cases. Typically, the dispute is argued in a secret dispute-settlement system, with an arbitrator making a final decision that cannot be appealed and it is **not made public**. Sometimes the firm supplying the arbitrators is on contract with the seller. One such firm gave 99.6 percent of its decisions in favor of the seller, First USA.

Investor complaints against securities brokers are often serious as they involve large sums, and the number of grievances is increasing. About **10,000** securities cases go to industry arbitration panels annually. Consumers **win just over half** the securities disputes which amounts to about $80 million annually. For details about going to arbitration, call (212-858-4400) the National Association of Securities Dealers Regulation (NASDR; www.nasdr.com). In general, claims must be filed within three years of investing in a security or one year of discovering a problem, whichever is less. The consumer-investor must also pay a $2,000 filing fee. Most cases are very slow and take 12 to 18 months to arbitrate, in contrast to 2 to 5 years to get a civil lawsuit before a judge.

Arbitration **should be impartial**, but sometimes it is not. Arbitration **should be voluntary** and at the discretion of consumers, not mandatory. It should be entered into after a dispute has arisen, not before. Consumer advocates want Congress to prohibit mandatory arbitration. They also are supporting a bill to require independent arbitrators in these disputes to place limits on the fees consumers have to pay to participate in an arbitration case, and to require that arbitration results be made public. Chances for passage are slim since the business community likes the status quo. Fortunately, some state courts are refusing to enforce binding arbitration clauses in consumer agreements, recognizing that buyers are being tricked into giving up important consumer rights.

Retirement Plans at Risk

There are **three types of retirement plans** in the United States and each is at risk. Not so much from fraud and deception, although these problems do persist. Assuming you do not get ripped off from some shyster stealing your money, the biggest risk is the likelihood that you will **not have enough money** at retirement.

Types of Retirement Plans

First, the oldest type of retirement plan is employer-sponsored **defined-benefit (DB)** retirement plan, and it covers about 25 percent of working adults. Here an employer sets up a companywide plan where the **employer bears the investment risk and gets to keep any excess profits**. Retirement payout is based on length of employment and final salary. For example, 20 years at a 1.5 percent retirement factor multiplied times an ending salary of $60,000 equals an annual pension of $20,000. This pension plan is "back-loaded," meaning that benefits build up sharply toward the end of a worker's career. Up to half the benefits are earned in the last five years on the job. DB plans provide retirement income as well as **survivors' benefits** to spouses if the worker-retiree selects that option before actually retiring. A DB plan may not be taken from one job to another, thus it best serves older workers who intend to be at one employer for many years.

Second, the newest type is the **cash balance (CB)** retirement plan. Here employers contribute a fixed amount of an employee's salary (perhaps 3 to 5 percent) to a cash balance account each year. Accounts earn a fixed rate of interest and benefits accrue **uniformly** over an employee's working life. The payout is a *lump sum* (that must be managed by the retiree) or an *annuity* (purchased from an insurance company that will make monthly payments). A cash balance plan is **portable**, so it can be moved to another employer, and this is of particular interest to younger, mobile workers.

Third is a **defined contribution(DC)** retirement plan. It is popularly known by derivative names like **401(k), 403(b),** or **457 plan**. Here employees *and* employers contribute to the accounts of each worker and the **employee makes the investment choices** among those offered through the employer. The **worker bears all the investment risk** and enjoys **all the returns**. The payout is usually a lump sum available at retirement that the former worker must manage through his or her years of retirement. For example, a worker might have accumulated $500,000 in a 401(k) plan and that lump sum can be used for retirement income. If the principal earned 8 percent, it would pay $40,000 annually. A defined contribution plan is **portable**, meaning it can be transferred from one job to another.

Many Risks Exist

The major risk is that after working many years in anticipation of a big pension it **will disappear**, and this can happen with all three of the retirement plans. For example, an employer that sponsors a DB plan may one day eliminate the plan and replace it with a cash balance plan. By converting to a CB plan, employers save big money. IBM immediately saved $200 million when it converted. Switching plans typically leaves some workers nearing retirement age with sharply reduced benefits. Hundreds of plan sponsors have converted to CB plans.

Both DB and CB plans are insured to some extent by the federal **Pension Benefit Guaranty Corporation** (PBGC), who insures the retirement incomes of 44 million workers and retirees. Still, risks remain. The PBGC is funded by company premium payments and investment income. If an employer insured by the PBGC (www.pbgc.gov) goes bankrupt, the agency takes over the remaining assets of the pension plan and they provide the employer's pensioners and current workers limited benefits. The PBGC pays a maximum benefit of $1,072 a month for multi-level employer plans and as much as $3,579 for single-employer plans. Highly paid workers who worked for a firm that goes bankrupt, therefore, will not receive their expected big retirement income from the PBGC.

Hundreds of DB plans are **underfunded** by the companies that run them, and some firms deliberately underfund their pension plans. The gap between employers' promises and the funds set aside to pay pensions is at least $60 billion. PBGC makes payments to 125,000 retirees from more than 1,500 bankrupt businesses, and last year they had a $3.6 shortfall.

Critics want the PBGC to **raise the premiums** it charges companies for pension insurance, especially for higher-risk employers who are not putting enough money away for future retirees. Well-known underfunded plans include Phillips Petroleum, ExxonMobil, Delphi Automotive, Conoco, Pharmacia, and United Airlines.

Another risk to DB plans occurs when a company's plan has a **surplus of assets** in the plan, or more money than needed to pay the claims of present and future retirees. The risk is that those moneys will be used to help finance someone else's effort to buy a company. Here usually the company officers and other private investors use the pension assets as collateral to finance the takeover. Such **leveraged buyouts** permit the takeover people to: (1) buy out companies with surplus pension plans; (2) change the pension plan from a defined-contribution to a cash balance; (3) enforce mandatory retirement on workers; (4) reinsure the pension plan beneficiaries with investments in guaranteed investment contracts that technically meet all legal obligations to workers and pensioners; and (5) break the company into pieces and sell its parts for high profits. Pensioners are often left having their checks slashed by **30 percent or more**.

DID YOU KNOW?
Divorced Women's Right to Ex-husband's Pension

About one-quarter of divorced older women (age 62+) receive retirement income directly from a former spouse's defined benefit pension because survivorship **rights are not automatic**. Details on how to collect a former spouse's pension may be found in *Your Pension Rights at Divorce, What Women Should Know* (Pension Rights Center, 918 16th Street, NW, Washington, DC 20006. The AARP (www.aarp.org) publishes *A Women's Guide to Pension Rights*. These rights do not pertain to defined contribution and cash balance plans.

The retirement plan that **most workers** have today, a defined-contribution plan, is **not covered by any insurance**. Since these plans are voluntary for employees, a gigantic risk is that a worker may **not elect to participate** in the retirement plan. Today, **one in four** workers who could participate in an employer-sponsored DC or CB plan does not. Overall, one-half of all workers say they have not yet begun to save for retirement, either through an employer-sponsored plan or a private plan.

Many DC plans are risky because they have invested lots of employee retirement money into **company stock**. If the company does well, the price of the stock will rise and lots of money will be available for people at retirement. Alternatively, if the fortunes of the firm decline so will the pension plan's assets.

Another risk to DC plans is that their success is partly based on the **employer making contributions** to each worker's plan. Some big companies, like Charles Schwab and Prudential Securities, are no longer making such contributions. The employer's promise to fund a DC plan is exactly that, a promise.

If the stock, bond and mutual fund investment selections within the worker's DC portfolio are profitable and perform well, there may be plenty of funds available for that person's retirement years. If the investments do poorly, however, an **insufficient amount or possibly even no money** will be available. Companies like Enron and WorldCom that went bankrupt in effect let their worker's DC plan investments evaporate. Even though workers must bear the full responsibility of their investment decisions, only 20 percent say their investment knowledge is "good." Four in ten workers say they have little or no knowledge. Two-thirds say they want professional financial advice to help them manage their retirement funds.

Fearing the possible loss in value of their retirement funds, many workers choose to invest a portion of their retirement money into what they think is a very conservative and safe investment called a **guaranteed investment contract (GIC)**. This is a contract backed by an insurance company's assets that is designed to pay the investor a fixed rate of return for a certain number of years. In this manner, GICs are similar in design to a certificate of deposit or annuity. GICs are backed **solely by an insurance company's assets**, and they are **not insured** by the federal government. In point of fact, GICs are not "guaranteed" because when an insurer goes bankrupt, the investors (including retirement plans that have purchased GICs) lose all or part of the principal. Fewer than half the states have a plan to step in and pay limited amounts of cash to GIC investors. Clearly, GICs are not what their name implies.

For most workers, **Social Security** will make up a portion of their retirement income. Social Security benefits for young workers, however, will be delayed until they are 67 years of age. Reduced Social Security retirement benefits are available for those who retire early, which is age 62 according to the rules. The Social Security system is solvent through the year 2041, after which benefits will outstrip what is collected in payroll taxes.

CONSUMER UPDATE:
Estimate Your Retirement Needs

There are many **Internet sites** that can help you estimate whether you are **saving enough** for retirement. To use them you need to (1) estimate how long you will live (average life expectancy now is 74 for men and 79 for women), (2) how much money you will need in retirement, and (3) how much you will earn on your investments. Check out the really **simple-to-use estimator** at the American Education Savings Council (www.asec.org). More comprehensive calculations can be determined using the Quicken Retirement Planner (www.quicken.com) as well as TrowePrice (www.troweprice.com), Fidelity (www.fideltiy.com) and Vanguard (www.vanguard.com)

Timeshares are *Not* Investments

Timeshare are sold with high-pressure, complete with gimmicks and prizes to entice the consumer and **shills** in the audience who are paid to say "Oh, what a wonderful bargain...where do I sign?" Many states now have cooling-off period laws, 3 to 10 days, during which consumers can change their minds about investing in timeshares.

Timesharing is often promoted as investment property, which is false. Profits for consumers are extremely rare. **Timesharing** is the use of a vacation home for a limited, preplanned time. About two million consumers own timeshares, and about 120,000 consumers a year are buying them. For $5,000 to $25,000 buyers can purchase one week's use of luxury vacation housing furnished right down to the salt and pepper shakers. Vacationers also pay an **annual maintenance fee** for each week of ownership, perhaps $500 a year, and it can rise significantly over time. Many people buy, falsely thinking that they are making a real estate investment that will appreciate in value. What they are really doing is making a decision on where to spend future vacations.

Some consumers buy timeshares because they believe that they can easily and inexpensively use an **exchange network** to trade for use at other properties in more exotic places. The largest timeshare exchange network business is Resort Condominiums. It charges a $300 initiation fee, a $199-a-year membership fee, and another $150 for each week of an exchange.

Timeshares have a terrible resale history. It is almost **impossible to resell** a timeshare, perhaps because you moved across the country or because your lifestyle changed. Resort Property Owners Association says that 58 percent of survey respondents had tried to sell their timeshares, but only 3 percent of them have succeeded, and the average resale took 4 ⅓ years.

Consumers sometimes wind up paying **substantial fees to advertise and trade** use of their properties. A large Florida seller of timeshares, Independent Timeshare Sales, reports that its commissions are 20 to 25 percent. At any point in time, about 60 percent of all timeshare owners are trying to sell. Even worse for the owner is that resale of timeshare properties is only 20 to 40 percent of the original price, reports Timeshare.com. Of course, once you buy a timeshare you will be occasionally hassled to upgrade to a bigger condo or **buy "points."** This is a new trend where you own a number of points rather than a certain week, and they can be spent at a number of resorts only for a few days at a time, rather than a week.

So-called **real estate liquidators** are scam artists that take advantage of people with hard-to-sell properties, such as timeshares and undeveloped land. The promise is to connect the owner with prospective buyers. Some operators tell owners that their nationwide computer network contains the names of many buyers who are interested in similar properties. Other promoters promise to sell the timeshare during the following twelve months for a price equal to or greater than the amount originally paid. Sometimes such sellers promise to give the property owner a $1,000 savings bond certificate if they fail to sell the property. (And from reading Chapter 4, you know that the corporate savings bond was issued by a nearly defunct corporation and is worthless.) After collecting a $250 to $1,000 **advance fee**, the promoters simply do not refund the money, even though property owners were "guaranteed a 100% refund" if a sale did not occur.

Timeshare purchasers should *only* buy **deeded timesharing** units because the buyer actually owns part of the property. **Non-deeded timesharing** is a purchase agreement that permits a limited, preplanned period right-to-use of certain property. Legally it is a vacation lease, license, or club membership that lasts only a specific number of years. When the lease runs out, often in 20 to 25 years, the non-deeded timesharing consumer has **zero legal claim** to anything.

Review and Summary of Key Terms and Concepts

1. List two examples in the **insurance consumer's bill of rights**.

2. Summarize how the insurance industry is **not competitive and poorly regulated**.

3. Distinguish between **anti-rebate** and **anti-group laws**.

4. Outline how collusion occurs between the auto insurance companies and some auto repair shops.

5. Summarize the problem with **uninsured motorists**.

6. Distinguish between the **fault** and the **no-fault auto insurance systems**.

7. List two **benefits of no-fault** insurance.

8. Summarize how the **pay-at-the-pump no-fault insurance** plan might work.

9. Explain how the **pay-per mile auto insurance plan** would work.

10. Explain what happens **when insurance companies go broke**.

11. Give two examples of investments that are not **federally insured**.

12. Offer three examples of **corporate fraud, thievery and avarice**.

13. Distinguish between a **commission-only financial planner** and a **fee-only financial planner**.

14. Give two examples of products sold in banks that are **not insured** by the FDIC.

15. Explain the concept of **mandatory arbitration** and why it is bad for consumers.

16. Distinguish between a **defined-benefit retiremetn plan** and a **defined-contribution retirement plan**.

17. Cite one **risk for consumers** saving for retirement in a defined-benefit plan and a defined-contribution plan.

18. What is a **guaranteed investment contract**?

19. Explain why **non-deeded timesharing** is not only not an investment, but also unsafe.

Useful Resources for Consumers

American Savings Education Council
www.asec.org

Employee Benefit Research Institute
www.ebri.org

Employee Benefits Security Administration
www.dol.gov/ebsa/welcome.html

First Gov for Consumers
www.consumer.gov/

International Association for Financial Planning
www.iafp.org

NASD Dispute Resolution
www.nasdadr.com

National Association of Insurance Commissioners
www.naic.org

National Association of Securities Dealers
www.nasdr.com

New York Stock Exchange
www.nyse.com

Pension Benefit Guaranty Corporation
www.pbgc.gov

Profit Sharing/401(k) Council of America
www.psca.org

Public Investors Arbitration Bar Association
www.piaba.org

"What Do You Think" Questions

1. Offer your reactions to the suggestion that the insurance industry is **noncompetitive and poorly regulated**.

2. Tell why you prefer one of the following reform proposals over the others: no-fault, **pay-at-the-pump no-fault**, **no pay no play**, and **pay-per mile**.

3. Give your reactions to the **fraud and thievery** in corporate America, and offer some suggestions to improve the situation.

4. There are some risks in the safety of **employer-sponsored retirement plans**. What suggestions can you offer to improve the likelihood that workers today will have the benefits they expect available at retirement?

Careers in Consumer Affairs

Career Opportunities in Consumer Affairs

C areer opportunities exist for professionally trained college graduates interested in the field of consumer affairs. This appendix describes consumer affairs as an academic area of study, typical curriculum requirements, expected competencies of graduates, job responsibilities, career development responsibilities, and career options.

Most people work and that's it. Many people also volunteer some of their time helping others. Choosing a career in consumer affairs helps achieves both goals.

Consumer affairs is an area of study that prepares students to reasonably advocate the consumer interest and help consumers improve their well-being. The primary responsibilities of **consumer affairs professionals (CAPS)** are to champion the consumer's viewpoint to their employing organization and to convey information about the organization's products and services to the consumer.

Although the consumer affairs area of study deals with concerns of business, it is people-oriented, with emphasis on the consumer perspective. It focuses on the human viewpoint in problem-solving. Consumer affairs majors are expected to have a keen interest in people and their quality of life.

Consumer affairs professionals are concerned with more than simply calculating the benefits and costs of alternatives. They also consider fairness, decency, kindness, compassion, and honor. Each student majoring in consumer affairs must identify his or her life mission and career aspirations, the answers to which are rooted in that person's values, goals, interests, and priorities. Majors are expected to develop clearer ideas about the way the world works and what needs to be done to make it better.

Job Responsibilities

The focus of work of consumer affairs professionals is on problems and issues that affect consumers. CAPs should be interested in prevention of customer complaints and changing the status quo for the better. The end result is to improve consumer welfare by positively affecting public policy, corporate behavior, and societal changes by working directly or indirectly with consumers and families.

Consumer affairs professionals often interact with consumers, corporations, social service agencies, government agencies, educators, and persons with limited incomes. Many large organizations employ consumer affairs professionals.

Major activities of consumer affairs professionals include responding to consumer inquiries and complaints; championing the interests of consumers within the organizational decision-making structures; developing promotional and informational programs; preparing leaflets and booklets on how to use products; monitoring and evaluating consumer trends; monitoring legislative issues; writing news releases, informational brochures, and newsletters; speaking to consumer, educational, professional, and government groups, as well as opinion leaders; helping others understand an employer's perspective (that of business, government, or a nonprofit agency); and being a change agent.

Career Development Opportunities

People who graduate from consumer affairs programs are qualified for employment in positions as consumer affairs professionals. Careers follow six primary paths: (1) complaint-handling, (2) complaint prevention, (3) customer service, (4) public relations, including information and education and lobbying, (5) community outreach, (6) and sales. Jobs for consumer affairs professionals exist in most large businesses and government agencies.

Entry-level Job Titles in Consumer Affairs

Typical entry-level job titles include customer service representative, consumer information and education specialist, consumer investigator, complaint mediator, product information specialist, quality assurance representative, consumer researcher, consumer writer, product testing specialist, human resources specialist, consumer service specialist, hospital patient representative, ombudsman, community reinvestment act officer, retail sales and management, restaurant management, securities sales, real estate sales, publicist, community relations representative, consumer communication specialist, insurance agent, insurance claims adjuster, insurance cost-containment specialist, cooperative extension agent, telemarketing sales, travel agent, loan officer, credit or financial counselor, financial planning assistant, income tax preparation specialist, entrepreneur, consumer education coordinator, public relations representative, lobbyist, legislative assistant, political staff assistant, and public information officer.

Entry-level Employers of Consumer Affairs Graduates

Typical employers for entry-level consumer affairs majors include public utility companies, Better Business Bureaus, Chambers of Commerce, non-profit community organizations (United Way, Community Chest, etc.), banks, savings and loan associations, credit unions, consumer credit counseling services, hospitals, marketing research firms, advertising firms, automobile dealerships, mortgage lenders, creditors, collection agencies, credit reporting organizations, supermarkets, personnel management firms, life insurance companies, property and casualty companies, financial planning firms, income tax preparation services, securities firms, mutual fund companies, advertising agencies, cooperative extension services, telemarketing firms, travel agencies, real estate firms, various retail businesses, government agencies (federal, state and local), and professional and trade associations.

Lifelong Career-Development Opportunities

Lifelong career-development opportunities exist for consumer affairs professionals. Advanced positions, which require several years of successful consumer affairs experience, include directing and training a consumer affairs staff, representing an organization at meetings, monitoring legislative and regulatory issues, addressing legislative hearings, coordinating research on consumer complaints, and reasonably advocating the consumer interest to top management within an organization. Top job titles in the consumer affairs profession include manager of consumer affairs, vice president for consumer affairs, vice president for global consumer affairs, and director-consumer affairs worldwide.

Career Options

Consumer affairs graduates are employed in business firms, government agencies, and nonprofit agencies. Consumer affairs positions are more likely to be found in large organizations rather than in smaller firms. Potential employers are located throughout the country, although the greatest number of employment opportunities are in urban areas.

Jobs in Business

Many employment positions are available in businesses concerned with manufacturing, processing, and marketing. Graduates often find employment in such industries as savings, investments, food, housing, retailing, entertainment, insurance, oil, agriculture, radio, television, journalism, travel, transportation, textiles, household appliances, labor, medical care, and credit. Graduates may work for business trade associations, such as the American Gas Association, National Turkey Federation, AARP, Better Business Bureau, or American Bankers Association. Some graduates work for regulated utilities, such as the telephone, water, gas, and electric industries.

Jobs in State and Local Government

Graduates may work for state and local government agencies, such as a county office of consumer affairs, state office of consumer affairs, housing authority, department on aging, weights and measures office, tourism, licensing, registration, bureau of automotive regulation, social services, energy agency, cooperative extension service, attorney general's office, insurance commission, financial institutions bureau, utilities commission, or for a legislator.

Jobs with the Federal Government

Employment opportunities are also available with the federal government working for members of Congress, as well as for various agencies, such as the Office of Management and Budget, Consumer Product Safety Commission, Food and Drug Administration, U.S. Department of Agriculture, Environmental Protection Agency, Occupational Safety and Health Administration, and National Highway Traffic Safety Administration.

Jobs in Federal Offices in Local Communities

Employment positions for consumer affairs majors are available in federal offices located in local communities, such as the Farmers Home Administration, the Housing and Urban Development Office, Army Community Services, Navy Family Services, Social Security, and an area energy office.

Jobs in Consumer and Public Interest Organizations

Other graduates may work for consumer and public interest organizations, such as Public Citizen, Consumer Federation of America, National Consumers League, Center for Auto Safety, Public Voice for Food and Policy, Common Cause, People for the Ethical Treatment of Animals, and U.S. Public Interest Research Group, or for a non-profit community services agency, solar energy center, legal services organization, or public interest research group.

Curriculum Requirements

Consumer affairs majors study the role of consumers in the economy and analyze the information needed for individuals and families to become more knowledgeable and assertive consumers. They seek answers to questions such as, "How can I get my money's worth?" "How can I contribute to improving communication and respect between consumers and producers?" and "How can I personally help improve the world in which I live?" The subject matter is taught from the consumer point of view, not from the perspective of marketing interests in consumption. For example, students learn which styles of nutritional information on food labels are most helpful to consumers rather than which format sells the most products.

The concepts and skills of the consumer affairs profession come from a range of academic disciplines and applied areas, including political science, law, finance, insurance, management, marketing, accounting, economics, family economics, psychology, sociology, credit, statistics, research methods, computer technology, nutrition, media, and communications. This broad range of knowledge is used by the professional to help consumers get the best products and services for their money, to promote the availability of choices for consumers, to assess consumer complaints and suggest fair solutions, and to help consumers better manage their money. The curriculum provides students with a liberal and practical education rather than a technical education.

Courses in the department offering the major in consumer affairs generally have a family perspective with which students can examine problems and issues to improve the level of living of individuals and families. Issues and problems are studied from the perspectives of consumers, businesses, and governments. Students learn a variety of terms, concepts, processes, and applications relevant to employment in careers as consumer affairs professionals.

Specialized course offerings in the consumer affairs major often include such titles as Consumer Rights, Consumer Protection, Family Finance, Budget and Debt Counseling, Debtor/Creditor Relationships, Resource Management, Family Economics, and Professional Seminar in Consumer Affairs.

Consumer affairs majors are provided a variety of in- and out-of-class learning experiences. Opportunities for self-development exist with student professional associations on campus, as well as relevant state and national organizations, such as the Consumer Educators of Michigan (CEM), Illinois Consumer Education Association (ICEA), American Council on Consumer

Interests (ACCI), Society of Consumer Affairs Professionals in Business (SOCAP), and National Association of Consumer Agency Administrators (NACAA).

Students are expected to develop independence and initiative. Because the curriculum is designed with the ultimate goal of developing skills and confidence, students progressing through the consumer affairs curriculum have increasing responsibility to individualize aspects of their educational program. Majors in consumer affairs often are required to complete an individual study experience, such as research, a field study, or an internship.

Competencies of Graduates

Students develop competencies that enable them upon graduation to: (1) make rational buying decisions, (2) efficiently resolve consumer problems, (3) advise people to manage resources more effectively, (4) be familiar with major problems and issues confronting consumer affairs professionals, (5) understand how to operate a consumer complaint-handling system, and (6) advocate the consumer interest to superiors in an organization.

Graduates of consumer affairs programs seek employment as consumer affairs professionals. Employers look for the ability to communicate effectively orally and in writing. They want employees who possess analytical decision-making skills and are able to take into consideration a number of complicated, subjective factors. CAPs should have a thorough knowledge of consumer-related problems and issues, utilize economics in analyzing alternatives, know survey research techniques, appreciate the American free-enterprise system, understand consumer behavior and public relations, appreciate the legislative and regulatory processes, and understand ways of affecting changes in legislation and public policy. They should also be able to plan, research, and develop consumer education and information materials, and implement such programs.

Graduates should be motivated, resourceful, and focused. Employers prefer those who are willing to work and demonstrate curiosity, dependability, open-mindedness, competence, confidence, leadership, and a positive professional attitude. CAPs need to see both the short- and long-term view of a situation. In addition, graduates should possess the desire to increase knowledge and skills and stay up-to-date in the field of consumer affairs.

Sample Letters for Employment

Two samples letters follow. One is to seek an internship and the other is to seek a job.

SAMPLE LETTER SEEKING INTERNSHIP

Return Address
Today's Date

Name
Address of Addressee

Dear Mr./Ms. XXXXX:

I am writing to inquire about an internship with your office this coming summer. I am currently a junior attending _____ college majoring in Consumer Affairs. This major provides a broad background in business and human relations. In addition, the major emphasizes the importance of supporting the consumer interest.

The courses in my major have helped prepare me to deal with the problems and challenges experienced by consumers. My courses in Consumer Affairs, particularly the class in Consumer Protection, has given focus to my desire to help promote the interests of consumers. My communications classes have taught me a variety of writing styles and interpersonal skills to use when dealing with others. In addition, I have strengths in the academic areas of consumer economics, credit, personal finance, family relations, economics, marketing and political science. For one of my upper-division classes, Professionalism in Consumer Affairs, we researched the importance of effectively handling consumer complaints. My studies have helped me develop a sense of professionalism and sharpened my ability to make rational decisions where the consumer interest is concerned.

Last summer, I worked as an office assistant for _____, a credit bureau. One of my duties was to perform credit checks on personal credit card accounts. This required that I deal with individuals by telephone to verify purchases, handle complaints, and determine account status. The previous summer I worked in retail sales for a furniture company, where I learned to deal with the public on a one-to-one basis listening to and analyzing their wants and needs while conveying the company's total quality management perspective to each sales contact. During the academic school year, I have worked 15 hours a week as an analyst in the Registrar's Office, mostly dealing with the confidential details of graduation analysis. These experiences, combined with the knowledge I have learned in my classes, have prepared me for an internship with _____.

I will contact you within two weeks to ensure that you have received this letter and the enclosed resume. I hope an interview can be arranged so that I might personally convey to you some idea of my abilities and interest in an internship at _____. I will require a salary to offset my living expenses over the summer. Should you have any questions, please feel free to communicate with me. I look forward to hearing from you soon.

Sincerely,

Your Name

Enclosure

SAMPLE LETTER SEEKING JOB

Return Address
Today's Date

Name
Address of Addressee

Dear Mr./Ms. XXXXX:

I am writing to pursue the opportunity of becoming a customer service representative with _____. My major at _____ college was Consumer Affairs.

My senior year at college has been very rewarding for me. I have sharpened my writing and public speaking skills in several ways. My greatest opportunity in this area came in February when I co-presented a paper with my academic advisor and professor _____, who has helped me in my professional development. The paper, "_____," was based on a class research project. It was presented at the _____ meeting and published in the conference proceedings. This year also afforded me the opportunity to serve as Vice President of the Consumer Interest Organization, a student group. In addition, I had the privilege of doing volunteer work helping to build homes for Habitat for Humanity.

For the past four years I have worked for different companies that ultimately are concerned with the same objective: customer satisfaction. Through my employment experiences as an office assistant, salesperson, analyst, and research assistant, I have been able to develop and enhance a number of job-related abilities. These include word processing, spreadsheet, financial software, organizational skills, technical writing, and platform speaking. My internship last summer with the Better Business Bureau enhanced my interpersonal and telephone skills, and I learned more about reasonably advocating the consumer interest. Also, my fluency in Spanish improved. My experience and education make me confident that I can be a successful employee at _____.

I expect to be in the _____ geographic area during the week of _____, and I would enjoy an opportunity to visit your office to discuss the possibilities of a position at _____. I look forward to hearing from you soon.

Sincerely,

Your Name

Enclosure

Index